W9-ATY-954

POLICE ADMINISTRATION

Gary W. Cordner
Eastern Kentucky University

Kathryn E. Scarborough
Eastern Kentucky University

Robert Sheehan

5th edition

LexisNexis™

anderson publishing
A member of the LexisNexis Group

Police Administration, Fifth Edition

Cordner, Gary W.
    Police Administration / Gary W. Cordner, Kathryn E. Scarborough, Robert Sheehan. -- 5th ed.
        p. cm.
    Includes index.
    ISBN 1-58360-550-9 (pbk.)

Cover design by Tin Box Studio, Inc.

EDITOR Elisabeth Roszmann Ebben
ACQUISITIONS EDITOR Michael C. Braswell

In memory of Robert Sheehan—pioneer police educator, philosopher, guide, and friend.

Preface

This book is written for students and practitioners interested in police administration. Although police administration is far from a simple undertaking, the subject matter of this book is purposely presented in the simplest possible terms. The difficulties inherent in managing a police department and assuring the quality delivery of police services to the public can be overwhelming. These challenges demand the best efforts of the best men and women who can be attracted to the law enforcement field. This is especially true in a free, democratic society in which the police are trusted to exercise great restraint in the use of their awesome powers.

For this edition we resisted the urge to add homeland security to the title of the book, just as with the fourth edition we resisted the urge to add community policing to the title of the book or to add a chapter or two on community policing. We have added a section on homeland security in the new "Contemporary Issues" chapter in deference to the importance of this critical new topic, and we have given increased attention throughout the book to such matters as the police intelligence function, information sharing, interagency cooperation, and communications interoperability.

The text opens with several basic considerations crucial to understanding the unique features of police administration. These include the development and environment of police administration, the nature of police work, police goals and objectives, police organizational tasks, and the role of the police executive. These basic considerations provide a foundation for more detailed exploration of modern police administration.

We then examine the challenging enterprise of police administration from several important perspectives, including a systems perspective; a traditional, structural perspective; a human behavioral perspective; and a strategic management perspective. The systems perspective, which permeates the entire text, emphasizes the interrelatedness among units and organizations, the influence of external conditions on systems, and the importance of feedback for correcting and improving performance. The traditional perspective highlights administrative principles, management functions, and the importance of written guidelines. The behavioral perspective stresses the human element in organizations, an element that is often overlooked or taken for granted. The strategic management perspective considers communications and information systems, evaluation of police performance, the strategies and tactics by which police work is accomplished, and prevailing and promising approaches to increasing the effectiveness of police agencies.

We think it is extremely beneficial to examine police administration from these multiple perspectives. Many texts adopt just one view, thereby ignoring important aspects of the subject. We hope our approach helps you appreciate the breadth and complexity of contemporary police administration. If you are interested in further exploring this complexity, each chapter includes a short suggested reading list.

Nine case studies are included at the end of the book. You may want to practice using the conceptual and theoretical tools introduced in the text to identify and analyze the organizational problems and situations presented in these cases.

Many fields of professional activity seek improvement and recognition by establishing standards. Extensive police standards were first promulgated more than two decades ago by the National Advisory Commission on Criminal Justice Standards and Goals and the American Bar Association Project on Standards for Criminal Justice. More recently, the Commission on Accreditation for Law Enforcement Agencies has identified standards for police adoption. We have inserted some of the standards from these sources throughout the text to acquaint you with the benchmarks that professionally recognized groups use in evaluating police departments.

We believe that the field of police administration today is vibrant and exciting. Many studies conducted over the last 30 years have provided useful information to expand theory and refine practice. New and innovative programs and policies have been developed and tested. Some of our most basic assumptions about crime, violence, policing, and police administration have been seriously challenged. In the 1990s, the community policing strategy caught the imagination of ordinary citizens, local officials, the U.S. Congress, and even the president of the United States.

Most recently, international terrorism has dramatically affected America's beliefs and expectations about policing and public safety, and given rise to the new construct "homeland security." The role of local police in homeland security will be evolving over the next several years. Traditional lines between local police, federal law enforcement, and the military may be blurred. Very important issues related to public protection and civil liberties will be at stake.

Underlying all this effort and activity are some important fundamental issues related to order and liberty in a free society. The police are at the vortex of all our hopes for a fair, just, and safe existence; police administration remains as honorable and challenging an undertaking as any that can be imagined.

Acknowledgments

We are grateful to all those who contributed to this book in one way or another: by reading the manuscript at its various stages of development and making valuable suggestions and contributions; by giving us direct editorial input; by shaping the attitudes and philosophies that we have taken with us into the book; and by encouraging us and being patient with us during the long period since we began the first edition of this book almost 30 years ago.

We want to thank the following individuals for the professional guidance and personal kindness they have shown: Cornelius Behan, Chief (ret.), Baltimore County (Maryland) Police Department; Edward Blessing, Chief (ret.), Easton (Maryland) Police Department; Ed Brodt, Eastern Kentucky University; Tim Bynum, Michigan State University; David Carter, Michigan State University; Derral Cheatwood, University of Texas–San Antonio; Pam Collins, Eastern Kentucky University; Ed Connors, Institute for Law and Justice; Steve Edwards, Bureau of Justice Assistance; Michael Gray, Wor-Wic Technical and Community College (Salisbury, Maryland); Jack Greene, Northeastern University; Donna Hale, Shippensburg University; David Hayeslip Jr., Urban Institute; Larry Hoover, Sam Houston State University; Dennis Kenney, John Jay College of Criminal Justice; Truett Ricks, Eastern Kentucky University (ret.); Cindy Shain, Eastern Kentucky University; Mitchell Smith, Rural Development Center; Mittie Southerland, Murray State University; Darrel Stephens, Charlotte-Mecklenburg (North Carolina) Police Department; William Tafoya, University of New Haven; Walter Tangel, International Association of Chiefs of Police; and Gerald Williams, University of Colorado at Denver.

We are very grateful for the continued assistance and encouragement provided by the Anderson Publishing Company, including Michael Braswell, Susan Braswell, Kelly Grondin, Gail Eccleston, and especially Elisabeth Ebben. We would especially like to acknowledge the long-standing contributions of Bill Simon, now retired from Anderson.

Finally, special recognition is due our families for their patience, understanding, and many sacrifices.

Thank you all very much.

Contents

Part Two
The Traditional Perspective

Chapter 5
Principles and Policies in the Police Organization

Chapter 6
Functions of Police Management

Chapter 7
The Police Executive   179

Part Four
The Strategic Management Perspective 289

Chapter 11
Information in the Police Organization 291

Chapter 12
Evaluating Police Performance

Chapter 13
Police Strategies and Tactics

Chapter 14
Police Organizational Improvement   397

Chapter 15
Contemporary Issues in Police Administration 429

Case Studies 449

BASIC CONSIDERATIONS

The four chapters in Part One serve as an introduction to the study of police administration as presented in this book. These chapters provide important background information and perspectives for anyone involved in police administration.

Chapter 1 considers the history and context of police administration. The police manager's job is greatly influenced by historical, social, political, legal, and democratic factors; an understanding and appreciation of these factors will help police managers adjust to their roles and be more effective. We stress that police executives need to develop community-oriented approaches to police administration to complement the community policing strategies and tactics being implemented by their officers.

Chapter 2 examines the nature of police work. Our rationale is that, to be successful, the organization and management of police departments must be consistent with the fundamental realities of police work. Some of these realities include danger, authority, and discretion. Many of the recurring problems encountered in police administration can be attributed to a lack of congruence between traditional administrative methods and the nature of the organization's basic work.

Chapter 3 focuses on police goals and systems. Police managers must have a keen awareness of their organizations' missions and goals so that efforts can be concentrated on attaining those ends. The systems approach is introduced because it helps us think logically and systematically about police administration; because it forces us to recognize that police departments are composed of interrelated subsystems; and because it emphasizes the interdependence of police agencies, other organizations, and the community.

Chapter 4 discusses 30 basic police subsystem tasks within the framework of operations, administration, and auxiliary services. The treatment of these numerous subsystem tasks is necessarily brief. Our intent is to impress upon the reader the number and variety of tasks that must be performed in a police organization if the attainment of goals and objectives is to be a realistic possibility.

Preceding each of the chapters is a list of learning objectives that identifies many of the important facts and concepts introduced in that chapter. The reader may want to refer to these learning objectives while reading each chapter or use them later on as a study guide. At the end of each chapter are discussion questions for the reader to consider and suggested readings for those who want to explore the subject matter in greater detail.

Introduction to Police Administration

1

Learning Objectives

- Cite the first two fundamental principles of Peelian reform.

- Contrast the political, professional, and community eras of American policing.

- Identify several reasons for the development of community policing during the last decade or two.

- Briefly summarize the social, political, and legal contexts of American police administration.

- Identify the four dimensions of community policing and the implications of each for police administration.

Police administration is primarily concerned with (1) the performance of management duties within police departments, and (2) the implementation of policies and programs related to crime, disorder, and public safety. Police administrators must focus internally on running their organizations and externally on problems in their communities. They must strive for efficiency in the performance of police duties and effectiveness in achieving the goals of policing. In their pursuit of efficiency and effectiveness, police administrators must abide by a variety of legal and ethical constraints, and they must also remain accountable for their actions and decisions.

Police administration does not take place within a vacuum—it has a history and a context. Particularly in a free society, it is important for police administrators to be aware of the social, legal, and political frameworks within which they operate.

The Development of Police Administration

The development of police administration had to await the development of organized policing. The year 1829 marks the origin of organized, paid, civilian policing as we currently know it. In that year, the Metropolitan Police Act became English law, culminating a long and emotional debate. Prior to that time, law enforcement in England and America had been the province of ordinary citizens, volunteers, night watchmen, private merchant police, soldiers, personal employees of justices of the peace, constables, sheriffs, and slave patrols. This informal and unorganized law enforcement approach, which had proved satisfactory for centuries, was overwhelmed by the Industrial Revolution, which spawned rapid urbanization and upwardly spiraling crime rates.

The Metropolitan Police Act of 1829 authorized Sir Robert Peel to establish a police force for the metropolitan London area, and 1,000 men were quickly hired. Where no police force at all had previously existed, there suddenly stood a large organization. The basic organizational and managerial problems faced by Peel and his police commissioners, Charles Rowan and Robert Mayne, were essentially the same as those faced by police chiefs today. How were they to let their officers know what was expected of them, how were they to coordinate the activities of all those officers, and how were they to make sure that directions and orders were followed?

Some of Peel's answers to these questions can be found in the fundamental principles of his Peelian Reform:

1. The police should be organized along military lines.
2. Securing and training proper persons is essential.
3. Police should be hired on a probationary basis.
4. The police should be under governmental control.
5. Police strength should be deployed by time and area.
6. Police headquarters should be centrally located.
7. Police record keeping is essential.[1]

The foundation of Peel's approach to police administration is in his first two principles. Although he felt strongly that the police and the military should be separate and distinct agencies, he turned to the military for his model of efficient organization. He also turned to many former military officers in recruiting his first police officers.

That Peel should borrow his organizational style from the military was not at all unusual. The military and the Church were actually the only large-scale organizations in existence at that time. Both were organized similarly, although their members bore different titles. Both were centralized; a few people held most of the power and made most of the decisions, whereas many people just did as they were told. In addition, both operated under a system of graded authority; for example, generals had full authority, colonels and majors had a little less, captains and lieutenants had less still, sergeants had only enough to direct their privates, and privates had none at all.

It was natural, then, that Peel should borrow the centralized organizational form of the military model. His personnel practices, though, were not copied from the military, which at that time was composed largely of debtors, criminals, and draftees, with officers drawn from the wealthy and aristocratic classes. The military was chronically in need of people and would accept anyone into its ranks. Peel, however, was highly selective in choosing his police. Only a small percentage of applicants was accepted, and a probationary period was used to weed out those whose performance was unsatisfactory. The standards of conduct were very rigid, so many officers were dismissed, especially in the early years of organizational development.

Peel's approach to police administration can thus be summed up as follows: (1) centralized organization with graded authority, and (2) selective and stringent personnel standards. He fashioned his approach in 1829, and in many communities we still fall short of implementing it.

The Political Era

One obstacle to the adoption of Peel's approach in the United States was the enduring view of police work as essentially undemanding physical labor. This widely held belief prevented the establishment of the rigorous personnel standards advocated by Peel. As a result, the pay and status derived from police work have tended to be low, and the job, until recently, has attracted mainly those whose job prospects elsewhere were bleak.

Stringent personnel standards in the early days of American policing were also subverted by the influence of local politics (see "Politics and the New York Police," p. 6). Local politics served as the vehicle for bringing immigrant groups into the American social structure, and police jobs were part of local political patronage. Initially, police work was the domain of certain politically powerful ethnic groups rather than a profession of highly qualified people who could meet rigid standards. Consequently, police officers were likely to be dismissed by their agencies not because of unsatisfactory performance but because they belonged to the wrong political party.

During the political era of American policing, decentralized organizational structures were favored over centralized ones.[2] In big-city police departments the real power and authority belonged to precinct captains, not to chiefs or commissioners. Detectives usually reported to these precinct captains rather than to a chief of detectives at headquarters. The reason for this decentralized approach was to protect local political influence over the police. Local political leaders ("ward bosses") picked their own precinct captains and expected them to be very responsive. A strong central headquarters might have interfered with this politically based system.

Politics and the New York Police

An important reason for the discrepancy between ideals and practice, in addition to public expectations of the police, was the force's involvement in partisan politics. Decentralization and political favoritism weakened discipline. Before 1853 patrolmen looked to local politicians for appointment and promotion. Consequently, they were less amenable to their superior officers' orders, and friction developed which "soon ripened into the bitterest hatred and enmity, and which were carried out of the department into the private walks of life." Policemen participated in political clubs, often resigning to work for the reelection of their aldermen, who left the positions vacant until they won the election and could reappoint the loyal patrolmen. Chief Matsell said that this politicking kept the department in "constant excitement." Discipline improved somewhat under the 1853 commission, which cut the tie to local aldermen and prohibited participation in political clubs. However, the commission had little chance to improve its effectiveness, for favoritism was rife under Mayor Fernando Wood, elected in 1854. Captains were not promoted from the ranks but "taken from the citizens, and placed over Lieutenants and Sergeants of ten years' experience, depressing the energies of the men."

Source: Wilbur R. Miller, *Cops and Bobbies: Police Authority in New York and London, 1830-1870* (Chicago: University of Chicago Press, 1977), p. 43.

The Professional Era

Although complaints about police abuses and inefficiency were common in the 1800s, widespread criticism of the political model of policing, including its decentralization and acceptance of mediocre personnel, did not emerge until the beginning of the twentieth century.[3] Since then, however, police practitioners, academics, and investigating commissions have decried the poor quality of police personnel; pointed out the need for intelligence, honesty, and sensitivity in police officers; called for stricter organizational controls; and thus reaffirmed Peel's philosophy.

Among the individuals most vocal and noteworthy in support of both centralized organization and higher police personnel standards were August Vollmer,[4] Bruce Smith,[5] and O.W. Wilson.[6] Each strongly believed police work to be a demanding and important function in a democratic society, requiring officers able to deal flexibly and creatively with a wide variety of situations. They agreed that physical power was an important attribute, but felt that good judgment, an even temperament, and other human qualities and skills were more important. They believed strongly in education, training, discipline, and the use of modern technology in policing. They and other leaders advocated a professional model of policing.

Supporting their views were the findings and recommendations of investigating commissions, most notably the Wickersham Commission in the 1930s and the President's Crime Commission in the 1960s. The Wickersham Commission found that the American police were totally substandard;[7] the President's Commission found that insufficient progress had been made from the 1930s to the 1960s.[8] Both found that the quality of police personnel was low in terms of carrying out the job to be done and in comparison to the rest of the population, and both called for substantial upgrading of police personnel.

Through the mid-1960s the need for better police personnel and stricter organizational controls dominated the literature and practice of police administration. Since then, however, other important issues—such as the poor state of police-community relations, the need for a more diverse police workforce, the ineffectiveness of traditional police strategies, and the need for more flexibility within police organizations—have come to the forefront. These other issues have arisen because of both the successes and the failures of the professional model of policing.[9]

The Community Era

In most major jurisdictions today, the need for intelligent, sensitive, flexible people in policing has been accepted. More well-educated people are being hired as police officers than was the case 30 or more years ago.[10] Over the long run, police salaries have been improving, along with occupational status. Police agencies are more selective when choosing their officers.

Quality is subjective, however. Many police departments, in their quest for higher-caliber personnel during the professional era, emphasized educational attainment, physical skills, appearance, conformity, abstinence from experimentation with drugs, and spotless police records. Use of such criteria sometimes made it more difficult for local people, women (with less upper-body strength, on average, than men), and members of minority groups (who, in some jurisdictions, are less likely to have attended college and more likely to have been arrested for minor offenses) to obtain police employment. The lack of these kinds of employees in turn created police-community relations problems for more than a few police agencies.

Questions also began to arise about the more centralized structures and stricter organizational controls that characterize the professional model.[11] The rigid, military approach no longer seems to fit the demanding, variable, discretion-laden nature of the police job. Nor does it seem appropriate for management of the better-educated, more knowledgeable police officers of today. Other kinds of organizations, in both the business and government sectors, have moved away from centralized, military forms of organization in favor of more flexible arrangements.

The professional model of policing has come under criticism on other fronts as well. The very idea of professionalism may encourage police officers to think of themselves as better than the average person. Separation of policing from politics, when taken to extremes, can result in police who are so independent of political control that they are no longer responsive or accountable to the public.

Perhaps most damaging to the professional model is the question of its effectiveness. During the model's heyday in the 1960s and 1970s, crime was not reduced, but instead increased more than in any other time in recent memory. Also, the key strategies of the professional model (preventive patrol, rapid response, and follow-up investigations) have each been found to be far less effective than originally thought (as explained in Chapter 13).[12]

Today, some observers are calling for further refinement of the professional model, while many others are calling for it to be augmented or replaced by a *community policing* model.[13] The community-oriented model advocates, among other things, more decentralized organizational structure, closer ties to the community, a stronger focus on prevention, and a problem-solving approach to police work.[14] This model supports the need for high-quality personnel, but emphasizes education and creativity over conformity, physical attributes, and unnecessarily rigid background characteristics.

Even the most fervent supporters of community-oriented policing (COP) see the continued necessity of some elements of the professional model, however. The need for high standards, thorough training, and sound organization and management in policing are widely accepted. If it is to be successful, COP will have to learn from and build upon the professional model. The ideas and information presented throughout this text are equally important whether one is primarily following the professional model or community model of policing.

The Social Context of Police Administration

Just as current police administration can be explained in part by its past, so too can its form and substance be explained in part by the social context within which policing operates. We have already mentioned, for example, that the low status of police work in America helped to explain the unsatisfactory quality of police applicants and thus the inability of police administrators to implement stringent personnel standards.

The police seem perpetually to be the brunt of scathing criticism—in recent years, this has been evident in the aftermath of such high-profile events as the Rodney King beating, the O.J. Simpson trial, the tragic conclusion of the Waco, Texas, stand-off, and the assault on Abner Louima. One reason for the apparently constant dissatisfaction with the police in American communities is the lack of agreement in society about what the objectives or role of policing should be. General agreement does not exist in society on the most important goals of policing, not to mention the means of attaining those goals.[15] In addition to the disagreement among people about what the police should be doing, individuals often change their opinions and priorities over time or in response to certain perceived emergencies, so that the unfathomable "will of the community" is always changing. As a result, even the police administrator who tries to provide the community with the type of police service that it desires is unlikely to escape criticism.

Consider, for example, Geoffrey Alpert and Roger Dunham's study of five diverse neighborhoods in Dade County, Florida (see "Community Conflict Over the Police"). One neighborhood, the Kendall area, ranked police officer *courtesy* and *demeanor* as its two most important concerns. Another neighborhood in the same jurisdiction, James Scott, ranked 15 other issues as more important—the biggest concern of this area's residents was police officer *appearance*. It is extremely difficult for one agency to satisfy such divergent interests.

Community Conflict Over the Police

A study of five racially and ethnically diverse neighborhoods in Dade County, Florida, illustrates the widely differing opinions and priorities of the police held by citizens. Survey respondents were asked to rate the importance of 20 police tasks and characteristics. The table below highlights some of the more interesting results.

Importance Rankings by Neighborhood

Tasks and Characteristics	Rolling Oaks	James Scott	1960 Cubans	1980 Cubans	Kendall Area
Knowledge	1st	13th	1st	4th	6th
Courtesy	5th	16th	4th	5th	1st
Appearance	6th	1st	15th	16th	10th
Human Relations	7th	17th	10th	7th	4th
Judgment	13th	2nd	5th	1st	3rd
Demeanor	15th	18th	6th	10th	2nd
Initiative	16th	4th	11th	8th	9th
No Personal Problems	18th	9th	7th	2nd	16th

Clearly, the Metropolitan Dade County Police Department faces a very difficult situation trying to please such diverse communities. While the social context of South Florida may be more complicated than in most other regions of the country, every police agency is confronted with the problem of conflicting demands and priorities.

Adapted from: Geoffrey P. Alpert and Roger G. Dunham, "Community Policing," *Journal of Police Science and Administration* 14, no. 3 (September 1986): 212-222.

The social implications and environment of policing have been high-lighted over the last 50 years in discussions and debates about police-community relations. Mass altercations in the 1960s between minority groups and the police, as well as between students and police, dramatically demonstrated that police relations with at least these communities were less than ideal. In urban areas, the estrangement of the police and the community extended beyond civil disorders to everyday policing, as many other groups seemed also to regard the police as an army of occupation.[16] The problem of police relations with these and other segments of the community made it clear that the police operate in a social system that they can neither take for granted nor totally control. Different community groups view the police differently and have varying notions of the priorities and objectives of law enforcement and criminal justice (see "Police Role in the Ghetto").

Police Role in the Ghetto

Police work in the ghetto encompasses a series of roles and/or responsibilities. The various attributes of the job can appear, at times, to be working at cross-purposes, but under closer examination the ambiguities of the police role in the ghetto bear definite societal intentions. On the one hand, the police are expected to represent the strong arm of the law; they must do battle with the ghetto's rugged individualism. But on the other hand, they must be able to show compassion and understanding to the public being served: the mother of the lost child, the victim of a crime. As to the other side of the ledger, ghetto residents may see the police as their oppressors, but at the same time the residents cannot do without the social services the police provide. In the absence of these services, the ghetto community would be hard-pressed to maintain social equilibrium. The police may be in adversary relations with the ghetto, but they are also a necessary linchpin of the community.

Source: Basil Wilson and John L. Cooper, "Ghetto Reflections and the Role of the Police Officer," *Journal of Police Science and Administration* 7, no. 1 (March 1979): 35, with permission of the International Association of Chiefs of Police.

Most recently, police-minority relations have been brought to the fore-front in discussions about "driving while black," racial profiling, and biased-based policing.[17] The fundamental issue in these discussions is whether the police have been fair and equitable when using their authority to stop, and sometimes search, individuals and vehicles. From a civil liberties and minority group perspective, it sometimes seems that police power to stop and search is used disproportionately against people of color. In return, police officials often assert that they are simply trying to address problems of crime, drugs, and gangs, often in response to urgent requests from minority and low-income neighborhoods. Finding common ground between these opposing perspectives has not been easy.

The new community policing model attempts to address such perplexing problems in several ways. Through closer contact with individual citizens and community groups, police are trying to stay attuned to the public's changing needs and priorities. Departments are also seeking a more representative workforce, including increasing numbers of civilians and volunteers to augment sworn officers. In addition, police are varying their enforcement strategies and programs from one neighborhood to the next, instead of applying one uniform approach throughout the entire community. Despite these new efforts, however, it remains difficult in heterogeneous communities to police in a way that satisfies all citizens. The same diversity that makes the United States such a vibrant and resilient country makes effective and responsive policing a major challenge. This challenge will only increase in the future as America's population becomes even more diverse.

The Political Context of Police Administration

Part of the environment of police administration is the governmental and political system. We have already noted that during its development American policing was closely tied to local politics and that this relationship had important consequences for police decisionmaking and police personnel standards. Although this undesirable political relationship is greatly diminished today, the political environment of police administration is still an important factor to consider in understanding and explaining police behavior, practices, and organizations.[18]

In our junior high school civics classes we all learned about the American government's system of checks and balances and separation of powers. The Founding Fathers dispersed authority among the legislative, executive, and judicial branches of government in order to prevent any one person or branch from becoming all-powerful. The legislative branch was assigned the roles of enacting laws and appropriating funds. The executive branch was given the tasks of implementing and enforcing the laws. The judicial branch was directed to review the constitutionality of legislative enactments and to adjudicate alleged violations of the laws.

The police are a part of the executive branch of government. Their role, then, is to enforce the laws enacted by the legislature and to refer alleged violations of those laws to the judiciary. In actual practice, of course, policing is considerably more complex and less mechanical than this description suggests. Police officers utilize discretion in such a way that they do not enforce all of the laws all of the time; their efforts are not universally reviewed by the courts; and many of their practices involve activities not related specifically to law enforcement. Nevertheless, it remains useful to keep in mind that the police make neither the laws nor the decision between the guilt or innocence of a suspect brought to court. These matters, though important to policing, are within the domain of other branches of the government.

Another important characteristic of our governmental system is federalism. Besides being distributed among different branches of government, power in our system is also dispersed through several levels of government. As a result, some functions are performed by the national government, some by the states, some by counties, some by local communities, and some are shared.

Policing in America is basically a local function, although the states and the national government are also involved with law enforcement and cannot be ignored. Three-quarters of our nation's one million-plus police protection employees work for local governments, and 90 percent of the 17,000 or so police agencies in this country are local police departments or sheriff's departments.[19] One consequence of the local character of American policing is that most of the country's law enforcement agencies are small—one-half have 10 or fewer sworn employees. Therefore, police administration in the United States frequently involves organizing and managing fairly small departments, a fact that is important to keep in mind, because the natural tendency when speaking of administration is to immediately think of large, complex organizations.[20]

With respect to objectives, priorities, and budgets, police administrators deal primarily with city councils, city managers, mayors, and other local executive and legislative units. State and national law enforcement organizations deal with state and national executive bodies, respectively. Even local police, however, have relationships with the state and national governments. The bulk of the law that most police enforce is state law enacted by state legislatures. Also, in many areas, the correctional and judicial systems, both of which are important to policing, are operated by counties and by states. Finally, since the 1960s, many local police administrators have had increased contacts with state and national government officials who control special anticrime funds, drug enforcement monies, and other federal funds used to augment local law enforcement budgets. In the 1990s, most of these federal funds were for the hiring of additional police officers to perform community policing duties in local communities.

Although the political environment of local police administration varies from agency to agency, some regional patterns can be discerned. In the Northeast, local city and town government is very strong and partisan. Police chiefs and other administrators are frequently changed after elections, and local partisan politics have a strong influence on day-to-day policing. In the West, by contrast, local politics are much more likely to be nonpartisan, with college-trained city managers who, like elected mayors in the East, exercise much of the authority. Police administrators in the West are more likely to be given authority and responsibility for everyday police operations, and "professional" police administration is more apparent. Moreover, in the West, and in the South, the county plays a larger role than elsewhere. In many rural areas, the elected county sheriff is the paramount law enforcement officer as well as one of the most prominent politicians.[21] Some counties also have county-wide police agencies serving under an appointed chief who is responsible to a county executive or county council. In other areas, however, particularly the Northeast, the county is an insignificant level of government, and frequently the sheriff is responsible only for serving civil court papers or running a county jail.

Thus, the political and governmental environment of police administration varies widely. Whatever the local circumstances, police administration is strongly influenced by these factors. Along with the historical and social contexts, the political context of police administration has important implications for the people, processes, and organization of policing.

The Legal Context of Police Administration

Although police work involves much more than just enforcing the law, police administration is constrained and affected by the law in a number of ways. For example, the criminal law defines what acts are crimes and what actions police officers may legally take in a variety of situations. Each year legislatures define new criminal acts, such as computer crime, stalking, hate crime, and carjacking, that fall within police jurisdiction. Legislatures also sometimes revise police authority, such as in permitting (or even mandating) warrantless arrests for misdemeanor spousal assault based solely on probable cause. In addition, the courts interpret and redefine the law continuously by their trial and appellate decisions.

One aspect of the law that is always in flux is constitutional law. At both the state and national levels, the courts interpret and reinterpret passages in constitutional law pertaining to limitations on police authority, such as search and seizure and interrogation of suspects. The courts also determine the precise meaning of individual rights that police officers must protect, such as the rights of assembly and free speech.

Police departments sometimes inherit new duties and responsibilities through legislation. Handgun waiting periods and registration laws, for example, frequently assign to police the task of checking the criminal records of handgun purchasers. Police are often required by new laws to conduct background checks on school bus drivers, day care providers, and others entrusted with the safety and well-being of children. Revised domestic violence legislation sometimes requires police officers to provide protection and transportation to spousal assault victims.

Even more common is for police administration to be constrained and regulated by law. In the personnel area, federal legislation protecting the employment rights of women, minorities, older workers, and the disabled has left most police administrators thoroughly confused about the types of hiring practices they can and cannot employ. Many traditional police practices related to roll calls, lunch breaks, on-call assignments, and special assignments have fallen afoul of the federal Fair Labor Standards Act. Police departments' internal disciplinary procedures in many jurisdictions are governed by a Police Officer's Bill of Rights enacted into state law. Laws also regulate the use of radio equipment, the maintenance of documentary records, the disposal of found and seized property, and myriad other matters.

Over the last two decades police administrators have become increasingly concerned with civil law, particularly civil liability.[22] Many police trainers, supervisors, and managers are now so worried about being sued that they suffer from "litigiphobia."[23] In the past, the police officer who made a false arrest, used excessive force, or failed to protect a crime victim might be sued; today, such a suit commonly includes others in the chain of command as defendants, alleging that they failed to properly train, direct, supervise, or control the officer. These kinds of civil suits are particularly effective if it can be shown that administrators encouraged or permitted a pattern of improper conduct to develop and continue.

Clearly, police administration takes place in a complex and changing legal environment. Although it is not yet the case that police administrators must be lawyers, they certainly need access to sound legal advice. And although police executives need not develop phobias about their civil liability, prudent risk management is warranted. The best protection is provided by thorough and systematic application of the modern principles of police administration presented in this text.

The Challenge of Police Administration in a Democratic Society

In discussing the historical, social, political, and legal contexts of police administration, we have skirted the most basic context of all: the democratic nature of our society. This one factor has tremendous implications for the ways in which we police our society, for the role of the police, and for police administration.

George Berkley has best described the difficult position of the police in a democratic society.[24] As he has noted, democracy is based on consensus among the members of the society; the police job starts when that consensus breaks down. Perfect democracy would have perfect consensus and, thus, no need for police. Also, in a democracy, the government is established to serve the people, to follow their demands, and to operate with their consent. Much of policing, however, involves making people behave against their wishes or prohibiting them from doing what they please. Related to this, a basic element of democracy is freedom, and much of the police job involves limiting or revoking freedom. An additional aspect of democracy is equality; however, citizens do not deal with the police on an equal basis. The police are armed and have the authority to demand cooperation from the public. So, in many ways, the exercise of policing is in direct conflict with the values of our democratic society.

These and other conflicts reflect our continuing pursuit of ordered liberty. In our society we basically believe that all people should be free to do as they please. However, we also recognize that the exercise of total freedom by one person necessarily limits the freedom available to others. The basic problem, then, becomes one of designing the boundaries on individual freedom. We see that individual freedom must be limited, but we want to limit it as little as possible. We have not found a neat equation for determining just how much to limit individual freedom, and so all of us have our own opinions on the matter, and our opinions change over time. None of this helps the police, who must make difficult decisions every day about limiting the freedom of individuals. Although we recognize that the police function has to be done, we basically do not like what the police do.

Police officers and police administrators quickly become aware of their less-than-exalted positions in society. Many of them take the dislike personally and become upset and frustrated because they know that they are trying to do the job the best way they know how. Police officials are also frequently scrutinized by the media and feel that their actions are portrayed unfairly. If police personnel have an understanding of their role in a democratic society, however, they will understand, and perhaps even appreciate, the dislike and distrust that are inherent factors in the policing process.

Police administrators are in an especially difficult position, because the public will hold them accountable for crime control, while at the same time distrusting them for the functions performed by their organizations. This distrust will be reflected in numerous constraints being placed on the measures available to the police for controlling crime. The police are required to obtain arrest and search warrants from the courts, they must advise suspects not to incriminate themselves, their use of electronic surveillance is severely restricted, and so on. Despite these constraints, the public still expects the police to control crime and holds the police administrator accountable for accomplishing that objective.

The police administrator truly is in a difficult position and should recognize it as such. Society cannot really make up its mind about what the police are supposed to accomplish or how they should accomplish it. A perfect democracy would not need the police, and so society accepts them only as a necessary evil. Society severely restricts the methods available to the police for controlling crime but still expects crime to be controlled. Somehow the police administrator has to operate and survive in this conflicting environment.

There are no easy answers to be given to police administrators. The job is a difficult one to perform well. Police administrators must constantly keep in mind that they are operating in a democratic society. They must understand (in fact, internalize) the democratic values of the society and the implications for their jobs and their organizations. Administrators must realize that the police are allowed to restrict freedom only so that the freedom of all can be protected and maximized. As Berkley has noted, "the police today are faced with the problem of improving their efficiency while, at the same time, maintaining democratic norms and values."[25] The solution to this difficult and perplexing problem must be democratic, moral, legal, and constitutional. One difficulty for the police administrator is that it must also be effective.

Community-Oriented Police Administration

In the modern era, the most promising and effective response to the difficult challenges of policing in a free society has been community policing (COP). The COP strategy, which has risen dramatically over the past decade or two, has some very important implications for police administration. To put it quite simply, if COP is a different way of doing policing, it may require a different approach to police administration—both a different approach to the internal role of running the police department and a different approach to the external role of dealing with the community and its problems. It is helpful to recognize four major dimensions of community policing,[26] and then consider their impact on police administration:

1. the philosophical dimension
2. the strategic dimension
3. the tactical dimension
4. the organizational dimension

The *philosophical dimension* includes the central ideas and beliefs underlying COP, such as the necessity of citizen input, the broad nature of the police function, and the need for police to provide tailored and personal service to the public. The police administrator's responsibility in this realm is to articulate the agency's philosophy of policing, communicate it to both employees and the community, persuade employees and citizens of its sensibility, and make sure that the philosophy really guides the actions of officers. This is a challenging mandate.

The *strategic dimension* provides the link between the broad ideas and beliefs that underlie COP and the specific programs and practices by which it is implemented. This dimension assures that agency policies, priorities, and resource allocation are consistent with the community-oriented philosophy. Three strategic elements of community policing are (1) alternative police operational strategies, (2) a sharper geographic focus, and (3) a stronger emphasis on prevention. Establishing strategic directions, and seeing that they really guide the police organization's policies, priorities, and decisions, is one of the central responsibilities of any police administrator. Changing the organization's priorities and allocation of resources is an important step in the process of implementing COP or any other new strategy.

The *tactical dimension* of community policing ultimately translates ideas, philosophies, and strategies into concrete programs, practices, and behaviors. Three of the most important tactical elements of COP are positive interactions with the public, partnerships, and a problem-oriented approach to police work. These nuts-and-bolts activities are primarily carried out by police officers, detectives, and other operational-level personnel, not by police administrators. Administrators, though, must assure that these kinds of activities really get implemented, especially if they are different from traditional methods of policing in a department. This may simply require good, sound traditional police management practice, or it may require innovative and different approaches to police administration that correspond better with the new and different activities associated with community policing.

The *organizational dimension* directly addresses the changes in police organization, administration, management, and supervision that might be required to support and facilitate the implementation of COP. Such changes may be necessary in at least three areas: structure (how authority, responsibility, and tasks are arranged in the police organization), management (the process of running the organization and dealing with employees), and information (the types of data and information that are needed, and the systems for providing that information). Many police departments have already discovered that how they are structured, how they are managed, and how they use information does not correspond very well with their new COP philosophy, strategies, and tactics. These and other agencies are currently searching for, and experimenting with, alternative organizational practices that provide a better "fit" with the new way that they want to do business—i.e., community policing.

Throughout this text we will be presenting information and techniques that are consistent with a community-oriented approach to police administration. These approaches build upon many of the traditional and fundamental principles of police administration and are consistent with the social, political, and legal contexts of policing discussed earlier in this chapter. In some cases we explicitly use the community-oriented label, but mostly we just try to present the best information and practices that we have found for conducting the challenging responsibility of police administration in a free society.

Ten Guiding Principles

Much of the remainder of this book is focused on the details of police administration, on successfully running a police organization. Just as it is easy in the real world to get caught up in handling day-to-day problems and crises, however, it is easy when studying a subject to get lost in the details and lose one's bearings. For that reason, we suggest that you periodically review the following 10 principles of policing and police administration in a democratic society. These principles should provide you with a solid framework for the study and practice of modern police administration. They are timeless and impervious to trends and fads—these principles can still be used 20 years from now, whether at that time we say we are doing community policing, professional policing, or just plain good policing for a democratic society.

1. The police are a general-purpose government agency that provides a wide variety of services to the community, including law enforcement and crime control.

2. The police get their authority from the law, the community, political superiors, and the police profession, and are ultimately responsible to each of these sources of authority.

3. The overriding objectives in every police action or decision must be the protection of life and property and the maintenance of order.

4. Protection of life is always the primary objective of policing; the relative importance of protecting property and maintaining order may vary from place to place and from time to time.

5. Law enforcement is not an objective of policing; rather, it is one method that is sometimes employed in the effort to protect life and property and maintain order.

6. The police are rightly constrained in the methods they can employ in pursuing their objectives; they must resist the temptation to employ unauthorized methods.

7. The police must treat each individual person and situation according to the particular circumstances encountered; but individualized treatment may not include discrimination on the basis of race, ethnicity, religion, gender, social class, or other improper criteria.

8. The police must be willing and capable of employing force when justified to achieve legitimate objectives, but the use of force must always be a last resort, and the police must strive to develop nonviolent methods of gaining cooperation.

9. Police must ultimately be guided by ethical and legal standards that may sometimes conflict with, and must supersede, organizational, community, and peer pressures.

10. The police are unavoidably associated with those in power; yet they have a special responsibility to protect both those furthest from power and the democratic political process itself.

Summary

This chapter helps lay a foundation for the rest of the book. It presents the historical, social, political, legal, and democratic contexts of American policing, as well as some implications of community policing and some timeless guiding principles so that you can gain a better appreciation of where police administration has been and what its present environment is like. These contexts exert important influences on the people, processes, and organization of policing. They make police administration in our society very challenging, to say the least.

Discussion Questions

1. Do you agree that in our society there is a lack of agreement about the goals and objectives of policing? What do you think are or should be the goals and objectives of the police? List them in order of importance.

2. What do you think is the proper role of politics with respect to policing?

3. Policing in America is a fragmented, primarily local function. Do you think it should be? Would you alter this arrangement in any way? What purposes does the fragmentation of policing serve?

4. The text says that in large measure policing conflicts with our democratic values. What is meant by that? Do you agree? Is that the way things should be? As a police officer, how would you personally deal with this conflict?

5. What is your perception of community policing, and what implications do you think COP has for how police departments should be organized and managed?

Notes

1. A.C. Germann, F.D. Day, and R.R.J. Gallati, *Introduction to Law Enforcement and Criminal Justice* (Springfield, IL: Charles C Thomas, 1969), pp. 54-55.

2. G.L. Kelling and M.H. Moore, "The Evolving Strategy of Policing," *Perspectives on Policing* No. 4. (Washington, DC: National Institute of Justice, 1988).

3. See C.B. Saunders Jr., *Upgrading the American Police: Education and Training for Better Law Enforcement* (Washington, DC: Brookings Institution, 1970).

4. A. Vollmer, *The Police and Modern Society* (Berkeley, CA: University of California Press, 1936).

5. B. Smith, *Police Systems in the United States* (New York, NY: Harper & Brothers, 1940).

6. O.W. Wilson, *Police Administration* (New York, NY: McGraw-Hill, 1950).

7. National Commission on Law Observance and Enforcement, *Report on Police* (Washington, DC: U.S. Government Printing Office, 1931).

8. President's Commission on Law Enforcement and Administration of Justice, *Task Force Report: The Police* (Washington, DC: U.S. Government Printing Office, 1967).

9. R.M. Fogelson, *Big-City Police* (Cambridge, MA: Harvard University Press, 1977).

10. D.L. Carter, A.D. Sapp, and D.W. Stephens, *The State of Police Education: Policy Direction for the Twenty-first Century* (Washington, DC: Police Executive Research Forum, 1989).

11. G.W. Cordner, "Open and Closed Models of Police Organizations: Traditions, Dilemmas, and Practical Considerations," *Journal of Police Science and Administration* 6, no. 1 (March 1978): 22-34; G.W. Cordner, "Written Rules and Regulations: Are They Necessary?" *FBI Law Enforcement Bulletin* (July 1989): 17-21.

12. See G.W. Cordner and D.C. Hale, eds., *What Works in Policing? Operations and Administration Examined* (Cincinnati, OH: Anderson, 1992).

13. M.H. Moore and R.C. Trojanowicz, "Corporate Strategies for Policing," *Perspectives on Policing* No. 6 (Washington, DC: National Institute of Justice, 1988).

14. Bureau of Justice Assistance, *Understanding Community Policing: A Framework for Action* (Washington, DC: Bureau of Justice Assistance, 1994).

15. J.Q. Wilson, "Dilemmas of Police Administration," *Public Administration Review* (September–October 1968): 407-417.

16. V.G. Strecher, *The Environment of Law Enforcement: A Community Relations Guide* (Englewood Cliffs, NJ: Prentice Hall, 1971).

17. L. Fridell, R. Lunney, D. Diamond, and B. Kubu, *Racially Biased Policing: A Principled Response* (Washington, DC: Police Executive Research Forum, 2001); M.E. Buerger and A. Farrell, "The Evidence of Racial Profiling: Interpreting Documented and Unofficial Sources," *Police Quarterly* 5, no. 3 (September 2002): 272-305.

18. K.D. Tunnell and L.K. Gaines, "Political Pressures and Influences on Police Executives: A Descriptive Analysis," in G.W. Cordner and D.J. Kenney, eds., *Managing Police Organizations* (Cincinnati, OH: Anderson, 1996), pp. 5-17.

19. M.J. Hickman and B.A. Reaves, *Local Police Departments, 1999* (Washington, DC: Bureau of Justice Statistics, 2001); B.A. Reaves and T.C. Hart, "Federal Law Enforcement Officers, 2000," *Bulletin* (Washington, DC: Bureau of Justice Statistics, 2001).

20. G.W. Cordner and K.E. Scarborough, "Operationalizing Community Policing in Rural America: Sense and Nonsense," in Q.C. Thurman and E.F. McGarrell, eds., *Community Policing in a Rural Setting*, Second Edition (Cincinnati, OH: Anderson, 2002).

21. D.N. Falcone and L.E. Wells, "The County Sheriff as a Distinctive Policing Modality," *American Journal of Police* 14, no. 3/4 (1995): 123-149.

22. V.E. Kappeler, *Critical Issues in Police Civil Liability*, Third Edition (Prospect Heights, IL: Waveland, 2001).

23. F. Scogin and S.L. Brodsky, "Fear of Litigation among Law Enforcement Officers," *American Journal of Police* 10, no. 1 (1991): 41-45.

24. G.E. Berkley, *The Democratic Policeman* (Boston, MA: Beacon Press, 1969).

25. Ibid., p. 19.

26. G.W. Cordner, "Community Policing: Elements and Effects," in G.P. Alpert and A. Piquero, eds., *Community Policing: Contemporary Readings*, Second Edition (Prospect Heights, IL: Waveland, 2000), pp. 45-62.

Suggested Reading

Fridell, Lorie, Robert Lunney, Drew Diamond, and Bruce Kubu. *Racially Biased Policing: A Principled Response*. Washington, DC: Police Executive Research Forum, 2001.

Gaines, Larry K. and Gary W. Cordner, eds. *Policing Perspectives: An Anthology*. Los Angeles, CA: Roxbury, 1999.

Jeffery T. Walker, ed. *Policing and the Law*. Upper Saddle River, NJ: Prentice Hall, 2002.

Walker, Samuel. *Popular Justice: A History of American Criminal Justice*. New York, NY: Oxford University Press, 1980.

Wilson, James Q. *Varieties of Police Behavior: The Management of Law and Order in Eight Communities*. Cambridge, MA: Harvard University Press, 1978.

The Nature of
Police Work

2

Learning Objectives

- Identify several explanations for the development of paid, full-time police forces in the early 1800s.

- Describe the evolution of police duties from the early 1800s to the present.

- Explain why it is inevitable that police officers have discretion in their law enforcement duties.

- Assess the evidence bearing on the question of whether police work is mainly crime control, order maintenance, or social service.

- Identify the core of the police role and the kinds of skills most relied upon by effective police officers.

Some managers and some authorities on management make the argument that "administration is administration," meaning that running a bakery, running a steel mill, running a baseball team, running a church, and running a police department all involve the same knowledge, skills, and abilities. This point of view has considerable merit. The manager of a bakery and a police chief both have to engage in planning if their organizations are to successfully achieve their objectives over a long period of time. The superintendent of a steel mill and a police chief both have to carefully organize resources and activities to be effective. The general manager of a baseball team and a police chief both must give generous attention to staffing in order to attract and retain the best possible personnel. The pastor of the parish and the police chief both concern themselves with directing and controlling their employees, as well as influencing others who look to them for guidance and comfort.

Administration is administration, up to a point. All managers perform similar functions, as described later in this text. All administration can be guided by some general principles. All managers must deal with the complexities of human behavior in organizations. It makes sense to have organizations such

23

as the American Management Association and the American Society for Public Administration, because managers of all kinds of organizations share common tasks, problems, and information needs.

However, there is a limit to the universality of management and administration. Most managers are expected to know something about the substance of what they are in charge of, beyond simply the process of management. Many managers, in fact, have considerable experience doing the kind of work that they now manage. Certainly it is the rare police chief, sheriff, or police commissioner who does not have experience "on the street" (although "lateral entry" out of college or from other professions into police command positions is common in other countries).[1]

Aside from the commonsense belief that managers should know something about what they are managing, there is a more fundamental limitation on the "administration is administration" viewpoint. It seems quite apparent that such administrative matters as the opportunity for realistic planning, the form of organizational structure that is most efficient, the applicability of technical personnel practices, and the means by which employee behavior can best be directed and controlled depend significantly on the nature of the work that is performed in the organization.[2] In other words, despite all the commonalities inherent in management of any kind, and thus the problems and tasks shared by bakery managers, steel mill superintendents, baseball team general managers, church pastors, and police chiefs, all of these administrators also have their own unique organizational situations that make their jobs somewhat different.

Our argument is that police administration is unique because police work is particularly different from most other kinds of work. Such characteristics of police work as discretion, authority, variety, ambiguity, and danger distinguish it greatly from what most people do for a living. Moreover, these characteristics of the work have profound implications for police organization and management. Police administration is not merely a subtopic or branch of public administration or business administration, although it can borrow considerably from those disciplines; because the nature of the work performed by police organizations is unusual and distinctive, the separate and distinct study of police administration is warranted.

This chapter is about the nature of police work and its effect on the nature of police administration.

The Evolution of Police Work

In some respects, police work as we know it today is little different from that performed by the first London bobbies in 1829 and the first New York cops in 1845. Police then dealt with alcoholics, inebriates, wayward children, thieves, and smugglers, as they do now. In other respects, of course, police work has changed dramatically. While modern police ride in automobiles and are in direct radio communication with their superiors at all times, the first police officers walked their beats and had only the most primitive methods of communication available, such as beating their nightsticks on the pavement or blowing their whistles.

Why were full-time, paid, organized police forces created in England and America in the early 1800s? It is clear that both countries were undergoing industrialization and urbanization, trends that were significantly changing social and economic conditions. Neighbor no longer knew neighbor. Most of the people one encountered were strangers. People worked long hours under the worst conditions in a factory for a low wage, instead of working the land for food to eat and barter. Many of the people who came to the cities looking for wage-paying jobs found an insufficient number of jobs available and remained unemployed. Parents working in factories no longer maintained the same level of supervision over children as they had back on the farm, and children in cities engaged in more serious mischief than those who had lived under more controlled conditions in rural settings.

One explanation for the formation of modern police forces sees them as the logical government response to the inevitable consequences of urbanization and industrialization. In essence, police forces were a natural development in the march of civilization. A more cynical interpretation views the creation of the police as an action taken by ruling elites to bring under control the working classes and other dangerous and subversive elements. In this view the police are seen as the repressive arm of the capitalists who fostered and benefited from industrialization.[3]

Another factor in the development of the police was the failure of the military to handle civil disorder effectively. Food riots, draft riots, and race riots were not uncommon in London as well as in American cities in the early years of industrialization. Prior to the establishment of police forces, such riots and other civil disturbances had to be dealt with by the military. Too often, the military either failed to take action out of sympathy for the protesters, or it took oppressive action, treating the riot or disturbance as a military encounter and leaving extensive casualties.

Regardless of the reasoning behind the creation of organized police forces, it is clear that the first police were much more significantly engaged in maintaining order than in investigating crimes. Among the many duties performed by police in the 1800s were:

1. controlling alcoholics, inebriates, vagrants, the disorderly, and the homeless;
2. controlling gambling, prostitution, and other forms of vice;
3. controlling riots, disturbances, and crowds;
4. watching for fires;
5. maintaining basic public health standards in the streets and other common areas;

6. inspecting businesses, taverns, and lodging houses; and

7. licensing peddlers, transportation for hire, and other forms of commerce.

Prevention of crime was generally accepted as one function of the police, along with order maintenance and the provision of various government services. Police were expected to prevent crime by diligently patrolling their assigned beats so that wrongdoers would be deterred by the fear of police discovery. Police patrolling was expected to create a sense of police "omnipresence," a sense that the police were everywhere, or at least might always be right around the corner.

The early police did not devote a major portion of their time and resources to the investigation of crimes already committed, or to the apprehension of those responsible for committing serious crimes. Crime victims commonly offered rewards for the return of stolen property or the capture of assailants, and these rewards were largely the province of private detectives, informers, and, frequently, perpetrators themselves. There was a clear distinction between patrol work and detective work; patrol work was performed by the public police forces, while investigative work remained in the private domain.

Gradually, however, the public police became more involved in crime investigation and criminal apprehension, to the point that by the 1950s and 1960s the public's image of the police was that of crime fighters. Clearly, the police also came to see themselves as crime fighters. Exactly how and why the police function changed from being almost exclusively order maintenance to being dominated by crime fighting is open to debate, but these may be some of the reasons:

1. The public's expectations with respect to order, safety, and protection have increased. The public demanded that its police provide better and more comprehensive services, including protection from crime.

2. The legal system has sought to gain greater adherence by the police to legal norms. The police became less influenced by community norms and more influenced by legal norms. This orientation naturally inclined the police toward a focus on crimes, which are violations of legal norms.

3. Police evolution took place within the context of the reform era in American government.[4] Police departments had to specify their functions and gather data to demonstrate their efficiency and effectiveness. Crime-related and enforcement-related activities were much easier to quantify and justify than more nebulous order-maintenance activities.

4. The police sought professional status. Investigating crimes seemed more professional than dealing with alcoholics, inebriates, vagrants, and prostitutes. The police could claim special skills as well as the need for special training for investigating crimes, much more so than for maintaining order. Special equipment and scientific methods were also part of criminal investigation and could be cited as evidence that police work was a profession.

5. Products of modern technology that the police were able to include in their work, such as automobiles, radios, telephones, and computers, are all more consistent with a crime-attack model of policing than with a more informal, order-maintenance model.

6. An action-oriented mandate such as crime fighting is more in keeping with American cultural expectations than a passive or reserved mandate tied to informal community norms for order maintenance.[5] Thus, the evolution of American policing toward crimefighting may have been inevitable.

7. The influence of the media on the public's image of police work has contributed to the crime fighting image. Newspaper, radio, and television presentations on police emphasize crime fighting over order maintenance, because crime fighting is both more newsworthy and more entertaining than the more mundane aspects of order maintenance. The police and the public are both greatly influenced by these portrayals.

In considering these points it is important to note that the actual nature of police work and its popular image are not identical. While it is clear that police forces have become more involved in crime investigation and criminal apprehension than was originally the case, with crime fighting perceived by the public to be the cornerstone of the police image, the actual extent to which modern police work involves crime-related activity is very much in question. We will address this issue shortly.

Some of the changes in police work since the mid-1800s are so obvious that they are frequently overlooked. Today's police officer, for example, typically gives considerable attention to the traffic function, including traffic direction, enforcement, and accident investigation. It is not likely, though, that a police officer in 1870 spent time issuing traffic tickets or running radar. That officer may have been concerned with wagon and coach traffic jams but probably dealt with them as public order problems rather than as infractions of a traffic code requiring enforcement activity.

Numerous other changes in the nature of police work have occurred. Over the years criminal law has expanded to meet new social and environmental demands; the police today have more laws to enforce than did their predecessors. In recent years, crime has become more organized, presenting new and different challenges and problems. In the last few decades, the problem of drug abuse has become widespread, and society has looked to law enforcement for a solution. Drug law enforcement requires special kinds of operational strategies and tactics, such as undercover work and controlled buys, that raise ethical dilemmas and risk "dirtying" the police image.[6] In addition, drug law enforcement has made the police the enemies of many otherwise law-abiding middle-class citizens, a new group of drug users whose support the police had traditionally been able to take for granted.

Community policing and problem-oriented policing have also affected the nature of police work. Some police officers now spend substantial time meeting with community groups, analyzing and solving problems, working in schools, and collaborating with other governmental agencies, and thus less time patrolling, responding to calls, and investigating individual crimes. This leads to police work that is more visible and personal than bureaucratic, 911-style policing and tends to be associated with generalist, rather than specialist, approaches to policing.[7] It may also raise the levels of education, social skills, analytical skills, and maturity needed by police officers to higher standards than in the past.

On the other hand, many aspects of police work seem relatively unchanged since the days of Sir Robert Peel. Husbands and wives continue to have quarrels, occasionally requiring police intervention. People drink too much alcohol and need help finding their way home. Some have no home and need assistance so that they will not freeze to death on very cold nights. Children still run away from home, sometimes with tragic consequences. Loud parties still have to be quieted so that the family next door with the new baby can get a little sleep. Police work then and now is partly a matter of using common sense and good judgment to help sort out the kinds of problems that naturally arise between and among people with differing values, goals, and lifestyles.

Police Discretion

Typically associated with the crime-fighting view of police work has been the idea that police work primarily involves law enforcement. This approach sees policing mainly in terms of legal norms. Police officers are perceived as technicians trained to apply the law to problems of crime and disorder. Further, their law enforcement actions and activities are later reviewed by prosecutors and judges, who as legal experts ensure that the law has been properly applied. This "civics" explanation of police work emphasizes that the police neither make the laws nor sit in judgment of law violators; they "merely" enforce the law.

When sociological and legal scholars began studying the police in the 1950s, however, they discovered that police work, as actually practiced, differed substantially from this simplistic "mere enforcement" description. A major study by the American Bar Foundation found, for example, that police exercised considerable discretion in deciding whether to arrest and prosecute when a law is violated; that police develop methods other than law enforcement to deal with law violation situations; and that much of the work that police do is never seen by the courts and, thus, is not reviewed by prosecutors and judges.[8] Numerous studies over the last three decades have documented that police officers operate with considerable discretion; they do not simply enforce the law. In fact, over the wide range of circumstances and situations that the police confront, they actually enforce the law rather infrequently.

Police Discretion

[S]ome cops will tell drinking youths to "call it an evening" because the neighbors are complaining. Others will just tell them to move. Still others will tell the kids to move and then give them suggestions on where to drink so they won't be in the vicinity of households that might complain. How an officer handles a call is very much a matter of his personal outlook. Some cops are very much against drinking in public. One cop almost goes into hysteria at the sight of an open beer can. This officer arrests for public drinking. Some officers think marijuana smoking is a step on the road to heroin, and they will arrest people for possession of pot. Others, even if they get a complaint that people are smoking marijuana, will not arrest. They'll just tell the people involved to "knock it off." To them, marijuana smoking is no big deal.

Source: Stephen Francis Coleman, *Street Cops* (Salem, WI: Sheffield, 1986), p. 142.

In his study of eight communities, James Q. Wilson found that a police officer's discretion varied somewhat depending on the type of situation encountered.[9] He found that police had great latitude in self-initiated law enforcement situations, such as traffic or drug violations, mainly because there is rarely a victim or complainant demanding that a certain kind of action be taken. In citizen-initiated law enforcement situations, however, the police have less discretion—partly because the police usually have no clues about who committed the crime and also because, if the offender can be identified, the preferences of the citizen-initiator will often influence the officer's decision to arrest.

The police generally have considerable discretion in dealing with order-maintenance problems, whether police- or citizen-initiated, although their discretion is not totally unconstrained. When police officers discover a disorderly situation, they can react to it in many ways, ranging from ignoring the problem to arresting the disorderly person (see "Police Discretion," above). In this police-initiated situation, with no complainant and very possibly no witnesses, the police officers have great discretion in making a "low visibility decision."[10] When a citizen reports the disorder, the police officer is somewhat constrained by that citizen's wishes. However, in many order-maintenance situations, both parties have legitimate claims, throwing the discretion in the police officer's lap.

Police work entails selecting which of several options is the best solution to the problem at hand. If police work simply involved enforcing the law whenever a violation was observed, it would require no common sense, judgment, or wisdom, and very little education or training. It would also be easy to manage. However, police officers inevitably exercise discretion, for several reasons:

1. a police officer who attempted to enforce all the laws all of the time would be in the station house and in court all of the time and thus would be of little use when problems arose in the community;

2. legislatures pass some laws that they clearly do not intend to have strictly enforced all of the time;

3. legislatures pass some laws that are vague, making it necessary for the police to interpret them and decide when to apply them;

4. most law violations are minor in nature (speeding one mile per hour over the limit, parking 13 inches from the curb) and do not require full enforcement;

5. full enforcement of all the laws all of the time would alienate the public and undermine support for the police and the legal system;

6. full enforcement of all laws all of the time would overwhelm the courts and the correctional system; and

7. the police have many duties to perform with limited resources; good judgment must therefore be used in the establishment of enforcement priorities.

Of course, it is also true that police officers are human beings, with their own likes and dislikes, values, priorities, and susceptibilities. Thus, police officers may let law violators go free out of sympathy, because they like them, because they hope to get something in return, or because they think a particular law is unimportant or ridiculous.[11]

Enforcement of the law is best understood as one means employed in police work, rather than as an end in itself.[12] Ideally, the ends pursued by police work are its proper goals: the protection of life and property and the maintenance of order. When police officers confront problem situations in which these proper ends are in jeopardy, one means they might choose to employ as a remedy is law enforcement. In most instances they will have other options as well, especially if they are skillful and resourceful police officers. They might, for example, use conflict resolution techniques or issue a warning. In some situations they will choose to enforce the law by issuing a citation or making an arrest because that seems the best way to protect life and property and to maintain order. The law should not always be enforced simply because it is the law. Police officers have other choices, other solutions to problems, that in many situations offer more goal attainment than would be achieved by enforcing the law.

The myth of full enforcement and the reality of discretion create ethical dilemmas for the police. Most police officers promise to uphold the law when they are sworn to duty, and the laws of many states mandate that officers shall arrest whenever they have sufficient evidence. Officers must recognize the legislative intent behind such language in order to avoid feeling that they are shirking their duties when they exercise their discretion not to enforce the law. To assist officers in resolving this problem, police codes of ethics should emphasize service to the public and commitment to the primary goals of protection of life and property and maintenance of order rather than emphasizing strict enforcement of the law.

Discretion introduces another ethical dilemma into police work. Police officers sometimes confront situations in which it seems that the protection of life and property or the maintenance of order can be achieved only through the use of illegal, immoral, or unethical methods.[13] For example, the only way to save a kidnapping victim's life might be to coerce his or her location from a suspect in custody, as in the famous movie *Dirty Harry*. Police officers, sworn both to protect life and to obey rules and laws, are sometimes confronted by "no win" circumstances such as these, in which every option seems to carry ethical costs. We can guide officers in such situations by insisting that they always obey the law, but what if a life is at stake and, thus, the law that the officers are considering "bending" does not seem quite as serious?

There are no ready solutions to the ethical problems inherent in police work. It is important, however, that the existence of such problems be recognized by police officers and by the public. These ethical dilemmas illustrate the demanding nature of police work and the need for wisdom in police officers.

Crime Control, Order Maintenance, or Social Service?

When scholarly research on the police began in the 1950s, and when it came of age in the 1960s, the popular image of police work emphasized crime fighting and law enforcement. Because social science often amounts to exploring and debunking popular conceptions and misconceptions, it is not surprising that much of the early research focused on the extent to which police work actually did *not* involve crime fighting and law enforcement. Perhaps it could have been predicted that these results would challenge the popular image of policing.

The cumulative effect of several studies conducted between 1964 and 1971 was to change the scholarly view of police work.[14] In textbooks, college courses, and police training programs, it became common to find police work described as primarily involving order maintenance, services, or social work. Probably because police officers had always realized that their popular image as crime fighters was inaccurate and misleading, many officers accepted these new descriptions of police work. Although the average citizen may still think of the police primarily as crime fighters, over a rather short period of time the image of police work held by police officers and by students of policing changed dramatically.

Though these studies performed a valuable function by challenging the crime-fighting image of police work, it was perhaps inevitable that their conclusions would be carried too far. By the late 1970s it had become common to find police chiefs and scholars downplaying and deemphasizing the crime-related and law enforcement aspects of police work. At least one of the pioneering researchers, James Q. Wilson, noted this disquieting development, confessing that he would "prefer the police to act and talk as if they *were* able to control crime"[15] (emphasis in original).

In retrospect, these early studies had a number of serious shortcomings that seriously undermined their findings and contributed to their misinterpretation.[16] In addition, it is important to recognize that much of police work takes shape in the eye of the beholder. A domestic argument between husband and wife, for example, might best seem to fit in the order maintenance category. However, if the responding officers are trained in crisis intervention or if they refer the couple for counseling, they arguably have provided a social service. On the other hand, if a husband is found to have assaulted his wife, it is arguably a crime-related matter. If the police make an arrest or even just assist the wife in swearing out a warrant, the matter becomes a law enforcement issue. The category to which this incident would have been assigned varied greatly from researcher to researcher, making it difficult and tenuous to draw any solid conclusions from the research taken in its totality.

The most valid study of patrol work, in our opinion, is the Police Services Study conducted in 1977.[17] This study examined patrol work in 60 different neighborhoods, with observers accompanying patrol officers on all shifts in 24 police departments. The observers collected information on each encounter between a police officer and a citizen, detailing nearly 6,000 encounters in all. The fact that this study included so many different police departments, and police-initiated as well as citizen-initiated activity, makes it very persuasive.

The Police Services Study found that 38 percent of police-citizen encounters dealt primarily with crime-related problems. Most of these were nonviolent crimes or incidents involving suspicious circumstances. The next most common kinds of encounters were disorder problems and traffic-related matters, each accounting for 22 percent of the total. Finally, 18 percent of the police-citizen encounters were primarily of a service nature.

Similar results were found in two more recent studies. In Minneapolis, 32 percent of calls handled by police were classified as conflict management, 30 percent as crime, and 19 percent as traffic.[18] In Wilmington, Delaware, 26 percent of total patrol time was devoted to criminal matters, while 50 percent of patrol officers' time spent on call handling and public contact was crime-related.[19]

Taking all of these studies into consideration, we think a middle-of-the-road position is advisable. It is obvious now that police work is not so completely dominated by crime fighting as its public image and media misrepresentations would suggest. However, it is equally clear that crime-related matters occupy an appreciable portion of the police workload. The available research conclusively demonstrates that those who have been arguing that police work has little or nothing to do with crime know little or nothing about police work.

Police Work and the Meaning of Justice

It may appear preposterous to assert that patrolmen have the power to determine the course of justice; patrolmen obviously do not make the laws, nor do they set policy within a police department. Indeed, the contemporary view holds that much of what patrolmen do is not connected with law enforcement and justice at all; rather, they are all-around social workers who keep the peace and provide services. Patrolmen direct traffic, manage domestic disputes, administer stern warnings to wayward juveniles, find lost children, talk suicidal people down from rooftops and perform a variety of incidental administrative chores. Such a view obscures their coercive role and the political consequences of their decisions. Patrolmen make most of the arrests for major felonies, all decisions to stop and interrogate, and decisions not to enforce the law or take action, particularly in the context of assaults. If and when the police deny legal protection to individuals, abridge due process or employ distinctions of race and class, it is patrolmen who do so. In short, patrolmen are profoundly involved with the most significant questions facing any political order: those pertaining to justice, order and equity. They necessarily trade in the recurring moral antinomies that accompany political choice, and through the exercise of discretion patrolmen define and redefine the meaning of justice.

Source: Michael K. Brown, *Working the Street: Police Discretion and the Dilemmas of Reform* (New York, NY: Russell Sage Foundation, 1981), pp. 6-7.

The Core of the Police Role

Thus far in this chapter we have reviewed the evolution of police work, the discovery of police discretion, and the controversy over the crime-relatedness of modern police work. Some of the more important points made have been these:

1. Police work initially had much more to do with maintaining order than with crime investigation.
2. Police work became more involved with crime fighting, and today, crime-related matters make up a substantial part of police work.
3. Police officers have considerable discretion in performing their crime-fighting, law enforcement, and order-maintenance duties.
4. Law enforcement is best understood as one means employed by police officers to solve problems, rather than as an end in itself.

Although law enforcement is but one method used by the police to respond to the variety of problems that are encountered in police work, it is the method that we most tend to associate with the police. While we realize that the police let many lawbreakers go and that much of police work involves disputes that the police solve informally, we also know that enforcing the law is, and always will be, a useful and vitally important police tool.

Canadian criminologists Clifford Shearing and Jeffrey Leon have discussed the centrality of law enforcement in the role or function of the police. They refer to the police "license and capability," or, in other words, the authority and power vested in the police. They argue forcefully that:

> any suggestion, on the basis of the fact that policemen seldom actually enforce the law or use physical force, that the police in reality serve a "social service" rather than a "law enforcement" function is clearly unfounded. Equally unfounded is any attempt to classify police activity into two classes, "social service" or "law enforcement."

> Because the symbolic backdrop of the police license and capability is always present whenever a police officer responds to a problem, he is always responding as a police officer and not as a social worker, whether amateur or professional. Indeed, the continual presence of the police license and capability militates against his ever being able to play the role of a social worker, as everyone (including the police officer) will know that ultimately he has access to the means uniquely accessible to police officers.[20]

The argument presented here is an important one for our discussion of the nature of police work. When reviewing the findings of studies of police tasks, citizen calls for police service, and police-citizen encounters, we run the risk of not seeing the forest for the trees. We need to look at the bigger picture, the function that police perform in the social and political systems. One approach to this is to ask what functions of the police are unique—functions that are not performed by other public agents.

According to Shearing and Leon, one of these functions is law enforcement. Egon Bittner has gone further and argued that the use of force is at the core of the police role. He notes that many kinds of public agents enforce laws, but it is the police we call when "something-ought-not-to-be-happening-and-about-which-something-ought-to-be-done-NOW!"[21] In doing something about such conditions, it is the police who can ultimately force compliance (see "Police Work and the Meaning of Justice," p. 33). They have the legal authority, the tools, the training, and the skills to coerce us into behaving differently. Stated more eloquently by Bittner, "the role of the police is best understood as a mechanism for the distribution of non-negotiably coercive force employed in accordance with the dictates of an intuitive grasp of situational exigencies."[22]

Bittner's argument does not imply that the police frequently use force against the public. The point is that the police "license and capability" to use force is always lurking in the background. In any particular situation, the police may attempt to counsel, refer, persuade, cajole, convince, or con citizens into changing their behavior, and in this respect they may seem to act as social workers. However, citizens reacting to the police know that, in the final analysis, the police can force them to cease and desist, if necessary by arrest; that is, police can use that ultimate power as leverage in gaining compliance.

Bittner's description of the role of the police contains some other important ingredients. "Non-negotiably coercive force" indicates that the police officer, not the citizen, decides whether to use force and how much force to use. Bittner's choice of the term "intuitive grasp" suggests that the police officer draws on common sense, judgment, and other personal resources when analyzing and acting on a situation, rather than on rules, training, or supervision. The officer considers primarily "situational exigencies," that is, the nature of the specific situation at hand. The officer does not rely on a predetermined plan of action, because no such plan could possibly cover the variety and complexity of situations that might arise.

To the ordinary citizen, common sense suggests that the function of the police may be defined very simply by reference to law enforcement and the use of force. However, over the last two decades, police officers and students of the police have emphasized the social service and order maintenance functions of the police. As we have shown, maintaining order, providing social services, and responding to crime-related problems all account for a sizable share of police activity. Yet, when we ask what sets the police apart from other government workers, it is their "license and capability"—their authority to enforce the law and their power to use force. As Shearing and Leon concluded, "the common sense view of the police as law enforcers and crime-fighters contains an important element of truth that has recently been obscured as a result of the interpretations that have been made of the findings of studies analyzing police activity."[23]

The Skill of Policing

Although the use of force is at the core of the police role, the police do not use force frequently. Similarly, although the police authority to enforce the law is an important factor in most situations that the police handle, the police have considerable discretion in deciding whether to invoke the law, and more often than not, they find other means for resolving problems.

The Police Services Study that was mentioned earlier in connection with the nature of police-citizen encounters also examined the specific actions that police officers took in those encounters.[24] Remember that this study included almost 6,000 police-citizen encounters from 60 different neighborhoods. The figures below indicate the proportion of all encounters in which police officers took each kind of action. (The figures add up to more than 100 percent because officers often took more than one type of action in an encounter.)

57%	Interviewed a witness or person requesting service
40%	Interrogated a suspect
29%	Conducted a search or inspection
28%	Lectured or threatened (other than threat of force)
27%	Gave information
23%	Gave reassurance
14%	Used force or threat of force
11%	Gave assistance
19%	Gave a ticket
18%	Used persuasion
15%	Made an arrest
12%	Gave medical help

The police invoked the law relatively rarely, making arrests in only five percent of the encounters and issuing tickets in less than one of 10 encounters. Officers used force or the threat of force in 14 percent of the encounters (with force actually used in five percent, most of this amounting only to handcuffing or taking a suspect by the arm). The use of force or its threat was about equally likely in situations involving crime, disorder, and traffic encounters, but very rare in service situations.

Perhaps the most interesting characteristic of police work revealed by the figures is the importance of communication skills. Five of the six most common actions taken by officers consisted entirely of talking and listening. These five were interviewing, interrogating, lecturing or threatening, giving information, and giving reassurance. It is primarily by communicating that police officers determine what is going on in any given situation, and it is primarily through communicating that an amicable solution is reached. Enforcing the law and using force often come into play only after communication tactics and informal solutions prove unsuccessful, although it should be noted that serious law violations may require immediate enforcement and very dangerous suspects may warrant immediate use of force.

This brings us to what we think is a tremendously important synopsis of the police role in our society:

1. the core of the police role involves law enforcement and the use of coercive force;
2. the primary skill of policing involves effectively handling problem situations while avoiding the use of force;
3. skillful police officers avoid the use of force primarily through effective, creative communication.[25]

We give our police officers considerable authority in enforcing the law and using force. The nature of police work demands that officers be given discretion in exercising this authority. Good police officers understand that enforcing the law and using force are means to an end, methods that may be used under some circumstances for solving problems. Generally they will search for other solutions first, mostly involving good communication: talking and listening. These officers are neither afraid nor reluctant to do their duty, they simply know a means from an end and understand their role. As Carl Klockars has put it, "using coercive force is never a good thing for professional police officers, but when they have used all their skills to avoid its use and something must be done, it is necessary."[26]

Management Implications

Now that we have discussed some important aspects of the nature of police work, what does it all mean for police administration? While the rest of this book takes up that question in some detail, we should consider a few important additional issues before we attempt to answer that question.

Perhaps more than anything else, the matter of police discretion complicates police administration. If police officers "merely" applied rules and laws in clear-cut situations, then police management would "merely" involve teaching those rules and laws and periodically checking to make sure that they were being applied correctly. Instead, police officers decide what action to take, based on what Bittner calls "an intuitive grasp of situational exigencies"; they use common sense and judgment to size up each problem situation and then choose a solution to the problem. Although they have rules and laws to draw upon, they are frequently expected to apply the rules and laws only as a last resort.

Adding to problems created by discretion, the situations that police are thrust into are often tense and dangerous. Decisions often have to be made quickly, with supervisors rarely present to give advice. Moreover, peoples' families and reputations, and sometimes their freedom and their very lives, are at stake; in other words, it really matters whether the officer makes a wise, intelligent, and compassionate decision.

The importance of the decisions that police officers make necessitates the establishment and enforcement of policies and procedures. There must be strict guidelines governing critical operational issues, such as, for example, the use of force (especially deadly force) and high-speed driving. At the same time, those "situational exigencies" referred to by Bittner necessitate that officers have some leeway to use judgment (discretion) because each situation is to some extent unique. Part of the skill of the police administrator is in the delicate balancing of these demands for rules and for discretion.[27]

The need to use discretion, coupled with the seriousness of the decisions that police officers make, has profound implications for police selection and training. Police agencies need to attract and hire the kinds of people who can be entrusted with such awesome responsibilities. Common sense, maturity, good judgment, wisdom, intelligence, communication ability, and command of emotions are as important as a strong back and, in many instances, much more important. Police training needs to address not only procedural rules and substantive laws, but also when and how to use them, when and how to avoid their use, and when and how to use force when force is appropriate. In addition, it needs to produce officers who can "innovate, solve problems, develop alliances, negotiate, and internalize the values of community policing."[28] Training needs to focus less on memorization and much more on "the particularities of police work as it is experienced by serving officers and . . . analyzing that experience and making it available to future police officers."[29]

Even the best classroom training is unlikely to fully prepare a police recruit for the wise exercise of police discretion. Not every kind of situation can be simulated in training, nor can every nuance of police response be duplicated. Further, some of the skills that officers might apply, especially creative communication skills, cannot be readily taught in brief classroom training sessions. For these reasons, much of police work has traditionally been learned on the job, usually from a skillful veteran police officer. This is one of the reasons why James Q. Wilson refers to police work as a craft rather than a profession.[30] Crafts are traditionally learned by way of apprenticeship, whereas professional preparation primarily involves formal classroom training. Once professionals have mastered their body of knowledge, their work is fairly straightforward application of that knowledge. Craftsmen, however, always have to adapt their skills to the materials and situations with which they work, with each outcome being somewhat unpredictable and a little bit different from any other (see "Science or Craft?").

Science or Craft?

[F]rom the point of view of the patrol officer, policing is more like a craft than a science, in that officers believe that they have important lessons to learn that are not reducible to principle and are not being taught through formal education. These lessons concern goals—which ones are reasonable; tactics—which ones ensure achievement of different goals in varying circumstances; and presence—how to cultivate a career-sustaining personality. "Experience-tested good sense," as one officer said, is what police must learn over the years.

What has not been grasped, however, is that even as policing at the present time is more craft than science, learning can take place, skills can be increased, and levels of expertise can be discerned. Officers themselves recognize this point when they talk about how they "learned" to become effective.

Source: David H. Bayley and Egon Bittner, "Learning the Skills of Policing," in Roger G. Dunham and Geoffrey P. Alpert, eds., *Critical Issues in Policing: Contemporary Readings*, Fourth Edition. (Prospect Heights, IL: Waveland, 2001), pp. 96-97.

What organizational structure and management style are appropriate for such an enterprise? If we were to judge by the typical police department, our answer would be a hierarchical, centralized organization with an authoritarian, punishment-oriented management style.[31] Some observers doubt, however, that this style of administration is best suited to manage workers (police officers) whose jobs involve making momentous life-and-death discretionary decisions, in unpredictable situations, without the benefit of supervisory advice.[32] We agree with these observers.

As you read on in the book about principles of administration, management functions, styles of leadership, and subsequent topics, review them against the characteristics and peculiarities of police work as we have presented them in this chapter.

Summary

This chapter has examined the nature of police work on the premise that police administration is different from other forms of administration, because police work is different from other forms of work. The evolution of police work from its early emphasis on peacekeeping to its more recent emphasis on crime fighting was discussed along with the debate about the extent to which modern police work actually is crime-related. Research clearly indicates that police work involves substantial crime-related and order-maintenance activities as well as traffic- and service-related functions.

The core of the police role revolves around law enforcement and the use of force, yet police officers have great discretion in enforcing the law and only infrequently use force. The skill of policing is in avoiding the use of force while still accomplishing the goals of protecting life and property and maintaining order. The principal means by which police officers get their jobs done without resorting to force involves communication: talking and listening, reasoning, reassuring, lecturing, persuading, convincing, and otherwise getting people to comply with the law and reduce their disorderliness. Because communication does not always produce the expected or hoped-for results, when police confront "something-that-ought-not-to-be-happening-and-about-which-something-ought-to-be-done-NOW," they must be willing and able to use force when and if it is justified and necessary.

Discussion Questions

1. The police have discretion when deciding whether to issue a ticket, whether to "check out" a suspicious person, and whether to arrest. Is this a good thing? Could police discretion be eliminated? Can it be controlled?

2. Do you agree with us that the media typically misrepresent the real nature of police work? What are the consequences of this misrepresentation? How does it affect the general public's perception of the police? Police self-perception?

3. The police do not often use force, and yet the use of force is at the core of their role. How do you explain this apparent contradiction? Could the police role be changed? Should it be changed?

4. Skillful police officers use communication to get cooperation from victims, witnesses, suspects, and other citizens, thus avoiding the use of force except when absolutely necessary. By what methods would you select the best communicators from among applicants for police jobs? How would you teach communication skills to police recruits and develop those skills among current police officers?

5. Various authorities have classified police officers as bureaucrats, as professionals, or as members of a craft. In which category do you think police work belongs? Why?

Notes

1. G. Berkley, *The Democratic Policeman* (Boston, MA: Beacon Press, 1969).

2. J. Woodward, *Management and Technology* (London: Her Majesty's Stationery Office, 1958); C. Perrow, *Complex Organizations: A Critical Essay*, Third Edition (New York, NY: McGraw-Hill, 1986).

3. P.K. Manning, *Police Work: The Social Organization of Policing*, Second Edition (Prospect Heights, IL: Waveland, 1997).

4. R.M. Fogelson, *Big-City Police* (Cambridge, MA: Harvard University Press, 1977).

5. P.K. Manning, "The Police: Mandate, Strategies and Appearances," in *Policing: A View from the Street*, P.K. Manning and J. Van Maanen, eds. (Santa Monica, CA: Goodyear, 1978).

6. J.Q. Wilson, *The Investigators: Managing FBI and Narcotics Agents* (New York, NY: Basic Books, 1978).

7. P.K. Manning, "Community-Based Policing," in G.P. Alpert and A. Piquero, eds., *Community Policing: Contemporary Readings*, Second Edition (Prospect Heights, IL: Waveland, 2000), pp. 23-34.

8. W.R. LaFave, *Arrest: The Decision to Take a Suspect into Custody* (Boston, MA: Little, Brown, 1965).

9. J.Q. Wilson, *Varieties of Police Behavior: The Management of Law and Order in Eight Communities* (Cambridge, MA: Harvard University Press, 1968), pp. 83-89.

10. J. Goldstein, "Police Discretion Not to Invoke the Criminal Justice Process: Low Visibility Decisions in the Administration of Justice," *Yale Law Journal* 69 (March 1960): 543-594.

11. S.F. Coleman, *Street Cops* (Salem, WI: Sheffield, 1986).

12. H. Goldstein, *Policing a Free Society* (Cambridge, MA: Ballinger, 1977).

13. C.B. Klockars, "The Dirty Harry Problem," *Annals of the American Academy of Political and Social Science* 452 (November 1980): 33-47.

14. M. Banton, *The Policeman in the Community* (New York, NY: Basic Books, 1964); J.H. Skolnick, *Justice without Trial: Law Enforcement in a Democratic Society* (New York, NY: John Wiley and Sons, 1966); Wilson, *Varieties of Police Behavior*; A.J. Reiss Jr., *The Police and the Public* (New Haven, CT: Yale University Press, 1971); T. Bercal, "Calls for Police Assistance," *American Behavioral Scientist* 13 (1970); J.A. Webster, "Police Task and Time Study," *Journal of Criminal Law, Criminology and Police Science* 61 (1970): 94-100.

15. Wilson, *Varieties of Police Behavior*, 1978 edition, p. x.

16. G.W. Cordner, "Police Patrol Work Load Studies: A Review and Critique," *Police Studies* 2 (1979): 50-60; J.F. Elliott, *Interception Patrol* (Springfield, IL: Charles C Thomas, 1973), p. 6; G.L. Kelling, T. Pate, D. Dieckman, and C.E. Brown, *The Kansas City Preventive Patrol Experiment: A Technical Report* (Washington, DC: Police Foundation, 1974), p. 500.

17. G.P. Whitaker, "What Is Patrol Work?" *Police Studies* 4 (1982): 13-22.

18. L. Sherman, *Repeat Calls to Police in Minneapolis* (Washington, DC: Crime Control Institute, 1987).

19. J.R. Greene and C.B. Klockars, "What Police Do," in *Thinking about Police: Contemporary Readings*, Second Edition, C.B. Klockars and S.D. Mastrofski, eds. (New York, NY: McGraw-Hill, 1991), pp. 273-284.

20. C.D. Shearing and J.S. Leon, "Reconsidering the Police Role: A Challenge to a Challenge of a Popular Conception," *Canadian Journal of Criminology and Corrections* 19 (1977): 342.

21. E. Bittner, "Florence Nightingale in Pursuit of Willie Sutton: A Theory of the Police," in *The Potential for Reform of Criminal Justice*, H. Jacob, ed. (Beverly Hills, CA: Sage, 1974), p. 30.

22. E. Bittner, *The Functions of the Police in Modern Society: A Review of Background Factors, Current Practices, and Possible Role Models* (Washington, DC: U.S. Government Printing Office, 1970), p. 46.

23. Shearing and Leon, "Reconsidering the Police Role," p. 343.

24. Whitaker, "What is Police Work?"

25. Bittner, *Functions of the Police*; W.K. Muir Jr., *Police: Streetcorner Politicians* (Chicago, IL: University of Chicago Press, 1977); C.B. Klockars, ed., *Thinking about Police: Contemporary Readings* (New York, NY: McGraw-Hill, 1983), pp. 227-231; Coleman, *Street Cops*.

26. Klockars, ibid., p. 231.

27. G.W. Cordner, "Written Rules and Regulations: Are They Necessary?" *FBI Law Enforcement Bulletin* (July 1989): 17-21; G.P. Alpert and W.C. Smith, "Developing Police Policy: An Evaluation of the Control Principle," in G.W. Cordner and D.J. Kenney, eds., *Managing Police Organizations* (Cincinnati, OH: Anderson, 1996), pp. 111-126.

28. F. Himelfarb, "RCMP Learning and Renewal: Building on Strengths," in Q.C. Thurman and E.F. McGarrell, eds., *Community Policing in a Rural Setting* (Cincinnati, OH: Anderson, 1997), p. 34.

29. D.H. Bayley and E. Bittner, "Learning the Skills of Policing," in *Critical Issues in Policing: Contemporary Readings*, Fourth Edition, R.G. Dunham and G.P. Alpert, eds. (Prospect Heights, IL: Waveland, 2001), p. 83.

30. J.Q. Wilson, "Dilemmas of Police Administration," *Public Administration Review* 28 (1968): 407-417.

31. G.B. Sandler and E. Mintz, "Police Organizations: Their Changing Internal and External Relationships," *Journal of Police Science and Administration* 2 (1974): 458; M.K. Brown, *Working the Street: Police Discretion and the Dilemmas of Reform* (New York, NY: Russell Sage Foundation, 1981).

32. R.A. Myren, "A Crisis in Police Management," *Journal of Criminal Law, Criminology and Police Science* 50 (1960): 600-604; Bittner, *Functions of the Police*; T.J. Cowper, "The Myth of the 'Military Model' of Leadership in Law Enforcement," *Police Quarterly* 3, no. 3 (September 2000): 228-246; M.E. Buerger, "Reenvisioning Police, Reinvigorating Policing: A Response to Thomas Cowper," *Police Quarterly* 3, no. 4 (December 2000): 451-464.

Suggested Reading

Bittner, Egon. *The Functions of the Police in Modern Society*. Washington, DC: U.S. Government Printing Office, 1970.

Lersch, Kim Michelle. *Policing and Misconduct*. Upper Saddle River, NJ: Prentice Hall, 2002.

Manning, Peter K. *Police Work: The Social Organization of Policing*, Second Edition. Prospect Heights, IL: Waveland, 1997.

Mawby, R.I., ed. *Policing across the World: Issues for the Twenty-first Century*. London: University College Press, 1999.

Waddington, P.A.J. *Policing Citizens: Authority and Rights*. London: University College Press, 1999.

Police Goals and Systems

3

Learning Objectives

- Identify three primary police goals.

- Identify eight primary police objectives.

- Explain the importance of efficiency, legality, equity, and accountability in guiding police actions and decisions.

- Identify the three primary characteristics of systems.

- Define feedback, explain its role in differentiating between open-loop and closed-loop systems, and explain the difference between open and closed systems.

One of the fundamental themes in this book is the systems approach to police administration. Basically, this approach emphasizes the interrelatedness that characterizes modern society and the necessity of viewing people, organizations, and processes as parts of larger systems. The systems approach, with its stress on interrelatedness, helps us to keep these external influencing factors in mind. And as the forces of change, complexity, and interdependence in our society continue to grow stronger, the need for the systems approach to organizing and managing will increase.

Any system, especially an organizational system, is created and maintained for a reason—to accomplish some kind of purpose. This chapter begins by discussing the purposes of police organizations—their missions, goals, and objectives—and then explains why we believe the systems approach to police administration is an extremely useful perspective from which to manage a police department. We hope this discussion will give you a useful framework for reading and thinking about the rest of the book, which deals with the behavior, processes, and organization entailed in police administration.

The Purposes of the Police

Organizations, including police departments, by their nature exist for a purpose. Schools have as their purpose the education of students; hospitals, the treatment of the sick and injured. The purpose of a private company in our capitalistic economic system is to make money for its owners. In a socialistic system, the same company's purpose might be to provide employment or some kind of product or service.

In actuality, of course, most organizations have multiple purposes. The most general statement of an organization's purpose is often called its *mission*. Slightly more specific purposes are termed *goals*; even more precise purposes are labeled *objectives*. These purposes should serve to guide the development of strategies, tactics, programs, tasks, policies, procedures, and rules, all of which in turn guide the behavior of members of the organization, as shown in Figure 3.1.

Figure 3.1
The Relationship between Overall Mission and Specific Organizational Behavior

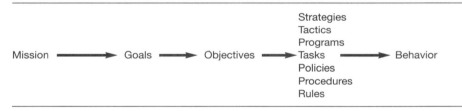

When this process works from left to right, as indicated by the arrows in Figure 3.1, management is following a rational and proactive path. If, on the other hand, the process works from right to left, management tends to be crisis-oriented and reactive. It is crucially important for any organization's executives to continuously focus attention on the purposes of the enterprise and to design strategies and tasks that will accomplish those purposes. However, strategies and tasks are often undertaken out of tradition or because they offer the path of least resistance. This tendency is common and must be resisted.

Another frequent source of misdirection arises because of the difference between official and unofficial purposes. For example, while the avowed purposes of a university might be the education of students and the production of new knowledge, the actual purpose might seem to be the accumulation of the maximum number of federal grants and contracts. Similarly, a hospital might officially exist for the purpose of treating the sick and injured, but in fact it might serve primarily to provide interesting and profitable work for surgeons and other medical specialists.

We point out this distinction between official and unofficial purposes as a kind of disclaimer. On the pages that follow, we present and discuss the mission, goals, and objectives of policing—these are the official purposes of the police, what police departments and police officers are *supposed* to be trying to achieve. Needless to say, many police agencies and officers are also guided by unofficial purposes. Such unofficial purposes can be as mundane as simply avoiding hard work, or as deviant and dangerous as making life miserable for minorities, creating dossiers on political activists, meting out "street justice," or collecting graft and corruption.[1] Unofficial purposes are as inevitable in police departments as in any other kind of organization. It is the police executive's responsibility to assure that official purposes remain supreme and that unofficial purposes do not substantially distract the organization (see "Values in Policing").

Values in Policing

All organizations have values. One can see these values expressed through the actions of the organization—the things that are taken seriously and the things that are rejected as irrelevant, inappropriate, or dangerous. Jokes, solemn understandings, and internal explanations for actions also express values.

Police departments are powerfully influenced by their values. The problem is that police departments, like many organizations, are guided by implicit values that are often at odds with explicit values. This breeds confusion, distrust, and cynicism rather than clarity, commitment, and high morale.

Source: Robert Wasserman and Mark H. Moore, "Values in Policing," *Perspectives on Policing* No. 8. (Washington, DC: National Institute of Justice, 1988), p. 1.

The Police Mission

The most general statement of the purpose of a police organization is usually its mission. The mission statement typically expresses the most important values that guide the department and the overall philosophy of the agency. The role of the mission statement is to "focus on the purpose of the organization, to call attention to what is important, and to set organizational goals to align practices with values."[2]

Some police departments rely on very succinct mission statements such as "To Serve and Protect," while others prefer lengthier and more elaborate statements. Most agencies do attempt to keep their mission statements reasonably brief so that officers can remember and be guided by them. There is no reason to expect or demand that all police agencies adopt the same formal mission statement, however—the core essence of policing may be constant throughout the country, but each community has different needs and each department has different capabilities.[3] Three sample mission statements are presented below:

> **Portland, Oregon**—The mission of the Portland Police Bureau is to maintain and improve community livability by working with all citizens to preserve life, maintain human rights, protect property, and promote individual responsibility, and community commitment.[4]

> **Houston, Texas**—The mission of the Houston Police Department is to enhance the quality of life in the City of Houston by working cooperatively with the public and within the framework of the United States Constitution to enforce the laws, preserve the peace, reduce fear, and provide for a safe environment.[5]

> **Madison, Wisconsin**—The mission of the Madison Police Department is to work in partnerships to create safer neighborhoods and preserve our special quality of life.[6]

These mission statements are not presented as ideal types, although they have much to recommend them. Rather, they are meant to illustrate the kinds of statements that police departments are adopting today to express their missions. Each police agency should carefully prepare its own mission statement that describes its unique role for the benefit of police employees and citizens.

Police Goals and Objectives

An organization's goals and objectives, though more specific, should be consistent with its mission and contribute to the accomplishment of its overall purpose. The number and variety of goals and objectives that a police department could adopt are almost limitless. The Portland Police Bureau, for example, identified six goals connected with its mission statement presented above.[7] In this chapter, we simply want to highlight three primary goals and eight primary objectives that are universally applicable to all police departments.

The three primary goals of any police department are:

1. to protect life;
2. to protect property; and
3. to maintain order.

In addition, there are eight primary objectives toward which police activities are directed in order to meet primary obligations:

1. to prevent and control conduct widely recognized as threatening to life and property;
2. to aid individuals who are in danger of physical harm;
3. to protect constitutional guarantees;
4. to facilitate the movement of people and vehicles;

5. to assist those who cannot care for themselves;
6. to resolve conflict;
7. to identify problems that have the potential for becoming more serious; and
8. to create and maintain a feeling of security in the community.[8]

Protecting life, protecting property, and maintaining order are primary police goals. A police department exists to guarantee to citizens that order will be maintained in society and that their lives and property will be protected by law. Unable and unprepared to take the law into their own hands, citizens look to the police for assistance in guarding themselves against unscrupulous elements that would disrupt and disturb their peace, violate their freedoms, threaten their existence, and steal or destroy their property. All citizens have the right to expect that their lives and property will be protected and that the community in which they live will be peaceful.

The right to peace and protection is a responsibility of government. The police department is the branch of government to which this responsibility is assigned. Therefore, it naturally follows that the maintenance of order and the protection of life and property are primary goals of any police department. This means that police departments must direct their energies and activities toward the accomplishment of these primary goals. To do less than this would be to neglect government's responsibility to the citizens and the taxpayers of the community.

Law Enforcement Agency Role

Standard 11.5.1   A written directive requires the formulation and annual updating of written goals and objectives for the agency and for each organizational component within the agency. Established goals and objectives are made available to all affected personnel.

Source: *Standards for Law Enforcement Agencies: The Standards Manual of the Law Enforcement Accreditation Program.* Fairfax, VA: Commission on Accreditation for Law Enforcement Agencies, Inc., 1999.

The eight primary police objectives are described below.

Preventing and Controlling Threatening Conduct. A key objective of the police is to prevent and control serious crime and other forms of behavior that threaten life and property. One fundamental element of this objective is that it is not limited to crime. Thus, police attention to issues such as dangerous driving practices (e.g., dump trucks using a residential street) or handgun safety is justified, and in fact recommended, because such matters involve threats to life and property, even if they are not in and of themselves serious crimes. Efforts to prevent crime and other forms of threatening behavior are just as important, and perhaps more important, than efforts at control after the fact. As necessary and satisfying as arrests and convictions are, citizens and the community as a whole benefit more when crimes are prevented.

Aiding Individuals in Danger of Harm. A second primary objective of the police is to aid people who have been crime victims or who are in danger of physical harm. In the past, police sometimes largely ignored the needs of crime victims, instead focusing solely on investigating crimes and apprehending offenders. But protecting lives and property includes helping them put their lives back together after being victimized. Moreover, protecting life requires that police proactively aid those in danger of harm, such as people who have been threatened, children susceptible to neglect or abuse, and people who have been victims of spousal assault or who fear for their safety. This objective reminds police that it is not satisfactory to wait until a serious crime has been committed; protecting people means keeping them from harm, not just mopping up after the fact.

Protecting Constitutional Guarantees. The United States Constitution and the state constitutions spell out the basic frameworks of government and the inalienable rights of all Americans. One of the main objectives of the police is to protect the functioning of government and to safeguard individual liberties. Thus, police often provide protection for governmental leaders, security for legislative and judicial deliberations, and supervision of elections. It is equally important that police exercise self-control so that the use of police power does not violate the rights of citizens, and they must protect citizens who are legally exercising their constitutional rights, such as freedom of assembly and freedom of speech. Citizens exercising these rights are frequently controversial, unpopular, and even hated. When popular opinion runs against such people, no one but the police can be counted upon to protect them and their liberties—a responsibility that underscores the importance of this primary police objective.

Facilitating the Movement of People and Vehicles. Although the freedom of movement is not to be found anywhere in the Bill of Rights, Americans certainly cherish their right to come and go as they please, without delay. As a primary police objective, this requires that police pay attention to pedestrian and vehicular traffic, not just from the standpoint of safety but also from the perspective of free and orderly movement. When the objective is met, citizens are able to go about their daily travels safely and smoothly. Thus, police must attend to various obstructions of sidewalks and roads, as well as traffic jams caused by excessive numbers of vehicles. In addition, police should involve themselves in zoning matters, development decisions, construction permits, site design, and traffic engineering so that land-use patterns and street layout are influenced by the objective of facilitating the movement of people and vehicles.

Assisting Those Who Cannot Care for Themselves. Because of the goals of protecting life and property and maintaining order, and because the police are open for business 24 hours a day in all kinds of weather, it is inevitable that the police are called upon to look after people who cannot or will not properly care for themselves. This includes young children, elderly citizens, the mentally ill, the homeless, and people who are intoxicated or under the influence of drugs. Police assistance to these people can only go so far, of course—police cannot raise other peoples' children, cure the mentally ill, or build houses for all the homeless people in this country. However, police can and often do provide or arrange temporary shelter and transportation for those in need. They also make referrals and provide information so that people can take advantage of programs and services available to them. During times when the economy is struggling, when social programs are underfunded, and when many citizens turn a cold shoulder to those less fortunate, police assistance is often the only option for those who cannot properly care for themselves. Thus, this objective becomes simply a humanitarian one, consistent with the police goal of protecting life.

Resolving Conflict. Another primary objective of the police is to resolve various kinds of conflicts. These include conflicts between individuals, such as domestic disputes, disputes between neighbors, and landlord-tenant arguments, as well as more generalized conflicts, such as those between rival gangs, neighborhoods, and racial groups. Resolution of such conflicts helps police attain their primary goal of maintaining order and may also contribute to the protection of life and property, because conflicts sometimes escalate into crime and violence. Police attempt to resolve conflicts primarily through mediation and negotiation;[9] enforcement of criminal laws is often an option, but unless a serious crime has been committed, arrest and trial rarely address the underlying conflict. Although some conflicts have such deep-rooted causes that police are unlikely to be able to resolve them, others are more superficial and amenable to negotiation. When police occupy the role of neutral arbiter and devote some time to conflict resolution, they often attain this important objective and prevent more serious harm from occurring.

Identifying Potentially Serious Problems. This objective also emphasizes the preventive role of policing. Police should always be on the lookout for problems and conditions that have the potential for becoming more serious and thus jeopardizing lives, property, and order. The range of such situations is very broad: trees and shrubs that obscure traffic signs or the visibility of drivers, short-duration walk lights that catch elderly pedestrians in the middle of the street, volunteer firefighters who drive too fast to the fire station when the siren goes off, real estate agents who are too casual in lending out keys to rental properties, day care providers who fail to conduct careful background checks on their employees, and so on. Whenever police identify such potentially serious problems and conditions, they have the responsibility to monitor them, correct them if possible, or refer them to the officials who can correct them. Sometimes police may even find it necessary to publicize such problems in order to garner public support to resolve them.

Creating and Maintaining a Feeling of Security. In addition to various objectives related to protecting life and property and maintaining order, the police also have the objective of making people feel safe. Why is this important? Many studies have shown that because of their fear of crime, people often stay home, avoid downtown areas, and greatly restrict their childrens' activities. Their quality of life is substantially affected because they do not feel safe.[10] Up to a point, these feelings may be based on real danger, in which case such precautions are wise and rational. Often, however, these fears far exceed the real danger when they do, people suffer unnecessarily, as do their communities. Thus, in addition to efforts to prevent and control crime and other threatening behavior, aid individuals in danger of harm, and identify potentially serious problems, police should take steps to create and maintain a well-informed sense of safety and security in the community. Creating such a feeling of security can reap further dividends if residents thereby increase their use of, and surveillance over, the community's sidewalks, streets, parks, and other common areas.

Other Important Values

Police work and police administration should be guided by the primary goals and objectives described above, as well as by a statement of the overall mission of the police department. The activities of police officers and police administrators should contribute either directly or indirectly to the attainment of the organization's mission, goals, and objectives. Whenever it is found that resources are being expended or efforts are being undertaken that are not connected to the department's mission, goals, and objectives, hard questions should be asked, because those resources and efforts may not be contributing to the true effectiveness of the agency.

Many of the most important values that should guide policing are explicitly or implicitly expressed in the police organization's mission, goals, and objectives. Four that deserve special emphasis at this point, because they were not directly discussed above, are efficiency, legality, equity, and accountability.

It goes without saying that police departments should strive to be effective—they should vigorously attempt to attain their primary goals and objectives. However, they must also use their resources wisely, getting the biggest possible bang for the buck—in other words, they should strive for *efficiency* too. As taxpayers, we are all interested in seeing that government spends our money carefully and without waste. We want our lives and property protected and our order maintained as economically as possible. This does not mean that police administrators must be shortsighted in their financial planning or that they must operate on a shoestring, but it does require an honest concern for efficiency in the expenditure of public funds.

Police officers and administrators must also exercise great care in assuring the *legality* of their actions. This can be difficult, given the incredible maze of criminal and civil law within which the police operate, as well as the frequent pressures from political leaders and the public to ignore the law in order to accomplish an objective more quickly or conveniently. In the long run, however, society and the police are best served when the police carefully operate within the law. Symbolically, as well, it is important that those who enforce the law also are seen to abide by it.

It is also quite important that police actions be fair and that police services be distributed in an equitable manner. *Equity* can be difficult to prove, of course, and to some extent it is subjective. It does not necessarily follow that all people or all neighborhoods must be treated equally, for example — that might require officers to treat armed felons and lost children exactly the same, or require police departments to devote the same amount of attention to high-crime and crime-free neighborhoods. Instead, equity requires that all actions be guided by principles of fairness so that decisions are equitable in light of the circumstances in each case. In addition, equity demands that actions taken in one instance be reasonable in comparison to actions taken in other instances.

Finally, in our constitutional and democratic system of government, the ultimate *accountability* of the police to the courts, political leaders, and the public must be unchallenged. In the short run, as discussed above with regard to legality, the police may sometimes need to resist improper external pressures. In the end, though, the police must answer for their actions and decisions. After all, the police are merely government officials appointed to carry out certain functions. They are not elected by the people or appointed for life, nor do they have the final authority of the judiciary or the people. The people may entrust the responsibility for policing to appointed officers and administrators and delegate substantial and awesome authority to them, but in a constitutional democracy, final authority for police matters remains with the courts and the people.

This can sometimes be a bitter pill to swallow, especially if judges and citizens seem to lack common sense and basic intelligence with regard to crime problems and police issues. Police officers and administrators would do well, though, to ask themselves whether they would really rather live in a society in which the police were not accountable for their use of power and authority. Such societies exist, and most of their citizens seem mainly interested in escaping to countries with more freedom and more control over their police. Police officials would also do well to take every opportunity to inform and educate the public about crime and police issues, and then to develop a healthy trust and respect for the public's long-term reasonableness and good sense.

The Systems Concept

As defined by Harold Koontz and Cyril O'Donnell, a system is "an assemblage of objects or functions united by some interaction or interdependence."[11] Inasmuch as all factors within a system relate to one another, the action of one factor results in a reaction of another. Your family, for example, is a system. If you, as a member of that family, borrow your parents' car and wreck it in an accident, you could logically expect your parents to react in some way to the incident. They might be angry; they might express feelings of relief that you were not hurt; or they might express no feelings at all and simply put in a call to the insurance company. Of one thing you can be certain—they will react in some way. That is, they will do or say something as a result of what you did. It is also likely that others in the family will react. Your brothers and sisters, grandparents, and possibly your aunts and uncles may do or say something as a result of your initial action. If your family were studied in terms of its actions and reactions, we would say that it was being studied from a systems perspective.

All things are systems. The more parts and functions they have, the more complicated they are. For example, an automobile engine is a system. Because it has more parts that interact and are interdependent, a jet engine is more complicated than an automobile engine. Almost anything you can think of is a system. The human body, a whooping crane, General Motors, American Airlines, the government of South Korea, Indiana University, the Hilton Hotel chain, the National Broadcasting Company, Howard Johnson restaurants, the Knights of Columbus, the Kentucky Derby, the Oshkosh Public Library, the Methodist Church, and the New York City Police Department are all systems. There are records systems, thoroughbred handicapping systems, health-care systems, and multinational economic systems.

Because systems imply interaction or interdependence between or among two or more objects or functions, all systems have subsystems. The sun, moon, Mercury, Venus, Mars, Jupiter, Saturn, Uranus, Neptune, Pluto, and Earth are all subsystems of the solar system. Each one of these subsystems may be regarded as a system in itself, comprising any number of subsystems that in turn may be individually studied as systems themselves. Thus, Earth, a subsystem of the solar system, is a system made up of the atmosphere, oceans, and land masses.

The United States is a system made up of 50 subsystems (i.e., states). Each of the 50 subsystems is also an individual system made of subsystems (counties, cities, towns, and villages), which also may be viewed as separate systems. Each of these units of government has subsystems: the legislative, executive, and judicial branches. The executive branch, when looked upon as a system, has several subsystems (e.g., the public works department, the water department, the sewer department, the recreation department, the school department, the health department, the fire department, and the police department). Each of these subsystems can also be studied as an individual system. The police department, for example, is a system made up of bureaus, divisions, units, squads, teams, and shifts. These subsystems interact and are interdependent. They are established to help the department meet its goals and objectives, just as the department is established to meet the goals and objectives of the executive branch of government.

This explanation of the systems concept is perhaps an oversimplification. When one considers that the subsystems of a police department are themselves systems made up of both human and inanimate factors (people, rules, regulations, policies, desks, chairs, radios, telephones, police cars, chemical sprays, jail cells, weapons, records, computers, typewriters, Breathalyzers, laboratories, booking desks, radar guns, first aid kits, cutting tools, cameras, helicopters, resuscitators, and much more), it becomes clear that police systems are extremely complex and involved. A single change in any one factor of the system will bring about changes in other factors. An action taken by an individual in the system will inevitably result in reactions by other individuals. Systems, therefore, are always changing. It is vital to the stability of any system that any changes within it contribute to its capabilities of meeting its goals and objectives.

In any system, such as a police department, in which people are assigned tasks within subsystems of the parent system, it must be recognized that these people, as individuals, are themselves also subsystems of the parent system. This complicates matters, because people must be dealt with not only as workers in subsystems, such as operations bureaus, detective divisions, and drug units, but also as individuals having different backgrounds, ideals, religious beliefs, values, philosophies, viewpoints, tolerances, and educations. Each individual, therefore, must be looked upon as a system. For example, think of yourself as a system. Your nervous system, skeletal system, digestive system, circulatory system, and respiratory system are all subsystems of the total system of you as an individual. You are also part of numerous parent systems: your family, your church, the organization for which you work, the college or university you attend, your government, and your neighborhood. Whatever you do affects one or more of your subsystems or parent systems.

Consider the chain reaction of processes that take place in your body when you eat food, have three alcoholic drinks, or run a mile. Consider the impact on your family if you were to be arrested, break your back in an automobile accident, or flunk out of college. What you do as a system has a tremendous impact on one or more of your parent systems and on one or more of your subsystems. But you, as a system, are much more complicated than your stomach, brain, heart, veins, and lungs might suggest. You are a human being with many goals and objectives. You are also unpredictable. You therefore tend to complicate systems in ways that are difficult to predict. In systems in which people, as well as things, are system factors, the job of systems management is a demanding, difficult, and challenging task.

The mix of all system and subsystem factors in the building of an organization designed to meet goals and objectives cannot be achieved by following any established blueprint or book of rules. The process of systems building is too dynamic to describe it in an exact or precise way.

Even the best systems builders make mistakes. Consider the case of Montana ranchers who, having been convinced that coyotes were menacing their grazing livestock, set out to destroy the animals by poisoning them. The coyotes, which were subsystems of the ranch operations, were preventing the ranchers from achieving system goals and objectives: raising livestock and earning a living. Yet aside from destroying cattle and sheep, the coyotes were making contributions to the balance of nature, unbeknownst to the ranchers, by keeping down the gopher population. Once the coyotes were destroyed, the number of gophers on the ranches increased astronomically. Herds of gophers burrowed all through the ranchers' grazing land, which then became overgrown with sagebrush. Because grazing livestock do not eat sagebrush, their food supply was diminished significantly, and they suffered accordingly, as did the ranchers.[12]

We may conclude that systems have three primary characteristics:

1.   they comprise subsystems that may be looked upon as systems in and of themselves;
2.   they are made up of factors that interact and/or are interdependent; and
3.   they are established for the purpose of meeting specific goals and objectives.

Inputs, Processes, Outputs, and Feedback

In addition to their primary characteristics, systems can also be described in terms of what they do. For example, many green plants take sunlight and water (inputs), perform photosynthesis (process), and produce oxygen and food (output). Similarly, a construction company takes various inputs (labor, lumber, brick, cement, and nails), processes them (carpentry and masonry), and produces an output (a house).

Besides inputs, processes, and outputs, most systems are also characterized by feedback. Feedback may be described as an input about how the output is doing. A foreman who criticizes a mason for bricking over a window space is delivering feedback (input) about the mason's results (output). Similarly, when a professor grades an examination and gives it back to a student, the professor is providing the student with information or feedback (input) about the quality of the student's work (output).

This process of feedback is essential to the proper functioning of any system. Without feedback, the system cannot know whether its outputs are good or bad, satisfactory or unsatisfactory, productive or unproductive. When a system continues to perform poorly, it must be assumed that feedback is not being provided to those in control, or, from a systems standpoint, to those who have the power to change inputs and processes for output improvements.

Feedback is what differentiates a closed-loop system from an open-loop system. In an *open-loop system*, no provision is made for feedback. The system functions in a one-way, cause-and-effect relationship,[13] as shown in Figure 3.2. In a *closed-loop system*, by contrast, provision is made for feedback (see Fig. 3.3). In other words, a closed-loop system provides for the introduction of information about how well or how poorly the system is working.

Figure 3.2
An Open-Loop System

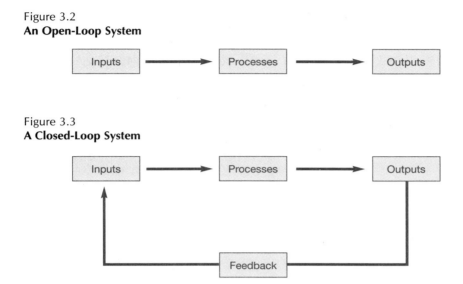

Figure 3.3
A Closed-Loop System

Types of Systems

Any system can be described in terms of the interrelatedness and interdependence of its subsystems; its functions of inputs, processes, and output; and whether it provides for feedback (closed-loop system) or does not (open-loop system). In addition to varying in these characteristics, systems may be described as being open or closed.[14]

Open and closed systems are distinctly different from one another. An open system is in contact with its environment; input and output are not restricted to factors directly related to the process involved. (Some additional characteristics of open systems are described in "Principles of Open Systems," p. 56) For example, in the construction illustration cited above, the weather, an external input, can either help or hinder the process, but it cannot be easily controlled. The output of the construction process, the house, might affect drainage in the area, the habitat of wildlife, or the social relationships of other people living in the neighborhood.

A closed system, by contrast, is not influenced by its environment, or at least is influenced very little. The solar system, which is a static structure in an ordered universe, is a good example of a closed system. Typhoons, atomic explosions, and intrusions by humans do not change its processes and outputs, although an intergalactic catastrophe might. Many machines, such as a wristwatch, are essentially closed systems, although most would certainly be affected by extreme events. If you have an old-fashioned watch with a winding stem, though, it is an example of an open system. Without external input (winding), it will run down and stop working.

Principles of Open Systems
Homeostasis: an open system seeks a steady state through self-regulation based on feedback.
Negative entropy: an open system sustains itself by importing energy from its environment.
Requisite variety: the internal regulatory mechanisms of an open system must be as diverse as the environment with which it is trying to deal.
Equifinality: in an open system there may be many different ways of achieving any particular goal.
System evolution: the capacity of an open system to evolve depends on an ability to move to more complex forms of differentiation and integration.

Adapted from Gareth Morgan, *Images of Organization*, Second Edition (Thousand Oaks, CA: Sage, 1997), pp. 40-41.

In this book we will be concerned with police organizations as systems. Because these systems are in part made up of people who are responsive to and influenced by their environments, they may be considered living systems. All living systems are open systems.[15]

Organizations as Systems

In 1956 Kenneth Boulding identified nine different levels of systems.[16] As adapted from his research, the nine levels, in order of their increasing complexity, are:

1. static systems—frameworks
2. simple dynamic systems—machines
3. cybernetic systems—thermostats
4. self-perpetuating systems—cells
5. genetic-societal systems—plants
6. animal systems—animals
7. human systems—people
8. social systems—organizations
9. transcendental systems—unknowns

Boulding maintained that beyond the second level we had little understanding of what really goes on in systems. Since 1956, however, much has been learned about the third and fourth levels—cancer research, for example, is at the fourth level, while human genome research going on today promises to advance our understanding of levels 5, 6, and 7.

Our efforts, though, to study organizations as systems (level 8) will be incomplete. Studying the control of organizations from a systems standpoint is four levels more complex than studying the control of cancer. This is not to say that we should not attempt the effort, but we must understand at the outset that we simply do not understand all of the interrelationships and factors that govern organizations as systems. The best we can do is depend on the confidence expressed by Felix Nigro that open-systems theory "represents an analytical framework believed to be the most effective for adequately describing what an organization is, how it functions and how it should function."[17]

The Police Organization as a System

Police departments are systems no more or less complex than other organizational systems. Police organizations consist of numerous involved, interdependent subsystems. The investigations division, or subsystem, for example, depends on the records division for arrest records, the patrol division for backup, the intelligence division for information on organized crime, the laboratory for scientific investigative assistance, the property unit for storage of evidence, the detention unit for the holding of prisoners, the maintenance division for servicing its vehicles, the communications division for radio contact, the supply unit for weapons and ammunition, the training division to keep up with the latest investigative techniques, the planning division to isolate high-crime areas, and the payroll unit to distribute paychecks. The work of the detectives who are assigned to the investigations division is made much more difficult, and sometimes impossible, when one or more of these divisions performs poorly or works in a way that is inconsistent with the goals and objectives of the organization.

The subsystems of police organizations may be studied from three different perspectives:

1.   the traditional, structural perspective
2.   the human perspective
3.   the strategic management perspective

The *traditional, structural perspective* sees the organization from the top, looking down. The subsystems in this perspective are those found on the traditional organization chart: for example, the patrol division, the investigations division, the traffic division, the communications division, and all other component parts of the organization. This perspective is also quite concerned with principles of administration and functions of management.

The *human perspective* views the organization from the bottom, looking up. Some subsystems involved in this perspective are leadership, individual police officers and their various characteristics (such as attitudes and motivation), and groups of officers.

The *strategic management perspective* focuses more on the technology of the organization (its techniques for performing basic functions) and its connection to the attainment of goals and objectives. In some ways this perspective takes a view of the organization from the side, looking across. Its subsystems are the flow of information, the flow of orders, the flow of communications, and the methods of performing and processing the organization's work.

All three perspectives are important. They are, in effect, vantage points from which to examine the organization. This text utilizes all three of these perspectives in order to provide the most comprehensive and thorough understanding of police organizations possible.

As with other systems, police organizations can be discussed in terms of inputs, processes, and outputs. Inputs include police officers, civilian personnel, modes of dress, equipment (such as patrol cars and two-way radios), rules and regulations, the law, and community values.

Outputs consist largely of organizational products intended to contribute to attaining primary and secondary goals and objectives. These include arrests, tickets, prosecutions, problems identified, conflicts resolved, and services delivered. The processes involved in police organizations are numerous and relate directly to particular inputs, inasmuch as each input must be processed. Consider, if you will, the single input of police officers. Processing includes such activities as recruiting, selecting, training, equipping, assigning, supervising, paying, and evaluating.

Many police departments fail to recognize as essential one of the most important aspects of the systems approach to police organization: *feedback*. For example, police chiefs occasionally initiate a new procedure. If they make no effort to determine whether their officers understand the new procedure, and if they fail to ascertain whether their officers are following it as a guideline in their work, they will lack feedback as to how their input (the new procedure) is actually being used (process) and whether it is having the desired result (output). Lack of feedback within an organization results in lack of organizational control. If chiefs fail to make provision for feedback, they will soon lose control over their entire organization. Feedback is that important.

Police management consultants have found that many police departments are open-loop systems characterized by a one-way cause-and-effect relationship. The effective delivery of police services (output) demands, however, that police organizations be administered on a closed-loop basis.

A specific example of input, process, output, and feedback may help to illustrate. Suppose that a police communications division receives a call from a citizen that a fight is in progress at Joe's Hot Dog and Hamburger Emporium. The call from the citizen is the input. The process is the communications division's receiving and evaluating the call and assigning one or more officers to service the complaint. The output is the arrival of the officer or officers at the scene and the actions they take to break up the fight. The feedback is the information the communications division receives about the disposition of the matter: there is no fight in progress at Joe's; there never was a fight; more help is needed to break up the fight; the fight has been broken up; or an arrest has been made. Figure 3.4 shows this sequence of events from a systems perspective.

This one illustration emphasizes the importance of feedback. Without feedback, the communications division would have no way of knowing if the processing of the call was correct, and no information would be available as to whether the output was appropriate. If many people had been injured in the fight, and if the communications division sent only one car to service the call, the process involved in evaluating calls of this nature should perhaps be modified through the introduction of new or different input into the system.

Figure 3.4
A Police Action as Input, Process, Output, and Feedback

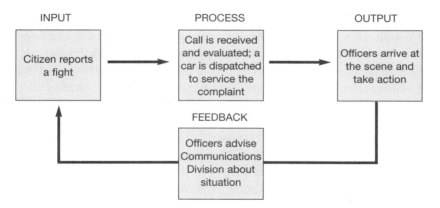

It is essential that the output (what happens at the scene) be described to the communications division (feedback) for consideration and study. It might be determined that the communications division failed to obtain sufficient information from the person who reported the fight. An effort could then be made to develop procedures by which better information could be taken from people who register complaints over the telephone, thus improving input. It is through feedback that corrective action is taken, thus providing effective output in the future.

In summary, police organizations are open systems in constant contact with their environments. They can be studied from structural, human, and strategic management perspectives, and they have inputs, processes, and outputs that can be identified. Like many other organizations serving the public, police organizations have a disturbing tendency to disregard the importance of feedback. In order to deliver services effectively, they must be constructed as closed-loop systems. Police organizations also have numerous subsystems that interact and are interdependent. They are discussed in detail in Chapter 4.

The Police in the Larger System

Earlier in this chapter we mentioned that police systems are subsystems of the executive branch of government. Equally important is the fact that police systems are also subsystems of the criminal justice system, which also has two other major subsystems: the courts and corrections. The fact that these three subsystems have often failed to consider their interdependence has been widely noted, even though each affects the others in a profound way.

The backlog of cases in the courts contributes significantly to increased police problems: serious offenders not held in jail because so many others are already there awaiting trial; physical evidence that must be stored for longer periods of time; witnesses whose memories fade, thus weakening cases; victims who become increasingly frustrated; and defendants who are allowed to plea bargain to greatly reduced charges and light sentences in order to dispose of their cases. Jail and prison overcrowding forces the courts to resort more readily to the use of probation, home detention, and other remedies when incarceration would be more appropriate. Similarly, police departments that are particularly successful in clearing crimes by arrest and in apprehending drug offenders are likely to overburden the courts and place severe strains on correctional systems, which are already bulging at the seams with clientele they are incapable of servicing properly. The courts respond by further delaying cases, and correctional systems respond by increasing the use of parole to make room for newly sentenced offenders. The assembly line and revolving door images fit nicely.

Clearly, police departments need to become more adept at collaborating with their fellow components of the criminal justice system, in order for the entire system to function more effectively. The development of community policing in recent years has encouraged some progress in this direction. In part, this has been because collaboration with all kinds of public and private organizations is seen as an important aspect of COP.[18] In addition, police officers and police departments have discovered that working more closely with juvenile services, probation, parole, community courts, drug courts, pretrial release, and other elements of the criminal justice system can contribute substantially to problem solving and crime control in specific neighborhoods and communities.[19]

Police departments are parts of other systems as well—for example, they are parts of the mental health, social services, and public safety systems. The latter system is a particularly important arena for police organizations, as it overlaps with the criminal justice system, but also includes fire protection and emergency medical agencies, plus, under certain circumstances, the military. Also, in recent decades the line between public and private responsibilities for, and authority over, safety, security, and crime prevention has become increasingly blurred.[20] This is very significant because it makes public/private cooperation and collaboration a more and more important concern for police departments. This makes the police agency's environment even more complex than it already was and demonstrates again that police organizations are open systems.

Summary

The purposes of the police—mission, goals, objectives, and other important values—were discussed in detail in this chapter. These purposes should guide police officers in the performance of their operational duties as well as police executives in conducting their administrative duties. Three primary goals of protecting life, protecting property, and maintaining order, and eight primary objectives were described along with the important concerns of efficiency, legality, and accountability. It is a major challenge for the police in a free society to remain efficient, legal, equitable, and accountable, while striving for effectiveness in the achievement of primary goals and objectives.

This chapter has also introduced the concept of systems and has demonstrated how the concept applies to police organization and management. One overriding theme of the systems concept is interdependence among subsystems—everything tends to affect everything else. Systems are also characterized by their relationships with their environments—police organizations are open systems because they react to environmental inputs and affect their environments with their outputs. Input, process, output, and feedback were stressed as essential elements of system design. Feedback, in particular, is crucial to the successful performance of any system, including a police department.

Discussion Questions

1. Which of the three police mission statements presented in the text do you prefer? Why? How are the three different?

2. How would you prioritize the eight primary police objectives presented in the text? Is it necessary to prioritize them? If you were a police chief, how would you go about prioritizing them for your community?

3. Feedback is a key concept in the study of systems. What forms of feedback are utilized in the classroom? On the job? In your personal relationships?

4. Why do you think that many systems, including organizations, fail to provide for and utilize feedback?

5. How is a police department influenced by the larger systems of which it is a part? How are those larger systems influenced by the police department? Would you say that police departments are more or less interdependent on other systems than most organizations?

Notes

1. V.E. Kappeler, R.D. Sluder, and G.P. Alpert, *Forces of Deviance: Understanding the Dark Side of Policing*, Second Edition, (Prospect Heights, IL: Waveland, 1998).

2. D.C. Couper and S.H. Lobitz, *Quality Policing: The Madison Experience* (Washington, DC: Police Executive Research Forum, 1991), p. 24.

3. M.H. Moore and D.W. Stephens, *Beyond Command and Control: The Strategic Management of Police Departments* (Washington, DC: Police Executive Research Forum, 1991), p. 29; A.Y. Jiao, "Degrees of Urbanism and Police Orientations: Testing Preferences for Different Policing Approaches across Urban, Suburban, and Rural Areas," *Police Quarterly* 4, no. 3 (September 2001): 361-387.

4. Portland Police Bureau, "2000-2002 Community Policing Strategic Plan." http://www.portlandpolice.com/PDFs/2000plan.pdf

5. Houston Police Online, http://www.ci.houston.tx.us/departme/police/mission.htm

6. Madison Police Department, http://www.ci.madison.wi.us/police/vision%20mission%20values.html.

7. Portland Police Bureau, "2000-2002 Community Policing Strategic Plan." http://www.portlandpolice.com/PDFs/2000plan.pdf

8. H. Goldstein, *Policing a Free Society* (Cambridge, MA: Ballinger, 1977), p. 35.

9. H. Goldstein, *Problem-Oriented Policing* (New York, NY: McGraw-Hill, 1990), pp. 111-114.

10. M.H. Moore and R.C. Trojanowicz, "Policing and the Fear of Crime," *Perspectives on Policing* No. 3. (Washington, DC: National Institute of Justice, 1988).

11. H. Koontz and C. O'Donnell, *Principles of Management: An Analysis of Managerial Functions*, Fourth Edition (New York, NY: McGraw-Hill, 1968), p. 43.

12. P.B. Sears, "Ecology, the Intricate Web of Life," in *As We Live and Breathe: The Challenge of Our Environment* (Washington, DC: National Geographic Society, 1971), as adapted in N. Greenwood and J.M.B. Edwards, *Human Environments and Natural Systems: A Conflict of Dominion* (North Scituate, MA: Duxbury Press, 1973), pp. 62-63.

13. Koontz and O'Donnell, *Principles of Management*, p. 43.

14. G. Morgan, *Images of Organization*, Second Edition (Thousand Oaks, CA: Sage, 1997).

15. R. Chin, "The Utility of System Models and Developmental Models for Practitioners," in *The Planning of Change: Readings in the Applied Behavioral Sciences* W.G. Bennis, K.D. Benne, and R. Chin, eds. (New York, NY: Holt, Rinehart and Winston, 1961), pp. 201-214.

16. K.E. Boulding, "General Systems Theory: The Skeleton of Science," *Management Science* 2, no. 3 (April 1956): 197-208.

17. F.A. Nigro, *Modern Public Administration*, Second Edition (New York, NY: Harper & Row, 1965), p. 100.

18. Bureau of Justice Assistance, *Understanding Community Policing: A Framework for Action* (Washington, DC: Bureau of Justice Assistance, 1994).

19. G. Berman and L. Paik, "Cop-Court Connection Takes on a New Look," *Community Links* 4, no. 2 (fall 1997): 6-7.

20. D. Bayley and C. Shearing, "The Future of Policing," *Law & Society Review* 30, no. 3 (1996): 585-606; J.R. Greene and R. Stokes, "Policing Business Districts: Problem Solving in a Different Context," in T.O. Shelley and A.C. Grant, eds., *Problem-Oriented Policing: Crime-Specific Problems, Critical Issues, and Making POP Work* (Washington, DC: Police Executive Research Forum, 1998), pp. 205-229.

Suggested Reading

Brodeur, Jean-Paul, ed. *How to Recognize Good Policing: Problems and Issues*. Thousand Oaks, CA: Sage, 1998.

Delattre, Edwin J. *Character and Cops: Ethics in Policing*, Fourth Edition. Washington, DC: American Enterprise Institute, 2002.

Goldstein, Herman. *Policing a Free Society*. Cambridge, MA: Ballinger, 1977.

Hoover, Larry T. ed., *Police Management: Issues and Perspectives*. Washington, DC: Police Executive Research Forum, 1992.

Morgan, Gareth. *Images of Organization*, Second Edition. Thousand Oaks, CA: Sage, 1997.

Police
Organizational Tasks

4

Learning Objectives

- Identify the three major subsystems of the police organization.

- Identify the relationship among operations, administration, and auxiliary services.

- Characterize police operational tasks and identify 10 such tasks.

- Characterize police administrative tasks and identify 10 such tasks.

- Characterize police auxiliary services tasks and identify 10 such tasks.

If you were asked to list the basic police tasks as they are portrayed in the media, you would probably think only of those that are closely related to the apprehension of criminal offenders. These are the tasks on which television and the movies focus. They are certainly the most exciting and interesting tasks that police officers perform, yet they represent only a small percentage of what police officers actually do. Who would want to watch a movie about directing traffic, planning, or maintaining police vehicles? Despite the relatively uninteresting nature of these and many other kinds of tasks, police organizations depend on them for the accomplishment of goals and objectives.

This chapter will briefly discuss 30 basic police organizational tasks. The exact number of tasks that the police perform is really not very important; we have identified 30 that we believe are important and should be discussed. The number is significant, though, in that it suggests there is a proliferation of tasks that must be performed in any police organization.

Some police departments are so large that separate units have been established to perform each task; others are so small that all tasks are performed by one person. The remaining police departments fall somewhere in the middle; for them, the major challenge is developing a logical and effective approach for grouping similar functions into operating units. (This management function, termed *organizing*, is discussed in Chapter 6.)

The three major subsystems of the police organization are:

1. operations
2. administration
3. auxiliary services

These three subsystems provide the framework for our discussion of the basic police tasks. The list below shows the tasks arranged within the subsystems of the police organization.

Operations	Administration	Auxiliary Services
Patrol	Personnel	Records
Traffic	Training	Communications
Criminal investigation	Planning and analysis	Property and evidence
Vice and drugs	Budget and finance	Laboratory
Organized crime	Legal assistance	Detention
Special operations	Information processing	Identification
Crime prevention	Public information	Alcohol testing
Juvenile services	Inspections	Facilities
Community services	Internal affairs	Equipment and supply
School services	Intelligence	Maintenance

The Operations Subsystem

Operations are activities that directly assist the public. The operations subsystem is the part of police work with which most people are familiar. Through the operations subsystem, police officers are deployed to take action, to fight crime, and to provide services to the public. The other two subsystems (administration and auxiliary services) exist to provide day-to-day and long-term services to personnel working within the operations subsystem.

The goals of the operations subsystem are identical to those of the entire police agency—primarily, maintaining order and protecting life and property. All work in which operations personnel are involved is directed toward the accomplishment of these primary organizational goals and the eight primary objectives discussed in Chapter 3. The tasks included within the operations subsystem are aimed directly at achieving one or more of these goals and objectives. These tasks are patrol, traffic, criminal investigation, vice and drugs, organized crime, special operations, crime prevention, juvenile services, community services, and school services.

Patrol

Patrol is commonly referred to as the backbone of the police service.[1] Patrol officers are normally the first to respond to crime scenes, accidents, and calls for service. In some instances, patrol officers handle the entire matter with which they are confronted; in others they conduct a preliminary investigation before turning the matter over to specialized personnel. Patrol officers are expected to be alert for crimes in progress, traffic violations, suspicious persons and circumstances, public property in need of repair, and anything else out of the ordinary. Patrol is also intended to prevent crime through its omnipresence, to keep in touch with the communit, and to be responsive to citizen needs and problems. One of the most important aims of patrol is to provide law-abiding citizens with a feeling of security so that they can conduct their affairs without fear of criminal interference. The patrol function maintains order and protects life and property on a continuous basis.

Merriam-Webster's *Collegiate Dictionary* defines patrol as "the action of traversing a district or beat or of going the rounds along a chain of guards for observation or the maintenance of security."[2] The police use several methods of traversing a district or beat: foot patrol, car patrol, motorcycle patrol, bike patrol, horse patrol, aircraft patrol, and marine patrol. Circumstances in each situation should dictate the means employed, and none should be used simply because of tradition or common practice.

The patrol task must be organized by time and location; that is, patrol personnel work shifts on a 24-hour basis and are assigned to beats so that the entire jurisdiction receives patrol coverage. Unfortunately, many police administrators assign personnel to patrol times and locations on the basis of tradition or whim; as a consequence, patrol personnel in many communities are not allocated to maximize their effectiveness.

Patrol personnel should be assigned according to patterns of crime and requests for service in the community they serve.[3] This is their business, and they should work when and where their business occurs. To do otherwise is to waste tax dollars and reduce the effectiveness of the police.

A celebrated study conducted in Kansas City, Missouri, raised some serious questions concerning the true value of motorized police patrol.[4] The experiment, conducted by the Police Foundation and the Kansas City Police Department, could find no real evidence that routine patrol deters crime, improves the delivery of services, or affects citizen feelings of security. These findings, although highly controversial, spurred further research into the effectiveness of police patrol and resulted in a rethinking of the patrol function.[5] Directed patrol and foot patrol gained some backing as effective supplements to motorized preventive patrol, while the evolving strategies of community policing and problem-oriented policing suggest replacing most patrolling with more focused activity.[6] We will look more closely at patrol research and tactics, including community and problem-oriented policing, in Chapter 13.

Traffic

The traffic task includes several subtasks relating to different police activities vis-à-vis motor vehicles. These subtasks include intersection control (traffic direction), traffic law enforcement, parking law enforcement, and traffic accident investigation.

Except for unusual situations at accident scenes or large gatherings, the task of intersection control is ordinarily a major concern only in urban or highly congested suburban areas. In such situations, the demands of intersection control can cause severe drains on police personnel. Many police departments employ civilian traffic controllers for intersection work as a cost-saving measure.

The traffic law enforcement subtask involves issuing citations for various motor vehicle violations; this activity is directed toward the reduction of accidents and of injuries and fatalities caused by accidents. Because many citizens come in contact with the police only as a result of having violated a traffic law, this activity has serious implications for the relationship between the police and the community; consequently, it must be performed with considerable care and courtesy. Traffic law enforcement should be based on careful analysis of traffic accident patterns so that the kinds of violations that cause accidents in certain locations at certain times are suppressed. This approach, which should be the basis for every police department's traffic law enforcement activities, is called *selective enforcement*.

One aspect of traffic law enforcement that has come to the forefront in recent years is the enforcement of drinking and driving laws. While a police officer in a resort town in the early 1970s, one of the authors worked in a very relaxed enforcement atmosphere. The prevailing attitude was that visitors came to the town to have a good time and that the police should refrain from interfering with their revelry by arresting drunk drivers. The town had a significant motor vehicle accident problem, but cracking down on Driving Under the Influence (DUI) violations was not considered to be a solution to the problem.

Less than 10 years later, attitudes in this resort community and elsewhere had changed dramatically. DUI enforcement is now a high priority in most police departments, and it is obvious today that such enforcement directly contributes to the protection of life and property. However, it took pressure from such groups as Mothers Against Drunk Driving (MADD) and Students Against Drunk Drivers (SADD) to get legislatures, courts, and police agencies to recognize the problem and alter their approach to it.

The use of radar by the police has proved to be an extremely effective deterrent to speeding. Radar gives the police a scientific tool for the strict enforcement of speed laws. Another technological development now gaining wider acceptance is the use of unmanned cameras for speed enforcement and intersection surveillance.

The enforcement of parking laws is designed to keep traffic moving, to keep fire hydrants clear of obstructions, to keep intersections unclogged, and to keep parking spaces free at meters and in front of businesses. In some large jurisdictions, this activity is performed primarily by civilians assigned exclusively to the task; in other jurisdictions, police officers perform the task as a part of their generalist function.

The subtask of traffic accident investigation is to determine the causes of motor vehicle accidents. In cases in which fault can be established, traffic accident investigators issue citations. Accident investigation, therefore, is an enforcement task. The task also provides input to the process of insurance claim settlement in jurisdictions where insurance claims are based on fault. Traffic accident investigation can, also focus on criminal law violations ranging from assault to manslaughter to murder. Finally, accident investigations can help identify types of driving behaviors that need to be discouraged through education and enforcement as well as dangerous roadway conditions that need to be corrected. It is an extremely important, specialized task that requires considerable training and insight.

In a small police department, intersection control, traffic law enforcement, parking law enforcement, and traffic accident investigation may all be performed by officers serving as generalist patrol officers. In a large department, each of these subtasks may be handled by a separate subunit of a traffic division. Some of these tasks can easily be performed by civilians; indeed, some of them can be performed better by civilians and at a much lower cost. A decision to create a specialized traffic division and to employ specialized civilian personnel should be based on the size of the organization and on the volume and patterns of traffic-related business.

Criminal Investigation

Criminal investigations, the actions taken by the police to identify and apprehend perpetrators of crimes, include such activities as crime scene investigations, interviewing, and interrogation. Ideally, they culminate in the criminal conviction of suspects, but most often they do not. The American police are successful in clearing by arrest (not conviction) only 20 percent of the serious crimes called to their attention.[7]

Detectives are the specialists in criminal investigation; they are not, however, its only practitioners. As a rule, officers assigned to the patrol function conduct all preliminary and minor investigations. Because all police departments have more officers assigned to the patrol subtask than to the criminal investigation subtask, patrol officers routinely shoulder a major part of investigative activity. Many police departments have adopted a policy stipulating that uniformed patrol officers should conduct investigations of all minor crimes, referring them to detectives only when they have reached a dead end in their efforts. This policy, which embodies the generalist patrol theory, allows detectives to concentrate on more serious crimes and, at the same time, provides for the handling of investigations of less serious offenses, for which most criminal investigation divisions have little time.

Figure 4.1
Crimes Cleared by Arrest, 2000

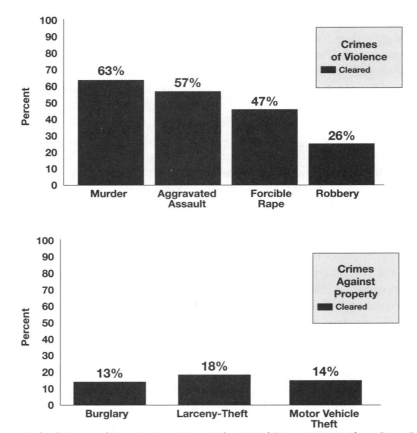

Source: Federal Bureau of Investigation, *Crime in the United States, 2000: Uniform Crime Reports.* Washington, DC: U.S. Government Printing Office, 2001.

Most police departments, no matter how committed to the generalist theory, find it necessary to assign some personnel solely to criminal investigation. The number of officers to assign to investigative activities is a point of contention in many municipal police agencies; 10 to 15 percent of sworn officers is a common rule of thumb.

Another common point of controversy is the degree of specialization needed in the criminal investigations division. Departments with the least specialization might use the general assignment approach, with all detectives handling all types of investigations; highly specialized departments might have a Crimes Against the Person Unit, with separate squads handling homicides, assaults, sex offenses, and robberies. A Crimes Against Property Unit might have specialized squads handling burglaries, auto thefts, and larcenies. The degree of specialization in any police agency must be based on local circumstances, taking into consideration such factors as the size of the department, the skills of its personnel, the patterns and amounts of its activities, and prevailing policies.

The actual effectiveness and productivity of detectives has been called into question by research over the last three decades. Studies have found that most crime clearances can be attributed to contributions by witnesses and patrol officers rather than to contributions by detectives.[8] In addition, it has been established through research that detectives spend most of their time in the office, on the telephone or doing routine paperwork, rather than out on the street meticulously searching for clues or interviewing informants, victims, and witnesses. The "detective mystique" seems highly overrated.[9]

As part of community policing, many larger police departments have decentralized their investigative units over the past decade. Following this approach, detectives are assigned to work under precinct captains or other area commanders rather than under a chief of detectives at headquarters. The aim of this approach is to help detectives become more knowledgeable about local neighborhood problems and to encourage them to work more closely with neighborhood residents and patrol officers.[10]

Vice and Drugs

The responsibility for vice regulation and drug enforcement has caused the police innumerable problems, largely because vice laws declare illegal a host of goods and services (i.e., gambling, prostitution, pornography) that are desired by a great number of citizens. The rationale for laws that forbid people to do much of what they might like to do is not that some unsuspecting stranger might be victimized, but rather that people must be protected from their own wants and desires.

Because there is so little consensus about the desirability and importance of vice laws, the enforcement of those laws places the police in a difficult position. The police understand that many people desire the goods and services curtailed by vice laws; they see that society in general is frequently indifferent to violations of vice laws. The police are not often sought out by aggrieved victims, as they are in the cases of rapes, robberies, and burglaries. They observe that the courts usually deal leniently with vice offenders (although harsher sentences for drug offenders have become more common since the 1980s). They further observe that vice and drugs generate large sums of money.

It is for these reasons that vice regulation and drug enforcement are at the heart of much of the public animosity toward the police and at the core of much police corruption. If the police strictly enforce all vice laws, the public as well as the purveyors of illegal goods and services become upset. If the police are lenient toward vice, the public assumes that they have been corrupted. In many cases this suspicion has proved to be well-founded; whether well-founded or not, however, the damage in terms of public support and respect is the same.

As long as vice and drug laws remain on the books and as long as vice regulation and drug enforcement remain the responsibility of the police, the police administrator will have to deal with these problems. Even in police circles, there is considerable confusion about the best methods to use in dealing with vice and drug problems. In recent years, though, it has become common to involve ordinary patrol officers in vice and drug enforcement rather than relegating it strictly to specialists. Police today frequently work closely with neighborhoods in identifying and combatting vice and drug problems. Police have also become creative in their use of such innovative techniques as sting operations, reverse stings, asset seizure, multiagency task forces, and civil nuisance abatement procedures.[11]

Organized Crime

Organized crime has always caused difficult organizational problems for the police, in part because of the extent of organized crime. Gambling, prostitution, pornography, narcotics, hijacking, and loan-sharking are the bread and butter of organized crime. However, the need to control the marketplace also gets organized crime involved with such crimes as murder, assault, robbery, theft, and extortion. Moreover, the process of laundering dirty profits involves various kinds of frauds and swindles, some of which affect legitimate business. Because each kind of criminal offense committed by organized crime may be investigated by a separate police subunit, the police often fail to see the big picture of organized crime at work.

In addition to the wide variety of offenses involved, the structure of organized crime acts to thwart traditional police efforts. The people who collect the bulk of the profits and who direct the operations of organized crime rarely commit observable offenses. Usually they order someone who orders someone else who orders someone else to commit a crime. Everything is done covertly through layers of organization designed to protect the leadership. These layers are reinforced by money, legal services, loyalty, and force. Despite numerous arrests of organized crime figures, the police are rarely able to bring syndicate bosses to the bar of justice.

One form of organized crime that gained increased attention in the 1990s was criminal gangs.[12] Gangs tend to be composed of youthful members, though not necessarily juveniles, and they are often territorially based, but not always. Some gangs exist simply to meet their members' social or protection needs, but most engage in some form of organized criminal activity, whether it be drug dealing, burglary, theft, or robbery.

In recent years the task force or strike force approach has had some success in combatting organized crime and gangs.[13] This approach is usually multijurisdictional, often taking in metropolitan areas, states, and regions. It involves investigators and prosecutors from local, state, and federal agencies. The approach is usually quite sophisticated and often makes use of financial and tax records, on the valid assumption that profits from organized crime are not usually reported to the Internal Revenue Service. Increased use has also been made of grand juries and of immunity, two techniques that when used in concert can force syndicate leaders and their underlings to choose between telling what they know or going to jail. The resources of the combined agencies at different levels of government make more credible the assurances of protection offered informants and prosecution witnesses.

Special Operations

One clear trend in modern policing has been the development of special capabilities to deal with particularly difficult situations. Prior to the 1970s, even the most complicated and dangerous situations were handled by regular patrol officers without the advantage of specialized training or equipment. The most these patrol officers could expect in the way of organizational assistance in the handling of a hostage situation, for example, would be the presence of a supervisor or commander at the scene.

Today, many police agencies have specially trained personnel for handling these kinds of situations, and all have access to such personnel, if only through their state police organizations. The range of situations calling for special operational capabilities is quite broad, but should probably include the following at a minimum:[14]

• armed confrontations	• executive protection
• hostage situations	• disaster response
• barricaded persons	• search and rescue
• suicide threats	• riots and civil disturbances
• bomb threats	• civil defense
• bomb disposal	• terrorist acts

Police agencies of different sizes arrange for the availability of special operations in different ways. Small departments may rely almost completely on larger neighbors (e.g., their county sheriff's department and the state police) or they may have a few officers with some special training and mutual aid agreements to fill in the gaps. Larger agencies are more likely to have full complements of specially trained officers for handling the entire range of situations that might occur. Even in most larger departments, though, these specially trained officers will probably have regular assignments in patrol or other units, while being subject to call-out when situations requiring their expertise occur. Only the largest police organizations have the demand and resources to justify full-time special operations units that do nothing but handle special situations.

Crime Prevention

Preventing crime is one of the primary objectives of the police service. It was traditionally thought that crime prevention was accomplished by having uniformed police officers in marked vehicles moving about the community to give the impression of police omnipresence. Statistics, however, would seem to prove otherwise. Traditional police methods have not been very successful in preventing crime.

Techniques developed in recent years mandate that the police concentrate on high-crime risks in attempts to increase the effort, increase the risk, or reduce the reward associated with crime.[15] In many instances dramatic decreases in crime rates can result. These techniques, referred to collectively as *situational crime prevention*, include improving security, locking devices, and construction; screening or barring doors and windows; providing more and better alarm systems and lighting; and teaching citizens and businesspeople how to secure their premises more effectively. Through Project Identification programs, many police departments loan marking tools to the general public so that citizens can mark valuable property in their homes and businesses; such programs increase the chances of recovering stolen property. Some police departments even provide special officers as security consultants to business and industry in an effort to prevent or reduce crime.

Another approach to crime prevention relies on mobilizing community support. Neighborhood Watch programs enlist the eyes and ears of residents, encouraging and training them to look out for each other and report suspicious activity to the police. Safe homes in each block are also designated and marked for the benefit of children who may be frightened, lost, or in the process of escaping from an attacker. Some communities have even established citizen patrols that attempt to deter crime and report suspicious activity.

The idea of crime prevention as a specialized activity is fairly new in police circles. The police have traditionally been prosecution-oriented, not prevention-oriented. They have gauged their success on clearances by arrest and successful prosecutions and, except for traditional preventive patrol, have placed little emphasis on preventing crimes. Learning from the successful experiences of security administrators, whose private-sector companies are much more interested in preventing thefts than in prosecuting offenders, the police have slowly come to realize that prosecutions alone are not an adequate measurement of police success. Controlling, reducing, and preventing crime are more viable yardsticks for measuring police effectiveness in dealing with crime. Citizens are far less interested in numbers of prosecutions than in rising crime rates. Police success in crime-related activities, therefore, should be predicated on crime reduction and not, as has been the traditional practice, on numbers of crime clearances and prosecutions.

It should be pointed out that the police are limited in what they can do to control crime. Not everyone understands this, and there are many who think that the police should be able to control all crime. This is not the case. The police are not responsible for social conditions that breed crime. They have no control over poverty, bad housing, poor health care, discrimination, child neglect, and inadequate education. The bitter fruit of these social conditions is crime. It is generally recognized that crime will not disappear, regardless of what the police do to prevent it, until the social conditions that cause it disappear. Given this reality, the most that the police can do is attempt to reduce crime, not eliminate it. Other forces and factors that cause crime can always be expected to be present in a democratic society that cherishes freedom and individual rights. Indeed, some say that crime is the price we pay for democracy. The responsibility of the police is to prevent crime to the degree that they reasonably can, and to refine their techniques for preventing crime in a social milieu that breeds it.

Juvenile Services

Police services for juveniles constitute a separate task because of the special legal and practical aspects of dealing with children. Juveniles are a clear and distinct subgroup of society, and their offenses are ordinarily handled more informally and with more leniency, although the tendency in recent years has been to become more strict. In addition, juveniles are usually dealt with by the criminal justice system as parts of family units rather than as free and responsible citizens. They are often tried in juvenile courts by special judges; when incarcerated, juveniles are placed in special institutions apart from adult offenders. There were 1.56 million arrests of persons under 18 years of age in 2000, representing 17 percent of all arrests made in the United States. In that year, juveniles were involved in 33 percent of all burglary arrests, 25 percent of robbery arrests, and 34 percent of motor vehicle theft arrests.[16]

Most large police departments have separate juvenile divisions, which are essential because of the factors outlined above and because of the enormity of the juvenile crime problem. In addition to getting referrals from other departmental divisions and units, the juvenile division may take a special interest in matters of child abuse and neglect, children in need of supervision, runaways, and truants. The juvenile division will also ordinarily coordinate relations among the police department, the juvenile courts, juvenile detention centers, and social service programs for juveniles.

The focus of the juvenile division is decidedly more on social welfare than on crime; for this reason, the juvenile division is often denigrated by police officers who fail to understand the importance of having some police officers involved in social welfare activities, especially as these relate to children. Social workers also tend to denigrate the work of juvenile divisions, claiming that the inexperience of police officers and their general lack of educational background should disqualify them from participation in social services activities. Yet if the police fail to become involved in helping children in trouble, even if only referring them to appropriate social welfare agencies, the children will probably receive no help whatsoever.

Juvenile Operations

Standard 44.1.1   A written directive establishes the agency's juvenile operations function, and includes, at a minimum, the following:

a.   a statement that the agency is committed to the development and perpetuation of programs designed to prevent and control juvenile delinquency; and

b.   a statement that the responsibility for participating in or supporting the agency's juvenile operations function is shared by all agency components and personnel.

Source: *Standards for Law Enforcement Agencies: The Standards Manual of the Law Enforcement Agency Accreditation Program.* Fairfax, VA: Commission on Accreditation for Law Enforcement Agencies, Inc., 1999.

Two of the most pressing problems confronting police departments today are the related problems of child abuse and missing children. While most police officers have always taken allegations of child abuse seriously, it is clear that society has only relatively recently awakened to the problem. On the other hand, many police officers often callously grumbled about taking a runaway child report, and some agencies even required that the child be missing for 24 hours before an investigation would commence. Public pressure has now caused police agencies to take missing children reports more seriously.

Community Services

There is a general recognition today that the police have a key role to play in the delivery of a variety of services to the community. By default, social service agencies have given to the police much of the routine, day-to-day responsibilities that were once considered solely within the province of social service agencies. What traditional social service agency operates 24 hours a day, seven days a week, 52 weeks a year? The police department is the only such agency in the community, and unlike many other social service agencies, the police still make house calls.

Depending on the nature of the service needed, the skills of individual police officers, and the policies of the departments in which they serve, the role of the police may be to: (1) provide the service themselves, (2) assist others in providing the service, or (3) refer the matter to another agency. If the appropriate social service agency is not open, it becomes the responsibility of the police to handle such matters. Police officers' qualifications to handle the wide variety of situations that come to their attention is secondary to the need to handle all matters that cannot be immediately referred to a social service agency. People who would completely divorce the police from all social welfare activities often fail to recognize that if such activities are not handled by the police, they will not be handled at all. Whether they like it or not, social workers who work 40 hours a week leave the other 128 hours for the police to service. At the very minimum, then, police probably handle two-thirds of all threshold social work in this country; when one considers that human trauma occurs more frequently at night, and often on weekends, that percentage undoubtedly rises. When people need immediate help, regardless of the circumstances, they call the police. Furthermore, they expect the police to respond right away and to alleviate the problem.

In addition to the kinds of services provided by individual patrol officers responding to calls from citizens, many agencies have created special programs to address critical needs in their communities. Among the kinds of formal community service programs that police departments frequently provide are school-based programs (such as Drug Abuse Resistance Education—DARE), recreational programs (such as Police Activities Leagues—PAL), victim-witness programs, and domestic violence programs.

Referral is a practice that even the smallest police department can adopt. All departments come in contact with various kinds of social problems that do not require arrest but that cry out for help and treatment. Such situations often involve people with substance abuse problems, people with mental illness, or homeless people.[17] If police officers know what social services are available in their communities and the kinds of assistance programs they offer, they have a viable and productive alternative to arrest. They do not, of course, have the authority to require participation in treatment programs, but their recommendations can be critical to troubled individuals who need help but do not know where to find it.

School Services

One of the biggest growth sectors for policing in the past decade has been school-based services and programs. In response to concerns about youth violence, school safety, drug abuse, and gangs, many police departments and school systems have begun working much more closely together than ever before. At least five different types of approaches can be identified—these are sometimes used separately or in combination.

Perhaps the most long-standing approach is to involve police officers in educational programs for youths. Since the 1950s, some police departments have presented Officer Friendly, Stranger Danger, and a variety of safety-oriented programs (household safety, pedestrian safety, bicycle safety) at the elementary school level and had officers give law-related talks to middle school and high school classes. More recently, the DARE program and GREAT (Gang Resistance Education and Training) have become popular. Police also sometimes participate with teachers in presentations on anger management and conflict resolution.[18]

Another model has been for the police to establish special programs within schools aimed at reducing crime and disorder problems on school grounds. For example, many jurisdictions have implemented special versions of the popular Crimestoppers and Crime Watch programs within their schools. Some schools have also worked with police to establish drug tip hotlines and Police Explorer programs.

A third approach is simply to create closer connections between regular police officers and schools. Some police departments use the Adopt-a-School program, in which individual patrol officers and detectives "adopt" a school to which they will pay special attention, in addition to their regular duties. These officers spend extra time in the school, perhaps by eating lunch in the school cafeteria on a regular basis, and generally serve as the police department's liaison to that school. Alternatively, many departments that are implementing community policing by giving patrol officers regular beat assignments insist that these officers treat any schools within their beats as particularly important clients. Following the adage that "police should be where the people are," these agencies encourage their officers to spend considerable time in their schools.

Yet another approach, and one that seems to be gaining momentum, is the utilization of School Resource Officers (SROs). These are police officers who are assigned full-time to work in the schools. SROs may participate in educational programs and other special programs in the schools but, in addition, the school is their "beat." That is, they provide all regular police services within the school, including patrol, investigation, and juvenile services, as well as special school-based programs. Proponents of this approach like the fact that these officers act like "real police," not just Officer Friendly, and that they provide a significant police presence in the school. That is, SROs do not just drop in to give a talk; they are on the premises during the entire school day.

Finally, a few police departments are attempting to engage school students directly in community policing and problem-solving activities.[19] This approach takes the view that the school is a community and that the students are its most numerous "residents," so it is important to involve them in improving the quality of life and level of safety. In some ways this is the most far-reaching model, because it tries to overcome the inherent limitations of a police-focused approach by harnessing the energy and talents of students, while at the same time preparing those students for later life, when they will also be expected to shoulder some of the responsibility for keeping their communities safe and orderly.

The Administration Subsystem

The tasks that constitute the *administration subsystem* (personnel, training, planning and analysis, budget and finance, legal assistance, information processing, public information, inspections, internal affairs, and intelligence) are performed not in direct assistance to the public, but for the benefit of the organization as a whole. The tasks of the administration subsystem have a more long-term application than do those of the auxiliary services subsystem. One way to differentiate administration tasks from auxiliary services tasks is to ask: "Does this task need to be performed around the clock?" Tasks that do not, such as planning and budget preparation, are generally considered administrative tasks; tasks that need to be performed continually, such as communications and identification, are usually categorized as auxiliary service tasks. Both types of tasks are of benefit to, or service to, the department as a whole; both types are primarily performed internally. Operational tasks, on the other hand, are performed externally. They are for the benefit of the public.

Personnel

The personnel function (including recruitment, selection, assignment, transfer, promotion, termination, and labor relations) has to do with who gets what jobs when and, very often, who gets what pay. It is, therefore, an extremely important task. Allen R. Janger has noted that modern personnel units have not been content in confining themselves to these activities and that they are becoming involved with management development, organization planning, personnel development, and personnel research.[20]

Police personnel development practices have often come under close scrutiny with respect to minority recruitment, selection, assignment, and promotion.[21] In numerous instances the federal courts have found entrance-level tests and job qualifications to be discriminatory against blacks, women, and Spanish-speaking Americans. More recently, attention has also focused on older citizens and disabled persons. Patterns of discrimination have also been identified in promotion and transfer practices.

Police personnel activities are frequently constrained not only by equal opportunity law but also by civil service systems, local government personnel departments, and state laws and regulations. Many police agencies have little or no control over their personnel systems, with hiring criteria, processes, and decisions administered by merit boards or civil service commissions.

This kind of structure helps reduce the amount of bias, personal influence, and political interference affecting police personnel matters, but it also inhibits police executives from assuring that personnel decisions contribute positively to the accomplishment of the overall police mission. A healthy balance should be sought between external regulation and police input to the police personnel function.

Standard 13.3
Minority Recruiting

Every police agency immediately should insure that it presents no artificial or arbitrary barriers (cultural or institutional) to discourage qualified individuals from seeking employment or from being employed as police officers.

1. Every police agency should engage in positive efforts to employ ethnic minority group members. When a substantial ethnic minority population resides within the jurisdiction, the police agency should take affirmative action to achieve a ratio of minority group employees in approximate proportion to the makeup of the population.

Source: National Advisory Commission on Criminal Justice Standards and Goals, Police (Washington, DC: U.S. Government Printing Office, 1973), p. 329.

Standard 13.6
Employment of Women

Every police agency should immediately insure that there exists no agency policy that discourages qualified women from seeking employment as sworn or civilian personnel or prevents them from realizing their full employment potential.

Source: National Advisory Commission on Criminal Justice Standards and Goals, Police (Washington, DC: U.S. Government Printing Office, 1973), p. 342.

An enduring police personnel issue concerns the desirability of higher education for police officers. Police reformers have advocated the hiring of college graduates for decades, and many police officers today have degrees or at least some college credits. Attempts to prove that college-educated police officers perform better have not universally succeeded, but most observers believe that the college experience makes officers more tolerant, more flexible, more understanding of different cultures, and more adept at problem solving.[22] Few police departments require higher education for police employment, but many agencies give applicants extra points for college; moreover, when final hiring decisions are reviewed, it seems clear that having a college degree is frequently an advantage in getting hired even when no formal reward for higher education is offered.

Training

The police training task can be broken down into a number of different approaches, including in-class and on-the-job training, academic and skills training, and recruit and in-service training. Instructors can be police personnel assigned to a training unit, general police personnel, supervisory personnel, command-level personnel, professional trainers, or college professors. The training can be conducted at a departmental or regional training academy, in roll-call sessions, on the street, in patrol cars, or at a college or university. The training might be for newly hired recruits, newly promoted officers, experienced officers, or even for a police chief.

Most small departments depend on the services of nearby larger departments or regional or state training academies. Almost all states require by law that recruits and newly appointed officers receive minimum amounts of training either before assuming their duties or during the first several months they are on the job. Such requirements, and the training commissions developed to satisfy them, have contributed significantly to upgrading police services in small communities.

Unless new police officers are thoroughly trained before they are on the job for any considerable length of time, they are likely to develop rigid habits and attitudes that will be difficult to alter. After recruit training, officers should be assigned to field training officers who will break them in on the job, showing recruits how their training is related to their work on the street.[23] Field training officers should be carefully chosen from among the best officers in the department. The early days of a new officer's career are crucial; they should be devoted to internalizing what he or she has learned from recruit training and reinforcing principles of good police practice.

When patrol officers are promoted to supervisory positions, they are usually unprepared for their new responsibilities. Just because they are capable police officers with considerable street experience and are well trained for police work does not necessarily mean that they will make good supervisors. The same holds true for administrative and management positions; a good supervisor does not automatically become a good administrator. The higher a police officer ascends in the hierarchical structure of the police department, the more training he or she needs to meet increased responsibilities. The training at each level must necessarily be different and must be designed to prepare officers for the work they will be expected to do on the level to which they have been advanced.

In-service personnel, whether generalists or specialists, need regular refresher training. Some police departments conduct daily roll-call training sessions. Others insist that their officers undergo one week of in-service training every year. Some departments do both. Regardless of how in-service training is accomplished, it is a must in a field as complex and involved as police work. How well or how poorly a police officer is trained relates directly to the success or failure of the entire organization in meeting its goals and objectives.

Field Training
Standard 33.4.3 A written directive establishes a field-training program for all newly sworn officers with a curriculum based on tasks of the most frequent assignments with provisions for the following: a.   field training of at least four weeks for trainees, during and/or after the required classroom training; b.   a selection process for field training officers; c.   supervision of field training officers; d.   liaison with the academy staff, if applicable; e.   training and in-service training of field training officers; f.   rotation of recruit field assignments; g.   guidelines for the evaluation of recruits by field training officers; and h.   reporting responsibilities of field training officers.

Source: *Standards for Law Enforcement Agencies: The Standards Manual of the Law Enforcement Agency Accreditation Program.* Fairfax, VA: Commission on Accreditation for Law Enforcement Agencies, Inc., 1999.

Planning and Analysis

Planning is preparing for the future in the hope that anticipation and preparation will lead to more effective coping with future events. Planning is a much underrated function in most police departments. Many police departments do no planning whatsoever; others, through their budgets, plan only for the coming year. The philosophy of "we'll cross that bridge when we come to it" is prevalent throughout the police field.

It is essential, however, that police organizations plan for such eventualities as civil disorder, natural disasters, and rises in crime and accident rates. They must also plan for change and the effects of such trends as energy depletion, rapid technological advancement, and population shifts. Everyday planning for personnel requirements, police officer deployment, and patrol concentration is also important in the planning process.

In order to plan effectively and to make informed decisions about operations, administration, and auxiliary services, police departments need to perform at least three types of analyses. One type is *crime and problem analysis*.[24] Departments must collect and analyze data on crime and related problems in the community in order to allocate officers to shifts, deploy them to beats, develop effective tactics, assign special units to problem areas, and generally to respond to the crime problem as effectively as possible. The data that must be collected on each crime include location, time, and very specific information on method of operation (MO). Analysis of these data mainly involves looking for patterns and trends. The most important aspect of crime and problem analysis is communicating findings to operational personnel for use in performing their work.

A second type of analysis crucial to police effectiveness is *operations analysis*. Operations analysis examines patrol, investigations, and other operational tasks and seeks to improve their effectiveness. For example, operations analysis uses crime analysis data and data on other aspects of patrol workload (such as service calls, investigations, arrests, and auto accidents) to determine whether patrol resources are allocated in proportion to workload. Operations analysis also includes examinations of traffic accidents and traffic citations in order to establish a selective traffic enforcement program designed to reduce accidents.

The third category of analytical activity is *administrative analysis*. This involves the study of internal procedures and practices for the purpose of identifying problem areas and making improvements. For example, many police departments have had to analyze their recruitment, selection, and training practices in order to eliminate practices that discriminated against women and minorities. Many departments have performed studies to determine the best chemical agents to utilize, the ideal ammunition to issue, the most effective soft body armor to purchase, and the most cost-efficient type of automobile for patrol work. The variety of administrative analyses that might be performed is nearly boundless.

Budget and Finance

This task involves the administration and handling of departmental money matters. It includes such activities as payroll, purchasing, budgeting, billing, accounting, and auditing.

Depending on the size of the department and local governmental practice, some of these activities are handled by the parent system. In all cases, however, the police are involved, to a greater or lesser degree, in all of these functions. In the case of budgeting, the police department usually has full responsibility for development of its budget. The budget is important in that it outlines police activities and programs for a given period of time, usually one year.

Many police administrators have little understanding of the budgeting process; their budgets tend to be the same each year, with minor increases or decreases depending on the state of the treasury. This kind of copycat budgeting provides for no evaluation of the actual desirability of various programs and budget categories and leaves no room for innovation. No effort is made to determine what kinds of expenditures might bring the organization closer to achieving its goals and objectives. As a rule, only incremental changes are made.

Two progressive approaches are the Planning-Programming Budgeting System (PPBS) and Zero-Based Budgeting (ZBB). These two systems attempt to force administrators to identify the goals and objectives of their organizations and then to move toward achieving goals and objectives on the basis of intelligently allotting available funding resources. PPBS and ZBB are means by which administrators weed out ineffective or superfluous programs and practices and then emphasize activities that lead their organizations toward their goals and objectives in better ways. They make budgeting an ongoing process that mandates the continuing evaluation of programs to determine their effectiveness and usefulness.

Neither PPBS nor ZBB is a panacea; most administrators find it difficult to evaluate their own programs objectively and resist change even in the face of facts. The true relevance of programs to departmental goals and objectives is often difficult to determine. In addition, budget review and appropriation committees of the parent governmental system, accustomed to working with traditional budgets, are frequently unimpressed with what they often view as the overly sophisticated nature of these new approaches. Despite these shortcomings, however, the Planning-Programming Budgeting System and Zero-Based Budgeting are helpful because they force police administrators to ask themselves whether they are making the best possible use of the public's tax dollars. These systems force administrators and reviewers to consider financial requests in light of actual goals and objectives and allow them to manage their organizations systematically through their budgets.

Legal Assistance

The legal assistance function includes, depending on the jurisdiction, training in legal matters, legal advice in policy formulation and planning, liaison with legislatures and the courts, departmental representation in civil proceedings, advice and direction for internal administrative hearings, and counsel on specific problems arising out of criminal cases.[25]

Additionally, in some jurisdictions the police prosecute their own cases in the lower courts without any assistance from a district attorney or a state's attorney. In such instances, legal assistance is of the utmost importance and is concerned primarily with aiding officers in the prosecution of criminal cases. A police department may designate a police officer who has had legal training as its prosecutor and legal advisor, or it may hire an attorney specifically for this purpose.

Because most police departments are not large enough to employ a full-time attorney, many small departments may band together on a regular basis to hire a legal advisor who is available to all of them on a full-time basis. Other departments retain counsel on a part-time basis.

Information Processing

Information is the lifeblood of many types of organizations, especially police departments. The task of processing information within police agencies includes a variety of secretarial, clerical, and data-processing duties. Today, computers and other information technology systems are typically utilized for information processing in police organizations, although much information is still processed verbally or in handwritten form.

Police communications and records systems are discussed in the next section on the auxiliary services subsystem, because they are needed to provide ongoing information and support to police officers in the field. Police departments also needed internal mechanisms that provide and process administrative information, however. Letters, memoranda, training bulletins, personnel orders, schedules, policies, procedures, and rules must be prepared and disseminated. Systems are also needed to keep track of expenditures, vehicle maintenance, officer training, departmental equipment and supplies, found property, evidence, and numerous other matters. In addition, police administrators need systems that provide them with information about how well the department is doing in meeting its primary goals and objectives—that is, with feedback to establish a closed-loop management system that corrects mistakes and keeps the organization on track toward efficiency and effectiveness.

The technology of information processing changes ever more rapidly in today's electronic age. In some police agencies, a significant amount of internal information sharing is now accomplished via e-mail, internet mailing lists, and an organizational intranet. More and more, of course, external information sharing is also electronic, utilizing e-mail, Web pages, and the Internet.

Public Information

Both public relations and press relations come under the subtask of public information. Keeping the public informed about police activities includes news about crime, media relations, features on police officers and programs, information on crime prevention and how to avoid being victimized by crime, public lectures on policing and explanations of policies, and procedures that affect the public. The public information function is important to the police because it gives them the opportunity to tell their story, to explain their position on controversial issues, and to respond in a meaningful way to public concerns.

A new method of disseminating public information is the Web page or home page on the Internet. Many police agencies today have their own home pages. Often these are fairly rudimentary, providing about the same information that is contained in the department's brochures or annual report. However, home pages can be used to post the latest information about crimes, wanted persons, and new police programs, as well as to solicit public input on important police-related issues. If police departments devote sufficient time and energy to keeping their home pages fresh and current, many citizens will avail themselves of this method of obtaining public information.

For the foreseeable future, though, most of the public will continue to receive their information about the police via the media. Unfortunately, many police officials find it difficult to relate to the media. Because of poor experiences with newspapers and television stations, some police officials see members of the media as enemies or, at the very least, antagonists. As a result, they make it difficult for reporters to get the news and sometimes exhibit open hostility toward the press. This creates a negative attitude on the part of media representatives toward the police and contributes to the development of what can easily become a vicious cycle of open warfare between the police and the press. Such a relationship works to the detriment of everyone concerned and negatively affects the image of the police.

It is essential for police administrators to cultivate good relations with the press.[26] Whether this is done through the formal establishment of a public information division, as in large departments, or through the careful handling of media relationships by the chief or a designated officer, as in small departments, it is important to understand that a positive policy needs to be developed within every police department for the handling of public information. Whoever is responsible for public information should make every possible effort to provide news on police activities as accurately and as quickly as possible. The designated public information officer should also encourage feature stories about the police department and cooperate fully in their development.

The police administrator must resist the temptation, albeit strong on occasion, to manipulate reporters and the news. The responsible police administrator cultivates healthy media relations not only because the media enhance the flow of news and information but also because they provide a line of communication between the police and the public that the police cannot afford to jeopardize. Media institutions are essential to the democratic process and serve as adversaries to governmental abuse. In the United States they are as much a part of the system of checks and balances as are any of the branches of government; as such, they must be respected and treated fairly. Thomas Jefferson once said that he would prefer the press with no government to the government with no press.

Public Information
Standard 54.1.1 The public information function shall include, at a minimum:

   a.   assisting news personnel in covering news stories at the scenes of incidents;

   b.   being available for on-call responses to the news media;

   c.   preparing and distributing agency news releases;

   d.   arranging for, and assisting at, news conferences;

   e.   coordinating and authorizing the release of information about victims, witnesses, and suspects;

   f.   assisting in crisis situations within the agency;

   g.   coordinating and authorizing the release of information concerning confidential agency investigations and operations; and

   h.   developing procedures for releasing information when other public service agencies are involved in a mutual effort.

Source: *Standards for Law Enforcement Agencies: The Standards Manual of the Law Enforcement Agency Accreditation Program.* Fairfax, VA: Commission on Accreditation for Law Enforcement Agencies, Inc., 1999.

Inspections

The aim of the inspections function is to ascertain adherence to direction. Persons handling this task systematically check the organization to determine how well policies, procedures, rules, and regulations are being followed.

Although larger departments need to establish specialized inspections units, it should be understood that in all police departments, regardless of size, every administrator and supervisory officer has inspection responsibilities. Each must attempt to learn how well subordinates adhere to directives and to control subordinates in this adherence.

In departments large enough to have a specialized inspections unit, the persons responsible for this function are not directly involved in the controlling process. They merely inspect the organization and report their findings, both good and bad, to the chief. If they discover any lack of adherence to directives, it is the chief who exercises the controlling function, not them. It is important to understand that in large departments the inspections function and the controlling function are different functions performed by different people. In departments not large enough to have an inspections unit, both the inspections and controlling functions are usually performed by the chief or by someone designated to do this on a part-time basis.

It is essential that the inspections function be administered on a totally professional, objective, and impartial basis. Under no circumstances should those assigned to inspections go about their work in a clandestine fashion. Officers should be advised that inspections is an ongoing function within the department and that all operational, administrative, and service subsystems will be examined to determine adherence to directives. It should also be understood that all positive as well as negative findings will be reported.

The inspections function will serve the chief as a secondary source of information to supplement information received through the regular chain of command. Many important matters that the chief should be aware of will, either purposely or inadvertently, never come to the attention of anyone at the command level. Some of these problems will be of such significance that they will negatively affect the entire organization if they are not identified and solved. A good inspections program will identify them. A good chief will solve them.

Officers who perform the inspection function are in a sense the chief's internal patrol unit. Whereas the regular patrol unit becomes involved with violations of the criminal law as committed by the general public, the inspections unit is interested in the enforcement of the department's internal laws, policies, procedures, rules, and regulations. Just as the personnel of the regular patrol unit must be regarded as fair and honest to be successful at their jobs and respected by the public, so too must inspections personnel have a reputation for fairness and integrity if they are to perform their function effectively and without creating excessive internal strife.

Internal Affairs

Internal affairs personnel investigate allegations of police misconduct and criminality. These investigations emanate from information received from the public, the police, and independently developed sources. The internal affairs function should always be a specialized function in large departments. In small departments the chief should be responsible for internal affairs.

The need to have the internal affairs function performed by the chief of police in small departments should be obvious. In such departments the chief is, as a general rule, the only sworn officer in the department who will not be reduced in rank and reassigned. The chief, therefore, is the only logical candidate; only the chief can handle such an assignment without having to fear its consequences at a later date. In highly political police departments, in which police chiefs change with the election of a new mayor or with the appointment of a new city manager, it is virtually impossible to establish viable internal affairs programs. This is especially so if police chiefs are recycled back into the organization with every change in political administration. Consequently, many departments, especially small ones, rely on an outside agency, such as the state police, to conduct particularly sensitive or serious internal investigations.

Several years ago, a presidential commission noted that "if the police are to maintain the respect and support of the public, they must deal openly and forcefully with misconduct within their own ranks whenever it occurs."[27] This can be accomplished only through the establishment of an internal affairs component that is designed to meet its obligations fully, which in some situations may even require proactive seeking out of corrupt officers rather than merely sitting back and waiting for allegations to investigate.[28] The people who guard the guards must be skilled investigators of unquestionable integrity.

A practice that has become more common in the last decade is external or "civilian" review of complaints against the police. A variety of models are now in existence, from ones in which nonpolice personnel conduct the investigations all the way to models in which the external board serves only as an avenue of appeal for those complainants who are not satisfied with the police handling of their case.[29] While still somewhat controversial among police officials, these external mechanisms for responding to police misconduct seem to be gaining popularity, probably because they offer the public some assurance that its complaints against the police will be taken seriously and not swept under a rug.

Intelligence

The gathering and analysis of information comprise the intelligence function within a police department. For the most part, it involves collecting and analyzing information that relates to the existence, scope, and impact of gangs, organized crime, drug trafficking, and terrorism.

Criminal Intelligence

Standard 51.1.1   If the agency performs an intelligence function, procedures must be established to ensure the legality and integrity of its operations, to include:

   a.   procedures for ensuring information collected is limited to criminal conduct and relates to activities that present a threat to the community;

   b.   descriptions of the types or quality of information that may be included in the system;

   c.   methods for purging out-of-date or incorrect information; and

   d.   procedures for the utilization of intelligence personnel and techniques.

Source: *Standards for Law Enforcement Agencies: The Standards Manual of the Law Enforcement Agency Accreditation Program.* Fairfax, VA: Commission on Accreditation for Law Enforcement Agencies, Inc., 1999.

Most intelligence units operate through the extensive use of informants and undercover employees. Officers assigned to the intelligence function usually serve in a staff capacity and rarely become involved operationally. In most departments intelligence personnel report directly to the chief, who makes tactical and strategic decisions based on the information and analyses provided.

Officers assigned to the intelligence function should be selected very carefully and should possess qualities of integrity that are completely above reproach. They should be experienced police officers who have served their apprenticeships as departmental investigators.

With the emergence of domestic and international terrorists openly dedicated to the violent overthrow of the government and to the destruction of the democratic process, the police intelligence function has become increasingly important and controversial. That the government and the society have a right and an obligation to defend themselves from such groups is not usually questioned, but of great and legitimate concern are decisions about which groups to investigate and what means of investigation should be used.

Many police agencies apparently closely monitored totally law-abiding groups during the 1960s and 1970s. The suspected "crimes" of these groups seem to have been nothing more than opposition to prevailing government policies, such as escalation of the Vietnam War. These groups were spied on (and in some instances had their mail illegally opened and their homes and offices burglarized) because they were political dissenters. The efforts of earlier political dissenters, such as John Adams, Thomas Paine, and George Washington, made political dissent legal and, indeed, important in our system of government. Police administrators must have a strong appreciation of this. They must be careful to differentiate between dissenters and truly violent opponents of the democratic process. The latter, but not the former, are worthy targets of police intelligence activity.

The Auxiliary Services Subsystem

We have described operations as activities performed in direct assistance to the public and administration as activities that are likely to be of long-term benefit to all units of the organization. The remaining activities constitute the *auxiliary services subsystem*. It should be noted that these activities also benefit other units within the department but on a more regular and frequent basis than administrative activities. Auxiliary services functions are usually available to assist the police officer on a 24-hour-a-day, 365-day-a-year basis; administrative functions are usually available eight hours a day, five days a week. Although it is sometimes difficult to distinguish between these two types of activities, it is useful to think of administrative services as long-range services available on a limited basis and of auxiliary services as direct services available on a continuing basis. The tasks included within the auxiliary services subsystem are records, communications, property and evidence, laboratory, detention, identification, alcohol testing, facilities, equipment and supply, and maintenance.

Records

The records task, a vitally important one for the police organization, furnishes the agency with a memory, enabling it to retrieve information long forgotten. It can provide information on wanted persons, unpaid parking tickets, last year's traffic accidents, crime patterns, and activity statistics.

The foundation of the records task is the reporting system. Some departments use one report form for almost all types of complaints; others have separate forms for different types of complaints. Regardless of the system used, each complaint should be assigned a unique complaint number for use in case control. All initial and follow-up reports on a given complaint should bear this number, enabling the records unit to maintain individual files on all investigations.

In addition to files of complaint reports, the records unit should ordinarily maintain files on arrests, warrants, traffic tickets, summonses, methods of operation, aliases, and mug shots. The records unit should also maintain cross-index files for the quick retrieval of information.

Medium and large police departments, as well as many small ones, have found it helpful to computerize their records systems, thereby giving them a capability of instant record retrieval. Many departments have now refined this process to the point of installing computer terminals in patrol cars, providing officers with laptop computers, or even issuing handheld palmtop computers, thus giving individual officers the opportunity to check immediately on such matters as suspicious persons and stolen vehicles they might come across in the course of their duties. The computerization of records has made police work more effective and efficient.

Access to departmental records must be available 24 hours a day. For the small department with limited personnel, this sometimes poses a severe problem, especially from a security standpoint. Because of the necessity to control access, records cannot be made available on a one-to-one basis to anyone in the department who happens to need them. Therefore, small departments must assign records officers who will be responsible for records for control purposes during given shifts. A strict system of accountability should be enforced in all such instances.

Communications

The communications function (call taking and dispatching) is integral to both operations and auxiliary service. In many instances, communications personnel handling incoming telephone calls are able to satisfy callers' needs directly, without having to refer matters further. When such services are provided to the public directly in this way, they are operational. But for the most part, communications personnel provide internal services that benefit police officers and assist them in their work. The bulk of their work is directed toward helping officers perform their tasks, and therefore they are generally looked on as being auxiliary service personnel.

Communications
Standard 81.1.2   A written directive requires that the agency's radio operations be conducted in accordance with Federal Communications Commission (FCC) procedures and requirements.
Standard 81.2.1   The agency provides 24-hour, toll-free telephone access for emergency calls for service.

Source: *Standards for Law Enforcement Agencies: The Standards Manual of the Law Enforcement Agency Accreditation Program.* Fairfax, VA: Commission on Accreditation for Law Enforcement Agencies, Inc., 1999.

As a vitally important police function, communications provides the link between the police and the public for the delivery of police services to the community at large. It should go without saying that people assigned to the communications task should be effective communicators who are receptive to and concerned about the public interest. When answering telephones, communications personnel must obtain as much accurate information as possible about complaints, so that proper responses can be chosen and responding units can be prepared for what is likely to await them. As dispatchers, communications personnel must be aware of the seriousness of all calls and assign appropriate numbers of officers and vehicles to accommodate needs and ensure officer safety. The communications unit is the brain of every police department; it receives information, processes it, and sends signals out into the system to be acted on.

Property and Evidence

This task encompasses the handling of all property for which the police are responsible (e.g., prisoners' property, recovered stolen property, lost property, confiscated property, departmental property, abandoned and towed vehicles, and evidence).

The handling of property, thought by some to be a simple warehouse operation, can be complicated and burdensome for the police administrator. In all cases, property must be protected in a systematic way. Although some items need to be stored for only short periods, others, such as perishable goods or narcotics evidence, need special care and continual surveillance. Honest attempts must be made to find owners of lost property; departmental property and equipment must be accounted for and maintained.

Property Management

Standard 84.1.2   All in-custody property and evidence is stored within designated, secure areas.

Standard 84.1.6   The following documented inspections, inventory and audits shall be completed:

a.   an inspection to determine adherence to procedures used for the control of property is conducted at least quarterly by the person responsible for the property and evidence control function or his/her designee;

b.   whenever the person responsible for the property and evidence control function is assigned to and/or transferred from the position, an inventory of property is conducted jointly by the newly designated property custodian and a designee of the CEO, to ensure that records are correct and properly annotated;

c.   an annual audit of property held by the agency is conducted by a supervisor not routinely or directly connected with control of property; and

d.   unannounced inspections of property storage areas are conducted as directed by the agency's chief executive officer.

Source: *Standards for Law Enforcement Agencies: The Standards Manual of the Law Enforcement Agency Accreditation Program.* Fairfax, VA: Commission on Accreditation for Law Enforcement Agencies, Inc., 1999.

Special procedures must be devised for the control of all property, and records must be maintained so that any single piece of property can be located at a moment's notice. A rigid system of security for the property storage area is essential for the protection of all property, and great pains must be taken to control property in the possession of the police.

Handling evidence is an especially difficult and important task, as the American public learned during the O.J. Simpson murder trial. In order for evidence to be admissible in court, it must be maintained within a chain of custody that guarantees it to be in the same condition as when it was seized by police. Each time a piece of evidence is passed, for whatever reason, from one person to another, the person taking possession becomes a link in the chain of custody. Officers responsible for property within a given police department must maintain records indicating the chain of custody and describing the purposes for which evidence has been passed from one person to another. Property officers must establish a system to maintain the integrity of evidence, always exerting caution that it is not altered or contaminated.

Laboratory

Sophistication in investigative activities requires the use of technology and science. Instead of relying solely on confessions to get convictions, which had been the traditional approach, the police now often rely on the development of scientific evidence through such techniques as DNA analysis and Automated Fingerprint Identification Systems (AFIS).[30] Physical evidence such as fibers, tool marks, tire tracks, bloodstains, and fingerprints are considered the most reliable of all forms of evidence; the examination and classification of such evidence rests with the laboratory.

Few police departments have the financial resources to maintain their own laboratories, although in recent years even the smallest police organizations have been able to train evidence technicians to perform some of the more routine scientific tasks. Most police departments rely on the facilities of regional or state laboratories, and many send evidence to the Federal Bureau of Investigation Laboratory in Washington, D.C., certainly one of the best police laboratories in the world.

Because physical evidence has come to play such an important role in the successful prosecution of cases, it is imperative for all police departments to rely on the laboratory for processing evidence. This requires all departments to either establish their own laboratories or develop working relations with other laboratories that have the capabilities of examining every conceivable type of evidence. In departments that do not have their own laboratories, one person is often designated as laboratory coordinating officer and given the responsibility for coordinating physical evidence examinations.

Detention

For most police departments the detention task usually involves the temporary confinement of arrested persons for short periods after their arrest. If the accused person is not released by the court after his or her arraignment or cannot raise the necessary bail for release, he or she is usually taken to a holding facility, often administered by the county, until trial. Incarceration in police lockups, therefore, is usually for short periods of time, and police jail populations are generally very transient.

Because our system of justice presumes the innocence of all persons charged and because our culture dictates that all human beings be treated with dignity, arrested persons in the custody of the police deserve fair and just treatment. Separate quarters for juvenile and female detainees must be provided. Detention areas should be clean and should give prisoners the opportunity to rest, wash, and use toilet facilities. Prisoners should be fed and housed in accordance with their needs; they should be protected from other prisoners, as well as from themselves at times. All personal property, including belts, shoelaces, neckties, matches, and cigarettes, should be temporarily confiscated. In order to prevent prisoner suicides, cells should be constantly monitored by closed-circuit television and by sound systems, and all cells should be constructed or reconstructed to be suicide-proof. Prisoners should also be checked periodically to prevent them from doing bodily harm to themselves. If prisoners need medical attention, it should be provided immediately. In short, in attempting to meet the needs of prisoners, the police should act responsibly.

Detention facilities should be secured and should be designed to prevent escape as well as any danger to police personnel. One officer should be placed in charge of all prisoners and held accountable for their care while in custody.

Identification

The identification task, which usually entails fingerprinting and photography, relates most notably to detention, records, and criminal investigation. Prisoners should be both fingerprinted and photographed immediately following arrest. Fingerprints are maintained as permanent records in local, state, and federal files. Photographs are usually maintained locally for future reference. Both are extremely useful in criminal investigations for identification purposes. Photographs are used to identify suspects and to record crime scenes in vivid detail; they are often useful in the prosecution of cases. Fingerprints also serve to identify suspects, sometimes providing the only link between a crime and a criminal. Modern AFIS systems have greatly improved the value of fingerprints, both for positive identification of prisoners using aliases and for suspect identification using latent fingerprints found at crime scenes.[31]

Large police departments usually have identification experts who are skilled in all aspects of fingerprinting and photography. Some departments equip all of their police vehicles with inexpensive cameras and require their patrol officers and detectives to do their own photographing. Some small departments also train one or more officers on each shift to handle fingerprinting, photography, and other technical crime scene services as a part of their normal patrol or investigative activities as the need arises.

For the proper investigation of major crimes, it is essential for all police departments to have available to them the resources of a truly professional police photographer and identifications expert. If such an expert is not locally available, the department should depend on the services of personnel available from regional identification facilities or from state police organizations.

Alcohol Testing

Because drunk driving causes so many automobile-accident injuries and fatalities, many police departments consider the apprehension and conviction of intoxicated drivers to be one of their highest priorities. In addition to an officer's observations of a defendant's driving behavior and condition, the results of an alcohol test can be compelling evidence of intoxication.

Several different methods can be used to test for the degree of intoxication, including the examination of the breath, blood, and urine. Because the breath test can be administered by a police officer trained in the operation of the testing equipment, it is the test most commonly used by police departments. Blood and urine tests involve laboratory analysis and have proved to be difficult methods for the police to use.

It is the policy of most police departments, both small and large, to train a number of officers on each shift to administer breath tests. The process is simple and can be learned in a short period. All police departments should be equipped for alcohol testing or should have the facilities for such testing available to them immediately.

Facilities

The police facilities task involves all aspects of the building or buildings in which a police department is housed. It encompasses the allocation and efficient use of space. The facilities task is designed to make the best possible use of available space, with full consideration given to the goals and objectives of the organization.

Because most police chiefs are not qualified as building superintendents or architects, the police facilities task has been poorly handled over the years. Yet the way space is used is of supreme importance in the implementation of police programs and in getting the work done. To this day, many police departments are cramped in abandoned city halls or in station houses built in the early 1900s. These ancient edifices often lack proper security, sanitary facilities, and rooms for lockers, roll calls, and interviews. Very often their layouts expose communications rooms to the public and necessitate the location of cell blocks down flights of stairs in basements that lack ventilation and over the years have become moldy and dirty.

The structural grouping of related police functions is one of the most important aspects of the facilities task. Subsystem components that depend on each other or are similar in nature should be located in close physical proximity. The communications and records sections, for example, should be close together, with consideration given to the necessity of locating records in an area accommodating public access while at the same time sealing off communications from the range of public view and hearing. Similarly, offices used for operational purposes, such as patrol and investigations, should be separate but at the same time near each other. In order to enhance prisoner safety, detention facilities should be located in or near an area that is staffed 24 hours a day.

Equipment and Supply

There is an almost endless variety of police equipment and supplies. Police equipment includes vehicles, bullhorns, searchlights, first aid kits, computers, firearms, cameras, uniforms, riot gear, radios, dogs, horses, microscopes, aircraft, boats, motorcycles, scooters, and bicycles. Supplies include items such as paper, forms, pens, gasoline, tires, fingerprint powder, bullets, bandages, and flashlight batteries.

Personnel responsible for the equipment and supply task are involved from purchasing through installation and disposal. They monitor equipment performance and evaluate departmental needs for new equipment. One of their more important functions is to develop an inventory system by which equipment and supplies can be controlled, replenished, and not lost or stolen. Every police department should calculate the rate of usage of each kind of supply item and flag items for repurchase when stocks have dwindled. Because good equipment and supplies are essential in the operation of every police department, this function must be performed expertly and must be looked on, as it oftentimes is not, as a specialized function requiring constant concern.

The personnel in charge of this responsibility should attempt to purchase equipment and supplies at the lowest possible cost. It is their obligation to establish bidding procedures, to put items out for bid, and to supervise the bidding process. In addition, to the degree possible, they should be required to enter into regional purchasing compacts with other police departments in their area in order to purchase equipment and supplies in quantity and therefore obtain the lowest possible unit costs.

Maintenance

Keeping police facilities clean and equipment repaired and functioning properly has a positive impact on the effectiveness of every police agency. Those who perform the maintenance task have this responsibility.

There is nothing more frustrating for a police officer than to be forced to work out of a dirty police facility with equipment that works only occasionally. In departments in which maintenance of facilities and equipment holds a low priority, the morale of police officers is likely to be low. In fact, one of the most frequent complaints voiced by police officers concerns the poor maintenance of the vehicles they drive.

Because most police chiefs do not regard maintenance as a police function per se, they rarely use good judgment in ensuring its performance at an acceptable level. Thus, in city after city, police cars operate at less than full spark plug capacity and have dented fenders, broken mirrors, and nonfunctioning lights. Very often, one finds oxygen tanks without oxygen, fire extinguishers in need of recharging, and first aid kits without bandages.

Many police chiefs find that it is more cost-effective to have maintenance service performed by outsiders on a contract basis. Some departments, for example, hire custodial services to maintain their buildings and hire private auto repair shops to maintain their vehicles. Because such services are provided on a competitive basis, outside service agencies are often found to perform them significantly better than departmental personnel assigned to this task. Most departments cannot afford full-time radio technicians, computer repairers, mechanics, and custodians. They can, however, afford to assign the responsibility for maintenance to someone within the department and hold that person accountable for the performance of the function. Although the maintenance function is not glamorous, it is nonetheless vital to the proper functioning of the organization.

Interdependence of Subsystem Tasks

The 30 basic police subsystem tasks discussed in this chapter must be performed in every police agency. If any one of these tasks is neglected or not performed, the job of providing good police services to the community will be impaired, often to a great degree. Inasmuch as each task is an integral part of the police system as a whole, the system itself as well as component subsystems will be affected adversely if any one of the subsystem tasks is performed poorly or not at all.

From an organizational standpoint, because all subsystem tasks are interrelated, all subsystem tasks are interdependent. Each relies on all of the others being performed well. When an organization fails to meet its goals and objectives, the failure can always be attributed to a breakdown in one or more subsystem tasks. Understanding the importance of these tasks is the first step in understanding the organization itself (i.e., the system). All of the organization's subsystem tasks are parts of the machinery that make the system run. Just as a worn tire, a faulty spark plug, or a sticky carburetor reduces the efficiency of an automobile, an inept patrol supervisor, an inadequately equipped laboratory, or a poorly planned budget reduces the efficiency of a police department. When all component parts of a system are working together in good order, the total system works in good order. Take away or damage one component part of the system, however, and you damage the whole system; it begins to break down. Systems that are put together poorly to begin with or lack the necessary parts to function stand little or no chance of achieving their goals and objectives.

Summary

In this chapter we have examined the most important basic police subsystem tasks, tasks that must be performed if police departments are to be viable. To suggest that these subsystem tasks are the only ones that police perform would be naive. Each subsystem task could in fact be looked on as an individual system in and of itself, with each task comprising numerous additional subsystems.

You should be aware that operations, administration, and auxiliary services are the three major subsystems of the police organization and that each comprises several additional important subsystem tasks that are essential to the system as a whole if it is to function properly. We have examined 30 of these subsystem tasks and have attempted to explain their importance and interdependence. In the last analysis, it is how well these tasks are performed that will determine a police department's success or failure.

Discussion Questions

1. When the subject of police work comes up, what kinds of activities come to mind? What are the implications for police work of the glamorized, fictional presentations seen by the public on television, in the movies, and in novels?

2. Juvenile services, community services, and crime prevention are often looked down on by police officers as not being "real police work." What is real police work? As a police manager, how would you go about elevating the status of such tasks?

3. When police recruits leave the training academy and hit the streets, they are frequently advised by more experienced officers to forget everything that they were taught, because it is not applicable to the real world. The recruits then learn from the "old salts" such things as sleeping on the job, accepting gratuities, quickly getting rid of service calls, and reporting on activities not actually performed. How can this cycle be broken? How can the department guarantee that the proper procedures taught in training classes are actually implemented?

4. An age-old problem concerns the responsibility for police abuses. If the investigation of police corruption and brutality is left to the police themselves, how can the public be sure that proper action is taken? If the responsibility is placed elsewhere, such as with a civilian review board, how can the police be convinced that they will be dealt with justly?

5. The police must collect intelligence about certain groups. Experience suggests that the police often exceed their proper role and use illegal means or collect intelligence on legal and nonviolent groups. How can these problems be resolved? Who should decide what means are proper and what groups should be investigated?

Notes

1. G.D. Eastman and E.M. Eastman, eds., *Municipal Police Administration*, Seventh Edition (Washington, DC: International City Management Association, 1971), p. 77.

2. *Merriam-Webster's Collegiate Dictionary*, Eleventh Edition (Springfield, MA: Merriam-Webster, 2003), p. 909.

3. M. Levine and J.T. McEwen, *Patrol Deployment* (Washington, DC: National Institute of Justice, 1986).

4. G.L. Kelling, T. Pate, D. Dieckman, and C.E. Brown, *The Kansas City Preventive Patrol Experiment: A Summary Report* (Washington, DC: Police Foundation, 1974).

5. G.W. Cordner and R.C. Trojanowicz, "Patrol," in *What Works in Policing? Operations and Administration Examined*, G.W. Cordner and D.C. Hale, eds. (Cincinnati, OH: Anderson, 1992), pp. 3-18.

6. G.L. Kelling and M.H. Moore, "The Evolving Strategy of Policing," *Perspectives on Policing* No. 4 (Washington, DC: National Institute of Justice, 1988).

7. Federal Bureau of Investigation, *Crime in the United States, 2000: Uniform Crime Reports* (Washington, DC: U.S. Government Printing Office, 2001).

8. P.W. Greenwood and J. Petersilia, *The Criminal Investigation Process* (Santa Monica, CA: RAND, 1975).

9. J.E. Eck, "Criminal Investigation," in *What Works in Policing?*, pp. 19-34.

10. C. Cosgrove, "Investigations in the Community Policing Context," in C.S. Brito and T. Allan, eds., *Problem-Oriented Policing: Crime-Specific Problems, Critical Issues, and Making POP Work*, Volume 2 (Washington, DC: Police Executive Research Forum, 1999), pp. 151-176.

11. D.W. Hayeslip Jr. and D.L. Weisel, "Local Level Drug Enforcement," in *What Works in Policing?* pp. 35-48.

12. M.W. Klein, "Attempting Gang Control by Suppression: The Misuse of Deterrence Principles," in L.K. Gaines and G.W. Cordner, eds., *Policing Perspectives: An Anthology* (Los Angeles, CA: Roxbury, 1999), pp. 269-282.

13. E. Magnuson, "Hitting the Mafia," *Time* (September 29, 1986): 16-22.

14. *Standards for Law Enforcement Agencies* (Fairfax, VA: Commission on Accreditation for Law Enforcement Agencies, 1998).

15. R.V. Clarke, ed., *Situational Crime Prevention: Successful Case Studies*, Second Edition (Guilderland, NY: Harrow and Heston, 1997), pp. 3-21.

16. Federal Bureau of Investigation, *Crime in the United States, 2001.*

17. P. Finn and M. Sullivan, "Police Response to Special Populations," *Research in Action* (Washington, DC: National Institute of Justice, 1988); Police Executive Research Forum, *The Police Response to People with Mental Illness: Trainers Guide and Model Policy* (Washington, DC: Police Executive Research Forum, 1997).

18. D. Crawford and R. Bodine, *The Handbook of Conflict Resolution Education: A Guide to Building Quality Programs in Schools* (Washington, DC: Office of Juvenile Justice and Delinquency Prevention, 1996).

19. D.J. Kenney and T.S. Watson, "Reducing Fear in the Schools: Managing Conflict through Student Problem Solving," *Education and Urban Society* 28, no. 4 (August 1996): 436-455.

20. A.R. Janger, "The Expanded Personnel Function," in Dale S. Beach, ed., *Managing People at Work: Readings in Personnel* (New York, NY: Macmillan, 1971), p. 34.

21. L.K. Gaines and V.E. Kappeler, "Selection and Testing," in *What Works in Policing?* pp. 107-123.

22. D.L. Carter, A.D. Sapp, and D.W. Stephens, *The State of Police Education: Policy Direction for the Twenty-first Century* (Washington, DC: Police Executive Research Forum, 1989).

23. M.S. McCampbell, "Field Training for Police Officers: State of the Art," in R.G. Dunham and G.P. Alpert, eds., *Critical Issues in Policing: Contemporary Readings*, Fourth Edition (Prospect Heights, IL: Waveland, 2001), pp. 107-116; G.F. Kaminsky, *The Field Training Concept in Criminal Justice Agencies* (Upper Saddle River, NJ: Prentice Hall, 2002).

24. M.M. Reuland, ed., *Information Management and Crime Analysis: Practitioners' Recipes for Success* (Washington, DC: Police Executive Research Forum, 1997).

25. President's Commission on Law Enforcement and Administration of Justice, *Task Force Report: The Police* (Washington, DC: U.S. Government Printing Office, 1967), pp. 63-65.

26. J.E. Guffey, "The Police and the Media: Proposals for Managing Conflict Productively," *American Journal of Police* 11, no. 1 (1992): 33-51; M. Motschall and L. Cao, "An Analysis of the Public Relations Role of the Police Public Information Officer," *Police Quarterly* 5, no. 2 (June 2002): 152-180.

27. President's Commission on Campus Unrest, *Report of the President's Commission on Campus Unrest* (Chicago, IL: Commerce Clearing House, 1970), pp. 5-8.

28. L.W. Sherman, *Scandal and Reform: Controlling Police Corruption* (Berkeley, CA: University of California, 1978).

29. S. Walker and V.W. Bumphus, "The Effectiveness of Civilian Review: Observations on Recent Trends and New Issues Regarding the Civilian Review of the Police," in G.W. Cordner and D.J. Kenney, eds., *Managing Police Organizations* (Cincinnati, OH: Anderson, 1996), pp. 45-65; P. Finn, *Citizen Review of Police: Approaches and Implementation* (Washington, DC: National Institute of Justice, 2001).

30. C.R. Swanson, N.C. Chamelin, and L. Territo, *Criminal Investigation*, Eighth Edition (Boston: McGraw-Hill, 2003), pp. 216-240.

31. D.J. Klug, J.L. Peterson, and D.A. Stoney, *Automated Fingerprint Identification Systems: Their Acquisition, Management, Performance, and Organizational Impact* (Washington, DC: National Institute of Justice, 1992).

Suggested Reading

Cordner, Gary W., Larry K. Gaines, and Victor E. Kappeler, eds., *Police Operations: Analysis and Evaluation*. Cincinnati, OH: Anderson Publishing Co., 1996.

Finn, Peter. *Citizen Review of Police: Approaches and Implementation*. Washington, DC: National Institute of Justice, 2001.

Geller, William A., and Darrell Stephens, eds., *Local Government Police Management*, Fourth Edition. Washington, DC: International City Management Association, 2003.

President's Commission on Law Enforcement and Administration of Justice. *Task Force Report: The Police*. Washington, DC: U.S. Government Printing Office, 1967.

Swanson, Charles R., Neil C. Chamelin, and Leonard Territo, *Criminal Investigation*, Eighth Edition. Boston, MA: McGraw-Hill, 2003.

THE TRADITIONAL PERSPECTIVE

The three chapters in Part Two address topics traditionally considered central to police administration. The discussions rely heavily on such matters as structures, principles, and functions. Although in some respects modern management has gone "beyond" these concerns (as Parts Three and Four will demonstrate), we feel strongly that the elements of traditional police administration are the building blocks for more advanced practices. To use a sports analogy, they are similar to the basketball fundamentals of passing, dribbling, and defensive position. The most sophisticated offensive and defensive schemes in basketball depend on such sound fundamentals. In the same fashion, police departments utilizing the most up-to-date organizational and managerial practices still depend in large measure on the sound application of traditional concepts of police administration.

Chapter 5 presents the basic principles of police organization and discusses the role of policies in police administration. Organizational principles are useful guidelines for organizing police work and police personnel. Although the applicability of the principles varies somewhat depending on department size, all police managers need a working familiarity with them. Policies, procedures, rules, and regulations provide the flow of direction from management to employees, and their enforcement is the police manager's basic means of control. Exercising effective direction and control is a particularly challenging aspect of police administration, because police officers have so much discretion in their decisionmaking in the field.

Chapter 6 considers six basic functions of police management: system building, planning, organizing, staffing, directing, and controlling. The first three of these functions are focused on creating and revising the structure and processes of the organization and are of particular concern to top managers. They are centrally concerned with "setting the stage" upon which managing, supervising, and actual work performance are carried out. The latter three functions—staffing, directing, and controlling—are heavily people-oriented. They are concerned with acquiring and utilizing the organization's human resources and making sure that employees both know what is expected of them and do what is expected of them.

In Chapter 7 we present an overview of the role of the police executive. Internal roles of managing and leading are discussed, as are external relations with political leaders, unions, the media, and the community. Several different styles of police executive behavior are considered. Emerging approaches that emphasize excellence and the "reinvention" of government are explored.

Principles and Policies in the Police Organization 5

This chapter addresses two related issues: (1) principles that guide the structure of the police organization, and (2) policies and procedures that guide police employees in their decisionmaking and actions. The information in this chapter lays the foundation for the discussion of the functions of police management presented in Chapter 6.

Authority, Responsibility, and Accountability

Any organization in which someone has authority over someone else is a hierarchy. Governments, corporations, families, fraternities, universities, and police departments are all hierarchies. Most organizations are hierarchical in some respects; some are more hierarchical than others. The greater the number of levels of supervisors or administrators an organization has, the more hierarchical the organization is. For example, Figure 5.1 shows that police department A is more hierarchical than department B, even though both have the same number of employees.

Figure 5.1
Two Seven-Member Police Departments.
Department A is More Hierarchical than Department B.

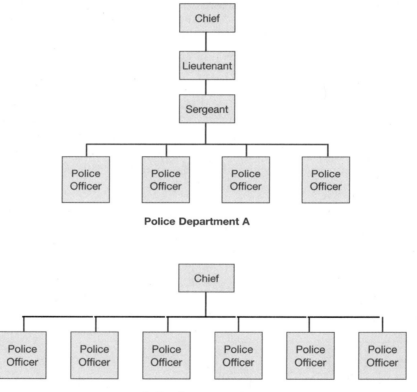

Typically, larger organizations are more hierarchical than smaller ones, simply because more employees require more supervisors, more supervisors require more mid-level managers, and so on. If too many levels of hierarchy are created, however, many different kinds of organizational problems can arise, such as delays in communication from the top of the organization to the bottom and lack of feedback at the top of the organization. Many organizations today, including police departments, are trying to become "flatter" by eliminating unnecessary levels of hierarchy.[1] As with most elements of organizational structure, balance is required—in this case, balance between the need for sufficient supervision and the desire to streamline the organizational structure as much as possible.

When we say someone is a person's boss, we generally mean that he or she has the authority to give the person orders. In terms of authority, the boss is the supervisor and has the power to command the subordinate. If the boss has the power to command the subordinate, it follows that the boss has the right, as well as the responsibility, to command the subordinate.

Besides bestowing on the boss the right and the responsibility to command, authority also gives the boss the right to make decisions and take actions. A police sergeant, for example, has the right as supervisor to approve a patrol officer's request to leave an assigned patrol area. The sergeant makes such a decision based on the responsibility to exercise delegated authority. The patrol officer, who by departmental policy is mandated to remain within a designated patrol area, has no authority to leave it without permission.

Authority and responsibility should be balanced in each position in the organization. It would not be fair to make an employee responsible for a function without also providing sufficient authority to make decisions and take actions in carrying out the function. By the same token, employees should not be given authority without commensurate responsibility, because of the possibility of abuse of that authority.

Authority and Responsibility
Standard 11.3.1   A written directive requires that:
a.   responsibility is accompanied by commensurate authority, and
b.   each employee is accountable for the use of delegated authority.

Source: *Standards for Law Enforcement Agencies: The Standards Manual of the Law Enforcement Agency Accreditation Program.* Fairfax, VA: Commission on Accreditation for Law Enforcement Agencies, Inc., 1999.

Police chiefs should never make the mistake of assuming that those to whom they have delegated authority will use it wisely. In order to minimize the ever-present possibility that delegated authority will be misused or abused, chiefs must institute a formal system for monitoring the activities of all officers who have been delegated authority. Such a system is based on the principle of accountability.

The principle of accountability means that all individuals to whom authority has been delegated must be held accountable for its use. It demands that action be taken if and when individuals exercise their authority improperly or irresponsibly. Further, it requires that a conscious effort be made to identify organization members who fail to use their authority, use too much authority, or use their authority improperly.

The police chief can monitor the use of authority by organization members in several ways. The basic way is through supervision within the chain of command. In addition, the inspections and internal affairs subsystem tasks described in Chapter 4 provide information about the use of authority throughout the department. The organization's information system should be designed to aid in monitoring performance, including use of authority. The performance appraisal process by which each employee's performance is periodically reviewed and evaluated is another important source of information.

The principle of accountability is put into effect through swift and certain action that is uniformly and fairly administered. All individuals should be treated alike, regardless of rank or position, and no favoritism should be shown in implementing the principle. Therefore, an action must be taken in every instance in which authority is misused or when it becomes apparent that an individual is shirking responsibility or not doing the job as assigned. Distinctions must be made, of course, between intentional acts and honest mistakes made by employees trying to do their jobs properly.

If a chief does not use the principle of accountability as a control device and takes no action, everyone tacitly understands that the department will condone certain improprieties under certain circumstances. When officers realize that they can misuse their authority or neglect their responsibilities with impunity, authority will be misused and responsibilities will not be met on a continuing basis throughout the organization.

In departments in which functions are poorly defined and little or no authority is delegated, it is impossible to put the principle of accountability into effect. In such organizations, authority, which is the glue that holds an organization together, becomes an administrative tool by which friends are rewarded and enemies are punished. Personalities, rather than organizational principles, take over the department and become the focal point around which the organization is administered. In such departments, an officer gets ahead by siding with the right people politically, not by doing the job. The job becomes incidental to personal priorities and prerogatives. The department becomes self-centered rather than community-centered.

Delegation of Authority

In a properly organized police department, the chief delegates authority for decisionmaking to people at all levels within the organization. Authority is the power to make decisions or to perform tasks. The ultimate authority in a police department lies with the chief, who must wisely and widely delegate authority to others so that decisions can be made and tasks performed.

Every person within an organization who is expected to perform a specific task should be delegated the necessary amount of authority to perform it well. In police departments in which chiefs do not understand this necessity, there will be few operational decisions made and little work accomplished. For example, when the chief of one small department was first appointed, there was only one other member of the department. Thirty years later, the department had more than 20 members. Although the chief was well-intentioned and had the best interests of the department and the town at heart, the department had grown so much that he was not able to adjust to the fact that he could no longer retain all authority and make all decisions in the department. He gave the one lieutenant and three sergeants little authority to make decisions and to assume command and supervisory responsibilities. As a result, the patrol officers' work was totally unsupervised. The sergeants were little more than patrol officers with three stripes on their sleeves and greatly resented the fact that the chief would not give them the authority to do their job. Both the town and the department suffered because of the chief's unwillingness to delegate his authority to others who needed it to do their work and meet their responsibilities.

The failure to delegate authority is not at all uncommon in police organizations. In many instances police chiefs simply do not understand the mechanics of the delegation process. In other cases, chiefs are unwilling to delegate authority, fearing that it will be abused by subordinates and reflect negatively on both the department and themselves. Many chiefs are aware that ultimate responsibility is theirs and, accordingly, are extremely cautious about allowing others within their organizations the opportunity to make mistakes that could prove to be embarrassing. Often, though, police chiefs are the least qualified people within their organizations to make decisions, because they are generally furthest removed from the people and the situations their decisions will affect.

The ironic aspect of this unwillingness to delegate authority is that it affects administrative matters more than operational matters. Police chiefs often refuse to delegate the authority for such actions as purchasing a tire to keep a patrol car on the road, issuing flashlight batteries, switching from summer-weight to winter-weight uniforms in the autumn, or making minor work schedule alterations. Yet the authority to use force or to take away a person's freedom is delegated to the lowest-ranking members of the organization, almost without a second thought. Perhaps it is because police chiefs realize that such awesome legal authority is so widely delegated that they jealously guard the limited administrative authority they have.

In delegating authority, chiefs should make absolutely certain that everyone within their departments has a precisely defined understanding not only of the authority he or she has been delegated, but also of the circumstances under which that authority may be used. In order to be sure that the person receiving delegated authority thoroughly understands it, it should be delegated in writing. Except for emergency situations, a chief of police should never delegate authority using only the spoken word. Confusion, forgetfulness, and misunderstandings can quickly dissipate authority that is not in writing.

Just as the chief has total authority over the entire police department, officers in high-ranking positions have more authority than those in lower ranks. Captains generally would have more authority than lieutenants; lieutenants, more authority than sergeants. A captain in charge of an operations bureau, for example, should have the authority to decide what priorities will be assigned to various types of investigations. The captain exercises authority by establishing these priorities responsibly in terms of a number of factors, which might include workload, seriousness of the offense, current crime problems, and availability of personnel. The captain might reasonably choose to delegate the authority to establish the priorities to the lieutenant in charge of the investigations division or retain the authority and establish the priorities personally. As a good administrator, the captain should probably delegate the authority to the lieutenant, spelling it out in writing. The lieutenant, however, should not delegate this authority to investigative sergeants. The lieutenant, with an overview of the entire investigations division, is in a much better position than the sergeants to establish investigative priorities.

Whenever feedback within a police system indicates that authority is being abused or that officers to whom authority has been delegated are not using it responsibly, that authority must be recovered or taken back. When they delegate authority, police chiefs must be fully aware that the delegation is never permanent. This must also be understood by everyone to whom authority is delegated. When a department is reorganized, when duties are rearranged or reassigned, and when departmental objectives, policies, and programs are modified, authority will inevitably be recovered.[2] The delegation of authority and the recovery of authority are continuing processes by which the organization is made more responsive to the interests of its clientele (citizens, in the case of a police department) and more productive in terms of its output (services).

If the concepts of authority, responsibility, and accountability are fully understood by everyone within a police department and if the chief follows some simple principles of organization in administering the agency, there should be no difficulty in using authority delegation as an organizational device to increase departmental efficiency and effectiveness.

The Authority-Level Principle

The authority-level principle is based on the premise that authority exists within an organization at all levels and that only decisions that cannot be made at a given level because of lack of authority should be referred upward for resolution. It is based on the assumption that within an organization there will be problems everywhere that must be solved continually if the organization is to meet its goals and objectives. Further, it dictates that "all decisions should be made as low as possible in an organization."[3]

In police departments in which functions have been improperly grouped, the chain of command is not in effect, and individuals at various ranks lack the authority to do their jobs, departmental personnel tend to either sweep problems under the rug or rely on the chief to make most of the decisions. Sweeping the problems under the rug is the easier of the two alternatives; the chief, lacking a viable chain of command, will in all likelihood never be advised that problems exist.

The authority-level principle is perhaps the most difficult principle of organization to put into effect. Weak command-level personnel and inept supervisors can be expected to avoid their problem-solving responsibilities and allow problems to fester into open sores. Insistence that problems that cannot be solved at lower levels be communicated upward is therefore essential. In police departments, this insistence should be procedurally formalized, with officers and managers at all levels mandated to write regular reports on problems that have surfaced that they lack the authority to solve themselves. This procedure was developed as a result of the work of Hrand Saxenian, a management consultant and former Harvard Business School professor who successfully applied it in working with business and industry. By writing down their problems and passing along their reports to the person within the organization to whom they report and from whom they receive their authority through the chain of command, they are in fact referring the problems upward for solution. When superiors receive reports outlining problems from subordinates, it is incumbent on them, if they have the necessary authority, to solve the problems themselves. If they lack the authority to solve the problems, they too are obliged in their regular reports to their superiors to list the problems that they lack the authority to solve personally. If such a system is put into effect, and if reports are kept by the department, accountability can be fixed on officers who are shirking their problem-solving responsibilities.

Most problems in most departments will probably be solved more informally. For example, a patrol officer who is having mechanical difficulties with a patrol vehicle should only need to mention this to the sergeant in order to have arrangements made for the vehicle's repair. If this problem is then solved, it would not be listed among the problems the sergeant outlined in his or her regular report. On the other hand, if the sergeant refuses to make arrangements to have the vehicle repaired, thereby refusing to make a decision on the matter, it would be the patrol officer's responsibility to list this as a problem in his or her report. By insisting that the patrol officer reduce this problem to writing, and by keeping the reports for a year, it will be a relatively easy matter for the lieutenant in charge of the shift, or for the captain in charge of operations, to fix accountability on the sergeant for not dealing with a problem for which authority had been delegated. Both the captain and the lieutenant should, by departmental policy, be required to make periodic spot checks on reports in an effort to find problems that their subordinates may be attempting to keep from them.

Although this example may seem to be a rather inconsequential matter, it should be understood that when combined with a number of other little problems, this problem can seriously impede the effectiveness of the patrol division. In one police department studied by one of the authors, minor problems similar to the one above seriously affected the morale of police officers and stood in the way of achieving departmental goals and objectives. Almost no problems were solved at the operating level, and no systems existed for referring problems upward. Although the department consisted of almost 200 police officers, it had a very loosely knit chain of command and no organization chart. If the chief was aware of the principle of accountability or of the authority-level principle, he was certainly not applying them to the management of the department. As a result, portable radios were in varying stages of disrepair, and many were missing. Police vehicles were poorly equipped and maintained. Several would have had difficulty passing state inspection; one had a nonfunctioning front headlight, another had a blown muffler. A patrol vehicle was once out of service for five days because no one assumed the responsibility of cleaning vomit from its rear floor rug. Patrol cars had no fire extinguishers or first aid kits. These and other problems remained unsolved because no one had the authority to solve them and because the chief was either unaware of or chose to ignore their existence. He simply did not know how to apply the basic principles of police organization to his department. He, the officers in his department, and the citizens in his community all suffered as a result of his inability to manage.

The authority-level principle, if it is applied consistently throughout the organization, will help to solve many problems that would otherwise go unsolved. It is a device that all police chiefs should utilize to the fullest extent if they expect their departments to meet their goals and objectives.

Key Organizational Principles

This section discusses several fundamental organizational principles: chain of command, unity of command, span of control, and grouping like functions. Along with the concepts of authority, responsibility, and accountability, these principles are used to help guide the structure of police organizations.

Chain of Command

Chain of command, also referred to as the *scalar principle*, is an organizational mechanism that establishes formal lines of communication within a police department. It is founded on the premise that the clearer the line of authority from the ultimate authority to every subordinate, the more effective decisionmaking and organizational communication will be. It establishes a vertical flow of information, directives, and orders downward through an organization. The chain of command establishes a direct path between every person in the department and the chief. The path may also be viewed as a two-way street whereby information may flow upward through the organization from subordinates through superiors and ultimately to the chief.

The schematic design that establishes the chain of command is the organization chart. Organization charts may be very simple or very complex, depending on department size. Regardless of their simplicity or complexity, however, they all show the relative positions of all subsystems within the police department. The organization chart in Figure 5.2, for example, shows a chain of command from chief to operations lieutenant to shift sergeant to patrol officer. In the same chart, the chain of command links the crime prevention officer and the chief directly.

Figure 5.2
Organization Chart for a 26-Member Police Department

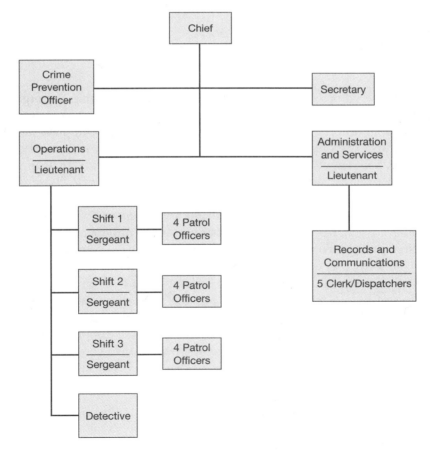

The chain of command is an invaluable organizational tool because it establishes formal communication links. If a department is to be properly organized, these communication links must be used by everyone within the organization to communicate formally. If the chain of command is not used for all formal communicating, serious organizational difficulties can be anticipated. For example, a chief of police who disregards the chain of command by issuing an order directly to a patrol officer is breaking the chain and dissipating the authority of all those within the chain who have varying degrees of authority over what the patrol officer does. If the chief makes a habit of issuing orders directly to patrol officers, they quickly learn that the chain of command is inconsequential in internal communications and that they, too, may disregard it in their efforts to communicate upward in the organization.

In applying the chain of command to the organizing of a police department, a chief should consider the fact that there are various levels of management, each with somewhat different functions. For our purposes, we can group these levels of management into three categories:

1. chief administrative level
2. command level
3. supervisory level

The chief administrative level, always the top level within the organization, consists of the chief and the chief's staff. The command level generally comprises all officers of the rank of lieutenant and above who have authority and overall responsibility for line or staff functions. The supervisory level consists of ranking officers below the rank of lieutenant who are assigned to supervisory duties. Most departments have sergeants, and many have corporals who fall into this category.

Ranking officers who neither command nor supervise line or operational functions are generally referred to as staff personnel. Although they hold rank and often perform important functions, they do not have command or supervisory authority over anyone. Most often staff personnel are assigned to higher levels of management. A lieutenant, for example, who is assigned to the operations bureau as legal advisor is in a staff position, not a command-level position, even though the work is performed at the command level. Another lieutenant assigned to the operations bureau might have the overall responsibility for running a patrol shift. Because the assignment would involve command responsibilities, this lieutenant would be considered to be in a command-level position.

Unity of Command

The principle of unity of command insists that the reporting relationship between subordinate and superior be on a one-to-one basis. A subordinate should not be expected to report to more than one superior or take orders from more than one superior.[4]

If a person is expected to take orders from more than one superior, tremendous confusion can result. A young boy whose father tells him to mow the lawn and whose mother tells him to wash the dishes instead will be wrong regardless of what he does. His parents have violated the principle of unity of command. They have both given the youngster orders, and they both expect him to follow through.

The consequences of this situation in a family setting are not disastrous. However, consider the case of a patrol officer who receives three different patrol assignments from the sergeant, lieutenant, and chief, respectively. Both the sergeant and the lieutenant will be upset by the chief's action, and the patrol officer will be totally frustrated: which of the three supervisors' orders should be followed?

This kind of problem must be taken into consideration when a police department is organized; departmental policy must stipulate that each officer takes orders from and reports directly to only one person: his or her immediate superior in the chain of command. If the chief wants to issue an order to a patrol officer, it must be understood by everyone that this can be done only through the chain. In this instance, the chief would tell the lieutenant how to assign the patrol officer, the lieutenant would tell the sergeant, and the sergeant, as the patrol officer's immediate superior, would issue the order to the officer.

Unity of Command

Standard 11.2.1   Each employee is accountable to only one supervisor at any given time.

Standard 12.1.2   A written directive establishes the command protocol for the following situations, at a minimum:

    a.   in the absence of the chief executive officer;

    b.   in exceptional situations;

    c.   in situations involving personnel of different functions engaged in a single operation; and

    d.   in normal day-to-day agency operations.

Standard 12.1.3   A written directive requires employees to obey any lawful order of a superior, including any order relayed from a superior by an employee of the same or lesser rank. The directive must also include procedures to be followed by an employee who receives a conflicting or unlawful order.

Source: *Standards for Law Enforcement Agencies: The Standards Manual of the Law Enforcement Agency Accreditation Program.* Fairfax, VA: Commission on Accreditation for Law Enforcement Agencies, Inc., 1999.

The principle of unity of command is a simple device that helps to avoid confusion in the issuance of orders. It makes all personnel within the organization more comfortable in their roles and more secure in terms of reporting relationships.

Practical necessities sometimes complicate unity of command, however. In the 26-member police department described in Figure 5.2, for example, the five clerk/dispatchers report to the lieutenant in charge of administration and services. Because they work shifts, though, the lieutenant frequently will not be on duty when they are. In this department, the on-duty clerk/dispatcher would typically be directly supervised by the on-duty patrol shift sergeant. Out of necessity, the clerk/dispatchers would be required to take orders from these patrol sergeants regarding, for example, when they could take their meal breaks. Ultimately, though, they would remain responsible to their superior in the chain of command, the lieutenant in charge of administration and services.

In situations such as these, which often arise in police agencies because they provide 24-hour-a-day service, two adjustments to the unity of command principle are required: (1) it must be clear to employees which supervisors have the authority to command them under what circumstances; and (2) at any given time, the employee should be expected to take orders from only one superior. With these adjustments, the principle of unity of command can be made compatible with the practical realities of police work.

Span of Control

The total number of subordinates reporting to a single superior is referred to as that superior's span of control. The chief who commands three captains has a span of control of three. The patrol sergeant who supervises the activities of nine patrol officers has a span of control of nine. The operations lieutenant in Figure 5.2 has a span of control of four—the three shift sergeants and the detective.

Early theorists believed that the proper number of persons within a span of control could be precisely established. Formulas were developed to "prove" that six or seven or some other number of people was the optimum number that could be supervised with ease. Over the years, however, it became apparent that the complexities of tasks and responsibilities, the skills of subordinates, and the talents of supervisors make it impossible to establish an ideal span of control. Rather, determining a given span of control is based on a subjective evaluation of the number of people a given supervisor can supervise effectively. Peter E. Drucker even suggests that a supervisor's span include a few more persons than he or she can closely supervise, thus making it impossible for a supervisor to do subordinates' work.[5]

It is useful to think of a span of control as narrowing progressively toward the top of the organization. Thus, a police chief has the smallest span of control. A good rule of thumb is that the span should be devised according to the degree of responsibility and authority that exists at a particular level in the hierarchy. The greater the degree of authority and responsibility that exists, the narrower the span of control.

Depending on circumstances, however, this general guideline need not always be followed. It is possible, for example, that a chief might have a span of control consisting of four captains, whereas a lieutenant who is in charge of a patrol shift in that department has responsibility over only three sergeants. As John R. Pfiffner and R. Vance Presthus point out, "there is no constant number applicable to every situation."[6] In short, span of control is an organizational supervisory tool that if used with care and revised through experience can contribute significantly to organizational solidarity.

Grouping Like Functions

Police officers have many basic responsibilities and work in a variety of ways. They direct traffic, intercede in family disputes, counsel youth, make arrests, drive patrol vehicles, conduct surveillances, enforce laws, write reports, maintain records, interrogate suspects, interview complainants and victims, testify in court, enforce parking regulations, investigate accidents, supervise subordinates, prepare budgets, provide for the safety of schoolchildren, give first aid, inspect liquor establishments, book prisoners, check doors and premises at night, collect and preserve evidence, perform Breathalyzer tests, deliver babies, and engage in myriad other functions that come within the purview of their mission. Their duties are many and are often conflicting.

Because a police organization cannot have a separate unit to perform each of the tasks listed above, it becomes necessary to combine them in some systematic way. The most useful way of grouping functions is through application of the principle of functional definition, which in police circles is usually referred to as grouping like functions. This principle holds that functions that are similar should be grouped together organizationally. Functions are similar when:

1. the same level of authority is required for their execution
2. responsibility for them is executed at the same time or in the same place
3. they require the same amount of training and/or degree of skill to be performed

It is through the grouping of similar functions that the various units within a police organization are formed. Suffice it to say that a chief of police should make a concerted effort to group similar tasks together logically within the organizational framework.

The chief should be guided not only by similarities in functions but also by the size of the department. In a department with one chief and four patrol officers, the chief would in all likelihood perform all administrative and auxiliary service functions as well as numerous operational tasks. The patrol officers would probably be assigned exclusively to operational responsibilities. In departments with more personnel available to perform specialized functions, any number of possibilities exists for grouping like functions.

You should note that the organization chart for a 26-member police department depicted in Figure 5.2 does not have a box for each and every one of the 30 police organizational tasks described in Chapter 4. Still, those tasks must be performed within this department, as in any other. Many of the 20 administrative and auxiliary services tasks, for example, would probably be performed by the chief or the lieutenant in command of administration and services. With respect to these and the operational tasks, the chief should be careful in delegating authority so that it is clear which tasks are the responsibility of which personnel.

Unless a conscious effort is made to group like functions in some systematic, logical way, officers within the department will eventually become confused over how they should perform assigned tasks. In one department, a sergeant assigned to the day shift was given responsibility for the safety of children as they traveled to and from school. In this position, the sergeant served as supervisor for more than 50 school crossing guards who assisted youngsters across busy city streets. That the sergeant and the crossing guards were placed organizationally in the same division was an appropriate grouping of similar functions.

The sergeant, however, was also assigned the task of inspecting the operations division's police vehicles at 8:00 A.M. Monday through Friday. These inspections usually lasted between 15 and 30 minutes. With schools opening at 8:30 A.M., the half hour between 8:00 and 8:30 was critical in terms of the sergeant's major responsibilities. His assignment to vehicle inspection at that time meant that he had to neglect his primary functions in order to perform a task very different from his major responsibilities.

In assigning the sergeant dissimilar functions, the chief violated the principle of functional definition; it was a serious violation because it was made at the peril of youngsters walking to school. Although important, the vehicle inspection function should have been performed by someone else, logically by someone assigned to the operations division. School safety and vehicle inspections are dissimilar functions and should not, unless the department is a small one, be performed by the same person or by the same group of persons. Although, depending on circumstances, the same level of authority may be required for their execution, the two tasks are not executed in the same place and do not require the same degree of skill or training to be performed.

A good rule of thumb in organizing a department is to group all operational duties, all administrative duties, and all auxiliary service duties separately. If a department is not large enough to accommodate these groupings, a distinction should be made organizationally between line and staff duties. *Line duties* are departmental functions that are operational in nature; *staff duties* are those performed within the administrative and auxiliary service components of the organization.

Over the last few years, in conjunction with growing interest in community policing, the criterion of "place," or geography, has become more important in grouping similar functions together. Departments that once gave greater emphasis to "time" in organizing patrol units (making the shift the primary building block of patrol operations) are now emphasizing place by creating beat teams and similar geographically focused units. In addition, departments that once organized largely on the basis of function (due to skill and training requirements of different specialized jobs) are now organizing more on the basis of geography. Under this model, for example, detectives report to an area commander rather than to a chief of detectives based at headquarters. Some departments have also reduced the number of functionally specialized jobs (detectives, traffic officers, etc.), arguing that neighborhood-based patrol officers can perform many of these functions, and can perform them more effectively due to their in-depth knowledge of their geographic areas of responsibility.

Grouping like functions inevitably raises the issue of specialization. In a five-member police agency, the patrol and investigative functions must be grouped together as similar functions and performed by the same people. A 30-member department, on the other hand, might lend itself to the establishment of both a patrol division and an investigations division. In a much larger department, where the availability of personnel would suggest further specialization, the patrol division might be subdivided into a number of subsystems to include a tactical unit, an emergency unit, a family crisis intervention unit, a helicopter unit, a scuba unit, a mounted unit, a canine unit, and a bomb unit. Similarly, the investigation division in the larger department could be subdivided into a vice unit, a narcotics unit, a shoplifting unit, a hotel unit, a stolen auto unit, a fraud unit, a homicide unit, a burglary unit, a robbery unit, and a liquor violations unit.

Care should be taken in determining the degree of specialization that should be introduced in any police department. Although traditional organization theorists tend to believe that effectiveness increases with specialization, this is not necessarily so. It was originally believed that the more concentrated the talents and energies of a worker, the greater the worker's productivity. The assembly line, the logical manifestation of this belief, revolutionized the manufacture of goods. In time, however, problems arose. Many workers became bored with the sameness of their routine. As boredom increased, so too did absenteeism and labor problems.

In police departments, specialization tends to deflect efforts away from meeting total organizational objectives and to concentrate efforts on attaining the narrower goals of the specialist's subunit. If a narcotics detective, for example, is paying an addict-informant for information, a real possibility exists that the informant may be committing burglaries to support his or her drug habit. Although the objectives of the narcotics detective may be satisfied by the information provided by the addict-informant, the overall goal of the department to decrease crime is not. The narcotics detective is, in fact, working against the overall goals and objectives of the department because the goals and objectives of the special unit seem to demand it. The tendency of subunits in an organization to pursue their own narrow objectives, regardless of the effect on overall organizational goals, is sometimes called *suboptimization*.

A related problem caused by specialization is that if some activity or function is assigned to a specific officer or unit, then the rest of the organization often feels that it is no longer responsible for that function. This happened in many police departments in the early stages of implementing community policing and problem-oriented policing.[7] Moreover, specialized officers and units can easily become isolated from the rest of the organization, which can impede communication, reduce effectiveness, and lead to misunderstandings and stereotyping.

Decisions about how much specialization there should be in organizing a police department are vitally important because they will directly influence the department's overall effectiveness. In departments with many specialized subunits, the chain of command becomes a less effective communication device. These units tend to work independently of one another. Information tends to be guarded on a unit-proprietary basis and not shared with the rest of the department. Detectives in some departments have been known to pocket arrest warrants in anticipation of making a major arrest themselves. Specialization tends to increase unit competition and negate departmental cohesiveness.

The problem of specialization versus generalization does not lend itself to an easy solution. Perhaps the best advice on the use of specialization in police organization came from Thomas Reddin, former chief of the Los Angeles Police Department. Reddin suggested that when specialization is considered to be absolutely necessary, personnel should be rotated frequently through specialized positions: "a good general rule to follow is to specialize if you must, generalize if you can."[8] This proposal seems to be an excellent rule to follow in organizing any police department.

Policies and Procedures

In the police field, policies, procedures, and rules and regulations are extremely important.[9] They are, in effect, statements that define role expectations for police officers. As previously pointed out, the police officer is given powers not granted to the ordinary citizen. Because they possess extraordinary powers, the police represent a potential threat to freedom. It can therefore be argued that the police need to be restrained by explicit and carefully defined directions that will guarantee they will play their roles in accordance with departmental rather than personal expectations. At the very least, the police in a democratic society should be expected to play their roles within the confines of legal constraints; they must certainly be expected to abide by the laws they are committed to enforce. In addition, because police departments are service-oriented public agencies that significantly affect public safety and public protection, they must work according to well-defined, specific guidelines designed to ensure that police officers will conform consistently to behavior that will enhance public protection (see "Establishment of Policy," below).

Standard 2.2
Establishment of Policy

Every police chief executive immediately should establish written policies in those areas of operations in which guidance is needed to direct agency employees toward the attainment of agency goals and objectives.

1. Every police chief executive should provide written policies in those areas in which direction is needed, including:

    a. General goals and objectives of the agency;

    b. Administrative matters;

    c. Community relations;

    d. Public and press relations;

    e. Personnel procedures and relations;

    f. Personal conduct of employees;

    g. Specific law enforcement operations with emphasis on such sensitive areas as the use of force, the use of lethal and nonlethal weapons, and arrest and custody; and

    h. Use of support services.

Source: National Advisory Commission on Criminal Justice Standards and Goals, *Police* (Washington, DC: U.S. Government Printing Office, 1973), p. 53.

One must also consider the fact that the police task is characterized by an enormous degree of discretion afforded individual officers in the exercise of their duties. The incredible variety of situations that police officers encounter, the omnipresence of danger in their work, their need to settle problems informally, and the variable personal skills that individual officers bring to their work all mitigate against narrow, unbending behavioral requirements.

The goal of any police chief must be to find the middle ground between unlimited discretion and total standardization (see "Police Discretion," p. 123

and "Structuring Discretion," p. 127). This is not an easy task, but it can be accomplished through an understanding of the proper applications of policies, procedures, and rules and regulations.

The case for clear behavioral guidelines in police organizations has been made time and again. In 1967 the President's Commission on Law Enforcement and Administration of Justice recommended that "police departments should develop and enunciate policies that give police personnel specific guidance for the common situations requiring exercise of police discretion."[10] In 1972 the American Bar Association asserted that "police discretion can best be structured and controlled through the process of administrative rulemaking by police agencies. Police administrators should therefore give the highest priority to the formulation of administrative rules governing the exercise of discretion."[11] In emphasizing the need for clear police policy, the Police Foundation pointed out in 1972 that "despite some progress in the last five years, police agencies still tend to keep major policies ambiguous and invisible rather than risk discussion and controversy by following overt administrative guidelines."[12]

Throughout the 1970s, many police departments promulgated policies and procedures in response to national and state efforts to establish standards for the law enforcement profession. The National Advisory Commission on Criminal Justice Standards and Goals published a lengthy volume in 1973.[13] Some of the Commission's standards were controversial. One standard, for example, established a college education requirement for police officers. Because of the controversial nature of some of the Commission's standards and because of the diversity of police practices around the country, some states formed their own commissions to establish police standards. The states of Washington and Virginia, for example, adopted their own standards that were incorporated into model policy and procedure manuals.

In the late 1970s and early 1980s, two additional stimuli for the development of standardized police guidelines appeared. One was the legal doctrine of civil liability, and the other was the creation of the Commission on Accreditation for Law Enforcement Agencies. Under the vicarious liability doctrine, police supervisors, administrators, and departments can be held financially liable if it can be demonstrated that a police officer has abused his or her authority as a result of not having been properly directed and/or controlled.[14] Police departments have thus been encouraged to develop precise guidelines addressing operational activities that could result in lawsuits.

The Commission on Accreditation produced a lengthy set of standards by which agencies could become accredited through the adoption of and adherence to certain relevant standards pertaining to law enforcement agencies within six size categories. The Commission was established through the efforts of four major police professional organizations: the International Association of Chiefs of Police; the National Organization of Black Law Enforcement Executives; the National Sheriffs' Association; and the Police Executive Research Forum. Most of the standards are stated in such a way that they identify procedures that must be covered by agency guidelines.[15] For example, Standard 35.1.4 states, "A written directive requires that non-probationary employees be advised in writing whenever their performance is deemed to be unsatisfactory and that the written notification be given to them at least 90 days prior to the end of the annual rating period."[16]

Standard 1.3
Police Discretion

1. Every police agency should acknowledge the existence of the broad range of administrative and operational discretion that is exercised by all police agencies and individual officers. That acknowledgment should take the form of comprehensive policy statements that publicly establish the limits of discretion, that provide guidelines for its exercise within those limits, and that eliminate discriminatory enforcement of the law.

2. Every police chief executive should establish policy that guides the exercise of discretion by police personnel in using arrest alternatives.

3. Every police chief executive should establish policy that limits the exercise of discretion by police personnel in conducting investigations, and that provides guidelines for the exercise of discretion within those limits.

4. Every police chief executive should establish policy that governs the exercise of discretion by police personnel in providing routine peacekeeping and other police services that, because of their frequent recurrence, lend themselves to the development of a uniform agency response.

Source: National Advisory Commission on Criminal Justice Standards and Goals, *Police* (Washington, DC: U.S. Government Printing Office, 1973), pp. 21-22.

As a result of these stimuli and the general evolution of police administration, most medium-sized and large police departments today have extensive and well-developed policies and procedures. Many small law enforcement agencies still lack adequate written guidelines, however.[17] An additional challenge is that policies and procedures must be regularly updated to reflect changes in the law and professional practice—too often, agencies adopt policies but then fail to keep them current and relevant. Good sources of up-to-date policies include the Commission on Accreditation, the International Association of Chiefs of Police, and the Police Executive Research Forum.[18]

The police role is much too ambiguous to become totally standardized, but it is also much too important to be left completely to the discretion of individual officers. The following discussions of policies, procedures, and rules and regulations should shed some light on the manner in which police chiefs can harness, but not choke, their employees.

Organizational Policy

Policies are more general than procedures, rules, or regulations. Policies are primarily guides to thinking rather than to action. They are especially important as guides to decisionmaking. Therefore, policies should reflect the purpose and philosophy of the organization and help interpret that purpose and philosophy for its members.

Harold Koontz and Cyril O'Donnell have identified four sources of organizational policy that help immeasurably in understanding the dimensions of what policy actually is:

1. originated policy
2. appealed policy
3. implied policy
4. externally imposed policy[19]

Originated policy emanates from within the organization itself, usually from top management, but often from other levels of management as well. Most of the policies found in a police department's policies and procedures manual are originated policies. Raymond O. Loen has identified five key stages in the development of originated policy:

1. define long-range purpose
2. define managing philosophy
3. define policies in areas in which repeated decisions are made
4. determine how policy will be enforced
5. specify how exceptions to policy will be handled[20]

Appealed policy also comes from within the organization. Somewhat like the common law, appealed policy develops haphazardly as decisions are appealed or simply passed up the chain of command. As with the law, unwritten and written precedents that gather force with time and use are established. These appealed policies are often confusing, conflicting, and uncoordinated.

Implied policy derives from the impression given by the organization's actions rather than its words. For example, if the expressed originated policy of a police department is that promotions are based on merit when in fact only the chief's friends get promoted, the implied policy is that it is not *what* you know that counts, it is *who* you know. Similarly, if a police department's official policy strictly limits the use of force by officers, but officers are informally encouraged to rough up prisoners, the implied policy creates a different impression and, indeed, dictates a different behavior than the originated policy.

Externally imposed policy originates outside of the organization. Three major sources of externally imposed policy for police departments are the courts, other governmental agencies, and employee organizations. The courts have imposed a variety of policies on police departments over the years, such as the requirement that employees accused of wrongdoing be treated according to due process considerations. The federal government has imposed the policy that personnel selection, assignment, and promotion will be made without discrimination according to race or sex. Employee unions are instrumental in establishing policy with respect to hours of work, pay, and grievance procedures. Such policies are all externally imposed.

Another important source of external input to police organizational policy is the community. Some police officials are inclined to resist such community input, but they should recognize that in a free and democratic society, the public is supposed to have substantial say in how their government, including the police, operates.[21] A balance has to be struck between appropriate citizen input and improper interference in day-to-day operations. Allowing and, in fact, encouraging community input at the policy-making level is a good way of achieving the right balance, because policies are broad statements of purpose and philosophy rather than narrow operational dictates.

Written Directives

Standard 12.2.1   The agency has a written directives system that includes, at a minimum, the following:

 a.   agency values and mission statement;

 b.   a policy statement that vests in the agency's chief executive officer the authority to issue, modify, or approve agency written directives;

 c.   identification of the persons or positions, other than the agency's chief executive officer, authorized to issue written directives;

 d.   a description of the written directives system format;

 e.   procedures for indexing, purging, updating, and revising directives;

 f   statements of agency policy;

 g   rules and regulations;

 h.   procedures for carrying out agency activities; and

 i.   procedures for review of proposed policies, procedures, rules, and regulations prior to their promulgation.

Source: *Standards for Law Enforcement Agencies: The Standards Manual of the Law Enforcement Agency Accreditation Program.* Fairfax, VA: Commission on Accreditation for Law Enforcement Agencies, Inc., 1999.

In order for an organization to develop coherent policy, the four types of policy must be consolidated. To this end, appealed policy must be recognized and then incorporated into originated policy. Implied policy should be minimized through the simple act of honoring originated policy. If originated policy is carefully adhered to by management, the development of implied policy will be severely hindered. Finally, the impact of externally imposed policy can be minimized by having comprehensive originated policy. When imposed, it must be accepted as binding and included in organizational policy. The police agency accreditation process, with its emphasis on self-study and continuing oversight, provides a very viable mechanism for developing and maintaining coherent written policy (see "Written Directives," p. 125).

With regard to the actual development of policies, several considerations are important.[22] Policies should reflect organizational goals, objectives, and plans. Under no circumstances should any policy exist that does not serve a useful purpose. Inasmuch as policies are guidelines for clear thinking and decisionmaking, they should be consistent. They should also be flexible so that they may be applied to varying situations and changing times.

Policies must be carefully distinguished from procedures and rules and regulations. Policies should also be committed to writing as a prerequisite, although not a guarantee, of clear thinking and understanding. All policies should be thoroughly explained to all personnel, and feedback should be sought to ensure understanding. Finally, policies should be controlled, added to, adjusted, and deleted according to the requirements of changing circumstances.

Organizational Procedures

Procedures are more specific than policies. As the means for carrying out policy, procedures are, in effect, guides to action. According to O.W. Wilson and Roy C. McLaren, a procedure is "more specific than a policy but less restrictive than a rule or regulation. . . . (It) describes a method of operation while still allowing some flexibility within limits."[23]

Most organizations abound in procedures. Police organizations, for example, have investigative procedures, patrol procedures, booking procedures, arrest procedures, radio procedures, filing procedures, roll-call procedures, sick-leave procedures, promotional procedures, evidence handling procedures, reporting procedures, and many more procedures that describe specific methods of operation. These procedures are action plans or designs for implementing policy. They are not totally inflexible, but they do describe rather detailed methods for carrying out policy.

Some procedures are mandated by the U.S. Supreme Court, which from time to time hands down decisions that provide procedural guidelines for all police departments to follow. For example, in *Tennessee v. Garner*, 53 U.S. 441 (1985), the Court established parameters within which the use of deadly force is justified. Prior to *Garner*, almost half the states in the United States

Structuring Discretion

Because police discretion has been covert and disavowed, no system exists for structuring and controlling it. So the police really suffer the worst of all worlds: they must exercise broad discretion behind a facade of performing in a ministerial fashion; and they are expected to realize a high level of equality and justice in their discretionary determinations though they have not been provided with the means most commonly relied upon in government to achieve these ends.

If discretion is to be exercised in an equitable manner, it must be structured; discretionary areas must be defined; policies must be developed and articulated; the official responsible for setting policies must be designated; opportunities must be afforded for citizens to react to policies before they are promulgated; systems of accountability must be established; forms of control must be instituted; and ample provisions must be made to enable persons affected by discretionary decisions to review the basis on which they were made.

There is plenty of room for narrowing discretion without eliminating it. The major challenge, in each area of police operations, is in deciding on the appropriate level of specificity for a given set of guidelines.

At a minimum it would seem desirable that discretion be narrowed to the point that all officers in the same agency are operating on the same wavelength. The limits on discretion should embody and convey the objectives, priorities, and operating philosophy of the agency. They should be sufficiently specific to enable an officer to make judgments in a wide variety of unpredictable circumstances in a manner that will win the approval of top administrators, that will be free of personal prejudices and biases, and that will achieve a reasonable degree of uniformity in handling similar incidents in the community.

As an example it would certainly be a major advance if a police administrator clarified his agency's objectives in handling minor disputes. If the prime objective is to resolve the dispute, as it should be, the efforts of the officer who attempts to do this through the use of a variety of different techniques will be legitimated and supported, and the officer who seeks only to make an arrest or who limits his concern to deciding whether an offense occurred will be expected to alter his behavior in order to conform. Here a policy could be more specific without becoming unduly restrictive.

Source: Herman Goldstein, *Policing a Free Society* (Cambridge, MA: Ballinger, 1977), pp. 110-112.

followed the common law rule, which held that deadly force could be used if necessary to apprehend a fleeing felon. *Garner* set forth a new procedure, which holds that deadly force is justified only when a "suspect threatens the officer with a weapon or there is probable cause to believe that (the suspect) has committed a crime involving the infliction or threatened infliction of serious physical harm." *Garner* therefore establishes a restrictive police procedure whereby "it remains constitutional for police officers to use deadly force to apprehend (certain) categories of fleeing felony suspects"[24] but severely limits by mandate the use of deadly force to apprehend others.

Koontz and O'Donnell have noted that in most organizations procedures generally multiply and become more exacting at lower organizational levels.[25] They ascribe this to the need for closer control, the advantages of detailed instructions, the reduced need for discretion, and the applicability of the philosophy that there is one best way to accomplish routine tasks. Although this theory may hold true in business organizations, it does not do so in police organizations. Police patrol officers operate at the lowest organizational level, yet their work is far from routine and requires enormous discretion. Because of this unusual characteristic of police organizations, James Q. Wilson, for one, has concluded that precise, positive guidance in the form of detailed procedures cannot realistically be made available in many circumstances.[26]

Loen has further pointed out that, in general, an abundance of standardized procedures tends to discourage initiative and imagination.[27] Stultifying procedures can unnecessarily complicate jobs and make it difficult to attract and keep capable and enterprising employees. On the other hand, procedures can decrease the time wasted in figuring out how to accomplish tasks and thereby increase productivity. They can also ensure a continuing level of quality output. Finally, good procedures can help cut training costs because they describe in an explicit way what actions an employee is expected to take.

As with policies, a middle ground must be sought in procedure development. One option is to think in terms of three categories of police activity: (1) those requiring strict procedural controls, (2) those requiring structured guidelines, and (3) those requiring only summary guidance.[28] The types of situations requiring strict controls are those that pose the greatest risk, such as use of force and pursuit driving.[29] In these situations, very serious harm can result if poor decisions are made. Both police officers and other subjects, including innocent bystanders, can suffer injury or death, and the department could suffer from lawsuits and negative publicity. Therefore, strict controls that attempt to minimize the chances of poor decisionmaking are certainly justified, even though they do limit police officer discretion and flexibility in decisionmaking.

The types of situations requiring structured guidelines are primarily those in which police officers have discretion in solving problems and enforcing the law. In these situations, officers need to retain substantial discretion in order to fashion tailor-made solutions to the wide array of unpredictable problems they are asked to handle. Without such discretion, officers would be too restricted in their options, and many citizens would be disappointed in the services that they received. Still, though, guidelines are needed. In domestic violence cases, for example, the department may strongly prefer that officers use the arrest option, unless very unusual circumstances are found, and may also mandate certain options, such as transporting the victim to a shelter whenever requested. An excerpt of structured guidelines from the Kentucky Model Domestic Violence Law Enforcement Policy is provided below.[30]

INTRODUCTION

Domestic violence is a serious crime against the individual and the community. The failure of any law enforcement officer to properly respond [to] and handle a domestic call, no matter how frequent, will expose individuals and the community to danger up to and including death. Because domestic violence can and does result in the death of individuals, every response to a domestic call, no matter how often, shall be treated the same as any other crime against a person.

Policy

Every officer shall:

1) *make an arrest when authorized by state law as the preferred response, instead of using dispute mediation, separation or other police intervention techniques;*

2) *treat all acts of domestic violence as criminal conduct;*

3) *respond with the same protection and sanctions for every domestic violence incident, regardless of race, religion, creed, national origin, gender, sexual orientation, disability, and socio-economic status, including cases where any of the alleged parties may be a law enforcement officer, public official or prominent citizen;*

4) *immediately report all known or suspected cases of domestic violence and abuse, adult abuse, or child abuse as required by state law; and*

5) *receive training on domestic violence as required by state law.*

Procedures

Whether or not an arrest has been made, if the officer has reason to suspect that a family member, member of an unmarried couple, or household member has been the victim of domestic violence, the officer is required to use all reasonable means necessary to prevent further domestic violence, including but not limited to:

1) *remaining at the scene as long as the officer reasonably suspects there is danger to the physical safety of the individuals present without the presence of a law enforcement officer;*

> 2) *assisting the victim to obtain medical treatment, including offering to transport, or arranging transportation of the victim to the nearest medical treatment facility capable of providing the necessary treatment; and*
>
> 3) *advising the victim of rights and services available.*

Situations requiring only summary guidance are those that are low-risk and relatively routine. They may still involve some use of discretion, but the range of options is smaller to begin with and less is at stake. Examples of such situations might include parking enforcement and telephone contacts with the public. Officers and other police department employees who engage in these activities need guidance in order to perform them correctly, but that guidance need not be overly detailed or restrictive.

Organizational Rules and Regulations

Rules and regulations are specific managerial guidelines that leave little or no room for discretion. They either require or prohibit specific behavior on the part of organizational employees. Whereas policies are guides to thinking, and procedures are guides to action, rules and regulations are mandates to action.

The requirements that uniformed officers wear their hats whenever they get out of their patrol vehicle, that they not smoke on the street, that they be in court 30 minutes prior to the opening of sessions to confer with prosecutors, that they not accept gratuities, that they take a specified time for lunch breaks, and that they appear for roll call are a few examples of rules and regulations. These requirements leave no room for discretion and mandate that specific actions be taken. There will, of course, always be instances in which some rules or regulations may be waived; however, these are few and far between. A regulation specifying that all officers appear for roll call, for example, might be waived by a commanding officer or a supervisor who, for whatever good reason, believes it necessary for certain officers to report directly to fixed posts rather than to stand roll call. Officers handling an emergency call during the 30 minutes prior to the opening of court could not be expected to leave the emergency situation before it is resolved just because rules and regulations require them to be in court 30 minutes prior to the opening of court. By and large, however, rules and regulations are mandates that police officers must follow.

Rules and regulations must be fair, reasonable, pertinent, and in keeping with the times. Therefore, they must be subject to change and must be updated periodically. The police department must be careful not to allow rules and regulations to interfere materially with an officer's use of discretion in unpredictable situations. They must apply only to specific situations that are essentially unchanging and predictable. Unless they are so limited, officers will be hampered in the performance of their duties and will come to regard rules and regulations as both bothersome and invalid.

Furthermore, the number of rules and regulations should be kept to a minimum because of their unbending and coercive nature.[31] If rules and regulations are allowed to proliferate unchecked, management is, in effect, saying to its employees, "We are telling you exactly what and what not to do because we do not have confidence in your abilities to act responsibly." If such a message is transmitted to employees, they must either acquiesce or rebel; in neither instance will they will remain active partners in the effort to accomplish organizational goals and objectives.

Once again, that elusive middle course must be sought. Some rules and regulations are obviously necessary. These should be confined strictly to nondiscretionary matters in which no behavioral latitude whatever can be granted. It should be the function of policies or procedures to govern activities in which behavioral latitudes may be allowed and in which interpretive discretion is essential. Management, then, must be careful not to overdo it when it comes to constrictive rules and regulations. On the other hand, it must be equally careful to establish precise, dogmatic canons affecting behavior that should, under all circumstances, be restricted. The achievement of a delicate balance between the two is essential to departmental stability. Whenever possible, management must allow for individual discretion and hence professional growth. As Thomas Reddin so aptly puts it:

> Certainly we must have rules, regulations, and procedures, and they should be followed. But, they are no substitutes for initiative and intelligence. The more a man is given an opportunity to make decisions and, in the process, to learn, the more rules and regulations will be followed.[32]

Formulation of Organizational Guidelines

The formulation of policies, procedures, and regulations for a police department has an important effect on not only the department but also individual police officers and the community in general. The manner in which these guidelines are developed can be as crucial as the guidelines themselves.

Several sources of organizational policy have already been noted. These reflect the fact that police departments are open systems, are affected by their environments, and receive inputs from external systems. Any given police department receives inputs from its parent governmental system, the community, the courts, employee groups, professional police organizations, and many other special and general interest groups.

Because the police administrator receives inputs from so many different quarters, it is unwise to develop policies, procedures, and rules and regulations without giving serious consideration to both external and internal constraints. There are three good reasons why guidelines should not be formulated as if the police administrator were operating in a vacuum (see "Method of Policymaking" and "Police Officer Contribution to Police Policy").

First, the police administrator must recognize that the police department is a part of the executive branch of a democratic government. People who are intensely involved in the selection of those who make the law can be expected to show tremendous interest in those who enforce it and to demand that police officers be responsive to their interests. Aware that their tax dollars pay police salaries, citizens expect some consideration in return. The police administrator must therefore take into consideration community input in the formulation of policies, procedures, and rules and regulations.

Standard 4.5
Method of Policymaking

In its development of procedures to openly formulate, implement and reevaluate police policy as necessary, each jurisdiction should be conscious of the need to effectively consult a representative cross-section of citizens in this process.

Source: American Bar Association Project on Standards for Criminal Justice, *The Urban Police Function*, Approved Draft (New York, NY: American Bar Association, 1973), p. 9.

Second, the police executive should seek employee "buy in" as guidelines are being developed. The only effective way of doing this is to involve those who will be affected by the guidelines in their development. This kind of democratic, participative involvement can help considerably in promoting guideline acceptance. This gives the members of the department a better understanding of the rationale behind the guidelines and a stake in their successful application.

Third, the involvement of numerous concerned parties in the formulation of guidelines is likely to result in better guidelines. Community involvement in policy formulation, for example, will almost invariably result in better policy, because it is much more likely to be universally accepted than is policy developed by the police alone. The involvement of organizational employees in the development of procedures will result in better procedures because it is the people who actually do the work who know the most about how it can best be done.

Police administrators should not be concerned that the involvement of the community and of organizational employees will be considered an abdication or usurpation of their authority. Their authority originates in the community, and they are expected to use it in the community's best interests. The community should have a say in determining what these interests are. Police administrators accomplish the goals and objectives they establish for their organizations through their employees, who should have their say in how these are best achieved. Meeting responsibilities by sharing authority is an indication of strength and wisdom, not abdication.[33]

Standard 6.2
Police Officer Contribution to Police Policy

Policemen, as individuals and as a group, have a proper professional interest in and can make significant contributions to the formulation and continuing review of local law enforcement policies within individual communities. Methods should be developed by police administrators, therefore, to ensure effective participation in the policy-making process by all ranks, including the patrolman who, because of his daily contact with operational problems and needs, has unique expertise to provide information on law enforcement policy issues.

Source: American Bar Association Project of Standards for Criminal Justice, *The Urban Police Function*, Approved Draft (New York, NY: American Bar Association, 1973), p. 12.

It is not sufficient to simply formulate policies and other types of guidelines—in fact, this can be thought of as just the first step in a four-step process:[34]

1. Establish policies that guide the most critical decisions made by personnel.
2. Make certain that personnel are trained in what these policies mean and how they apply to them.
3. Hold personnel accountable for abiding by policy.
4. Continually review policies to ensure that they are responsive to community needs and that they hold personnel properly accountable as new problems are identified.

Discipline

Who will investigate acts of misfeasance and malfeasance by the police? As the Romans put it 20 centuries ago, *Quis custodiet ipsos custodes?* (Who will guard the guardians?), a question that has plagued governments since they were first organized.

If guidelines are established for the purpose of controlling personnel in their official operational duties, then routine supervision, as well as uncompromising inspections and internal affairs programs, must be designed to ferret out those who would willfully or incompetently violate fundamental organizational commandments. We discussed the inspections and internal affairs functions in Chapter 4, as well as civilian review options, but did not emphasize the importance of discipline in their implementation. These all-important functions are needed to ensure compliance with official organizational guidelines, and discipline is needed to put teeth into compliance enforcement.

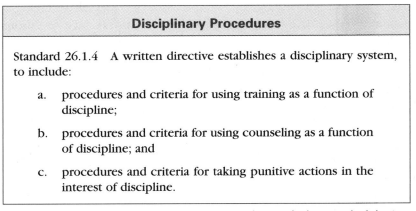

Disciplinary Procedures

Standard 26.1.4   A written directive establishes a disciplinary system, to include:

   a. procedures and criteria for using training as a function of discipline;

   b. procedures and criteria for using counseling as a function of discipline; and

   c. procedures and criteria for taking punitive actions in the interest of discipline.

Source: *Standards for Law Enforcement Agencies: The Standards Manual of the Law Enforcement Agency Accreditation Program.* Fairfax, VA: Commission on Accreditation for Law Enforcement Agencies, Inc., 1999.

Traditionally, discipline in law enforcement agencies was confined to the exercise of seven possible options: oral reprimand, written reprimand, punishment duty (work without pay), transfer, suspension, termination, and prosecution. Officers could be disciplined with little or no consideration for their constitutional rights and in many instances were disciplined in an arbitrary and capricious manner. Because of some outrageously unfair disciplinary practices, the courts and the National Labor Relations Board outlawed numerous unfair labor practices and provided officers relief in the courts (i.e., the NLRB decision in the *Garcia* case, which outlawed punishment duty and the United States Supreme Court decision in *Patsy v. Florida Board of Regents*, which guaranteed persons in the process of being disciplined the right to initiate litigation in the federal courts for violation of their civil rights "without exhausting administrative remedies provided under state law").[35] Many states also passed "Police Officer Bill of Rights" statutes. The establishment of new and rather restrictive legal constraints on a police chief's heretofore unilateral disciplinary prerogatives sent a signal to police managers throughout the nation that in the future great care should be taken to exercise their disciplinary responsibilities within solidly established legal parameters designed to assure an absolute guarantee of fairness, equity, and constitutional protection.

This mandated change in disciplinary procedure has forced police administrators to adopt a more positive and constructive attitude toward the disciplinary process with an emphasis on training, guidance, and correction fully as important, if not more important, than punishment.[36] This kind of change has also been encouraged by police unions and fraternal associations.

It is also becoming more common in police discipline decisions to distinguish between errors and rule violations that are inadvertent or well-intentioned and those that are intentional and committed for personal or malicious reasons. Police departments have even gone so far as to promise their officers that honest, reasonable mistakes will not be punished. Certainly, an agency that wants to encourage extra effort and creativity from its officers will quickly negate any enthusiasm and trust if it punishes minor rule violations or those that have been made in good faith.[37]

In considering disciplinary measures, the police manager must now carefully weigh disciplinary objectives and employee relations as well as legal issues and constraints before taking disciplinary action. In all but the most blatantly serious situations, every effort should be made to place emphasis on redemption, rehabilitation, and reform, not punishment. When punishment is required, departments generally follow the principle of progressive discipline, with specified ranges of punishment for first and subsequent violations of various rules. The objective is to treat individual employees fairly, while at the same time sending a convincing message throughout the organization that failure to follow directives will not generally be tolerated.

Summary

This chapter has presented the basic principles of police organization. It should be noted that these principles are means to ends (meeting departmental goals and objectives) and are not ends in themselves. They are not all intended to be universally applicable within all organizations all of the time; Therefore, their use should be situational and dependent on the character of the police organization and the quality of its personnel. Just as builders need blueprints to build houses, so too police chiefs need organizational principles to build police departments. If they judiciously use these basic principles in organizing their departments, they can be certain that their organizations will be constructed in solid fashion, capable of meeting their responsibilities and achieving their goals and objectives.

There is a great need for clear policies, procedures, and rules and regulations in police departments. Conformity to such guidelines is important, and therefore they must be well-defined and understandable. Much of police work is routine and easily standardized. Parts of the job that are not routine are much too important to be left completely to the discretion of the individual police officer. On the other hand, discretion exists and must be structured and controlled. Deciding what parts of the job are routine and what parts of the job are not becomes critical for the police administrator. The administrator's overall success may very well be predicated on his or her ability to make such decisions and to deal with disciplinary matters in a constructive manner within established legal parameters.

Another way to think about this situation is to recognize that police managers need to control their employees and, at the same time, empower them. Striking the right balance between control and empowerment is a big part of the police manager's job. Erring too far in either direction is likely to cause severe organizational problems. One set of questions adopted by the Carrollton (Texas) Police Department for officers to consider when making decisions, as a device to empower employees without losing control, is presented below:[38]

1. Is it ethical?
2. Is it legal?
3. Is it the right thing to do for the community?
4. Is it the right thing for the Carrollton Police Department?
5. Is it within our policies and values?
6. Is it something you can take responsibility for, and be proud of?

If the answer to all of these questions is yes, then it is a good decision and it should be implemented.

Discussion Questions

1. Think of the organizations to which you belong—for example, family, school, employment, voluntary, and others. Are any of them not hierarchical? Which are the most, and the least, hierarchical?

2. Many managers never learn how to delegate authority. Because they have no confidence in their subordinates, they try to do everything themselves and get worn out in the process. Do you know managers like this? How do their subordinates react to the unwillingness to delegate? How would you explain such managerial behavior? How would you change it?

3. Many organizations use specialization to create units and positions through which they can rotate personnel. This is thought to be pleasing to employees, because they can transfer from one position to another when they get bored. On the other hand, specialized jobs may become boring more quickly than generalist jobs because they are so narrowly defined. So in one respect specialization contributes to boredom, and in another respect it seems to combat it. How do you explain this apparent contradiction? How would you resolve it as chief of police?

4. The authority-level principle seeks problem resolution at the organizational level where authority exists for such resolution. It is a principle that attempts to overcome both buck passing and problem hiding. It seems simple, and yet it is very difficult to implement. Why?

5. We recommend that police administrators seek input from the community and police employees when developing organizational guidelines. Do you agree with this recommendation? How would you carry it out? How can a police administrator, when developing organization guidelines, take community interests into consideration and yet remain impartial and objective?

Cases

Three of the cases at the end of this text are pertinent to the principles of organization presented in Chapter 6. You should analyze "Case 1: The Energetic Chief," "Case 2: The Peripatetic Sergeant," and "Case 4: The Chief Who Played King" from the standpoint of the basic principles of police organization. This chapter's discussion of policies, procedures, rules, regulations, and discipline can be used to examine three cases at the back of the text: "Case 1: The Energetic Chief," "Case 2: The Peripatetic Sergeant," and "Case 3: The Yuletide Remembrance."

Notes

1. G.W. Cordner, "Community Policing: Elements and Effects," in G.P. Alpert and A. Piquero, eds., *Community Policing: Contemporary Readings*, Second Edition (Prospect Heights, IL: Waveland, 2000), pp. 45-62.

2. H. Koontz and C. O'Donnell, *Principles of Management: An Analysis of Managerial Functions*, Fourth Edition (New York, NY: McGraw-Hill, 1968), pp. 69-70.

3. R. Townsend, *Up the Organization* (New York, NY: Knopf, 1970), p. 45.

4. O.W. Wilson and R.C. McLaren, *Police Administration*, Fourth Edition (New York: McGraw-Hill, 1977), pp. 80-81.

5. P.F. Drucker, *The Practice of Management* (New York, NY: Harper & Brothers, 1954), p. 139.

6. J.M. Pfiffner and R. Presthus, *Public Administration* (New York, NY: Ronald Press, 1967), p. 190.

7. E.F. McGarrell, E. Langston, and D. Richardson, "Implementation Issues: The Specialized Unit or Department-Wide Community Policing," in Q.C. Thurman and E.F. McGarrell, eds., *Community Policing in a Rural Setting* (Cincinnati, OH: Anderson, 1997), pp. 59-64.

8. T. Reddin, "Are You Oriented to Hold Them? A Searching Look at Police Management," *Police Chief* 33, no. 3 (March 1966): 12-20.

9. G.P. Alpert and W.C. Smith, "Developing Police Policy: An Evaluation of the Control Principle," in G.W. Cordner and D.J. Kenney, eds., *Managing Police Organizations* (Cincinnati, OH: Anderson, 1996), pp. 111-126.

10. President's Commission on Law Enforcement and Administration of Justice, *The Challenge of Crime in a Free Society* (New York, NY: Avon Books, 1968), p. 267.

11. Advisory Committee on the Police Function of the American Bar Association Project on Standards for Criminal Justice, *The Urban Police Function*, Approved Draft (New York, NY: American Bar Association, 1973), p. 8.

12. *Experiments in Police Improvement: A Progress Report* (Washington, DC: Police Foundation, 1972), pp. 14-15.

13. National Advisory Commission on Criminal Justice Standards and Goals, *Police* (Washington, DC: U.S. Government Printing Office, 1973).

14. V.E. Kappeler, *Critical Issues in Police Civil Liability*, Second Edition (Prospect Heights, IL: Waveland, 1997).

15. S.D. Mastrofski, "Police Agency Accreditation: The Prospects of Reform," *American Journal of Police* 5, no. 2 (fall 1986): 45-81.

16. *Standards for Law Enforcement Agencies* (Fairfax, VA: Commission on Accreditation for Law Enforcement Agencies, 1998).

17. V.E. Kappeler, "Police Use of Force and Citizen Complaint Policies and Practices in Kentucky: A Statewide Survey and Content Analysis," presentation to the Kentucky Criminal Justice Council, 2002.

18. See www.calea.org, www.iacp.org and www.policeforum.org.

19. H. Koontz and C. O'Donnell, *Principles of Management: An Analysis of Managerial Functions* (New York, NY: McGraw-Hill, 1968), pp. 178-188.

20. R.O. Loen, *Manage More by Doing Less* (New York, NY: McGraw-Hill, 1971), pp. 86-89.

21. Cordner, *Community Policing*.

22. Koontz and O'Donnell, *Principles of Management*, p. 88.

23. O.W. Wilson and R.C. McLaren, *Police Administration*, Third Edition. (New York, NY: McGraw-Hill, 1972), p. 130.

24. J.J. Fyfe, "The Supreme Court's New Rules for Police Use of Deadly Force," *Criminal Law Bulletin* 22, no. 1 (January/February 1986): 62.

25. Koontz and O'Donnell, *Principles of Management*, p. 88.

26. J.Q. Wilson, *Varieties of Police Behavior: The Management of Law and Order in Eight Communities* (Cambridge, MA: Harvard University Press, 1968), pp. 278-279.

27. Loen, *Manage More*, pp. 91-92.

28. Alpert and Smith, "Developing Police Policy."

29. G.P. Alpert, D.J. Kenney, R.G. Dunham, and W.C. Smith, *Police Pursuits: What We Know* (Washington, DC: Police Executive Research Forum, 2000).

30. "Model Domestic Violence Law Enforcement Policy" (Frankfort, KY: Governor's Council on Domestic Violence, 1996).

31. G.W. Cordner, "Written Rules and Regulations: Are They Necessary?" *FBI Law Enforcement Bulletin* (July 1989): 17-21.

32. Reddin, "Are You Oriented," p. 17.

33. L.P. Brown, "Police-Community Power Sharing," in William A. Geller, ed., *Police Leadership in America: Crisis and Opportunity* (New York, NY: Praeger, 1985), pp. 70-83.

34. J.J. Fyfe, J.R. Greene, W.F. Walsh, O.W. Wilson, and R.C. McClaren, *Police Administration*, Fifth Edition. (New York, NY: McGraw-Hill, 1997), p. 490.

35. J.E. Scuro Jr., "Legal Issues Affecting the Police Administrator," *The Police Chief* (March 1985): 99.

36. G.W. Garner, "The Supervisor's Role in Discipline," *Law and Order* (March 1984): 41.

37. M.K. Sparrow, M.H. Moore, and D.M. Kennedy, *Beyond 911: A New Era for Policing* (New York, NY: Basic Books, 1990).

38. D. Carter and G. Cordner, "Merging Community-Oriented and Crime-Specific Policing: Problem-Oriented Approaches," *TELEMASP Bulletin* (Huntsville, TX: Law Enforcement Management Institute, 1998).

Suggested Reading

Alpert, Geoffrey P., Dennis Jay Kenney, Roger G. Dunham, and William C. Smith. *Police Pursuits: What We Know*. Washington, DC: Police Executive Research Forum, 2000.

Geller, William A. and Michael S. Scott. *Deadly Force: What We Know—A Practitioner's Desk Reference on Police-Involved Shootings*. Washington, DC: Police Executive Research Forum, 1992.

Kappeler, Victor E. *Critical Issues in Police Civil Liability*, Third Edition. Prospect Heights, IL: Waveland, 2001.

Standards for Law Enforcement Agencies: The Standards Manual of the Law Enforcement Agency Accreditation Program. Fairfax, VA: Commission on Accreditation for Law Enforcement Agencies, Inc., 1999.

Zhao, Jihong. *Why Police Organizations Change: A Study of Community-Oriented Policing*. Washington, DC: Police Executive Research Forum, 1996.

Functions of Police Management

6

Learning Objectives

- Cite the six basic functions of police management.

- Identify the three management functions that are primarily performed by top-level managers.

- Explain the importance of system learning for organizational effectiveness.

- Identify the five steps in the planning process.

- Identify four types of police plans.

- Identify six separate staffing functions.

- Explain the importance of "prevailing mythology" for recruitment.

- Identify four major activities within the training function.

- Distinguish assessment centers from other techniques used in the promotion process.

- Identify four activities that comprise the directing function.

What do people who are called managers do? What are their primary responsibilities? A review of the literature on management functions shows that authorities have different answers to these questions. Acronyms such as POD-SCORB (Planning, Organizing, Directing, Staffing, Coordinating, Reporting, Budgeting)[1] and POSTBECPIRD (Planning, Organizing, Staffing, Training, Budgeting, Equipment, Coordination, Public Information, Reporting, Directing)[2] have been proposed by management theorists in order to define management functions. Leonard R. Sayles identifies three basic managerial functions: participation in external work flows through lateral interaction, leading, and monitoring.[3] George D. Eastman and Esther M. Eastman see the functions of management as planning, organizing, assembling resources, directing, and controlling.[4] Harold Koontz and Cyril O'Donnell agree, but substitute the word "staffing" for the term "assembling resources."[5]

In this chapter we will discuss six basic police management functions:

1. system building
2. planning
3. organizing
4. staffing
5. directing
6. controlling

Performing these management functions skillfully and knowledgeably is critically important. Aside from the obvious benefits accruing to departmental professionalism and stability, the legal concept of vicarious liability has placed significantly greater demands on police managers.[6] In instances in which police chiefs or other police managers improperly perform certain management functions, or negligently fail to perform those functions, they can be sued for improperly discharging the duties of their offices.[7] The growth of the concept of vicarious liability serves as a reminder of the importance of proper performance of police management functions and adds a measure of accountability not previously experienced by most police managers.

Management Functions by Level in the Organization

To some extent, each and every manager in the police organization performs the six management functions of system building, planning, organizing, staffing, directing, and controlling. However, the relative importance of the functions varies, depending on the manager's level in the police organization.

Managers at the chief administrative level in a police agency are obviously responsible for the successful performance of all six management functions. It is their responsibility to ensure that the department achieves its goals and objectives as fully as possible, that the department abides by the law and is responsive to its community. Police chiefs, in particular, can never delegate responsibility for any of the six management functions. Responsibility for the six is uniquely theirs.

By the same token, police chiefs must delegate authority, including managerial authority. Except in the smallest departments, chiefs must delegate some of the authority and some of the work involved in system building, planning, organizing, staffing, directing, and controlling to subordinate managers at the command and supervisory levels.

Delegation of authority to lower levels of management to perform the three functions of staffing, directing, and controlling is essential. This is not to say that these functions are any less important than the other three but, rather, that they are more appropriately performed by subordinate managers. The staffing function should be assigned to a command-level manager (except in small agencies, in which the chief will perform most staffing tasks). Directing and controlling are the basic elements of every manager's job throughout the police department. Every commander and every supervisor must be primarily concerned with making certain that subordinates know how to perform their jobs and that they perform them effectively and productively.

These three functions (staffing, directing, and controlling) can be thought of as operating the organization, as making sure that the organization runs according to design. They primarily depend upon managers' technical and human skills, that is, on their expertise in doing the work of the organization and their skills in dealing with people. The other three functions (system building, planning, and organizing) are more concerned with formulating and constructing the design of the organization in the first place. These latter three functions, therefore, are less amenable to delegation. Setting up the overall departmental design and deciding on goals and priorities and how best to achieve them are functions best performed at the chief administrative level in the police agency. These functions depend heavily on conceptual skills—"the ability to see the enterprise as a whole" and to see "how changes in any one part affect all the others."[8]

System Building

In the ideal organizational setting, in which the systems approach to management has traditionally been applied, it might not be necessary to address system building as a separate management function. However, in the police field, in which little attention has been given to managing from the systems perspective, it is essential for administrators to realize that many police problems have evolved solely because police administrators have developed their organizations without paying attention to systems concepts.

The systems theory is so foreign to police administrators generally and so basic to the development of sound organizations universally that special emphasis needs to be placed on system building: what it is and how it can be used. Although some good police administrators build good systems instinctively, few really have understood all of the ramifications of what they have been doing. System building has been isolated in this chapter as one of the six primary management functions because the other five primary functions are totally dependent on it for their implementation.

In part, system building means simply constructing coherent systems that take inputs, process them, and produce outputs that meet the goals and objectives of the police department. Other management functions are concerned with pieces of this responsibility. Staffing, for example, attempts to ensure that the organization has the numbers and kinds of people needed as employees to process inputs into outputs by doing the work of the agency. Directing is concerned with making sure that employees know what they are supposed to do and how to do it. What distinguishes system building is its focus on the entire management system and its application of systems concepts.

Carrying out the management function of system building requires that the police executive give considerable attention to four interrelated systems concepts: the interdependence of elements in a system; the organizational environment; the key role played by feedback; and the need for ongoing adaptation, learning, and change.

Interdependence

The various parts of a system are interdependent; each affects the other. Consequently, a change made in one part of a system is likely to have impact on other parts. In addition, because police departments are open systems, changes occurring outside the organization are likely to affect the police system's inputs, processes, and outputs. An important managerial responsibility is to anticipate and manage these interactive effects so that the effectiveness of the police agency is not hampered.

Sometimes it is obvious that new inputs or changes in the environment are likely to affect the police organization. Major changes in inputs include new employees, budget cuts, a new police facility, or new types of information made available by developing technology. Environmental changes could include newly elected political officials, a downturn in the economy, annexation of additional land area, or new laws passed by the legislature. Most police managers could and would anticipate that changes of this magnitude might affect various parts of the police organizational system. Hopefully, these managers would then take the necessary actions to keep their systems functioning as effectively as possible.

Sometimes, relatively insignificant changes can have surprising effects. One competent police chief who managed his department from a systems perspective learned very quickly the importance of seemingly insignificant factors when he decided that it would be in the best interests of departmental efficiency if he moved the office of a civilian employee from one area of the police station to another. His decision was made purely on the basis of a need to utilize space more effectively; the decision was made in keeping with the goals and objectives he had established for his department. The civilian employee was a responsible person who had complete authority over the department's fiscal affairs. When the chief announced that her office was to be changed, she construed the move as a personal affront, a reflection on her abilities, and an attempt to downgrade her status. She became extremely emotional and expressed her outrage to family and friends. Her husband became so concerned about her condition that he came to the police station and personally registered a complaint with the chief. The woman's work suffered as a result, and she sought employment elsewhere.

After much deliberation, the chief finally decided to reverse the original order to move the woman's office and made every conceivable effort to explain a mistake for which he took total blame. The woman is now satisfied, her work output better than ever, and her feelings toward the chief warm and friendly.

In another department, this one much smaller, the hiring of several zealous young officers over a two- to three-year period gradually changed the personnel makeup of the agency and its operational style. What had been a service-oriented and community-oriented police agency became a much more legalistic and enforcement-oriented one. Had this gradual evolution matched corresponding changes in the community or its political leadership, the effects might have been positive. In this instance, however, police-community conflict developed, and the chief eventually became discredited and lost his job. He either misjudged the needs of his community or failed to monitor and manage the effects on his agency caused by new inputs to the system.

Environment

As open systems, police organizations interact with their environments. Changes in the police organizational environment can have important effects on police system functioning, as noted above; thus, a crucial aspect of system building and police administration involves managing these effects. In addition, police executives should seek out positive inputs from their environments; constantly monitor changes in the environment; and, when possible, seek to modify the environment for the benefit of their communities and police departments.

Among the inputs that police departments need from their environments are fiscal resources, material goods, job applicants, new ideas, and community and political support. Part of system building, then, involves seeking fiscal resources through the budget process, grants, and other sources; obtaining needed equipment and, on occasion, encouraging research and development efforts to produce better equipment; attracting sufficient numbers of the best possible applicants for sworn and civilian positions; searching out new concepts, techniques, and ideas, and bringing them into the police organization; and developing and sustaining moral support and active assistance within the community and among the political leadership. Performing these aspects of system building helps contribute to healthy system functioning by maintaining a steady flow of new energy into the system.

To secure these kinds of inputs for their organizations, and to anticipate external changes that might affect their organizations, police executives should constantly monitor their environments. This means that they, or their staffs, should keep up with changes in the community, technological developments, social changes, legislative proposals, and political trends. They must also keep abreast of developments within the field of policing by reading the literature, belonging to professional associations, attending professional meetings, and keeping in touch with colleagues who themselves are well-informed. Their objective should be to take advantage of new developments, adapt when possible, and, at the very least, prevent their departments from being surprised or embarrassed by important changes in the environment. Even when it is not possible for the police agency to avoid being affected adversely by some change in the environment, it is useful to appear well-informed and to have the opportunity to minimize any negative effects.

Sometimes organizations can take a more proactive role by modifying, rather than merely adapting to, their environments. They may be able to develop support in the community for new strategies of policing, head off serious budget cuts, or press for needed legislation. One police chief, believing that career criminals were getting off too lightly, systematically championed a tougher approach to handling repeat offenders. He convinced the state to allocate funds for experimental programs, and he convinced other criminal justice officials in his area to cooperate with the police department on a coordinated new initiative. In this instance, this police chief went beyond merely reacting to or adapting to his organization's environment—he was able to change the environment itself in a way that benefitted the community and the police department.[9]

Feedback

Construction of closed-loop systems that provide feedback is an essential aspect of the system-building function of police management. It is also probably the most neglected aspect. Police executives, like most other people, tend to stop short of acquiring authoritative feedback, sometimes out of laziness or because they really do not want to know exactly how things are going. It is much easier for a police manager to sit back and take an "if it ain't broke, don't fix it" attitude than it is to aggressively seek feedback, some of which may point out the shortcomings of his or her own actions.

Any individual or organization truly concerned about effectiveness, excellence, quality, and serving the customer will have an unquenchable thirst for feedback. Feedback provides the information that is needed to determine which organizational systems are operating properly and which are not. With feedback, executives can routinely correct systems that are not working properly, reward those that are, and generally keep the enterprise on course.

What this means for police managers is that they must build and maintain systems that provide feedback. Mechanisms for providing feedback vary with each system but include information systems, program evaluations, performance appraisals, inspections, internal affairs, customer surveys, and "management by walking around."[10] The use of feedback information is typically within the context of one of the other management functions—to exercise control over improper conduct, for example, to provide clearer direction to employees, or to reorganize in order to facilitate better coordination. Managers can only know that these kinds of actions are necessary, however, when systems have been built in such a way that they provide ongoing feedback.

Change and Organizational Learning

Many capable police chiefs have exerted tremendous efforts in order to build sound organizational systems in their departments, only to discover serious problems within a very few years. What these chiefs failed to understand was that system building, like all of police administration, is a continuing process. It is never completed. The world surrounding a police agency is always changing, as are the people within the police department. The shifts and duties that once satisfied a young patrol officer may not satisfy him as he grows older. The knowledge and skills of a police manager may evolve as she matures, gains experience, and receives additional training. Ideas change within the police profession regarding the most effective operational strategies, the viability of civilian review boards, the proper limits on high-speed pursuits, and other important matters. The community changes. Politics change. Society changes.

Because the police system and its environment are dynamic rather than static, a key aspect of system building is designing systems that can change, adapt to changing circumstances, and learn from their experiences.[11] Most people get better with age—they gain experience and knowledge and become wiser and more savvy. Organizations can do the same and for even longer periods of time if properly designed and maintained.

Two considerations pertinent to system change and adaptation have already been discussed—the environment and feedback. An additional consideration is system learning. The most effective systems are ones in which lessons are learned and not forgotten, and in which lessons learned in one part of the system are shared throughout the system.[12] The former condition, avoiding memory loss, is achieved when lessons are embodied in formal systems and written policies and preserved in histories, diaries, slogans, and files. Sharing of lessons can be accomplished through cooperation, teamwork, newsletters, and training.[13]

Over the long term, the most effective organizations will have these properties:

1. positive interchanges with their environments;
2. continuous monitoring of their environments;
3. proactive modification of their environments;
4. systematic feedback;
5. ongoing adaptation to internal and external changes;
6. shared learning among elements of the organization; and
7. mechanisms to preserve and update system learning.

One of the primary functions of police management is to build systems within the police organization that have these kinds of properties. When successfully done, police agencies will not only function effectively, they will also adapt over time to maintain their effectiveness.

Planning

Planning is a future-oriented management function. One plans in order to prepare for the future. Organizations plan so that when a decision has to be made or an action taken they will be prepared. The decision or action itself tends to be driven by a short-term focus—employees ask themselves, "What should we do right now?" If effective planning has previously taken place, though, a longer-term perspective has already helped shape the kinds of choices that employees will make.

Much of our future activity is planned either by us or by someone else. Your course in police administration was planned by your instructor. It was planned or scheduled to meet at a certain time on certain days of the week by the dean of your college. It is probably within your plans to graduate from college and to be successful in your career. Perhaps you plan to get married and have a family. One day you may plan to buy a home. You may even plan for your own children to go to college. Plans are preparations for future expectations. They are the means by which you will meet your goals and objectives.

Planning is perhaps the most cerebral aspect of management. It requires a certain amount of foresight and creativity and a willingness to set aside some time for thought and reflection. Unfortunately, ours tends to be an action-oriented, quick-fix kind of culture. Consequently, people and organizations often confront problems only when they have become crises. The old adage, "I'll cross that bridge when I come to it," is the attitude of those who place a low priority on planning. The good planner arrives at the bridge and crosses with no difficulty. The poor planner arrives at the river at the wrong spot, with no bridge in sight.

Effective planning is especially crucial for the police. The protection of lives and property and the maintenance of order in the community depend on the police being in the right place at the right time, taking proper actions. In our complex and rapidly changing society, only careful planning can make this possible. For example, if a police administrator has not properly staffed patrol shifts, there is a distinct possibility that not all calls for service can be handled. In one Eastern city with a population of 360,000 people, 15,000 calls for service per year went unanswered because of a lack of available personnel during peak workload times. This was a serious matter that reflected poor planning; it had serious consequences for the citizens of the city.

Planning frequently begins with the identification of a problem. The problem may be identified by a patrol officer, the chief, a clerk in the records division, a citizen, or by anyone else, either inside or outside the organization. If the authority-level principle has been applied to the department, the planning involved in solving many problems will be relatively simple and will not require the attention of specialized planners or a planning unit. Planning is an important part of every supervisor's and manager's job. Only problems that require extensive research and cannot be solved at any working level within the police department should be referred to the planning unit, which should be responsible for studying specific problems that are not easily solved and presenting solutions to these problems in the form of plans that can be either accepted or rejected by the chief.

The planning unit itself should have very broad responsibilities and should be involved in studying every aspect of the department. It should periodically examine every procedure and every operation within the department to determine if these are operating effectively and efficiently. It should be self-starting, proceeding on its own without waiting for direction from the chief, but in no way precluding such involvement should the chief wish to provide guidance.

An excellent vehicle for undertaking an organizational self-assessment is the accreditation program run by the Commission on Accreditation for Law Enforcement Agencies (CALEA).[14] Even if a department elects not to take part in the formal accreditation program, the standards promulgated by CALEA provide useful benchmarks by which to judge the department's current practices.[15]

Questions such as the following might be asked when examining procedures and operations:

1. Is this really necessary?
2. Should this be eliminated?
3. How could this be done better?
4. Could this be done less expensively?
5. If a change were made, what would the result be?
6. Has another police department found a way of doing this better?

The Planning Process

Regardless of whether planning is conducted by a separate planning unit or by an individual police manager, the planning process comprises five steps:

1. Ends analysis
2. Forecasting
3. Means analysis
4. Implementation
5. Evaluation

The first step, *ends analysis*, focuses either on the kinds of problems described above or on missions, goals, and objectives. Whichever is the case, ends analysis simply identifies the purpose of the planning exercise—the problem that needs to be solved or the goal that needs to be achieved. Problems are sometimes identified by organizational members and sometimes by members of the community or other representatives of the police agency's environment. Similarly, goals may be devised by the police department or they may be thrust onto the department from outside. Problems and goals may be well-defined or vague, well understood or poorly understood. An important aspect of ends analysis is to gather as much information about the problem or goal situation as possible. This involves analyzing the situation in order to describe it (who, what, when, where, how) and, if possible, explain it (why).

Once problems or goals have been identified in the planning process, an important next step to undertake is *forecasting*. This is the point at which planning becomes explicitly future-oriented. Planners must recognize that while problems exist in the present, problem solutions will be implemented and goals will be achieved in the future. Thus, planners should seek information about the future context within which their forecasted solutions will be applied. One good resource for police planners at this forecasting stage is the Society of Police Futurists International.[16]

Oftentimes plans will be implemented just a few days or weeks into the future, in which case it may be reasonable to assume that little will have changed. However, other plans have longer duration. Suppose, for example, that a police department's deployment plans are revised annually. These plans deploy patrol resources around the community based on the previous year's workload. If, in drawing up these plans, planners were to ignore a new shopping mall about to be completed or serious impending budget cuts, their deployment plans for the upcoming year would be seriously flawed. The entire department's efforts to protect life and property and maintain order might be jeopardized.

Once ends have been identified and forecasting has taken place, alternatives must be explored and studied (*means analysis*). Every aspect of a matter must be thoroughly researched and considered before a final plan is devised. It is crucial to conduct a wide search for alternative solutions. Existing alternatives can sometimes be found within the organization; more often, other police departments can be located that have already developed and tested alternatives in response to similar problems or goal situations. Wise police planners take maximum advantage of the efforts and experiences of other agencies in order to avoid spending considerable time "reinventing the wheel."[17] These existing alternatives can be uncovered through personal contacts, professional organizations, published material, and the Internet. The Police Abstract Listing Service operated by the International Association of Law Enforcement Planners (IALEP) is a particularly good resource.[18]

Once alternatives have been chosen and put in the form of a strategy, policy, program, or plan, they must be systematically implemented and carefully evaluated. *Implementation* is often overlooked to the detriment of much perfectly good planning; many well-developed and carefully thought out police programs and plans have either failed or never been tried due to lack of implementation.[19] What is required for implementation is simply the remaining management functions of organizing, staffing, directing, and controlling. Many times, however, as soon as the design of the program or plan is completed, the police organization's attention turns to the next problem or goal, and only later do managers realize that implementation was a failure.

Finally, *evaluation* of the planning product provides information about whether the problem was solved, whether the goal was achieved, and whether adjustments are needed. Simply stated, evaluation is feedback to close the loop of the planning system. With feedback, rational adjustments and decisions can be made.[20] Without it, the police organization is just hoping that things will turn out all right.

Types of Police Plans

It is important to realize that planning is primarily a process—it is an ongoing process of ends analysis, forecasting, means analysis, implementation, evaluation, and more planning. It is somewhat risky to present information on types of plans, because you may be diverted into thinking that the plan marks the end of the planning process. In fact, the plan has value only to the extent that it affects real-world actions, and even then the process continues as the actions are evaluated and the planning process begins anew.

Nevertheless, plans do exist in police agencies and should be recognized. Because police work is enormously varied, there is potentially a wide range of types of police plans. Four basic types are:[21]

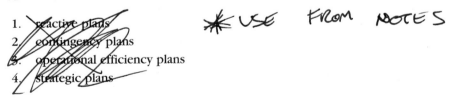

1. reactive plans
2. contingency plans
3. operational efficiency plans
4. strategic plans

※ USE FROM NOTES

Reactive plans are probably more common in police departments, and in most other kinds of organizations, than any other type. Reactive planning occurs in response to a crisis or a decision forced on the department from the outside. Police agencies have recently been engaging in reactive planning, for example, in response to federal legislation governing employment of disabled and older persons.[22] Departments have no choice but to plan for how they will adhere to these laws.

Contingency plans vary in their breadth and focus but have in common an attempt to prepare in advance for possible occurrences. A plan to deal with burglars caught in a building, using our earlier example, would be a contingency plan. This kind of plan is often formalized as a policy, procedure, or special operations order. Other kinds of contingency plans typically deal with natural and human-caused disasters; these types of situations call for massive coordinated responses that are difficult to make up on the spot. Contingency plans can also be more administrative in nature, such as a plan for the possibility of a major budget cut.

Operational efficiency plans seek to improve routine operations. Some are prepared on a regular basis, such as annual allocation and deployment plans that utilize workload information to determine how best to utilize patrol resources. Others are prepared on more of a special basis, such as a plan to increase the collection and submission of fingerprint evidence by patrol officers and detectives. Operational efficiency plans may be developed in response to perceived problems in the organization or simply as part of an ongoing effort to improve efficiency and effectiveness.

Strategic plans are the broadest of the four types of police plans and usually have the longest time horizon. They deal with the police organization's mission and primary goals and objectives and attempt to spell out an overall strategy for accomplishing them.[23] Strategic plans provide a picture of the kind of organization the police department wants to be and a roadmap for getting there.[24] This picture and map help the members of the organization and the community understand where they are and why certain practices and changes are being undertaken. Good strategic plans that are well communicated help police executives fulfill some of their most important and most difficult leadership responsibilities. They provide the "big picture" that many people, police officers included, sometimes have a hard time grasping.

Organizing

Organizing is the process involved in putting together the subsystems of an organization in order to achieve maximum efficiency, effectiveness, and productivity in meeting organizational goals and objectives. The subsystems of any organization must be arranged so that they can work well with one another. In police organizations the key organizer is the chief of police. A chief who is unable to organize the police department properly, using the systems approach as a basis for organizational efforts, will achieve little success in meeting goals and objectives. As James Mooney and Alan Reilly have pointed out, "it is inconceivable that a poor organizer can make a good manager."[25]

Organizing is not a simple process. It takes time, effort, and energy. It also takes skill, considerable patience, and a willingness to apply organizational principles to the process of organizing. Inevitably, it also requires a balancing act between competing interests: centralization versus decentralization of authority; specialists versus generalists; flatter hierarchies versus wider spans of control; unity of command versus practical necessities; formal versus informal communications; and so on. There are not many universal rules to follow to resolve these issues, only the kinds of general organizational principles presented in Chapter 5.

Organizing must be done by people who fully understand what the organizing inputs are. In one classic example, a small New England town of 12,000 people retained a police management consulting organization to study its police department. The organization assigned one of its most competent consultants to the job, a former police chief whose experience had been concentrated in Midwestern and Western cities. Never having worked in New England before, the consultant was unaware of the New Englanders' pride in their town meeting form of government, which makes every voter a member of the legislative branch of town government. Unlike cities where power is vested in a city council, New England towns were founded on the premise that everyone should have a say in local government. This prerogative is something not to be trifled with. Looking at the police department as a subsystem of local government, the consultant reasoned, based on his previous experience in government, that the organization of the police department could not be improved until improvements were made in local government, which he perceived to be about as inefficient as any government he had ever seen. One of his major recommendations, therefore, was that the town be turned into a city, and he pointed out the advantages of the city form of government. In his efforts to organize the police department, his lack of knowledge of New Englanders as a major part of the organizing process made him a laughingstock throughout the town and seriously impeded efforts to organize the police department properly.

The nature of jobs to be performed is also an important input to the organizing process. Each job must be carefully assessed and placed into a position within the organization where, grouped together with other similar functions, it can be performed most effectively. Specific jobs are the basis for the establishment of bureaus, divisions, units, squads, teams, and other subgroupings.

In organizing a police department, the objectives of the organization must be kept clearly in mind by the organizer. Although all police departments have the maintenance of order and the protection of life and property as primary goals, the priorities and exact content of their other goals and objectives might differ. For example, the kinds of noncriminal regulations enforced by the police might differ greatly from community to community. In cities and towns that have private ambulance service or ambulance service provided by the fire department, the police are relieved considerably of responsibility in serving the needs of the sick and injured. In jurisdictions where numerous social services are available to citizens, the services that need to be supplied by the police are drastically reduced. Organization, therefore, is a situational process that depends on the accurate identification of varying organization inputs. The process depends on the application of the basic principles of police organization (see Chapter 5). This involves providing for the grouping of like functions, assigning functions to appropriate subsystems, delegating authority, and coordinating overall effort.[26]

The output of the organizing process is the organization itself. It includes grouped functions, delegated authority, assigned activities, and overall coordination. Mooney and Reilly call organization "the form of every human association for the attainment of common purpose, relating duties, and functions in a coordinated scheme."[27]

Feedback on the organization itself can vary considerably. In the broadest sense, the effectiveness of the organization can be measured in terms of its accomplishment of goals and objectives. In a narrower sense, its effectiveness can be gauged in terms of whether workers have the necessary authority to do their jobs, whether they exhibit confusion over the identity of their immediate superiors, or whether, within units, each worker's tasks are relatively similar.

In order for continuous feedback to be made available to the organizer, or the chief, it must be understood by everyone from the chief on down that the organization in its present form is not sacred. Even if everyone believes the unlikely assumption that the organization is functioning perfectly today, the possibility of its malfunctioning tomorrow is entirely likely. System inputs (people, jobs, goals, and objectives) change. Furthermore, they change frequently. In order to accommodate these changes in input, the organization must be regularly scrutinized for signs that it is no longer suitable for the accomplishment of its objectives. The process of scrutinization must be designed so that the results (feedback) are introduced as input to the organizer.

It must also be understood that the organization is much more than a chart on the wall. Organizations should not be thought of as simple, unchanging groups of homogeneous people working together with computer-like efficiency. Rather, as Harold J. Leavitt suggests, organizations are "rich, volatile, complicated but understandable systems of tasks, structures, tools and people in states of continuous change."[28]

Staffing

Staffing involves the functions of recruiting, selecting, training, assigning, promoting, and terminating. These functions are often performed by a police department's personnel division; they are of such extreme importance, however, that they come within the purview of the police chief's major duties.

As with all other basic functions of police management, staffing should be examined from a systems standpoint. Inputs to the staffing function are of three types. The *people* input includes both present employees as well as candidates for job openings. The *jobs input* involves the positions presently held by employees plus job openings. The *objectives input* is the standard or standards used to measure the performance expected from present and prospective employees.

The output of all staffing function activities (recruitment, selection, training, placement, promotion, and termination) is the staff itself. The staff does the work of the organization; through its efforts, the organization either fails or succeeds. The importance of staffing should be apparent; it may well be the most important aspect of the police administrative process.

Feedback in the staffing function is the evaluative tool by which the performance of people within an organization is measured. The methods used to achieve such feedback are often the subject of considerable controversy. In police departments not administered from a systems perspective, little or no effort is made to evaluate performance. Departments managed with a high degree of systems emphasis use some extremely complex and sophisticated performance evaluation procedures and various kinds of quantitative and qualitative evaluative methods.

By emphasizing factors of performance that are relevant to the department's goals and objectives, the police administrator is indirectly exerting a degree of control over the organization. In effect, the administrator is saying, "These are activities that I consider to be important; if you perform these activities well, you will be rewarded." A well-designed performance evaluation system, therefore, will be built around the department's goals, objectives, and strategies—today, these systems should reflect the community policing strategy being adopted by many departments.[29] If it is to be a viable system, it will attempt to isolate criteria that can be objectively evaluated. Furthermore, everyone within the department should be fully apprised of exactly what these criteria are and precisely how they will be applied and weighted in the evaluating process. This matter of evaluating police performance is so important that we will consider it in more detail in Chapter 12.

Finally, in this discussion of feedback as an important element in the staffing function, some consideration should be given to the need that police departments have to evaluate personnel strength requirements—that is, to determine how many sworn officers and other types of employees are needed. All too often in the past, the number of police officers needed in particular assignments or in specified geographical areas has been predicated on political and sometimes even emotional factors. By conducting a personnel requirements survey, based on actual activity and the time needed to service it, a department will be armed with information that can be fed back into the staffing process as new input so that assignment adjustments can be made in terms of the department's actual needs.

The inputs of people, jobs, and objectives are processed through recruitment, selection, training, placement, promotion, and termination to produce staff. Feedback is provided through performance evaluation of staff members and analysis of staff requirements. Although many aspects of the staffing function legitimately belong to the department's personnel division, others are either the direct or indirect responsibility of each and every supervisor and manager.

Recruitment

The first stage of the staffing process is recruitment. Somehow a police department must induce individuals to apply for position openings. Generally, there are three categories of people who seek employment with a given organization:

1. people who are very interested in the position and who are eager to obtain it;
2. people who are not very interested in the position and who see it as one employment alternative among many; and
3. people who have no real interest in the position and who, because of their marketability, see it as their only employment alternative.[30]

Although one might assume that people in the first category would tend to perform better on the job than those in the other two groups, research fails to support such a contention. There is no simple correlation between reasons for seeking employment and applicants' subsequent performance. It is clear, however, that the image of an organization is one important factor in attracting numerous applicants. Indeed, some police departments seem to discourage applicants from applying. The low esteem in which police are held in some communities and the fictitious image of the TV cop are also factors in keeping qualified applicants away. Saul W. Gellerman refers to this phenomenon as a "prevailing mythology" and suggests to the organization that it "prevents much of the available labor pool from passing through its evaluation process and compels it to make its selection from a much narrower segment of the population."[31]

The critical nature of this "prevailing mythology" for police recruiting should be a matter of concern to every police administrator—especially in this era of community policing. The arbitrary establishment of height, weight, eyesight, and other physical requirements is but one example of how the police service has effectively eliminated from consideration countless prospective candidates. Physical requirements in many police jurisdictions have been established at a level much higher than requirements for entrance into West Point, Annapolis, and the Air Force Academy.

The ludicrousness of this situation is evidenced by the experience of a young college student who was one of more than 1,000 applicants who applied for 100 openings in a state police organization. The young man successfully passed written, oral, and physical strength tests; he had only a physical examination to pass in order to be accepted into the service. In looking over the organization's physical requirements, he noticed that it was necessary to have 28 teeth; he discovered, much to his amazement, that he had only 27. Panic-stricken, he discussed his problem with one of his police science instructors, a retired state police captain. The instructor called the state police physician who would be conducting the physical examination and asked whether a waiver could be obtained. The physician said no, but suggested that the man's dentist make a one-tooth plate for him. The young man followed the suggestion and wore the plate on the day of the examination. He passed the physical with no difficulty and was appointed as a trooper. The twenty-eighth tooth was never worn again and to this day remains in a bureau drawer, a reminder of a ridiculous physical requirement that could have cost him his job and the state police an otherwise highly acceptable candidate.

Federal legislation, including the Americans with Disabilities Act, has severely constrained police use of arbitrary and indefensible physical standards in employment decisions.[32] Even more than in the past, police agencies are now required to demonstrate that physical requirements are genuinely job-related. Police departments must also now make "reasonable accommodations" for disabled employees and applicants. Although this legislation is still being interpreted by the courts, it seems likely that the ultimate effect will simply be to make the police employment process more fair and less arbitrary. In the long run this should benefit police agencies as well as individual applicants.

In addition to attracting a large number of job applicants, police departments must also engage in targeted recruitment. For example, many departments have few minority group employees in relation to the minority populations of the communities involved and must actively recruit such applicants to overcome past discrimination, whether overt or de facto. Such targeted recruiting may, in some instances, be court ordered. Targeted recruiting is an important component of any affirmative action program if a police department is sincere in its efforts to increase employment of women, racial or ethnic minorities, and other groups of protected workers.

One focus of targeted police recruiting over the past 25 years has been higher education. This emphasis has succeeded in raising the average educational level of police officers in the United States from little more than a high school degree to nearly two years of college.[33] What was once considered a rather radical idea—that police officers should be college-educated—is now largely taken for granted. Few police departments absolutely require applicants to have higher education, but many give preference to applicants with college degrees and offer educational incentives to their current employees. Applicants without any college education can still compete for positions in most police agencies, but more and more they find themselves at a distinct disadvantage. The federal government has recently created a funding program, the Police Corps, that pays for all the costs of four years of college (up to a total of $30,000) in return for a four-year commitment to work in local policing.[34]

Selection

The process of choosing from among applicants is called "selection." Every applicant for almost any type of job expects to be accepted or rejected as the result of some type of selection process.[35] One theory of the selection process emphasizes the person; accordingly, the most mature, intelligent, stable applicant should be selected, without particular regard for the position to be filled. Hrand Saxenian, a former professor at the Harvard Business School and a prominent management consultant, is one outstanding advocate of this theory. To Saxenian, maturity is the single most important criterion in the selection process. He has attempted, with some success, to measure maturity by determining the extent to which persons express their own feelings and convictions with consideration for the thoughts and feelings of others.[36]

In an experiment conducted with one large state police organization, Saxenian, using his own unique system for determining maturity, interviewed all 50 recruits undergoing 12 weeks of training at the police academy. Each recruit was interviewed for less than 30 minutes. The recruits were then ranked for maturity from 1 to 50 according to Saxenian's system of measurement. At the end of the 12-week training period, the academy staff ranked the recruits from 1 to 50 on the basis of their overall performance while in training. The two sets of rankings were remarkably similar and statistically showed a very high degree of correlation.

Follow-up studies several years later verified the statistical validity of Saxenian's original findings. The recruits singled out by Saxenian as being the most mature were by far the best performers. The rationale behind the theory of emphasizing the person in the selection process is that the right individual can be trained for the job easily enough once he or she has been selected.

Another theory of the selection process emphasizes the job to be filled rather than the person selected to fill it. The advocates of this theory believe that some jobs require particular skills and abilities that cannot be easily learned. The major problem with this approach is the difficulty of testing for these skills and abilities. One could say, for example, that order maintenance depends on an innate ability to manage conflict. Some officers are much more naturally inclined toward peacekeeping responsibilities than are others. The problem arises in the development of a testing instrument to predetermine which applicants have ability in this sensitive area of concern. Little significant effort has been made in the police field to validate entrance-level testing. Until this is done to the satisfaction of police administrators everywhere, problems will persist in the attempt to find applicants who can be neatly fitted into specialized job slots.

One major problem with the job-oriented approach is that it tends to emphasize mechanical and quantifiable aspects of the job. Typically, a job analysis is performed to determine the content of the job and the knowledge, abilities, skills, and other characteristics needed to perform the job. This is a well-established procedure in the personnel field, but it works better if the job is clearly defined and routine. Police work, with all its ambiguity and complexity, is not a good candidate for the procedure. Police job analyses have usually resulted in selection criteria that emphasize physical traits (body strength to overpower a prisoner), mechanical skills (high-speed driving), and rudimentary knowledge (reading and writing), rather than such personal characteristics as maturity and good judgment. The former are easier to quantify, measure, and defend in court, but perhaps are less important to real success in police work.[37] Recently, in an effort to overcome this problem and also support community policing, at least two states (Arizona and Kentucky) have conducted police job analyses that incorporated systematic input from citizens about the types of police officers and police work preferred by the community. This represents a positive development with the potential to affect both police selection and police training.

Both selection-process theories have merit. The wide variety of duties that police officers perform, coupled with the innumerable talents and abilities needed to perform them, suggest that the entrance-level selection process must necessarily focus both on the person and on the job. Police administrators in recent years have begun to place more emphasis on selecting personnel on personal qualities such as common sense, intelligence, ability to verbalize, good judgment, and maturity. It is assumed, with considerable justification, that an applicant with these basic characteristics can be trained to perform the endless number of tasks that a police officer is expected to perform. Most job skills are learned after an applicant is accepted as a police officer, not before.

The psychological screening of applicants has recently become a major part of the selection process in a number of police departments.[38] Because police work is a difficult, demanding, and stressful occupation, it is becoming increasingly evident that applicants who are stress-prone should be identified early in the selection process and screened out. Although much more empirical research is needed before we can easily identify such people, we do know that those people who have not learned "healthy coping behaviors"[39] (such as continuing involvement in regular exercise and participation in hobbies and sports) are prime candidates for stress. We also know that unhealthy coping (such as smoking, excessive drinking, lack of exercise, limited non-job-related interests, and inordinate amounts of television watching) are stress indicators that can and should be determined during the selection process. The hiring of individuals who are not stress-prone is an important key factor in the selection process.

While police selection methods in the professional era tended to emphasize "screening out" applicants with background or psychological problems, a stronger effort is being made under community policing to "screen in" applicants with particularly desirable characteristics.[40] Such desirable traits include higher education, varied life experience, cognitive problem-solving skills, communication skills (including listening), and good interpersonal relations (such as empathy and respect for others).

Besides the particular mix of skills and qualities on which police departments base their selection decisions, there are important considerations that transcend traditional police practices. Numerous police departments have been required by the federal courts to develop affirmative action programs to hire more minority group members and women. The courts found that some selection criteria, including some physical requirements and entrance-level testing, were discriminatory when not clearly job-related.[41] It is important for police administrators to understand that, regardless of their own predispositions with respect to hiring practices, federally established selection guidelines must be followed and their own selection processes adjusted accordingly. There is every reason to believe that personnel carefully selected on the basis of equal opportunity/affirmative action programs will significantly strengthen police staffs, giving the police a better capability of dealing with all segments of the population. The best way for a police department to avoid discriminatory hiring practices is to fully adopt the philosophy of the Police Foundation, which contends that "it is clearly desirable, consistent with America's democratic principles, that police agencies have a healthy balance of people representing the range of citizenry in the communities those agencies serve."[42]

Training

Once selected, a new employee enters the training stage of the staffing process. Loen has identified four major activities:

1. a basic orientation, outlining organizational goals and objectives;
2. a planned, scheduled training program aimed at teaching new personnel how to perform tasks expected of them;
3. an organized in-service training effort directed toward upgrading personnel; and
4. a self-development training program designed to encourage personnel to develop themselves professionally.[43]

The first two of these activities are generally referred to as "recruit training" and typically involve both in-class and on-the-job training (often called "field training"). Many police departments are too small to support their own recruit training programs, and therefore send newly hired officers to regional or state academies. In-service training is provided to a greater or lesser degree by many departments—more progressive police agencies provide at least one week of in-service training a year for each police officer, and most states require at least one week every two years. Some departments take advantage of excellent in-service training courses offered by organizations such as state and regional training academies, the International Association of Chiefs of Police, the Federal Bureau of Investigation, the Federal Law Enforcement Training Center, the Traffic Institute of Northwestern University, and the Southern Police Institute at the University of Louisville. In-service police training is available extensively almost everywhere. A department need only take advantage of the wide range of training opportunities.

The fourth training activity, self-development, was strongly encouraged in the 1960s and 1970s through the establishment of the Law Enforcement Education Program (LEEP) of the Law Enforcement Assistance Administration, a federally funded effort that paid the tuition of more than 100,000 in-service police officers who attended colleges and universities throughout the nation. As these federal funds became less available, police administrators and educators were challenged to devise new programs to encourage employees to further develop themselves.

Training is an important part of the staffing process; it is concerned with molding selected job applicants into knowledgeable, skilled, committed employees of the organization and remolding current employees. Training is also a basic component of the directing function of management, which, as explained in a later section, is concerned with making sure that employees know what to do and how to do it.

Assignment

Once trained at the orientation and recruit levels, the employee must be assigned to a job within the organization. The nature of the job in which the trained recruit is placed ordinarily requires little choice for most police departments, because most new police employees usually begin their careers as patrol officers. This tradition has changed very little since Sir Robert Peel established the first metropolitan police department in London in 1829. However, in larger police departments, the assignment of rookies may involve some choice as to the locations of their assignment. Some departments assign officers to districts in which they live; others intentionally assign officers away from their places of residence. Some assignments are made on the basis of race and ethnicity. For example, black and Spanish-speaking officers may be assigned to predominantly black and Spanish-speaking neighborhoods, respectively.

Although there are vastly conflicting philosophies regarding assignments, the placing of individuals within any organization is an extremely important staffing function. Individuals who are improperly assigned can negatively affect the organization's effort to meet its goals and objectives.

Assignment should be regarded as a continuing staffing process. Those responsible for the staffing function should continually assess assignment output through feedback in order to make staffing adjustments or personnel transfers. Very few police officers spend their entire careers in the positions to which they were assigned as rookies. Although many may remain at the patrol officer rank throughout their careers, most will probably be transferred from district to district within the community or to specialized duties within the organization. The transfer of personnel should be looked on as a healthy application of the systems concept to the police management function. It should never be anticipated that everyone placed in every position will always be best suited to perform in that position.

Although long-term beat assignments for patrol officers are preferred under community policing, there is also much to be said for regular, periodic shifting of personnel. It not only develops more well-rounded employees, but by rechallenging them to learn new and more interesting jobs, it also lessens the likelihood that they will stagnate in one position. Transfers also become necessary in problem situations. Some employees simply may not be able to perform in a particular area of the community or in a particular job. Disputes between coworkers or between subordinates and superiors may be insoluble except through transfers. However, when personality problems impede an organization from meeting its goals and objectives, great care should be taken in using transfer as the solution. In such cases, transfers should be used only as a last resort, especially when feedback indicates that transfers would only move problems from one subsystem of the organization to another. Therefore, transfers should be made only if it appears likely that they will positively affect system output.

Promotion

Promotion as a staffing activity is a transfer upward in rank. The methods used by police departments to determine who will be promoted vary tremendously; there is no consistent police promotion pattern anywhere in the United States. Police promotional systems usually include one or more of the following evaluative techniques:

1.   written examinations
2.   oral interviews
3.   experience (sometimes called "longevity")
4.   past performance evaluation
5.   assessment centers

As a rule, various percentage weights are assigned to each evaluative technique. These will vary from department to department, depending on which criteria the department's administrator regards as most important.

Police departments that use only one or two of these techniques in their promotional systems can anticipate having problems in the administration of the promotional process. It is not recommended, for example, that promotions would be based solely on the outcome of a written examination. This, however, is the case in many police departments, and it is why so many police departments have problems with their promotional systems. Departments that fail to use multiple techniques, with published weighted values assigned to each criterion, impede the successful output of the staffing process, which in turn hinders their efforts to meet goals and objectives. Problems arising from the promoting process that are not being fed back into the staffing process as new inputs provide proof that most police departments do not look at staffing from a systems perspective. The value of the systems approach to any process of police management, including promoting and staffing, is that problems will be identified through feedback and that systems will be improved through new input.

Of the five evaluative criteria discussed here, perhaps the most promising is the fifth: the assessment center. This method uses simulated real-life situations designed to place the person being evaluated into a milieu in which he or she will have a full opportunity to exhibit job-related skills closely identified with the position to be filled. Although assessment centers can be utilized in the selection process,[44] they are most frequently used in the police field for promotional purposes and for the testing of managerial competence[45] and the viability of first-line supervision. As a promotional device, the assessment center is a multidimensional evaluation approach that, typically over a period of two or three days,[46] places the candidate for promotion in a variety of anxiety-laden roles and positions in which the candidate's prioritizing and decision-making capabilities, as well as his or her ability to articulate orally and in writing, are closely tested and minutely examined under the most realistic conditions possible. For example, one evaluation, known as the "in-basket exercise," requires a candidate to assume the role of a police supervisor and to carry out a series of difficult simulated assignments in a limited period of time.[47] After submitting a written report on the rationale for actions taken and being orally interviewed on positions taken, the candidate is evaluated on a whole range of characteristics and tasks pertinent to the job. Other role-playing simulations might include placing a candidate in a police manager's role at a press conference called to deal with a controversial issue or having the candidate counsel a problem subordinate. There is literally no end of simulations that can be easily designed and validated to test skills in this manner.

Termination

The final staffing activity, terminating, may occur on the employee's own initiative through normal retirement, early retirement, or resignation. It may also occur at the department's direction through forced retirements, forced resignations, or firings. Terminations may be based on sickness, injury, or death. Table 6.1 shows the various kinds of special and routine decisions made in the termination process by both the police department and the employee. When the department makes termination decisions, regardless of whether they are special or routine decisions, the department is engaging in the terminating process.

Table 6.1
Special and Routine Decisions Made in the Termination Process

Source of Decisions	Special Decisions	Routine Decisions
Department	Forced retirements Forced resignations Firings	Retirements due to sickness or injury Terminations due to death
Employee	Voluntary resignations	Normal retirement Early but voluntary retirements

An employee's voluntary retirement is usually the cause of much rejoicing and is regarded as the happy ending to many years of productive employment. By reaching retirement age or by choosing to retire early, the employee leaves the police department with the realization that he or she performed adequately for a considerable period of time.

When a police department fires employees or forces them to resign or retire, it is telling them, in effect, that they are no longer useful to the organization in its attempts to meet its goals and objectives. Such an action will necessarily affect the entire system and cause severe subsystem reactions. These reactions may be either positive or negative. When an employee is fired or forced to resign or retire as the result of an internal investigation that uncovered corruption or incompetence, the effect on the system should be positive. When an employee is forced out of a department based on inconclusive evidence of corruption or incompetence, it should be anticipated that the effect on the system will be negative. In the former instance, the action taken by the department serves notice to all other employees that corruption or incompetence will not be tolerated by the department. In the latter instance, action against the employee serves notice to all other employees that the same rules of evidence that are applied generally throughout the criminal justice system are not applicable to them, thus creating a morale problem that the department could very well do without in its efforts to meet its goals and objectives.

The voluntary resignation of an employee short of retirement age is usually regarded as a setback for the department. When a police officer resigns, the department loses not only its investment in the individual but also an experienced employee. Although many employees terminate voluntarily for personal reasons beyond the control of the police department, such as sickness, injury, or a better-paying position, others terminate voluntarily because of dissatisfaction with their jobs or because of departmental organizational problems with which they cannot cope. Still others quit because they are disinterested in their jobs, cannot get along with people, or find it difficult to make a long-term commitment to one employer. Voluntary terminations should be expected. Large numbers of voluntary terminations, however, should be a signal to people involved in the staffing function that something is seriously wrong with the department. To assess this condition, many police departments annually calculate their turnover rate, the percentage of employees who leave the agency during the preceding year.

The voluntary resignation or involuntary termination of an employee, besides being a waste for both the department and the individual concerned, may in all likelihood also be substantial proof of a breakdown somewhere in the staffing function, most probably in selection, training, or placement. Those responsible for staffing should therefore be required to carefully examine all aspects and all ramifications of involuntary termination in an effort to improve staffing input with respect to the termination process. Application of the systems approach is one way to get at and solve organizational problems that stem from management deficiencies. Exit interviews with terminated employees are useful in getting feedback on staffing problems. If an organization's selection, training, and assignment processes can be refined so that most problems are eliminated through the adjustment and change of systems inputs, a department can improve its turnover rate and avoid many involuntary terminations.

Directing

Think for a moment of motion picture directors and what they do. Their job is directing; they tell the actors and actresses to speak their lines, what movements to make before the cameras, and what emotions to display. They show their camera crews what angles, lenses, and filters to use. They establish filming schedules. They direct the activities of people involved in casting, costumes, and makeup. Their job involves telling people what to do, when to do it, and how to do it. They call the shots. They do this by bringing together all of the talents they have at their disposal and orchestrating them as best they can into what will become the final production, a motion picture.

This job may seem to be a simple process. It is not. Consider some of its complications. Actors and actresses are professionals in their own right and some of them may be more highly paid than the directors. They may refuse to comply with shooting schedules or refuse to take direction. Other members of the crew may have technical disagreements with the directors, or they may simply misunderstand their directions. In other instances, personality conflicts between the directors and their employees may impede progress. Problems involving sickness, injury, substance abuse, family, and just plain irresponsibility will contribute to delaying production and are likely to be costly.

In the directing function, managers develop and disseminate directives and provide leadership, guidance, coaching, coordination, and encouragement. Subordinates receive and act on those directives. Subordinates bring with them differing skills, abilities, knowledge, attitudes, perceptions, and levels of motivation. Objectives guide the purposefulness of the process. If directing fails to point an organization toward the accomplishment of its goals and objectives, it serves no useful purpose.

The output of the directing process, in general terms, is direction. In more specific terms, the outputs are policies, procedures, rules, regulations, general orders, special orders, personal orders, training curricula, training bulletins, advice, suggestions, encouragement, and persuasion.

Feedback to the directing function comes from evaluation of the extent to which directives (orders, rules, regulations, policies, and procedures) are understood and followed. Because dissemination and reception of directives involve the intricate processes of communication and perception, it is essential that the output of the directing process (direction) be carefully evaluated on a continuing basis so that any directives that are improperly communicated or misunderstood can be redesigned as new input and redisseminated through the directing process.

Some types of directives lend themselves to immediate feedback. For example, in issuing a personal order to a patrol officer to leave the police station immediately to answer a burglary-in-progress call, a sergeant will learn within a matter of seconds whether the patrol officer understands the order. Similarly, in discussing a newly disseminated general order with patrol officers at roll call, a sergeant can learn from their responses whether they understand the content of the order. However, most feedback to the directing process is not such a simple matter. Several months might go by before officers encounter a situation in which a new directive should be applied. If they have forgotten the directive, they will improvise as best they can under the circumstances but may not necessarily perform according to the method prescribed by the department through the directive. If they misunderstood the intent of the directive when it was issued, chances are good that they will perform in a manner not consistent with departmental procedure. Supervisors must be alert to such possibilities and advise their superiors when directives, for whatever reason, are not being followed. Therefore, supervisors are key people in providing feedback to keep the loop closed in the directing process. If supervisors fail to provide information for evaluation and new input, the department will likely be unaware that its directives are not being followed and will be lulled into a false sense of security about the activities of its officers.

There is no quicker way for a police department to degenerate organizationally than to allow the directing process to function in open-loop fashion. Departments that fail to approach the directing process from a closed-loop systems perspective actually encourage their police officers to defy directives and to handle all situations through a process that the President's Crime Commission referred to as "unarticulated improvisation."[48] This means, in effect, that police officers will handle situations according to their own individual judgments and whims and not according to the articulated policies of their own departments. This results in laws being enforced indiscriminately and services being provided haphazardly. The resultant inconsistencies in levels of enforcement and levels of services negatively affect the police generally and the individual department particularly. Although this may be a "comfortable approach," as the Commission put it, for the officers involved, it is organizationally chaotic and flies in the face of the systems approach to good management. As an alternative, the Commission recommended a different process, which is "systematic, intelligent, articulate and responsive to external controls appropriate in a democratic society."[49] The only way to achieve this is to keep the loop closed in the directing process.

Although feedback from supervisors is probably the single most important factor in keeping the loop closed in the directing process, other methods should also be used. One such method is the test. When a directive is issued, all employees governed by the directive should be tested on their understanding of its specifics. The test can be either written or oral; the written test, however, is more advantageous because it affords a better opportunity to examine in depth the individual's reception and perception of the directive. Moreover, an individual forced to describe the directive in written form is more likely to remember it than if the description is given orally. In addition, the answers on a written test can be reviewed by a number of people, thereby reducing the possibility of perception errors on the part of reviewers. If the test indicates that the directive is generally misunderstood, it can be used as an evaluative criterion that can be fed back into the directing process as new input, which would probably result in having the directive rewritten and redisseminated. If the directive is misunderstood only slightly or by only a few officers, it might be more prudent to design a roll-call training session or even a series of such training sessions to explain the directive. Testing should be an ongoing feedback mechanism and should be discontinued only when management is assured that a given directive is fully understood.

Informal conversations with police officers themselves can also be helpful. One former chief of police in a large West Coast city devoted one-half day per week to informal interviews with individual officers. This proved to be an effective feedback device and gave the chief an opportunity he would not otherwise have had to learn in what ways his own direction output was ineffective. Other chiefs and lower-level police managers simply engage in "walking-around management" by regularly spending some time observing their employees in the performance of their duties and by talking frequently with the police department's customers.[50]

By closing the loop of the directing process through feedback and by introducing corrective input into the system, police administrators can exercise their prerogatives and meet their responsibilities as the directors of their organizations. The process of directing involves the following activities:

1. development
2. dissemination
3. reception
4. action

These are the activities that, when affected by variables and constraints, make directing such a complex task.

Development

The development of directives involves considerable planning and a careful analysis of organizational goals and objectives. Because directives tell people what to do, they must be designed in accordance with what the organization itself wants to accomplish through the people it employs. People are the instrumentality by which the organization functions. It is only through the direction of people that the organization accomplishes what it sets out to do. Deciding what directives should be developed, therefore, is an important part of the directing process.

How should directives be developed? Although this is clearly a management responsibility, input from two groups is extremely valuable. First, it is a good idea to involve employees in the development of directives, because they are probably more knowledgeable about the practical realities of the work setting than most managers. Involving employees at this stage also makes it more likely that they will understand and comply with the directives that are ultimately developed. Second, it is desirable to engage the community in the development of some types of directives—those that most directly affect the public, such as personnel selection guidelines, complaint review procedures, and use of force policies. A central tenet of community policing is that in a free society citizens should have such opportunities to shape the style and manner of policing in their communities. An additional benefit of such citizen participation is usually an increase in trust and confidence in the police.

It is also important to consider, in the development stage of directing, what skills, abilities, and knowledge employees need and how best to fill those needs. Formal training may be required or one-on-one coaching may be more appropriate. Sometimes employees have the necessary tools but lack the will, commitment, or motivation to perform properly. In these instances the directing function should focus on providing encouragement, incentives, and leadership. Chapters 8 through 10 are devoted to the human aspects of management that come into play when carrying out the directing function.

Dissemination

Directives are disseminated, or communicated, from superiors to subordinates; they are also disseminated as part of recruit and in-service training. The process of communicating directives to those who are expected to follow them and act on them is an involved and complex procedure. Literally millions of people in the world earn their living by either communicating with people or telling people how to communicate with one another. Communication is an art practiced by many but mastered by few. It is the primary vehicle for the dissemination of directives.

Interpersonal communication is discussed in Chapter 8. The flow of communications within the police organization is further examined in Chapter 11.

Reception

The reception of directives involves individual perception, a matter as difficult to analyze as it is to predict. Nations have gone to war, businesses have gone bankrupt, and people have committed suicide because of faulty perception. Huge bureaucracies such as the Central Intelligence Agency and the KGB existed for decades almost solely to provide their respective governments with accurate perceptions of foreign powers. Political candidates and large corporations expend tremendous energy and sometimes substantial sums of money in efforts to perceive accurately what voters are thinking and what they want. Pollsters such as Gallup and Harris are widely read and generally relied on to provide perceptions of various trends that are occurring and always changing in society.

Yet even the most astute professionals frequently perceive incorrectly. The Ford Motor Company was guilty of inaccurate perception when it conceived the Edsel. Neville Chamberlain was guilty of inaccurate perception when he chose to trust Adolf Hitler. Every financial expert in the United States, except for Roger Babson, was guilty of inaccurate perception in failing to predict the stock market crash of 1929. How often have you personally made an innocent remark to someone that was taken the wrong way?

Action

The action taken as a result of directives depends on a number of factors, including the effectiveness of the dissemination and reception processes, group dynamics, leadership, values, attitudes, and motivation. Taken as a whole, the process of directing is tied up with the psychology of human behavior, which itself is an academic discipline. The better one understands the pragmatics of human behavior, human relationships, and human interaction, the better director one becomes. If one cannot understand and deal with behavior of human beings pragmatically and without illusions, one should not be involved in the directing process.

Controlling

The management function of controlling is closely related to directing. Whereas directing is involved in communicating what should be done, controlling is involved with ensuring that what should be done *is done*. If directing is the making and communicating of rules, controlling is enforcing rules.

Controlling as a management function is somewhat broader, however, than simple rule enforcement. It includes functions that might not generally be looked on as control devices. Budgeting, for example, is one way in which an organization uses the allocation of money to control its subsystems. Another control mechanism is the gathering and evaluation of statistics, a means by which an organization learns about the effectiveness of its operation and thereby controls its activities. Controlling is designed essentially to make certain that an organization and its component parts adhere to established directives.

A significant gap between the way functions are performed and the way they are supposed to be performed is an indication that the controlling function is not serving its purpose. It may also indicate a failure of the directing function; in such instances, employees simply do not understand directives. It may further indicate that prevailing directives are not consistent with organizational goals and objectives, presenting employees with a choice between doing what they have been told to do and what they honestly judge is best for the organization. Each of these possibilities must be kept in mind by police managers who administer their organizations from a systems perspective and who are responsible for directing and controlling.

Controlling involves influencing behavior. Numerous methods are used to influence behavior: rewards, punishments, threats, promises, and cajoling (see "The Control Principle," p. 172). In general, most police departments make little effort to influence the behavior of police officers through established techniques designed to effect control. This is probably because it is generally assumed by people who are unfamiliar with behavior modification techniques that the modification of behavior is an impossible task. Unfortunately for the police service, the major behavior modification technique used consistently by most police chiefs is punishment, at best a negative technique that usually creates serious morale problems.

The influencing of human behavior is a difficult, complex, and involved process. Most parents are thoroughly familiar with problems inherent in the process. Although they have almost total authority over their children, especially in the younger years, they often find it impossible to control their behavior and to have them act according to parental expectations. Parents' failures in controlling their children are disruptive to the family and harmful to the children themselves. Testing their parents to see how much they can get away with is not uncommon among children; it is, in fact, a continuing process. Consider how much more difficult it is to control an entire organization. In an organization comprising hundreds of people, the controlling function is quite involved and requires a concerted effort. If one is to achieve any degree of success in controlling people within large organizations, it is absolutely essential that a variety or continuum of techniques be employed[51] and that a closed-loop systems approach be used in the process.

Behavior modification techniques must be used intelligently to motivate people to perform effectively. These techniques are used to motivate people to do what you expect them to do, what they are directed to do. Once a directive is issued, there is no guarantee that an individual will automatically be predisposed to follow it, even if he or she understands it. In most organizations, the tendency is just the opposite—the tendency is called beating the system. People must somehow be motivated to follow directives if the organization for which they work is to meet its goals and objectives. Because it is essential for people in organizations to follow directives, the methods used to modify their behavior so that they will be willing to perform their jobs as expected must be carefully designed and implemented.

Of the many behavior-modification methods used, the two most important for police administrators to consider are reward and recognition, both of which are easy to develop and implement. Reward and recognition might take the form of pay increments for work well done, promotions, public recognition, days off, favorable assignments, and special awards. Even a pat on the back for a job well done should not be underestimated as a motivational factor.

Recognition is perhaps the most compelling behavior modifier of all. People who do good work should be recognized for their contributions. Recognition gives an individual a sense of organizational belongingness. It is nonmonetary pay for a job well done. It says to the officer, "We recognize your worth, and we place great value on your being an important part of the organization." It provides a tremendous incentive for the officer to want to continue to perform effectively. The officer feels a part of the organization team and is therefore motivated to follow directives in an effort to help the organization meet its goals and objectives.

Police departments that fail to realize the importance of reward and recognition as behavior modifiers cannot possibly meet their goals and objectives and will be constantly plagued by large numbers of officers attempting to beat the system. The system has to be geared to recognize the need that all people have to feel important. It must consciously devise as many methods as possible to make people feel important. If not, employees will feel that the system does not recognize their talents and contributions and that regardless of how well they do their work, nobody really cares. This contributes to an "organization be damned" philosophy, a feeling of uselessness, and a commitment to do as little work as possible just to get by.

Decisions made by individual officers with respect to actions taken often depend largely, and sometimes solely, on the sense of belonging that officers have toward their department. If they are comfortable in their positions and feel that their department recognizes what they do, chances are excellent that they will do their jobs to the best of their abilities and be organizationally productive in terms of goals and objectives. Because police officers often work alone with little direct supervision, their activities are extremely difficult to control. An assembly line worker with a hovering supervisor is much easier to control than a police officer who might see a supervisor only once or twice during an entire tour of duty. It is therefore important to realize that controlling a police officer involves the application of highly refined motivational devices. The mechanisms of reward and recognition as behavior modifiers, when properly applied, can make the difference between meeting or not meeting organizational goals and objectives.

It would be unfair to leave you with the impression that other behavior modification devices should be totally discarded in favor of reward and recognition. Punishment, for example, can be effective as a behavior modifier if used fairly, consistently and not to the exclusion of other behavior modifiers. However, punishment should be used only as a last resort. Realistically, it must be understood that some people are difficult to motivate except through punishment. The effort to motivate people through other means should always be made and punishment used only if everything else fails. Depending on the seriousness of the infraction, everyone should probably be given a second chance, and perhaps even a third, before the administrator resorts to punishment. When an infraction occurs, a subtle threat or even a direct promise to take action should the infraction reoccur might very well serve to motivate the individual sufficiently. The best method for effecting control within any organization is through the sensible application of as many motivational techniques as possible. These techniques, working in concert with one another, can effectively motivate people to follow directives, to do their jobs, and to meet organizational goals and objectives.

The output of the controlling process is control. If every employee always acted in exact accordance with organizational directives, absolute control would exist. In order for this to happen, perfect communication would have to exist within the organization; every directive would have to be completely understood by every employee; and every employee would have to agree that every directive issued was consonant with organizational as well as personal goals and objectives. Considering that some people are more motivated, more conscientious, and more talented than others, one should conclude that in an organization of any size, absolute control cannot exist.

The Control Principle

Police activities range from low-criticality to high-criticality and low-frequency to high-frequency. Police officials must identify which activities require strict control-oriented policies and which require only summary guidance. In other words, the style of policy will vary according to a continuum of control. In addition, there must be training to the policy, control and supervision of the activities and a system of discipline that holds the officers and agency accountable for the behavior.

Source: Geoffrey P. Alpert and William C. Smith, "Developing Police Policy: An Evaluation of the Control Principle," in Gary W. Cordner and Dennis Jay Kenney, eds., *Managing Police Organizations* (Cincinnati, OH: Anderson, 1996), p. 124.

The evaluation of the effectiveness of established control mechanisms provides feedback for the controlling function. The feedback of supervisors who observe their officers at work and who review their reports is critical to the controlling process. Informal feedback from officers themselves and from the public can also be helpful.

Large departments have specialized inspection divisions that make periodic checks throughout their organizations in an effort to determine the degree to which directives are being followed.[52] Inspections exist primarily to provide feedback in the controlling process. Their very existence, however, is a control mechanism in and of itself that ensures a certain degree of compliance with departmental directives. Even in the smallest police departments the inspection function can be performed by the chief or a trusted associate. It is an excellent feedback device.

The departmental audit is another mechanism that is frequently used to provide feedback on control output. Audits can be performed to determine conformity to almost any type of organizational directive. Some departments rely on independent outside consultants to study all aspects of the degree to which control over all activities is exercised. Such organizations as the International Association of Chiefs of Police and the Police Executive Research Forum have been widely used for this purpose.

The establishment of an internal affairs division is another useful feedback device. These divisions investigate internally such matters as police impropriety, brutality, corruption, and malfeasance. Aside from being a response to citizen interest in having the police police themselves, internal affairs divisions provide a strong incentive for police officers to comply with organizational directives, particularly to directives relating to behavior that borders on being improper or criminal. The results of internal affairs investigations should always be fed back into the controlling function as new input.

As with all management functions, the importance of feedback cannot be stressed too strongly. No chief of police, especially one several levels removed from operational components, can assume that directives are being followed; if the job of management is not approached from a systems perspective, the chief can be almost certain that directives are not being followed.

The controlling function of management, much like the directing function, is concerned largely with the psychology of human behavior, a subject that will be treated more fully in subsequent chapters.

Summary

This chapter has discussed six primary functions of management: system building, planning, organizing, staffing, directing, and controlling. The first three are the particular responsibility of top-level police managers, while the second three are among the standard responsibilities of virtually all managers in police agencies, from first-line supervisors through the chief executive. Each function is extremely intricate and could be the subject of a separate volume. We have discussed these functions within the framework of systems theory. We urge you to retain the systems concept as a frame of mind and as an important point of reference. By regularly searching for the inputs, processes, outputs, and feedback in management activities, you will become more adept at analyzing and building systems. Or, to put it another way, you will become more adept at managing.

Discussion Questions

1. What specific steps can police agencies take to enhance system learning? What happens to the store of knowledge and experience in a police department when key members retire after long careers? How could their knowledge and experience be "saved" by the agency?

2. Some people argue that planning is a wasteful activity, because they believe that the future is either preordained or too unpredictable to prepare for. Do you agree with these people? Does planning serve any useful purpose?

3. African Americans, women, and other groups have traditionally been underrepresented in police organizations. Why do you think this has been the case? How would you correct this situation?

4. Police departments have traditionally required their employees to retire once they reach a certain age, say 55 years old. Do you think this is fair to employees? What should police agencies do with older officers who do not want to retire? As a citizen, how would you feel if you were in trouble and the police officer who responded to your call for assistance was 65 or 70 years old?

5. Some authorities have proposed that police officers should be chosen only from among those people possessing college degrees. Do you agree with this position? If you do, how would you answer the criticism that many otherwise well-qualified people have been excluded from consideration? What about the argument that college is not as available to poor people and thus they would be unfairly discriminated against by a college degree requirement? On the other side of the coin, if you do not favor the requirement, what consideration would you give to those people who do have the degree? Would you offer promotional advantages, extra money, or special positions?

Cases

Three of the cases at the end of this text present situations that can be analyzed in light of the information presented in Chapter 6. You should examine the performance of management functions in "Case 1: The Energetic Chief," "Case 2: The Peripatetic Sergeant," and "Case 4: The Chief Who Played King."

Notes

1. L. Gulick, "The Theory of Organization," in *Papers on the Science of Administration*, L. Gulick and L. Urwick, eds. (New York, NY: Institute of Public Administration, 1937), p. 13.

2. R.L. Holcomb, ed., *Municipal Police Administration* (Chicago: International City Management Association, 1961), p. 77.

3. L.R. Sayles, *Managerial Behavior: Administration in Complex Organizations* (New York, NY: McGraw-Hill, 1964), pp. 49-54.

4. G.D. Eastman, "Police Management," in *Municipal Police Administration*, Sixth Edition, G.D. Eastman and E.M. Eastman, eds. (Washington, DC: International City Management Association, 1969), p. 37.

5. H. Koontz and C. O'Donnell, *Principles of Management: An Analysis of Managerial Functions* (New York, NY: McGraw-Hill, 1964).

6. W.W. Schmidt, "Section 1983 and the Changing Face of Police Management," in *Police Leadership in America: Crisis and Opportunity*, W.A. Geller, ed. (New York, NY: Praeger, 1985), pp. 226-236.

7. V.E. Kappeler, *Critical Issues in Police Civil Liability*, Third Edition (Prospect Heights, IL: Waveland, 2001).

8. R.L. Katz, "Skills of an Effective Administrator," *Harvard Business Review* (September–October 1974): 26.

9. The Baltimore County Repeat Offender Planning Project (Baltimore, MD: University of Baltimore, 1983).

10. T.J. Peters and R.H. Waterman Jr., *In Search of Excellence: Lessons from America's Best-Run Companies* (New York, NY: Harper & Row, 1982).

11. P.M. Senge, *The Fifth Discipline: The Art and Practice of the Learning Organization*, rev. ed. (New York, NY: Doubleday, 1994); W.A. Geller, "Suppose We Were Really Serious about Police Departments Becoming 'Learning Organizations'," *NIJ Journal* 234 (December 1997): 2-8; L.F. Alarid, "Law Enforcement Departments as Learning Organizations: Argyris's Theory as a Framework for Implementing Community-Oriented Policing," *Police Quarterly* 2, no. 3 (September 1999): 321-337.

12. D. Ogle, "A Model for Strategic Planning," in *Strategic Planning for Police*, D. Ogle, ed. (Ottawa: Canadian Police College, 1991), pp. 14-15.

13. R. Stata, "Organizational Learning," *Sloan Management Review* (spring 1989).

14. G.L. Williams, *Making the Grade: The Benefits of Law Enforcement Accreditation* (Washington, DC: Police Executive Research Forum, 1989).

15. *Standards for Law Enforcement Agencies* (Fairfax, VA: Commission on Accreditation for Law Enforcement Agencies, 1998).

16. The Society of Police Futurists International can be found on the Internet at www.police-futurists.org.

17. J.K. Hudzik and G.W. Cordner, *Planning in Criminal Justice Organizations and Systems* (New York, NY: Macmillan, 1983).

18. The International Association of Law Enforcement Planners can be found on the Internet at www.ialep.org/

19. J.R. Greene, W.T. Bergman, and E.J. McLaughlin, "Implementing Community Policing: Cultural and Structural Change in Police Organizations," in D.P. Rosenbaum, ed., *The Challenge of Community Policing: Testing the Promises* (Thousand Oaks, CA: Sage, 1994), pp. 92-109.

20. T.D. Cook, "Lessons Learned in Evaluation Over the Past 25 Years," in E. Chelimsky and W.R. Shadish, eds., *Evaluation for the 21st Century: A Handbook* (Thousand Oaks, CA: Sage, 1997), pp. 30-52.

21. G.W. Cordner, C.B. Fraser, and C. Wexler, "Research, Planning, and Implementation," in *Local Government Police Management*, Third Edition, W.A. Geller, ed. (Washington, DC: International City Management Association, 1991), pp. 333-362.

22. T.D. Schneid and L.K. Gaines, "The Americans with Disabilities Act: Implications for Police Administrators," in D.J. Kenney and G.W. Cordner, eds., *Managing Police Personnel* (Cincinnati, OH: Anderson, 1996), pp. 43-52.

23. R.R. Roberg and J.J. Krichoff, "Applying Strategic Management Methods to Law Enforcement: Two Case Studies," *American Journal of Police* 4,2 (fall 1985): 133-151; J. Zurcher and J.B. Hudak, "How to Build A Crystal Ball: Strategic Planning for Police Agencies," *Police Chief* (February 1987): 20-29.

24. J.R. Greene, "The Road to Community Policing in Los Angeles," in G.P. Alpert and A. Piquero, eds., *Community Policing: Contemporary Readings* (Prospect Heights, IL: Waveland, 1998), pp. 123-158.

25. J.D. Mooney and A.C. Reilly, *Onward Industry! The Principles of Organization and Their Significance to Modern Industry* (New York, NY: Harper Brothers, 1931), pp. 9-11, 12-17, as quoted in E. Dale, ed., *Readings in Management: Landmarks and New Frontiers* (New York, NY: McGraw-Hill, 1965), p. 155.

26. Koontz and O'Donnell, *Principles of Management*, p. 227.

27. Mooney and Reilly, *Onward Industry!*, p. 155.

28. H.J. Leavitt, *Managerial Psychology: An Introduction to Individuals, Pairs, and Groups in Organizations* (Chicago, IL: University of Chicago Press, 1972), p. 250.

29. T.N. Oettmeier and M.A. Wycoff, *Personnel Performance Evaluations in the Community Policing Context* (Washington, DC: Police Executive Research Forum, 1997).

30. S.W. Gellerman, *Motivation and Productivity* (New York, NY: American Management Association, 1963), p. 238.

31. Ibid., p. 240.

32. T.D. Schneid and L.K. Gaines, "The Americans with Disabilities Act: Implications for Police Administrators," *American Journal of Police* 10, no. 1 (1991): 47-58.

33. D.L. Carter, A.D. Sapp, and D.W. Stephens, *The State of Police Education: Policy Direction for the 21st Century* (Washington, DC: Police Executive Research Forum, 1989).

34. Information on the Police Corps program can be found on the Internet at www.usdoj. gov/cops/corps.htm.

35. E. Burbeck and A. Furnham, "Police Officer Selection: A Critical Review of the Literature," *Journal of Police Science and Administration* 13, no. 1 (March 1985), p. 58.

36. H. Saxenian, "To Select a Leader," *MIT Technology Review* 72, no. 7 (May 1970): 55-61.

37. G.W. Cordner, "Job Analysis and the Police: Benefits and Limitations," *Journal of Police Science and Administration* 8, no. 3 (September 1980): 355-362.

38. G.C. Hargrave and J.G. Brewer, "A Psychological Skills Analysis for California Peace Officers," *Police Chief* (February 1986): 34; V.B. Lord and N. Schoeps, "Identifying Psychological Attributes of Community-Oriented, Problem-Solving Police Officers," *Police Quarterly* 3, no. 2 (June 2000): 172-190; T. Ho, "The Interrelationships of Psychological Testing, Psychologists' Recommendations, and Police Departments' Recruitment Decisions," *Police Quarterly* 4, no. 3 (September 2001): 318-342.

39. J.W. White, P.S. Lawrence, C. Biggerstaff, and T.D. Gubb, "Factors of Stress among Police Officers," *Criminal Justice and Behavior* 12, no. 1 (March 1985): 120; J.D.K. Aaron, "Stress and Coping in Police Officers," *Police Quarterly* 3, no. 4 (December 2000): 438-450.

40. E. Metchik, "An Analysis of the 'Screening Out' Model of Police Officer Selection," *Police Quarterly* 2, no. 1 (March 1999): 79-95.

41. L.K. Gaines and V.E. Kappeler, "Selection and Testing," in *What Works in Policing? Operations and Administration Examined*, G.W. Cordner and D.C. Hale, eds. (Cincinnati, OH: Anderson, 1992), pp. 107-123.

42. *Experiments in Police Improvement: A Progress Report* (Washington, DC: Police Foundation, 1972), p. 13.

43. R.O. Loen, *Manage More by Doing Less* (New York, NY: McGraw-Hill, 1971), pp. 126-131.

44. D.A. Kent, C.R. Wall, and R.L. Bailey, "Assessment Centers: A New Approach to Police Personnel Decisions," *Police Chief* (June 1974): 72.

45. P.F. D'Arcy, "In New York City Assessment Center Program Helps to Test Managerial Competence," *Police Chief* (December 1974): 52.

46. C.L. Quarles, "A Validation Study of a Police Managerial Assessment Center," *American Journal of Police* 4, no. 1 (1985): 80.

47. C.D. Buracker, "The Assessment Center: Is It the Answer?" *FBI Law Enforcement Bulletin* (February 1980): 15.

48. President's Commission on Law Enforcement and Administration of Justice, *Task Force Report: The Police* (Washington, DC: U.S. Government Printing Office, 1967), p.18.

49. Ibid.

50. Peters and Waterman, *In Search of Excellence*.

51. G.P. Alpert and W.C. Smith, "Developing Police Policy: An Evaluation of the Control Principle," in G.W. Cordner and D.J. Kenney, eds., *Managing Police Organizations* (Cincinnati, OH: Anderson, 1996), pp. 111-126.

52. P.V. Murphy and G. Caplan, "Fostering Integrity," in *Local Government Police Management*, Third Edition. W.A. Geller, ed. (Washington, DC: International City Management Association, 1991), pp. 239-271.

Suggested Reading

Barlow, David E., and Melissa Hickman Barlow. *Police in a Multicultural Society: An American Story*. Prospect Heights, IL: Waveland, 2000.

Geller, William A., and Guy Swanger. *Managing Innovation in Policing: The Untapped Potential of the Middle Manager*. Washington, DC: Police Executive Research Forum, 1995.

Heidensohn, Frances, and Jennifer M. Brown. *Gender and Policing: Comparative Perspectives*. London: Palgrave Macmillan, 2000.

Kenney, Dennis Jay and Gary W. Cordner, eds. *Managing Police Personnel*. Cincinnati, OH: Anderson, 1996.

Strecher, Victor G. *Planning Community Policing: Goal-Specific Cases and Exercises*. Prospect Heights, IL: Waveland, 1997.

The Police Executive 7

Learning Objectives

- Identify and contrast the two basic roles of the police executive.

- Explain the difference between managing and leading.

- Identify eight principles for organizational excellence.

- Identify 10 principles for reinventing government.

- Explain the difference between "Politics" and "politics," and the proper influence of each on police administration.

- Explain the historical benefit that civil service reform brought to police administration, and describe some modern problems caused by civil service agencies.

- Identify three models for police media relations, the pros and cons of each, and the basic principle that should guide police relations with the media.

- Explain why police labor relations often put the police executive in a difficult "in-the-middle" position.

- Identify four police executive styles.

- Identify the police executive style that is least often exhibited and most in need today.

In this chapter we review the duties and responsibilities of the police executive. We frequently use the term police chief in this chapter and throughout the text; most of the information presented, however, will be just as applicable to other police executives, including police commissioners, superintendents, directors, chief constables, sheriffs, and all other heads of police agencies, regardless of title.

In earlier chapters, we examined in considerable detail such topics as police goals, systems, and subsystem tasks. In this chapter we discuss the fundamental roles played by police executives and some common styles or patterns of police executive behavior. We also present some contemporary views on organizational improvement, including approaches that emphasize excellence and the "reinvention" of government.

Characteristics of Police Executives

The Police Executive Research Forum (PERF), an association of police leaders, conducted a nationwide survey in 1997 of police chief executives (other than sheriffs) serving jurisdictions with populations greater than 50,000. This survey provided an interesting snapshot of the people in charge of police agencies in larger American jurisdictions as well as some of the conditions of their employment. Among their findings were these:[1]

- 81.6 percent were Caucasian, 10.9 percent were African American, and 4.7 percent were Hispanic
- 99.2 percent were men
- 67.6 percent were in the 46-55 age category
- 87.2 percent had at least a bachelor's degree, and more than 50 percent had graduate degrees
- the average tenure of the chiefs who served immediately before them was 4.9 years
- 82.4 percent had at least 16 years of police experience before obtaining their first chief's position
- 56.7 percent were promoted to the chief's position from within the same department
- about 60 percent of the chiefs report to a city or county manager, whereas 39 percent report to a mayor or other elected official(s)
- 26.5 percent reported having an employment contract or agreement

National data like these have not been collected again since 1997, but it seems likely that this picture shows several important trends: greater numbers of minority police executives (25 years ago there were few, if any), much higher educational levels, increased use of employment contracts, and perhaps some increase in the appointment of "outside" chiefs—those who come from other agencies, as opposed to being promoted from within. The most disappointing finding is the near absence of women police chief executives. Since women began entering police agencies in significant numbers more than 25 years ago and now represent about 13 percent of all sworn officers in the United States, we would expect that the proportion of major-jurisdiction police chief executives who are women would be greater than just 1 percent. We would also expect women to occupy more than just 7.3 percent of command-level police positions and 9.6 percent of supervisory positions in large municipal organizations, with women of color representing only 1.6 percent of command positions and 3.1 percent of supervisory positions. Even more discouraging is that women in small and rural agencies hold only 3.4 percent of command positions and 4.6 percent of supervisory positions, with women of color representing less than 1 percent of both command positions and supervisory positions. Current trends seem to indicate that instead of the numbers of women in leadership positions increasing in police organizations, the numbers of women are either stagnant or in some cases decreasing. [2]

Recent research has examined the tenure and turnover of police executives. While only a preliminary exploratory study, Fred Rainguet and Mary Dodge interviewed 10 former and incumbent chiefs to identify reasons that these executives gave for leaving their organizations.[3] These chiefs worked for municipal police agencies with an average of 5.1 years service as chief. Small, medium, and large organizations were all represented in this small sample. Each chief had some college education ranging from an associate's degree to a doctorate. The data revealed that health concerns, stress, politics, and personnel issues affected the short tenure of those interviewed. While the results of this work must be viewed with caution due to its small sample size and limited generalizability, the issues of concern cited by the respondents should be recognized as potentially affecting one's career, especially as he or she moves up the ranks.

The Two Basic Roles of the Police Executive

The police executive has two basic roles. The first involves internal matters in the police organization and focuses on the organization itself, including such concerns as employees, tasks, rules, supervision, jobs, collective bargaining, workload, efficiency, and budget. In this role the police executive is concerned with making sure that the organization functions correctly. The executive is at the helm of the system and must assure that inputs, processes, outputs, and feedback are properly combined so that the system achieves its goals.

The second basic role of the police executive is an externally oriented role. You will recall that police organizations are open systems. As such, they interact with their environments. The environments of police organizations present all kinds of demands, including both routine and unusual requests for police services; inquiries concerning police handling of specific incidents; directives from the judiciary; and state-mandated minimum requirements for police training. The police executive personally receives many of these demands and requests from the environment and is responsible for the organization's reaction. More generally, the police executive is responsible for managing the interaction between the organization and the environment so that the system's goal attainment is not impeded.

The internal and external roles of the police executive are equally important. It is obviously crucial that the police chief pay close attention to the inner workings of the police department. This internally directed role clearly fits everyone's concept of a manager's duties and responsibilities. The importance of the external role, however, is somewhat less obvious. As we have pointed out, a police department is an open system and is affected by its environment. Job applicants, the criminal law, money to pay police employees, and requests for police assistance all come to the police department from the environment. The parent government system, the criminal justice system, the community, and the media are major aspects of the police organization's environment. For the organization to be successful, police executives must give as much attention to relations with these elements of the environment as they give to managing the inner workings of their agencies.

Failure to perform either role adequately can ruin a police chief and his or her police department. Problems of internal management may result in low productivity, poor morale, substandard personnel and equipment, sloppy work, and such abuses as brutality and corruption. As a result of poor internal management, the system can be expected to fail to attain its goals. In the police context, this means substandard protection of life and property and inadequate maintenance of order.

Internal and External Roles

A police chief must be a team player. From the chief's perspective, there are two teams: city hall and the police department. Many people in a police department like to see the department as separate from city hall, but it's not. The chief has got to be the bridge between these two teams because he's the only one who plays on both. The chief cannot afford to be seen by the council as just another cop, nor can he afford to be seen by his department as a lackey of city government.

Source: Chief Tom Nichols, Lubbock (Texas) Police Department, as quoted in Michael S. Scott, *Managing for Success: A Police Chief's Survival Guide* (Washington, DC: Police Executive Research Forum, 1986), p. 49.

Failure to properly manage the police organization's interaction with the environment will also result in poor goal attainment. If a police executive alienates city hall, for example, it is likely that police budget requests will be jeopardized and funding will be less than adequate for peak police performance (see "Internal and External Roles," above). The police executive who interacts poorly with the media is unlikely to develop an image for the department that enhances citizen respect and support. If relations with prosecutors and the courts are not cultivated, police efforts to curtail crime can be undermined.

In the next two sections of this chapter, we will examine these two police executive roles, one internally focused and one externally focused.

The Internal Role

The internally oriented role of the police chief involves running the police organization itself. One way to picture this role is to imagine the police chief viewing the organization through the systems perspective, focusing his or her attention downward on the inner workings of the department. The internal role is concerned with everything that takes place within the boundaries of the organization.

Although this internal role of the police executive certainly fits the traditional concept of a manager's duties and responsibilities, some police chiefs virtually ignore the role. For example, in one 200-person, midwestern police department, the chief was found to be almost totally preoccupied with external relations. This was partly the chief's fault and partly the fault of the city government administration, which required the chief to serve on citywide budget, personnel, and labor relations committees. Because the chief was actively involved in various community groups, he was well regarded both by the community and his political superiors; however, he was a virtual stranger to police department employees. The internal administration of the department was left completely to the chief's subordinates. If the chief had talented and loyal deputies, this arrangement might have worked out reasonably well. However, in this city the chief's absence resulted in the police department being mismanaged almost to the point of being unmanaged. No one really commanded the department, making sure that the system worked correctly. Some individuals in the department did their best, but others did as they pleased, and no one took corrective action to keep the system on track. The result was departmental chaos.

In the following two subsections we will look at two related aspects of the internal role of the police executive: managing and leading.

Managing

Managing can be thought of as "making sure that the job is done correctly." Managers work with and through other people in guiding their organizations toward the achievement of goals. Managers have the authority to direct the work of others in their organizations, and they are responsible for achieving desired outcomes.

In systems terms, managing involves creating and guiding the system so that goals are attained. In the police system, managers are concerned with inputs such as money, employees, equipment, and information, as well as with outputs such as arrests, reports, and services to the public. Managers are responsible for obtaining the inputs, for designing and directing organizational processes, and for inspecting and improving outputs. Managers must also arrange for feedback about the operation of the system, so that inputs, processes, and outputs can be evaluated, corrected, and improved in order to achieve organizational goals and objectives: the maximum protection of life and property and maintenance of order.

In Chapter 4, we highlighted the most important organizational processes found in police departments. We identified and discussed 30 such processes, from patrol to internal affairs to detention. These are the specific processes that police managers must establish and oversee in order to turn inputs into desired outputs.

In Chapter 5, we presented a number of principles of organization that are valuable guidelines for the police manager. The police manager cannot personally do all of the work of the organization or make all of its decisions. This is particularly true of organizations such as police departments, which are open for business 24 hours a day, every day of the year. Thus, police managers must delegate authority and work throughout the organization. They must also logically organize the many tasks, processes, and subunits in their police departments. The principles presented in Chapter 6 can aid the police executive in these matters of authority delegation and task organization.

In Chapter 6, we considered the basic functions of management, the fundamental duties that all managers, including police executives, must perform. These functions are system building, planning, organizing, staffing, directing, and controlling.

Leading

To a large extent, managing a police organization involves managing people. Unlike some systems, in which inputs and processes are primarily raw materials such as machines, money, or information, police systems are labor-intensive. Police departments spend in excess of 80 percent of their budgets on employee salaries and benefits,[4] and virtually all of the work of police organizations is performed by people rather than by machines.

Managing people introduces complications not encountered in managing raw materials, machines, money, or information. People have feelings, ideas, and personal goals. People vary tremendously, are not always consistent, and cannot be completely understood. People change, and yet they frequently resist change. The so-called human element really takes management out of the realm of science and into the realm of practical affairs. In Chapters 8 and 9, we look closely at some theories and concepts of individual and group behavior in police organizations, freely admitting that the extent of our knowledge about such matters is decidedly limited.

Directing and controlling employees, making sure that they know what to do and how to do it, and supervising their work to assure that it is done correctly are basic components of management. Successful police executives must go beyond the basic components, however, to attain lasting organizational productivity. Beyond simple adherence to job specifications and organizational rules, the police executive must reach out for the hearts and minds of employees. This involves leadership, an ability that is somewhat different from management ability (see "Managing and Leading," below).

Managing and Leading

Chief officers must be more than mere managers performing the routine administration of a large organization. These officers must be dynamic leaders creating vision and purpose; driving change in an environment of flux, where resistance will present itself and must be overcome. In seeking to provide this transformational leadership there must be a consciousness of the legal obligations placed upon the police to maintain the "rule of law" and so regulate society. Equally there must be an awareness of the rights of the individual based upon national and international law.

The balance which has to be achieved is a very fine one. Decision makers within the police service are like circus performers walking a "tight rope" with people tugging at the rope. There is a large audience viewing from different perspectives demanding a high degree of performance; some hope for failure, others complain that the balancing act is not very good with only a few leaving satisfied. The most critical point for the police is not to fall off the "wire" through loss of balance as a result of the tugging at the rope. Effective strategic thinking and planning will minimize this risk.

Source: Norman S.J. Baxter, *Policing the Line: The Development of a Theoretical Model for the Policing of Conflict* (Aldershot, England: Ashgate, 2001), pp. 137-138.

Leading involves showing the way, in most instances by example or by exhortation. Leaders help people in their organizations understand how their efforts contribute to valuable outputs. They help them picture goals worth striving for. They reinforce values that contribute to organizational success. Leaders help encourage commitment to values, ethics, integrity, principles, and goals, rather than minimum performance designed simply to satisfy rules and supervisors.[5]

As part of the internal role of the police executive, leadership is discussed further in Chapter 10. You will find that leaders vary in personal characteristics and in leadership styles. Despite our limited understanding of what makes a good leader, the importance of leadership in police organizations is evident. Police officers perform extremely sensitive duties with little supervision and a great deal of discretion. In a sense, their actual work performance is only marginally directed and controlled by the organization. In the absence of strong direction and control, the organization's best chance for achieving desired behavior is through employee commitment to well-established professional values and goals; it is through leadership that police executives must seek that commitment.

Thus far, we have discussed leadership in terms of leading people; we have emphasized that this dimension of leadership is an important activity for the police executive. A second dimension of leadership involves leading the organization as a whole. Earlier we described management as making sure that the job is done correctly. In this vein, leadership involves making sure that the correct job is done. To make a similar analogy, management is involved with guiding a system so that it stays on track, but leadership is involved with laying the track in the first place.

The police executive's leadership role, in other words, includes charting the course of the organization. The executive must give serious consideration to the organization's goals, objectives, and priorities. There is little value in being on track if that track does not take the organization toward goal attainment. This dimension of the police executive's role that involves leading the organization itself toward the right destination is one that cannot be delegated and probably will not be performed at all unless given high personal priority by the executive.

The Pursuit of Excellence

The purpose behind managing and leading is to make the police organization as efficient and effective as possible and to maximize its goal attainment with whatever resources are available. In the police field it is sometimes difficult to measure effectiveness and goal attainment.[6] For example, how do you measure the current state of order maintenance? And even if you could find some indicators of how orderly a community was, how would you establish the correct or best level of orderliness? Some citizens want the community to be very quiet and controlled, while others prefer conditions that are exciting and dynamic, or in some instances, wild and crazy.

Because of such measurement problems and difficulties in divining the community's will, police management sometimes gives up trying to attain positive goals and instead concentrates on avoiding certain well-known evils, especially corruption and similar embarrassing conditions.[7] Inasmuch as many more police chiefs have lost their jobs due to scandal rather than ineffectiveness, this makes good sense for survival-minded police executives.

In the absence of clear and measurable goals, another alternative is to emphasize quality services. The police executive can focus on process and output, making the quality of these as high as possible, trusting that the eventual outcomes will concomitantly improve. Because police departments do not have a quantitative criterion, such as profit, by which to finally judge their performance, it may well be wise for police executives to focus their own attention, as well as that of their employees, on maintaining high-quality services.[8]

Equally important to a focus on quality is an emphasis on excellence. Through leadership and management the police executive should reward excellence within the organization, seeking to encourage each employee to do his or her best. The cumulation of efforts can gain the organization a reputation for excellence, for performing at the highest level of achievement with limited resources.

Thomas Peters and Robert Waterman Jr. studied American businesses and drew some conclusions about what separated the most successful companies from the rest.[9] Although their research was based on the management of private corporations, their conclusions about the causes of organizational excellence are certainly relevant to police agencies. They are summarized below.

1. In the best organizations Peters and Waterman found a bias for action. Though analytical in their decisionmaking, these organizations leaned toward experimentation and willingness to take risks in seeking organizational improvements.

2. The best organizations stay close to their clientele. They emphasize client satisfaction and actually listen intently to client ideas and suggestions.

3. These organizations permit internal autonomy and entrepreneurship. They delegate authority and encourage their employees to grow and develop.

4. Excellent organizations stress productivity through people. They treat their employees with respect. They value employees as sources of ideas, not just as machinelike resources.

5. Executives in the best organizations stay closely in touch with the organization's work and workers. These executives avoid becoming so caught up in long-range planning and other administrative tasks that they lose touch with the organization's basic operations. They also keep an ear to the ground to monitor the attitudes and values of employees, and take a personal leadership role in maintaining commitment to the organization's goals and values.

6. The best organizations avoid branching off into activity sectors that are unfamiliar or very different from their basic functions and services; they stick to what they know best.

7. The most successful organizations favor lean staffs and simple structures. They keep the bulk of their people close to the action, directly involved in providing services to clients.

8. Finally, excellent organizations are both centralized and decentralized. While autonomy is widely granted and authority widely delegated, nearly fanatical commitment to the organization's core values is emphasized. In addition, high standards of performance are established, and accountability to these standards and to core values is strictly enforced.[10]

While these prescriptions for organizational excellence are far from startling, any sober analysis of the present condition of American law enforcement agencies would find many of them at odds with almost all of the eight characteristics of successful companies. Rather than demonstrating a bias for action and experimentation, for example, many police organizations seem to suffer from stifling inertia. Only in the last 20 years have a few police agencies begun to experiment with new work modes and methods.[11] Sadly, some of these experiments have met with heated criticism. To some police officials it almost verged on professional sacrilege to even question the efficacy, value, and utility of traditional police methods and practices, let alone introduce new tactics and strategies.

For a variety of reasons, modern police organizations also often fail to keep in close touch with their clientele. Telephones, radios, and police cars have altered the patterns of contact between police and the public. Though the police respond to calls for assistance, they rarely, if ever, engage in dialogue with the public about the overall quality of police services and how to improve them. The professional model of policing emphasized that, as carefully selected and highly trained experts, professional police officers are the best judges of how the community should be policed. Such professional arrogance and defensiveness separated the police from the people and precluded community involvement in police system improvement.

Oddly enough, modern police organizations do allow their employees considerable autonomy; they do their best, however, to deny it and to give exactly the opposite impression.[12] Hence, most people believe that the police are closely supervised and controlled. This is not the case. Ordinary police officers perform the basic work of the organization with a great deal of autonomy and discretion. In the process they make many mistakes, but they also develop creative responses to difficult problems.

Police executives typically deny the existence of discretion, partly because they find it difficult to justify and partly because admitting its existence might bring demands for accountability in its control.[13] By establishing and enforcing great numbers of rules and regulations, police executives create the impression that police officers work under severely controlled conditions. On close examination, however, these rules can be seen to affect peripheral matters, such as when the uniform hat must be worn or whose approval of overtime is required, rather than the actual performance of police duties.

Most police agencies demonstrate little respect for the intelligence, creativity, and integrity of their employees. Police departments are typically managed as punishment-centered bureaucracies, with heavy emphasis on management by fear and strict discipline.[14] This management style clearly implies to employees that executives see them as lazy and incompetent. In such situations it is not surprising that labor relations are characterized by distrust and conflict.

Perhaps the single most common criticism of police executives by police officers is that executives have lost touch with police work on the street, that they do not remember what it is really like out there. While sometimes this criticism is just childish whining, it often contains a kernel of insight. Most police management training over the last few decades has emphasized to newly promoted executives that they are now police managers, not police officers. Many police executives are so conscious of their new management role that they avoid any real contact with actual police work. In the process, they often become proficient at acting like managers while gradually losing contact with the police organization's very purpose for existing, its goals and objectives, and its everyday bread-and-butter operations. Besides leading to a loss of respect from employees, this tendency also leads to the deterioration of individual and organizational performance because executives are no longer paying attention to what really matters.

Many police departments, especially larger ones, have fallen prey to over-specialization and staff proliferation. As a result, although the patrol force may still be referred to as the "backbone" of the police department, fewer and fewer resources are devoted to patrol and other basic operations. One study a few years ago found that smaller police agencies kept a substantially greater proportion of their employees assigned to direct services to the public than did larger police departments.[15] In large organizations, subunits are always clamoring for more people; overtime, staff, and special units tend to grow at the expense of patrol and investigations.

We have painted modern police organizations with a rather broad brush in the preceding paragraphs. As there are approximately 17,000 police agencies in the United States alone, any generalizations are tenuous at best. Excellent police departments exist, as do very poor ones. In our experience, though, most police agencies fall far short of excellence. The characteristics of police organizations described above, however harshly presented, accurately represent the status and condition of many police departments across this country.

Police executives are in a position to correct these pervasive problems and improve the delivery of police services by their organizations. The characteristics of excellent companies discovered by Peters and Waterman provide some useful guidelines for police organizational improvement. Police executives should use them in conjunction with the theories and principles of management and leadership presented throughout this book.

Reinventing Government

In their book *Reinventing Government*,[16] David Osborne and Ted Gaebler argue strongly that while there are many things wrong with the way we currently run government agencies, there are also important differences between public administration and private-sector management. They recommend a set of new principles for providing public services that embody an entrepreneurial spirit yet recognize the public nature of government enterprises. They also report on the current application of these principles in government agencies, including police departments, all over the country. These principles, which are quite compatible with those pertaining to organizational excellence, are summarized below.

1. *Government should steer more than row.* Government's main responsibility is to see that services are provided but not necessarily to provide all services itself. The roles of catalyst and facilitator can be more appropriate for government than the role of provider.

2. *Government should empower citizens and communities instead of just serving them.* Helping people become self-reliant has more long-term value than making people dependent. When citizens coproduce government services, those services are more effective and cheaper.

3. *Government should encourage competition rather than monopoly.* Competition can lead to greater efficiency, more responsiveness, and more innovation as well as foster morale and pride among public employees.

4. *Government should be mission-driven, not rule-driven.* Accomplishing missions and goals is the ultimate purpose, not adhering to laws, rules, or procedures. Missions should be well understood and they should guide the operation of the agency.

5. *Government should be results-oriented and focused on outcomes, not inputs.* How hard the government works and how many pieces of paper it processes is not what really matters. What matters are outcomes: how well children are educated, how safe communities are, and so on.

6. *Government should serve its customers, not its own bureaucracy.* Government needs to measure citizen satisfaction with its services and use such information to make improvements and corrections.

7. *Government should earn money as well as spend it.* By charging fees and using other methods, government agencies can take in revenue to help offset their expenditure of tax dollars. This is particularly important whenever public animosity toward taxes runs high.

8. *Government should prevent as well as cure.* Correcting conditions that give rise to problems is more efficient and effective than continually reacting to the problems with short-term, band-aid solutions. Deal with the disease, not just the symptoms.

9. *Government should decentralize and adopt more participative styles of management and leadership.* Workers always know more about their jobs and about how to improve efficiency and effectiveness than staff analysts or bosses. Relying on workers and trusting them will help get them involved in reinventing government.

10. *Government should leverage change through the marketplace, not just by creating public programs.* Through a combination of regulations and incentives, the private sector can be encouraged to contribute to the accomplishment of public missions and goals.

In recent research, Gennaro Vito and Julie Kunselman surveyed police middle managers to examine their perceptions of the principles of reinventing government. [17] The researchers chose this group because middle managers would be those most likely to implement these principles, so their support would be critical. They found that the managers most supported the principles of community-owned government, customer-driven government, and decentralized government, which the authors contend reflect community policing ideals. Those principles that managers thought were the least beneficial were enterprising government, competitive government, and results-oriented government. Although broad support for the principles was cautious, the notion of reinventing government could be especially useful in organizations making the transition to community policing.

The External Role

The externally oriented role of the police chief involves managing the organization's interaction with its environment. As open systems, police departments interact with their environments, receiving all kinds of environmental inputs and having effects on their environments with myriad outputs. The overall effects of these interactions can be positive or negative or both. The police chief must deal with all of these.

One aspect of the police executive's external role is that of official organizational representative. The police executive serves as the department's spokesperson in official communications with a variety of governmental and community groups. The executive also represents the agency at functions, on committees, and before political, private sector, and administrative bodies. In a symbolic sense, the executive epitomizes the image of the police department.

One of the most important external responsibilities of the police chief involves securing the resources necessary for effective departmental performance. The police department's resources (employees, equipment, and funding available for performing tasks and achieving goals) are allocated by people and organizations in the department's environment. Most of the department's resources are made available through its budget. Budget decisions are made by elected political leaders and by bureaucrats working for executive and legislative agencies in the police organization's environment. Some additional resources may be available from other governmental agencies and from private groups and foundations. These fiscal sources are also located in the environment of the police organization. The effectiveness of any police agency depends on the availability of adequate resources and, thus, on the police executive's ability to obtain these resources from funding organizations located in the environment of the police agency.

Another significant dimension of the police executive's external role involves protecting the police agency from environmentally generated threats. Such threats can arise in the form of arbitrary laws, unfair administrative decisions, constraining policies, bad publicity, public criticism, new technology, and degenerating social conditions. Any developments of this nature could threaten the safety of police officers and the ability of the organization to protect life and property and maintain order. The executive must protect the police organization from all unwarranted attacks from the outside, being careful not to be overly defensive in attempting to protect the status quo and the self-interests of the department and its members. The best way to avoid knee-jerk defensiveness is for the executive to evaluate all threatening inputs in terms of their effect on the police department's attainment of primary goals. The executive's task is to defend the organization against genuine attacks and threats, not to resist any and all changes.

When changes do occur in the environment of a police agency, the executive's responsibility is to monitor and analyze them so that the agency can successfully adapt. Open systems not only have environments, but they also have changing environments. The systems that survive and improve are those that continually adapt to their changing environments. Social conditions, economics, demographics, politics, values, customs, technology, laws, policies, and regulations are just a few of the characteristics of the environment that can change. Police departments today face computer crimes that were once unimaginable, are regulated by state training commissions that did not exist a few decades ago, and must abide by legal procedures that often change at a moment's notice. In recent memory, police departments competed vigorously for federal funds granted by the Law Enforcement Assistance Administration (LEAA), an agency that was created, attained annual budgets of hundreds of millions of dollars, and then was abolished, all in less than 15 years. Now, substantial federal funding is once again available, this time from the Office of Community Oriented Policing (OCOPS). Police organizations that successfully adapt to changes such as these provide better services and protection to their communities. Guiding this adaptation process is a critical part of the police executive's external role.

The external role of the police executive includes serving as the official representative of the agency, obtaining agency resources, protecting the agency against threats, and assuring that the agency successfully adapts to its changing environment. In a nutshell, the external role involves managing the department's interaction with its environment, a vast and complicated region that we shall explore.

Politics

A major objective of both the reform era in American government and the police professionalization movement was to insulate police departments from politics. This objective was intended to eliminate the overwhelming infusion of partisan politics in police administration, a legacy that had endured during the first century of American policing. During that period, police personnel decisions and enforcement decisions were commonly dictated by whichever political party happened to be in power, a situation that led to uneven enforcement of the law, substandard police personnel, considerable corruption, organizational chaos, and general ineffectiveness.

By the same token, there is a strong positive tradition of constructive political influence over police matters in this country. One of the oldest and most traditional of law enforcement positions, that of sheriff,[18] is filled by election. Prosecutors are also elected in many jurisdictions. Police chiefs are generally appointed rather than elected, but they are usually appointed by and serve at the pleasure of elected officials. Finally, the extreme decentralization of American policing reflects our desire that police departments be closely tied to political and community interests and that they be held politically accountable for their actions. Politics is one of the primary instruments that a democratic society uses to keep police power in check.

Police executives must continually wrestle with society's ambivalence between political control over the police and police independence.[19] Inappropriate political interference will usually be perceived as pressure on police executives. They must decide how to respond to requests and demands from political and community interests.

One important distinction for the police executive to make is the distinction between *Politics* and *politics*.[20] Politics with a capital "P" (the use of partisan political influence on police department decisions) is generally unhealthy. On the other hand, politics with a small "p" refers to a manner of governance, the science of politics, intended to serve the will of the people. As a part of the executive branch of government, police departments are required to serve the public. The police executive answers to appointed and elected officials who are accountable to the community for their actions. It is proper and, indeed, healthy for police agencies to be influenced by this variety of politics. As one police chief put it, "policing and police administration should avoid party or partisan politics but should embrace politics and political action in the highest sense of those terms."[21]

To help police executives make the distinction between appropriate and inappropriate kinds of political influence, Patrick V. Murphy, who headed police departments in New York City; Detroit; Washington, D.C.; and Syracuse, has suggested some negotiable and nonnegotiable issues.[22] He lists the most important areas in which the police executive needs independence as personnel matters, discipline, and prohibition against partisan political activity by police agency members. Other areas in which the chief should seek independence, but which are not as crucial, are control over budgeting and resource allocation, control over media relations, and the availability of within-agency legal advice. Matters over which Murphy thinks police executive independence can be negotiable include the chief's terms of employment, the chief's role in making decisions and policies in nonpolice but related government matters (such as traffic engineering or zoning), and the chief's degree of independence in police policymaking.

The extent and effect of political influence on the police executive depends on government structure, political culture, and the particular relationship between the police chief and political superiors.[23] In jurisdictions with nonpartisan elections and strong city manager forms of government, the police executive is often completely free of partisan political interference. To the extent that the governing principles are rationality and efficiency rather than partisan politics, the chief will probably enjoy considerable independence. In jurisdictions with partisan elections and strong-mayor forms of government, the police chief will more likely have to contend with partisan political pressures.

The police chief's relationship with the mayor, council president, city manager, or whoever supervises the police department is crucial. One mayor has noted that "if the chief and the mayor are on the same general wavelength in understanding and commitment, the chief should be able to proceed with a minimum of involvement by the mayor."[24] This mayor also points out that the intelligent police executive will be familiar with the mayor's law enforcement priorities, will avoid intruding on politicians' "turf" unless important police matters are involved, and will not generate more controversies than those that naturally arise as a result of the police role in our society. The police chief who abides by these understandings is more likely to be trusted by politicians and given independence in police matters.

The classic distinction between policy and administration is perhaps the best shorthand explanation of the proper relationship between politics and policing. It is through the political process that broad police policy is established (enforcement priorities, funding levels, and appointment of the police chief). Within this broad policy, the police executive deserves substantial independence in administration of the police department. Broad policy is formulated through politics but implemented through police administration. Politicians and community groups "should provide guidance on direction and priorities, but they ought not become involved in developing detailed instructions on how policies are to be implemented."[25] Under this system, the politician "does not actually run the police department; rather, he ensures police department compliance with obligations imposed by authorities higher than the municipality (federal constitution, state law), as well as police department receptivity to input from more localized interest (neighborhood groups and the like)."[26]

The precise police/politics relationship will vary from community to community; it would be wrong for us to impose too binding a prescription for the proper relationship. But, as discussed in this section, there are some matters over which the police executive should insist on independence. Certainly, police executives need to carefully develop and nurture their relationships with their political superiors, showing sensitivity to the legitimate concerns of political leaders but resisting inappropriate interference.

Other Government Agencies

Police departments interact with a host of government agencies. Interaction arises when the police department needs the services of another agency, or vice versa. The police executive can enhance this interaction through effective communication, formulation of policies and procedures, and the creation of an atmosphere of cooperation. Interaction also occurs in the budget process when resources are being allocated to the police department and other government agencies. This interaction is inevitably competitive, because one agency's gain is every other agency's loss. Yet another kind of interaction is of a regulatory nature. A number of government agencies (such as police training commissions, civil service commissions, and the Equal Employment Opportunity Commission) establish and enforce regulations that affect and constrain the police department. The police executive's management of this type of interaction guides the department's adaptation to changes and may also ultimately influence the content of the regulations and their enforcement.

Civil service is a governmental agency that affects many police departments. In jurisdictions covered by civil service or institutionalized merit systems, police personnel matters such as recruitment, selection, and promotion are generally under the control of the civil service agency rather than the police department. One study found that 85 percent of police agencies in medium- and large-sized cities were governed by some degree of civil service regulation.[27] Degree of control varied from simple oversight to total control in which the civil service agency determined selection criteria, tested applicants, and dictated to the police department which applicants to hire.

Civil service systems began for the same reasons that the police professionalization movement began. Before civil service, it was common for police officers to be hired on the basis of their political connections and personal friendships rather than on the basis of any objective qualifications for the job. Civil service commissions seek to protect "personnel practices from adverse political influences and to ensure that some measure of fairness and rationality is brought to the personnel process."[28] This objective has largely been achieved. In many jurisdictions today, however, civil service systems have become bureaucratic impediments to police personnel improvement.[29] Civil service systems frequently interfere with the police executive's need to examine, hire, promote, and terminate employees, often taking months to accomplish what could be done internally in a day. Whenever feasible, the police executive should insist on control over personnel processes and decisions. Civil service oversight and broad personnel policymaking are acceptable, but civil service control is not. A management concern over which police executives have less justification and opportunity for control is budgeting. In every jurisdiction, political leaders make the final decisions about how much money to allocate to each government agency. These political leaders are generally advised by budget bureaus, city managers, and other watchdog administrative officials. Police executives can usually present arguments and rationale in support of their budgets during the budget formulation process. The final decisions, however, are always out of their hands and are always politically made.

Police executives should seek to maximize the influence they have in the budgeting process. To the extent that police executives are trusted and respected by administrative and political officials, their arguments and requests will have credibility. In addition, budget requests that are rational and supported by convincing documentation are more likely to be given consideration than those that are extravagant and poorly documented. One study found that budget decisionmakers today are more likely to demand empirical justifications for police department and other public agency budget requests than in years past.[30]

In an attempt to exert control over budgetary matters, one type of influence that the police executive has available for use is political influence. The police chief usually has the opportunity to generate public pressure in support of police interests and even to grant small but legitimate favors to political decisionmakers. The police chief should not tread this path lightly, however. Once the police executive gets political, the battle lines will be drawn and the executive and the entire department will be open to political interference. The professional and nonpolitical image of the police chief, often so valuable, will be lost. Generally, the police executive should refrain completely from exercising even the most legitimate varieties of political influence unless the welfare of the department and the protection of the community clearly necessitate such drastic action. Relationships between the chief and governmental agencies that decide budgetary matters should never be allowed to place the police department in a position where it is vulnerable to inappropriate political interference or corruption.

Almost all states now have police training commissions that establish minimum recruit and in-service training requirements for police officers. A few states also set selection standards for police officers and require state certification. These kinds of training and selection regulations have obvious merit and affect police departments in a positive way. They serve to make police departments more professional and more responsive to the public interest.

The police work with a number of other government agencies in the provision of service to the public. Fire departments and rescue/ambulance squads join the police in providing emergency services. A variety of social service agencies, such as child protective services, welfare departments, and senior citizen agencies, call the police or are called by the police for assistance. Police departments also often find it necessary to cooperate with public works departments, utility companies, highway departments, and parks and recreation departments. In disaster situations, police departments must work with emergency management agencies, the Red Cross, and the National Guard. In addition, police agencies at all levels of government must work together. Municipal, county, and state police must cooperate with one another, and all three work with federal police and investigative agencies. Assuring cooperative and successful interaction with all of these agencies is a responsibility of the police executive.

Interagency collaboration is seen as particularly important within the framework of community policing and problem solving.[31] Police agencies today recognize that they alone cannot effectively control crime and disorder.

Moreover, police departments have discovered that many of the problems that neighborhood residents cite as their greatest safety-related concerns are things like abandoned buildings and vehicles, poorly maintained streets and sidewalks, poor lighting in public places, trash, litter, graffiti, and similar "quality of life" issues. Clearly, in order for the police to respond to these types of safety-related concerns, collaboration with other government agencies is required, unless officers themselves want to begin performing sanitation and public works duties on a regular basis.

Criminal Justice Agencies

Whether you prefer to think of police, courts, and corrections as comprising a criminal justice system or a nonsystem, the agencies within the process obviously interact. At the front end of the system, the police have a tremendous effect on other criminal justice agencies, particularly in terms of the quantity and quality of cases they generate in the courts. Police departments, in turn, are affected by actions taken by the other agencies in the system. Prosecutors determine whether arrests proceed to the courts, and prosecutorial policies guide police enforcement decisions. The courts decide guilt, innocence, and punishment in cases initiated by the police, and also make more sweeping decisions about the legality and propriety of police tactics. Jails and prisons aid the police by maintaining custody of arrested and convicted persons and sometimes need police assistance during disturbances and escapes. Probation and parole agencies often share information with the police about released persons in the community; their decisions whether to seek revocation of probation or parole for violators are of great interest to the police. In general, the more or less effective the rest of the criminal justice system is in dealing with offenders, the easier or harder, respectively, the task of the police.

While the police executive has no authority to demand particular actions of other criminal justice agencies, he or she can take a leadership role in encouraging improvement of the system and cooperation among its member agencies. The police chief is one of the most visible of criminal justice agency heads and in most jurisdictions probably enjoys more support and respect than most other criminal justice administrators. Corrections agencies rarely attract much public attention, and even less public support. At one time judges were held in extremely high regard by most citizens, but public support and respect for the judiciary have eroded.

An example of criminal justice interagency cooperation led by a police executive is provided by the Repeat Offender Program Experiment (ROPE) project in Baltimore County, Maryland. The impetus for establishing the project came largely from county police chief Neil Behan, an enlightened and dedicated police executive. A small planning grant from the state was obtained, and a steering committee was formed, comprised of the chief, the county prosecutor, the head of the state parole and probation agency, representatives of state corrections and juvenile services agencies, and the county criminal justice coordinator; the committee was chaired by the county manager.

The committee's work began on the assumption that repeat offenders were not being adequately treated by the county's criminal justice system and that this was a major problem for the county. Not much data was available, however, to support the assumptions or, indeed, to define the problem adequately. The committee hired a consultant to research the problem, to identify it definitively, and to assist the committee in designing a satisfactory solution. Each of the agencies represented on the steering committee opened its records to the consultant and assisted in data collection. As the problem was defined and the consultant's attention turned to solutions, he sought direction and input, including program suggestions, from members of the committee as well as from operational personnel in their agencies.

Because each agency had been represented in the research and planning processes, more consensus was achieved among steering committee members than would have ordinarily been expected from people with such differing roles and constituencies. Agreeing on a final program of action was not easy and required negotiation and compromise; a consensus was reached, however, and a program was established, one that each represented agency agreed to support with resources and involvement. After the program was implemented, the steering committee continued to meet periodically to monitor progress and make changes when necessary.

Complete cooperation among criminal justice agencies is not always possible, and in some instances may not be desirable, because parts of the process are adversarial. In the ROPE project, for example, judges declined to be steering committee members, although their views and concerns were sought and considered by the consultant and the committee. During the implementation of ROPE, the main stumbling block was judicial resistance to mandatory sentences for repeat violent offenders. Nevertheless, the ROPE project did succeed in focusing criminal justice resources and attention on repeat offenders, resulting in stronger cases, more convictions, longer sentences, better treatment, and more intensive community supervision. The success of the project was made possible by an unusual degree of cooperation among criminal justice agencies and was largely due to the innovative organizational efforts of the county police chief.[32]

The Media

The media are important components of a police agency's environment, because they control much of the information that the public learns about the police agency. The media present information about the police to the public in the form of news, investigative reports, feature stories, public service announcements, and entertainment. The content of these messages and the manner of their presentation greatly affect public views of the police (see "Media Relations," below). The police executive must recognize that the media, sometimes referred to as the "fourth estate," play an important role in our system of government. The Founding Fathers distrusted government authority and provided for freedom of the press as a check against government abuses. Although reporters' demands can at times be a nuisance and an imposition to the police executive, it should be understood that the public has a right to know about police activities in a free society and that it is the media that has the responsibility for keeping the public informed.

It is in the police department's best interests for the police executive to establish good relations with media representatives and to provide procedures for dissemination of news information. If the police executive is open and honest with reporters, police-press relations will become less adversarial and reporters will be more likely to consider the department's viewpoint on controversial or embarrassing issues and news stories. As one observer noted, "You're not going to control the media, but you do in fact influence their thinking if you work with them on a regular basis."[33]

Media Relations

When questioned, the chiefs we interviewed stressed the importance of good media relations. When asked to rank on a scale of 1 to 10 the importance of communication with the media as compared with other features of the police chief job, the median score given by the 25 chiefs was 8.5, with six giving media communication a top rank of 10. No chief responded with a ranking below 7. To test police chiefs' responsiveness to media, we asked the following: If three office phones were ringing and their secretary told them that the calls were from the mayor, a member of city council and a reporter, which call would they answer first? One chief chuckled at the question and gave an answer that expressed the consensus of the group. "I'd pick up the mayor's call first," he said. "But I'd also figure that the mayor was calling me about what I was going to say to the reporter."

Source: Jerome H. Skolnick and Candace McCoy, "Police Accountability and the Media," in *Police Leadership in America: Crisis and Opportunity*, William A. Geller, ed. (New York, NY: Praeger, 1985), p. 113.

For the dissemination of news information, police departments can select one of three basic models:

1. the police executive handles all media relations personally;
2. the police executive delegates media relations responsibility to a specific individual or unit within the department; or
3. the police executive authorizes every employee to release news information and answer media questions.

The first model gives the executive the most control over information released to the media but can consume much of the executive's valuable time and also denies other members of the department the experience of media relations. The second model relieves the executive of the responsibility, while still allowing him or her to maintain control over the release of information. The third approach is the most risky in the sense that the opportunities for inappropriate comments and improper release of information are increased. However, allowing all officers to handle media relations shows confidence in employees, gives them useful experience, gives the media greater opportunities for firsthand accounts of events, and may contribute to reducing the typical police antipathy toward the media.

One sensible approach is to permit all officers to release information and answer questions concerning routine incidents, accidents, and arrests. Media questions pertaining to administrative matters, police policies, sensitive investigations, or any controversial issues, on the other hand, should be referred to a media relations specialist, if the department is large enough to employ one, or to the top executive. Much more important than the particular procedure that is used to disseminate information, however, is total departmental cooperation in media relations. Every officer in the department, from the chief executive on down, must foster good media relations, not only to satisfy the public's right to know, but also to encourage the media to portray the police department in the most positive way possible. As one former reporter noted, "Chiefs should remember that they have a lot of power in that they have at their control data. Data is news. How you shape the data—honestly, obviously—can have enormous impact."[34]

The Community

The community is an element of the police organizational environment. For the working police officer, the community generates police activity (law violations and calls for service) and provides the setting within which police work must be performed. For the police executive, the community represents a source of both support and complaints and, most importantly, is the final arbiter of the quality of police services and the effectiveness of the police department. In today's community policing environment, the community is also seen as a valuable partner of the police department in efforts to control crime and disorder and improve the level of safety and quality of life in the community.

The police executive primarily encounters the community in the form of organized community groups. By meeting regularly with groups such as business and citizen associations; church and youth groups; Rotary, Kiwanis, and Lions Clubs; the Chamber of Commerce; the PTA; and the NAACP, the police executive can establish open lines of communication with influential community interest groups. Such meetings give the executive the opportunity to present and explain publicly the police department's viewpoint; the executive, in turn, is exposed to a variety of community concerns, interests, and viewpoints (see "Getting Out into the Community," below).

Traditionally, police executives emphasized their public relations role vis-à-vis the community; they saw their task as telling and selling, or promoting the police department's viewpoint to the community. With the advent of an institutionalized approach to police-community relations in the 1960s, the police for the first time became interested in soliciting community views and sincerely engaging in a real problem-solving dialogue with the community. This new approach to communication helped police executives fulfill their role of guiding their organizations' adaptations to their environments.

Getting Out into the Community

In communicating with the community, show real empathy. Don't hit them with statistics to show them why their concerns shouldn't exist. They do exist and their perceptions are all that matter. Get to know the neighborhoods very well. Listen to people. And do something about their problems. Remember, what's important in one neighborhood, may not be in another. So be discriminating and attentive. Make those speeches. Get out into the community directly. Show your face. Let them know you are the chief for all of them. It's not how good you think you are, it's how good they think you are that matters.

Source: Commissioner Bishop Robinson, Baltimore Police Department, as quoted in Michael S. Scott, *Managing for Success: The Police Chief's Survival Guide* (Washington, DC: Police Executive Research Forum, 1986), p. 46.

In recent years some police executives have sought to move beyond the police-community relations format in order to take up leadership positions in their communities. These executives are not reverting to telling and selling and promoting the police department's product, but are drawing on their positions, reputations, and expertise to influence community attitudes and behaviors. For example, police chiefs who want to alter the style and role of their police officers can build community support to counteract internal opposition and criticism.[35] Police chiefs can also educate the public about the many causes of crime and the inability of the police, acting alone and on their own, to control crime. They can "take the lead in addressing broadened local social service needs that could, if neglected, produce greater crime problems."[36]

Police executives should adopt this kind of proactive leadership role in the community. Their positions give them the opportunity and the credibility needed to affect community attitudes and actions. Top executives of other organizations, public and private, have historically served as community leaders. Police chiefs should do the same, particularly when issues of crime and related social problems are at stake. In so doing, the police executive has the opportunity to shape the police department's environment instead of merely adapting to it.[37] According to one highly regarded police chief, "initiating positive interaction with the community generally results in increased citizen support, higher morale in the workforce, protection against or insulation from many hostile external forces, and increased resources."[38]

Police Unions

Although police unions and employee associations are made up of members of the organization and thus might be thought of as internal system factors, the police executive deals with them as collectivities and confronts them more as interest groups than as employees. In this sense, labor relations more accurately reflect the police executive's external role than his or her internal role. Still, it is obvious that the executive's performance of the internal role (managing and leading employees) greatly affects labor relations.

The existence and influence of police unions and employee associations vary greatly around the country. In the South, in particular, police executives rarely have unions or strong employee associations to contend with. In the industrialized Northeast, virtually every police department is unionized. In general, large police departments are more likely to be unionized than small departments, but, again, geographic variation is evident.

Almost all police unions engage in collective bargaining, while some employee associations serve as little more than social clubs. The kinds of issues that unions and police executives tangle over can range from salaries and fringe benefits to so-called management prerogatives, including such matters as assignments, shift schedules, overtime, promotion, and discipline, to mention only a few. Traditionally under the control of the police executive, these prerogatives are now a part of the collective bargaining process in unionized departments, and many of them are controlled by contractual agreement rather than by police executive order. Some observers regard this kind of union activity as threatening to the police department's ability to protect the community and provide quality services.[39] Other observers, however, blame management instability and incompetence for such union activity, and see employee influence over traditional management prerogatives as a positive trend.[40]

While the precise extent of police unionism and collective bargaining is not known, one study that examined changes in police labor contracts in medium- and large-sized cities from 1981 to 1991 sheds some light on the kinds of issues covered by labor contracts.[41] The list below provides a sample of the kinds of clauses and provisions that were found in the police labor contracts examined:

	1981	1991
Strong or comprehensive management rights clause	24%	37%
Maintenance of standards and benefits required	29%	8%
Grievances resolved by arbitration	92%	83%
Full management right to set staffing requirements	36%	42%
Exclusive management right to establish rules and regulations	36%	53%
Seniority as exclusive determinant of personnel decisions	39%	10%

For the most part, the typical police labor contract did not tie the hands of the police executive, but did introduce some constraints. The trend seems clearly in the direction of strengthening management's position with respect to the internal administration of the police organization. It may have been the case that most of police unions' efforts during this period were focused on wage and benefit issues rather than on employee relations or management rights issues. But it also seems that police management has become more sophisticated in the area of labor relations and better able to protect its interests. Overall, "one may conclude that the police collective bargaining process is stabilizing. Management's seat at the collective bargaining table is increasingly one of true negotiation rather than reaction."[42]

Because the existence and strength of police unions varies considerably among jurisdictions, it is difficult to prescribe the proper labor relations role for the police executive. Certainly, the police chief who treats employees with respect and who stays in touch with day-to-day operations and problems is more likely to enjoy a positive relationship with the employees' union or association (see "Working with the Union," p. 204). When it comes to collective bargaining, the police chief should either serve as the department's representative on matters of working conditions and management prerogative, or at the very least have veto power over such matters.[43] Otherwise, the city manager or labor lawyer bargaining on behalf of the police department may unwittingly bargain away crucial management authority.

The police executive is in the awkward position in collective bargaining of needing to protect management authority against union encroachment while at the same time demonstrating respect for employees and support for their wage and benefit positions. The police executive is in the middle—both an adversary and an advocate who must in conscience put aside personal proclivities and consider all proposals in terms of their effects on the police department's ability to protect life and property and maintain order. The best justification for supporting or opposing union demands rests on the effects such support or opposition would have on the police department's attainment of its goals and objectives. In the long run, the police executive who acts in conscience and in the best interests of the police organization should gain the support of the community and of police employees.

Working with the Union

One of the benefits of regular, open dialogue with the union is that you don't waste time posturing before getting to business. The union leaders may be sufficiently impressed with this communication that they won't feel compelled to work actively against you. Allowing the union representatives to participate at staff meetings and on task forces also gives them the opportunity to see how you operate. They may then recognize the conflicting pressures you face and not see you as an enemy of the rank and file.

Accord the union leaders all the dignity and respect they deserve. Invite them to participate in ceremonial affairs with you. Participate in some of their ceremonies. Even if you don't allow the union leaders to participate in management affairs, make sure they are informed early of your decisions. Don't force them to learn what's going on in their police department by reading the newspapers. They have to answer questions about management decisions from the officers, so be sure they have all the information they need to do so accurately.

Source: Michael S. Scott, *Managing for Success: A Police Chief's Survival Guide* (Washington, DC: Police Executive Research Forum, 1986), pp. 38-39.

The Fraternal Order of Police (FOP), which is an employee association, not a union, is "committed to improving the working conditions of law enforcement officers and safety of those we serve through education, legislation, information, community involvement, and employee representation."[44] The organization's mission is broad and includes activities ranging from providing legal defense for law enforcement officers to supporting police families through counseling. It is not uncommon to find the FOP working closely with police unions in addressing common issues of interest. While the power of the FOP compared to unions is questionable, police managers must recognize the potential power of this external influence and respond accordingly.

Police Executive Styles

In the performance of their internal and external roles, police executives make numerous decisions and handle all kinds of problems. Executives vary on a number of matters, including how they allocate their time and the relative importance they attach to internal and external responsibilities. Consequently, police executive behavior can take many forms. In the following sections we identify and briefly describe four police executive styles. It should be noted that while some police executives exhibit just one style, others represent combinations of two or more styles.

The Administrator

The administrator style emphasizes the internal role of the police executive as well as the managing aspects and manifestations of that role. The administrator concentrates on planning, organizing, staffing, directing, and controlling the police organization. The administrator adheres to the professional model of police administration, with a belief in police autonomy and great faith in education, training, and technology as methods for police improvement. The administrator believes that as a police executive, he or she is a manager first and a police officer only a distant second.

There are advantages and disadvantages of the administrator style. The strong belief in police autonomy and consequent lack of attention to the external role of the police executive can lead to trouble with elected officials, unions, the community, and the media. The emphasis on the managing role can reap internal benefits, especially in greater control and efficiency, but the positive results can be short-lived if they are made at the expense of relations with employees and the public. The administrator also tends to focus on internal procedures rather than on actual work products, thereby creating an organization that looks and acts efficient but fails to satisfy its clientele or achieve its goals.

The Top Cop

The top cop style, like the administrator style, emphasizes the internal role of the police executive but focuses more on leading than on managing. The top cop is heavily involved in police operations, often commanding the troops in the field or taking charge of the more interesting and most important investigations. Through example as much as by other means, the top cop demonstrates to police officers what behaviors and attitudes are most highly valued by the organization.

Top cops are more likely than administrators to be liked and respected by police employees, although this depends heavily on their operational abilities. If top cops fail or act incompetently in field command or investigations, they quickly lose the respect of their troops. In addition, executives adopting the top cop style can sometimes be resented by police managers and police officers who interpret their involvement in police operations as an indication of a lack of confidence in subordinates.

If the top cop neglects the more mundane, routine aspects of management, as is likely to be the case, the police department will gradually become more disorganized and less efficient. The top cop's effect on external relations is harder to predict. Some politicians, media representatives, and community members may be put in such awe by the top cop style that the organization will benefit. On the other hand, the police executive adhering to the top cop style will not generally spend much time or expend much energy on external relations and will inevitably alienate some people. The top cop, for example, would be more likely to lead a narcotics raid than attend a dinner meeting of the Lion's Club.

The Politician

The politician emphasizes the external role of the police executive over the internal role. The politician is likely to leave the internal administration of the police department to subordinate managers and to view the chief's role as primarily externally oriented. The executive adopting this style might prefer to lead a narcotics raid rather than attend a Lion's Club meeting, but would sublimate personal preferences in favor of attending the meeting. The politician would attend the meeting on the assumption that the meeting would provide opportunities to garner departmental support.

By neglecting internal administration and leadership, the executive adopting the politician style leaves such matters in the hands of subordinates. Even if the subordinates are talented and capable, in all likelihood they will manage the organization less than satisfactorily in the absence of the chief executive, whose authority and leadership are needed on a continuing basis to provide organizational guidance and stability.

The politician's approach to external relations emphasizes protecting the police department's interests by meeting with community and governmental groups and political leaders, by defending the organization from any and all external threats, and by constantly courting resource constituencies for support. By paying so much attention and committing so much time to external forces, the politician is frequently successful in gaining both fiscal and community support for the police agency. The executive adhering to the political style is rarely caught by surprise because of external developments that might affect either the police department or the executive. The clever politician executive avoids making enemies and is adept at surviving fluctuations in the political climate.

The Statesman

The statesman emphasizes leadership—among the troops, throughout the entire organization, and in the community. The statesman recognizes the aspects of the police executive's responsibilities that can be carried out by no one else. While not ignoring the internal management of the department, the statesman delegates most management tasks and concentrates on charting the overall course of the organization and influencing the core values of employees. The statesman also delegates some externally oriented tasks in order to concentrate on serious threats to the organization and to provide leadership in the community.

The essence of the statesman style involves being "a leader of a democracy, someone who can transcend the current values of the day and lead both police and the public into accepting a better set of values and strategies for policing."[45] Police organizations are involved in controversial, emotional, honor-and-dishonor, life-and-death matters. Police officers and citizens frequently become frustrated and confused by the ethical and practical issues at stake and are often inclined to support drastic remedies for the problems of the day. Police executives who act as statesmen seek to temper momentary fears and frustrations, chart a course for the long haul, and reinforce by example and exhortation the core values underlying our democratic, free society.[46]

As admirable and necessary as the statesman style may seem, it can have its limitations. The lofty concerns of the statesman can sometimes deflect attention from the day-to-day operations of the police department and the subsequent quality of services received by the public. Personally or through subordinates, the statesman executive must assure that basic services do not deteriorate while high ideals are being stressed. Similarly, the statesman executive runs the risk of losing touch with reality, or at least seeming to have lost touch with the opinions of police employees and the community. To impress these constituencies and to avoid becoming irrelevant or out-of-touch, the statesman may occasionally be forced to return to the streets to demonstrate competent police operational skills. The statesman may also lose credibility with police officers and the public by espousing ideas and values too far removed from the norm. In some situations the shock value of radically different ideas can be employed to overcome inertia and challenge hidden assumptions, but the executive using this strategy runs the risk of being labeled a radical. An alternative strategy is to encourage gradual change over a long period. This approach is safer for the police executive but less likely to bring about immediate changes. The choice can be a difficult one.

A case can be made for the value of each of these styles. The best police executive probably would adopt a mixture of the four styles. The most effective style depends on the situation. Factors such as the capabilities of subordinate managers, the political climate, the militancy of the police union, and the particular strengths and weaknesses of the police department all go into determining which style or which blend of styles is most effective in any situation.

Although in any isolated, particularized or unique situation, the administrator, the top cop, or the politician might be the most successful style, what American police service needs most today is more statesmen. Of the four styles, the statesman, unfortunately, is found least often in police departments.

Summary

The police executive fills two basic roles—one is focused internally on running the organization; the other is focused externally on relations with the environment of the organization. The two basic components of the internal role are managing and leading. An emphasis on the pursuit of excellence and on the reinvention of government was recommended as a guide to performing the internal role. The external role of the police executive includes representing the organization, securing resources, defending the department against threats, and guiding the agency's adaptation to changes in its environment. Important components of the police organizational environment include politics, other government agencies, criminal justice agencies, the media, the community, and police unions.

In the performance of their internal and external roles, police executives exhibit four styles of management behavior: the administrator, the top cop, the politician, and the statesman. The style most appropriate and effective depends upon the situation, but the statesman style is probably the rarest and the most needed in contemporary law enforcement.

Discussion Questions

1. In this chapter we cite the findings of a recent study of management practices in private corporations. Are these applicable to police administration? To what extent can the lessons learned in business administration and public administration be applied to police administration? What similarities and differences do you see?

2. A few years ago, one of the most popular bumper stickers read "KEEP THE POLICE OUT OF POLITICS, AND POLITICS OUT OF THE POLICE." Why do you think it was so popular? Should politics and the police be completely separated?

3. Police unionism is controversial. Should police be allowed to unionize? Should they be allowed to affiliate with other labor unions, such as the Teamsters? As workers, how can police officers protect their rights except through unionization? Under what circumstances should police be allowed to go on strike? To engage in work slowdowns? To conduct "votes of no confidence" against their police chiefs?

4. Which police executive style would you be most likely to adopt? Why? What styles have been exhibited by police chiefs that you have observed?

5. What do you think of the relative importance of education and experience as qualifications for police chiefs? How much of each would you require of police chief applicants?

Cases

Two of the case studies at the end of this text pertain to information presented in Chapter 7. You might want to consider the internal and external roles and the executive styles displayed by Harold Nubby in "Case 1: The Energetic Chief" and by Luke Grinnel in "Case 4: The Chief Who Played King."

Notes

1. "Police Executive Survey," mimeo (Washington, DC: Police Executive Research Forum, 1998).

2. "Equality Denied: The Status of Women in Policing, 2001," mimeo (Los Angeles, CA: National Center for Women and Policing, 2002).

3. F.W. Rainguet and M. Dodge, "The Problems of Police Chiefs: An Examination of the Issues in Tenure and Turnover, " *Police Quarterly* 4, no. 3 (September 2001): 268-288.

4. J.F. Heaphy, *Police Practices: The General Administrative Survey* (Washington, DC: Police Foundation, 1978).

5. U.S. Department of Justice, *Police Integrity: Public Service with Honor* (Washington, DC: U.S. Department of Justice, 1997).

6. T.V. Brady, "Measuring What Matters: Measures of Crime, Fear, and Disorder," *Research in Action* (Washington, DC: National Institute of Justice, 1996).

7. J.Q. Wilson, *The Investigators: Managing FBI and Narcotics Agents* (New York, NY: Basic Books, 1978).

8. L.T. Hoover, ed., *Quantifying Quality in Policing* (Washington, DC: Police Executive Research Forum, 1996).

9. T.J. Peters and R.H. Waterman Jr., *In Search of Excellence: Lessons from America's Best-Run Companies* (New York, NY: Harper & Row, 1982).

10. Ibid., pp. 13-16.

11. J.Q. Wilson, "Police Research and Experimentation," in *Progress in Policing: Essays on Change,* R.A. Stauffenberger, ed. (Cambridge, MA: Ballinger, 1980), pp. 129-152.

12. G.W. Sykes, "The Myth of Reform: The Functional Limits of Police Accountability in a Liberal Society," *Justice Quarterly* 2, no. 1 (March 1985): 51-66.

13. H. Goldstein, *Policing a Free Society* (Cambridge, MA: Ballinger, 1977), pp. 106-116.

14. E. Bittner, *The Functions of the Police in Modern Society* (Washington, DC: U.S. Government Printing Office, 1970); M.K. Brown, *Working the Street: Police Discretion and the Dilemmas of Reform* (New York, NY: Russell Sage Foundation, 1981); V. Franz and D.M. Jones, "Perceptions of Organizational Performance in Suburban Police Departments: A Critique of the Military Model," *Journal of Police Science and Administration* 15, no. 2 (June 1987): 153-161.

15. E. Ostrom, R.B. Parks, and G.P. Whitaker, "Police Agency Size: Some Evidence on Its Effects," *Police Studies* 1, no. 1 (March 1978): 34-46.

16. D. Osborne and T. Gaebler, *Reinventing Government: How the Entrepreneurial Spirit is Transforming the Public Sector* (Reading, MA: Addison-Wesley, 1992).

17. G.F. Vito and J. Kunselman, "Reinventing Government: The Views of Police Middle Managers," *Police Quarterly* 3, no. 3 (2000): 315-330.

18. D.N. Falcone and L.E. Wells, "The County Sheriff as a Distinctive Policing Modality," *American Journal of Police* 14, no. 3/4 (1995): 123-149.

19. K.D. Tunnell and L.K. Gaines, "Political Pressures and Influences on Police Executives: A Descriptive Analysis," in G.W. Cordner and D.J. Kenney, eds., *Managing Police Organizations* (Cincinnati, OH: Anderson, 1996), pp. 5-17.

20. W.H. Hudnut III, "The Police and the Polis: A Mayor's Perspective," in *Police Leadership in America: Crisis and Opportunity*, W.A. Geller, ed. (New York, NY: Praeger, 1985), p. 20.

21. R.J. Brzeczek, "Chief-Mayor Relations: The View from the Chief's Chair," in Geller, *Police Leadership*, p. 48.

22. P.V. Murphy, "The Prospective Chief's Negotiation of Authority with the Mayor," in Geller, *Police Leadership*, pp. 33-39.

23. J.Q. Wilson, *Varieties of Police Behavior: The Management of Law and Order in Eight Communities* (Cambridge, MA: Harvard University Press, 1968).

24. D.M. Fraser, "Politics and Police Leadership: A View from City Hall," in Geller, *Police Leadership*, p. 43.

25. Goldstein, *Policing a Free Society*, p. 150.

26. Brzeczek, "Chief-Mayor Relations," p. 52.

27. G.W. Greisinger, J.S. Slovak, and J.L. Molkup, *Police Personnel Practices in Forty-two American Cities* (Washington, DC: Public Administration Service, 1978).

28. J.H. Burpo, *Police Unions in the Civil Service Setting* (Washington, DC: Public Administration Service, 1979), p. 2.

29. G.W. Greisinger, J.S. Slovak, and J.L. Molkup, *Civil Service Systems: Their Impact on Police Administration* (Washington, DC: Public Administration Service, 1979), p. v.

30. G.W. Cordner, J.R. Greene, and T.S. Bynum, "Police Human Resource Planning," in *Managing Police Work: Issues and Analysis*, J.R. Greene, ed. (Beverly Hills, CA: Sage, 1982), pp. 53-74.

31. Bureau of Justice Assistance, *Understanding Community Policing: A Framework for Action* (Washington, DC: Bureau of Justice Assistance, 1994).

32. G.W. Cordner, *The Baltimore County Repeat Offender Planning Project* (Baltimore, MD: University of Baltimore, 1983).

33. M. Clark, quoted in "Measuring What Matters: Developing Measures of What the Police Do," *Research in Action* (Washington, DC: National Institute of Justice, 1997), p. 13.

34. A. Benson, quoted in ibid.

35. R.C. Davis, "Organizing the Community for Improved Policing," in Geller, *Police Leadership*, pp. 84-95.

36. L.P. Brown, "Police-Community Power Sharing," in Geller, *Police Leadership*, p. 71.

37. A.J. Reiss, Jr., "Shaping and Serving the Community: The Role of the Police Chief Executive," in Geller, *Police Leadership*, p. 68.

38. Davis, "Organizing the Community," p. 85.

39. A.V. Bouza, "Police Unions: Paper Tigers or Roaring Lions?" in Geller, *Police Leadership*, pp. 241-280.

40. R.B. Kliesmet, "The Chief and the Union: May the Force Be with You," in Geller, *Police Leadership*, pp. 281-285.

41. D.L. Carter and A.D. Sapp, "A Comparative Analysis of Clauses in Police Collective Bargaining Agreements as Indicators of Change in Labor Relations," in Cordner and Kenney, *Managing Police Organizations*, pp. 19-43.

42. Ibid., p. 40.

43. A.H. Andrews, Jr., "Structuring the Political Independence of the Police Chief," in Geller, *Police Leadership*, pp. 5-19.

44. S. Zahurak and J. Ruiz, "The Fraternal Order of Police: A Study in Transmogrification," *Police Forum* 12, no. 3 (July 2002): 1-13.

45. L.W. Sherman, "The Police Executive as Statesman," in Geller, *Police Leadership*, p. 462.

46. K.A. Betsalel, "Police Leadership and the Reconciliation of Police-Minority Relations," in Cordner and Kenney, *Managing Police Organizations*, pp. 67-78.

Suggested Reading

Cordner, Gary W., and Dennis Jay Kenney, eds. *Managing Police Organizations*. Cincinnati, OH: Anderson, 1996.

International City Management Association and Police Executive Research Forum. *Selecting a Police Chief: A Handbook for Local Government*. Washington, DC: Police Executive Research Forum, 1999.

Kirchoff, William, Charlotte Lansinger, and James Burack. *Command Performance: Career Guide for Police Executives*. Washington, DC: Police Executive Research Forum, 1999.

Osborne, David, and Ted Gaebler. *Reinventing Government: How the Entrepreneurial Spirit Is Transforming the Public Sector*. Reading, MA: Addison-Wesley, 1992.

Peters, Thomas J., and Robert H. Waterman Jr. *In Search of Excellence: Lessons from America's Best-Run Companies*. New York, NY: Harper & Row, 1982.

THE HUMAN PERSPECTIVE

The three chapters in Part Three discuss the human, or behavioral, perspective on police administration. The importance of this behaviorial approach was recognized several decades ago by business and industrial managers who observed that people at work do not always produce with machine-like regularity and efficiency. Since that revelation, management has come increasingly to be viewed as a people-oriented function in terms of both managers and those managed. Management is often now described as the business of getting things done with and through people. Certainly this description of management in general closely fits the tasks and purposes of police administration.

In Chapter 8, the behavior of individuals in organizations is discussed. The primary aspects of organizational behavior presented in this chapter are attitudes, roles, self-concept, motivation, perception, and communication. We attempt to provide some clues for understanding why people behave as they do in organized settings. Such understanding can be very helpful to the manager charged with the responsibility for directing and controlling people at work.

Chapter 9 addresses organizational behavior in terms of groups rather than individuals. The approach in this chapter is basically sociological, as compared with the more nearly psychological discussion of individual behavior. This chapter supplements the previous one so that, taken together, Chapters 8 and 9 should provide considerable insight into the behavior of people in organizations.

Chapter 10 discusses leadership, one of the most critical and elusive elements in management. The differences between management and leadership are sketched; although the two concepts are closely related, we stress that they are not identical. A number of functions, styles, and theories of leadership are presented; we emphasize, though, that the intangible quality of leadership makes it difficult to analyze and categorize. Unfortunately, definitive instructions for developing leadership talents that apply in all situations have not yet been discovered and in all likelihood never will be.

The Individual in the Police Organization

8

Learning Objectives

- Characterize the relationship between attitudes and behavior.

- Explain why attitudes are so difficult to change.

- Differentiate between behavior modification and sensitivity education.

- Characterize the relationship between self-concept and behavior.

- Cite the findings of the Hawthorne studies.

- Describe Maslow's hierarchy of needs.

- Describe the role of feedback in perception.

- Differentiate between one-way and two-way communication.

- State the only advantage of one-way communication.

- Cite the advantages and disadvantages of written and oral messages.

This chapter introduces the fundamentals of human behavior in organizational settings. Factors that mold and inspire individual behavior and affect interaction between and among individuals are discussed.

An understanding of human behavior is extremely important for police managers, because every aspect of organization and management involves people. Police managers must understand and successfully deal with the behavior of citizens, their subordinates, their peers, and their superiors. They must influence the behavior of others while at the same time understanding and controlling their own behavior.

Human behavior is the most intricate and involved input to the management process. There are innumerable explanations for human behavior. Most people make subjective judgments all the time as to why other people behave the way they do. People tend to perceive what others do from their own peculiar perspectives, failing to consider or appreciate differing values, motives, or perceptions. Unless they are well grounded in behavioral theory, individuals' subjective evaluations of what others do and say may be erroneous.

This chapter is not intended to provide a comprehensive understanding of human behavior; we provide little more than a basic overview of the subject matter. Explaining human behavior in police organizations is a difficult task; human behavior is too dynamic to lend itself easily to description or explanation. This presentation is therefore limited to what we believe to be the most important factors that affect human behavior in organizations. Discussion of these factors will be based on the premise that behavior, as an open system, is influenced by all kinds of outside environmental forces that interact with the internal characteristics of the individual.

The Individual as a Subsystem

The individual is the basic subsystem of the organization. In structural terms, individuals are grouped to form bureaus, staffs, divisions, units, squads, and teams, which together make up the formal organization. Individuals do the work, pass the information, and communicate in the organization. Individuals also create informal groups, which combine to form a powerful informal organization. It is individuals who provide leadership and make the decisions in the organization.

As pointed out in Chapter 3, an individual consists of numerous interdependent subsystems, each of which may be considered a system in and of itself. In physiological terms, an individual has muscular, skeletal, nervous, sexual, digestive, circulatory, and respiratory systems; in psychological terms, emotional, value, ethical, moral, religious, and motivational systems. Each of these interdependent systems is a subsystem of the whole individual, and each works in concert with the others to influence the individual's behavior.

In addition to internal subsystem influences, the individual is influenced by external subsystems and systems of which he or she is a part: among them, the governmental system, the political system, the religious system, the family system, and the organizational work system. The dynamic interdependence between human and organizational systems accounts in large part for the complexities of human behavior.

There are so many interdependent variables involved in the process of human behavior that it is virtually impossible to understand them all and to predict accurately how they will affect one another. Voluminous research conducted on this subject by medical and social scientists has failed to reduce human behavior to an exact science. However, physiology, psychology, and sociology, when considered in terms of the systems perspective and as applied to the organizational setting, provide some substantial and worthwhile insight to human behavior. Our discussion of human behavior, borrowed from these disciplines, will focus on the following six major aspects of organizational behavior:

1. attitudes
2. roles
3. self-concept
4. motivation
5. perception
6. communication

Each aspect will be more fully discussed in terms of the various ways they impact interdependently on individual human behavior within the police organizational setting.

Attitudes

Norman Maier describes an attitude as a psychological "mental set," that represents "a predisposition to form certain opinions."[1] Similarly, Robert E. Worden defines an attitude as "a constellation of beliefs, sentiments, and behavior tendencies concerning some object."[2] Attitudes may be ideals, values, sentiments, thoughts, ideas, concepts, feelings, beliefs, and assumptions.

Attitudes affect people's perceptions, behavior, and events. People with different attitudes will form different opinions of the people with whom they associate. They will also evaluate events and activities in which they are involved differently, depending on their attitudes. They will perceive their fellow workers, their commanding officers, the citizens of their communities, their pay, the way they are treated, and everything they do according to their preconceived opinions or attitudes. In short, attitudes are what people are predisposed to bring to everything in which they become involved.

The relationship between attitudes and behavior, however, is not a direct one.[3] For example, some people have the attitude that their work is boring, yet they still work. Some police officers believe that their sergeants are incapable of supervising, yet they follow orders. Others believe that their police chiefs deserve their best efforts each and every day, but nonetheless find themselves coasting in their jobs. Although how people behave has a great deal to do with their attitude, behavior is also influenced by many other factors.

The classic example of the indirect relationship between attitude and behavior is the relationship between prejudice (attitude) and discrimination (behavior). All of us have prejudices, or preconceived notions, about groups of people. People tend to form attitudes about individuals on the basis of the groups to which they belong. In terms of racial prejudice, for example, whites' attitudes about individual African Americans are often based on what they think they know about black people in general. For various reasons, however, whites' behavior toward blacks may not flow directly from their prejudices. A white store owner who does not like blacks may still act friendly toward black customers because he or she needs their business. Similarly, a businessman who believes that women are not as competent as men may still employ women, thinking that it is only fair or because a union or the government requires it.

In his study of police-community contacts in large cities conducted in the mid-1960s for the President's Crime Commission, Albert Reiss found very little evidence of discriminatory behavior on the part of white police toward black people.[4] However, he did find that the white police officers he studied had very prejudicial attitudes toward blacks. Similarly, Stephen Coleman found that the police officers he studied were very prejudiced, but that their attitudes did not often directly translate into brutality or illegal arrests of blacks.[5] The effect of the prejudiced attitudes was more subtle, as officers were more likely to be suspicious of black citizens and less likely to be friendly or respectful toward blacks. So again, although attitudes have an important influence on behavior, the relationship is not as simple or direct as one might think.

From an organizational point of view, an important set of attitudes are those toward work and authority. Some people express the attitude that work is enjoyable and should be done well, while others look at work simply as a means to an end, a contract in which they trade their time and energy for money to spend on their real pleasures. Similarly, some people accept the legitimacy of organizational authority without question, while others spend a major portion of their time undermining their bosses' authority. Despite these variations, though, most people willingly join organizations, work, and develop at least some commitment to their places of employment. These basic social norms, often taken for granted, make collective action and organizational control possible.[6]

Figure 8.1 shows the behaving process as well as its inputs and outputs from a systems perspective. Attitude, it should be noted, is but one of six system inputs that influence behaving. Behaving is a process affected by each input interacting with the others, with no single input having a consistently higher or lower weighted value. Considering the variables associated with each input, behaving must be looked at as an extraordinarily involved process. It is clear then that the relationship between attitude and behavior is not direct.

In fact, when describing behavior in systems terms, Edgar F. Huse and James L. Bowditch do not include attitudes as input.[7] Instead, they classify attitudes as steering mechanisms in the behaving process; factors that influence and direct tasks, problems, relevance, and rewards as each of these bears on eventual behavioral output. They believe that attitudes, which are not perfectly responsive or accurate, impart only general tendencies to behavior.

The development of a person's attitudes is influenced by such factors as family, gender, age, race, ethnicity, economic and social status, education, intelligence, and place of residence. Attitudes are also influenced by myriad other factors that are unique to a given person. Each person's set of attitudes, therefore, is different from every other person's. Even in a closely knit family, in which one might expect similar attitudes to prevail, the members' differences in attitudes are likely to be remarkable and can often be easily identified.

Figure 8.1
Behavior from a Systems Perspective

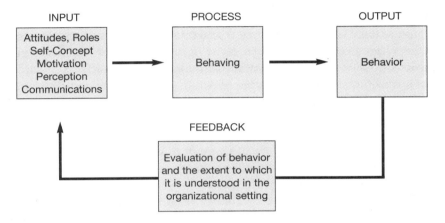

Individuals usually have fairly elaborate rationales with which they explain and justify their attitudes to themselves and to others. People even tend to associate with others who have similar attitudes; this is a means by which individuals reinforce their own attitudes. Living becomes a more comfortable experience if a person can be surrounded by people who agree with him or her. Thus, few conservative Republicans associate socially with liberal Democrats. Pro-choice advocates and antiabortionists find little solace in one another. People with different attitudes are often psychologically threatened by one another; the sacredness of one's own attitudes is a personal domain in which the individual encourages little or no interference. However, behind the "rational" explanations for one's attitudes are strong emotional reasons. Because a person becomes emotionally attached to his or her attitudes through years of conditioning and experience, attitudes are extremely difficult to change.

The traditional route to behavioral change has been by way of attitudinal change. Because of the strong emotional aspect of attitudes, however, this route has often failed. By contrast, some of the contemporary methods of behavioral change bypass attitudes altogether and concentrate on the relationship between behavior and reward. This relationship is referred to as *behavioral modification*; it assumes that behavior can be changed through reward and punishment. Because behavior modification evades confrontation with attitudes, many behavioral scientists believe it to be tantamount to brainwashing; others see it as the only sensible method available to get around strongly held individual attitudes in moving forward toward the goal of organizational productivity. Individually held attitudes can be major stumbling blocks in attempting to achieve goals and objectives and must somehow be dealt with in the process.

A good example of police behavioral change that is not dependent on attitude change pertains to the use of deadly force. Many police departments have recently made their policies and procedures on discharging firearms much more restrictive. Officers have been carefully informed of the limited circumstances in which use of their firearms is permitted. The penalties for unauthorized use of force have been increased, and procedures for investigating police shootings have been tightened. The focus of the entire effort has been on the behavior of police use of firearms; the attitudes of police officers toward the use of force or toward different types of people have not been targeted, at least not directly. The available evidence indicates that this behavior modification approach has succeeded in substantially reducing police use of firearms (without any increased danger to police officers, it should be added).[8]

Behavior modification achieved through punishment and reward conditioning is not the only effective method that can be used in dealing with attitudes. Although the process involved is prolonged and difficult, attitudes can be changed. The method most commonly used to change attitudes is *sensitivity training*, which is designed primarily to force an individual to face the irrationality involved in his or her own attitudinal shortcomings. Although it is called "training," it is much more of an educational process than a training process. Training is designed to teach a person how to do something; education is designed to provide an intellectual base for individual behavior. Sensitivity education, then, offers an individual an opportunity to examine his or her own attitudes intellectually. It may also offer individuals information about other groups of people, in the form of cultural awareness or cultural diversity education.

If a person's attitudes are to change, it is essential that he or she be forced to examine critically and objectively the rationales used to support them. This is indeed a difficult and delicate process. For an individual to come to the realization, for example, that his or her long-held negative attitudes about Catholics, Muslims, blacks, homosexuals, or homeless people are without foundation and based on ignorance can be an extremely traumatic experience. The skilled sensitivity educator, dealing with the dynamics of human behavior in the classroom, can bring about this realization only if there is sufficient time to deal effectively with the natural resistance that is inevitable in getting people to face their own attitudinal inadequacies.

Sensitivity education is directed toward getting people to see themselves as they are and as other people see them. Because attitudes develop over a period of many years and are so strongly reinforced, they are likely to be rigid and difficult to change. This whole educational process is complicated by the fact that some attitudes are reasonable and valid and can be supported by facts. Everyone, then, has a mixture of reasonable and unreasonable attitudes.

People find it impossible to confront their own shortcomings because they are unwilling to admit, either to themselves or to others, that they might be wrong. Pride and a misguided sense of self-preservation unconsciously stand in the way of approaching one's own inadequacies, and this hinders people professionally and impedes personal growth. Very few people have the character, understanding, and inner strength to ask of others, "What's wrong with me?" and to be receptive to the answers without being personally threatened.

It is human nature to see oneself not as one is, but as one would like to be. In order to change one's attitudes toward self and others, a person must undergo an experience that very carefully and slowly leads to the realization that many of one's attitudes may be based on false reasoning. This is something that cannot be taught directly; in fact, any attempt to intrude on one's attitudes may be looked on as an invasion of privacy.

Sensitivity education avoids direct confrontation with attitudinal inadequacies. There is no attempt to teach individuals anything about their shortcomings directly. Rather, the sensitivity educator gradually forces individuals to examine themselves and their attitudes in light of the facts and to come to a personal realization that they have been wrong and that they must change. The sensitivity educational experience provides them with the support and encouragement necessary to confront these facts. They are never told that their attitudes are faulty; they come to this conclusion themselves. They are never told to change their attitudes; they change their attitudes themselves on the basis of having undergone this experience. What really happens is that their attitudes change as they become more sensitive to themselves and others.

Aside from sensitivity education, the cumulative effect of everyday experience can sometimes change attitudes, as can a single powerful experience. Police officer attitudes, for example, are definitely affected by work experiences (see "Police Attitudes and Police Personality," p. 222). Police officers often become more suspicious of others, more cynical about the human condition, and more politically conservative, especially during their first few years in the profession.[9] Officers may also become more racially prejudiced, particularly if they work in areas where suspects and troublemakers seem to disproportionately represent one racial or ethnic group.

In principle, at least, more positive attitudinal changes should also result from everyday experience. A case in point may be police officers' racial prejudices. Some observers believe that the one factor most likely to reduce police prejudice is the increased employment of African American and other minority police officers. In the view of Herman Goldstein, "no training program can possibly work as well as this day-to-day contact among peers to break down the barriers and hostilities between different cultures."[10]

Police Attitudes and Police Personality

Most police officers conclude that they have been affected by their career in the police service and that they have changed at both the level of personality and at the level of social attitudes.

First, the level of personality changes: in general, there is a gradual increase in the level of self-confidence and assertiveness. One inspector summarized his experiences very succinctly: "When I first joined I was inhibited and had difficulties dealing with 'new' people. Now I'm not afraid of anyone."

There is usually a rather profound emotional "hardening." Different officers experience this in different ways, but most admit (and admit this sadly) that they have developed a protective shell which insulates them from the emotional upheavals caused by some of the dreadful experiences they have had to undergo. Suspiciousness, cynicism and skepticism may not be bad qualities to have as operational police officers. Indeed, they may well be necessary to assist in the process of being operationally competent. These feelings are problematic when they extend beyond immediate police work into all aspects of the officer's life.

Officers feel that they become either more or less dogmatic. There is probably a complex interaction between individual personality dynamics and social experience. Some officers, so irritated by the world they see about them, wish for a powerful cleansing of society. They become intolerant, bigoted and punitive. Others become more broad-minded and compassionate and blame not individuals but an iniquitous social history and/or social environment for the behaviors they observe.

Initially most officers experience a widening of horizons. Closely allied to this breadth of social experience is a loss of naiveté.

Police officers find themselves adhering to various norms within the police subculture. These norms include a derogation of the social services and the liberal "do-gooders," a distrust or even blatant dislike of ethnic minorities, a vilification of certain types of offender (especially the sex offender), a dislike of theory (and ivory-tower intellectuals), and a positive regard for common sense and the "practical man." Finally, adherents to the police culture also support a rather traditional masculine set of outlooks on the world.

Source: K. Robert C. Adlam, "The Police Personality: Psychological Consequences of Being a Police Officer," *Journal of Police Science and Administration* 10, no. 3 (September 1982): 347-348, with permission of the International Association of Chiefs of Police.

Joining work experiences as a profound influence on police officers' attitudes is peer pressure. Young police officers crave acceptance from their more experienced colleagues; adopting and displaying the "right" attitude is one prerequisite of initiation into the police subculture. Rookie officers also tend to adopt the dominant attitudes of their peers, because those attitudes help make sense of the danger, hostility, fear, violence, and authority in their new world. The influences of work experience and peer pressure are extremely powerful, and it is rare that a police officer's attitudes would not significantly change after only a few years in police work.

A major challenge for police managers is to harness these powerful peer influences so that young officers' attitudes change positively rather than negatively. Although distrust and cynicism are among the common effects of police work and the police culture on young officers, it is also possible for officers to remain optimists or become realists but avoid developing into pessimists or cynics.[11] Carefully chosen field training officers can help young officers interpret their early experiences, while sergeants should regard tending to the moral development of their subordinates as a very important aspect of their responsibilities.

Roles

In much the same way that actors in a motion picture assume certain characteristics of behavior that conform to the roles they are playing, all human beings are similarly responsive to what they perceive to be the necessity for playing their real-life roles according to accepted behavior.

Everyone is involved in playing many roles simultaneously. This presents somewhat of a problem, because the roles played are often very different from one another, with each role demanding a different kind of behavior. For example, a woman may be a mother, wife, daughter, sister, aunt, cousin, member of a choir, police officer, Methodist, Democrat, Southerner, golfer, soccer fan, and amateur photographer. These roles, all of which influence the woman's behavior, are all played differently according to the way they are perceived.

The fact is that people differ greatly in how they play similar roles. Some mothers work outside the home; others do not. Some husbands outwardly manifest affection for their wives; others do not. Some daughters feel a responsibility to visit their aging parents frequently; others feel no such responsibility. Finally, some police officers see themselves as tough, hard-line crime fighters; others see themselves as professional, service-oriented public servants.

The way that people play their roles depends not only on the expectations of others as these expectations are individually perceived, but also on the way other people play their own roles. Role conflict may result in differing role expectations. However, it is important to point out that it is possible to resolve role conflicts through adjustment. Adjustment, or mutually agreed-upon role change, sometimes involves major changes in attitude and behavior, changes that are extremely difficult to accomplish.

The effect of roles on behavior varies according to the situation. Some roles guide behavior in virtually every situation, whereas others apply only in specific circumstances.[12] Sex roles, for example, influence behavior in a wide range of situations: in most instances, they have a much stronger impact than many of the other roles that people play. The fact that a person is a woman will probably influence her behavior to a much greater degree than will her membership in Toastmasters or the Democratic Party.

The role of police officer seems to be one that strongly influences those who play it. For some it is more of a "calling" than a job. The authority that police are given, the danger they face, the social stigma that attaches to them, and the isolation from "civilians" that often develops, all contribute to a strong sense of identification with fellow police and with the police role, however it is conceived.[13] The strength of the police officer role also may carry over into other roles and aspects of life. Police officers are often said to act like cops even when interacting with their families and to react with suspicion and cynicism in everyday social settings. In part, this may be fueled by the common view that "police officers are always on duty, 24 hours a day."

Police officers vary widely in how they view their police role, but five major types have been identified. These role types differ on several dimensions, including particularistic versus universalistic values, outcome versus process orientation,[14] aggressiveness, selectivity,[15] perspective, morality of coercion,[16] and emphasis on due process versus social order.[17] The five resulting types are professionals, tough cops, clean-beat crime fighters, problem solvers, and avoiders.[18]

Professionals are willing to use coercive police authority when necessary but are not inclined to overuse it. They define the police role in broad terms and look for varied ways of accomplishing legitimate objectives. They have empathy for the people they have to deal with and can imagine themselves experiencing other people's problems. Professionals understand the limits on their own ability to solve other people's problems, though, and are thus able to do their best without being overly frustrated or tormented. They generally retain positive views toward both police work and the public.

Tough cops are enthusiastic about using police authority and generally believe that the people they deal with deserve what they get. Instead of looking into various options for solving problems, they jump quickly to the use of coercive authority, without too much concern for its legality. They lack empathy for other people, and typically adopt an "us versus them" mentality. Tough cops blame the continuance of crime and disorder problems on lack of support from the community, the courts, and their own administrators. They usually develop quite negative attitudes toward just about everything and everybody except their fellow tough cops.

Clean-beat crime fighters share many attitudes and beliefs with tough cops, but they are more willing to stay within the rules and the law. In this respect they are more process-oriented, whereas tough cops are more outcome-oriented. Clean-beat crime fighters see their role primarily as law enforcement, and believe that systematic and thorough application of the law will lead to a safer and more orderly community. They often experience frustration, either because their efforts to enforce the law aggressively are thwarted by administrators and the community, or because their enforcement efforts fail to deter law violators to the extent they had expected.

Problem solvers share empathy and a broad view of the police role with the professionals, but are more conflicted over the use of coercive authority. They want to be a positive influence on individuals and the community and see law enforcement and the use of force as negative influences. They emphasize delivering services, collaborating with citizens, and resolving conflict, and they avoid the use of authority. In some communities these problem solvers experience considerable success and public support, but in others they can get frustrated if their efforts are not successful or appreciated. Moreover, if their dislike of using authority is extreme, they may either fail to perform effectively in critical situations, or if they use authority despite their dislike for it, they may become tormented by self-doubt or even guilt.

Finally, the *avoiders* lack both empathy for other people and a willingness to use force to solve problems. These officers go out of their way to avoid difficult situations, as their label implies. They tend to shirk their duties, are not very productive, and try to attract as little attention as possible. These avoiders often cannot be reached on the police radio, never arrive first at the scene of a serious incident, and engage in little proactive policing. Basically, they seem to care about little more than surviving until their retirement starts.

Police managers should be attuned to these different conceptions of the police role. In the recruitment and selection of new employees, managers should seek individuals who are already inclined toward the type of police role that the department prefers. In recruit and field training, strong efforts should be devoted toward molding young officers in appropriate roles and discouraging support for inappropriate roles. Supervision and management should reward appropriate behavior and discourage the types of behavior associated with unsatisfactory role conceptions. The leadership of the department should articulate and reinforce the particular conception of the police role that is considered most appropriate for the community and the department.

Self-Concept

Self-concept, another determinant of behavior in organizations, is defined as the image a person has not only of self, but also of ideal self: how he or she would like to be. Both aspects of this definition have important effects on the ways people act in organized situations.

A person's self-concept develops through interaction with other people. People learn who they are by watching how other people react to them.[19] Other people's behavior toward a person is the mirror in which one sees oneself; this behavior provides the database from which a person forms his or her own self-concepts. Thus, your own self-concept is formed in part by how other people behave toward you.

By carefully watching and analyzing the behavior of others, a person also learns what must be done in order to get more favorable reactions from others. In the process, one develops an ideal self-concept, comparing present self with ideal self. If an individual's ideal self-concept is too far removed from his or her real potential to achieve it, he or she may develop feelings of inadequacy and failure. On the other hand, if no one seems to expect much, people are likely to develop too narrow or too conservative ideal self-concepts and, consequently, never reach their potential.

Some people enter police work either because their conception of the role of the police fits their self-concept or because being a police officer coincides with elements of their ideal self-concept. How well their career choice works out depends on these conceptions and on individual capabilities. One person may be big and strong and choose police work because it seems to present plenty of opportunities for commanding and authoritative behavior. This person may be capable of playing the role as perceived, but may nevertheless be frustrated if the nature of police work turns out to be different from what is anticipated. Another person might seek strength and authority in his or her ideal self in an effort to compensate for a recognized sense of weakness or inadequacy. This person might choose policing as a means of achieving the ideal and might fail for the lack of the physical and mental toughness that police work sometimes demands.

Other people might go into policing because they see it as a helping profession and because their ideal self-concept includes notions of charity and service. Such people could easily become frustrated if the good deeds performed in the course of their work do not seem to significantly improve people's lives, or even if the recipients of their help do not always seem grateful.

These examples illustrate some of the problems related to self-concept and ideal self that can be associated with a police career; however, they are not meant to suggest that such problems are inevitable. These problems are probably most often encountered in extreme cases. Individuals with inaccurate conceptions of their present selves or unrealistic conceptions of their ideal selves may be most susceptible to the kinds of problems described above and perhaps are not good candidates to fill the police role. Nor are those who expect a police career to contribute too dramatically to improvements in present self-concept or achievement of ideal self likely to make successful and satisfied police officers.

Because work is an important aspect of a person's self-concept, superiors are important participants in one's effort to achieve an ideal self-concept. By accurately appraising subordinates in terms of who they think they are and what they think they can become, a police chief is in a good position to understand their behavior and to make a positive contribution toward their personal and professional development. By carefully providing them with information about their progress toward achieving ideal self-concept goals and by encouraging them in every possible way to establish reasonable and justifiable ideals, a police chief can be assured of better work performance and greater productivity for the organization as a whole.

The relationship between behavior and self-concept is direct. As a general rule, most people evaluate situations and choose behaviors on the basis of how they think their self-concepts will be affected. Thus, behavior perceived as satisfying or enhancing ideal self-concepts is chosen; behavior perceived as damaging to ideal self-concepts is rejected.

Individual behavioral problems are likely to arise when either or both of the following conditions prevail:

1. individuals are incorrect in choosing behavior that they believe will enhance their ideal self-concepts; and
2. individuals are incapable of exercising behavior that they believe will enhance their ideal self-concepts.

In the first instance, inaccurate perception of the facts involved in the situation may be blamed for an individual's choosing behavior that negatively affects self-concept. The young, idealistic police rookie, for example, who behaves on the job according to policies and procedures learned at the academy may abruptly discover that such behavior is not condoned by the dominant police subculture. The high school class clown whose behavior is reinforced by both teachers and students in the old home town may learn that similar behavioral patterns are unacceptable in the college or university milieu. Behavior predicated on inaccurate perception can have a devastating effect on the individual's ideal self-concept.

In the second instance, a person who is incapable of exercising behavior that will enhance ideal self-concept can become extremely frustrated over his or her inadequacies. The youngster who is uncoordinated and therefore a poor athlete can have his or her self-concept ruined by growing up in a neighborhood where the peer group places a high value on being a good athlete. The police officer whose ideal self demands and gets respect from everyone may be crushed if unable to achieve such a reputation on the streets and in the squad room.

Individuals who are able to cope with these frustrations often do so by overcompensating for what they perceive to be their own inadequacies. If an individual's efforts to overcompensate can be directed toward healthy and productive ends, a great deal can be achieved in making the individual a worthwhile contributor to society in general and to the organization for which he or she works in particular. It is management's responsibility to improve an individual employee's self-concept by providing realistic and reachable goals and objectives with which the individual employee can be comfortable and that will serve to enhance ideal self-concept.

Motivation

One of the more important aspects of human behavior in organizations is motivation. Motivation refers to motives, or what makes the individual behave in a certain way. It involves the "why?" question in human behavior. The answer, as might be suspected, is not an easy one.

Because we are interested in police officers who work in organizational settings, our primary concern here is what motivates people to work? Theories that attempt to describe the process abound. Huse and Bowditch have outlined four general models of motivational systems: the force and coercion model, the economic/machine model, the affection/affiliation model, and the growth–open system model.[20]

Force and Coercion Model

According to the force and coercion model, human beings work because they have to in order to avoid pain and punishment. The parent who says to his or her child, "Learn your spelling words before supper or you can't watch television tonight," is attempting to create motivation based on this model. Students who take required courses in which they are not interested, study in order to pass: examinations for the courses are constructed in order to force and coerce students to study. The once widespread institutions of serfdom and slavery were based on total compliance with the force and coercion model.

In American society, forcing and coercing behavior are regarded as distasteful. For this reason, and because force and coercion generally tend to debase human beings, this model has become the least popular motivational method. It is also the least effective; it encourages only the very minimum amount of work necessary to avoid punishment. It also breeds resentment and causes morale problems. In extreme cases this resentment and loss of morale can turn into open rebellion and even organizational sabotage.

Although motivation based on force and coercion is generally out of favor in progressive businesses and government agencies, it is not uncommon to find that employees and their bosses in an organization disagree about the motivational model in use. This is certainly true in many police departments. In a study of 64 police agencies in Illinois, for example, operational and supervisory personnel reported that motivation was sought primarily by way of threats, fear, and coercion, while administrators claimed to be emphasizing higher-level needs to motivate their employees.[21]

There are instances in policing, however, when force and coercion are the only methods that can be used to motivate desired behavior. If the dominant police subculture dictates role expectations that are diametrically opposed to organizational goals and objectives, and if dominant police subcultural behavior conflicts with departmental policies, a police administrator might have to resort to force and coercion in order to maintain organizational stability. In situations in which police officers are protected by outmoded civil service regulations, tenure, or strong union backing, force and coercion may very well be the only means by which a police administrator can demand behavior consistent with the police department's goals and objectives.

Economic/Machine Model

The economic/machine model suggests that human beings work in order to obtain the tangible rewards that employment offers. In the carrot-and-stick approach to motivation, the economic/machine model would represent the carrot, whereas the force and coercion model would represent the stick. According to the former theory, work is nothing more than a means to an end; it implies that if somehow everyone immediately became wealthy, no more work would be done.

The police chief who subscribes fully to the thesis of the economic/machine model views police officers basically as machines designed to produce solely for pragmatic reasons. The chief is not particularly concerned about departmental employees except in terms of their performance and productivity. The main concern is efficiency, getting maximum return for minimum investment on a cost-effective basis. Although efficiency is important, especially in terms of prudent expenditure of the taxpayer's dollar, it cannot be looked on as the only basis on which to deal with workers.

Affective/Affiliation Model

Through the *Hawthorne studies*, a classic motivational research effort, it became apparent that immediate economic reward was not the only reason for individual productivity.[22] These studies demonstrated that social and psychological factors in the work setting have considerable effect on performance. Specifically, the studies found that the output of workers improved significantly when they were made to feel important and when they were consulted about job decisions.

These findings are at the heart of the affective/affiliation model of motivation. In other words, workers may be motivated to work because of their social needs, their need to work harmoniously with other people.

Growth–Open System Model

The growth–open system model of motivation grew out of the Hawthorne studies and their subsequent findings. This model incorporates much of the philosophy on which the economic/machine model is based; in addition, it gives consideration to those social and psychological forces (affective/affiliation model) that influence work behavior. This combination of the two other models is an open system, because it recognizes and stresses that the work situation cannot be insulated from the outside world; it emphasizes the fact that the individual at work must be looked on as a human being influenced by the environment.

A central theme of the growth–open system model of motivation is that people work in order to satisfy certain human needs. Maslow has identified a five-level hierarchy of these needs. An adaptation of *Maslow's hierarchy* follows:

1. basic needs (food, clothing, shelter)
2. security needs (protection against physical and psychological threats to an individual's well-being)
3. social needs (love, friendship, camaraderie, acceptance)
4. self-concept needs (recognition, respect, esteem)
5. ideal self needs (fulfilling individual potential and achieving ideal self-concept)[23]

After satisfying basic and security needs, an individual progressively seeks to satisfy higher-level needs (social, self-concept, and ideal self needs). In other words, people fill their needs step-by-step in the hierarchy, moving from level to level. When one level of needs has been satisfied, it generally ceases to have strong motivational value. If a person feels secure physically and psychologically (Level 2) and has satisfied social and self-concept needs (Levels 3 and 4), any additional motivation will probably derive from Maslow's fifth hierarchical level.

In the United States today, the basic needs of the great majority of employed workers are satisfied. Police pay scales in most jurisdictions within the United States are sufficient to meet police officers' most basic needs. Consequently, according to Maslow's theory, basic needs no longer have significant motivational value for police officers. Therefore, the police department that seeks to motivate its employees primarily through salary increases and other lower-level incentives is applying a motivational technique that has little value.

In reality, this is only partially true. Many police officers, like other workers, have fulfilled their basic needs but feel insecure about those needs being met in the future; the strength of police unions is a manifestation of this insecurity. The threat of having fulfilled needs cut off at any one of the five hierarchical levels is in itself a strong motivational force; only when that threat dissipates does an individual cease to be motivated at any given level.

Certainly, many people are still strongly motivated by pay incentives even though they may also be responsive to factors higher in Maslow's hierarchy. Harold Leavitt, for example, has noted that "wages and salary are not just money. They are indicators of progress, worth, and status. And they are equity measures, too, telling us whether our treatment relative to others and to our own performance is right and proper."[24]

The issue of equity raised by Leavitt is an important determinant of work motivation. Workers are interested in being treated fairly.[25] They compare themselves to others in terms of how they are treated by management and the organization. If an employee perceives his or her own treatment as inequitable in comparison to the treatment of others, satisfaction and productivity may be negatively affected. Interestingly, some studies have found that inequity works both ways; that is, both individuals who perceive themselves as undercompensated and those who think they are overcompensated reduce their work effort and commitment to the organization.[26]

When choosing specific actions and their overall level of work effort, employees are also guided by what they see as the probabilities of their actions leading to desired outcomes. This is termed *expectancy theory*.[27] A police officer deciding whether to attend night college classes, for example, might weigh the following considerations:

1. the probability of successfully completing the classes
2. the probability of obtaining a degree
3. the probability that completing the classes or a degree would benefit his or her police career

The combination of these probabilities or expectancies would strongly influence the officer's decision whether to enroll in the college classes. In addition, the value of the outcomes would be considered. If the probabilities were low but the officer highly valued the college degree or the possible career benefit, he or she might enroll despite the odds. On the other hand, some officers might decide against enrolling, even though their probabilities of success were high, because they placed little value on college education and career advancement.

The growth-open system model of motivation emphasizes the factors of attitudes, roles, self-concept, and human growth to be considered in attempting to achieve organizational goals and objectives. This model holds that human beings are neither machines to be directed and controlled nor totally free decisionmakers operating in a vacuum. The model maintains that behavior in work settings is a result of complex and interrelated motives that are not easily identifiable. Essentially, it recognizes that both behavior and motivation for behavior are open systems. As open systems, behavior and motivation have inputs, outputs, processes, and feedback, all of which are very personal to the individual and all of which are influenced by outside environmental factors.

A Modest Theory of Motivation

In discussing attitudes, roles, self-concept, and motivation, we have been seeking a better understanding of human behavior, especially in organized work settings. Such an understanding is elusive and difficult to conceptualize, because each person's behavior is unique and complicated. It is relatively easy to develop theories and models that explain behavior in a general sense, but these models often break down when applied to particular individuals. We must conclude, therefore, that there are no absolutes, no concrete principles that allow us to predict or to understand completely the behavior of others. Although Maslow's hierarchy of needs is a useful theory to explain much of the behavior that occurs in organizations, there are people with more money and status than they could ever possibly exhaust who are still highly motivated to attain more of each.

Anthony Athos and Robert Coffey have described what we will call a modest theory of human behavior, which allows for a wide latitude of conscious and unconscious perceptions of self and situation and which seems almost universal in its applicability.[28] This theory makes no attempt to be as prescriptive as a mathematical formula or, indeed, as definitive as the other models discussed; it is nonetheless helpful in providing insights into behavior inexplicable through the application of other models. The three elements that make up this theory can be summarized as follows:

1. A person's self-concept is determined by self-perception, perception being influenced by both conscious and subconscious factors.
2. A person's individual frame of reference is predicated on the way he or she perceives the world at any given time (including people, places, and things in the immediate environment) in combination with self-perception in a particular setting.
3. A person behaves in order to protect or enhance his or her feelings of security or adequacy in any given situation.[29]

If one uses this theory as a model, all behavior is logical, and all behavior can be explained. This theory is an extremely important concept to bear in mind when trying to understand behavior that is difficult to understand or that does not seem to conform to the norm. It provides a rationale for the contention that all behavior is logical and that individuals who are behaving in particular ways are doing so according to what they think is best for them in particular situations as they see the situations. A person's behavior may seem irrational or even self-destructive, but for the person exhibiting it, that behavior makes sense.

The theory makes allowances for differences between the way individuals see things and the way things really are. This difference is a product of perception.

Perception

People learn about other people, places, and things through information gathered by the sensory organs. The database for perception is the individual's own way of seeing, hearing, touching, tasting, and smelling the environment. Most police officers learn quickly about the importance of differences in perception. It is common to interview two witnesses of the same incident only to obtain accounts with little similarity. Often, after interviewing two drivers involved in an automobile accident, it is hard to believe that they are describing the same accident. It is not unusual to interview a complainant in an order-maintenance situation and be ready to apply the full force of the law to the offending party, only to discover that the other side of the story is every bit as believable and deserving of consideration. Admittedly, some of these differences are due to intentional lying, but quite frequently each participant is telling the whole truth as he or she perceives it.

People behave differently from one another in part because their sensory organs have varying capabilities. For example, the information gathered by people with excellent eyesight differs from that gathered by people with poor eyesight. The behavior of these two groups is based on different information.

Although no one can perfectly analyze the effect of sensory limitations on perception, and hence on behavior, it is safe to assume that perception and behavior are influenced to a remarkable degree by such limitations. The behavior of a person walking in the dark along a narrow, lonely road who hears a car approaching at a fast rate of speed would differ greatly from the behavior of a person who fails to hear the car; one would jump out of the way, and the other would continue walking. Most sensory information needs to be interpreted before it can be used to design appropriate behavior. This interpretation of sensory data is perception.

Some of the perceptual process is carried out mechanically by the sensory organs. Your eyes, for example, sort out and arrange a steady flow of light so that you can see objects, people, color, and movement. This mechanical interpretation is important, although people tend to take it for granted, becoming aware of it only when something such as an optical illusion deceives them.

Some perception is based on fairly straightforward learning. As your eyes present you with visual data on objects, for example, you learn to see and differentiate chairs, tables, books, automobiles, and a great number of other commonplace items. You learn to interpret the visual image of an object with four wooden vertical legs and a rectangular wooden top as a table, something on which to eat a meal, play Monopoly, or study. In other words, you learn to perceive the object as a table, and you perceive it in terms of the varying ways you relate to it or use it.

Perception involves your own peculiar interpretation of sensory information; it includes both mechanical and learning processes. However, the combination of these two processes is not enough to explain the wide variety of ways in which people interpret identical situations. Marcus Alexis and Charles Z. Wilson point out that "the information gathering function is not a sequence of purely mechanical, routine physiological processes. Personalities and social needs are intricately woven into how people see things."[30]

To a large extent, then, people see things in terms of their attitudes, roles, self-concepts, and motivation (see "Police Perception and the Symbolic Assailant," p. 235). A police officer may perceive a drug addict as a criminal. To a doctor, the person is sick or perhaps a patient; to a psychologist, an addict with an emotional problem; to a drug dealer, a customer; to a parent, a child who is unable to cope with the stresses of society. In all instances, the drug addict is the same person but is perceived differently by different people playing different social roles. In each example, the personal attitudes held by the perceivers with respect to drug addicts and drug addiction would further differentiate their perceptions.

Similarly, a person's self-perception as a result of interaction with others may be a behavioral determinant. A person who has a concept of self as being intelligent may perceive going to school and taking examinations as enjoyable, rewarding experiences; a person who has consistently failed in academic studies, on the other hand, may perceive himself or herself to be considerably less intelligent, fear school, and freeze when taking examinations.

Each person behaves so as to protect or enhance his or her perceived self-concept. It is important to understand that the way in which another person perceives a situation and subsequently behaves on the basis of that perception is likely to be different from the way you perceive the same situation and subsequently behave on the basis of your perception. In a very real sense, your own perceptions obstruct your abilities to understand behavior in others. People tend to believe that other people should perceive and behave in exactly the same way that they do. The administrator must overcome this tendency in order to deal effectively with the various kinds of behavior one can expect from individuals within an organization.

In addition, administrators must realize that perception is a selective process through which people accept or reject in automatic fashion what best or least suits their needs. Leavitt tells us that "people perceive what they think will help satisfy needs; ignore what is disturbing; and again perceive disturbances that persist and increase."[31] Perception controls interpretation of sensory information, blocks out bothersome information, and accents pleasing information.

Another important aspect of perception is that it can be made more accurate through the utilization of feedback. A child who perceives a red-hot coal to be inviting and touches it gets immediate feedback in the form of pain; the pain "says" that the perception was inaccurate and that the child had better change that perception before being tempted again to touch a red-hot coal. Chances are excellent that the child will change as indicated.

Police Perception and the Symbolic Assailant

The policeman, because his work requires him to be occupied continually with potential violence, develops a perceptual shorthand to identify certain kinds of people as symbolic assailants, that is, persons who use gesture, language and attire that the policeman has come to recognize as a prelude to violence. This does not mean that violence by the symbolic assailant is necessarily predictable. On the contrary, the policeman responds to the vague indication of danger suggested by appearance. Like the animals of the experimental psychologist, the policeman finds the threat of random damage more compelling than a predetermined and inevitable punishment.

Nor, to qualify for the status of symbolic assailant, need an individual ever have used violence. A man backing out of a jewelry store with a gun in one hand and jewelry in the other would qualify even if the gun were a toy and he had never in his life fired a real pistol. To the policeman in the situation, the man's personal history is momentarily immaterial. There is only one relevant sign: a gun, signifying danger. Similarly, a young man may suggest the threat of violence to the policeman by his manner of walking or "strutting," the insolence in the demeanor being registered by the policeman as a possible preamble to later attack. Signs vary from area to area, but a youth dressed in a black leather jacket and motorcycle boots is sure to draw at least a suspicious glance from a policeman.

Source: Jerome H. Skolnick, *Justice without Trial: Law Enforcement in a Democratic Society* (New York, NY: John Wiley, 1966), pp. 45–46.

Unfortunately, feedback is not usually this direct and immediate. The administrator who sincerely wants to improve perception must always actively seek information to either substantiate or correct initial perceptions of people and situations. There must be an awareness that perceptions may be inaccurate and that subordinates, individually and collectively, may perceive situations differently. Additionally, the good administrator must understand that varying perceptions are major causes of behavioral differences among people.

Communication

The attitudes, roles, self-concepts, motivation, and perceptions of others become known primarily through communication. Two people learn about each other through the communication process. It is through this process that people attempt to influence the behavior of others. Communication is the medium through which a police manager conducts day-to-day activities.

It has become fashionable in recent years to attribute any kind of organizational deficiency to faulty communication or to gaps in communication. People who are likely to use communication as a scapegoat for all organizational difficulties do not fully appreciate or understand human behavior as it is affected by attitudes, roles, self-concept, motivation, and perception. To say simply that an organization has communication problems, without considering that other aspects of organizational behavior affect communication, is an oversimplification that cannot be easily justified. This is not to say, however, that poor communication does not cause problems; it does, just as all of the other five aspects of organizational behavior cause problems.

For the purposes of our discussion here, communication simply means the way in which information is exchanged. Communication can be oral, verbal, or nonverbal. Oral communication occurs through the use of the spoken word. Verbal communication too is based on words and can be either written or oral. Nonverbal communication, in contrast, takes place without any use of words.

People tend to be much more aware of oral and verbal communication, although in actuality a great deal of information that is neither written nor spoken is received and transmitted. Gestures, facial expressions, and body language are a few examples of nonverbal communication.

Different effects can be achieved through nonverbal communication even though the same medium of communication is used. If you are driving down the street and see a friend, you are likely to tap your horn two or three times, smile, and wave. If, on the other hand, you are driving down the street and are abruptly cut off by a driver you do not know, you are likely to lean hard on the horn two or three times, grimace, and possibly even make an unfriendly gesture. In both situations you communicate nonverbally; in the first instance, you use the horn to communicate friendship; in the second, you communicate anger. Both recipients probably fully understand your nonverbal messages, even though not a single word was spoken.

The ability to receive nonverbal communication is especially dependent on the powers of observation. In the examples given above, one need not have acute powers of observation to understand the intended messages. Not all nonverbal communication is so obvious, though much of it is very subtle and extremely difficult to interpret. People who have superior powers of observation and who understand the importance of nonverbal communication are much more adept than others at picking it up and in interpreting it correctly.

Whether the message is verbal or nonverbal, the information received is useless if the recipient is unable to interpret it accurately. Such interpretation involves perception. Physiological capacities, attitudes, roles, self-concepts, and motivations combine to determine how accurately a person receives information. Two individuals may receive the same message but perceive it differently. Faulty perception, therefore, is a main cause of organizational communication problems.

Increasingly, another challenge to communication, both within a police organization and between the organization and its community, is language. Only a few decades ago, most police departments could conduct all of their business in English, with perhaps only an occasional need for a translator. Today, many police agencies frequently need the capacity to communicate in Spanish, and some departments face a variety of languages on a regular basis. Thus, police officers and police executives can no longer take for granted that effective communication requires only careful listening and speaking in the English language.

Most of a police chief's communication is verbal, either written or oral. The chief transmits information to subordinates and superiors and receives information from many other people. Communication is, in fact, the medium of management. It is the device by which management transmits and receives all information essential to organizational stability and well-being. Inasmuch as people speak to one another more often than they write to one another, most organizational communication is oral.

Oral, verbal, and nonverbal communication can be either one-way or two-way. One-way communication involves the transmission of information; the reception of such information may or may not occur. Two-way communication involves: (1) the transmission and reception of information and (2) a retransmission of the information by the receiver to the transmitter, confirming the fact that the communication is fully understood. In two-way communication, the receiver is required to indicate what he or she perceived the message to be. The transmitter learns through this process whether the intended message was accurately received.

From a systems perspective, the essential difference between one-way and two-way communication is that the latter provides for feedback, a necessary element in maintaining a closed-loop system. In two-way communication, the transmitter gets information (feedback) about the quality of the attempt to communicate, learning whether success was achieved in getting the message across. Two-way communication, therefore, has a distinct advantage over one-way communication: accuracy. Because accuracy is essential to the communication process, a police chief should utilize two-way communication whenever possible. Because a recipient's accurate perception of a message as well as the confirmation of that fact are necessary elements if communication is to take place, it can be logically argued that two-way communication is the only real form of communication and that one-way communication totally misses the mark.[32]

The only apparent advantage of one-way communication is that it is faster. If one considers the time lost as a result of organizational problems created by faulty communication, however, one-way communication is not a time saver in the long run. One-way communication serves a valid purpose in policing only in emergency situations that require immediate action and in which a commanding officer has no time to evaluate through feedback whether orders are understood. It is only in such emergency situations that one-way communication becomes preferable to two-way communication—and even then, only when absolutely necessary.

Notwithstanding its obvious faults, one-way communication is frequently used by most people. There are numerous reasons for this. People find it difficult to understand that others do not perceive in exactly the same way that they do. Others are totally unaware that people perceive differently. One-way communication is easier and quicker. It also spares one the embarrassment of learning that he or she did not transmit and receive information perfectly.

Using one-way communication lets a person blithely assume that everyone understands everything he or she has written and said, and vice versa. Although these are comforting assumptions and may make people feel effective as communicators, nothing could be further from reality; people who make such assumptions are living in a dream world. Using two-way communication, on the other hand, provides a constant reminder of the fallibility and imperfections in communicating; all people are imperfect communicators. In two-way communication these problems can be overcome by recognizing them for what they are, which gives people the opportunity to become better communicators.

Both one-way and two-way communication can involve either writing or speaking; in some instances, they can involve both. Written messages generally have the advantages of being more carefully formulated and more permanent. Oral messages, however, are speedier and permit immediate feedback. On the negative side, written messages are more expensive and more time-consuming; if they are poorly written, conveying unintended ideas and questionable information, they accomplish little. Oral messages may have similar negative effects if the receiver is at all hesitant in asking questions to clarify meaning.[33]

The formal structure of communication as a system within the organizational framework will be discussed in Chapter 11. Here, we are more concerned with communication as an interpersonal activity; as such, it requires technical proficiency in formulating and interpreting messages as well as an understanding of and a commitment to two-way communication processes. The latter requirement is every bit as important as the former. Even the most perfectly worded message can be misunderstood. Feedback is the only technique available that can ensure the transmitter and the receiver that they have the same perception with respect to the meaning of a given message.

One study found that 72 percent of a police officer's time is spent in some form of communication activity.[34] This percentage for police chiefs would probably be even higher; most of a police chief's time is spent communicating. Success in management is clearly related to success in communicating. The police chief who is a poor communicator can never become a successful police manager. Peter Drucker tells us that "the manager's . . . effectiveness depends on his ability to listen and to read, on his ability to speak and to write. He needs skill in getting his thinking across to other people as well as skill in finding out what other people are after."[35] In short, the effective manager needs to be an effective communicator.

Summary

This chapter has emphasized the importance of attitudes, roles, self-concept, motivation, perception, and communication as elements of human behavior in organizational settings. These are just a few, but by far the most important, elements involved in human behavior. Controlling and manipulating human behavior in police organizations is an exceedingly complex task; a police manager's job would be an easy one if human behavior were less complex.

The police manager who is interested in reaching an objective understanding of the behavior of others must first come to a point of self-understanding and must develop an awareness of his or her own attitudes, roles, self-concepts, motivations, perceptions, and communication talents, and understand that his or her own behavior is determined largely by these factors. Only then can the police manager really understand fully why others behave as they do.

Discussion Questions

1. Try to identify your prejudices. Are they rational or irrational, in your opinion? Try to figure out how and when you developed them.

2. What roles do you play? Try to put them in rank order from most important to least important. Are there situations in which your least important roles become very important?

3. Using Maslow's hierarchy, what would you say are the needs most important to you in your present situation? Would your answer have been different five or 10 years ago? How do you think you would answer this question 10 years from now?

4. Because of their role, in what ways do police officers perceive things differently from other people?

5. How conscientious are you in maintaining two-way communication? How important do you think two-way communication is for the police manager?

Cases

This chapter presented a number of concepts pertaining to individual behavior in police organizations. You might want to use those concepts to analyze police officer behavior in "Case 1: The Energetic Chief," "Case 2: The Peripatetic Sergeant," and "Case 3: The Yuletide Remembrance" at the back of this text. In addition, "Case 5: Cod Bay," "Case 6: Tulane City," and "Case 7: Rixton" can each be analyzed from the standpoint of police roles.

Notes

1. N.R.F. Maier, *Psychology in Industrial Organizations,* Fourth Edition (Boston, MA: Houghton Mifflin, 1973), p. 42.

2. R.E. Worden, "Police Officers' Belief Systems: A Framework for Analysis," in D.J. Kenney and G.W. Cordner, eds., *Managing Police Personnel* (Cincinnati, OH: Anderson, 1996), p. 139.

3. S.P. Robbins, *Organizational Behavior: Concepts, Controversies, Applications*, Ninth Edition (Upper Saddle River, NJ: Prentice Hall, 2000).

4. A.J. Reiss Jr., *The Police and the Public* (New Haven, CT: Yale University Press, 1971).

5. S.F. Coleman, *Street Cops* (Salem, WI: Sheffield, 1986), pp. 145-148.

6. H.A. Simon, *Administrative Behavior: A Study of Decision-Making Processes in Administrative Organizations,* Third Edition (New York, NY: The Free Press, 1976).

7. E.F. Huse and J.L. Bowditch, *Behavior in Organizations: A Systems Approach to Managing*, Second Edition (Reading, MA: Addison-Wesley, 1977), p. 75.

8. J.J. Fyfe, "Administrative Interventions on Police Shooting Discretion," *Journal of Criminal Justice* 7 (1979): 313-335.

9. J.H. Skolnick, *Justice without Trial: Law Enforcement in a Democratic Society* (New York, NY: John Wiley, 1966).

10. H. Goldstein, *Policing a Free Society* (Cambridge, MA: Ballinger, 1977), p. 271.

11. W.K. Muir Jr., *Police: Streetcorner Politicians* (Chicago, IL: University of Chicago, 1977).

12. A.G. Athos and R.E. Coffey, *Behavior in Organizations: A Multidimensional View* (Englewood Cliffs, NJ: Prentice Hall, 1968), p. 155.

13. J. Van Maanen, "Kinsmen in Repose: Occupational Perspectives of Patrolmen," in *Policing: A View from the Street*, P.K. Manning and J. Van Maanen, eds. (New York, NY: Random House, 1978).

14. S. White, "A Perspective on Police Professionalization," *Law & Society* Review 7 (fall 1972): 61-85.

15. M. Brown, *Working the Street: Police Discretion and the Dilemmas of Reform* (New York, NY: Russell Sage Foundation, 1981).

16. J. Broderick, *Police in a Time of Change,* Second Edition (Prospect Heights, IL: Waveland, 1987).

17. Muir, *Police.*

18. Worden, "Police Officers' Belief Systems," pp. 140-147.

19. C.H. Cooley, *Human Nature and the Social Order*, rev. ed. (New York, NY: Scribner's, 1922), p.184.

20. Huse and Bowditch, *Behavior in Organizations*, pp. 80-100.

21. J.H. Auten, "Police Management in Illinois: 1983," *Journal of Police Science and Administration* 13, no. 4 (December 1985): 325-337.

22. F.J. Roethlisberger and W.J. Dickson, *Management and the Worker: An Account of a Research Program Conducted by the Western Electric Company*, Hawthorne Works, Chicago (Cambridge, MA: Harvard University Press, 1939).

23. A.H. Maslow, *Motivation and Personality* (New York, NY: Harper & Brothers, 1954).

24. H.J. Leavitt, *Managerial Psychology: An Introduction to Individuals, Pairs, and Groups in Organizations* (Chicago, IL: University of Chicago Press, 1972), p. 182.

25. E.E. Lawler III, *Motivation in Work Organizations* (Monterey, CA: Brooks/Cole, 1973), pp. 17-18.

26. J.S. Adams, "Inequity in Social Exchange," in R.M. Steers and L.W. Porter, eds., *Motivation and Work Behavior* (New York, NY: McGraw-Hill, 1975), pp. 138-154.

27. D.A. Nadler, J.R. Hackman, and E.E. Lawler III, *Managing Organizational Behavior* (Boston, MA: Little, Brown, 1979), pp. 31-38.

28. Athos and Coffey, *Behavior in Organizations*, p. 154.

29. Ibid.

30. M. Alexis and C.Z. Wilson, *Organizational Decision Making* (Englewood Cliffs, NJ: Prentice Hall, 1967), p. 69.

31. Leavitt, *Managerial Psychology*, p. 25.

32. W. Scholz, *Communication in the Business Organization* (Englewood Cliffs, NJ: Prentice Hall, 1962), p. 32.

33. H. Koontz and C. O'Donnell, *Principles of Management: An Analysis of Managerial Functions* (New York, NY: McGraw-Hill, 1968), pp. 607-608.

34. T.R. Cheatham and K.V. Erickson, "Law Enforcement Communication Contacts," *Police Chief* 12, no. 3 (March 1975): 49.

35. P.F. Drucker, *The Practice of Management* (New York, NY: Harper & Brothers, 1954), p. 346.

Suggested Reading

Black, Donald J. *The Manners and Customs of the Police*. New York, NY: Academic Press, 1980.

Kappeler, Victor E., Richard D. Sluder, and Geoffrey P. Alpert. *Forces of Deviance: Understanding the Dark Side of Policing*, Second Edition. Prospect Heights, IL: Waveland, 1998.

Robbins, Stephen P. *Organizational Behavior*, Ninth Edition. Upper Saddle River, NJ: Prentice Hall, 2001.

Vila, Bryan, and Cynthia Morris. *The Role of Police in American Society: A Documentary History*. Westport, CT: Greenwood Press, 1999.

Zemke, Ron, Raines, Claire, and Bob Filipczak, *Generations at Work: Managing the Clash of Veterans, Boomers, Xers, and Nexters in Your Workforce*. New York, NY: American Management Association, 2000.

Groups in the Police Organization

9

Learning Objectives

- Differentiate between activities and interactions.

- Characterize emergent-system behavior in terms of positive and/or negative influence on the organization.

- Characterize the likelihood of an emergent system developing in an organization.

- Characterize the relationship between group cohesiveness and productivity.

- Identify the likelihood of conflict within and between groups.

In Chapter 8 we discussed the individual in the police organization, with a view toward gaining some understanding of the complexities of human behavior. We talked about such things as attitudes, roles, self-concept, motivation, perception, and communication. An understanding of these aspects of human behavior is critical for the police manager, whose whole job involves getting things done through other people in the organization. In this chapter we will continue the discussion of human behavior in organizational settings, but from a slightly different perspective. Here we will focus on groups rather than individuals, and their implications for organizational behavior and management. More specifically, we will describe the police organizational culture, how this impacts individual behavior, and what implications this might have for police managers.

The discipline of sociology, which is the study of groups and group behavior, characterizes humans as social beings and studies them as such. Sociologists generally reject the premise that humans are loners, rugged individualists who operate independently of their fellow human beings. Instead, sociologists argue that people form groups and that much of a person's identity is based on group membership. They claim that what people do and how they behave is influenced by the group or groups to which they belong. Beth

Hess, Elizabeth Markson and Peter Stein define sociology as "the study of human behaviour, group life, and of societies . . . of both the outside forces and the ways in which experience is given meaning by people in interaction with others."[1] Sociological studies provide tremendous insight into how groups affect individual behavior, a matter of great importance to anyone studying police organizations and the individuals who comprise them.

The organization itself is a group, a formal configuration to which managers, supervisors, and workers all belong. If the organization is large, there will be many subgroups within it, each subgroup comprising employees who also belong to the larger organization. Employees are likely to also belong to a number of outside groups that have nothing to do with the organization that employs them. Except for cloistered nuns and contemplative monks, this rule applies almost universally. In some cases, outside as well as inside groups influence employee behavior and thereby affect job performance and attitude.

Groups and subgroups tend to develop their own cultures that guide their members' behavior (see "Organizational Culture," p. 245). These cultures include such characteristics as norms, roles, and status.[2] Over time, some group members come to identify so strongly with the group that their individual values and beliefs change to fit those of the group. The desire to belong and be accepted by the group, in combination with peer pressure, can exert a strong conforming influence on individuals. This conforming group influence is probably at least as strong in police departments as in other types of organizations. Of primary consideration then is the influence of the police organization's culture and its effects on the functioning of the organization.

The police organizational culture is frequently referred to as the *police subculture*. Some authors contend that the police subculture dominates the organization and individual behavior within the organization. While in principle the notion of the police subculture makes sense from a sociological perspective, we feel that this term does not adequately depict what is going on in the police organization. Perhaps the police subculture is simply a vocational culture, created by virtue of the unique characteristics of police work. What may be more useful for examining group behavior in police organizations is a focus on subgroups in addition to the police subculture.

Subgroups may be formal or informal. Some formal subgroups are formed as a result of the functions of people working together, as in a particular unit such as the detective bureau or traffic division. Other subgroups are formed as a result of administrative organization, for example, those in management and supervisory positions, and those other workers in the organization. Informal subgroups that exist in the police organization are frequently socially based and sometimes affected by shift work. For example, a uniformed patrol shift that works days may frequently associate in the evenings not only as a means of social activity but also as a means of maintaining their work relationships outside of the workplace.

It is critical for the police manager to understand that subgroups, both formal and informal, are composed of individuals who have, or tend to develop, similar values and norms. This means that collectively these individuals can have a significant impact on the organization, either positive or negative. A police manager must be able to either subvert negative effects of subgroup behavior or harness positive effects of group behavior, whichever a situation merits.

Groups in Police Organizations

Because most police work is performed by officers working alone or in pairs, the need for direct cooperation in work performance is not as great in a police department as in, for example, an army battalion or a coal mine. Police do not typically do their work in groups except in special operations situations or major case investigations. However, police officers still tend to identify strongly with their entire group of fellow employees or with subgroups within the police organization, which again, may be formally or informally organized. These groups inevitably have significant effects on how individual police officers think and act, and thereby affect organizational behavior as well.

The 24-hour-a-day nature of the police business generally requires that patrol officers be divided into shifts or squads; these formal organizational subunits often become separate and influential groups. It is not unusual to discover that these patrol squads have distinct personalities, with differing values, beliefs, and norms that lead to substantially varying behaviors. Police departments large enough to have separate precincts or district stations also frequently find that a similar phenomenon develops. The same may be true of specialized units such as detective divisions or juvenile bureaus.

Organizational Culture

Every organizational culture is different for several reasons. First, what has worked repeatedly for one organization does not for another, so the basic assumptions differ. Second, an organization's culture is shaped by many factors, including, for example, the societal culture in which it resides; its technologies, markets, and competition; and the personality of its founder(s) or most dominant early leaders. Some organizational cultures are more distinctive than others. Some organizations have strong, unified, pervasive cultures, whereas others have weaker cultures; some organizational cultures are quite pervasive, whereas others have many subcultures in different functional or geographic areas.

Source: J. Steven Ott, *The Organizational Culture Perspective* (Pacific Grove, CA: Brooks/Cole, 1989), p. 3.

One of the authors observed dramatic subgroup differences in a police department that was called upon to handle numerous noise complaints, usually in the form of calls about loud parties. One patrol shift approached most of these calls from a negotiating standpoint, trying to convince partyers to be quieter, to move indoors, and to close down at a reasonable hour. The approach was friendly and relaxed. Another patrol shift took a much more legalistic and combative stance. At every opportunity, partyers were arrested for drinking in public or disorderly conduct. Partyers' cars were ticketed or towed whenever possible. The antagonism and conflict caused by this approach often resulted in additional arrests for interfering with a police officer and for resisting arrest. Pitched battles sometimes broke out.

The primary causes of this dramatic divergence between two patrol shifts in discharging their order-maintenance function were differences between the two shift commanders. One was a talker and negotiator who believed in resolving conflicts peacefully and informally. He trained and led his subordinates accordingly. The other shift commander took a much more legalistic approach, loved a good fight, and had little regard for young people having fun late at night. He selected shift members in his own image and rewarded them for emulating his behavior.

This extreme inconsistency between subgroups should not be permitted when it subjects the public to such unpredictable and capricious police behavior. Top police managers must be conscious of the different groups that exist or develop in their organizations. In particular, they need to be sensitive to the norms, values, and behaviors that are supported within the overall group and within subgroups (see "Police Culture"). Some differences between groups will be inevitable, as will be differences between group norms and official departmental values and policies. Harmful conflicts between groups must be avoided, and everything possible should be done to encourage group norms that support rather than impede the organization's accomplishment of its goals and mission.

Perhaps the two most common subgroups in police organizations are "street cops" and "management cops."[3] Sharp divisions between workers and management are common in many organizations, but the cleavage is especially deep in police departments. This is partly because of the skepticism and cynicism that are common traits among police organization members—police officers tend to be cynical toward their bosses just as they are cynical toward the courts, politicians, and just about everyone else. Also, though, a significant part of police management's role is to control the exercise of authority by police officers. This control focus of management collides directly with both officers' desires for autonomy and their beliefs about what it takes to do effective police work. So management and officers often feel as though they are pitted against each other not only in the typical labor/management sense but also in the effort to reduce crime and disorder. This becomes particularly divisive whenever officers perceive management controls as threatening their safety out on the streets.

Another division between subgroups in modern policing often occurs in departments that have specialist officers or units implementing community policing.[4] These specialists frequently resent the lack of cooperation they get from other officers in the organization. Even more commonly, other officers deride these specialists as "kiddie cops" and complain that COP officers fail to do their share of work by handling calls and taking enforcement action. To some degree, this conflict is typical of that surrounding many types of specialization. It is exacerbated, however, by the fact that many traditionalist police officers do not believe that community policing is an effective or appropriate strategy. Thus, this particular split between policing subgroups reflects some fundamental disagreements about the police mission, what works in policing, and the future of police work. With increasing acceptance of COP and the adoption of the principles by the entire organization versus a small unit or individual officers, this division is less prevalent today.

Other subgroups in police organizations are often defined by gender, race, and ethnicity. Because female police officers are still relatively few in number and because they frequently encounter discrimination and harassment within police departments,[5] the formation of subgroups is not surprising. In fact, the degree to which policewomen seem integrated within other groups, such as patrol squads or the "street cop" group generally, is more surprising and a testament to the practical necessity in policing of obtaining acceptance by one's peers. The same can be said for racial and ethnic minority groups within police agencies. Male members of these groups have not faced the "masculinity tests" that have confronted policewomen, but they have often had to deal with prejudice and discrimination.

Elements of Behavior in Groups

One highly respected sociological theorist, George C. Homans, developed a systems theory of groups that is solidly based on observable behavior and readily applicable to groups within organizations.[6] His theoretical approach is compatible with our viewpoint on the systems approach to organization and management. Homans found that everyday behavior can be classified in terms of three elementary forms: activities, sentiments, and interactions.

Activities are what people do alone. Activities also include what people do with other people when reaction or feedback from these other people is nonexistent or at least not an important aspect of the activity. Observable activities might include walking, writing, sewing, typing, sleeping, stamp collecting, shaving, praying, bicycling, woodworking, bird watching, swimming, and jogging. These behaviors would be classified as activities whether the person engaged in them alone or with other people whose presence did not influence his or her behavior through reaction or feedback. Another example of an activity is the lecture method of teaching, in which the instructor presents information without allowing discussion or questions.

People in police organizations perform a wide variety of activities. Operational duties such as "shaking doors" to see if they are secure, administrative duties such as counting parking revenue, and many other police organizational functions are essentially activities. They are activities because the reaction of others is not ordinarily an integral part of these duties.

Sentiments are feelings and beliefs and are observable in the sense that they are expressed directly or indirectly in the statements and behavior of the individual. They include attitudes, roles, self-concept, and motivation, which were all discussed in the last chapter. Observable sentiments might include attitudes toward work and supervisors; feelings of alienation, anger, sadness, satisfaction, friendship, pity, embarrassment, lust, understanding, sympathy, and contrition; and religious beliefs. Everyone harbors his or her own sentiments, not all of which are clearly observable. This is no less true in the police organization than in any other.

Some observers make a distinction between sentiments that people will articulate or admit to, calling them beliefs and values, and underlying assumptions that truly guide behavior whether people are aware of them or not.[7] Police officers, for example, may consciously believe in due process of law but actually operate on the basis of an underlying assumption that offenders need to be punished no matter what the courts might decide. Alternatively, officers might espouse the view that anybody who works any harder than they absolutely have to is a fool, while they in fact act on a deeper belief in the value of hard work and the obligation to do one's best at all times.

Interaction is activity among and between people; it is the actions people take toward, for, and with other people wherein the resulting reactions of other people provide feedback information that becomes a part of the ongoing behavior. Some observable interactions are making love, playing basketball, riding a tandem bicycle, participating in a conversation, taking part in a committee meeting, attending a cocktail party, and leading a parent-teacher discussion group. In each case, the individual's behavior is necessarily directed toward one or more other persons, forcing some response that becomes a factor in the individual's continuing behavior. Note that the substantive behaviors in activities and interactions can be essentially the same. For example, one can play basketball with a group in such a way that it is an activity, by ignoring the presence of others and refusing to interact. So it is not really the behavior as such but the manner in which it is "enacted" that differentiates activities from interactions.

Police work and police organizational behavior are replete with interaction. Patrol officers regularly interact with their supervisors, other patrol officers, dispatchers, crime victims, witnesses, suspects, traffic violators, and numerous other people. Police managers interact with their subordinates, peers, superiors, and with various representatives of the general public. Records clerks interact with people who want public information (such as lawyers, employers, and traffic accident victims), police officers who want information, those who supply information, and their supervisors. Interaction is an extremely common mode of behavior in most organizations, particularly in those reliant on information, such as police departments.

Police Culture

Culture covers a lot of intellectual and emotional territory. Police organizational structures, policies, behaviors, arrest patterns, corruption, education, training practices, attitudes toward suspects and citizens, forms of patrol, and all other areas of police work—the whole ball of wax—are witnessed and practiced through the lens of culture. All areas of police work have meaning of some kind to cops, and as every reformer and chief who has sought to change any organization knows, these meanings tend to bind together in sentiments and values impossible to analytically separate and individually change.

Carried in the minds of street cops who work together, culture enables a wide variety of police activities to link together in ways that are, though not systematic, sensible enough to give meanings to different kinds of situations in which cops find themselves. Organizational traditions are customary ways of doing things, and they take on common-sense value that cannot be changed easily or frivolously. This is why many insiders say that efforts to change the police, whether the change concerns traditional ideas of patrol, getting officers to talk about corrupt fellow officers, even changing the type of weapons they carry, must first win the hearts and minds of its officers. Until advocates of police change recognize the importance of culture, they will continue to be as surprised as they have been for the past 100 years at the profound limitations of reform efforts to yield real and enduring changes.

Source: John P. Crank, *Understanding Police Culture* (Cincinnati, OH: Anderson, 1998), p. 6.

The elements of behavior in groups, then, are activities, sentiments, and interactions. An activity is an acted-out behavior that ignores other people and is conducted without benefit of reaction or feedback. A sentiment is an attitude that is directly expressed or one that can be indirectly inferred from observable behavior. An interaction is an acted-out behavior that involves more than one person, with the reaction of one person to the behavior of another influencing subsequent behavior. In Homans's view, all aspects of behavior in groups can be classified in terms of these three behavioral elements.

Basic Aspects of the Group Social System

The elements of behavior in groups just discussed use the individual as the frame of reference. Individual behavior was classified in terms of the three elements. Building on these, we can identify three basic aspects of the group social system: the required system, the personal system, and the emergent system.[8] These aspects of the group social system look at behavior in groups from the point of view of the group.

The *required system* is composed of activities, sentiments, and interactions that are necessary for group survival. This refers essentially to the mandates of the job itself and to the required tasks that must be performed in order for the job to be productive and remain worthwhile and viable. Part of the required system of a police organization, for example, includes activities such as writing reports and retrieving records, sentiments such as believing in the concept of due process of law, and interactions such as questioning witnesses and settling disputes. If the police system falls short in any aspect of the required system, its chances of accomplishing its goals and objectives are severely diminished.

The *personal system* comprises all of the personal predispositions that members of an organization bring to the workplace. However much management would like its employees to be blank slates or automatons, waiting to be programmed for the job at hand, in the real world people come already equipped with deeply entrenched ideas, expectations, values, beliefs, attitudes, prejudices, and feelings. All of these elements of the personal system have an important, though imprecise, influence on the behavior of people at work in organizations. In police organizations, for example, many members have in their personal systems deep ethnic, religious, and racial prejudices and attitudes that often run counter to the stated policies and legal requirements of the organization for which they work. Although their prejudices and attitudes may not always be reflected in their official behavior, they nonetheless become a factor in the group social system.

The *emergent system* is composed of the total of the behavior in the group setting that is not required for the group's survival. It is the result of the collision that occurs when the personal system impinges on the required system. The personal needs of the members of an organization, as expressed by their ideas, feelings, and values, are rarely satisfied within the purely job-related activities and interactions of the required system. While at work, people are usually not content with just silently, steadily working. Their personal systems make them want to talk, take breaks, work slowly sometimes and quickly other times, and behave in many other ways that are not strictly in accordance with the required system.

Emergent-system behavior is sometimes counterproductive to the pursuit of organizational goals and objectives (see "Peer-Group Pressure and Police Corruption," p. 251). In a police organization, for example, the emergent activity of "cooping" (sleeping on the job), the emergent sentiment that free restaurant food is a fringe benefit of the police officer's job, and the emergent interaction of addressing ethnic-group members with derogatory slurs all will have a negative impact on organizational effectiveness. These are all behaviors not demanded by the required system, which makes them emergent, and by their nature they retard the organization's attainment of its goals and objectives.

There are two important considerations about the emergent system. First, its development is inevitable. Given human nature and the complexities of individuals, no organization can exercise the degree of control necessary to eliminate it. Second, the emergent system is not necessarily the negative influence that the examples above might suggest. Emergent interaction, for example, might result in improvements in the required system. Frequently, worthwhile and profitable suggestions are received by management from members of the organization who are not generally encouraged or required to contribute to the organization beyond their own narrow scopes of interest. An individual with special knowledge or insight, a commitment to efficiency and effectiveness, and a dedication to the organization might very well make a contribution in the form of emergent interaction that benefits the required system and the organization as a whole.

Peer-Group Pressure and Police Corruption

Many of the committees investigating police corruption of the past described very vividly how officers were socialized into corrupt practices, in other words, how they responded to peer pressure to become corrupt. Therefore, the essence of the problem in controlling and preventing police corruption involves developing peer group attitudes that are intolerant of corruption. To be sure, the organization must still have an internal affairs unit and other organizational procedures which will combine with peer group pressure to reinforce the concept that corruption within the organization will not be tolerated. However, the most important factor in the prevention of police corruption will be the rank-and-file attitude of police officers' condemning corruption as being wrong and contrary to their own code of behavior.

Source: Joseph D. McNamara, "The Impact of Bureaucracy on Attempts to Prevent Police Corruption," in Arthur Niederhoffer and Abraham S. Blumberg, *The Ambivalent Force: Perspectives on Police*, Second Edition (Hinsdale, IL: Dryden, 1976), p. 155.

As an example of emergent behavior that is not necessarily counterproductive, one of the authors, while a police patrol officer, submitted to his chief a proposal for an antiburglary program. This was emergent behavior because the author's assignment was to the patrol division, with no planning or program-development responsibilities. The chief responded cordially that the proposed program was a good one but that it would never work because of public apathy. A year later, the chief asked the author and another patrol officer to explore outside funding possibilities for an antiburglary program he was devising, and another year later the program was initiated with federal funding. The chief's antiburglary program looked quite familiar to the author. The emergent behavior of submitting the program proposal had resulted in an innovative program that contributed to the organization's attainment of its goals and objectives. The route may have been circuitous, but the result was positive.

Emergent System Development

The emergent system is composed of all of the behavior in the group or organization that is not necessitated by the required system. It is all the behavior, then, that is not required in getting the work done and in ensuring the survival of the group. Because these activities, sentiments, and interactions of the emergent system are "extras" and are not required, they are not taught in training or addressed in general-orders manuals. Individually, they are brought to the workplace by the people employed there. Collectively, in terms of the emergent system of the group, these behaviors develop over time. This development of the group emergent system can be described in terms of three identifiable characteristics: elaboration, differentiation, and standardization.[9]

Elaboration is the initial stage of development of the emergent system; members of the group develop activities, sentiments, and interactions not mandated by the required system. This process is generated, as previously mentioned, by the inability of the required system to satisfy all of the personal needs of the members of the group as expressed by their ideas and values.

Imagine a police recruit training class, for example. On their first day of training the recruits do not know one another, are in a strange environment where the rules are unknown, and are very eager to impress. In the first session of the training class an instructor will probably advise the recruits of the procedures and rules and regulations by which they will be expected to abide. These will essentially constitute the required system of the training class. Gradually, the recruits will develop additional behaviors. Some may cheat on exams. Especially in physical or firearms training, some recruits who are proficient may give unrequired assistance to other recruits who are having a difficult time. These and many other kinds of behaviors may develop even though the required system does not mandate them.

Differentiation refers to the process whereby the activities, sentiments, and interactions of the emergent system become valued differently. Some behavior is seen as furthering the formal and informal interests of the group; this behavior is highly valued. Other behavior is perceived as hindering the formal and informal interest of the group; as might be expected, this behavior is looked on as being objectionable and is likely to be suppressed.

In our example about recruit training, it is easy to imagine differentiation following the elaboration of emergent-system behaviors. Talking to instructors during breaks is often perceived as furthering individual but not group interests; as a result, the recruit class might come to value this behavior negatively, so recruits who engaged in it would be labeled as "apple polishers" or worse, and the behavior would be held against them. On the other hand, if a majority of the recruits were genuinely apprehensive about exams, cheating might come to be valued highly, because many would participate in it and gain an advantage. Thus, cheating could be seen as contributing to group interests.

Differentiation also includes the rank relationships between and among people in the group, the so-called pecking order. Rank within the emergent system may or may not be associated with formal rank in the required system of the organization. A police union leader, for example, may hold high rank in the emergent system and low rank in the required system. Similarly, status in the police recruit training class may or may not be related to formal success on exams.

While the activities, sentiments, and interactions of the emergent system are being differentiated according to their perceived value to the group, *standardization* is also occurring. As various behaviors are becoming identified as having value, most group members will tend to gravitate toward those behaviors. Norms develop in the emergent system that give group members clues and provide them with guidelines on which to base their behavior in certain situations—for example, norms develop concerning output limitations. In a police organization, the emergent system might adopt a norm that regulates the number of moving violation citations (traffic tickets) issued by patrol officers during a given period. This norm would be adopted on the basis of experience; it would satisfy the minimum standards of the required system, and it would not put a particularly heavy burden on any member of the group.

Why would such a norm develop? Without it, different officers might be writing widely varying numbers of tickets. Management would see that some officers were writing many tickets and would want to know why other officers were writing so few. Management might penalize those who wrote tickets infrequently and come to expect all officers to write as many as were written by the zealous officers. Output limitation norms thus develop. Pressure is brought to bear on the zealous ticket writers and the absolute goldbricks, encouraging each type to adhere more closely to the group norm. If they fail to conform, in all likelihood they will be ostracized by the group, which would have the effect of making their work lives very difficult. This is particularly true in policing, where the support and assistance of fellow workers can be lifesaving. As a result, emergent systems in police organizations tend to have strong norms. It is accurate to say that emergent-system standardization is well developed in most police organizations.

In his study of police discretion, Michael K. Brown found that the two core values in the police emergent system were loyalty and individualism.[10] Police officers demand loyalty from one another, sometimes to the extreme of lying to cover up illegal or improper actions. In return for accepting the value of loyalty, officers are granted considerable leeway by their peers in the performance of their duties. Through the processes of elaboration, differentiation, and standardization, these two values attained high standing in the police emergent system.

The pressure on police officers to conform to emergent system norms and values can be intense.[11] The physical well-being of police officers sometimes depends on prompt assistance from fellow officers; this provides a strong motive to conform to the emergent system in order to be accepted and thus entitled to unswerving loyalty and immediate backup assistance. Similarly, officers gain psychological benefits from acceptance into the emergent-system culture. Officers who fail to adopt important emergent-system norms and values are often ostracized, especially if the norms and values are seriously deviant. Thus, the officer who refuses to sleep or drink on duty is not likely to be accepted into an emergent system that supports such behavior and may be targeted for harassment or worse if he or she cannot be trusted to cover up peer deviance. The celebrated case of New York police officer Frank Serpico dramatically illustrated the potential consequences of refusing to conform to emergent system norms.[12] The behavior of officers in the highly publicized brutality cases in Los Angeles and New York in recent years, whether in terms of officer participation in beatings or simply standing by and later helping to cover up such acts, is further evidence of the influence of peer pressure to conform to the norms and values of the police group culture.

Consequences of the Emergent System

We have noted that the development of the emergent system in any organization or group is inevitable and that the emergent system can have both positive and negative effects. In addition, we have discussed the process of emergent-system development, which includes elaboration, differentiation, and standardization. Next, we will mention three important consequences of the development of the emergent system that are of concern to administrators. As pointed out by Anthony Athos and Robert Coffey, these consequences are productivity, satisfaction, and growth.[13]

Productivity is the output of the labor contributed by members of the organization. It involves both the quality and the quantity of the services that the organization is in business to provide. It should be obvious that productivity is the basic concern of the required system and that it is greatly influenced by the emergent system. As mentioned earlier, the emergent system frequently develops norms of output limitation; these often compete directly with the productivity standards of the required system. Other emergent-system norms, such as those supporting sleeping on duty, accepting bribes, or brutalizing prisoners, also reduce the efficiency and effectiveness of the police organization. Conversely, activities, sentiments, and interactions spawned by the emergent system can positively contribute to productivity, as in the case of officers who voluntarily create a police athletic league or lead a drive to collect food for the needy at Christmastime.

Satisfaction involves how the members of the group feel about their work, the personal relationships and interactions they experience at work, and the rewards and costs associated with their group membership. Satisfaction depends on the makeup of the personal system of the group member, his or her position in the required system and rank in the emergent system, and the prevailing norms of the emergent system, among other things.

Emergent groups within organizations can have complicated effects on satisfaction. On one hand, membership in such groups can provide employees with satisfying experiences, thus enriching their organizational lives. On the other hand, if the emergent group is in conflict with other subgroups or with management, satisfaction can suffer. This seems to happen particularly often in police organizations, where morale always seems to be low. Officers will typically report general satisfaction with their work and their colleagues but express complaints about management, working conditions, politicians, and the community. Often, these complaints seem to be expressions of group sentiments more than strongly held individual views.

Growth involves both individual group members and the group social system. It implies change for the better. Individuals who cease to grow and groups that become stagnant experience a decline in creativity, enthusiasm, fresh ideas, and commitment. Growth for the individual means learning new concepts, experiencing new ideas, confronting new situations, meeting new people, perfecting skills, and continuing in the process of maturation. Growth for the group means growth for its members, increases in physical size, continued development of the required system, and improvements in productivity and satisfaction.

Successful administrators must be concerned about all three of these consequences. If they neglect productivity, the primary concern of the required system, it is impossible for the organization to achieve its goals and objectives. If they neglect satisfaction, the emergent system will provide it, often to the detriment of productivity, through its own activities, sentiments, interactions, ranks, and norms, which may not support the organizational culture. If they neglect growth, their organizations will not be prepared to deal with the changes that the future is sure to bring.

These concerns are critical for the police manager, who must constantly monitor productivity, especially in these times of limited resources. In doing so, however, the manager cannot ignore the matter of satisfaction. We all know of wonderful programs and ideas, in policing and other pursuits, that were sabotaged on implementation by the workers who were expected to put the ideas into action. This kind of failure is often the result of single-minded attention to productivity and inattention to satisfaction. By the same token, satisfaction is not a guarantee of high productivity. Police managers must maintain a strong concern for both at the same time—a difficult (but not impossible) task.[14] They must also show an interest in individual and group growth. They can do this by encouraging comment and criticism, strongly supporting education and training, and demonstrating a willingness to try different approaches to problem solving and decisionmaking.

A study of the emergent system in an organization can provide insight into the caliber and climate of its management. If the emergent system is clearly at odds with the required system, as demonstrated by strong output-limitation norms, highly divergent rank structures, and hostile management-employee relations, it is likely that management is concerned solely about productivity, to the exclusion of growth and satisfaction. If, on the other hand, the emergent and required systems are in complete harmony (an indication that management is neglecting the mandates of the required system), productivity is likely to be extremely low. At both extremes, severe management problems are likely. To avoid these kinds of situations and problems, the manager must learn to emphasize productivity, satisfaction, and growth simultaneously. Again, this is not a simple matter, but it is the ideal toward which managers must strive.

Group Cohesiveness and Productivity

It is often assumed, incorrectly, that there is a positive relationship between group cohesiveness and productivity. Empirical research has consistently shown that no such relationship exists.[15] Some cohesive groups are productive, whereas others are not; some loosely knit groups are productive, whereas others are not.

Cohesiveness refers to the feelings of closeness and camaraderie that bind the members of a group together. It is the glue that holds the people of an organization together, working in the common interest. Cohesiveness is demonstrated by how well the group members get along with one another, how strongly they identify with the group, and the extent to which the norms of the group are accepted and followed. Two key indicators of cohesiveness within an organization are employee turnover and attendance. To some extent, cohesiveness is related to satisfaction; the more cohesive groups are, the more their members tend to be satisfied.

The relationship between cohesiveness and productivity depends on the similarity between the goals and objectives of the required system and those of the emergent system. If the goals are divergent, then cohesiveness within the group will tend to support the emergent system and its output limitation norms; this inevitably results in a curtailment of productivity (see "Cohesiveness and Performance," p. 257). If the goals of the emergent and required systems are similar, however, a lack of cohesiveness within the group will not necessarily hinder productivity.

The complexity of the relationship among cohesiveness, satisfaction, and productivity can certainly be found in police organizations. "Poor morale" has to be one of the most commonly identified characteristics of police agencies.[16] Sometimes this poor morale, or low job satisfaction, is accompanied by a high degree of cohesiveness among street-level officers, reflecting conflict with management, the courts, or the public. In some police departments the opposite is so: poor morale is associated with little or no cohesiveness among street-level police officers. To take the possibilities a step further, some police organizations with low morale are nevertheless productive and effective, while others are inefficient and unprofessional. Just as with the baseball examples, the relationships that exist among cohesiveness, satisfaction, and productivity are not as straightforward as might be expected.

Cohesiveness and Performance

For most urban police recruits, the first real contact with the police subculture occurs at the academy. Surrounded by forty to fifty contemporaries, the recruit is introduced to the harsh and often arbitrary discipline of the organization. Absolute obedience to departmental rules, rigorous physical training, dull lectures devoted to various technical aspects of the organization and a ritualistic concern for detail characterize the academy. Only the recruit's classmates aid his struggle to avoid punishments and provide him an outlet from the long days.

The main result of such stress training is that the recruit soon learns it is his peer group rather than the "brass" which will support him and which he, in turn, must support. For example, the newcomers adopt covering tactics to shield the tardy colleague, develop cribbing techniques to pass exams and become proficient at constructing consensual ad hoc explanations of a fellow-recruit's mistake. Furthermore, the long hours, new friends and ordeal aspects of the recruit school serve to detach the newcomer from his old attitudes and acquaintances. In short, the academy impresses upon the recruit that he must now identify with a new group: his fellow officers.

Source: John Van Maanen, "Observations on the Making of Policemen," in Peter K. Manning and John Van Maanen, eds., *Policing: A View from the Street* (New York, NY: Random House, 1978), pp. 296, 299.

Varieties of Intergroup Behavior

In addition to the relationships that exist between and among individual members of a group, a study of groups would be incomplete if it did not include the relationships between and among groups themselves. These relationships can run the gamut from perfect cooperation to bitter conflict. There are three basic factors involved in this spectrum of intergroup behavior: cooperation, competition, and conflict.

Cooperation refers to situations in which groups involved with one another lend assistance whenever needed, share information, and generally work together toward a common goal. Cooperation allows the groups to be more productive and effective than they would be if they worked alone. Cooperation, however, is not always a positive factor and does not always provide the spark that ignites groups to superior performance. Athos and Coffey note that cooperation can lead to contentment and that "unlike contented cows, contented groups do not always achieve the best possible results."[17] Cooperation, then, can lead to groups becoming lethargic and can negatively affect group productivity.

Competition is a factor that fits into the American creed somewhere between Kansas in August and blueberry pie. It is a cherished American value and the basis of the American economic system. It is understood that groups in competition vie with one another in order to achieve greater productivity, win, or accumulate greater portions of available resources. In some instances, competition can spur groups on to increased effort. On the other hand, the desire to win and the fear of losing can produce harmful effects among the competing groups. The ends may come to be seen as justifying the means, for example, and the fear of failure may prevent some groups from entering the competition at all.

Conflict occurs as the result of competition for limited resources and rewards. It also arises between and among groups with incompatible goals and objectives. Groups in conflict tend to become more internally cohesive, distrust one another, characterize themselves positively in every respect, and stereotype competing groups as negative in every respect. Edgar F. Huse and James L. Bowditch point out that such competition and conflict can be useful only in a clear win/lose situation in which the groups involved are independent of one another, such as in the case of two advertising agencies competing for a particular account.[18] Where the groups involved are interdependent, as are two divisions of one organization, the winning group will be adversely affected by the failure of the losing group. In such an instance, victory will always be accompanied by defeat.

Intergroup behavior involving police organizations is rarely of a win/lose variety, because police organizations are independent of very few groups in society. Even in dealing with organized criminal groups, a "victory" for the police would be accompanied by losses. Useful sources of information would be eliminated, known patterns of criminal activity would be replaced by more unpredictable patterns, and some controls on particular types of criminal activity would be removed.

Police organizations are even more interdependent with more legitimate groups in society. Police competition for funds with other criminal justice agencies and social service agencies illustrates this. If the police were to "win" the competition with these other organizations for the limited resources available, it would certainly be a defeat for them in the long run.

The criminal justice system, except for the police, would be unable to operate efficiently or effectively, so suspected criminals would not be convicted, restrained, reformed, rehabilitated, or reintegrated into society in any meaningful manner. Moreover, the more general social service system would be unable to serve its clientele in a fashion designed to solve human problems. As a result, the social climate and the criminal justice system would deteriorate, causing severe problems for the police, all because they "won" the competition for resources.

These two examples are not meant to imply that the police should leave organized crime alone and turn their budgets over to other organizations. They are simply offered as examples of the possible consequences of an all-out competitive approach in a highly interdependent society. With respect to the organized crime illustration, the potential losses may be negligible when compared to the benefits of eliminating the problems. With respect to the other criminal justice and social service organizations, a healthy mixture of competition and cooperation may be a preferred approach to the issue of resource allocation. The same can be said for competition among different law enforcement agencies. Several agencies may be investigating related crimes, for example; some competition can be useful, but not if it prevents these agencies from cooperating and sharing information needed to solve crimes. The FBI was notorious for many years in successfully seeking information from local police agencies and using that information to enhance its own image while giving little or no information and cooperation in return.[19] Similarly, various law enforcement agencies have competed viciously over the years to control and dominate drug enforcement efforts.

The critical importance of cooperation among police agencies is perhaps best illustrated by the phenomenon of serial murder. Often, each of a serial murderer's crimes is committed in a different jurisdiction, sometimes spanning states or even the entire country. Without extensive cooperation among police agencies, each department might perceive its murder case as an isolated incident and never recognize the pattern among the multiple offenses. Only through cooperation would any of the agencies have a reasonable chance of identifying and apprehending the murderer. Steven A. Egger has referred to the traditional failure of police departments to foster such cooperation as *linkage blindness*.[20] The Violent Criminal Apprehension Program coordinated by the FBI[21] and various regional investigative programs[22] is a current effort to reduce linkage blindness and encourage cooperation in the investigation of serial crime. In light of recent terrorist activities, too, the need for coordination among law enforcement agencies has become even more apparent and will likely increase in the coming years.

One unfortunate by-product of competition is that relations among law enforcement agencies can degenerate into hostile conflict. In one recent instance, a state police agency investigated a municipal police department for suspected violations of automatic weapons laws. The municipal police chief was so enraged by this intrusion that he ordered his officers to ticket any illegally parked state police cars they observed, regardless of circumstances; he also forbade any cooperation with the state agency. This occurred in a rural area, where the state police were an important law enforcement presence, and between agencies that ordinarily work quite closely together.

Intergroup behavior involving groups within police organizations is also rarely of a win/lose variety. Competition to solve a criminal case may lead to an unwillingness to share information between, for example, the patrol and detective divisions. Each wants so badly to solve the case personally that everyone loses sight of organizational goals and objectives. In such a situation the pooling of information might well lead to an early solution, but the fear of not getting credit often prevents such cooperation. It is still possible, though, for the competitive atmosphere to spur investigative efforts. The police manager must attempt to maintain a healthy balance between competition and cooperation.

Production competition among groups within a police department is common. For example, patrol squads sometimes compete for numbers of arrests or tickets issued. This competition can emanate from patrol officers themselves but more frequently results from pressure exerted by commanders who are evaluated in terms of their squads' productivity. In general, such production competition can be healthy and can increase productivity. However, in the police context, an administrator has to be careful when pressuring officers to produce tickets, arrests, or other quantitative indicators. Situations have occurred in which police officers have made "technical" arrests, most often bad arrests, in order to satisfy their superiors. The same can be said for traffic tickets. The police administrator must attach a qualitative dimension to any quantitative productivity pressure in order to avoid citizen harassment and the deprivation of personal rights all in the name of production competition.

Conflict among groups is inevitable. This includes conflict among groups in a single organization (see "Perception and Group Conflict"). The challenge for the administrator is to manage conflict so as to minimize its negative consequences. The best way to accomplish this is to keep conflict out in the open, attempt to reduce stereotyping, move people internally on a frequent basis from group to group, actively seek input on conflict resolution from everyone involved, encourage group interaction, and seek participation from the members of individual groups on the establishment of organizational goals and objectives.[23] In other words, attempt to manage conflict by actively promoting cohesiveness in the required system.

Summary

It is impossible to understand human behavior without taking into consideration the influence of groups on people. Human behavior can be classified in terms of activities, sentiments, and interactions. The interdependence of these elements of behavior is reflected in the group social system, which is made up of the required, personal, and emergent systems. The emergent system develops because of the inability of the required system to satisfy all of the personal needs of group members. The development of the emergent system involves three identifiable characteristics: elaboration, differentiation, and standardization. The relationship between the required and emergent systems, and particularly the degree of congruence between their respective goals and objectives, influences productivity, satisfaction, and growth as well as the cohesiveness of the group. Group cohesiveness is also influenced by intergroup relations, which are characterized by cooperation, competition, and conflict.

The police administrator must understand the concepts presented in this chapter as well as their implications for the police organization in order to work successfully with the various groups that comprise the police department and the rest of society.

Discussion Questions

1. Think about the classroom situation in terms of group characteristics. What are the required and emergent systems?

2. In the text we argue that the influence of the emergent system on the organization can be either positive or negative. What is the influence of the emergent system in the classroom?

3. In your school and/or work career, have you encountered output-limitation norms? In what situation? How did you react to them? How would you react as a manager?

4. Describe some groups with which you are familiar in terms of their cohesiveness. Then assess their productivity. What seems to be the relationship between cohesiveness and productivity in these groups?

5. In the text we claim that conflict in organizations is inevitable. As a manager, how would you deal with it?

Cases

This chapter introduced a number of concepts pertaining to group behavior in police organizations. These concepts should prove useful for understanding the situations presented in "Case 1: The Energetic Chief" and "Case 3: The Yuletide Remembrance," at the back of this text. In addition, you might want to examine "Case 5: Cod Bay," "Case 6: Tulane City," and "Case 7: Rixton" from the perspective of police culture and values.

Notes

1. B.B. Hess, E.W. Markson, and P.J. Stein, *Sociology*, Third Edition (New York, NY: Macmillan, 1988), p. 3.

2. S.P. Robbins, *Organizational Behavior: Concepts, Controversies, and Applications*, Third Edition (Englewood Cliffs, NJ: Prentice Hall, 1986), pp. 169-199.

3. E. Reuss-Ianni, *Two Cultures of Policing: Street Cops and Management Cops* (New Brunswick, NJ: Transaction, 1983).

4. E.F. McGarrell, E. Langston, and D. Richardson, "Implementation Issues: The Specialized Unit or Department-Wide Community Policing?" in Q.C. Thurman and E.F. McGarrell, eds., *Community Policing in a Rural Setting* (Cincinnati, OH: Anderson, 1997), pp. 59-64.

5. D.C. Hale and S.M. Wyland, "Dragons and Dinosaurs: The Plight of Patrol Women," in L.K. Gaines and G.W. Cordner, eds., *Policing Perspectives: An Anthology* (Los Angeles, CA: Roxbury, 1999), pp. 450-458.

6. G.C. Homans, *The Human Group* (New York, NY: Harcourt, 1950).

7. J.S. Ott, *The Organizational Culture Perspective* (Pacific Grove, CA: Brooks/Cole, 1989), p. 44.

8. A.G. Athos and R.E. Coffey, *Behavior in Organizations: A Multidimensional View* (Englewood Cliffs, NJ: Prentice Hall, 1968).

9. Homans, *Human Group*.

10. M.K. Brown, *Working the Street: Police Discretion and the Dilemmas of Reform* (New York, NY: Russell Sage Foundation, 1981), pp. 82-86.

11. S.F. Coleman, *Street Cops* (Salem, WI: Sheffield, 1986), pp. 201-212.

12. P. Maas, *Serpico* (New York, NY: Bantam, 1972).

13. Athos and Coffey, *Behavior in Organizations*.

14. R. Blake and J.S. Mouton, *The New Managerial Grid* (Houston, TX: Gulf, 1978).

15. C.R. Shepherd, *Small Groups; Some Sociological Perspectives* (San Francisco, CA: Chandler, 1964), pp. 85-96.

16. V. Franz and D.M. Jones, "Perceptions of Organizational Performance in Suburban Police Departments: A Critique of the Military Model," *Journal of Police Science and Administration* 15, no. 2 (June 1987): 153-161.

17. Athos and Coffey, *Behavior in Organizations*, p. 207.

18. E.F. Huse and J.L. Bowditch, *Behavior in Organizations: A Systems Approach to Managing*, Second Edition (Reading, MA: Addison-Wesley, 1977), pp. 203-204.

19. J.Q. Wilson, *The Investigators: Managing FBI and Narcotics Agents* (New York, NY: Basic, 1978).

20. S.A. Egger, "A Working Definition of Serial Murder and the Reduction of Linkage Blindness," *Journal of Police Science and Administration* 12, no. 3 (September 1984): 348-357.

21. J.B. Howlett, K.A. Hanfland, and R.K. Ressler, "The Violent Criminal Apprehension Program (VICAP): A Progress Report," *FBI Law Enforcement Bulletin* (December 1986): 14-22.

22. P.R. Brooks, M.J. Devine, T.J. Green, B.L. Hart, and M.D. Moore, "Serial Murder: A Criminal Justice Response," *Police Chief* (June 1987): 37-45.

23. Huse and Bowditch, *Behavior in Organizations*, pp. 210-213.

Suggested Reading

Crank, John P. *Understanding Police Culture*. Cincinnati, OH: Anderson, 1998.

Drummond, Douglas S. *Police Culture*. Beverly Hills, CA: Sage, 1976.

Jaffee, David. *Organization Theory: Tension and Change*. Boston, MA: McGraw-Hill, 2001.

Reuss-Ianni, Elizabeth. *Two Cultures of Policing: Street Cops and Management Cops*. New Brunswick, NJ: Transaction, 1983.

Roberg, Roy, John Crank, and Jack Kuykendall. *Police and Society*, Second Edition. Los Angeles, CA: Roxbury, 2000.

Leadership in the Police Organization

10

Learning Objectives

- Differentiate among the terms *manager*, *formal leader*, and *complete leader*.

- Identify the three basic leadership functions.

- Cite the factor that separates managers from leaders.

- Cite the five sources of influence.

- Characterize the police manager's access to reward power.

- Cite five general styles of leadership.

- Cite the findings of studies that attempted to identify the personality traits and other personal characteristics that separate good leaders from bad ones.

- Characterize Fiedler's situational model of effective leadership.

- Distinguish between the managerial grid and Hersey and Blanchard's situational theory of leadership.

- Describe emotional intelligence as it might be applied to policing.

- Identify some of the environmental factors that constrain the police leader.

Leadership is a difficult concept to define. To some, leadership is a science that can be mastered through study and practice. Others regard it as an art and maintain that leaders are born, not made. Some believe that leaders are respected and admired by their followers. Others believe that they are feared. It is not uncommon for people to believe that real leaders can be identified by their abilities to take charge in all situations. Others believe that leadership talents pertain only to certain groups and that different group members will emerge in leadership roles in different situations in accordance with formal credentials, proven expertise, charisma, and range of contacts.

None of these perceptions of leadership is completely right or completely wrong. Because leadership involves a complex combination of activities and behaviors,[1] it is not easily defined, described, or categorized. Any attempt to understand what a leader is must focus on functions, sources, styles, and theories of leadership, the topics discussed in this chapter.

Police Managers and Police Leaders

[A] police administrator must be fully aware of the sensitive and delicate nature of the police function . . . he must attach a high value to protecting constitutional guarantees of free speech, due process, and freedom from unreasonable search and seizure. He must fully appreciate the need for various systems to assure accountability on the part of the police to the body politic. He must be knowledgeable regarding the legislative process, the functioning of the criminal justice system and the operation of the various other systems which the police employ. He must be well informed about different categories of deviant conduct, the range of behavioral problems of concern to the police and the dynamics of the various political and social movements in our society. He must be conversant with the major issues of current public interest that involve the police and be articulate in discussing them in the public forum.

Beyond these basic requirements, a leader in the police field is often expected to rescue an agency that has been drifting without clear objectives and principles for years. He is the central figure in any attempts to effect significant changes in the organization and staffing of the agency and in the form of services it provides. This requires a great deal more than traditional managerial skill. He must be aware of the need for change and committed to achieving it. He must be open, challenging, curious and innovative. He must be sufficiently confident of his capacity and sufficiently secure in his position to take risks and to conduct experiments. He must be unflagging in his determination. He must have a masterful capacity to relate well to the various elements that comprise his community so as to win support for his programs, as well as an equally effective ability to relate to his own personnel, eliciting their best performance and coordinating their efforts toward his pre-established goals.

Source: Herman Goldstein, *Policing a Free Society* (Cambridge, MA: Ballinger, 1977), pp. 227-228.

Leadership is an extremely important concept for the police administrator to understand. In the police field, leadership is crucial. As new organizational patterns emerge, the police attempt to adjust to rapid social change, and they are required to handle an ever increasing and diverse range of social problems. The Police Foundation has noted that "progressive police leadership is essential both in terms of sensing the need for change and in managing the process of change."[2] Few observers, though, give police leaders uniformly high marks. Several years ago, A.C. Germann noted:

> Police leadership decisions, today, tend to preserve the status quo and enshrine the archaic. Somehow, in the police establishment, leadership must be developed that is open, willing to listen, willing to change even the most revered attitude or practice. Most current police leadership does not have the breadth of vision, perspective, or motivation to do what must be done.[3]

Since Germann made his assessment, police leadership has improved considerably. In Herman Goldstein's view, during the tumultuous 1960s and 1970s, many police leaders showed more vision and sensitivity than did their mayors and other government administrators.[4] Evidence of the existence of sophisticated police leadership in the United States in recent years can be found in the book *Police Leadership in America*, written largely by police chiefs.[5] However, the overall state of leadership in this country's 17,000-plus police departments remains much less than satisfactory. In fact, one recent assessment concluded that "executive leadership has been 'structured' out of police administration,"[6] because top executives are so consumed with day-to-day management routines and crises.

The Police Leader as a Subsystem

One of the most important factors to consider in discussing leadership is that the leader is an individual whose behavior is influenced by numerous variables. Thus, as an individual, the police leader's behavior is influenced by attitudes, roles, self-concept, motivation, perception, and communication abilities.

A leader, like other individuals, also participates in a number of groups. So a leader may not only lead groups, but may also be a nonleading member of other groups, including those made up of leaders. A chief of police, for example, might be a president of the parent/teacher's association, president of the state association of chiefs of police, a Rotarian, and a member of the International Association of Chiefs of Police. Aspects of group behavior and interaction, including conformity, cohesiveness, output limitation, cooperation, competition, and conflict, all have their influence on the leader.

A police chief is a formal leader; that is, the chief has been designated as the person in charge and has been granted authority to command the people assigned to the police department. All other police managers are formal leaders, too. The sergeant has formal authority with respect to commanding a squad or platoon, the shift commander has formal authority with respect to all the patrol officers and patrol sergeants working during a given tour of duty, and the director of the planning and research division has formal authority with respect to the members assigned to that division.

The terms "formal leader" and "manager" are similar; in fact, all managers are formal leaders. However, a formal leader is not necessarily a complete leader. There is considerably more to leadership than simply being given authority and being designated as the formal leader (see "Police Managers and Police Leaders," p. 266).

The Functions of Leadership

Just as the terms "leader" and "police manager" are not synonymous, the functions of the leader and the police manager are not identical. In Chapter 6 we grouped the basic functions of police management into the categories of system building, planning, organizing, staffing, directing, and controlling. Here we will discuss leadership in terms of the following three functions:

1. definition of structure
2. coordination control
3. goal and norm clarification

Definition of Structure

This leadership function is similar to the management functions of system building, planning, organizing, and staffing. One of the principal tasks of a leader is to arrange people and jobs for the accomplishment of goals and objectives or, more simply, for the purpose of getting things done, defining the structure.

In a sandlot baseball game, for example, the team leader will assign the players their positions in the field and their places in the batting order. Similarly, the leader of a crime scene search will indicate the types of evidence to look for, the search method to be used, and the particular assignments of the personnel involved. In both instances, the leaders define the structures of the tasks to be performed so that the members of their groups will have a better idea of what to do and how to do it.

A police patrol sergeant regularly exercises definition of structure when assigning officers to patrol areas. The investigative supervisor performs the same function when assigning cases to detectives. These examples are relatively minor in scope, however, when compared with the definition of structure of command-level police managers, especially the chief of police.

Upper-level managers make the basic organizing, staffing, and system-building decisions that establish limits on the definition-of-structure decisions of lower-level managers. In terms of patrol personnel allocation, for example, the upper-level managers determine how many officers there will be in the patrol division, how they will be distributed by shifts and squads, what methods and techniques of patrol will be utilized, and how the patrol areas will be drawn. Although lower-level patrol managers normally assign individual officers to their patrol areas, they perform the definition-of-structure function with less authority and on a much smaller scale than do upper-level managers.

Coordination Control

This leadership function includes the management functions of directing and controlling and involves most of the leader's routine decisionmaking. Relations with other groups, coordination of the efforts of the people in the group, and supervision of the work of the group members are all part of coordination control.

Leaders of musical groups, for example, are responsible for seeing to it that the music of the individual musicians harmonizes into good group sounds. They will also decide what music to play and what engagements to accept. In making these and other day-to-day decisions, the leaders are providing coordination control.

As another example, the leader of a police union is expected to schedule and run the organization's meetings, make routine decisions that cannot be delayed until a meeting is held, maintain contact with other police unions, and represent the union in dealings with management. No matter how democratically this or any other group may be structured, someone will always be needed to provide coordination control.

Coordination control is exercised by police managers at all levels, but, to a significant extent, lower-level managers determine how effectively this leadership function is carried out. In theory, upper-level managers issue most of the directives and are responsible for controlling the organization. However, because they are few in number and cannot be everywhere at once, upper-level police managers depend on lieutenants and, particularly, sergeants to implement organizational direction and control. Sergeants interpret directives for their squads and largely determine what control measures will be initiated. Sergeants perform most of the supervision in the organization, represent their squads in relations with other organizational subunits, and are also responsible for coordinating the efforts of the individuals in their groups. So in contrast to the leadership function of definition of structure, coordination control is more closely associated with lower-level police managers than with upper-level ones.

Goal and Norm Clarification

This function of leadership is both the most important and the most difficult to provide. It is through this function that the leader assists the group in defining acceptable and unacceptable behavior and developing the objectives of group activity. The leader must articulate and reinforce the group's mission and key values, convince others (group members and outsiders) of the legitimacy and importance of the mission, and impart to group members a vision that they can understand and believe in. The leader goes beyond the manager's concerns for productivity and efficiency and tries to gain employee commitment and dedication to the ideals of the organization. Leaders are concerned as much with determining what their organizations should do as with overseeing what is done. Their focus is as much on charting the group's course as on simply following it (see "Shaping Organizational Values," p. 271).

In performing this function, the leader often cannot simply impose personal desires on the group, but must be sensitive to the goals and norms of individual group members and attempt to clarify and synthesize them into group goals and norms. This is a difficult function to perform; sometimes the most effective method available to leaders is to demonstrate through their own behavior the goals and norms they perceive to be, or think should be, the goals and norms of the group. This is generally referred to as *leading by example*. When the late President John F. Kennedy wanted Americans to become more conscious of physical fitness, for example, he was photographed swimming and playing touch football. Through his own behavior he attempted to influence the physical exercise norms of the American people.

Sometimes goal and norm clarification is required for organizations to overcome debilitating conflicts. For some years in San Jose, California, racial conflict seemed to be the police department's most serious problem.[7] Community leaders criticized the department's insensitivity and lack of minority employees. The police department, in turn, complained about lack of cooperation in the minority community and resisted affirmative action programs on the grounds of maintaining high personnel standards. The conflict, which dragged on for years, was defined as law enforcement and professionalism versus minority rights. A new police chief, however, was slowly able to transform the debate. He reminded all parties of the greater mission of the police agency—protecting life and property and maintaining order. He convinced them that this mission required high professional standards and a police department both representative of, and working closely with, its community. He helped them see that their conflict was detrimental to the police department and the community, whereas cooperation might make it possible to satisfy both groups. The chief essentially redefined the situation in such a way that the disputants were able to recognize their mutual interests instead of focusing on their differences.

In Chapters 8 and 9 we pointed out that the way police officers view their jobs and their responsibilities is not always based on organizational policy. Instead, police officers are often left on their own to define their roles, which they may do individually or with the assistance of established cultures and subcultures. Role expectations developed in this manner may or may not agree with those held by the chief and other police managers.

When role expectations are developed by individual police officers, management has defaulted on its leadership role. It may still be managing by providing definition of structure and coordination control, but it is not leading. It has turned over the important leadership function of goal and norm clarification to individual officers; in essence, the organization has told its members to lead themselves.

It is no wonder, then, that police officers turn to their colleagues for goal and norm clarification. The police culture (or its subcultures) takes up the function of defining role expectations. Its leaders effectively become the organization's leaders, at least with respect to this one leadership function.

Shaping Organizational Values

An effective leader must be the master of two ends of the spectrum: ideas at the highest level of abstraction and actions at the most mundane level of detail. The value-shaping leader is concerned, on the one hand, with soaring, lofty visions that will generate excitement and enthusiasm for tens or hundreds of thousands of people. That's where the pathfinding role is critically important. On the other hand, it seems the only way to instill enthusiasm is through scores of daily events, with the value-shaping manager becoming an implementer par excellence. In this role, the leader is a bug for detail and directly instills values through deeds rather than words: no opportunity is too small. So it is at once attention to ideas and attention to detail.

Attention to ideas (pathfinding and soaring visions) would seem to suggest rare, imposing men writing on stone tablets. But, our colleagues Phillips and Kennedy, who looked at how leaders shape values, imply that this is not the case: "Success in instilling values appears to have had little to do with charismatic personality. Rather, it derived from obvious, sincere, sustained personal commitment to the values the leaders sought to implant, coupled with extraordinary persistence in reinforcing those values. None of the men we studied relied on personal magnetism. All *made* themselves into effective leaders." [Emphasis in original.]

Source: Thomas J. Peters and Robert H. Waterman Jr., *In Search of Excellence: Lessons from America's Best-Run Companies* (New York, NY: Harper & Row, 1982), pp. 287-288.

This process has occurred not only in police organizations but in many other organizations as well. It illustrates that effective managing is relatively common, as compared with effective leading, which is relatively uncommon. The function of goal and norm clarification separates the leaders from the managers.

In hierarchical organizations, the relative importance of the three leadership functions varies according to level. That is, the most important function for the leader of the entire organization will differ from the most important function for the leader of an organizational division consisting of only a few people. In general, the function of definition of structure becomes more important as one goes up in the organization, whereas coordination control becomes more important as one goes down in the organization. The importance of goal and norm clarification does not vary as widely, but it remains as a vital function for leaders at all levels.

Sources of Influence

Leadership involves influencing the behavior of others. It is through the use of influence that a leader attempts to coordinate and control, define structure, and clarify goals and norms. The sources of this influence will be discussed in terms of the following five categories of power:

1. position power
2. coercion power
3. reward power
4. expert power
5. charisma power[8]

Position Power

Position power is a source of influence that is completely independent of the individual leader. It flows directly from the position held by the leader and accrues to any person who occupies the leadership position. When a person vacates the position, the influence is left behind for the successor.

The authority of police officers to regulate human behavior in certain situations is an example of position power. When they are sworn in, police officers are granted powers not held by other citizens. When they leave the job, they lose these powers; they have them only as long as they remain police officers.

Other holders of position power are basketball referees, baseball umpires, mayors, corporate executives, judges, ship captains, and police chiefs. Within all organizations, position power is delegated to all kinds of positions in the form of authority. Position power is a basic source of authority and influence for police managers. Through such administrative principles as division of labor and delegation of authority, police management positions inherit power. Thus, the patrol sergeant's authority to assign squad members to patrol areas originates in the position, not the person. Similarly, the authority of the operations commander to coordinate the activities of the patrol, investigations, and traffic divisions comes from the position, not the person.

Coercion Power

Coercion power is based on the threat or actual delivery of punishment. This source of influence may be vested in the position held by the leader, or it may be a personal attribute of the leader.

Police managers acquire coercion power through their control functions. Patrol sergeants coerce their subordinates by assigning unpopular patrol areas as punishment for behavior they do not appreciate, and they can also recommend more severe punishments. Upper-level managers, though more removed from the basic operations of the organization, have greater coercion power, in the form of harsher punishments. In theory at least, the police chief has the most coercion power, inasmuch as only the chief has the authority to punish everyone else.

Coercion power in police organizations can also be personal in origin. Some police managers are feared because of their size, temper, or scathing tongue, though they might rarely use the coercion power of their position. Nonmanagerial personnel may also exercise coercion power within the police organization. Such use may be for personal gain or retribution, but it may also be exercised on behalf of the organization, the dominant culture, or a subculture. It may be used on behalf of the organization—for example, to bring into line a fellow officer who is giving the department a bad name by taking bribes, lying in court, or roughing up suspects. Coercion power may also be used on behalf of the dominant subculture to coerce an officer who refuses to participate in corrupt, dishonest, or brutal activities.[9]

Reward Power

Reward power is based on the ability of the leader to bestow rewards on other group members. As with coercion power, reward power may be an inherent characteristic of the position held by the leader. To a lesser degree, it may simply be a device developed by the leader to distribute rewards.

The leader of a political machine, for example, traditionally wields influence in the form of government jobs and contracts to reward supporters; although the morality and ethics of such rewards are often questioned, the fact remains that jobs and contracts are used as a source of power by many political leaders. Political leaders who are independently wealthy or who have financial support from large numbers of contributors might choose to pay supporters for their services and thus reward them for their loyalty and their assistance. Similarly, an employer who gives employees bonuses or salary increments is using reward power as a source of influence.

One of the difficulties of police management, and of public administration generally, is the relative unavailability of rewards. Police managers ordinarily cannot reward good performance with bonuses, salary increases, or even promotions. Civil service regulations and the realities of public finance prohibit such gestures, for the most part. For rewards, police managers can offer little more than a handshake and a pat on the back.

These kinds of rewards are not without value, however. Most people appreciate recognition and like being told that they have done a good job. In addition, modest benefits such as desirable assignments, days off, first choice of vacation times, recognition awards, and new equipment and supplies may sometimes be used by the police manager to reward good performance.

Expert Power

Expert power is a source of influence that derives from the skill, knowledge, and expertise of the leader. It is based on the leader's ability to accomplish difficult tasks that others would be either unable or unwilling to perform. Although the position held by the leader might serve to identify the expert, the influence the leader has comes directly from innate and learned talents.

At the scene where an explosive device has been found, for example, bomb disposal technicians will very likely assume leadership because of their special training and skill. Even if they are the lowest-ranking officers at the scene, their expert power will give them considerable influence over everyone else present, regardless of their ranks or positions.

When officers or managers in staff positions want to exert influence on line operations, they often have to rely on expert power. Members of the planning and research unit who have discovered a pattern of criminal activity, for example, would rely on their expertise to try to convince the chief, the operations commander, patrol sergeants, and patrol officers to base future activities on their findings. The extent to which these individuals altered their work behavior as a result of these findings would depend on how much expert power they believed the members of the planning and analysis unit possessed. An important consideration in this judgment would be the success or failure of operational activities based on the findings and directions of the crime analysts.[10] If their discovery turned out to be inaccurate or false, their expert power would diminish. On the other hand, if criminal apprehensions were made and crimes cleared as a result of their findings, their expert power would be strongly enhanced.

Charisma Power

Charisma power is influence drawn from the leader's personality, reputation, integrity, attractiveness, values, and general reputation. Some leaders have influence over other people because of an almost ethereal quality about them that makes others want to believe in them and follow them.

Among the outstanding examples of charismatic leaders in recent history are Mahatma Gandhi and Martin Luther King Jr. Both developed tremendous influence over large numbers of people even though their source of influence was restricted solely to charisma power. They had no significant position power, no expert power, and no capabilities to coerce or reward their followers; yet there was something about them as individuals that caused literally millions of people to believe in them and to follow them.

Styles of Leadership

The manner in which the leader exercises power and influence in order to carry out leadership functions is often referred to as *leadership style*. Certainly every leader's style is unique; it may even differ somewhat from situation to situation. For purposes of discussion here, we will define five general styles of leadership:

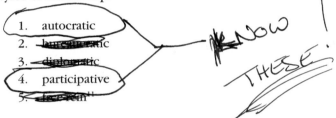

1. autocratic
2. bureaucratic
3. diplomatic
4. participative
5. free-rein

Autocratic Style

The autocratic, or authoritarian, leader makes decisions and carries them out according to his or her own personal beliefs, without regard to precedent, rules and regulations, or the opinions of others. Autocratic leadership has the advantage of speedy decisionmaking. It works well if most group members attempt to avoid responsibilities. It has the disadvantage of being associated with one-way communication and its attendant shortcomings. Inasmuch as the leader makes all decisions personally, this style will be unsuccessful if the leader is not an expert in a wide range of areas. The autocratic leader is almost always resented by those in the group who believe that they have something to contribute and who think that they should be consulted in decisionmaking. The autocratic leader is almost always seen as a liability.[12]

Bureaucratic Style

Bureaucratic leaders operate by the book, basing every move on a careful examination of the policies, procedures, rules and regulations, general orders, and other directives in effect in the organization. If they have any doubt as to the proper course of action, bureaucratic-style leaders will first consult their superiors or someone else likely to know the correct way to proceed. Bureaucratic leadership is consistent and fair; similar situations will be treated similarly.

The basic shortcoming of this leadership style is that it is not at all flexible. Operation by the book limits the leader's ability to adapt to changing circumstances and to react to the nuances and mitigating factors present in all situations. This kind of inflexibility often leads to resentment, because the people involved dislike not being treated as individuals.

Diplomatic Style

Diplomatic leaders make most of their decisions without consulting anyone. After decisions are made, though, they attempt to soft-sell them to the group, using gentle methods of persuasion and appeals to reason. By explaining to a group the reasoning behind a decision, a diplomatic leader often gets the group's cooperation in the execution of the decision. The group is likely to interpret the leader's efforts as a show of respect for its membership and abide by the decision as an expression of appreciation. On the other hand, if the leader does a poor job of selling the decision to the group, his or her efforts may seem to be an insincere gesture and will probably be resented. Diplomatic leaders also run the risk that some group members may view their efforts to explain their decisions as signs of weakness and insecurity.

Participative Style

The participative leader consults group members before decisions are made; in some cases group members may even make the decisions themselves. In either instance, the members' inputs influence the decision-making process. As a result, there is ordinarily more support for the decision among the group members. There is also more information available for those making the decision, including information from the grassroots level, where the decision will probably be carried out. Additionally, participation by group members contributes to their own personal and professional growth, making them better suited for future decision-making positions.

This style has the disadvantage of being time-consuming, however. It is also likely to establish cliques within groups, which can cause morale problems and even hinder the decision-making process. Furthermore, it provides leaders with a device by which they can avoid their own responsibilities. Finally, group members who are consulted and have their ideas rejected can become extremely resentful of the leader and eventually cause his or her downfall.

Free-Rein Style

Free-rein leaders exercise a minimum of direction and control over their groups; they attempt to avoid making decisions whenever possible. Some group members are comfortable and productive in this kind of laissez-faire environment. Because individual group members are called on to make many of their own decisions, significant individual growth is possible. Professional people usually work well within this kind of setting. On the other hand, some people cannot operate effectively in such an unstructured situation. Because the free-rein style of leadership provides for little control over the activities of group members, the risks involved are high.

One research study surveyed all members of one police department in an attempt to identify the most preferred style of leadership and management.[13] The choices available to respondents on each item of the survey represented the full range of leadership styles. The study found that the choice of all ranks was a diplomatic/participative style of leadership. This style was characterized by supportive (helping) relationships, substantial trust, delegated decision-making authority, and moderate interaction up and down the hierarchy.

Another study focused on 64 police agencies in Illinois.[14] When asked what management philosophy was currently in use in their police departments, an overwhelming majority (81%) of operational police officers identified the autocratic style. Administrators from the same police departments, however, thought that the participative style was most commonly used. Not surprisingly, then, perceptions of leadership in police organizations differed between those at the bottom and those at the top of the hierarchy. When asked to select the philosophy that they would prefer in their departments, though, both operational personnel and administrators identified the participative style. An even more recent study from Ohio produced similar findings.[15]

Theories of Leadership

Which kind of leader is likely to be most successful? This question has drawn the attention of a large number of behavioral researchers and theorists. Early efforts to answer the question tended to focus on leader traits, such as personality or physical characteristics. These studies compared the effectiveness of attractive and unattractive leaders, tall and short leaders, introverted and extroverted leaders, friendly and distant leaders, and leaders with similarly contrasting traits. Jennings summed up these research efforts by stating that "fifty years of study have failed to produce one personality trait or set of qualities that can be used to discriminate between leaders and nonleaders."[16]

Once leader traits were ruled out as the primary factor in leadership effectiveness, attention turned to leader behavior. This avenue of study sought to identify the most successful leadership style. Initial efforts focused on two contrasting styles: task-oriented leadership versus relationship-oriented leadership. The task-oriented leader emphasizes task performance by setting production quotas, supervising and correcting workers, and generally ignoring all other considerations. The relationship-oriented leader, on the other hand, shows concern for the needs of workers, checks on their welfare, and generally tries to motivate through satisfaction of higher-level needs.

Research comparing the effectiveness of task-oriented and relationship-oriented leadership was inconclusive. Some studies supported the use of the task-oriented style, while others recommended the relationship-oriented style. Still others found no differences in the effectiveness of the two styles. As a result of this confusion, researchers were obliged to proceed in two directions: (1) a more careful elaboration of leadership styles, and (2) consideration that leader success might be contingent on situational factors.

Fiedler's Situational Theory

One of the first situational theories of leadership effectiveness was advanced by Fred E. Fiedler.[17] He sought to determine the kinds of situations in which task-oriented leadership would be most successful and those in which a relationship-oriented style would be most effective. His research led him to identify three critical situational factors:

1.   leader-member relations
2.   task structure
3.   position power

Fiedler characterized situations in terms of whether leader-member relations were good or bad, task structure was clear or vague, and whether the position power of the leader was strong or weak. He found that when all factors were positive (when leader-member relations were good, task structures were clear, and position power was strong), the task-oriented leader was more successful. When all factors were negative (when leader-member relations were poor, task structures vague, and position power was weak), the task-oriented style again was more successful. However, when the factors were mixed, the relationship-oriented leader was more likely to be successful.

Fiedler recommended that leaders use his theory to analyze their own unique situations and then to choose the more effective leadership style. He also suggested that, within an organization, leaders could be appointed to positions based on the suitability of their styles for the situations at hand. Whether these practical applications of his theory are completely justified is debatable, but his research does demonstrate that the answer to the question "Which kind of leader is likely to be the most successful?" is clear. It all depends on the situation.

The Blake/Mouton Grid

While Fiedler was examining the kinds of situations in which task-oriented or relationship-oriented leadership would be most successful, Robert R. Blake and Jane S. Mouton were challenging the task-versus-relationship dichotomy itself.[18] They pointed out that in the traditional dichotomy, more task orientation necessitated less relationship orientation and vice versa. They devised the novel and startling argument that task and relationship orientation might be independent behaviors that interact to form a managerial style, rather than competing behaviors, as posited by the traditional approach. In their view, a leader's behavior could vary from strong task orientation to weak task orientation and could also vary, independently, from strong relationship orientation to weak relationship orientation. Their theory is graphically represented by the Leadership Grid shown in Figure 10.1.

Figure 10.1
The Leadership Grid® Figure

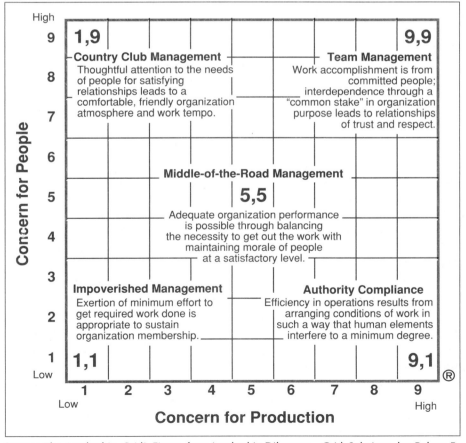

The grid identifies five leadership styles. The 1,9 style, which incorporates strong relationship orientation and weak task orientation, is identical to Fiedler's relationship-oriented style and similar to the diplomatic style discussed earlier in the chapter. The 9,1 style, which emphasizes tasks over relationships, is identical to Fiedler's task-oriented leadership style and similar to the autocratic style previously described.

Besides these two styles, which match Fiedler's, three additional leadership styles are identified in the figure. The 1,1 style is characterized by weak task and relationship orientation and is similar to what we earlier termed "free-rein leadership." The 5,5 style evidences moderate task and relationship orientation, much as the bureaucratic leadership style presented earlier. The 9,9-style leader demonstrates strong concern for both tasks and relationships and is closest to the participative style previously discussed. More recently, Blake and Mouton have identified two additional styles—the paternalistic or "father knows best" style, in which reward is promised for compliance and punishment is threatened for noncompliance, and the opportunistic or "what's in it for me?" style, in which the style utilized depends on which style the leader feels will return him or her the greatest benefit.

Having identified these seven leadership styles, Blake and Mouton leave no question that they regard the 9,9 style as being most effective. In their view, the leader who shows a high degree of concern for employees and relationships, and at the same time a high degree of concern for task performance, will be most successful.

Hersey and Blanchard's Theory

By arguing as they do that the 9,9 style is best, Blake and Mouton seem to ignore the situational theories advocated by Fiedler and others. While the Leadership Grid advanced leadership theory by destroying the task/relationship dichotomy, they seem to have taken a step backward in advocating a one-best-way style regardless of differences in leadership situations.

Paul Hersey and Kenneth Blanchard have attempted an interesting merger of the managerial grid and situational theory,[19] as depicted in Figure 10.2. Under the grid, they have added a situational dimension they term *task-related maturity*. They define this dimension as the extent to which followers (employees, subordinates, group members) have mastered task-related skills and knowledge, as well as the extent to which they are committed to the organization's goals and values. Followers who have mastered their tasks and are committed to the organization score high on task-related maturity, while those who are still learning their tasks and show little or no commitment to the organization score low on task-related maturity.

Figure 10.2
Hersey and Blanchard's Situational Model

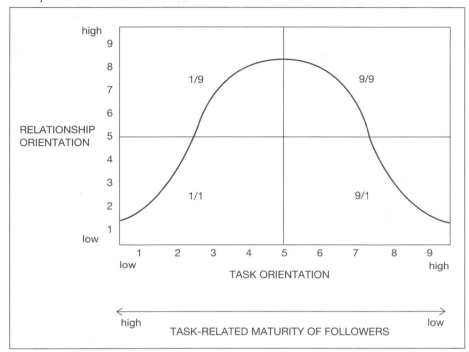

Source: Paul Hersey and Kenneth H. Blanchard, *Management of Organizational Behavior: Utilizing Human Resources*, Fourth Edition (Englewood Cliffs, NJ: Prentice Hall, 1982), p. 152. Adapted by permission.

Hersey and Blanchard argue that the most successful leadership style will be the one that best matches the task-related maturity of followers. Because this factor (followers' task-related maturity) can be expected to vary from one situation to another, the most effective leadership style will also vary, depending on the situation. In addition, because followers' task-related maturity may change over time, such as when they become more skilled at their tasks, the best leadership style for a particular group may also change over time.

According to Hersey and Blanchard, a task-oriented leadership style is most effective when followers' task-related maturity is very low. In this kind of situation the leader must supply structure, direction, and control, because followers are not skilled at their tasks or committed to high productivity. The leader must show followers what to do, supervise their performance, correct their mistakes, and perhaps "crack the whip" to get their attention and efforts.

As followers' task-related maturity increases, the best leadership style becomes less task-oriented and more relationship-oriented. The 9,9 leadership style, with high concern for tasks and relationships, is recommended when followers are low to average in task-related maturity. When followers are above average in task-related maturity, the 1,9 style, emphasizing concern for relationships over concern for tasks, is suggested. Finally, when followers are characterized by very high task-related maturity, Hersey and Blanchard recommend the 1,1, or free-rein, leadership style. In this situation the followers are experts in task performance and highly committed to the organization; leaders need do little more than coordinate activities and protect followers from unnecessary distractions.

This theory has much to offer, because it incorporates situational factors and avoids the task/relationship dichotomy. Its attractiveness is enhanced by its compatibility with the observations of experienced consultants and managers. For example, Raymond Loen suggests the following guidelines:

1. Use the autocratic style if you are an expert and in all emergency situations.
2. Use the participative style only when group members are extremely capable.
3. Use the free-rein style when group members are capable of being productive when working independently.[20]

Most current thinking, whether in the general field of management or specifically in police administration,[21] supports a contingency or situational model of managerial and leadership effectiveness; the kind of leadership that will be most successful will vary from one situation to another. We think that the theory advanced by Hersey and Blanchard is the most useful and practical situational theory of leadership presently available.

Emotional Intelligence

Daniel Goleman proposes that while technical skills and high IQ are important qualities in leaders, emotional intelligence is imperative for quality leadership.[22] His research indicates that most effective leaders have high degrees of emotional intelligence. In related research, David McClellan found that a correlation exists between emotional intelligence and high performance.[23] In other words, those leaders who had high degrees of emotional intelligence also outperformed others that were similarly situated.

Emotional intelligence consists of five components that culminate in the keystone of the concept, which is "awareness of one's own feelings as they occur."[24] The five components that make up emotional intelligence are self-awareness, self-regulation, motivation, empathy, and social skill. *Self-awareness* is a critical awareness of one's emotions, strengths, weaknesses, needs, and drives, with an acute understanding of how these impact self-perception, others' perceptions, and their job performance. *Self-regulation* is being in control of one's feelings and impulses—those who are masters of their emotions. *Motivation* is the want and desire to achieve for simply the satisfaction of achievement versus some external reward such as notoriety. *Empathy*, often easily recognized, is the thoughtful consideration of others' feelings in decision-making. Finally, *social skill* is "friendliness with a purpose" that enables leaders to direct people in ways you desire.[25]

Can emotional intelligence be learned? Goleman indicates that while research indicates there is a genetic component to emotional intelligence, nurture plays a significant role as well. He also contends that emotional intelligence increases with age or maturity. Goleman proposes that traditional methods of increasing characteristics such as emotional intelligence are not sufficient alone, but that an individual's sincere desire and concerted effort are more important. While emotional intelligence may have not been considered a crucial element of police leadership to date, it is worthy of consideration for managers not only for their own self-improvement but for developing leadership skills in their employees as well.

In a later work, *Primal Leadership*, Daniel P. Goleman, Richard Boyatzis, and Annie McKee take Goleman's premises from *Emotional Intelligence* and describe what they call a "resonant leader."[26] A resonant leader is one who has not only acute self-awareness and social awareness, but also the ability to use these in dealing with his or her employees. Empathy, which is achieved through self-awareness and social awareness, is of extreme importance to the leader in dealing with his or her employees. By being empathetic, leaders are able to motivate people and spread enthusiasm about the work of the organization. According to the authors, leaders who exhibit empathy can be especially effective in service occupations or those that require extensive dealings with the public, such as policing.

Goleman, Boyatzis, and McKee also stress the importance of a leader letting employees see who he or she really is—letting emotions show. For example, they advocate the use of humor in the workplace under certain circumstances, to engage people and to contribute to a calming work environment. While we might not typically view humor as useful in the police organization setting, consideration of new practices such as these is noteworthy. Most of the research that Goleman and his colleagues have undertaken has been in the corporate setting. Looking at the applicability of emotional intelligence to police leadership, however, may well be worth our time and efforts.

The Environment of Police Leadership

Leadership, as an element of human behavior, is an open system, influenced by and having influence on its environment. It would be much simpler to understand and easier to provide if it were exercised in a vacuum, but this is not the case.

Standard 7.7
Importance of Police Administration

In addition to directing the day-to-day operations of his agency, the police administrator has the responsibility to exert leadership in seeking to improve the quality of police service and in seeking to solve community-wide problems of concern to the police. The position of chief should be recognized as being among the most important and most demanding positions in the hierarchy of governmental officials.

Source: American Bar Association Project on Standards for Criminal Justice, *The Urban Police Function* (New York, NY: American Bar Association, 1973), pp. 14-15.

In performing leadership functions, police managers are constrained by external factors. In defining the structures of their organizations, they are limited by budgetary considerations. Moreover, political pressures often dictate their allocation of personnel and their design of patrol areas. Coordination control is greatly restricted by the natural human desire to avoid and evade direction and control. Goal and norm clarification has as its boundaries the goals and norms of the entire society, and within these limits, police cultures and subcultures further constrain the influence of the manager.

The position power available to police managers is determined by their superiors and thus is susceptible to change. Even the chief has superiors (e.g., the mayor, city manager, city council, public safety director) who can alter the power of the chief's position. Coercion power, the ability and/or authority to punish, is strictly limited by civil service regulations, due process guarantees, and the criminal law. Reward power, as we noted earlier, is also limited by civil service and the budget. Expert and charisma power are more clearly vested in the person, but nevertheless their exercise is also constrained by human, organizational, and political factors.

These are some of the reasons why leadership is difficult to provide in police organizations. Police leaders operate in an environment that includes the constraining influences of politics, law, other interdependent agencies, police fraternal organizations and unions, budgets, and human behavior (an important point discussed earlier in Chapter 7). It is not an easy task to provide definition of structure, coordination control, and, particularly, goal and norm clarification in such an environment.

Summary

At the outset of this chapter we indicated that leadership is not easily defined, described, or categorized. There are a number of functions that leaders perform, a number of ways they go about performing them, and a number of theories about which ways are the best. Although it has been the subject of considerable research over the years, leadership remains one aspect of human behavior about which not much is known.

Lao-Tzu, a sage in ancient China, said something about leadership; although his research design is not clear, we still take him at his word:

> As for the best leaders, the people do not notice their existence. The next best, the people honor and praise. The next, the people fear; and the next, the people hate . . . . When the best leader's work is done the people say, "We did it ourselves."[27]

Discussion Questions

1. Do you think that leaders are born or made? Why? Do you think that the best leaders are loved, respected, or feared?

2. What is the condition of leadership in organizations with which you are personally familiar?

3. Compare the following officials in terms of sources of influence: police officer, patrol sergeant, patrol captain, chief of police, mayor, judge, prison warden, probation officer, assembly-line supervisor, and company president.

4. Identify some charismatic leaders. What gives them their power?

5. Analyze your present work situation according to the three critical factors in Fiedler's theory. Which kind of leader does the situation seem to call for? Does the present leader operate that way? Is the present leader successful? What leadership style is suggested according to Hersey and Blanchard's theory?

Cases

The subject of this chapter was leadership in the police organization. Three case studies at the end of this book, "Case 1: The Energetic Chief," "Case 3: The Yuletide Remembrance," and "Case 4: The Chief Who Played King," present leadership situations that can be analyzed using theories and concepts from the chapter. Compare and contrast the three in terms of leadership functions and styles of leadership.

Notes

1. J. Kuykendall and P.C. Unsinger, "The Leadership Styles of Police Managers," *Journal of Criminal Justice* 10 (1982): 311.

2. *Experiments in Police Improvement: A Progress Report* (Washington, DC: Police Foundation, 1972), p.18.

3. A.C. Germann, "Changing the Police: The Impossible Dream?" Reprinted by special permission of Northwestern University School of Law, *Journal of Criminal Law, Criminology and Police Science* 62 (1971): 417.

4. H. Goldstein, *Policing a Free Society* (Cambridge, MA: Ballinger, 1977), p. 229.

5. W.A. Geller, ed., *Police Leadership in America: Crisis and Opportunity* (New York, NY: Praeger, 1985).

6. N.H. Stamper, *Removing Managerial Barriers to Effective Police Leadership* (Washington, DC: Police Executive Research Forum, 1992), p. x.

7. K. Betsalel, "Police Leadership and the Reconciliation of Police-Minority Relations." *American Journal of Police* 9, no. 2 (1990): 63-76.

8. J. French and B. Haven, "The Basis of Social Power," in *Group Dynamics: Research and Theory*, Third Edition, D. Cartwright and A. Zander, eds. (New York, NY: Harper & Row, 1968).

9. An excellent example of this is in P. Maas, *Serpico* (New York, NY: Bantam Books, 1972).

10. G.W. Cordner, "The Effects of Directed Patrol: A Natural Quasi-Experiment in Pontiac," in *Contemporary Issues in Law Enforcement*, J.J. Fyfe, ed. (Beverly Hills, CA: Sage, 1981).

11. J. Owens, "The Art of Leadership," *Personnel Journal* 52, no. 5 (May 1973): 393.

12. R.L. Parker, "Autocratic Police Administration: An Outmoded Concept," *Law and Order* (May 1986): 33.

13. R. Reams, J. Kuykendall, and D. Burns, "Police Management Systems: What Is an Appropriate Model?" *Journal of Police Science and Administration* 3, no. 4 (December 1975): 475-481.

14. J.H. Auten, "Police Management in Illinois, 1983," *Journal of Police Science and Administration* 13, no. 4 (December 1985): 325-337.

15. J.H. Witte, L.F. Travis, and R.H. Langworthy, "Participatory Management in Law Enforcement," *American Journal of Police* 9, no. 4 (1990).

16. E.E. Jennings, "The Anatomy of Leadership," *Management of Personnel Quarterly* 1, no. 1 (autumn 1961): 2.

17. F. Fiedler, "Engineer the Job to Fit the Manager," *Harvard Business Review* 43, no. 5 (September–October 1965): 115-122.

18. R.R. Blake and A.A. McCanse, *The Managerial Grid III: The Key to Leadership Excellence* (Houston, TX: Gulf, 1985).

19. P. Hersey and K.H. Blanchard, *Management of Organizational Behavior: Utilizing Human Resources*, Fourth Edition (Englewood Cliffs, NJ: Prentice Hall, 1982).

20. R.O. Loen, *Manage More by Doing Less* (New York, NY: McGraw-Hill, 1971), p.111.

21. J.L. Kuykendall, "Police Managerial Styles: A Grid Analysis," *American Journal of Police* 4, no. 1 (1985): 61.

22. D. Goleman, *Emotional Intelligence* (New York, NY: Bantam, 1995).

23. D. Goleman, "What Makes a Leader?" *Harvard Business Review* (November–December 1998): 93-102.

24. Goleman, *Emotional Intelligence*, p. 46.

25. Goleman, "What Makes a Leader?" p. 101.

26. D. Goleman, R. Boyatzis, and A. McKee, *Primal Leadership: Realizing the Power of Emotional Intelligence* (Boston, MA: Harvard Business School Press, 2002).

27. Quoted in R. Townsend, *Up the Organization* (New York, NY: Knopf, 1970), p. 99.

Suggested Reading

Geller, William A., ed. *Police Leadership in America: Crisis and Opportunity*. New York, NY: Praeger, 1985.

Goleman, Daniel, Richard Boyatzis, and Annie McKee. *Primal Leadership: Realizing the Power of Emotional Intelliegence*. Boston, MA: Harvard Business School Press, 2002.

Hegelsen, Sally. *The Female Advantage: Women's Ways of Leadership*. New York, NY: Doubleday/Currency, 1990.

Hersey, Paul. *The Situational Leader*. Escondido, CA: Center for Leadership Studies, 1997.

Stamper, Norman H. *Removing Managerial Barriers to Effective Police Leadership*. Washington, DC: Police Executive Research Forum, 1992.

THE STRATEGIC MANAGEMENT PERSPECTIVE

The five chapters of Part Four discuss the strategic management perspective of police administration. This perspective emphasizes work tasks, organizational interactions, and outcomes, rather than structures or human behavior. It tends to look across the organization instead of taking the top-down view of the traditional perspective or the bottom-up view of the human perspective. The strategic management perspective is particularly focused on finding the most effective ways of carrying out the organization's work and accomplishing the organization's mission.

Chapter 11 addresses communication and information in the police organization and their relationship to decisionmaking. Information is probably the most important resource utilized by a police department. All sorts of management and operational activities and decisions depend on the timely availability of pertinent information. In order to ensure the accuracy and availability of such information, police agencies employ several types of information systems and engage in a variety of information analysis techniques. By conceptualizing police administration in terms of information-based decisionmaking, new insights into the process of directing and controlling police officers can be achieved.

Chapter 12 discusses the measurement and evaluation of police performance. This subject is crucial; we must first be able to measure performance before we can determine whether it is improving or deteriorating. As it turns out, measuring police performance is exceedingly difficult; a variety of measurement issues and problems are discussed. We conclude that perfection in measuring police performance cannot be achieved, but that some reasonably accurate and informative methods are available. Measurement and evaluation of individual-level, program-level, and organizational-level police performance are examined.

Chapter 13 examines the most important strategies and tactics adopted by police agencies. These strategies and tactics represent the principal methods by which the police attempt to perform their work and achieve their goals. A number of major studies in the 1970s called into question the effectiveness of many traditional police practices. Since then, a variety of alternative strategies and tactics have been implemented; although some of these alternative methods seem promising, police agencies continue to search for demonstrably effective new work methods.

In Chapter 14, a substantial number of approaches to police organizational improvement are presented. Within each of this text's perspectives on police administration (the traditional perspective, the human perspective, and the strategic management perspective), promising ideas and programs for improving police performance can be found. The most effective police departments, though, will be those that integrate the three perspectives and adopt multiple approaches to organizational improvement. These police agencies and their executives will achieve the greatest success in protecting life and property and maintaining order, while operating within the difficult role assigned to the police in a democratic society.

Chapter 15 discusses several contemporary themes and issues in modern police administration. The focus is on critical issues that are facing police organizations at the start of the twenty-first century, as well as issues looming on the horizon. We live in a fast-changing world. Police executives have the responsibility for identifying and anticipating social, political, and technological changes that are taking place in society, and then preparing their organizations for those changes. Looking ahead and preparing for the future is not an exact science, of course, but it is a very important management activity that is not always given the attention it deserves.

Information in the Police Organization

11

Learning Objectives

- Differentiate between formal and informal organizations.

- Identify the main barrier to effective downward communications.

- Cite the basic obstacle to effective lateral communications.

- Identify six categories of decisions made in police organizations.

- Distinguish among operations, command and control, and management information systems in police organizations.

- Identify four kinds of information analysis often found in police departments.

- Identify the basic purpose of crime analysis.

- Explain the distinction between crime analysis and intelligence analysis.

- Explain why police decisionmaking can never be totally rational.

- Explain the information-oriented perspective on police management direction and control.

In Chapter 8 we discussed communication as an important element of human behavior; we said, in effect, that communication works in concert with roles, attitudes, self-concept, motivation, and perception to produce behavior. We further indicated that communication is an involved and complex function for individuals to perform and that it is not often performed well.

If communication from one individual to another is a problem, consider the possibilities for difficulty in attempting to communicate with large numbers of people. In the organizational setting there are countless situations in which one individual must communicate with several others, groups of individuals must communicate with other groups, and groups must communicate with individuals. Seriously complicating these processes of communication are the many diverse roles played by individuals: superiors, subordinates, peers, group members, and competitors. These roles, in turn, influence the motivations of the participants and serve to impede good communication. Organizational communication, therefore, is even more complex than interpersonal communication.

Communication is critical for transmitting information among people in organizations. Information is needed at all levels in organizations for problem solving, planning, and decisionmaking. Police officers need information to make arrest decisions, supervisors need information to make scheduling decisions, and commanders need information to allocate personnel and choose strategies (see "Communication in the Police Organization," p. 293). All organizations, including police departments, need information and communications systems that provide employees with the information they need to effectively perform their duties.

Organizational Communication

Organizational communication is much more than a simple compilation of all of the interpersonal communication that takes place between and among members of an organization. It cannot be explained solely on the basis of the principles of interpersonal communication discussed in Chapter 8. Although these have a direct bearing on organizational communication, they must be considered in terms of some other organizational concepts.

William Scholz has maintained that "communication in an organization must be viewed as a system."[1] After discussing the channels, directions, and barriers of organizational communication, we will focus on communication and information systems as they provide information for police decisionmaking. Both interpersonal and organizational communications depend on feedback to ensure accuracy in the transmission and receipt of messages.

Communication Channels

In many organizations the best sources of information are secretaries. They type memoranda and letters, take notes at meetings, place and receive telephone calls, answer questions when the boss is absent, and open most of the mail. They are key participants in a number of communication processes, and they have access to a great amount of information. People within the organization who want to get information without going through official channels can probably get the information they want if they know the right secretary.

Communication in the Police Organization

Like other organizations, police departments depend upon communication structure and flow for defining and meeting the goals of the organization. However, it can by argued that information-sharing among workers is even more important in police departments than in most other bureaucracies. A police department is compelled by its very function to maintain a high volume of communication flowing both horizontally and vertically in the organization. The mandate of the police function is to be cognizant of and regulate citizen behavior, particularly activities citizens typically try to keep from the eyes of the public, or at least the eyes of the police. Thus, against the odds, the police officer is highly dependent not only on the gathering of information from outside sources, but also on the sharing and integration of information among workers. In addition, the police officer's willingness to communicate is critical for authority, for by the very nature of the patrol officer's task, supervisory control can often be exercised only after information has been communicated.

Source: Chris M. Dunning and Ellen Hochstedler, "Satisfaction with Communication in a Police Organization," in Jack R. Greene, ed., *Managing Police Work: Issues and Analysis* (Beverly Hills, CA: Sage, 1982), p. 142.

Anyone who has ever served in the armed forces knows that sergeants, not generals, win wars. This, of course, is a facetious way of saying that much of what is accomplished in organizations is accomplished in unofficial ways. In the military, sergeants are the people who have the information and who are usually in a position to act on it. Many a soldier who knew the right sergeant could find out what was going on, have orders changed, and be sent to an exotic assignment; information unofficially obtained and put to the right use can be extremely useful.

In similar fashion, people who work skillfully within an organization can often get their messages through to someone else in the organization in an unofficial way. A police officer who is displeased with the sergeant, for example, can relay that displeasure to the chief simply by talking about the sergeant in front of the right people; the right people, in this instance, are those who have access to the chief and who are likely to spread disparaging remarks.

These are examples of how unofficial communication can affect people within an organization. The formal organization chart establishes formal communicative relationships between and among superiors and subordinates and between and among peers at the same organizational levels. The organization that confines itself solely to these official communication channels will, in effect, starve its people from information. What happens in most organizations is that an informal organization develops for the purpose of facilitating unofficial communications (see Fig. 11.1). Organization members at all levels eventually learn to get the information they need; they learn to do this without going through official channels and without upsetting the formal organization.

Figure 11.1
The Informal Organization

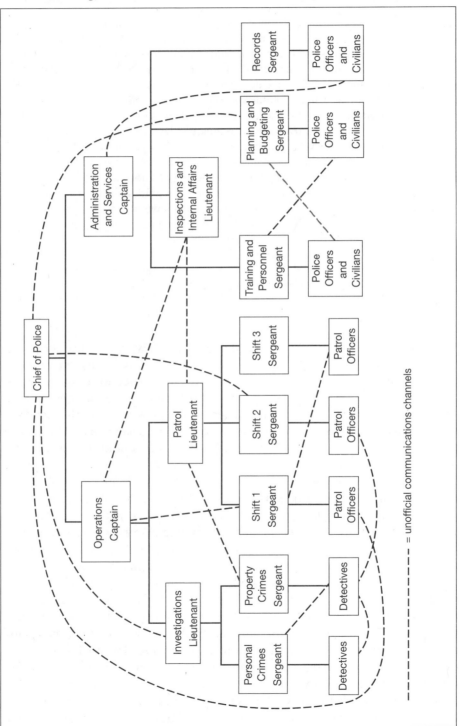

As might be expected, the unofficial communication channels that develop are often more efficient and effective than officially established channels. Unofficial communication channels are usually capable of passing information along more quickly; they can skip entire levels of the organization and avoid the red tape that the formal organization imposes on the communication process. The content of messages unofficially delivered is often clearer than the content of official messages; unofficial messages do not have to be shrouded in official language or be designed to please readers along official communication channels.

Although unofficial communication channels are essentially neutral structures, their existence can exert both positive and negative influences on the organization as a whole. They can serve to enforce output-limitation norms, spread rumors, pilfer confidential information, and generally create organizational turmoil. On the other side of the coin, unofficial communication channels have prevented many an organization from collapsing and disintegrating. They alert superiors to problems that middle managers do not recognize, choose to ignore, or attempt to hide. They provide information to decision-makers when official communication channels are clogged. They allow competent people with incompetent supervisors to do their jobs, and they facilitate speedy communication in crisis when official communication channels are too slow even if they are working.

Many police chiefs instinctively fight the informal organization, failing to recognize that it has probably developed because of the shortcomings of the formal organization, a matter that embarrasses them and affects their self-concepts. Secure and resourceful chiefs will recognize organizational inadequacies as the reason for the development of unofficial communication channels and will revise the structures and procedures of the formal organization so that efficient unofficial communication channels are absorbed into the formal organization. If they are unable to do this, they should at least attempt to recognize the value of these channels for the communication of information vital to the stability of their organizations. As Thomas Whitehead has noted, "if some department is in fact habitually obtaining information from another by unofficial means, this rather suggests that the information is found useful, and a few procedures for obtaining it with less trouble might be devised."[2]

Communication Directions and Barriers

Communications in a formal organization can go up, down, or across (see Fig. 11.2). Downward communications go from supervisor to subordinate down the chain of command. Upward communications go from subordinate to supervisor up the chain of command. All other communications go laterally across the organization.

Downward is the most traditional and accepted direction of organizational communication. Downward is the direction in which orders are given and authority is exercised. It is the direction in which police chiefs, command-level personnel, and supervisory personnel communicate with and through their subordinates.

Figure 11.2
Directions of Organizational Communication

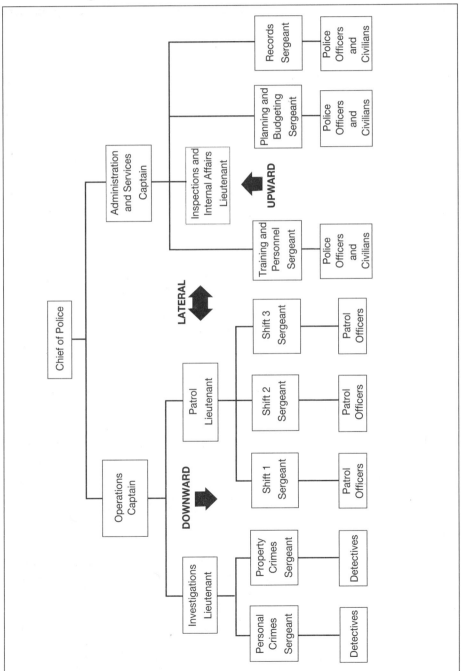

The main barrier to effective downward communication is the chain of command. According to this principle of management, a police chief who wishes to get a message to a patrol officer at the operational level must transmit that message down the chain of command, through each level of management. A police chief who wants to tell a patrol officer to dress more neatly, for example, must give the message to the proper captain, who in turn gives it to the proper lieutenant, who gives it to the proper sergeant, who gives the message to the patrol officer. Passing as it does through so many people, the message is likely to become distorted. Each person within the chain of command perceives the message differently, interprets its meaning differently, and transmits it with varying accuracy. In addition, because each person in the chain is in an authority position with respect to the next recipient of the message, each tends to add his or her own contribution. With so many perceptions, interpretations, transmissions, and personal contributions involved, it is the rare message that finally arrives at its destination intact.

Upward communications undergo this same distortion as they pass through levels of the organization, but they are beset by many other distorting forces as well, largely because upward communications go directly against the grain of organizational authority. In upward communications, employees are giving supervisors information that may eventually be used in evaluating or otherwise managing them. If the information is accurately communicated, it could reflect adversely on either the employee or the quality of his or her performance. Upward communications, therefore, are likely to be distorted at their inception.

It has been noted that supervisors generally tend to think that their subordinates feel free to discuss problems with them, whereas a much smaller percentage of subordinates believe that such an open relationship actually exists.[3] Employees often feel that it is dangerous for them to express their true feelings, that to disagree with their superiors will negatively affect their chances for promotions, that management is not really interested in their welfare, and that they will not be rewarded for good ideas.[4] Norman R.F. Maier has suggested that although supervisors regard their jobs as positions of responsibility, subordinates view their supervisors' jobs as positions of power.[5] Because of apprehension about how supervisors will use their powers, subordinates attempt to keep them in the dark, cover up problems, avoid taking chances, protect one another, and generally play it safe.[6]

Jack Gonzales and John Rothchild have identified four common organizational techniques that further thwart upward communication:

1. Banish or otherwise decimate whistle-blowers and boat rockers: employees who expose intolerable conditions, corruption, incompetence, and other problems in the organization.
2. Place safe and loyal employees above and below troublemakers in the organization's hierarchy, thus effectively silencing them.

3. Ask questions, the answers to which are predetermined, giving management an appearance of being concerned about problems without actually confronting them.

4. Decline to inform management about what is actually going on because of a belief that management would probably not understand anyway, or worse, that management might try to become directly involved and, thus, further complicate matters.[7]

Gonzales and Rothchild conclude that "from an agency perspective, the bureaucrat's main job is not only to hide facts from the public, but also to keep them from fellow bureaucrats up the line."[8] The very nature of organizations almost precludes effective upward communication.

Lateral communications are organizational communications that do not go up or down the chain of command. They may be between line and staff units, coequal units, employees within a particular unit, or even between different organizations. Although they are extremely important elements in the communicative process, lateral communications are often overlooked. With organizations performing more complex operations every day, managers at all levels are less able to coordinate their subordinates via the chain of command. The more complex an organization becomes, the greater the need for lateral communications among subordinates, so that all involved can know exactly how their particular work fits into the organization and where they fit on the team.

The nature of hierarchical organization is an obstacle to lateral communications. All hierarchies operate on the principle of *vertical authority*, authority that comes down from the top through communications. In lateral communications, authority is absent; its place is taken by persuasion. Moreover, hierarchies encourage specialization, a factor that is detrimental to lateral communications, inasmuch as specialists usually have their own frames of reference, loyalties, and languages. Additionally, the general division of the hierarchy into subunits is a barrier to lateral communications, with each subunit fighting for a larger share of organizational resources and a more prominent organizational position in the relative scheme of things. The huge size of many modern organizations makes it difficult for any unit to ascertain who has the information it needs or who needs the information it has.[9]

One must also consider the basic problems involved in communication between any two individuals in addition to the obstacles with respect to downward, upward, and lateral communications. Most organizational communications boil down to series of interpersonal communications being conducted within the organizational milieu and affected by organizational communication channels, directions, and barriers. As we have pointed out, feedback is the primary device used to clear the lines of interpersonal communications so that the communicating parties can be aware of whether they understand one another and whether messages have been received as sent.

Because interpersonal communications are major factors in organizational communications, feedback is also an essential element in keeping organizational communication lines unclogged. Other recommended practices are the use of simplified language, active listening, and emotional control.[10]

The Importance of Information

The substance of communications is information. Regardless of whether the direction is downward, upward, or lateral, what is communicated is information.

Information is an extremely important resource in any organization. Accurate information is needed at every organizational level. Without accurate information, good decisions cannot be made, good plans cannot be formulated, and good strategies and tactics cannot be devised; in general, no one can perform the job satisfactorily if accurate information is unavailable. Especially with respect to governmental service organizations, "the flow of information is the critical element. Information must flow to the key decision points where action is taken with regard to a service to be performed."[11]

Information gets from one place to another in an organization through communications. The messages containing the information can be written or oral. Of great importance, however, is whether the communications system carrying the messages is open-loop or closed-loop. If the communications system is open-loop, providing for no feedback and no evaluation of messages, the organization will be run on the basis of information that could be inaccurate or misperceived. If the communication system is closed-loop, providing for feedback and evaluation of messages, the organization will be run on the basis of accurate information. Thus, the necessity for a closed-loop communications system is obvious.

One of the most important tasks for any organizational administrator, therefore, is the development of a good, closed-loop communications and information system. Such a system is a fundamental and necessary factor for organizational effectiveness and stability. If administrators are deprived of information about how their organizations are running, they will be unable to run them properly. Their communications and information systems must be designed so that communications barriers are minimized, problems are identified quickly, and reliable information is available to decisionmakers. The creation and maintenance of such a system can be difficult, costly, and time-consuming, but the results invariably make the effort worthwhile.

Information and Police Decisionmaking

Much of police work and police administration can be viewed as decisionmaking. At any level in the police organization, decisionmaking involves choosing from among alternatives. Ideally, in each case the alternative selected will be that which promises the most complete solution of the problem at hand or the most complete attainment of the goals and objectives of the police department. Selection of alternatives is made difficult whenever uncertainty and ambiguity characterize the decision-making situation; herein lies one of the major challenges facing police administration, because police decisionmaking is almost always characterized by substantial uncertainty and ambiguity. The only way to minimize these conditions is by providing information that reduces uncertainty and clarifies goals, problems, and alternatives.

Before we examine methods of providing such information for police decisionmaking, we need to look more closely at the kinds of decisions involved in police work and police administration.

Street-Level Decisions

The largest number of police officers are those assigned to patrol duties. They are the officers who receive the lowest pay and are afforded the lowest status. In the performance of their duties, patrol officers make some of the most important decisions imaginable, decisions that involve restricting freedom and, in some instances, even the taking of life. When making decisions such as these, patrol officers operate with a great amount of discretion. Supervisors are rarely present when important decisions must be made, time is usually of the essence, and policies and procedures rarely provide strong positive guidance.

Concern for police discretion and decisionmaking has understandably focused primarily on the decision to arrest, because it is a frequent police decision that has far-reaching consequences for citizens. However, street-level police officers make a variety of other kinds of decisions in the course of their work:

1. Upon observing suspicious circumstances, they decide whether and how to intervene. They might ignore a situation, inquire casually, formally stop and frisk, employ force, or adopt another of the infinite variety of possible interventions.
2. Having intervened in a situation, police officers must choose a disposition. One choice may be arrest, but other options may also be available, including formal summons, referral to another agency (social service, mental health, juvenile services), mediation, warning, or doing nothing.[12]
3. Having arrested a person, police officers may have discretion in booking and charging, including release without charge, choosing what charges to place, deciding how thoroughly to search a person and his or her effects, and determining whether the person remains in jail overnight.

4. Patrol officers and detectives have discretion when deciding how thoroughly to investigate a reported crime and what investigative methods to employ.[13] Decisions about whether to employ such methods as polygraph examinations, undercover operations, or electronic surveillance have important consequences.

5. When responding to an emergency call or pursuing a traffic or criminal violator, police officers decide how fast to drive and whether to violate normal traffic laws and safety rules. These decisions may affect the likelihood of apprehending a violator or taking effective action at the scene of an emergency. They certainly affect the safety of police officers, violators, other motorists, passengers, and pedestrians.

6. When intervening in suspicious circumstances, disorderly situations, and crimes in progress, police officers decide whether to use force and how much to use. The implications of these decisions are obvious.

7. While on routine patrol, police officers decide how to utilize their uncommitted time. Some officers drive constantly, while others park. Some officers seek out trouble spots, while others avoid trouble. Some officers emphasize traffic enforcement, while others focus on burglary prevention, juveniles, or drug violations.[14]

8. When engaged in problem-solving activity,[15] police officers decide which of various alternative responses to a problem will be implemented. They decide whether to collaborate with community groups and other government agencies, and whether to pursue such powerful responses as nuisance abatement and civil forfeiture.

9. Police officers make a variety of other decisions that are not trivial to the people involved: whether to ticket, warn, or ignore a parking or traffic violation; whether to tow a vehicle in response to a parking violation; whether to contact the media to report an arrest or accident; whether to arrest in response to a computer "hit" that may be invalid; and whether to seize property only tangentially related to a crime under investigation.

Of all the decisions made in the police organization, street-level decisions are the most dramatic and have the most immediate impact on our lives. Decisions made at other organizational levels, however, are important and may also have profound effects on police performance, crime control, and the quality of services provided to the community.

Supervisory Decisions

Patrol and investigative supervisors make a variety of important decisions in two general categories: utilization of their subordinates to handle workload, and management of their subordinates. In the first category, patrol supervisors assign officers to beats, supervise the handling of major incidents, and direct activities in response to perceived crime and public order problems. A patrol supervisor might have to decide whether to assign an aggressive officer to a volatile neighborhood; whether to grant or cancel leave in accordance with manpower considerations; whether to permit a patrol officer to conduct an extended investigation of a reported crime; whether to handle a tactical problem with regular patrol units or call for specialized assistance; or whether to assign some officers to directed patrol duties in response to a particular crime trend. An investigative supervisor must make decisions about personnel utilization, case assignment, and utilization of special investigative methods. Examples of these decisions include how many detectives to assign to a major case; which detective to assign to a sensitive investigation; whether to authorize payments to an informant; and whether to permit a dangerous undercover assignment.

Police supervisors also make more routine management decisions. They decide which of their subordinates to recommend for promotion; whether to initiate formal disciplinary proceedings in response to an alleged infraction of the rules; whether any subordinates are in need of special training or retraining; and whether to argue for more resources during the budget process. Though not terribly dramatic when compared to a police officer's decision whether to arrest a citizen, these management-oriented supervisory decisions affect subordinates, agency performance, and, thus, agency effectiveness. These kinds of decisions can also affect the supervisor's and the police department's financial liability, should a subordinate commit a wrongful act or fail to perform a necessary act.

Allocation Decisions

A major set of decisions confronting police administrators pertains to the allocation of police resources. This kind of decision in police departments has traditionally been conceived largely in terms of *patrol allocation*. The default decision in patrol allocation is to assign equal numbers of officers to work the different days of the week and different times of the day. Alternatively, patrol manpower can be differentially allocated by times, days, and shifts, in accordance with workload, response time objectives, deterrence capabilities, and community engagement opportunities. Police administrators make these patrol allocation decisions, whether by design or by default.

Patrol allocation decisions are actually only one subset of police allocation decisionmaking. The principal decision concerns the allocation of resources among subsystems and units, of which patrol is traditionally the largest. The allocation decision involves distributing resources among the operations, administration, and auxiliary services subsystems as well as among the many functions subsumed within each. The police chief has to make such decisions as whether to have a juvenile unit and, if so, how many personnel to assign to it; how many personnel to assign to community services; and whether to have detectives on duty around the clock or only during the day shift.

Allocation decisions have a major impact on the police department's accomplishment of its goals and objectives. Consciously or implicitly, they reflect the police organization's values and priorities. They determine the resources available to handle different types of problems as they arise. The fact that allocation decisions in many departments are made on the basis of politics, community pressures, and police tradition in no way detracts from their importance.

Strategic and Tactical Decisions

Another category of decisionmaking in police agencies concerns the tactics and strategies employed in the performance of police operational duties. Historically, police administrators have given relatively little attention to this type of decision. Having allocated resources to patrol and investigations, police chiefs left the design of strategies and tactics to others. In some instances, supervisors attempted to direct the activities of their subordinates, but frequently it was left to the discretion of patrol officers and detectives to choose their own tactics. Under these circumstances, it was not unusual to find tremendous variation in tactics and enforcement styles within departments and even between patrol officers working the same beats.

Until recently, the traditional failure of police managers to make strategic and tactical decisions has masked the very existence of this kind of decision. With the advent of government fiscal problems and the development of planning-oriented police programs, however, the desirability of strategic decision making has become evident.[16] Given limited resources and a set of goals to be pursued, it is important for police administrators to adopt strategies and tactics that make optimum use of available resources. While the nature of police work may necessitate leaving considerable discretion in the hands of police officers, that discretion need not include total freedom in choosing tactics and strategies. Police administrators have the responsibility for overall organizational performance and the obligation to relate resources to the accomplishment of the organization's primary goals. It is therefore incumbent on them to make strategic decisions rather than deferring to the unarticulated, improvised, and sometimes questionable decisions of individual police officers.

Some of the strategic and tactical choices available to police administrators are discussed in Chapter 13. The task of the police administrator is to choose a combination of strategies and tactics that makes efficient use of resources, fits the community's problems and expectations, and yields the maximum amount of goal attainment.

Policy Decisions

Another set of decisions made by police administrators involves policy decisions. These decisions concern written policies that guide police officer decisionmaking, as well as the organization's general stance toward community issues and problems. Both written and unwritten policies are important reflections of the police department's values and priorities and, as such, represent important decisions for police administrators.

Most police departments promulgate written policies to cover a wide range of matters, but the most important subjects for policy coverage are police officer decisions that affect the lives, property, and freedom of citizens. Police administrators must choose policies that guide officers in their decisions to arrest, to use force, to engage in high-speed driving, or to make other street-level choices affecting life and freedom. Despite the operational reality of discretion, "police officers need administrative guidelines that are developed for the purpose of assisting them in making appropriate decisions as they carry out their work."[17] Police policies, procedures, rules, and regulations were discussed in Chapter 5.

Police administrators also make decisions about the organization's overall stance or policy toward community problems and issues. For example, decisions must be made about the police department's policy toward such crimes as gambling, prostitution, and drug possession. Similarly, a police department must have policies concerning media relations, cooperation with other law enforcement agencies, and collaboration with outside researchers. Frequently, the term "policy" is used to describe a department's philosophy or style, as in "it is our policy to work closely with the community" or "it is our policy to strictly enforce the law." These broad forms of policy may seem so vague as to be mere platitudes, but they represent one of the most significant ways in which the police organization transmits guidance to police officers.[18] For this reason, it is extremely important for police administrators to choose and communicate such policies carefully, rather than to permit them to be set by custom and tradition and transmitted through the filter of the police subculture.

Administrative Decisions

Finally, a whole host of administrative decisions are required in the course of managing a police organization. The management functions of system building, planning, organizing, staffing, directing, and controlling all involve substantial decisionmaking. Decisions must be made about qualifications for employment, which applicants to hire, which employees to promote, and which employees to terminate. Decisions are required concerning the length and content of recruit training, field training, and in-service training. Managers must make budgeting decisions, purchasing decisions, disciplinary decisions, and scheduling decisions. Organizational structure decisions pertaining to centralization, specialization, grouping like functions, delegation of authority, and span of control must be made.

The street-level decisions of patrol officers and detectives have an immediate impact on citizens; the discretionary character of such decisions frequently causes considerable notoriety. Police supervisors and administrators also make numerous decisions, as we have shown, and many of these allocation, strategic, tactical, policy, and administrative decisions have a significant bearing on the activities of street-level police officers and on the effectiveness of the police organization as a whole. When police administrators make these kinds of decisions, they rarely face the time constraints, danger, hostility, and situational unpredictability that confront patrol officers and detectives. On the other hand, administrators are required to juggle political and organizational pressures, resource constraints, and externally imposed policies while having to make difficult choices characterized by uncertainty and ambiguity.[19] Because police decisions at street and administrative levels have important consequences and are characterized by uncertainty, it is critically important that as much information as possible be made available for consideration in the decision-making process.

Police Information Systems

Due to the nature of their activities, police officers and police organizations collect a great amount of information. The records rooms and computer systems of a large police department contain significant amounts of information. All the file cabinets and computers, in turn, may not contain as much information as the heads of a few police officers.

To be useful for decisionmaking, information must be made available in a usable form to the decisionmaker at the time the decision has to be made. To achieve this, several steps must be taken:

- Data Collection—information must initially be obtained, with due concern for its reliability and validity

- Data Collation—information must be sifted, labeled, categorized, and otherwise manipulated so that its relevance to problems and decisions is identified

- Analysis/Interpretation—information must be tabulated, analyzed, and synthesized to reveal patterns, trends, and generalizations

- Dissemination—methods must be developed to communicate information and analyses to decisionmakers

- Feedback and Evaluation—a closed-loop system must be maintained to provide feedback on the validity and usefulness of information and analyses

The kind of information needed depends largely on the type of decision to be made. Police officers facing an arrest decision may need information about the incident that has occurred, about the people involved, about the law, and about the alternatives that are available for dealing with the situation. A police chief facing a patrol allocation decision, on the other hand, needs information about police workload by time of day, day of week, and location. In the following sections we will discuss three general types of police information systems: operations information systems, command and control systems, and management information systems.

Operations Information Systems

Operations information systems are systems that provide information to patrol officers, detectives, and other employees engaged in direct service to the public. The kinds of decisions being made by these police employees are primarily street-level decisions. Information is needed to make choices about whether and how to intervene in suspicious circumstances, what disposition to make following intervention, and what tactics to employ during routine patrol. The specific types of information that are required might include whether a person is wanted by the law; whether an item of property is stolen; whether a vehicle is properly registered; whether a violator has a prior record; whether a particular store window was previously broken; or whether a burglary under investigation fits the pattern of previously reported burglaries.

Some of the means by which operations information is provided in police departments are so routine that we are apt to overlook them when considering information systems. The police communications system and police records system are key components of the operations information system. Using the radio, a patrol officer who has noticed a broken store window can inquire whether the damage has previously been noticed and reported. Another officer, hearing the question over the radio, may have the information that is needed, or the information may be found in a records log or activity summary at the communications center. If the required information is not available from these sources, the radio dispatcher can use the telephone to call the store owner and determine whether the patrol officer has discovered a fresh incident or one that had previously been reported. In this scenario, the radio system, other officers listening on the radio, the dispatcher, communications center records and the telephone are all part of an operations information system that can obtain needed information for the patrol officer.

Other unobtrusive components of police operations information systems are the manuals that transmit training, policies, procedures, rules, and regulations. These manuals contain information about proper and improper methods of handling various kinds of situations. To the extent that police officers have learned the contents of the manuals, the information has been internalized, and reference to the manuals may not be necessary. Most police manuals are so voluminous, however, that few officers succeed in completely mastering them. To the extent that needed information can be retrieved from the manuals quickly, they can serve as useful information systems. However, if they are poorly organized and too bulky to carry into the field, as is often the case, the manuals lose their value as sources of information for street-level decisionmaking.

Today, some police departments make their manuals available to officers electronically, for example, by loading them into laptop computers that officers use for report writing and other duties.[20] This technique not only makes the manuals available in lighter and less bulky form, but also makes it possible for officers to use the computer's keyword searching capabilities when looking for information on a particular topic, such as drug evidence processing or seizure of abandoned vehicles.

Much of the information that police officers need for street-level decisions is stored in the records of the police department, in other police departments, and in motor vehicle registry agencies. It would be difficult for a police officer to check by radio or telephone with all 17,000 American police departments to determine whether a suspect was wanted or an item of property was stolen. Fortunately, the development of computers has made it feasible to link such information from all over the country. Most states have statewide law enforcement information systems that receive and disseminate information on wanted persons, stolen property, and criminal records. These systems are linked by the National Crime Information Center (NCIC).

An officer following a suspicious vehicle can use the police radio to run a check on the vehicle's license tag number, for example. Many departments have now gone a step further and installed computer terminals or laptop computers in patrol cars so that officers can make direct inquiries into operational information systems without having to go through a dispatcher and voice-radio communications. These kinds of systems directly support street-level decisionmaking.[21]

Another form of information useful for street-level police officers focuses on the nature of crime, traffic, and public order problems. When deciding how to utilize their patrol time, officers can benefit from information about crime trends and patterns, hot spots, repeat call locations, traffic accident patterns, and other problems occurring on their beats. Many police departments distribute activity bulletins to make officers aware of conditions on their beats; such bulletins are disseminated with the expectation that officers will use the information contained therein when allocating their time and choosing their patrol tactics. This kind of information is also valuable for detectives whose case-by-case focus sometimes prevents them from seeing geographic patterns and similarities in method of operation among several cases under investigation.

A common denominator for this type of information is location—systems that assist with the collection and dissemination of location-oriented data are termed *Geographic Information Systems (GIS)*. Police departments today are investing heavily in developing better GIS capacities (including, but not limited to, computer mapping) so that location-oriented information can be produced more efficiently and accurately. Within the context of community policing, especially, GIS capabilities have significant promise for making police information systems more useful for both street officers and police managers.[22]

Command and Control Systems

Command and control systems provide information to supervisors, commanders, and communications personnel to aid them in decisions concerning workload distribution, assignment of calls, and supervision of operations personnel. These systems can also provide administrators with information useful in making allocation, strategic, and tactical decisions.

The basic component of a police command and control system is the radio, often assisted today by a computer. Via the police radio, officers respond to calls, report their arrival, report their departure and respond to queries concerning their location and status. Patrol supervisors can direct their subordinates to certain locations, direct them to perform certain tasks, and question them about various matters over the radio. Messages received over the radio provide dispatchers with information about which patrol units are in and out of service and which units are closest to the scene of a reported incident. During a critical incident such as a high-speed chase or a crime in progress, the radio system provides the mechanism for coordination and control.

A number of technological innovations have enhanced the capabilities of police command and control systems. For example, computer-aided dispatch systems have been introduced to systematize and speed up the flow of information from complainant to police telephone operator to police radio dispatcher to responding patrol unit. Among the features of these systems are the following:

- verifying reported location by determining if it is a valid address

- assuring that operators obtain all necessary information from complainants

- determining in which patrol beat the incident is located

- assigning case numbers and priorities to calls

- reporting previous calls at the location

- routing calls to the appropriate dispatcher

- recommending patrol units for assignment to the call, based on location of the call and status of patrol units in the area

- recording time of dispatch, time of arrival, and time cleared

- keeping track of incident status and patrol unit status[23]

Another recent technological innovation is automatic vehicle monitoring. This kind of system automatically and continuously reports police vehicle location and status to the communication center.[24] This information can aid the dispatcher or computer-aided dispatching system when selecting patrol units to respond to calls and can also help dispatchers and supervisors keep track of patrol units. This feature can contribute significantly to officer safety if officers get into situations where they need assistance but cannot report their locations for some reason. Automatic vehicle monitoring may also deter patrol officers from wandering out of their assigned areas.

Advanced telephone reporting systems (911 systems) are another component of police command and control systems. Besides providing information more rapidly from complainants, enhanced versions of these systems can immediately inform police telephone operators of the telephone number from which a call to the police is being made as well as the location of the telephone. This information can be helpful for verifying the authenticity of the report, establishing the correct location of the incident, contacting the complainant for more information, and quickly dispatching patrol units to the scene.

Police command and control systems also provide information pertinent to decisions about allocation, strategies, and tactics. Basic information on total police workload, including numbers of incidents, types of incidents, day and time of incidents, location of incidents, time required to handle incidents, numbers of units required to handle incidents, and response time to incidents, is all produced through the command and control system. It may be reflected in dispatch cards and activity summaries, or it may be automatically collected and tabulated as part of computer-aided dispatching. However er collected, this information is crucial for allocation and strategic decisions. Analysis of this information is often termed *operations analysis* and will be discussed in a later section of this chapter.

Management Information Systems

Management information systems are systems that provide information needed for supervisory, allocation, strategic, tactical, policy, and administrative decisions. The command and control systems discussed in the last section are to some extent management information systems, but they also serve important operational functions and so are classified separately.

Some of the specific types of management information systems found in police departments include the following:

- personnel information systems[25]

- warrant control information systems[26]

- equipment inventory systems

- evidence and property control systems

- booking information systems

- detention information systems

- case tracking systems

- financial information systems

- fleet maintenance information systems[27]

These and other police management information systems may or may not be computerized. The issue of computerization depends primarily on the amount of data that must be handled by the system in order to provide the manager with the information needed for decisionmaking. A police department with a two-vehicle fleet probably does not need a computerized fleet mainte-nance information system, but it does need some kind of information system to keep track of vehicle maintenance performed, vehicle problems, and scheduled preventive maintenance so that the manager responsible for vehicle mainte-nance can make informed decisions about tune-ups, oil changes, tires, batter-ies, minor repairs, maintenance vendors, and vehicle replacement.

The concept underlying management information systems is simple. It is necessary to identify the decisions required of managers as well as the infor-mation they need to make informed decisions. The task of the information system is simply to provide the necessary information to managers when they need it. Often, the hardest part of developing an information system is getting managers to identify the information they need. The mechanics of getting the information may be complex, but this can usually be accomplished once the relevant decisions and information are identified.[28]

The real value of a management information system is that it routinely and continuously provides needed information. In the absence of such sys-tems, managers confronting decisions may or may not have the time and wherewithal to gather the information they need. With such systems, the information is readily available.

Numerous companies sell information technology systems for police departments. These systems vary to some extent in their emphasis on oper-ations information, command and control, management information, and mere record keeping. Vendors can be located at any police chiefs' meeting or in the pages of *Police Chief* magazine. Before purchasing such systems, however, police administrators should carefully think about the decisions they have to make and the information they need to make those decisions wisely. These purchasing decisions should be made carefully not only because computer systems are expensive but also because (1) technology changes rapidly, (2) the most technologically advanced system is not neces-sarily the most effective for any particular police department, and (3) much of the available information comes from vendors, whose vested interest is in promoting their systems more than in meeting the department's needs.[29]

Analysis of Police Information

Some information useful for police decisionmaking, such as the existence of an arrest warrant for a certain person, need only be stored, retrievable, and cross-indexed. Other information, however, must be aggregated, tabulated, correlated, or otherwise analyzed in order to be of real utility in decisionmaking. In the sections that follow, we discuss several of the most common forms of analysis conducted in support of police decisionmaking. These are by no means the only types of analysis that are conducted, but simply the most common.

Crime Analysis

Crime analysis is a type of police problem analysis. All organizations, to some extent, analyze the problems they confront as a means of gaining a better understanding of the problems and their solutions. Because crime is the most serious problem faced by the police, it is not surprising that crime analysis occupies a central role among the various types of police analysis.

Crime Analysis

Standard 15.1.1   A written directive establishes crime analysis procedures to include:

    a.   specification of source documents from which crime analysis data elements are extracted;

    b.   analysis of crime data;

    c.   documentation of the temporal and geographic distribution of selected crimes;

    d.   the distribution of crime analysis information;

    e.   feedback analysis; and

    f.   briefing the agency's chief executive officer on crime patterns and trends.

Source: *Standards for Law Enforcement Agencies: The Standards Manual of the Law Enforcement Agency Accreditation Program.* Fairfax, VA: Commission on Accreditation for Law Enforcement Agencies, Inc., 1999.

The basic purpose of crime analysis is to "identify, describe, and disseminate information concerning crime patterns and problems."[30] Crime analysis begins with data collection and collation. Crime reports, dispatch records, and activity summaries are scoured for specific information about crimes reported, suspicious persons identified by patrol officers, and suspects identified through investigation. Crime analysis particularly focuses on precise information about location, time of occurrence, and method of operation. This information is arranged in manual, semi-automated, or computerized files for ease of retrieval.

The analysis of these crime data primarily involves looking for patterns and trends. Similar methods of operation may be noted in two or more crimes, a geographic pattern may be observed, or a preponderance of certain types of crime on certain days or at certain times may be evident. A suspect or arrestee in one case may possibly be linked by method of operation, geography, or timing to other unsolved crimes. Some patterns may lead to predictions about the time or place of next occurrence, while others merely suggest areas that should be watched.

The dissemination of crime analysis information is typically achieved through hot sheets, bulletins, and maps. These devices summarize information and conclusions about crimes, patterns, and trends. In departments that utilize the directed patrol strategy, crime analysis information is disseminated as part of the instructions for directed assignments. In some police agencies, crime analysis personnel even design the directed patrol assignments, based on their analysis of crime data.[31]

Crime analysis information can be useful at various levels in the police organization.[32] Street-level decisions about whether to intervene in suspicious situations, what locations to target with uncommitted patrol time, and what tactics to use during patrol can benefit from crime analysis information. It has been observed, however, that "crime bulletins and statistical analyses, issued without supplemental personal contact, tend to be regarded at the field level as irrelevant due to lack of credibility, delay of receipt of the information or simple redundancy regarding what the officers already know."[33] This observation highlights the requirement that experienced police officers be included in the crime analysis process, that analysis not depend completely on written reports as sources of information, and that dissemination be timely. The dissemination of crime analysis information to operational personnel is an example of lateral communications that must overcome the barriers typical of that direction of organizational communication.

Police supervisors can utilize crime analysis information to better understand crime and service demands facing their shift or district. They can use the information when assigning personnel to beats and when deploying any special resources that may be available. They can also use crime analysis to direct the tactics of their subordinates.[34]

Police administrators can benefit from crime analysis information primarily when making allocation, strategic, and tactical decisions; when responding to outside requests for information; and when engaging in planning. The nature of the community's crime problems is obviously an important input to decisions about the allocation of police resources among different organizational units. Similarly, when deciding whether to utilize such strategies and tactics as directed patrol, foot patrol, decoy squads, or sting operations, information about crime problems is crucial. Such information is also frequently requested by political leaders, community groups, and the media for a variety of legitimate purposes. In addition, when police administrators are engaged in budgeting and planning for the future, information about crime problems and crime trends is valuable.[35]

During the last two decades, crime analysis units have become institutionalized in most large police departments. Most recently, federal funds from the National Institute of Justice and the Office of Community Oriented Policing Services have been used to encourage refinements in police crime analysis, especially in the area of computerized mapping.[36] In a large number of police departments, however, crime analysis information is still underutilized. Many crime analysis units spew out daily, weekly, and monthly reports without regard to the decision-making needs of, or crime analysis utilization by, police officers, supervisors, and administrators. In these departments, crime analysis needs to be more fully integrated with operations, command and control, and management information systems. Crime analysis must be tied to the real information needs of the department's decisionmakers.[37]

Other Types of Problem Analysis

Crime analysis is but one type of police problem analysis. Most police departments, for example, conduct some analysis of traffic accidents in order to identify hazardous intersections and types of violations that cause accidents. This information can be used for designing a selective traffic enforcement program, for directing the activities of patrol units, for public education, and for traffic engineering improvements. For state police agencies with major traffic enforcement responsibilities, this type of analysis may be more important than crime analysis. However, almost all police agencies have some traffic responsibilities and can better serve their communities by basing traffic-related operations and decisions on analysis of accident and violation data.

Police departments should also analyze service and order-maintenance problems in the same fashion as they analyze crime and traffic problems. Traditionally, police departments have not looked for patterns and trends in service and public order problems as they have in crime and traffic accidents, perhaps in the belief that the former occurred randomly or without conscious design. However, such problems as disorderly intoxication, panhandling, vandalism, domestic disputes, and gang intimidation may very well reveal patterns or trends if analyzed.[38] Similarly, police departments that provide ambulance services, bank escorts, and assistance to disabled motorists may find patterns and trends in these activities. Even discovering the locations, frequency, and magnitude of such services may be important information for allocation or policy decisions.[39]

Traffic Analysis

Standard 61.1.1 A written directive governs the agency's selective traffic enforcement activities, to include procedures for:

a. analysis of traffic crashes;

b. analysis of traffic enforcement activities;

c. implementation of selective enforcement techniques and procedures;

d. deployment of traffic enforcement personnel; and

e. evaluation of selective traffic enforcement activities.

Source: *Standards for Law Enforcement Agencies: The Standards Manual of the Law Enforcement Agency Accreditation Program.* Fairfax, VA: Commission on Accreditation for Law Enforcement Agencies, Inc., 1999.

Another type of police problem analysis focuses on the problem of fear of crime. It has long been recognized that fear of crime is not perfectly correlated with crime itself.[40] A geographic area with little crime may exhibit high fear, fear may increase while crime decreases, or citizens may fear specific crimes that do not actually threaten them. Recently, some police departments have begun to try to reduce fear of crime, independently of their efforts to reduce crime itself.[41] These efforts can only proceed on the basis of information about fear: information that police agencies have not typically collected or analyzed. In order to gather such information, departments have had to approach citizens with surveys, questionnaires, and interviews. This information can then be used to identify particularly fearful neighborhoods as well as the sources of their fear. In turn, tactics can be employed to treat the sources of that fear with the hope of minimizing citizen concern about crime.[42]

Operations Analysis

Operations analysis differs from crime analysis in that it is focused mainly on the police department's operations rather than on crime or any other specific community problem. It is oriented toward efficiency and effectiveness and provides input primarily to allocation, strategic, and tactical decisions. Operations analysis uses some of the same information as crime analysis, but for the larger purpose of matching allocation and strategies to workload and organizational goals rather than for the narrower purpose of directing patrol officers and detectives in accomplishing prevention and apprehension objectives.

The most common target of operations analysis is patrol allocation and deployment. Patrol involves the largest portion of police department resources and provides the bulk of services to the public. Among the major issues involved in patrol allocation are:

- Determining the number of patrol units to have on duty in each of the department's geographic commands; this may vary by time of day, day of week, or season of the year.

- Designing patrol beats.

- Developing policy for dispatching and redeploying of patrol units.

- Scheduling patrol personnel to match variations in the number of units needed on duty.[43]

In order to clarify these patrol allocation issues, operations data must be collected and analyzed. First, different categories of patrol workload must be identified; these include calls for service, officer-initiated activities, and administrative activities. For each activity, a variety of information must be collected, to include at a minimum:

- type of call or activity

- time reported

- time consumed

- day of week

- month

- location

- number of units assigned

Analysis of these data will reveal patrol workload and its variations by time of day, day of week, season, and location. The analysis can be performed manually, mechanically, partially by computer, or completely by computer.[44] The results of the analysis can then be used to allocate patrol resources proportionally to workload, to minimize response times to emergency calls, to distribute directed patrol time according to crime incidence, to maximize apprehension or prevention capabilities, or to hone the efficiency of other patrol-related techniques or activities according to almost any other criteria. The patrol allocation analysis merely provides information about workload and perhaps about the consequences of different allocation alternatives; the allocation decisionmaker uses this information in conjunction with such other factors as union contract specifications and political considerations in selecting the alternative that best achieves the primary goals of the organization.

Investigative work should also be the target of operations analysis. Information on each case assigned for follow-up investigation can be collected and analyzed, focusing on caseload size, time utilization, case clearance effectiveness, and case variations by time and location. Determinations eventually have to be made about the number of personnel assigned to investigations, their scheduling, and whether to employ formal case screening.[45] The latter practice involves identifying the most solvable cases and focusing investigative resources on them. The basis for this case screening practice is analysis of the case characteristics that predict whether a case will be solved.[46]

The matter of investigative case screening illustrates the applicability of operations analysis to strategic and tactical decisions as well as to allocation decisions. In the patrol sphere, operations analysis can identify the extent of patrol time available for directed patrol assignments or document the current utilization of aggressive patrol tactics through analysis of officer-initiated activity. Allocation decisions pertain to the amount of resources applied, while strategic and tactical decisions pertain to the tasks accomplished with those resources; both kinds of decisions demand information of the sort supplied by operations analysis.

Intelligence Analysis

Intelligence analysis involves the collection, collation, analysis, and dissemination of information concerning organized crime and criminals, including traditional organized crime syndicates, drug traffickers, and terrorists. Whereas crime analysis focuses on ordinary crime, intelligence analysis focuses on organized crime and terrorism.

The sources of intelligence information are widespread and include patrol officers, detectives, informants, undercover agents, witnesses, ordinary citizens, trial transcripts, commission hearings, license applications, newspaper and magazine articles, physical and electronic surveillance, and police records.[47] All this information must be evaluated for reliability and validity, assessed for value, filed and cross-referenced, and then analyzed for trends and patterns. Often the mere identification of an organized network of criminals represents valuable information and the first step toward effective enforcement.

Information from intelligence analysis is particularly useful to tactical and investigative units with specific responsibilities for addressing organized crime, drug trafficking, and terrorism. In addition, this information is needed by administrators when making allocation, strategic, tactical, and policy decisions. Often overlooked in the intelligence analysis process, however, are patrol officers. These officers are often in possession of more information about suspicious activity and associations among criminals than any other members of the police department; they may also be in the best position to use intelligence information, at least against street-level organized crime.

Revelations of police misconduct in intelligence gathering during the 1960s and 1970s seriously stunted the development of the intelligence analysis function in American policing. During that era, many police agencies collated and stored information on people whose only "crimes" were opposition to the Vietnam War or support for civil rights. Following the disclosure of these abuses of police authority, some police departments voluntarily ceased their intelligence-gathering activities; others were forced to curtail their activities by political supervisors or by the courts.

The events of September 11, 2001, have once again demonstrated the absolute necessity for police intelligence gathering and analysis. Without performing such activities, police departments cannot compete with terrorists and organized criminals. By the same token, however, "it is mandatory that a police department recognize that special care and precaution must be taken in intelligence to avoid interfering with or impairing the constitutional rights of citizens to maintain their privacy, to speak and dissent freely, to write and to publish, and to associate privately and publicly for any lawful purpose."[48] Police intelligence gathering must be limited to genuinely dangerous criminals and never applied to mere political dissidents. As wisely noted by one observer, "no other aspect of a police department's duties requires such detached and sensitive judgments by individual police officers as does intelligence" and "in no other kind of police work is reverence for the law more demanding and demanded."[49]

Implications of Community Policing

The widespread implementation of community policing over the past two decades has brought some additional types of police decisions, information needs, and analysis requirements to the forefront.[50] In addition, perhaps most importantly, community policing has highlighted a new set of information users—the community. Today, as police departments think about the types of information that need to be made available, and consider the users of that information, they have to remember to include those community residents and community groups who collaborate with police officers in identifying, analyzing, and solving problems.

Table 11.1 illustrates some of the more important informational differences between professional-era policing and community policing. As these differences become more widely recognized and institutionalized within policing, police information systems will need to be substantially enhanced and expanded.

Rational Police Decisionmaking

Throughout this chapter we have discussed the importance of information for police decisionmaking at various levels in the organization. We have also described several systems for providing such information, as well as a number of types of analysis often conducted to make information more meaningful and useful. Our entire presentation has been based on the assumption that police managers can, should, and will use information to make informed decisions. In effect, we have assumed the existence of a significant degree of rationality in police decisionmaking.

Table 11.1
New Information Requirements for Community Policing

Information Domains	Information Usage Patterns	
	Professional Era	**Community Policing**
Community Interface	One-way flow of incident-oriented, reactive information; narrow range of information (just the facts); mainly limited to officers and detectives gathering raw data from crime victims and other complainants	Two-way flow of information; proactive and problem-oriented information emphasized; wide range of information desired; all levels need both raw data and analysis; much greater emphasis on providing information to the community
Inter-Organizational Linkages	Little information sharing among police and other government agencies and nongovernmental organizations; not seen as relevant or important	Substantial information sharing; crucial to effective collaborative problem solving; information needed by line-level problem solvers, partners, managers, and executives
Work-Group Facilitation	Not seen as very important; incident-oriented policing primarily an individual-level activity	Problem solving and geographic focus raise the importance of work groups; officers and detectives need information to coordinate and collaborate with others; supervisors need more information to coordinate their subordinates under conditions of functional diversity and temporal complexity
Environmental Scanning	Not seen as very important; primarily an executive-level activity; generally limited to serious crime issues and major developments within the policing profession	Important at all levels of the organization; a wide range of issues are seen as relevant (crime, disorder, drugs, fear, new technology, professional developments, etc.); an important area for analysis, not just raw data
Problem Orientation	Focus on incidents, not problems	Policing and partnerships focus primarily on problem solving; raw data and analysis needed for problem identification, problem analysis, search for responses, and assessment; data and analyses needed by police at all levels and by external partners
Area Accountability	Accountability primarily temporal (by shift) or functional (patrol, investigations); no real geographic focus or accountability	Accountability primarily geographic; data and analysis need to be geographically oriented; needed by police at all levels and by external partners
Strategic Management	Commanders and executives rely on a narrow range of information (crime, calls for service) to analyze service demands and allocate resources; police management primarily defensive, reactive, tactical	Police management more complex; wider range of relevant objectives (crime control, order maintenance, fear reduction, public satisfaction, integrity, accountability); wider range of programs, policies, tactics, and strategies seen as viable; thus, a more strategic approach is needed, which requires increased information

Adapted from Terence Dunworth, Gary Cordner, Jack Greene, Timothy Bynum, Scott Decker, Thomas Rich, Shawn Ward, and Vince Webb. *Police Department Information Systems Technology Enhancement Project (ISTEP)*. Washington, DC: Office of Community Oriented Policing Services, 2000, pp. 12-13.

In this last section of the chapter, we address the issue of rational decisionmaking as well as the issue of police organizational control through influences on police officer and police manager decisionmaking.

Bounded Rationality

For several reasons, police decisionmaking, whether at the street level or at the level of the police chief, cannot be completely rational. To make a totally rational decision, one would need a clear and unambiguous goal, complete familiarity with every conceivable alternative for achieving the goal, exact information about the consequences of each and every conceivable alternative, and a complete understanding of all variables involved. As soon as a goal becomes vague and multiple goals are presented, rational decisionmaking becomes much more difficult to achieve. As soon as one limits the number of conceivable alternatives to be considered, because of lack of imagination or lack of time, the possibility of overlooking the best alternative(s) is introduced. When knowledge about variables is limited and when information about the consequences of alternatives is inexact or unavailable, as is always the case, it becomes impossible to guarantee the selection of the best alternative.

Police decisionmaking is not alone in facing these limitations on rationality. Virtually all decisionmaking is at best subjectively rational in that "it maximizes attainment relative to the actual knowledge of the subject."[51] Police departments share with other public agencies the absence of clear goals; in fact, "we turn to government in part precisely because we wish to attain vague, complex, controversial, hard-to-produce objectives (clear, easily attained, noncontroversial goals are more often than not left to the market or to private arrangements)."[52] In addition, police agencies share with many other organizations a lack of proven methods for attaining their goals as well as decidedly incomplete information about the effects of current practices and alternatives.

In addition to these fundamental limits on rational decisionmaking, there exist what might be termed *dynamic limits*. Street-level police decisionmaking is inevitably affected by changing and dynamic factors such as the race, sex, social class, culture, and demeanor of victims and suspects. Allocation and policy decisions are affected by community pressures, budgetary considerations, union contracts, civil service regulations, and a variety of other dynamic political factors. Most important decisionmaking, whether in police departments or other kinds of organizations, is affected by such nonstatic considerations.

Because of such fundamental and practical limitations on police decisionmaking, some observers might be inclined to dismiss the intrinsic value and importance of information. To these observers, police decisionmaking is a matter of judgment, common sense, and politics rather than a matter of information and analysis. They are partially correct. Street-level police decisions will always be affected by "situational exigencies"[53] that may not conform to rational criteria; similarly, allocation and policy decisions will always be affected by budgetary and political considerations. Yet acknowledgment of these realities does not eliminate the need for accurate, objective, and reliable information. Police officers will always need information about suspects, operational methodologies, and departmental rules and procedures. Police administrators will always need information to allocate resources efficiently within budgetary and political constraints.

Although the rationality of police decisionmaking is inevitably limited, it is in the public interest that such decisionmaking be as rational as possible. One of the principal methods for enhancing decision-making rationality is through the provision of accurate, objective, and reliable information. Therefore, police information systems and police analysis capabilities have an important role to play despite pragmatic real-world limitations on police decision-making rationality.

Controlling Decisionmaking

In order to assure the continuing stability of the police organization, it is necessary to exert influence over the decisionmaking of employees. The primary goals of the organization will be achieved to the extent that decisionmakers choose alternatives that maximize attainment of those goals. The police chief's task in promoting good decisionmaking can be seen as attempting to influence all members of the organization in such a way that they will make the choices that the chief would make if he or she could be present at the time each decision is made.

How does a chief achieve this? First, it is necessary that all decisionmakers pursue established goals and objectives and adhere to organizational values. This requires knowledge of established goals and values and a willingness to pursue them. Employees are informed of goals and values through training, socialization, and organizational policies. Employee willingness to pursue goals and abide by values is developed through selection and socialization, encouraged through rewards, and coerced through discipline and the authority structure of the organization.

Rational police decisionmaking also requires that employees select the best alternatives for achieving established goals. That is, employees must not only have good intentions, they must also choose effective methods. This requires knowledge, information, and rational thinking. Knowledge and information are transmitted through training, procedures, rules, regulations, and information systems. Through classroom and field training, an attempt is made to teach employees how to use this knowledge and information logically, intelligently, and rationally. To a large extent, police departments also rely on selection to identify applicants who already possess these information-processing capabilities.

Police departments can influence their employees' decisionmaking by providing good and useful information. When employees are aware of and committed to the organization's goals and are intellectually capable of using information rationally, the information available to them becomes the key ingredient in decisionmaking. Investigative decisions about whether to follow up on reported crimes can be made based on organizationally relevant criteria; supervisory decisions about whether to employ directed patrol during a particular shift can be based on crime analysis information; and patrol officer decisions about whether to arrest or refer juvenile vandals can be made according to their records, established policy, and legal (rather than extralegal) factors.

This information-oriented perspective on police management direction and control is useful to keep in mind.[54] Traditionally, control in police organizations was thought to be achieved through the formal hierarchy of authority. This view does have some validity, but it implies the existence of direct supervisory control over police officers that is not consistent with the reality of police operations or, indeed, police discretion.

Another approach to direction and control in police organizations stresses the influence that the community has over police actions. Citizens decide when to summon the police, exert influence over police dispositions of their complaints, set limits of acceptable police behavior, and influence police administration through their elected political leaders.

The third view of direction and control in police organizations, based on information and decisionmaking, is frequently not recognized and is significantly less appreciated than the formal authority and community pressure approaches described in the above two paragraphs. In many respects this view provides a closer fit with the nature of police work and police organizations that require large amounts of good decisionmaking on a continuing basis; and information is the key ingredient in that decisionmaking. This focus on information as the key ingredient in decisionmaking and on decisionmaking as the central activity of police work deserves wider recognition among police managers and greater attention from those involved in police research.

Summary

Although organizational communication reflects all of the complexities of interpersonal communication, it is made even more complex by its organizational context. Communications in organizations follow informal channels more frequently than they follow the formal chain of command. Upward, downward, and lateral communications are each impeded by different organizational barriers.

Communications carry information that is needed in organizations for effective decisionmaking. Police departments are characterized by important street-level, supervisory, allocation, strategic, tactical, policy, and administrative decisions. These decisions are supported by operations information systems, command and control systems, and management information systems. These systems provide specific pieces of information for decisionmaking in conjunction with crime analysis, analysis of other types of problems, operations analysis, and intelligence analysis. In recent years, community policing has introduced new types of decisions, creating the need for new categories of information and analysis, and also introducing community residents and other external partners as new and important users of police information.

The rationality of all decisionmaking, including police decisionmaking, is hindered by cognitive and practical limitations. Nevertheless, effectiveness and productivity depend on decisionmaking that is as rational as possible; one key to enhancing the rationality of police decisionmaking is careful attention to providing decisionmakers with the accurate, objective, and reliable information they need when they need it.

Discussion Questions

1. What roles are played by official and unofficial communications in organizations with which you are familiar? By the formal and informal organizations?

2. Why do supervisors think that subordinates feel free to communicate upward to them, when in fact most subordinates fear such communication?

3. Think of communications and information flow in organizations with which you are familiar. Is the flow open- or closed-loop in nature? Do decisionmakers know whether their information is accurate? Do decisionmakers find out about the effects of their decisions? Do order issuers know whether their orders are understood? Do they find out whether their orders are carried out?

4. What do you think will be the long-range impact of computers and other information-processing technology on police work and police administration? What has been the impact so far?

5. What do you think are the primary methods by which police organizations actually control their employees' decisionmaking?

Notes

1. W. Scholz, *Communication in the Business Organization* (Englewood Cliffs, NJ: Prentice Hall, 1962), p. 33.

2. T.N. Whitehead, *Leadership in a Free Society* (Cambridge, MA: Harvard University Press, 1936), p. 78.

3. R. Likert, *New Patterns of Management* (New York, NY: McGraw-Hill, 1961), pp. 46-47.

4. A. Vogel, "Why Don't Employees Speak Up?" *Personnel Administration* (May–June 1967): 20-22.

5. N.R.F. Maier, *Psychology in Industrial Organizations*, Fourth Edition (Boston, MA: Houghton Mifflin, 1973), p. 582.

6. Ibid.

7. J. Gonzales and J. Rothchild, "The Shriver Prescription: How the Government Can Find Out What It's Doing," *Washington Monthly* (November 1972): 37-39.

8. Ibid., p. 36.

9. F.A. Nigro, *Modern Public Administration* (New York, NY: Harper & Row, 1965), pp. 197-199.

10. S.P. Robbins, *Organizational Behavior*, Third Edition (Englewood Cliffs, NJ: Prentice Hall, 1986), pp. 214-215.

11. R.A. Johnson, F.E. Kast, and J.E. Rosenzweig, "Designing Management Systems," *Business Quarterly* (summer 1964), as quoted in P.P. Schoderbek, ed., *Management Systems* (New York, NY: Wiley, 1967), p. 117.

12. H. Goldstein, *Policing a Free Society* (Cambridge, MA: Ballinger, 1977), pp. 94-100.

13. Ibid.; see also T.S. Bynum, G.W. Cordner, and J.R. Greene, "Victim and Offense Characteristics: Impact on Police Investigative Decision-Making," *Criminology* 20, no. 3-4 (November 1982): 301-318.

14. G.W. Cordner, "While on Routine Patrol: What the Police Do When They're Not Doing Anything," *American Journal of Police* 1, no. 2 (1982): 94-112.

15. H. Goldstein, *Problem-Oriented Policing* (New York, NY: McGraw-Hill, 1990).

16. C.H. Levine, "Strategic Management," in J.J. Fyfe, ed., *Police Management Today: Issues and Case Studies* (Washington, DC: International City Management Association, 1985); M.H. Moore and R.C. Trojanowicz, "Corporate Strategies for Policing," *Perspectives on Policing* No. 6 (Washington, DC: National Institute of Justice, 1988).

17. L.P. Brown, "Police Use of Deadly Force: Policy Considerations," in R.N. Brenner and M. Kravitz, eds., *A Community Concern: Police Use of Deadly Force* (Washington, DC: U.S. Government Printing Office, 1979), p. 24.

18. J.Q. Wilson, *Varieties of Police Behavior: The Management of Law and Order in Eight Communities* (Cambridge, MA: Harvard University Press, 1968).

19. P. Engstad and M. Lioy, eds., *Report of the Proceedings: Workshop on Police Productivity and Performance* (Ottawa, ONT: Ministry of the Solicitor General of Canada, 1978), pp. 262-264.

20. D. Carter, "Networking Information for Law Enforcement: Creative Applications of Internet Protocols," *TELEMASP Bulletin* 7, no. 3 (Huntsville, TX: Law Enforcement Management Institute, 2000).

21. K. Layne, "A Case Study of In-Car Terminals in the Las Vegas Metropolitan Police Department," *Police Computer Review* 1, no. 1 (1992): 1-7; National Institute of Justice, "Toward the Paperless Police Department: The Use of Laptop Computers," *Research in Brief* (Washington, DC: National Institute of Justice, 1993).

22. K. Harries, *Geographic Factors in Policing* (Washington, DC: Police Executive Research Forum, 1990); C.R. Block, M. Dabdoub, and S. Fregly, eds., *Crime Analysis through Computer Mapping* (Washington, DC: Police Executive Research Forum, 1995).

23. K.W. Colton, M.L. Brandeau, and J.M. Tien, *A National Assessment of Police Command, Control, and Communications Systems* (Washington, DC: National Institute of Justice, 1983), pp. 37-49.

24. G.C. Larson and J.W. Simon, "Evaluation of a Police Automatic Vehicle Monitoring (AVM) System: A Study of the St. Louis Experience 1976-1977" (Washington, DC: U.S. Government Printing Office, 1979).

25. W.F. Cascio, *Police Personnel Management Information Systems: The Dallas and Dade County Experiences* (Washington, DC: Police Foundation, 1977).

26. J.P. Gannon, R.P. Grassie, J.W. Burrows, and W.D. Wallace, *Managing Criminal Warrants* (Washington, DC: U.S. Government Printing Office, 1978).

27. E. Hernandez Jr., *Police Handbook for Applying the Systems Approach and Computer Technology* (El Toro, CA: Frontline Publications, 1982).

28. W. Archambeault, "Emerging Issues in the Use of Microcomputers as Management Tools in Criminal Justice Administration," in J. Waldron, B. Archambeault, W. Archambeault, L. Carsone, J. Conser, and C. Sutton, *Microcomputers in Criminal Justice: Current Issues and Applications* (Cincinnati, OH: Anderson, 1987), pp. 110-111.

29. T. Dunworth, G. Cordner, J. Greene, T. Bynum, S. Decker, T. Rich, S. Ward, and V. Webb. *Police Department Information Systems Technology Enhancement Project (ISTEP).* (Washington, DC: Office of Community Oriented Policing Services, 2000).

30. G.H. Reinier, T.J. Sweeney, R.V. Waymire, F.A. Newton III, R.G. Grassie, S.M. White, and W.D. Wallace, *Integrated Criminal Apprehension Program: Crime Analysis Operations Manual* (Washington, DC: Law Enforcement Assistance Administration, 1977), p. 1-9.

31. G.W. Cordner, "The Effects of Directed Patrol: A Natural Quasi-Experiment in Pontiac," in J.J. Fyfe, ed., *Contemporary Issues in Law Enforcement* (Beverly Hills, CA: Sage, 1981).

32. M.M. Reuland, ed., *Information Management and Crime Analysis: Practitioners' Recipes for Success* (Washington, DC: Police Executive Research Forum, 1997).

33. G.H. Reinier, M.R. Greenlee, M.H. Gibbens, and S.P. Marshall, *Crime Analysis in Support of Patrol* (Washington, DC: U.S. Government Printing Office, 1977), p. 26.

34. Reinier et al., *Integrated Criminal Apprehension Program*, pp. 1-10 to 1-13.

35. R.G. Grassie, R.V. Waymire, J.W. Burrows, C.L.R. Anderson, and W.D. Wallace, *Integrated Criminal Apprehension Program: Crime Analysis Executive Manual* (Washington, DC: Law Enforcement Assistance Administration, 1977), pp. 1-16 to 1-23.

36. T.F. Rich, "The Use of Computerized Mapping in Crime Control and Prevention," *Research in Action* (Washington, DC: National Institute of Justice, 1995).

37. M.J. Levine and J.T. McEwen, *Patrol Deployment* (Washington, DC: National Institute of Justice, 1985), p. 7.

38. W. Spelman and J.E. Eck, "Problem-Oriented Policing," *Research in Brief* (National Institute of Justice, October 1986).

39. Levine and McEwen, *Patrol Deployment*, p. 5; and L.W. Sherman, *Repeat Calls to Police in Minneapolis* (Washington, DC: Crime Control Institute, 1987).

40. W.G. Skogan and M.G. Maxfield, *Coping with Crime: Individual and Neighborhood Reactions* (Beverly Hills, CA: Sage, 1981).

41. P.B. Taft Jr., *Fighting Fear: The Baltimore County C.O.P.E. Project* (Washington, DC: Police Executive Research Forum, 1986).

42. G.W. Cordner, "Fear of Crime and the Police: An Evaluation of a Fear-Reduction Strategy," *Journal of Police Science and Administration* 14, no. 3 (September 1986): 223-233; R.K. Higdon and P.G. Huber, *How to Fight Fear: The Citizen Oriented Police Enforcement Program Package* (Washington, DC: Police Executive Research Forum, 1987).

43. J.M. Chaiken, *Patrol Allocation Methodology for Police Departments* (Washington, DC: U.S. Government Printing Office, 1977), p. v.

44. R.G. Grassie and J.A. Hollister, *Integrated Criminal Apprehension Program: A Preliminary Guideline Manual for Patrol Operations Analysis* (Washington, DC: Law Enforcement Assistance Administration, 1977).

45. D.F. Cawley, H.J. Miron, W.J. Araujo, R. Wasserman, T.A. Mannello, and Y. Huffman, *Managing Criminal Investigations: Manual* (Washington, DC: U.S. Government Printing Office, 1977).

46. J.E. Eck, *Managing Case Assignments: The Burglary Investigation Decision Model Replication* (Washington, DC: Police Executive Research Forum, 1979).

47. R.G. Grassie and T.D. Crowe, *Integrated Criminal Apprehension Program: Program Implementation Guide* (Washington, DC: Law Enforcement Assistance Administration, 1978), pp. 3-3 to 3-5.

48. J.B. Wolf, *The Police Intelligence System*, Second Edition (New York, NY: John Jay Press, 1978), p. 5.

49. Ibid., pp. 5-6.

50. G.W. Cordner, "Community Policing: Elements and Effects," in G.P. Alpert and A. Piquero, eds., *Community Policing: Contemporary Readings*, Second Edition (Prospect Heights, IL: Waveland, 2000), pp. 45-62.

51. H.A. Simon, *Administrative Behavior: A Study of Decision-Making Processes in Administrative Organizations*, Third Edition (New York, NY: Free Press, 1976), p. 76.

52. J.Q. Wilson, *The Investigators: Managing FBI and Narcotics Agents* (New York, NY: Basic Books, 1978), p. 204.

53. E. Bittner, *The Functions of the Police in Modern Society* (Washington, DC: U.S. Government Printing Office, 1972).

54. E.S. Fairchild, "Organizational Structure and Control of Discretion in Police Operations," *Policy Studies Journal* 7 (1978): 442-449.

Suggested Reading

Dunworth, Terrence, Gary Cordner, Jack Greene, Timothy Bynum, Scott Decker, Thomas Rich, Shawn Ward, and Vince Webb. *Police Department Information Systems Technology Enhancement Project (ISTEP)*. Washington, DC: Office of Community Oriented Policing Services, 2000.

Levine, Margaret J., and J. Thomas McEwen. *Patrol Deployment*. Washington, DC: National Institute of Justice, 1985.

National Law Enforcement and Corrections Technology Center. *A Guide for Applying Information Technology in Law Enforcement*. Washington, DC: National Institute of Justice, 2001.

Reuland, Melissa Miller, ed. *Information Management and Crime Analysis*. Washington, DC: Police Executive Research Forum, 1997.

Schwabe, William, Lois M. Davis, and Brian A. Jackson. *Challenges and Choices for Crime-Fighting Technology: Federal Support of State and Local Law Enforcement*. Santa Monica, CA: RAND, 2001.

Evaluating Police Peformance

12

Learning Objectives

- Identify the best way to reduce the problems that vague goals cause for police performance measurement.

- Discuss the relative merits of objective and subjective measures of police performance.

- Explain the difference between reliability and validity in measuring police performance.

- Identify three purposes served by individual performance appraisals.

- Identify several methods of reducing employee dissatisfaction with performance appraisals.

- Explain the difference between absolute and relative methods of evaluating individual performance.

- Explain the halo, leniency, and career effects that sometimes interfere with performance appraisal.

- Distinguish between monitoring and evaluation.

- Identify the traditional method of evaluating overall police agency performance.

- Identify three recommended components of a comprehensive police agency performance evaluation system.

Later in the book we discuss various approaches to police organizational improvement. Prior to that, we need to discuss methods that can be used for measuring agency performance. Without such measurement devices, we will not know when the organization needs improvement; we will not know what aspects of the organization need improvement the most; and, following the implementation of changes, we will not know whether improvements have been achieved. The concept of improvement implies a need for information about current levels of performance as well as measurement of changes that occur following the adoption of new strategies and programs.

The need for measurement of individual performance is equally important. Organizations need to evaluate individual performance in order to provide feedback to employees about their work behavior and to provide information to management for staffing, directing, and controlling decisions.

Productivity is a critical element of organizational improvement. Presidents of the United States, corporate leaders, and police chiefs all recognize the economic and political importance of increasing the productivity of their respective business and government organizations. Such increases in productivity require performance measurement. Without such measurement, low productivity cannot be recognized and productivity increases would go unnoticed.

The focus of this chapter is on measuring and evaluating police performance as a prerequisite to police improvement. We examine performance evaluation as it pertains to individual police officer performance, the performance of police strategies and programs, and the overall performance of the entire police organization. First, we discuss the role of performance evaluation as well as some important issues that make the measurement of police performance particularly complex.

The Importance of Evaluating Police Performance

A number of different individuals and groups need information about the quality of police performance. Police supervisors need such information in order to accurately complete annual or semiannual performance appraisals of their subordinates. Police executives need such information when deciding which officers to promote, demote, assign to special units, and terminate. The police chief needs such information in order to assess the performance of unit and division commanders and to evaluate strategies, tactics, and programs. Internal management of police organizations depends heavily on information about levels of performance. With such information, police administrators can contribute to organizational improvement by "working smarter, not harder."[1]

Other officials also need such information. Political and administrative officials, including mayors, city managers, city councils, and their counterparts in towns, townships, boroughs, counties, and states, need information on police performance when making budget and policy decisions and when evaluating the performance of police chiefs. These officials have an overall responsibility to their communities to provide quality police protection at a reasonable cost; they can meet their responsibilities only if they have accurate information about the performance of their police departments. In general, "evaluating the effectiveness of programs in meeting public objectives is an essential component of state and local government management."[2]

Police performance information is also needed by others. The federal government, for example, through the Bureau of Justice Assistance, the National Institute of Justice, and the Office of Community Oriented Policing Services, has sought to fund innovative police projects as a means of improving police performance. In order to carry out this function, funding agencies need information about the effects of these innovative strategies, tactics, and programs; additionally, they need to measure police performance in order to document successful efforts and organizational improvements for Congress. Local, regional, and state planning agencies similarly need information on police performance for problem identification, grant applications, budget review, and evaluation of new projects. In addition, police associations such as the International Association of Chiefs of Police, the National Sheriff's Association, and the Police Executive Research Forum need information on police performance to aid them in representing the interests of their constituents, in disseminating innovations, and in providing advice to member police agencies.

Finally, citizens need to know how well their police departments are performing. One highly respected police chief's advice to the public is that "it is both your right and your obligation as a citizen to probe your police agency, ask the questions and decide for yourself if your community's public safety needs are being met."[3] While most citizens may lack a great deal of expertise in performance measurement and police work, they are both the consumers of police services and the final judges of the caliber of police performance.

The following is a list of uses for information pertaining to police performance.

1. By identifying current levels of performance, measurement can indicate the existence of particular problems.
2. When performance is measured over time, such measurement can indicate progress or lack of progress in improving performance.
3. When collected by geographical areas within a jurisdiction, performance data can help identify areas in particular need of attention.
4. Measurement can serve as a basis for evaluating specific activities. Measurement may indicate personnel who need special attention or activities, such as training or selection, that need to be modified.
5. Measurements of existing performance can provide agencies with the information necessary to set performance targets. Actual performance can subsequently be compared to the targets to indicate degrees of accomplishment.
6. Performance incentives for both managerial and nonmanagerial employees might be established.
7. Measurement data can be used for in-depth performance studies on ways to improve specific aspects of performance.

8. Performance measurement information can be used as a method to account for police operations to the public. Accountability is becoming a growing national concern and refers not only to the legal use of funds but also to the broader question of what is actually being accomplished by the police.[4]

The importance of measuring and evaluating performance of and within government agencies has been strongly stressed in the discipline of public administration for many years. As government agency administrators, police chiefs need to emphasize performance measurement in order to achieve efficiency and effectiveness in police operations. They also need to assure that their police departments can effectively compete for resources, influence policy decisions, and establish reputations for professionalism within the local government arena. Ultimately, a police chief's survival in the contemporary setting as well as in the future may very likely depend on his or her ability to develop meaningful systems for measuring and evaluating police performance.[5]

Issues in Police Performance Measurement

We have sought to explain the importance of performance evaluation for police administration and to describe some of the uses to which such information can be put. We also need to clarify some of the difficult problems that are encountered in measuring and evaluating police performance. It is in the best interests of the public and the police that the most relevant and reliable methods for measuring such performance be identified and developed.

In the sections that follow, the most difficult issues confronting police performance measurement and evaluation are discussed.

Goals and Criteria

Measuring performance requires decisions about what to measure; this is especially so because it is virtually impossible to measure every conceivable aspect of the activities of an individual or of an organization. Deciding what to measure requires choices about what is most important among the many activities performed. Unfortunately, there is considerable disagreement about the relative importance of different aspects of policing; this disagreement complicates performance measurement.[6] Some citizens and police officials are satisfied to measure such elements of crime control as arrests, case clearances, and crime rates; on the surface these would seem to represent the more important features of policing.[7] Others believe that police adherence to due process of the law and to constitutional prerogatives is what should be measured,[8] because to them this represents the best indication of successful police work. Still others suggest measuring citizen satisfaction with police services—this assumption is based on the premise that citizens are the best judges of police performance.[9]

Such blatant differences of opinion reflect the vagueness of broad police goals and the lack of consensus in our society about specific police objectives and their relative priorities. Citizens disagree about the criteria and indicators of effective or ineffective police performance and thus about what represents improved police performance.

The best way to reduce this problem as it affects performance measurement is to employ multiple measures.[10] The practice in many communities of evaluating the police department solely on the basis of increases or decreases in the crime rate or of increases or decreases in crime clearance rates is obviously deficient. Evaluating the police department solely on the basis of violation of constitutional rights would be equally inappropriate. A much more sensible and valid evaluative approach would be to identify several components of police performance (multiple measures), as reflected in differing viewpoints on the police function, and then to measure performance in each of these areas.[11]

Objective and Subjective Measures

Another difficult issue in police performance measurement and evaluation concerns the relative usefulness of objective and subjective measures. Objective measures, such as numbers of arrests or amount of crime, have the value of precision; they are therefore easier to defend when questioned. The measurement of subjective criteria, such as citizen satisfaction with the police department or an officer's judgment, is generally more susceptible to error and thus more open to question and challenge.

Because of these characteristics of objective and subjective measures, some police administrators are inclined to minimize subjective measures and rely heavily on objective measures. This tendency should be tempered by several considerations. First, many organizations fall prey to measuring what is easy to measure rather than what is important. Police departments often do this by counting arrests, citations, warnings, reported crimes, case clearances, and total calls for service. Although such activities should be measured, it is inappropriate to measure these activities to the exclusion of others.

If only easily measurable objective indicators are employed, the police department will then be evaluated on the basis of what is easy to measure, not what is important to measure. The same will be true if such measures are used to evaluate individual police officers. Aside from the fact that this practice may lead to inaccurate evaluations of individual and organizational police performance, it is also likely that performance itself, over time, will be influenced by questionable measures. That is, individual police officers will adjust their behavior so as to conform to the measures and, in similar fashion, the entire organization will adapt its performance to the questionable measures being employed. Consequently, performance criteria originally selected because of the ease of their measurement may become, in effect, the goals of the police department and the objectives of its individual members.

Clearly, police administrators need to think first about the important aspects of police performance before selecting appropriate measures to use. As explained previously, it is essential to include multiple aspects of performance as well as to employ multiple measures of performance. The choice between objective and subjective measures should then be made on the basis of identifying the best indicators of each component of performance. Some aspects of performance lend themselves easily to objective measures; others can be best measured subjectively.

It is important to recognize that a number of measures that purport to be objective lack precision. The use of reported crimes as a measure of the actual amount of crime, for example, has serious limitations. The case clearance rate, a seemingly objective measure of investigative performance, is susceptible to substantial manipulation by individual detectives and by police departments generally. Because of such measurement inadequacies, the actual difference between objective and subjective measures is not as great as might be expected.

Quantity versus Quality

The issue of quantity versus quality is closely related to the objective/subjective issue and to the tendency to measure whatever is easiest to measure. Quantity of performance is generally easier to measure, and more susceptible to objective measurement, than quality of performance. Quantities are also easier than quality to summarize and communicate. Numbers of traffic tickets are readily measured, summarized, and presented, for example, whereas it would be much more difficult to measure and express the quality of a police officer's or a police department's traffic enforcement performance.

There are, however, some excellent subjective measures of quality of performance.[12] Citizens' evaluations of the quality of police service and supervisors' evaluations of the quality of police officers' reports are good examples. Sometimes objective measures can also reflect quality. The number of traffic tickets issued for hazardous moving violations, the ticket conviction rate, or the total amount in fines generated by traffic tickets might come closer to measuring traffic enforcement quality than the mere number of tickets issued. The percentage of a police officer's reports returned for corrections is an objective alternative to a supervisor's summary evaluation of report writing as a means of measuring report writing quality.

The key consideration in evaluating performance is an initial determination of the important factors involved in performing a particular activity followed by a careful choice of measures that reflect excellence in the performance of that activity. There is also much to be said for the use of quantitative and qualitative measures in concert, for a system of multiple measures of police performance, and for the use of both objective and subjective measures in combination.

Reliability and Validity

Once significant components of police performance are identified and measures are selected, the task of collecting data and actually measuring performance begins. The issues of reliability and validity of data need to be thoughtfully and skillfully addressed. Carefully crafted measures of police performance are of little real value unless accurate data can be collected to determine how individuals or organizations score on the measures.

Performance data about an activity is reliable to the extent that repeated or independent measurement yields the same score. If all detectives in one police department use the same rules for determining whether a case can be cleared, for example, then case clearance rates may be reliable measures. On the other hand, if some detectives stray from the rules and clear a case strictly on the basis of linking the method of operation in that case to a subject arrested for another crime, without any other evidence of that suspect's involvement, then case clearance data in that department will be unreliable. Similarly, subjective supervisory evaluations of a police officer's judgment would be unreliable if several supervisors rating the same officer for the same period assigned different scores.

The validity of data is the extent to which it accurately represents actual performance. Data may be reliable without being valid. If all detectives in a department cleared cases when they could link method of operation to a subject already in custody for another crime, the case clearance rates would be reliable, because each detective's decisions would be governed by the same rules. The data would not be valid, however, because the clearance rates would be based on cases that should not have been cleared. If a police department used the same procedures for counting crimes year after year, the reported crime rate would be a reliable measure of the amount of crime, although it would not be a valid or accurate measure of the true amount of crime (because many crimes are never reported to the police).

Reliable measures that may not be valid are sometimes adequate for limited purposes. Reported crimes provide a good example. It is misleading to use reported crimes as a measure of the true amount of crime. It is also misleading to compare two or more police departments in terms of reported crime; their citizens may be differentially inclined to report crimes, or the departments may vary in their counting practices. On the other hand, the number of reported crimes may be one good indicator of police workload as well as a reasonable indicator of crime changes from year to year in a particular community. Likewise, it would not be valid to compare Supervisor A's evaluation of Officer A's judgment to Supervisor B's evaluation of Officer B's judgment if they were using different measuring devices. However, it would be reasonable to compare Supervisor A's evaluations of his or her 10 subordinates and conclude that Officer A has the best, worst, or average judgment among the group; in this instance, Supervisor A would be using the same measuring device for all 10 subordinates.

In measuring police performance, every effort should be made to obtain reliable and valid data. When the data being employed have limitations, these should be recognized and called to the attention of anyone who uses the performance measures for evaluation. All data have limitations; in order to work effectively with data and use them properly, it is necessary to be fully aware of these limitations and to be cognizant of these limitations when taking actions predicated on data analysis.

Cause and Effect

Police departments have traditionally, albeit naively, been evaluated by citizens, political leaders, and police administrators on the basis of shifts in crime rates. Decreases in reported crime have often been incorrectly taken as evidence of police effectiveness, while increases have been improperly perceived as indicating a lack of effectiveness. This traditional approach is unreasonable because the cause-and-effect relationship between police performance and amount of crime is not precisely known. We do know, however, that the crime rate is affected by a variety of social, economic, and organizational influences, of which police performance is but one of many. If the crime rate were to increase because of worsening economic conditions, it would be unfair to blame the police and give them a negative evaluation. Similarly, if the crime rate were to drop because of the aging of the population, it would be unreasonable to give credit to the police for the downward trend and, concomitantly, to reward the police with a positive evaluation.

When evaluating an individual, a program, or an organization in terms of the effects of performance, it is necessary to demonstrate the connection between performance and effects. Few police departments would consider it reasonable to evaluate individual officers on the basis of crime rates on their beats because of the limited impact that one officer would have in such isolated situations and because of the many other situational and circumstantial factors that could affect the crime rate.

On the other hand, a police department strategy aimed at reducing specific types of crime in specific areas might logically be evaluated on the basis of how it affected the rate of specific crimes in the specific area. Such an evaluation would necessarily require the linking of performance and effects, because extraneous factors could intervene. If an area with a particularly high rate of burglary was targeted for directed patrol, for example, and the burglary rate in that area was observed to decrease, a careful analysis would be necessary in order to attribute the decrease to the directed patrol strategy. It might have been the case that detectives had arrested the responsible burglars a few days before the directed patrol strategy was initiated. Alternatively, the burglars might have decided, independently of any police department efforts, that enough burglaries had been committed in the area and that it was time to move on to another area. Only through careful analysis can alternative explanations such as these be ruled out, thus providing support for the claim that the police action caused the observed effect.[13]

Routine evaluations of a police agency's performance are not particularly amenable to rigorous experimental design, but some principles of research methods can be employed. Consider, for example, the criterion of citizen satisfaction as a means of evaluating police performance. A police department could annually survey a random sample of citizens in order to measure citizen satisfaction with the department. Survey questions could probe aspects of satisfaction such as satisfaction with response time to calls, satisfaction with the actions taken by police officers, and satisfaction with the courtesy displayed by officers. If, during a particular year, response time became slower and citizen satisfaction with response time decreased, it would be reasonable to infer cause and effect. Similarly, if response time became slower but citizen satisfaction with response increased, it would be reasonable to credit the effect to a new program of call prioritization in which police telephone operators explained to citizens why response to their calls would not be immediate.

Scientists have established strict rules for linking cause and effect; police administrators, however, must still make allocation decisions, formulate policies, and implement strategies based on their best judgments of the effects of different actions. These judgments, however, need to be backed up as much as possible by valid knowledge. Such knowledge results from research, experimentation, and careful analysis. Ultimately, the more we know about the effects of various kinds of police performance, the better able we will be to make informed decisions that will have a positive effect on the way police officers protect and serve.

Individual Performance Appraisal

Most police organizations periodically evaluate the performance of individual police officers and other employees. Studies reported in 1973, 1978, and 1990 all found that about 80 percent of police departments utilized formal performance evaluation of police officer personnel.[14] These evaluations, or performance appraisals, are typically conducted once or twice a year. More frequent appraisals are sometimes conducted during police officers' probationary periods. Appraisals of individual performance serve three general purposes: they provide information for personnel research; they provide input to staffing decisions; and they provide feedback to employees.[15]

Performance appraisal data are needed in order to test the validity of selection and promotion methods. If employees who scored high on selection tests later receive high performance appraisals, the validity of the selection tests is confirmed. On the other hand, if selection test scores and performance appraisals are not positively correlated, the validity of the selection tests is questionable. Selection test validation is important for two reasons: (1) validity assures that the tests select the candidates who will do the best job; and (2) validity assures that the tests do not arbitrarily discriminate on the basis of race, sex, or other irrelevant criteria. Valid tests are needed to guarantee equal employment opportunity and top-quality personnel.

Staffing decisions relating to promotion, assignment, demotion, and termination all depend on information about individual performance. In addition, employees need periodic feedback on how well they are performing. Supervisors should continuously provide subordinates with this kind of information on an informal basis, but the formal performance appraisal process assures that supervisors periodically take stock, assess performance, inform subordinates of their standing, and counsel subordinates on shortcomings and ways of improving.

Many managers intensely dislike having to conduct performance appraisals.[16] There are a number of reasons for this, including dissatisfaction with the particular forms and systems in use, lack of information on which to base appraisals, uneasiness about giving negative evaluations, and lack of skill in communicating appraisals to subordinates. Consequently, many managers conduct the appraisals in a perfunctory manner, often viewing them as a necessary but onerous chore. This is unfortunate, because the results of performance appraisals have an important influence on a variety of organizational decisions.

Employees also often express dissatisfaction with performance appraisals. While most employees say they desire information about how well they are doing, they are generally not satisfied with the particular performance appraisal system in use in their organization. Common employee complaints about appraisal systems center on the arbitrariness, irrelevancy, or inaccuracy of performance criteria, as well as on supervisors' unwillingness or inability to meaningfully discuss the results of appraisals.

There are several ways of reducing supervisory and subordinate dissatisfaction with performance appraisals. One valuable approach is to focus appraisal as much as possible on performance rather than on personality. Performance is what really matters for organizational effectiveness; while an employee's personality may sometimes affect morale and have a bearing on organizational climate, personality is not nearly as relevant as performance. Personality should be considered only as it affects the employee's performance, the performance of coworkers, and relations with individual citizens and the public at large.

A useful approach in promoting acceptance of a performance evaluation system is to characterize the process, as much as possible, as an analysis rather than as an evaluation. *Evaluation* suggests a process of assessing good and bad points and tends to increase the defensiveness of the person being evaluated. The person's value is being examined, which is threatening to most people. *Analysis*, on the other hand, has a more neutral and detached connotation. All organizational activities are routinely analyzed in order to make improvements. It is assumed that any activity or any aspect of performance can be improved and that the purpose of analysis is to discover areas for improvement.

Another method that can enhance satisfaction with performance appraisal is careful training for those who do the evaluating.[17] Too often, supervisors complete evaluations without sufficient understanding of the rationale underlying the process or the specific methods and criteria being used. Undergoing evaluation is traumatic enough without adding supervisory confusion to the situation. With careful training, a police department can assure that each rater understands the system and that all raters have the same understanding of evaluation criteria.

Performance Evaluation

Standard 35.1.1   A written directive defines the agency's performance evaluation system and includes at a minimum:

    a.   measurement definitions;

    b.   procedures for use of forms;

    c.   rater responsibilities; and

    d.   rater training.

Standard 35.1.2   A written directive requires a performance evaluation of each employee be conducted and documented at least annually.

Standard 35.1.3   A written directive requires a written performance evaluation report on all entry-level probationary employees at least quarterly.

Source: *Standards for Law Enforcement Agencies: The Standards Manual of the Law Enforcement Agency Accreditation Program.* Fairfax, VA: Commission on Accreditation for Law Enforcement Agencies, Inc., 1999.

Engaging the subordinate in the process of analyzing performance also encourages acceptance of the performance evaluation system. Subordinates can periodically review their own performance, identify areas in need of improvement, and suggest ways of doing better. The supervisor must still play a role in this process, assuring that self-analysis is candid and accurate and helping subordinates establish goals for improvement; to the extent that subordinates can objectively assess their own performance, many of the usual complaints about performance appraisal disappear.[18] Subordinates can also participate in the evaluation of their supervisor's performance.[19]

Several other considerations are important for individual performance appraisal. One is the choice between absolute and relative methods of appraisal.[20] *Absolute methods* require that each employee's performance be measured against an absolute standard. These standards can be objective (e.g., completes reports by the end of the shift) or subjective (e.g., uses sound judgment when handling disputes). *Relative methods*, by contrast, require comparisons between and among employees. Instead of independently rating the soundness of each employee's judgment, for example, a relative appraisal might simply involve ranking employees from best to worst on the soundness of their judgments.

Both absolute and relative methods have their drawbacks. Supervisors are generally better able to make relative judgments ("Officer A has more initiative than Officer B") than absolute appraisals ("Is Officer A's initiative superior, good, satisfactory, poor, or very poor?"). Thus, relative methods probably yield more reliable information. However, relative methods make it difficult to compare individuals in different organizational units. Officer A may have the most initiative among the officers in Squad 1, but how he or she compares to the officers in Squad 2 is difficult to determine. Though we might want to consider Officer A the equal of the officer with the greatest initiative on Squad 2, Officer A's initiative might actually be average or low when considered in the context of Squad 2. Thus, relative methods generally provide more reliable but sometimes less useful information.

Another important issue in individual performance appraisal is the choice between objective and subjective measures. This issue was discussed earlier with respect to performance measurement in general. Basically, objective measures are easier to define and defend and therefore are less subject to bias by the supervisor doing the rating. On the other hand, it is rare when all of the principal criteria of good job performance can be measured objectively. One expert observed that "most supervisors would agree that the difference between good and bad patrol officers is most apparent in the intangibles (e.g., such qualities as initiative or attitude), which cannot be counted but must be judged by supervisors or others familiar with the performance."[21] As pointed out earlier, the best solution to the debate about objective versus subjective measures is to employ multiple measures of job performance.

An issue that has only recently received attention in police circles is the possibility of evaluating employees on different criteria at different points in their careers. One interesting suggestion is to adjust appraisals according to three career stages: (1) early in their careers, employees could be evaluated primarily on whether they have developed the knowledge, skills, and abilities needed to do the job effectively; (2) once these capabilities have been demonstrated, then evaluation could concentrate on whether employees are exerting appropriate effort; and (3) once capabilities and effort have been demonstrated, then evaluation could focus on results.[22] In this latter stage, supervisors would be most concerned with the subordinate's accomplishments, paying less attention to how they were achieved. This approach to performance evaluation corresponds nicely to the situational approach to leadership discussed in Chapter 10.

Another issue often overlooked concerns the selection of the person or persons who will actually do the evaluating. In most organizations, employees are evaluated by their immediate supervisors. Occasionally, however, several supervisors may be familiar with an employee's performance; in such a situation, a combined evaluation by the several supervisors would be feasible. A combined evaluation would be more accurate, because more information would be brought into the process. Another possibility is peer evaluation. Each employee within an organizational unit can be rated by his or her fellow employees. Although this approach is controversial because it does not follow the hierarchy of authority and because it allows employees who compete with one another to evaluate one another, it may provide the most accurate appraisals in situations in which one's fellow employees have the most information about one's performance. This method of peer ratings has been employed successfully in police departments.[23]

A final potential evaluator of police officer performance is the public.[24] Quite a few agencies currently conduct citizen surveys to determine satisfaction with police service. For the most part, these surveys are used to evaluate overall agency performance rather than individual performance. In principle, however, a police department could evaluate an individual officer by surveying citizens who had contact with that officer during the rating period. This approach would be quite controversial and should be used with great care, because the role of the police inevitably puts officers into antagonistic relations with some citizens. Although controversial, rating by citizens has intuitive appeal, especially within the context of community policing, because citizens often have the most direct knowledge of how police officers behaved in a situation and because ultimately the public must be satisfied that the police are performing effectively.

Timothy Oettmeier and Mary Ann Wycoff have recently offered 10 suggestions for police departments that are considering revising their performance evaluation systems.[25]

1. Performance evaluations are not bad in and of themselves. Frustration comes from how the process is administered and the lack of suitable performance criteria.
2. Officers want feedback and a permanent record of their accomplishments and performance.
3. Officers often feel they are doing more than they are receiving credit for, given the typical narrow design of their evaluation instruments and performance criteria.
4. The goals and structure of the organization should be decided before new performance measurement is developed. Form follows function.

5. There should be separate forms for different assignments (unless law prohibits).

6. Administrative convenience should not be a primary criterion in the redesign. The goal of the performance evaluation should dictate the way in which it is conducted.

7. Any significant alteration of past practices is likely to cause some dissatisfaction among supervisors. It is likely that this, too, shall pass as the new process becomes familiar.

8. Performance evaluation should be reprioritized as a critical supervisory responsibility. Without overreacting to sergeants' concerns, managers should be responsive. Removing meaningless administrative duties from sergeants allows them to spend more time verifying officer performance. In time, what was once considered drastic will become routine, provided it is perceived as having practical value to the supervisor.

9. Citizen involvement is central to performance evaluation. Citizens can be a good source of information about an officer's style and adequacy of effort, as well as community satisfaction with results. They also can provide valuable feedback about the status of neighborhood conditions. They should not, however, be put in a position of judging the appropriateness of an officer's decisions.

10. The process should be as simple as reasonably possible. This will increase both acceptance and the probability that the information will actually be utilized.

Methods of Performance Appraisal

There are a substantial number of specific devices and methods employed for evaluating individual performance in organizations. We discuss the work production, rating scale, rank ordering, paired comparison, forced distribution, checklist, forced choice, and critical incident methods in the following sections.

Work Production Methods. Most police departments routinely collect information on the numbers of arrests, tickets, and reports completed by each officer and use this information for evaluative purposes. Some departments rely completely on this method of appraisal; some use this method in addition to another appraisal method; and some simply use work production information as the basis for appraisal judgments about work quantity and quality.

An elaborate work production method was developed for the Englewood (Colorado) Police Department.[26] Twenty-three separate work products were identified, including several types of arrests and investigations. Each product was then assigned a weight according to its contribution to organizational effectiveness and the amount of time consumed. On a monthly basis, each officer's score was calculated based on number of work products and their weights. These scores were then adjusted to account for the number of days worked by each officer. Finally, each officer's adjusted score was compared to other officers in the same units, in order to arrive at a performance rating expressed as a percentage above or below the unit average.

The method used in Englewood was relative in that officers were rated each month in comparison to their unit average rather than in comparison to an absolute standard of good performance. The method was objective in that readily quantifiable and verifiable work products were measured. Through the use of a large number of work products with differing weights, the method sought to measure quality as well as quantity. Because of the nature of the measures employed, the data used for measuring work products could be expected to be both reliable and valid.

The main drawback of any work production approach to performance appraisal is the inability of objective measures to represent all important aspects of performance. The Englewood system, for example, almost completely ignored all but enforcement activity. Objective measures of service quality, effectiveness in resolving disputes, initiative and judgment are much more difficult, if not impossible, to develop. Total reliance on objective measures leads to the problem of measuring only what is easy to measure and the consequent problem of encouraging only the performance that is measured by the appraisal system.

Rating Scales. Rating scales are frequently used to appraise individual job performance. Employees may be rated on objective measures, but usually rating scales call for subjective judgments by supervisors. For example, a supervisor may be required to rate each employee's initiative as superior, above average, average, below average, or well below average. Alternatively, initiative could be rated as excellent, satisfactory, or unsatisfactory; on a scale of 1=poor to 10=excellent; or according to any other desired response scale.

Rating scales can be either relative or absolute. When the possible rating responses revolve around the term "average," as in the first example above, the ratings are relative, at least in principle. Actually, if the supervisor rated according to the unit's average, the ratings would be relative, whereas if the supervisor rated according to a general standard of average performance, the ratings would essentially be absolute. For the most part, rating scales are an absolute method of performance appraisal, when responses range from poor to excellent or from unsatisfactory to superior. Some rating scales range from well below standards to far above standards to make their absolute nature clear.

The major drawback of rating scales is the subjective judgment required of supervisors. It is certainly difficult to rate employee initiative, judgment, work quality, and similar nebulous aspects of performance on the typical types of response scales described above. For this reason, many police departments have chosen to utilize *behaviorally anchored rating scales (BARS)*.[27] An example of one BARS measure developed for police department use is presented in Figure 12.1. Notice that the labels attached to different points on the rating scale are specific to the measure and that they refer to behaviors.

The specific scale anchors are intended to make the supervisory ratings more reliable; supervisors might have different conceptions of what constitutes "superior" or "above average" judgment/decisiveness, whereas specific anchors encourage more accurate and precise shared perceptions. The use of behavioral anchors encourages supervisors to focus on performance rather than on personality.

Because rating scales are so widely used, it is important to recognize some specific problems with them.[28] One is the so-called *halo effect*. Supervisors tend to let their rating of an employee on one measure affect that employee's ratings on other measures. Employees typically receive all superior ratings or all average ratings. Studies of performance indicate that in reality each employee typically has strong points and weak points, but the halo effect tends to erase these differences.

While the halo effect tends to produce consistently generalized individual ratings (e.g., Officer A is rated above average on all measures), the problem of *central tendency* results in all employees receiving similar ratings (e.g., all officers are rated above average). It is not unusual when using a rating system that produces overall scores on a 1 to 100 scale, for example, to find all, or nearly all, employees within 5 to 10 points of each other. One cause of the central tendency problem is the common practice of requiring supervisors to provide written explanations whenever they issue a very high or very low rating. This practice encourages supervisors to confine their ratings within a range that does not require written documentation.

A related evaluative limitation that contributes to the central tendency problem is the phenomenon of *supervisor leniency*. Most supervisors are extremely reluctant to hurt an employee's feelings and therefore tend to avoid the inevitable conflict that would result from a very low rating. Also, in some organizations there is a tacit or implied understanding that even a moderately low evaluation can effectively ruin an employee's career; consequently, ratings are typically inflated.

Finally, the problem of *career effect* has an impact on rating scales. This limitation pertains to changes in employee performance from year to year. Ratings are expected to gradually improve during the early years of a police career, but in most instances, once a high rating is achieved it tends to persist. Studies of police performance indicate, however, that actual performance is not always so steady;[29] police officers can have good years and off years, much like athletes.

Although most of these problems are inherent in the use of rating scales, the use of BARS provides a partial remedy to these limitations by reducing the degree of judgment required from the supervisor.[30] Additionally, raters can be trained to be more objective and to resist tendencies toward partiality. A hybrid method sometimes employed to improve objectivity is to limit the number of officers who can receive a given rating. For example, supervisors would be required to rate no more than 30 percent of their subordinates as above average or superior on each measure.

We have discussed rating scales at some length because of their importance as a management tool and because their use is so widespread. The remaining evaluative methods we shall address (many of which were developed to overcome the problems of rating scales) are less widely used, but are important and certainly relevant and worthy of consideration.

Figure 12.1
Example of a Behaviorally Anchored Rating Scale (BARS)

Officer's Name _____

_____ Check if this work dimension is not applicable to officers in your work group.

JUDGMENT/DECISIVENESS   Willingness and ability to make well thought out, appropriate decisions.

HIGH   ———— 10

The examples to the right are examples of behavior of individual officers who are usually rated HIGH on Judgment/Decisiveness.

Makes own judgments based on what he/she knows and stands by decisions.   ———— 9
Thinks things over, weighs alternatives, and then acts.
Notices potentially dangerous situations before trouble occurs.   ———— 8
Observes situations and calls for assistance when necessary.
    ———— 7

AVERAGE

The examples to the right are examples of behavior of individual officers who are usually rated AVERAGE on Judgment/ Decisiveness.

Sticks to the letter of the law even if leniency would be a better solution.   ———— 6
Follows orders, but doesn't question or contribute information that might change appropriateness of order.
Sometimes doesn't consider   ———— 5
alternatives when making a decision.
Has trouble distinguishing serious and nonserious calls.   ———— 4

LOW

The examples to the right are examples of behavior of individual officers who are usually rated LOW on Judgment/Decisiveness.

Officer avoids responsibility for decisions by making few, if any.   ———— 3
Always or almost always calls supervisor to make decisions.
Ignores a problem if no supervisor is   ———— 2
available.
Has to be instructed step-by-step on how to handle a complaint.   ———— 1

COMMENTS (If your rating on Judgment/Decisiveness is based on behaviors not listed above, list those behaviors below.)

Rank Ordering. An alternative to rating each employee according to various scales is to rank order employees from best to worst. This can be done on one global measure simply by having each supervisor identify his or her best employee, next best employee, and so on down the line to the worst employee. Rank ordering can also be done on a number of specific evaluative criteria. For example, subordinates can be ranked from best to worst on such qualities as judgment, initiative, and job skills, adding their numerical scores to give them an overall ranking.

Rank ordering is a relative method of performance appraisal. It tends to produce reliable rankings of subordinates within a particular unit, but making meaningful comparisons among employees in different units is difficult, if not impossible.

Paired Comparisons. Another relative method of performance evaluation utilizes paired comparisons of subordinates. The supervisor considers each pair of subordinates and chooses which of the two is the better performer, either on a global measure or on several specific measures. With three subordinates, for example, the supervisor would compare Officer A with Officer B, Officer B with Officer C, and Officer A with Officer C. The employee's rating is determined by the number of favorable comparisons.

Paired comparisons provide even more reliable information than rank ordering. In effect, paired comparisons involve multiple rank orderings of pairs of employees; ranking just two employees is easier than ranking eight or 10. Because it is a relative method of appraising performance, paired comparisons have the same limitations as rank ordering. In addition, the use of paired comparisons can be unwieldy if the number of people to be rated or the number of rating measures is large. If a supervisor had 12 subordinates, for example, 66 paired comparisons would be required for each measure used.

Forced Distribution. Another method of performance appraisal is the forced distribution method. Whether applied to an overall global evaluation or to specific measures, this method requires supervisors to put certain percentages of their subordinates into different categories of performance. Typically, a distribution similar to a normal curve is required. The distribution below approximates a normal curve:

10% very good
20% good
40% satisfactory
20% poor
10% very poor

This method has the drawback of inhibiting comparisons between and among employees in different units of the organization. The worst employee in one unit could be better than the best employee in another, but the forced distribution method would not provide that information. Supervisors may also resent using the forced distribution method, because it constrains their rating freedom and requires them to give poor ratings to subordinates who may deserve better but must be so categorized due to the rigidity of the system.

Checklists. A popular alternative to rating scales that permits comparisons among employees in different units is the checklist method. One form of this method requires the supervisor to check a list of statements or behaviors that best describe the employee's performance. No rating scales or points are attached to the checklist; thus, most of the problems inherent in the use of rating scales are either reduced or eliminated because the supervisor has no knowledge of how each item on the checklist will affect the employee's rating. Scoring is calculated by someone other than the supervisor through the use of a scoring key that assigns positive and negative values to the statements that have been checked.

A modified version of the checklist utilizes response scales. Instead of simply choosing whether to check a statement such as "this officer treats citizens with respect," the supervisor responds to each statement by checking "always," "very often," "fairly often," "occasionally," or "never." This method obtains a response on each measure while continuing to withhold from the supervisor information about the effect of each response on the employee's overall numerical evaluation.

Although checklists overcome some of the common problems associated with rating scales, they have one serious drawback. Because supervisors are not involved in the actual scoring of the evaluation, and because they are unaware of the relative weights assigned to different statements and behaviors, they are unable to provide accurate feedback on matters of performance to employees. Because feedback and counseling are important benefits of performance appraisal, this deficiency is a serious limitation.

Forced Choice. Another variation of the checklist method is the forced choice method. This evaluative technique, used by the Ohio State Highway Patrol since the early 1960s,[31] provides sets of four statements from which the supervisor must select the statement that best describes the subordinate or the statement that least describes the subordinate. Each alternative statement is assigned a numerical value that is unknown to the supervisor doing the appraising. This method has the same advantages and disadvantages as checklists in general but is even more complicated to score and thus less beneficial for providing useful feedback to employees.

Critical Incidents. The final approach to performance appraisal focuses specifically on critical incidents; that is, on specific instances of job performance that are critical to the success of the organization. In police work such incidents could include controlling violent offenders, handling tense domestic disputes, reacting to verbal provocation, or delivering death notification messages. When using this approach, the supervisor records each subordinate's performances during critical incidents. At the end of a rating period, the supervisor has a list of performance descriptions for each employee. These descriptions can be used as the basis for judgments on overall performance or as data on which to base ratings on specific criteria such as judgment or sensitivity.

The latter use of critical incidents as data for ratings on specific criteria is preferable. Because police supervisors actually have quite limited opportunities for observing subordinate performance in critical incidents, it would be tenuous at best to derive an overall evaluation from a few glimpses of performance. On the other hand, records of critical incident performance can be used as data to support ratings in any of the performance appraisal methods we have described. In fact, one of the keys to making performance appraisal successful is for supervisors to keep careful records on performance to support their ratings of subordinates; records of performance during incidents that are critical to the organization's success are particularly relevant for employee performance appraisal.

Other Considerations

The foregoing discussion demonstrates that there exists a wide variety of performance appraisal methods, each of which has benefits and limitations. There is no perfect system or even best system. How, then, should an organization proceed to establish a viable, useful, fair, and equitable performance appraisal system? The best advice is as follows:[32]

1. Determine why an appraisal system is needed. The relative need for information to support staffing decisions, employee feedback, and personnel research affects the desirability of different methods.

2. Determine the important components of the jobs included in the performance appraisal system. Employees should be appraised on the most important aspects of their jobs, not on the least important or irrelevant aspects.

3. Evaluate the various performance appraisal methods in terms of Steps 1 and 2; determine which methods are best suited to the types of jobs to be appraised and to the information needs of the organization.

4. Provide opportunities for those who will do the appraising (supervisors) and those who will be appraised (subordinates) to have input into and to participate in the development of the appraisal system.

5. Employ multiple measures. Consider both quantity and quality, and employ both objective and subjective evaluative measures. Focus on performance, not on personality.

6. Train those who will do the appraising. Make sure they understand the process and the measures to be used. Instruct them to hoard information to support their appraisals.

7. Treat all appraisals as useful estimates of performance that include some degree of error. Do not base staffing decisions on any one appraisal.

8. Periodically evaluate the appraisal system and make adjustments as necessary. Monitor the field of applied personnel psychology to keep up-to-date on developments in performance appraisal.

Organizations that follow this advice should be successful in their performance appraisals. Evaluating individual performance, especially when such evaluations are used as input to important staffing decisions, is inevitably a source of some conflict and dissatisfaction. It is a necessary activity, however; as long as it is based carefully and conscientiously on performance of important activities, performance appraisal can contribute meaningfully to organizational effectiveness.

Evaluating Programs and Strategies

Police administrators need information about the effectiveness of programs and strategies in order to make informed policy, allocation, strategic, and tactical decisions. Formal evaluations are most often necessary to judge the effectiveness of new programs and strategies, and to help decide whether they should be continued, revised, or scrapped. However, even long-standing practices need to be monitored and analyzed to assure continued effectiveness and efficiency.

In the following sections we discuss some important considerations that affect the evaluation of police programs and strategies.

Input, Process, Output, and Outcome

Police programs and strategies are generally intended to have effects on community problems and conditions. For example, aggressive patrol is intended to reduce street crime, residential target hardening is intended to reduce burglary and theft, and crisis intervention is intended to reduce conflict and violence in police encounters with people experiencing mental illness crises. These effects are *outcomes*. They are the desired results or consequences of the program or strategy.

When a program or strategy has a desired outcome, part of its evaluation should include determining whether the desired outcome was achieved. Obviously, a program or strategy could not be considered successful unless the intended outcome was successfully met. More than simply establishing whether the desired outcome came about, however, an evaluation must also attempt to determine whether the program or strategy caused the outcome. This is far and away the most difficult task in evaluation.

Earlier we discussed the problems encountered in trying to establish cause-and-effect relationships. Careful use of scientific methods such as control groups and experimentation is required. These methods are well developed, but their application to real-life situations is difficult and sometimes risky. Consider the celebrated Kansas City Preventive Patrol Experiment, for example.[33] In that study, all preventive patrolling was removed from five patrol beats in the city for an entire year. Had serious problems developed in those beats (they did not), the police chief would certainly have been exposed to scathing criticism, at the least. It was politically risky to conduct the experiment and also administratively difficult to direct and control patrol officers in such a way that the experimental conditions were maintained.

In order to establish cause and effect, evaluations must measure inputs, processes, and outputs as well as outcomes. In order to successfully evaluate aggressive patrol,[34] for example, an evaluation would need to determine the amount of resources devoted to the strategy, the methods employed to carry it out, and the immediate outputs resulting. This information is needed to document the implementation of the strategy. It is important because the full implementation of the strategy is a prerequisite to it having its intended effects. A frequent explanation for the failure of a program or strategy to have its intended effects is that it was never fully implemented in the first place.

An evaluation of an aggressive patrol strategy might uncover any of the following circumstances:

1. Aggressive patrol was implemented, but street crime stayed the same or increased.
2. Aggressive patrol was implemented, and street crime decreased.
3. Aggressive patrol was never implemented, and street crime stayed the same or increased.
4. Aggressive patrol was never implemented, but street crime decreased.

The conclusions to be drawn from these four scenarios differ dramatically.[35] The best case is Scenario 2, which is consistent with strategy expectations and might indicate that aggressive patrol caused the crime decrease if experimental conditions were carefully observed. Scenario 1 suggests that, contrary to expectations, aggressive patrol did not deter street crime. The third and fourth scenarios are important for illustrating the importance of documenting implementation. In Scenario 3 the failure to decrease crime would have led us to believe that the aggressive patrol strategy failed, had we not established that the strategy was never implemented in the first place. In Scenario 4 we would have been inclined to declare the strategy a success, had we not observed that it was never put into place.

Implementation failure can involve failure to invest the necessary resources to make the strategy operational, failure to utilize the resources as intended, or failure to obtain expected immediate outputs. In the preceding example, the implementation of aggressive patrol might have been inadequate because too few officers were assigned to carry out the strategy, because officers failed to patrol aggressively by making frequent motor vehicle and suspicious person stops, or because the frequent stops did not produce many arrests. For an evaluation to establish implementation failure and to pinpoint why a strategy or program was not fully implemented, information must be collected on inputs, processes, and outputs.

Monitoring

Because of the need to determine as precisely as possible what causes desired outcomes, the evaluation of programs and strategies generally requires the use of the scientific method. However, a less scientific but nevertheless important approach to analyzing programs and strategies exists; it is called *monitoring*. Monitoring simply involves systematic collection of information about program and strategy inputs, processes, outputs, and outcomes. Monitoring does not permit managers to draw valid conclusions about cause and effect, but it does allow them to determine whether programs and strategies are being implemented as intended. Monitoring also can provide information about the status of crime, citizen satisfaction, and other outcome indicators. Basically, monitoring can provide all the benefits of evaluation except the discovery of cause-and-effect relationships.

An example of the importance of program monitoring was provided during the early stages of the Citizen Oriented Police Enforcement (COPE) project in Baltimore County, Maryland.[36] Three squads of 15 officers each had been created and given the mission of reducing fear of crime in targeted neighborhoods. Initially, the squads were given considerable latitude in designing their tactics. During the first year of the COPE project, the squads tended to rely rather heavily on saturation patrol tactics in the targeted neighborhoods. This tendency was detected by the police department's monitoring system, which collected information on COPE officers' activities and allocation of time to various tasks. Because the department's management expected COPE to incorporate substantial public contact into their tactics, the monitoring system's information indicated an implementation problem. The department reacted to the information by encouraging and guiding the COPE units toward more citizen-oriented tactics. Thus, the monitoring system played a crucial role in the successful evolution of the COPE project.

Ideally, monitoring can be accomplished through the utilization of the operational and management information systems described in Chapter 11. Monitoring of some new programs and strategies, however, may require information not routinely available. In these instances, special data collection, analysis, and information systems may have to be created. Once new programs and strategies become institutionalized, arrangements should be made to incorporate information for their monitoring so that such information will be routinely available to managers.

Inside versus Outside Evaluation

While monitoring can generally be performed through established organizational processes, evaluation of programs and strategies sometimes requires outside assistance. This circumstance may arise when an evaluation requires skills and expertise not available within the department. For example, the evaluation of the COPE project in Baltimore County was focused in part on fear of crime, because COPE's mission was fear reduction. Although the Baltimore County Police Department had a systematic monitoring and information system, it had no experience in collecting or analyzing information on fear of crime. Consequently, a consultant was retained to assist in developing methods for measuring fear of crime and evaluating the project's effects on fear.[37]

Outside evaluation is also recommended whenever a neutral, unbiased assessment is particularly necessary. Evaluations conducted by members of the police department can be totally objective, but there always exists the possibility of organizational pressure being applied in an effort to influence findings and conclusions. Additionally, an inside assessment rarely carries the same credibility as an outside evaluation. Thus, when an especially controversial or expensive program is to be evaluated, it is generally better to have the evaluation performed by specialists who are not members of the police department.

Up until the early 1970s, systematic, comprehensive evaluations of government programs and strategies were only rarely conducted.[38] Since then, however, the value of such evaluations has become widely recognized, evaluation methods have improved, and the number of people trained to perform evaluations has increased greatly. This trend is mirrored within police administration; numerous evaluations of all kinds of police programs and strategies have been performed in the last 30 years. Although not all evaluations have provided unambiguous and useful information, overall, the increased utilization of evaluations in the police service has provided a substantial amount of valuable information for use in police planning and decisionmaking.

Evaluating Overall Organizational Performance

Police administrators, political leaders, and citizens all need to know how well their police departments are performing. They need to know how their police departments compare to accepted standards, how they compare to other departments, how their performance this year compares to their performance last year, and how their performance compares to public expectations. Although these seem like reasonable and simple needs, they are not easily met.

Traditionally, police departments were evaluated on the basis of a few statistics collected as part of the national Uniform Crime Report (UCR) published annually by the FBI. These statistics include the number of reported serious crimes, the serious crime rate (the number of reported crimes per 1,000 population), the number of arrests, the value of recovered stolen property, and the serious crime clearance rate (the proportion of reported serious crimes that are classified as solved). Although all of these statistics have value, their adequacy as indicators of police performance has been and should be seriously questioned. The number of reported crimes, for example, is not a valid measure of the true amount of crime, and it can easily be manipulated by police department reporting practices. The number of arrests provides no information about quality of arrests, about the appropriateness of arrest decisions, or about whether the arrests resulted in prosecutions and convictions. The case clearance rate is based solely on arrests. It is easily manipulated and does not depend on conviction, recovery of property, or victim satisfaction.

During the 1960s and 1970s, several national commissions attempted to establish standards by which police agency performance could be assessed. Among these were the President's Commission on Law Enforcement and Administration of Justice, the National Advisory Commission on Civil Disorders, the National Commission on the Causes and Prevention of Violence, the President's Commission on Campus Unrest, the American Bar Association Standards Relating to the Urban Police Function, and the National Advisory Commission on Criminal Justice Standards and Goals. In general, the reports of these commissions argued that "the pursuit of criminals and the obsession with the crime rate to the exclusion of other valued aspects of policing were wrong-headed and counterproductive."[39] In addition to emphasizing crime control, the commissions stressed the importance of measuring police performance in terms of service, order maintenance, and good relations with citizens.

A more recent effort to create standards is the Law Enforcement Agency Accreditation Program.[40] This program includes a large number of standards that must be met by police agencies seeking accreditation. The standards are almost entirely focused on inputs and processes rather than on outputs or outcomes.[41] The standards require departments to have policies concerning the use of discretion, for example, but the content of those policies is not prescribed. Nor must departments achieve any particular levels of crime solving or citizen satisfaction in order to become accredited. Thus, the accreditation standards have limited value for assessing the effectiveness of police agency performance, although they do provide useful guides for assessing the thoroughness of police administrative practices.[42]

An approach to police agency evaluation that stresses characteristics of the police organization rather than crime rates or response times was suggested by David C. Couper, former chief of police of Madison, Wisconsin. In a monograph titled "How to Rate Your Local Police," Couper argued that answers to the following questions tell more about the quality of a police department than do quantitative measures of performance. He advised citizens to ask:[43]

- What kind of a person is the chief?
- What tone does the chief set for the agency?
- Does the chief articulate the policies of the agency clearly and understandably?
- Does the police agency have a clear sense of its objectives?
- Are there written policies for all operational practices?
- Does the police agency select the best qualified individuals to be police officers?
- Does the police agency provide high-quality training for its officers?
- Does the police agency reinforce the minimum requirements for a good police officer?
- Does the police agency guide, train, and supervise police officers in the restraint of the use of force?
- Is the police agency willing to investigate and discipline officers engaging in misconduct?
- Do police officers respect individual rights?
- Does the police agency address crime and order problems by using all community resources?
- Does the police agency cooperate and coordinate with neighboring law enforcement agencies and with other agencies in the criminal justice system?
- Does the police agency communicate well with the public?
- How does the police agency approach the media?

Performance evaluation approaches based on administrative standards and on qualitative issues provide much useful information by which to judge police agencies, but we are inevitably also interested in measures of effectiveness in solving problems and achieving objectives. One major project that attempted to create systems for measuring and evaluating police agency effectiveness was affiliated with the National Commission on Productivity appointed in 1970.[44] The commission sought to develop measures of police agency productivity that would be meaningful and practical, focusing particularly on patrol performance and crime control measures. A number of interesting performance measures were developed; three are presented in Figure 12.2.

Performance Measure A in Figure 12.2 would indicate the proportion of all patrol officers who were assigned to street patrol duties. This measure would be a reflection of resource utilization and could be monitored from year to year in one police department or used to compare two or more departments. In addition, national averages or standards could be developed for this measure, providing a useful guide for assessing any agency's utilization of resources.

Performance Measure B would provide useful information for evaluating an agency's response times to different types of calls for service. It could indicate, for example, the percentage of all emergency calls responded to in less than five minutes (a common standard) or the percentage of low-priority calls responded to in less than 30 minutes. By such measures, a police agency could monitor its response times so as to be alerted whenever a sizable proportion of calls were being responded to more slowly than desired.

Performance Measure C provides a productivity indicator of arrest quality. The numerator, by counting only arrests that survive initial judicial screening, weeds out arrests that are not supported by sufficient evidence. By using a denominator of "total patrol man-years," the measure becomes a productivity indicator. It reports arrests by amount of time invested rather than merely number of arrests. Thus, arrests might increase from one year to the next; however, if more patrol resources had been made available, the productivity measure might decline.

Figure 12.2
Measures of Police Agency Productivity

Performance Measure A

$$\frac{\text{Patrol Officers Assigned to Street Patrol Work}}{\text{Total Patrol Officers}}$$

Performance Measure B

$$\frac{\text{Number of Calls of a Given Type Responded to in Under "x" Minutes}}{\text{Total Calls of That Type}}$$

Performance Measure C

$$\frac{\text{Patrol Arrests Surviving the First Judicial Screening}}{\text{Total Patrol Man-Years}}$$

Adapted from Harry P. Hatry, "Wrestling with Police Crime Control Productivity Measurement," in Joan L. Wolfle and John F. Heaphy, eds., *Readings on Productivity in Policing* (Washington, DC: Police Foundation, 1975), pp. 93-96.

Although the efforts of the productivity commission can be criticized for focusing primarily on crime control measures and for relying on aspects of performance that could be readily quantified, the measures that were developed are more refined and sensitive than such traditional indicators as numbers of arrests and numbers of reported crimes. In addition to comparing outputs and results to inputs invested, some significant qualitative considerations were included in the measures. These represented some meaningful advances in measuring police agency performance.

A more comprehensive set of performance measures was developed by the American Justice Institute's National Project on *Police Program Performance Measures (PPPM)*. The PPPM system includes 65 effectiveness measures that pertain to police performance in five general areas and 19 detailed subareas:[45]

1. Crime Prevention
   a. Part I crimes (personal)
   b. Part I crimes (property)
   c. Part II crimes (selected)

2. Crime Control
   a. Public reporting to police
   b. Case closure (solution)
   c. Case preparation and testimony
   d. Stolen property return
   e. Constitutional propriety
   f. Custody of prisoners

3. Conflict Resolution
   a. Interpersonal conflict
   b. Intergroup conflict
   c. Personal stress

4. General Service
   a. Traffic
   b. Miscellaneous services (to the public)
   c. Communications with the public
   d. Auxiliary services (to other agencies)

5. Police Administration
   a. Police integrity
   b. Community leadership
   c. Coordination with other agencies

The PPPM system is the most comprehensive approach to police agency performance measurement and evaluation available. It does have its limitations, however. Some of the measures require data, such as the following, that are not readily available or easily obtained:

E3.1.1 Proportion of interpersonal conflict incidents in which there was an escalation, subsequent to police intervention, including:

additional deaths or injuries;

increased property damage; or

invocation of additional or more significant criminal circumstances than would originally have been applied.[46]

This is clearly a worthy measure of police success in handling interpersonal conflict situations. However, it would require special data-collection efforts just to identify instances of additional injuries and property damage occurring subsequent to police intervention, not to mention escalation in "criminal circumstances." Moreover, the determination of criminal circumstances beyond those that "would have originally been applied" would require very difficult judgment calls by those measuring the performance. Because of these difficulties, the reliability and validity of such data would be open to question.

In addition to official police department records, the PPPM system utilizes victimization surveys to supplement reported crime figures, surveys of citizen satisfaction with police services, and expert judgments of police practices. Obtaining information from these sources, although certainly important, takes time and incurs costs. A police department would have to be fully committed to performance measurement and evaluation for the PPPM system to be a feasible alternative to other, less accurate evaluative procedures.

Despite the complexity of implementing more refined performance and productivity measures, progress has been made in recent years. For example, the Thames Valley Police Department in England uses more than 20 indicators in its annual reports, including the following:

1. Percent of victims of violent crimes who were satisfied with police service.
2. Percent of emergency telephone calls answered within 10 seconds.
3. Percent of nonemergency telephone calls answered within 20 seconds.[47]

Similarly, a recent report from the Police Executive Research Forum suggests using 21 statistical indicators reflecting seven performance dimensions to gauge the overall effectiveness of a police organization (see Table 12.1).[48] These indicators and dimensions reflect a broad and mature understanding of the multiple goals and objectives of police agencies.

We have discussed several approaches to police agency evaluation in this section. Consistent with our earlier admonition to utilize multiple measures whenever measuring and evaluating performance, our suggestion is to incorporate several approaches into any serious attempt to assess police agency performance. In particular, three components are recommended:

1. A police department's administrative practices can be compared to the Law Enforcement Agency Accreditation Program's standards.

2. A police department's operational effectiveness can be assessed through the use of some set of quantitative measures of performance and productivity.

3. Qualitative considerations can be addressed by answering questions similar to those posed by Chief David C. Couper.

The combination of these three approaches assures a comprehensive assessment that includes objective and subjective measures; quantitative and qualitative considerations; and attention to inputs, processes, outputs, and outcomes.

Table 12.1
Statistical Measures of Police Organizational Performance

Performance Dimensions	Statistical Indicators
Reduce criminal victimization	Reported crime rates Victimization rates
Call offenders to account	Clearance rates Conviction rates
Reduce fear and enhance personal security	Reported changes in levels of fear Reported changes in self-defense measures
Guarantee safety in public spaces	Traffic fatalities, injuries, and damage Increased utilization of parks and public spaces Increased property values
Use financial resources fairly, efficiently, and effectively	Cost per citizen Deployment efficiency/fairness Scheduling efficiency Budget compliance Overtime expenditures Civilianization
Use force and authority fairly, efficiently, and effectively	Citizen complaints Settlements in liability suits Police shootings
Satisfy customer demands/achieve legitimacy with those policed	Satisfaction with police services Response times Citizen perceptions of fairness

Adapted from M. Moore, D. Thacher, A. Dodge, and T. Moore, *Recognizing Value in Policing: The Challenge of Measuring Police Performance* (Washington, DC: Police Executive Research Forum, 2002).

Summary

Performance evaluation is crucial to police administration and police improvement. Unless performance is regularly evaluated, administrators, political leaders, and citizens lack necessary information about the effectiveness of police services in their communities. Through evaluation, all concerned parties can know how their police departments compare to accepted standards, where problems and shortcomings exist, and whether performance is improving or deteriorating. It is a sad commentary on American police systems that in most communities this information is available only in the form of hunches and guesses.

Police performance evaluation is needed at three levels: individual performance appraisal, evaluation of programs and strategies, and evaluation of overall organizational performance. At all levels, some difficult problems in measuring police performance are encountered. Among these problems are vague and conflicting goals, choosing between objective and subjective measures of performance, balancing quantity and quality, obtaining performance data that are reliable and valid, and determining whether outcomes were caused by actions taken.

Individual performance appraisal provides information for three basic purposes: for staffing decisions, for feedback to employees, and for personnel research. Both supervisors and subordinates are typically dissatisfied with performance appraisal processes, partly because of deficient and inaccurate methods of appraisal and partly because the process in and of itself is personally threatening. Because the variety of different methods available for appraising individual performance is wide, managers can perhaps reduce this dissatisfaction among their employees. However, managers should not expect to achieve complete satisfaction with individual performance appraisal, regardless of the methods utilized.

Evaluating programs and strategies involves: (1) determining whether they achieve their objectives and (2) monitoring their implementation. Routine monitoring can readily be accomplished through an organization's information systems and chain of command, but rigorous evaluation most often requires outside assistance. Only through such rigorous evaluation can the effects of strategies and programs be determined. Accurate, reliable information about the effects of police practices is needed continually by police administrators for allocation, policy, strategic, and tactical decisionmaking.

Finally, citizens, political officials, and police administrators need information with which to judge overall police agency performance. Traditional methods that rely completely on crime and arrest statistics are inadequate. A more comprehensive approach should include accepted standards of police practice; sensitive quantitative measures that assess quality as well as quantity; and subjective judgments about the style, philosophy, and quality of police services, police policies, and police administration.

Discussion Questions

1. According to Chief Couper, "it is both your right and your obligation as a citizen to probe your police agency, ask the questions and decide for yourself if your community's public safety needs are being met." Do you agree with his view? By what methods can the public obtain and analyze such information? What should the public do once it obtains answers to its questions?

2. Have you ever worked in organizations beset by the quantity-versus-quality dilemma? What measures of productivity were used? How can organizations measure the quality of their performance?

3. What methods of individual performance appraisal have been used in organizations with which you are familiar? Were the methods liked or disliked by employees? By raters? Do you think the methods achieved their purpose of accurately distinguishing among workers according to their performance?

4. Which of the methods of individual performance appraisal do you think is best suited for use in police departments? Why?

5. What do you think are the most appropriate indicators of overall police agency performance? Why?

Notes

1. J.K. Stewart, "Research and the Police Administrator: Working Smarter, Not Harder," in W.A. Geller, ed., *Police Leadership in America: Crisis and Opportunity* (New York, NY: Praeger, 1985), pp. 371-382.

2. H.P. Hatry, R.E. Winnie, and D.M. Fisk, *Practical Program Evaluation for State and Local Government Officials* (Washington, DC: Urban Institute, 1973), p. 1.

3. D.C. Couper, *How to Rate Your Local Police* (Washington, DC: Police Executive Research Forum, 1983), p. 24.

4. Adapted from H.P. Hatry, "Wrestling with Police Crime Control Productivity Measurement," in J.L. Wolfle and J.F. Heaphy, eds., *Readings on Productivity in Policing* (Washington, DC: Police Foundation, 1975), p. 87.

5. M. Moore, D. Thacher, A. Dodge, and T. Moore, *Recognizing Value in Policing: The Challenge of Measuring Police Performance* (Washington, DC: Police Executive Research Forum, 2002).

6. "Measuring What Matters: Developing Measures of What the Police Do," *Research in Action* (Washington, DC: National Institute of Justice, 1997).

7. G.L. Kelling, "Defining the Bottom Line in Policing: Organizational Philosophy and Accountability," in L.T. Hoover, ed., *Quantifying Quality in Policing* (Washington, DC: Police Executive Research Forum, 1996), pp. 23-36.

8. J.R. Hepburn, "Crime Control, Due Process, and the Measurement of Police Performance," *Journal of Police Science and Administration* 9,1 (March 1981): 88-98.

9. G.P. Whitaker, ed., *Understanding Police Agency Performance* (Washington, DC: U.S. Government Printing Office, 1984), pp. 111-147.

10. D.H. Bayley, "Measuring Overall Effectiveness," in Hoover, *Quantifying Quality*, pp. 37-54.

11. G.T. Marx, "Alternative Measures of Police Performance," in R.C. Larson, ed., *Police Accountability: Performance Measures and Unionism* (Lexington, MA: Lexington Books, 1978), pp. 15-32.

12. "Potential Quality Measures for Law Enforcement," in Hoover, *Quantifying Quality*, pp. 263-273.

13. D.T. Campbell and J.C. Stanley, *Experimental and Quasi-Experimental Designs for Research* (Chicago, IL: Rand McNally, 1963).

14. T. Eisenberg, D.A. Kent, and C.R. Wall, *Police Personnel Practices in State and Local Governments* (Washington, DC: International Association of Chiefs of Police and Police Foundation, 1973), p. 30; G.W. Greisinger, J.S. Slovak, and J.J. Molkup, *Police Personnel Practices in Forty-Two American Cities* (Washington, DC: Public Administration Service, 1978), p. 19; W.F. Walsh, "Performance Evaluation in Small and Medium Police Departments: A Supervisory Perspective," *American Journal of Police* 9, no. 4 (1990): 93-109.

15. F.J. Landy, *Performance Appraisal in Police Departments* (Washington, DC: Police Foundation, 1977), pp. 4-5.

16. D. McGregor, "An Uneasy Look at Performance Appraisal," *Harvard Business Review* 35,3 (1957): 89-94; Walsh, "Performance Evaluation."

17. W.C. Lawther, "Successful Training for Police Performance Evaluation Systems," *Journal of Police Science and Administration* 12, no. 1 (March 1984): 41-46.

18. McGregor, "An Uneasy Look."

19. G.M. McEvoy, "Using Subordinate Appraisals of Managers to Predict Performance and Promotions: One Agency's Experience," *Journal of Police Science and Administration* 15, no. 2 (June 1987): 118-124.

20. W.F. Cascio, *Applied Psychology in Personnel Management* (Reston, VA: Reston, 1978), pp. 322-336.

21. Landy, *Performance Appraisal*, p. 6.

22. T.N. Oettmeier and M.A. Wycoff, *Personnel Performance Evaluations in the Community Policing Context* (Washington, DC: Community Policing Consortium, 1997).

23. K.G. Love, "Accurate Evaluation of Police Officer Performance through the Judgment of Fellow Officers: Fact or Fiction?" *Journal of Police Science and Administration* 9, no. 2 (June 1981): 143-149.

24. T.N. Oettmeier and M.A. Wycoff, "Police Performance in the Nineties: Practitioner Perspectives," in G.W. Cordner and D.J. Kenney, eds., *Managing Police Organizations* (Cincinnati, OH: Anderson, 1996), pp. 131-156.

25. Oettmeier and Wycoff, 1997, "Police Performance."

26. J.R. Vaughn, "Police Officer Productivity Assessment Program," *Journal of Police Science and Administration* 9, no. 4 (December 1981): 412-427.

27. F.J. Landy and C.V. Goodin, "Performance Appraisal," in O.G. Stahl and R.A. Staufenberger, eds., *Police Personnel Administration* (North Scituate, MA: Duxbury, 1974), pp. 180-181.

28. Landy, *Performance Appraisal*, pp. 11, 13.

29. E.C. Froemel, "Objective and Subjective Measures of Police Officer Performance," in C.D. Spielberger, ed., *Police Selection and Evaluation: Issues and Techniques* (Washington, DC: Hemisphere, 1979), pp. 87-111.

30. D.E. Bradley and R.D. Pursley, "Behaviorally Anchored Rating Scales for Patrol Officer Performance Appraisal: Development and Evaluation," *Journal of Police Science and Administration* 15, no. 1 (March 1987): 37-45.

31. Landy and Goodin, "Performance Appraisal," pp. 181-182.

32. Adapted from Landy and Goodin, "Performance Appraisal," pp. 183-184; T. Caplow, *Managing an Organization* (New York, NY: Holt, Rinehart and Winston, 1983), pp. 136-137.

33. G.L. Kelling, T. Pate, D. Dieckman, and C.E. Brown, *The Kansas City Preventive Patrol Experiment: A Summary Report* (Washington, DC: Police Foundation, 1974).

34. G.W. Cordner and D.J. Kenney, "Tactical Patrol Evaluation," in L.T. Hoover, ed., *Police Program Evaluation* (Washington, DC: Police Executive Research Forum, 1998), pp. 15-55.

35. J.E. Eck, *Assessing Responses to Problems: An Introductory Guide for Police Problem-Solvers* (Washington, DC: Office of Community Oriented Policing Services, 2002).

36. G.W. Cordner, *The Baltimore County Citizen-Oriented Police Enforcement (COPE) Project: Final Evaluation* (Baltimore, MD: Criminal Justice Department, University of Baltimore, 1985).

37. R.K. Higdon and P.G. Huber, *How to Fight Fear: The Citizen-Oriented Police Enforcement Program Package* (Washington, DC: Police Executive Research Forum, 1987).

38. Hatry et al., *Practical Program Evaluation*, pp. 7-21.

39. G.P. Whitaker, S. Mastrofski, E. Ostrom, R.B. Parks, and S.L. Percy, *Basic Issues in Police Performance* (Washington, DC: National Institute of Justice, 1982), p. 4.

40. *Standards for Law Enforcement Agencies* (Fairfax, VA: Commission on Accreditation for Law Enforcement Agencies, Inc., 1998).

41. S.D. Mastrofski, "Police Agency Accreditation: The Prospects of Reform," *American Journal of Police* 5,2 (fall 1986): 45-81.

42. G.W. Cordner and G.L. Williams, "Community Policing and Police Agency Accreditation," in L.K. Gaines and G.W. Cordner, eds., *Policing Perspectives: An Anthology* (Los Angeles, CA: Roxbury, 1999), pp. 372-379.

43. Couper, *How to Rate Your Local Police*.

44. *Productivity in Police Services*, Report of the Advisory Group on Productivity in Law Enforcement (Washington, DC: National Commission on Productivity, 1973).

45. M.W. O'Neill, J.A. Needle, and R.T. Galvin, "Appraising the Performance of Police Agencies: The PPPM System," *Journal of Police Science and Administration* 8, no. 3 (September 1980): 257.

46. Ibid., p. 259.

47. Moore et al., *Recognizing Value*, pp. 134-135.

48. Ibid., p. 132.

Suggested Reading

Couper, David C. *How to Rate Your Local Police*. Washington, DC: Police Executive Research Forum, 1983.

Eck, John E. *Assessing Responses to Problems: An Introductory Guide for Police Problem-Solvers*. Washington, DC: Office of Community Oriented Policing Services, 2002.

Hoover, Larry T., ed. *Police Program Evaluation*. Washington, DC: Police Executive Research Forum, 1998.

Moore, Mark, with David Thacher, Andrea Dodge, and Tobias Moore. *Recognizing Value in Policing: The Challenge of Measuring Police Performance*. Washington, DC: Police Executive Research Forum, 2002.

Rossi, Peter H., Howard E. Freeman, and Mark W. Lipsey. *Evaluation: A Systematic Approach*, Sixth Edition. Thousand Oaks, CA: Sage, 1999.

Police Strategies and Tactics

13

Learning Objectives

- Identify the three cornerstones of modern police strategy for dealing with crime.

- Summarize the findings of the Kansas City Preventive Patrol Experiment.

- Summarize the findings of research on the effects of police response time.

- Summarize the findings of research on the effectiveness of detective follow-up investigations.

- Distinguish between reactive and proactive repeat offender programs.

- Explain the rationale underlying differential responses to calls for service.

- Distinguish between the police-community relations programs of the 1960s and 1970s and community policing of the 1980s and 1990s.

- Explain how problem-oriented policing differs from traditional single-complaint policing.

- Describe how the police response to domestic violence has evolved over the last two decades.

- Describe how the police response to missing children has changed in recent years.

Any analytical approach to organizations focuses naturally on the methods used to perform the basic work of the organization. These work methods are sometimes referred to as *tasks* or as *organizational technology*. The use of the term "technology" in this context does not imply highly sophisticated or complicated methods or equipment, but simply the techniques, whether simple or complex, employed to perform the organization's work. Assembly line manufacturing, for example, is a basic organizational technology in which each worker performs a single specialized task on a product as it moves by on the assembly line, resulting in the finished product having been worked on by many specialized employees. If, instead, each worker assembled a complete product, performing all the various tasks necessary to finish the product, we would recognize that a different organizational technology was in use, even though the product was the same.

In this chapter we look analytically at police organizational technology. Traditional police terminology refers to tactics and strategies, which are simply combinations of specific tasks and general approaches to achieving police organizational objectives. We will identify the most commonly utilized police strategies and tactics and assess the available evidence about their effectiveness. Since the early 1970s there have been a tremendous number of studies aimed at evaluating and analyzing police strategies and tactics.

In a rational approach to police administration, managers should carefully design work tasks and organize them into tactics and strategies in such a way that the organization's goals of protecting life and property and maintaining order are maximally attained. This chapter is intended to introduce the reader to a rational approach, while at the same time identifying constraints that limit such an approach. One constraint is the vagueness of the police goal of maintaining order. While all citizens may favor orderliness in the abstract, differences of opinion emerge about whether a particular party, outdoor concert, or adult bookstore is orderly or disorderly. The police goals of protecting life and property are clearer, but public conflict is evoked over the propriety of methods of protection, such as eavesdropping, aggressive patrol, or the death penalty.[1] Even if the goals were clearer and there was less controversy about law enforcement methods, we still lack a great deal of knowledge about what methods to employ to achieve which goals.

The lack of agreement in our society about the proper degree of order to be maintained, and about proper methods for enforcing the law, poses serious constraints on police administration. The situation directly impinges on what James Q. Wilson sees as the three prerequisites for rational management.

> First, the goals must be sufficiently operational so that one can make a reasonably unambiguous judgment as to whether the desired state of affairs has actually been brought into being.
>
> Second, the organization must have the technology to achieve its goal.
>
> Third, the organization must be reasonably free to apply a suitable technology to a given objective.[2]

Because police goals are vague, the effects of police strategies are not precisely known, and the police are restricted in the strategies they can employ, police administration tends to become as much survival- and constraint-oriented as goal- and task-oriented. Police chiefs have traditionally been more concerned about avoiding scandals than about improving services and attaining goals. This, however, may be changing in the modern era, especially given new confidence among police administrators that they *can* have a significant impact on crime.[3] As Wilson notes, "constraints do not uniquely determine how administrators shall behave, they only reduce significantly the room to maneuver."[4]

Crime Control Strategies

Most police officers are assigned to the patrol function. At the beginning of their eight-hour workday, they are assigned to patrol areas, often called *beats*. Each officer patrols his or her beat until assigned a call by the police dispatcher. The officer responds promptly to the call; it could be a crime, a traffic accident, or a neighborhood dispute. The officer is expected to handle the call. This may involve writing a report, conducting a preliminary investigation, giving first aid, directing traffic, arresting or ticketing a citizen, breaking up an argument, giving advice, providing information, or even getting a cat out of a tree. As soon as the officer finishes handling the call, he or she returns to patrolling until the next call. If the call involves a crime or other serious matter, sometime later a detective may conduct a follow-up investigation to try to identify and arrest a perpetrator or recover stolen property.

This brief description includes the three cornerstones of traditional police strategy for dealing with crime: preventive patrol, immediate response to calls, and follow-up investigation. Each is examined in the sections that follow.

Preventive Patrol

Most police officers are assigned to patrol duties, with much of their time spent on routine patrol. Typically, only about one-half of patrol time is consumed by handling calls and performing administrative chores.[5] The larger portion is spent patrolling, that is, riding around in the patrol car, sitting in the parked patrol car, or patrolling on foot. Some police officers see this part of their workday as wasted or downtime, time waiting for something to happen.

Patrolling, however, does have important purposes and is an operational necessity. In 1829 Sir Robert Peel perceived the police as a preventive force, with uniformed officers on patrol as the primary mechanism of prevention. To this day, the strategy is termed *preventive patrol* by many. In 1967 the President's Commission on Law Enforcement and Administration of Justice found that "preventive patrol (the continued scrutiny of the community by visible and mobile policemen) is universally thought of as the best method of controlling crime that is available to the police."[6]

Patrolling relies on omnipresence and unpredictability (see "Police Patrol," below). Officers on patrol are expected to prevent crime by giving the impression that they are omnipresent—that they are everywhere. Because it is not actually possible to be omnipresent, officers are expected to patrol unpredictably so that at any moment they might be right around the corner. This unpredictable patrolling is often referred to as *random patrol*.

Another purpose of patrolling is to apprehend those who perpetrate crimes and commit disorderly acts. Unpredictable patrol and patrol of areas of high crime incidence improves the chances of an officer stumbling upon a crime in progress. In addition, the apprehension of violators can be an excellent preventive tool if potential and would-be violators are given the impression that the risk of capture is great.

Police Patrol

Like most things, the most satisfactory method of patrol is a combination of two extremes; combining the two, using the best of each, parts of both, depending on the situation. Thus, for general police patrol, the best system is to patrol so that everyone knows you are on the job, yet patrol so that no one knows where you will be next. A police chief of many years of experience expresses this very well by telling his men to be "systematically unsystematic." That is, do not follow any fixed route or schedule that a criminal might observe, but at the same time see that you cover all of your beat in such a way as to give adequate protection. This is not easy. The easiest way to operate, of course, is to lay out a route and schedule so that you need not think about what you are doing. Yet, remember that while this is the easiest way for you, it is also the easiest way for the criminals. There is nothing they like better than a police officer who is so systematic that they know that he visits a certain point, say the back door of a drug store, every night at say, 11:36, 12:03, 12:49, 1:32.

Few officers have so little interest or intelligence that they will knowingly use such a regular schedule, but far too many officers have fallen into certain regular habits without realizing it.

Source: Richard L. Holcomb, *Police Patrol* (Springfield, IL: Charles C Thomas, 1948), p. 19.

Police officers on patrol are also required to look for and correct any dangerous or threatening conditions on their beats. Historically, watching for fires was a central purpose of nighttime patrolling. Today, patrol officers are expected to check for damaged street signs, broken traffic signals, potholes, downed wires, unsupervised young children, flooding, and other community safety hazards.

There is also an operational necessity underlying the patrolling strategy. In order to be ready to respond immediately to a citizen's call for service, a patrol officer must essentially be doing nothing at the time the call is dispatched.[7] This is referred to as the *availability factor*. At any given moment, there must be patrol officers patrolling and available to respond to calls.

Patrol officers traditionally have enjoyed great freedom in determining how they patrol. Each patrol officer is limited to a beat and must handle in expeditious fashion all calls that are dispatched on that beat. Within the beat, during the four hours each workday that, on average, are not consumed by handling calls, patrol officers are given considerable leeway. As a result, they differ tremendously in how they patrol their beats.[8] Some concentrate on trouble-prone areas; others hide. Some make numerous traffic enforcement stops; others make none. Some drive only the main streets; others patrol residential areas. Little or no instruction or direction is generally given to patrol officers about how best to allocate their patrol time.

Although some in the police field have long regarded routine patrol as a waste of time and others have strongly defended it as the backbone of modern policing, it was not until the early 1970s that the strategy's effectiveness was rigorously tested.

The Kansas City Preventive Patrol Experiment. During 1972 and 1973, the Kansas City Police Department and the Police Foundation conducted a remarkable experiment to test the effects of routine preventive patrol.[9] The experiment has been both influential and controversial. One of the most interesting features of the study is that it was proposed by a task force of Kansas City police officers and not, as might have been expected, by outside researchers.

Experimental conditions in the Kansas City study were maintained for an entire year. Included in the study were 15 patrol beats in the city's South Patrol Division. Five of these beats were assigned to a control group with no changes in normal patrol staffing or tactics. Five other beats were chosen as reactive beats, with all preventive patrolling eliminated. Although outside patrol units handled calls in these reactive beats, the units left the beats once the calls were cleared. The final five beats in the experiment were proactive beats, in which two to three times the usual level of preventive patrolling was provided.

Prior to the outset of the experiment, researchers collected data on reported crime, arrests, response time, citizen attitudes, and citizen and business victimization for each of the 15 beats in the study. They collected similar data after the conclusion of the year-long experiment. During the experiment, the activities of the police officers assigned to the beats were observed and monitored.

When the study was finished, the researchers concluded "that decreasing or increasing routine preventive patrol within the range tested in (the) experiment had no effect on crime, citizen fear of crime, community attitudes toward the police on the delivery of police service, police response time or traffic accidents."[10] In fact, citizens in the experimental areas were completely unaware that any changes had been made in the levels of patrolling.

The study did have its limitations, however. For example, the use of patrol beats as the unit of analysis meant that the overall analysis was based on only 15 cases or research "subjects." Consequently, only very substantial differences among control, reactive, and proactive beats stood a chance of being statistically significant. In other words, the methodological design of the study was biased in the direction of finding no differences attributable to the varying levels of patrol.[11] This probably did not matter much, though, because not only was there a lack of statistically significant differences among the beats, there were also virtually no patterns among the nonsignificant differences that would suggest that any of the three categories of beats was better or worse off for having more or less preventive patrol for a year.

The actual differences in levels of patrolling among the control, reactive, and proactive beats were not as definitive or as clear-cut as the researchers had intended them to be. While routine patrolling was controlled and monitored, other operational units of the police department were not. Special police units, for example, were free to roam and to operate in any of the beats as they saw fit. In addition, reactive units responding to calls in their reactive beats were forced to drive through their beat areas going to and from the calls; this resulted in a substantial police presence that researchers were unable to eliminate from the reactive areas.

Additionally, there was no way to determine if reactive beat residents were able to differentiate between patrol units observed throughout the city and patrol units seen close to home. Furthermore, some critics have suggested that Kansas City is not sufficiently representative of urban America for the results of the study to be widely applicable, and others have criticized the study on the basis of its limited (one- year) duration.

Despite these criticisms and limitations, the Kansas City study has become widely respected by both researchers and police executives. While the study did not result in the elimination of preventive patrol, as some had predicted, it did set the stage for further experimentation with alternative patrol strategies and tactics. The Kansas City study demonstrated convincingly that police chiefs could try alternative patrol tactics without fearing that reduced preventive patrolling would result in calamity. The study did not give police chiefs any final answers about what new tactics to employ, but it did give them the opportunity to try something new and different.

Immediate Response to Calls

Studies of the effects of police response time also gave police administrators a license to innovate. As mentioned earlier, immediate police response to calls has been a cornerstone of modern police strategy. Technological developments, especially the telephone and the police radio, greatly aided police in their efforts to reduce response time. The adoption of the 911 emergency telephone system was aimed at making it easier for citizens to contact the police quickly. Computer systems were developed to design beats for optimal response time and to aid dispatchers in assigning calls to the nearest available patrol units.

Many police departments continually monitor their average response times to calls and, in part, base requests for additional personnel on the need to keep response times within an acceptable range. There is a tendency on the part of police officials, elected leaders, and citizens to make the following assumptions with regard to the advantages of rapid response:

1. It improves the odds of catching the offender at the scene or nearby;
2. It enhances the opportunity of the police to identify witnesses;
3. It provides for the immediate gathering of physical evidence;
4. It permits the police to administer lifesaving first aid quickly;
5. It enhances a police department's image and reputation, thereby serving a crime prevention function;
6. It creates citizen satisfaction.

Several studies have examined the extent to which rapid police response actually produces these desired outcomes; for the most part, findings have not been very supportive of the assumptions. The earliest studies found that quick response made an arrest more likely but emphasized that only extremely short response times were likely to be productive.[12] When police response time was one or two minutes, a desirable outcome was likely; improvements in these response times of even 15 to 30 seconds greatly improved the likelihood of a successful outcome. On the other hand, when response time exceeded three or four minutes, success probabilities dropped off sharply, and modest reductions in response time mattered very little.

Two later studies produced even less promising findings.[13] These studies looked more carefully at response time itself and at the different types of situations that give rise to calls for police assistance. One important finding was that citizens often delay after an incident occurs before calling the police. Sometimes a telephone was not available, or the victim was physically prevented from calling the police. In other instances the victim was temporarily disoriented, frightened, ashamed, or even apathetic. It was not unusual for crime victims to call their parents, their doctor, their minister, or even their insurance company before calling the police. Average citizen delay in calling the police for serious crimes was found in these studies to be between five and 10 minutes.

In previous studies and in police administration practice, response time had always been measured from the time that the police department was notified of the crime or incident (usually via a telephone call from a citizen) until the time the first patrol unit arrived at the scene. The time it took the citizen to call the police in the first place had not been part of response time measurement. However, the likelihood of catching an offender at the scene, locating a witness, or rendering lifesaving first aid actually depends on the length of time from *occurrence* to police arrival, not on the length of time from the call to the police until police arrival. The realization that citizens often delay for several minutes before calling the police puts response time in a different light and suggests that rapid response may not be as significant as once thought.

An important distinction was also made in the later studies between involvement crimes and discovery crimes. *Involvement crimes* are those experienced by a victim or witness while they are occurring. Robberies and assaults are by definition involvement crimes; the victim is involved and personally threatened. Burglaries and thefts, on the other hand, are not usually discovered until after the fact. They are not usually involvement crimes. When a victim or witness becomes aware of the crime only after it has occurred, it is referred to as a *discovery crime*.

The distinction between involvement and discovery crimes is an important factor in any consideration of police response time. With involvement crimes, rapid police response might be productive if citizen delay has not been too long. With discovery crimes, however, rapid police response is unlikely to matter, because the time of occurrence in all likelihood would have been a long time before the call to the police. Frequently, the actual time of occurrence is hours or sometimes even days earlier, making even instantaneous police arrival irrelevant.[14]

Given these considerations, it is not surprising that we conclude that police response time is not usually a crucial factor in arresting offenders and gathering evidence. In their careful study of response time in four cities, William Spelman and Dale K. Brown found the following:

> Rapid police response may be unnecessary for three out of every four serious crimes reported to police. The traditional practice of immediate response to all reports of serious crimes currently leads to on-scene arrests in only 29 of every 1,000 cases. By implementing innovative programs, police may be able to increase this response-related arrest rate to 50 or even 60 per 1,000, but there is little hope that further increases can be generated.[15]

This study found that median citizen delay in reporting involvement crimes ranged from four to five and one-half minutes. Delay was about 10 minutes for discovery crimes. Involvement crimes reported in progress had a response-related arrest probability of 35 percent; those reported within a few seconds, 18 percent; those reported one minute after the fact, 10 percent; and those reported within one to five minutes, 7 percent. Involvement crimes for which citizen reporting was delayed beyond five minutes had extremely low response-related arrest likelihoods. Response-related arrest probabilities for discovery crimes were even lower. In sum, "police response time had no effect on the chances of on-scene arrest in 70 to 85 percent of Part I crimes because they were discovered after they had occurred and had no effect on 50 percent to 60 percent of the rest because they were reported too slowly."[16]

Despite these limitations on the effectiveness of rapid police response, some police executives are eager to promise immediate response time because they believe the public demands it. The research has indicated, however, that citizen satisfaction depends not so much on rapid police response as on whether the police arrive within a reasonable amount of time.[17] Moreover, citizen expectations of reasonable response time are affected by what they are told when they call the police. If they are told that an officer will be there immediately, then a five-minute delay seems endless. On the other hand, if the citizen is informed that other urgent matters must be handled first and that an officer will arrive within 30 minutes, then a response anytime within that 30 minutes is typically satisfactory to the citizen.

When violent crimes, personal injury traffic accidents, and other emergencies are reported immediately to the police, rapid response serves a very important purpose. Being able to administer first aid quickly is an unquestionable advantage of rapid response to emergency calls and serves in a significant way in helping the police achieve their goal of protecting lives.

The police response time research indicates that immediate police response is desirable for a subset of all calls but is not necessary in every case. As with the Kansas City Preventive Patrol Experiment, the response time research demonstrates that current practice is not entirely effective and suggests an opportunity to revise and innovate. The development of new response strategies, as well as new patrol strategies, deserves to be a high priority in police research and planning.

Follow-Up Investigations

Most police departments assign 10 to 20 percent of their personnel to the investigative or detective function.[18] This function follows preliminary investigations conducted by patrol officers; hence, such investigations are referred to as *follow-up investigations*. It should be recognized, of course, that some detective work, especially vice-related activity (narcotics, gambling, prostitution), is instigative as opposed to follow-up in nature.[19] In such cases, a detective poses as a customer or as a criminal in order to instigate criminal activity, always being careful not to illegally entrap the person or persons who are the object of the investigation. Most detective work, however, involves follow-up activity, investigating crimes after they have occurred and focusing on discovering how the crimes were committed and who committed them.

Follow-up investigations are the third cornerstone of modern police crime control strategy. A follow-up investigation is typically conducted by a detective within a day or, at the very most, within a few days of the preliminary investigation. Except in the smallest of police departments, almost every reported serious crime is assigned to a detective for a follow-up investigation. In large departments detectives specialize in certain kinds of cases, such as burglary, robbery, arson or homicide; in small agencies, detectives are generalists and work on a variety of cases.

Because detectives work in plain clothes, because they are given wide latitude in handling their cases, and because they are free of the responsibility of responding to routine calls for service, they have historically enjoyed much higher status than patrol officers. This so-called detective mystique has been reinforced by countless short stories, novels, movies, and television programs depicting the investigative exploits of the detective. While patrol officers are often portrayed as the dull foot soldiers and report takers of modern police work, detectives are characterized as smart, tough, individualistic, and even mysterious.

Detective Work

Part of the mystique of detective operations is the impression that a detective has difficult-to-come-by qualifications and skills, that investigating crime is a real science, that a detective does much more important work than other police officers, that all detective work is exciting and that a good detective can solve any crime. It borders on heresy to point out that, in fact, much of what detectives do consists of very routine and rather elementary chores, including much paper processing; that a good deal of their work is not only not exciting, it is downright boring; that the situations they confront are often less challenging and less demanding than those handled by patrolling police officers; that it is arguable whether special skills and knowledge are required for detective work; that a considerable amount of detective work is actually undertaken on a hit-or-miss basis; and that the capacity of detectives to solve crimes is greatly exaggerated.

This is not meant to imply that what detectives do has no value. In a large number of cases, good detective work identifies the perpetrator and results in an apprehension. The dogged determination and resourcefulness of some detectives in solving cases are extremely impressive. But, in the context of the totality of police operations, the cases detectives solve account for a much smaller part of police business than is commonly realized. This is so because, in case after case, there is literally nothing to go on: no physical evidence, no description of the offender, no witness and often no cooperation, even from the victim.

Source: Herman Goldstein, *Policing a Free Society* (Cambridge, MA: Ballinger, 1977), pp. 55-56.

Recent studies clearly demonstrate that the detective mystique is a myth and that detectives deserve far less credit than they have been given for the work that they do. Looking at investigative work critically, it is first important to point out that only about one in five serious reported crimes is ever solved. Moreover,

> The single most important determinant of whether or not a case will be solved is the information the victim supplies to the immediately responding patrol officer. If information that uniquely identifies the perpetrator is not presented at the time the crime is reported, the perpetrator, by and large, will not be subsequently identified.

> Of those cases that are ultimately cleared but in which the perpetrator is not identifiable at the time of the initial police incident report, almost all are cleared as a result of routine police procedures.[20]

These findings indicate that victims, witnesses, and patrol officers solve more cases than detectives. Research also indicates that case clearances attributable to detectives more frequently result from routine investigative activity than from any direct efforts or special work input contributed by detectives (see "Detective Work," p. 372). Examinations of how detectives typically spend their time also chips away at their mystique.

> Our data consistently reveal that an investigator's time is largely consumed in reviewing reports, documenting files, and attempting to locate and interview victims on cases that experience shows will not be solved. For cases that are solved (i.e., a suspect is identified), an investigator spends more time in post-clearance processing than he does in identifying the perpetrator.[21]

In sum, detectives spend most of their time in the office reading, writing, and talking on the telephone. They spend little time doing the things that fictional detectives are famous for: searching for clues, prying information out of informants, questioning suspects, interviewing witnesses and victims, conducting surveillances, and tracking down perpetrators. For better or for worse, modern detective work has largely been bureaucratized.[22]

Research also indicates that physical evidence is rarely the only basis for identifying a suspect, that most police departments collect much more physical evidence that can be processed and analyzed, and that deficiencies exist in investigative thoroughness:

> In a relatively few departments do investigators consistently and thoroughly document the key evidentiary facts that reasonably assure that the prosecutor can obtain a conviction on the most serious applicable charges.

> Police failure to document a case investigation thoroughly may
> have contributed to a higher case dismissal rate and a weakening of
> the prosecutor's plea bargaining position.[23]

With respect to operational deficiencies, studies of detective work close-ly parallel those of preventive patrol and immediate response to calls: pre-ventive patrol cannot be shown to prevent; immediate response is not really immediate and is often unnecessary; and follow-up investigations are fre-quently futile, often merely duplicating preliminary patrol investigations. Starting in the late 1970s and continuing to the present, an important aspect of research and development in policing has been the search for more effec-tive crime control strategies and tactics.

Refinements

In each traditional area—patrol, rapid response, and investigations—sig-nificant refinements have been achieved since the landmark studies described above. For the most part, refinements in each area have empha-sized developing more targeted strategies and tactics that focus police resources where they can be most effective. The landmark studies have come to be interpreted as demonstrating that (1) spreading patrol evenly over the entire jurisdiction, (2) trying to respond rapidly to every crime report, and (3) throwing a detective at every crime case simply are not very effective approaches. The studies also demonstrate that substantial police resources can safely and responsibly be reallocated away from strict adherence to these traditional approaches and toward other, more effective strategies and tactics.

Patrol Refinements. One of the first programs to arise out of the "noth-ing works" disarray caused by early research findings, especially those of the Kansas City study, was *Managing Patrol Operations (MPO)*.[24] MPO was a fed-erally funded initiative of the Law Enforcement Assistance Administration (LEAA) that encouraged police agencies to adopt or improve rational patrol allo-cation methods, careful workload analysis, crime analysis, and directed patrol.

Directed patrol differs from routine preventive patrol in the use of uncommitted patrolling time. In directed patrol officers are given instruc-tions or directions to follow when they are not busy handling calls. These instructions are usually based on analysis of recent crime incidents and pat-terns and can be fairly general ("be on the lookout for subjects loitering sus-piciously in the area of car dealerships") or very specific ("At 11:00 P.M. park in the 200 block of Vine Street, walk across Broadway and then north one block to the Volvo/Honda dealerships. Approach quietly and observe from the perimeter for five minutes. If no suspicious activity is observed, proceed to check the lot and buildings. After completing the check, remain on the premises for 10 additional minutes before departing.").

The rationale behind directed patrol is to make patrolling as rational and informed as possible. Directed patrol is the opposite of random patrol. Directed patrol assignments attempt to guide patrol officers to locations where certain kinds of activities such as crimes and accidents are likely to occur, to give them tactics that may be used to prevent or detect target crimes, and to provide them with suspect and method information to increase the chances of prevention or detection. As police departments have improved their crime analysis capabilities and gotten better at identifying "hot spots," the credibility of directed patrol has been enhanced.

Studies of directed patrol have yielded promising results. One small study in California reported crime decreases during a directed patrol project, but the design of the study made it difficult to conclusively attribute the decreases to the strategy.[25] A later study in Pontiac, Michigan, found some evidence that target crimes were reduced by directed patrol; the findings indicated that the tactics employed during directed assignments, rather than the amount of time devoted to directed patrol, had the greater effect on crime.[26] In Minneapolis, the assignment of patrol officers to spend time at "hot spots" failed to reduce serious crime but did have an impact on disorder. In this case, mere visibility seemed to have caused the modest effect on disorder, as the officers' activities at the hot spots were unstructured and not very substantial.[27] The most recent study, in Indianapolis, found that directed patrol focused on firearms violations was successful in reducing the incidence of firearms-related crimes in the targeted area and that "focusing on individuals and situations where the police have some degree of suspicion of criminal behavior was more effective than casting a broad net over a neighborhood."[28]

Besides providing more direction to patrol, many police departments have adopted a more active or aggressive approach to patrolling. This essentially involves a higher degree of intervention by patrol officers, such as stopping numerous cars for traffic violations, checking out suspicious people, using every legal opportunity to search for drugs and weapons, and frequently checking for outstanding warrants.[29] The rationale underlying aggressive patrol is that these police interventions will result in apprehensions, interruptions of criminal activity, and prevention of crime. The main drawback is that aggressive patrol, if not properly and legally practiced, unnecessarily thrusts the police into many peoples' lives, thereby having an intimidating and chilling effect on the law-abiding public and causing civil libertarians legitimate concerns about the abuse of police power. It has also been suggested that the tactic more frequently places police officers into dangerous situations that could result in injury or death.

A study in San Diego tested the effects of an element of aggressive patrol known as *field interrogation*, which was defined as "a contact initiated by a patrol officer who stops, questions and sometimes searches a citizen because the officer has reasonable suspicion that the subject may have committed, may be committing, or may be about to commit a crime."[30] In the study, field interrogation (FI) activity was suspended for nine months in one experimental area but maintained at normal levels in two control areas. Suppressible crime in the experimental (no-FI) area increased by a substantial amount, while remaining about the same in the control areas. With the resumption of FI activity in the experimental area, the incidence of suppressible crime returned to approximately its preexperimental level.

Two studies of a cross-section of the largest American cities produced comparable findings. One study used the number of traffic citations issued as a measure of patrol aggressiveness and a sophisticated mathematical model to determine the relationship between aggressive patrol and the robbery crime rate. The analysis suggested that aggressive patrol contributes to a higher robbery arrest ratio, which in turn leads to a lower robbery crime rate.[31] A similar study, which used expert judgments (ratings by observers knowledgeable about police practices around the country) of police departments' "adherence to norms of efficiency and legalism" as a measure of patrol aggressiveness, produced comparable findings.[32]

A more recent study in Kansas City demonstrated the value of aggressive patrol in identifying individuals illegally carrying firearms.[33] Officers saturating a target area were successful in seizing substantially more weapons than other officers patrolling routinely in a control area, and the result was a significant decrease in gun crime in the target area. Target area residents also became less fearful of crime and more satisfied with their neighborhood, compared to control area residents. When the crackdown was stopped in the target area, gun crime increased.

Rapid Response Refinements. A number of studies challenged the importance of immediate response to calls for service and paved the way for a new approach, often termed *differential responses to calls for service.*[34] Stated simply, *differential responses* advocates abandoning the traditional practice of immediately responding to all calls for service, substituting the principle of matching the response to the call. Under this program, some calls are handled over the telephone, by appointment, by delayed patrol response, or by immediate non-sworn police response, thus reducing and managing the workload of the sworn patrol force.

Reducing and managing the patrol workload provides opportunities for alternative strategies and allocation decisions. More time may be devoted to directed patrol, preliminary patrol investigations, or crime prevention activities. Some patrol resources might be redistributed to investigations or other functions. In addition, more patrol officers will be available to respond en masse to crimes in progress and emergencies, perhaps improving patrol apprehension effectiveness.

Successful implementation of the differential response program requires planning and, in particular, skilled communications personnel. Police telephone operators are required to assess the nature of each incoming call and determine the appropriate response mode. Categories are established in advance (see Figure 13.1), but operators must still diagnose the endless variety of calls for police service and make decisions about seriousness and immediacy. Operators must also explain to callers with low-priority problems why the police will not appear immediately at their doorsteps. Research has shown that most complainants will accept such explanations if they are politely and logically presented, but experience suggests that providing such explanations goes beyond the traditional role of police communications personnel and will require training and supervision.

Figure 13.1
General Differential Response Model

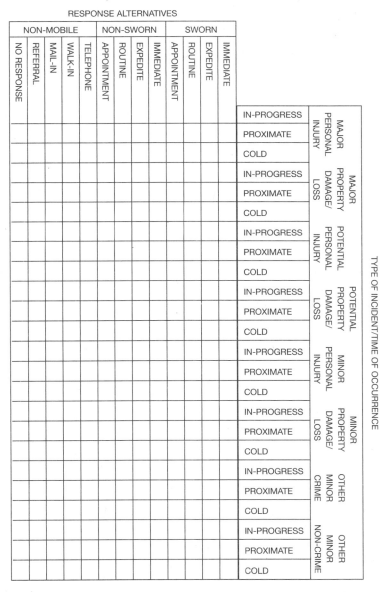

Source: Michael T. Farmer, ed., *Differential Police Response Strategies* (Washington, DC: Police Executive Research Forum, 1981), p. 6.

Tests of the differential responses program have yielded promising results.[35] Several police departments have successfully implemented the program and diverted up to 50 percent of calls to alternative responses without suffering any reductions in citizen satisfaction. Some difficulties are usually encountered with communications personnel early in the program, including hesitancy in choosing alternative responses, but these dwindle with experience. The program succeeds in releasing patrol resources for other, more productive strategies; the challenge is to identify the more productive strategies.

Investigative Refinements. As MPO arose largely from the wake of the Kansas City study, so *Managing Criminal Investigations (MCI)* arose in response to the RAND study of criminal investigations. MCI was a federally funded program of investigative improvement that included such components as solvability factors, case screening, case enhancement, and police/prosecutor coordination.[36] The first step in MCI was often the redesign of crime reports, highlighting important evidentiary items called *solvability factors*. The new report form, along with special training, was intended to encourage patrol officers to be investigators rather than mere report takers. When patrol reports were forwarded to the detective division, case screening could then take place based on the presence or absence of solvability factors. Police could screen out cases in which few or no solvability factors had been uncovered by the preliminary patrol investigation—that is, not those assigned for follow-up investigation. Because many cases are characterized by little or no evidence, the portion of cases screened out would be considerable. Detectives could then reallocate their time to those cases that are potentially solvable and to postarrest case enhancement.

Some MCI programs use quantitative formulas to determine whether a case should be assigned for follow-up investigation.[37] Studies have identified the solvability factors that best predict whether a case will be solved and the probability of case solution, given different amounts of evidence available following preliminary patrol investigation. A checklist or scoring system can be applied to each case to decide its eligibility for further investigation. Research conducted by numerous police departments has demonstrated that scoring systems successfully screen out low-probability cases and identify promising cases.[38] Some cases are so serious in nature or so important for other reasons that they deserve follow-up investigation regardless of their potential solvability following preliminary investigation.

Another investigative refinement was to refocus attention on offenders rather than offenses. This is called the *repeat offender approach*. The rationale behind this approach rests on research indicating that a few very active criminal offenders account for a disproportionate amount of criminal activity.

The reactive type of repeat offender program focuses on offenders already arrested. Prior records of arrestees are examined to identify repeat offenders, especially those who meet the criteria of subsequent offender laws enacted in many states. When an arrestee is found who meets the criteria, specially trained, highly skilled detectives review the arrest, enhance the prosecution through additional investigation, shepherd the case through the courts, and collect the necessary records to document prior convictions. In this way the case is kept from falling through the cracks in the court system, inappropriate plea bargaining is avoided, and the full weight of legal sanctions is brought to bear on the repeat offender.[39]

Some police departments also utilize more proactive repeat offender tactics, including extensive surveillance of suspected active repeaters. In general, this is an expensive undertaking because it takes several officers to conduct a continuing surveillance. Only very active offenders are likely to merit such an investment. A study in Washington, D.C., however, found that a proactive repeat offender unit was successful in arresting targeted offenders and that offenders who were apprehended had prior records that were much longer than average. The tactics of this unit included conducting surveillances of active offenders, locating wanted serious offenders, acting on tips from informants, and employing decoy and sting-type methods.[40] A similar study conducted in Phoenix focused on a mixed proactive/reactive model. Suspected repeat offenders were identified to police department personnel, so that some proactive work could take place, but the primary tactic was to seek additional evidence and conduct extensive background checks after repeat offenders were arrested, which was usually during the course of routine police business.[41] This study found that targeted repeat offenders were slightly more likely to be arrested than nontargeted ones, but more importantly, they were more likely to get prison sentences, and their sentences were on average 18 months longer than those given to nontargeted repeat offenders.

Problem-Oriented Policing

As described above, most of the refinements to preventive patrol, rapid response, and follow-up investigation since the 1970s have emphasized taking a more targeted approach by concentrating police resources on specific locations, specific types of calls and cases, and specific offenders. But the actual methods employed have not changed very much—for the most part, what has been targeted and concentrated is visible police authority and enforcement action. Since the 1980s, though, another targeted approach, called *problem-oriented policing,* has gained popularity.

Simply put, problem-oriented policing (POP) posits that police should focus more attention on *problems*, as opposed to *incidents*.[42] Problems may be recognizable as collections of incidents related in some way (such as by occurring at the same location) or as underlying conditions that give rise to incidents, crimes, disorder, and other substantive community issues that people expect the police to handle. By focusing more on problems than on incidents, police can address causes rather than mere symptoms and, consequently, have a greater impact. The public health analogy is often used to illustrate this difference in conceptualizing the police role, with its emphasis on prevention and taking a proactive approach. This analogy is useful, too, because it reminds us that even with a strong public health approach, people still get sick and need medical attention—that is, police still need to respond to calls and make arrests, even as POP prevents some problems and reduces the demand for reactive policing.

One of the most fundamental tenets of POP is that law enforcement—(using the criminal law)—should be understood as one *means* of policing, rather than as the end or goal of policing or even its raison d'etre. This is much more than a subtle shift in terminology. It emphasizes that police pursue large and critically important societal goals—controlling crime, protecting people, reducing fear, maintaining order. In every instance, police should choose those lawful and ethical means that yield the most efficient and effective achievement of these ends. Sometimes this may involve enforcement of the criminal law, and sometimes it may not. Thus, the words "policing" and "law enforcement" are not synonymous, and law enforcement is not the only—or even necessarily the principal—technique of policing.

In place of overreliance on the criminal law, POP recommends a rational and analytical approach to problem solving using a process best known in police circles as the *SARA model* (scanning, analysis, response, assessment).[43] According to this approach, police should continually scan their areas of responsibility, drawing on a variety of sources of information in order to identify apparent problems. Next, they should carefully analyze those problems in order to verify, describe, and explain them. Only after this analysis stage should police turn their attention to responses, and when they do, they should identify and consider a wide range of responses before narrowing their focus down to the most promising alternatives. After implementing these responses, they should then carefully assess impact in order to determine whether they need to try something else, and also to document lessons learned for the benefit of future problem-solving efforts.

POP analysis and responses are often focused on the three sides of the "crime triangle"—offenders, victims, and locations. Arguably, all three are needed for crimes or other problems to occur. Thus, analysis of these three factors should shed light on the nature of the problem and why it is occurring when and where it is. In addition, given the nature of a triangle, pulling out any one side should cause it to collapse—this encourages problem solvers to focus attention on responses that might affect offenders, victims, or locations. Finally, the inside of the triangle is the domain of "guardians." These are people who have a stake in protecting, monitoring, controlling, or improving offenders, victims, or locations. Problem solvers should look for guardians who can contribute to the implementation of responses and the overall effectiveness of the POP effort.

Early POP field tests were conducted in Baltimore County, Maryland,[44] and Newport News, Virginia.[45] POP has been greatly popularized through two articles in the *Atlantic Monthly* magazine[46] and further diffused through its association with community policing.[47] There are many specific examples and case studies of problem solving now available[48] and a few empirical studies of POP in practice.[49] An exhaustive retrospective and assessment has recently been published by one of Herman Goldstein's protégés, Michael Scott.[50] The consensus of 15-plus years of experience is that problem-oriented policing is an effective strategy for dealing with both crime- and noncrime-related problems at both the neighborhood and citywide levels.

Community Relations Strategies

As already described in this chapter, police strategies and tactics aimed at reducing crime have undergone a great deal of research and refinement since the early 1970s. At the same time, substantial research and development activity has also been focused on another major concern of the police, improving relations with the community. For the most part, developments in this area have occurred separately from crime control efforts, although some see community policing as the logical culmination of both streams of development.

Public Relations

In the 1950s and 1960s, many police departments established community relations units in response to perceived problems in police-community relations. Initially, these community relations units engaged mostly in public relations by presenting the police point of view to the community. This one-sided approach was soon recognized as inadequate and expanded to provide the community with a forum for expressing its views to the police. The two-way police-community relations philosophy emphasized the importance of communication and mutual understanding.

In the 1970s it became apparent that police-community relations officers and units were not effective in guaranteeing smooth relations between a community and its police department. A community experiences its police department through the actions of patrol officers and detectives more so than through the presentations of a few community relations specialists. Efforts were undertaken to train patrol officers in community relations and crime prevention techniques and to make them more knowledgeable about community characteristics and problems.[51] Team policing programs were also implemented, in part as a means of improving police responsiveness to community concerns.[52]

Crime Prevention

Early police efforts at public relations and community relations naturally evolved toward crime prevention, in part because of the public's thirst for information about how to protect themselves and their families. This was ironic in the sense that police efforts to improve community relations led the public to ask for information about how best to control crime. Because of this history, crime prevention as a police strategy refers not so much to preventive patrol as to special programs designed to make citizens, homes, and businesses more difficult to victimize. Organizationally, crime prevention units are often combined with community services and community relations units rather than with patrol or investigations.

One method, called *target hardening*, seeks improvements in doors, windows, locks, alarms, lighting, and landscaping that make illegal entry into homes and businesses more difficult and more time-consuming. Another method is to train citizens to avoid threatening situations and to react correctly when attacked or threatened. Still other methods encourage citizens to watch out for their neighbors' property and even to patrol their own neighborhoods.

Some police departments assign one or more officers to crime prevention duties. These officers then specialize in performing security surveys, giving public crime prevention lectures and presentations, and organizing community participation in crime prevention programs. Other departments have chosen to assign crime prevention duties to all patrol officers. Under this model, each officer is responsible for crime prevention duties on his or her beat.

The effects of crime prevention programs have not been conclusively established. Many police executives in recent years, however, have attributed crime decreases to community participation in crime prevention programs. Target hardening and increased community participation in crime prevention certainly contribute to crime reduction, and evidence is available that crime prevention programs at least make citizens feel safer and more willing to report suspicious activity.[53] On the other hand, the current tendency is to oversell community crime prevention as the solution to every community's crime and fear of crime problems. Yet some communities may not be receptive to such programs; citizen participation is frequently difficult to maintain over extended periods, and some programs may have unintended side effects such as increased fear among some participants.[54]

An increasingly popular approach that closely parallels problem-oriented policing is *situational crime prevention*.[55] This approach emphasizes the necessity of tailoring crime prevention responses to the specific characteristics of the crime problem being addressed—it rejects any one-size-fits-all thinking. It also focuses primarily on reducing opportunities for crime by, for example, increasing the effort required to commit offenses, increasing the risk of being detected, and reducing the reward should the offense be consummated. Situational crime prevention has achieved substantial success when targeted at a wide variety of types of offenses, including auto theft, shoplifting, thefts from vending machines, assaults at bus stops, and robberies at convenience stores.

Foot Patrol

Many observers now believe that the abandonment of foot patrol by most American police departments by the mid-1900s changed the nature of police work and negatively affected police-citizen relations. Officers assigned to large patrol car beats do not develop the intimate understanding of and cordial relationship with the community that foot patrol officers assigned to small beats develop. Officers on foot are in a position to relate more intimately with citizens than officers driving by in cars.

The results of two research studies, together with the development of small police radios, gave a boost to the resurgence of foot patrol starting in the 1980s. Originally, the police car was needed to house the bulky two-way radio. Today, foot patrol officers carry tiny, lightweight radios that enable them to handle calls promptly and to request information or assistance whenever needed. They are never out of touch and they are always available.

An experimental study conducted in Newark, New Jersey, was unable to demonstrate that either adding or removing foot patrol affected crime in any way.[56] This finding mirrored what had been found in Kansas City regarding motorized patrol. Citizens involved in the foot patrol study, however, were less fearful of crime and more satisfied with foot patrol service than with motor patrol. In addition, citizens were aware of additions and deletions of foot patrol in their neighborhoods, a finding that stands in stark contrast to the results of the Kansas City study, in which citizens did not perceive changes in the levels of motorized patrol. A second major foot patrol research program in Flint, Michigan, reported findings that were similar to the Newark findings, except that crime decreased too.[57]

These studies were widely interpreted as demonstrating that even if foot patrol did not decrease crime, at least it made citizens feel safer and led to improvements in police-community relations. Why the difference between motorized patrol and foot patrol? In what has come to be known as the "broken windows" thesis, foot patrol officers pay more attention to disorderly behavior and to minor offenses than do motor patrol officers.[58] Moreover, they are in a better position to manage their beats—to understand what constitutes threatening or inappropriate behavior, to observe it, and to correct it. Foot patrol officers are likely to pay more attention to derelicts, petty thieves, disorderly persons, vagrants, panhandlers, noisy juveniles, and street people, who, although not committing serious crimes, cause concern and fear among many citizens. Failure to control even the most minor aberrant activities on the street contributes to neighborhood fears. Foot patrol officers have more opportunity than motor patrol officers to control street disorder and reassure ordinary citizens.

Geography plays a large role in determining the viability of foot patrol as a police strategy. The more densely populated an area, the more the citizenry will travel on foot and the more street disorder there will be. The more densely populated an area, the more likely that foot patrol can be effectively used as a police strategy. While foot patrol may never again become the dominant police strategy it once was, it can play a large role in contributing police services to many communities.

Community Policing

Starting in the 1980s an even broader approach than community relations and foot patrol began developing. More police departments began employing foot patrol as a central component of their operational strategy rather than as a novelty or as an accommodation to downtown business interests. Crime prevention programs became more reliant on community involvement, as in neighborhood watch, community patrol, and crime-stoppers programs. Police departments began making increased use of civilians and volunteers in various aspects of policing and made permanent geographic assignment an important element of patrol deployment. This came to be called *community policing*, entailing a substantial change in police thinking, "one where police strategy and tactics are adapted to fit the needs and requirements of the different communities the department serves, where there is a diversification of the kinds of programs and services on the basis of community needs and demands for police services and where there is considerable involvement of the community with police in reaching their objectives."[59]

Research on the effectiveness of community policing has yielded mixed results. Foot patrol seems to make citizens feel safer, but it may not have much of an effect on the amount of crime.[60] A small study in Houston, Texas, that involved patrol officers visiting households to solicit viewpoints and information did report both crime and fear decreases in the study area.[61] A study of community constables in England, however, found that the constables actually spent very little of their time in direct contact with citizens, despite role expectations that emphasized community contact.[62] An ongoing study of department-wide community policing in Chicago has similarly discovered some officer resistance to working closely with citizens, but nevertheless has yielded promising effects on public satisfaction, fear, disorder, and crime.[63]

A study in Baltimore County, Maryland, provided some insight on the mixed results from community-oriented policing.[64] Three squads of 15 officers each were created, initially for the purpose of reducing fear of crime in target neighborhoods. These squads were designated as *Citizen-Oriented Police Enforcement* (COPE) units. During the first phase of COPE evolution, the units primarily employed preventive patrol tactics and based their analyses of neighborhood problems largely on crime analysis information. This phase of COPE was not truly community-oriented, and it was not very successful. Citizen awareness of COPE presence and reductions in community fear were minimal at best.

During the second phase of the COPE project, police-citizen contact was substantially increased. Police officers increased their canvassing of households, seeking information about citizen fears and concerns. COPE officers also made widespread use of crime prevention tactics, including home security surveys and community meetings, instead of relying so greatly on preventive patrol. With increased citizen contact, COPE's effects on fear improved, as did citizen awareness of COPE's presence.

COPE officers increased their citizen contact during the second phase of the project; in the process they became more aware of community concerns, but they did not make thorough use of this information. That is, after gathering information about the community's problems, COPE officers largely ignored that information, instead routinely implementing crime prevention and patrol as their solution to any and all problems. Thus, this second phase of COPE, although it incorporated substantial community contact, was not truly community-oriented or community-responsive.

COPE became genuinely community-oriented during its third phase. COPE officers adopted a process whereby they collected information from community residents and other sources before deciding what tactics to adopt. With information in hand, COPE officers analyzed the situation in a given target neighborhood and then chose the tactics most likely to solve the problems and improve the situation. In some situations, crime prevention tactics seemed most likely to succeed, but in other situations, other tactics, such as surveillance, saturation patrol, or a focus on repeat offenders seemed better suited to the problems at hand. The COPE units became increasingly more adept at gathering information, from community residents, analyzing that information, and designing good-fit solutions. This style of policing was community-oriented; citizens were heavily involved with COPE officers in problem identification and, to a lesser degree, problem solution. Not coincidentally, citizen satisfaction with the police, reductions in fear, and reductions in reported crimes in target neighborhoods were greatest during this third phase of the COPE project.

Besides being community-oriented, in its third phase the Baltimore County COPE project provided an example of problem-oriented policing. In its first and second phases, the COPE project had fallen victim to tradition and a one-size-fits-all tendency. Despite having an atypical police objective (the reduction of fear of crime), and despite gathering information from police and community sources about problems in target neighborhoods, when it came time to implement solutions the COPE units had resorted only to traditional, comfortable methods. The COPE response to problems was limited to the conventional repertoire of police strategies and tactics. Even when choosing among these few options, the COPE units failed to employ a problem-oriented approach. In the first phase of the project, preventive and saturation patrol were used predominantly, because officers were more familiar with these methods than any others. In the second phase, crime prevention tactics were emphasized, because the COPE units had been reminded of their citizen-oriented mandate and because security surveys and community meetings seemed the most convenient methods for achieving citizen contact. In neither phase were methods chosen because they were deemed the most effective responses to specific community problems and concerns.

The third phase of COPE adopted the problem-oriented approach. As described, the COPE units became more adept at collecting information about situations in target communities, using that information to identify and analyze problems, and considering a wide range of alternative responses before choosing those most likely to succeed. One clear change in this phase of COPE was a greater utilization of other government agencies and private resources to solve community problems.[65] If a vacant lot was at the center of neighborhood problems, COPE officers marshaled park and recreation, zoning, sanitation, and other public agencies to address the problematic conditions or force the property's owner to make improvements. If broken street-lighting concerned neighborhood residents, COPE pressured the electric company, apartment complex management, or whoever else had the authority to correct the problem. If a particular individual or group was terrorizing neighborhood residents, COPE adopted enforcement tactics to address the problem directly. The important innovation in this problem-oriented phase of COPE was the selection of methods based on analysis of problems rather than mindless utilization of comfortable, familiar methods without regard to the nature of the specific problems being addressed.

The third phase of COPE illustrates the possible confluence of the two major streams of development of police strategies, one focused on improving crime control and the other on improving community relations. Community policing seems to be the most effective strategy in the arsenal for improving police relations with the community. When combined with problem-oriented policing, it also seems to have great merit for improving the crime control effectiveness of policing.

Specific Problems and Issues

To this point we have discussed police strategies that are relatively broad approaches to providing police services and pursuing police objectives. In our examination of some of these strategies we have noted that the available research is sometimes inconclusive or inconsistent. This is due in part to the complexities of the strategies themselves. It is difficult to attribute effects to a strategy that has several components and that is implemented differently by different police departments.

In addition to broad strategies for controlling crime and improving community relations, police departments adopt specific strategies and tactics to deal with specific problems. In the remainder of this chapter we touch on just a few significant examples of these specific problems and issues.

Domestic Violence

Arguments and disputes between and among family members, particularly between husbands and wives, are a relatively common target of police intervention. Domestic disputes are one of the most frequent types of calls assigned to patrol officers, and one of the least liked. These disputes can sometimes be dangerous; in most instances they are difficult to resolve. Almost all police officers have experienced situations in which the disputing parties turned their anger on the police or when a husband or wife insisted on the arrest of a spouse only to refuse to press charges the following morning.

In the 1970s police attention was directed toward developing crisis intervention and conflict management skills for handling domestic disputes.[66] Patrol officers were trained in counseling techniques, and procedures were instituted to refer disputants to appropriate social agencies for treatment of their underlying problems. Some large departments created crisis intervention units to relieve patrol officers of the burden of handling domestic disputes. In general, the emphasis was on diverting family members away from the legal system and into health, welfare, and social systems.

Later in the 1970s, concerned feminists and others who were sensitive to the issue of domestic violence began to criticize the police for not adequately protecting women in domestic dispute situations. When domestic disputes erupt in violence, women are usually the victims. Critics complained that the police, whether out of their zeal to utilize referral to social agencies, their tendency to identify with husbands, their desire to avoid the work involved in arrests, or their apathy, were failing to provide women with equal protection of the law as provided by the Constitution.[67] Battered spouse programs and shelters produced numbers of vocal, articulate victims of domestic violence who felt that the police had abandoned them.

In response to these criticisms, many states passed laws toughening spousal assault penalties, laws empowering police officers to make misdemeanor probable cause arrests in spousal assault situations, and laws mandating police protection of spousal assault victims. Initial research supported the more legalistic approach to dealing with domestic violence, reporting that arrest of the assailant was the single most effective short-term method of preventing additional violence.[68] Subsequent studies, however, have produced mixed and sometimes conflicting findings.[69] At present, the legalistic approach to domestic violence cannot claim strong support from research for the proposition that it works best; it remains in place, though, supported by legislation and greater social awareness of the harm caused by domestic violence.

Perhaps most promising are community-policing and problem-solving approaches. For example, when officers in Charlotte-Mecklenburg, North Carolina, analyzed domestic violence cases, they found several interesting factors: many abusers were on probation or parole for other offenses; many abusers had previously committed "indicator" crimes against their partners, such as harassment, trespassing, and vandalism; and many couples had previously come to police attention, but it was not always discovered through repeat call analysis of home addresses (because incidents may have occurred at previous addresses or at places of work). Based on these discoveries, officers began compiling more complete databases on victims and assailants, they began targeting indicator crimes in hopes of heading off more violent episodes, they began coordinating more closely with social service agencies and prosecutors, and they implemented a Police Watch program to focus more attention and pressure on assailants and those engaged in indicator crimes. Initial results have been promising.[70]

Missing Children

Another problem for which police tactics and procedures have changed considerably in recent years is that of runaways and missing children. In the past, many, if not most, police departments took a lackadaisical approach to the problem. Departments often refused to take an official report until the child had been missing for at least 24 hours, in effect assuming that the child had run away and would return shortly. If the child remained missing for a day, a patrol officer would complete a report and perhaps enter the missing person in the computer information system. Little investigative effort would be expended unless there was strong evidence of foul play. If investigators were assigned to missing person cases, they were often the least experienced and least skillful of all detectives.

The documentation of child kidnapping cases, the apparent growth of the missing children problem and growing awareness of related problems of child abuse and child exploitation have now combined to force police departments to assign the highest priority to missing children reports. Reports are taken immediately and investigations begun promptly. State and federal investigative agencies have been ordered to perform investigative and coordinative functions. Missing children cases now receive as much or more publicity as almost any kind of crime, and public pressure on police departments to solve missing children cases can be intense. Most recently, programs such as Code Adam and the Amber Alert system have been developed to help solicit the community's participation in locating missing children more quickly.[71]

Drug Control

Few aspects of police work arouse such strong feelings as drug control strategies. Some citizens regard drug abuse as a tremendous problem and urge the police to take an all-out enforcement approach. Others who also regard it as a very serious problem would rather see an emphasis on education, prevention, and treatment. Still others think drug problems are over-exaggerated.

Within the enforcement realm, citizens have widely differing opinions about whether police should use specific tactics, such as drug-sniffing dogs, consent searches, surveillance, informants, and undercover operations. Concerns also develop about the equity of enforcement actions, which inevitably target public and street-corner violations more than private and country-club violations, resulting in a disproportionate impact on young and minority offenders.

Traditionally, efforts to control drug abuse have fallen into two categories—demand reduction and supply reduction. *Demand reduction* includes education and prevention, as well as enforcement targeted at drug users. *Supply reduction* includes crop eradication, alternative crop subsidies, control over prescription drugs and chemicals, antismuggling efforts, and various enforcement activities aimed at low-level and high-level drug sellers. A third general approach is harm reduction. This approach does not focus so much on trying to eliminate drug abuse as on trying to identify the worst harms associated with drugs and then looking for ways to minimize those harms. Often, this harm-reduction approach is advocated by those who argue in favor of medicalizing the drug problem rather than criminalizing it.

Most citizens, even if they personally lean toward education, prevention, treatment, harm reduction, or some other nonenforcement approach, expect the police to take action if a crack house or methamphetamine lab shows up next door. Police departments have been most successful in addressing neighborhood-level and street-level drug problems when taking a community policing and problem-oriented policing approach.[72] The community policing approach leads officers to work with the community, other government agencies, and nongovernmental organizations in identifying and tackling specific drug problems. These other entities can often provide information, resources, and even authority (e.g., by working with probation officers or code enforcement officers) to help solve the problem. The POP approach encourages officers to gather and analyze information first, to use the crime triangle to identify leverage points that can be exploited to reduce the problem, and to consider a wide array of traditional and nontraditional responses.

Summary

In this chapter we have reviewed a number of police strategies and tactics. Together these strategies and tactics comprise the police organizational technology—that is, the dominant methods by which police work is performed and police objectives are pursued. As we have seen, police strategies and tactics have changed over the years in response to changes in society, public pressures, and research. Police executives must continually reassess their organizational technology and make adjustments to improve the attainment of the goals of protecting life and property and maintaining order.

The three cornerstones of traditional police crime control strategy are routine preventive patrol, immediate response to calls, and follow-up investigations of reported crimes. As discussed in this chapter, major research studies have challenged the effectiveness of these strategies, leading both to refinements and to new approaches such as problem-oriented policing. On a parallel track, police departments have also sought more effective strategies for improving their relations with the community. Currently, community policing is seen as the most effective strategy for improved police-community relations, and, in combination with problem-oriented policing, as a promising approach to crime control as well. More variation is found in police strategies and tactics for dealing with specific problems and issues, although community policing and problem solving still often surface as effective approaches.

Discussion Questions

1. What are your personal beliefs about the preventive effects of police patrol? The theory of patrol is that it prevents crime; why doesn't it?

2. Why aren't detectives more successful at solving crimes? Given their relative lack of success, how do you account for the "detective mystique"?

3. Why do you think that foot patrol is more effective than motor patrol in reassuring citizens and making them feel safe? To what extent can we replace motor patrol with foot patrol in today's society?

4. Aggressive patrol produces arrests and may deter crime, but it also leads to more police intrusion in the lives of citizens. Do you favor its use? How would you balance the competing interests of civil liberties and crime control?

5. As a police chief, what policies and procedures would you institute to guide your officers in handling domestic violence cases? How much discretion would you leave in the officers' hands? How would you respond to pressure from women's rights and men's rights groups?

Notes

1. J.Q. Wilson, "Dilemmas of Police Administration," *Public Administration Review* (September/October 1968): 407-417.

2. J.Q. Wilson, *The Investigators: Managing FBI and Narcotics Agents* (New York, NY: Basic Books, 1978), p. 203.

3. W. Bratton with P. Knobler, *Turnaround: How America's Top Cop Reversed the Crime Epidemic* (New York, NY: Random House, 1998).

4. Wilson, *The Investigators*, p. 204.

5. G.P. Whitaker, "What Is Patrol Work?" *Police Studies* 4, no. 4 (winter 1982): 13-17.

6. President's Commission on Law Enforcement and Administration of Justice, *The Challenge of Crime in a Free Society* (New York, NY: Avon Books, 1968), p. 295.

7. J.Q. Wilson, *Varieties of Police Behavior: The Management of Law and Order in Eight Communities* (Cambridge, MA: Harvard University Press, 1968), p. 26.

8. G.W. Cordner, "While on Routine Patrol: What the Police Do When They're Not Doing Anything," *American Journal of Police* 1, no. 2 (1982): 94-112.

9. G.L. Kelling, T. Pate, D. Dieckman, and C.E. Brown, *The Kansas City Preventive Patrol Experiment: A Summary Report* (Washington, DC: Police Foundation, 1974).

10. Ibid., p. 16.

11. L.W. Sherman, "Policing Communities: What Works?" in *Communities and Crime*, A.J. Reiss Jr. and M. Tonry, eds. (Chicago, IL: University of Chicago Press, 1986), p. 359.

12. H.H. Isaacs, "A Study of Communications, Crimes, and Arrests in a Metropolitan Police Department," in *Task Force Report: Science and Technology* (Washington, DC: U.S. Government Printing Office, 1967); C. Clawson and S.K. Chang, "The Relationship of Response Delays and Arrest Rates," *Journal of Police Science and Administration* 5 (1977): 53-68; D.P. Tarr, "Analysis of Response Delays and Arrest Rates," *Journal of Police Science and Administration* 6 (1978): 429-451.

13. Kansas City Police Department, *Response Time Analysis: Executive Summary* (Washington, DC: U.S. Government Printing Office, 1978); W. Spelman and D.K. Brown, *Calling the Police: Citizen Reporting of Serious Crime* (Washington, DC: Police Executive Research Forum, 1981).

14. G.W. Cordner, J.R. Greene, and T.S. Bynum, "The Sooner the Better: Some Effects of Police Response Time," in *Police at Work: Policy Issues and Analysis*, R.R. Bennett, ed. (Beverly Hills, CA: Sage, 1983).

15. Spelman and Brown, Calling the Police, p.xix.

16. Ibid., p. 72.

17. T. Pate, A. Ferrara, R.A. Bowers, and J. Lorence, *Police Response Time: Its Determinants and Effects* (Washington, DC: Police Foundation, 1976).

18. J.F. Heaphy, ed., *Police Practices: The General Administrative Survey* (Washington, DC: Police Foundation, 1978).

19. Wilson, *The Investigators*.

20. P.W. Greenwood and J. Petersilia, *The Criminal Investigation Process Volume I: Summary and Policy Implications* (Santa Monica, CA: RAND, 1975), p. vii.

21. Ibid.

22. J.L. Kuykendall, "The Municipal Police Detective: An Historical Analysis," *Criminology* 24, no. 1 (February 1986): 175-201.

23. Greenwood and Petersilia, *Criminal Investigation Process*, pp. viii-ix.

24. D.F. Cawley and H.J. Miron, *Managing Patrol Operations: Manual* (Washington, DC: U.S. Government Printing Office, 1977).

25. J.W. Warren, M.L. Forst, and M.M. Estrella, "Directed Patrol: An Experiment That Worked," *Police Chief* (July 1979): 48-49, 78.

26. G.W. Cordner, "The Effects of Directed Patrol: A Natural Quasi-Experiment in Pontiac," in *Contemporary Issues in Law Enforcement*, J.J. Fyfe ed., (Beverly Hills, CA: Sage, 1981).

27. L.W. Sherman and D. Weisburd, "General Deterrent Effects of Police Patrol in Crime 'Hot Spots': A Randomized, Controlled Trial," *Justice Quarterly* 12, no. 4 (December 1995): 625-648.

28. E.F. McGarrell, S. Chermak, and A. Weiss, *Targeting Firearms Violence through Directed Police Patrol* (Indianapolis, IN: Hudson Institute, 1999), p. viii.

29. G.W. Cordner, "Evaluating Tactical Patrol," in L.T. Hoover, ed., *Quantifying Quality in Policing* (Washington, DC: Police Executive Research Forum, 1996), pp. 185-206.

30. J.E. Boydstun, *San Diego Field Interrogation: Final Report* (Washington, DC: Police Foundation, 1975).

31. J.Q. Wilson and B. Boland, *The Effect of the Police on Crime* (Washington, DC: U.S. Government Printing Office, 1979).

32. J.Q. Wilson and B. Boland, "Crime," in *The Urban Predicament*, W. Gorham and N. Glazer, eds. (Washington, DC: Urban Institute, 1976).

33. L.W. Sherman, J.W. Shaw, and D.P. Rogan, "The Kansas City Gun Experiment," *Research in Brief* (Washington, DC: National Institute of Justice, 1995).

34. M.T. Farmer, ed., *Differential Police Response Strategies* (Washington, DC: Police Executive Research Forum, 1981).

35. M.F. Cahn and J.M. Tien, *An Alternative Approach in Police Response: The Wilmington Management of Demand Program* (Cambridge, MA: Public Systems Evaluation, 1981); and J.T. McEwen, E.F. Connors III, and M.I. Cohen, *Evaluation of the Differential Police Responses Field Test* (Washington, DC: U.S. Government Printing Office, 1986); R.E. Worden, "Toward Equity and Efficiency in Law Enforcement: Differential Police Response," *American Journal of Police* 12, no. 1 (1993): 1-32.

36. D.F. Cawley, H.J. Miron, W.J. Araujo, R. Wasserman, T.A. Mannello, and Y. Huffman, *Managing Criminal Investigations: Manual* (Washington, DC: U.S. Government Printing Office, 1977).

37. B. Greenberg, C.V. Elliott, L.P. Kraft, and H.S. Proctor, *Felony Investigation Decision Model: An Analysis of Investigative Elements of Information* (Washington, DC: U.S. Government Printing Office, 1977).

38. J.E. Eck, *Managing Case Assignments: The Burglary Investigation Decision Model Replication* (Washington, DC: Police Executive Research Forum, 1979).

39. "The Baltimore County Repeat Offender Planning Project" (Towson, MD: Baltimore County Criminal Justice Coordinator, April 1983).

40. S.E. Martin and L.W. Sherman, "Selective Apprehension: A Police Strategy for Repeat Offenders," *Criminology* 24, no. 1 (February 1986): 155-173.

41. A.F. Abrahamse, P.A. Ebener, P.W. Greenwood, and T.E. Kosin, "An Experimental Evaluation of the Phoenix Repeat Offender Program," *Justice Quarterly* 8, no. 2 (1991): 141-168.

42. H. Goldstein, *Problem-Oriented Policing* (New York, NY: McGraw-Hill, 1990).

43. J.E. Eck and W. Spelman. *Problem-Solving: Problem-Oriented Policing in Newport News* (Washington, DC: Police Executive Research Forum, 1987).

44. G. Cordner, "Fear of Crime and the Police: An Evaluation of a Fear-Reduction Strategy," *Journal of Police Science and Administration* 14 (1986): 223-233; G. Cordner, "A Problem-Oriented Approach to Community-Oriented Policing," in J.Greene and S. Mastrofski, eds., *Community Policing: Rhetoric or Reality* (New York, NY: Praeger, 1988), pp. 135-152.

45. Eck and Spelman, *Problem-Solving*.

46. J.Q. Wilson and G.L. Kelling, "Broken Windows: The Police and Neighborhood Safety," *Atlantic Monthly* (March 1982): 29-38; J.Q. Wilson and G.L. Kelling, "Making Neighborhoods Safe," *Atlantic Monthly* (February 1989): 46-52.

47. H. Goldstein, "Toward Community-Oriented Policing: Potential, Basic Requirements and Threshold Questions," *Crime & Delinquency* 33, no. 1 (1987): 6-30.

48. R. Sampson and M. Scott, *Tackling Crime and Other Public-Safety Problems: Case Studies in Problem-Solving* (Washington, DC: U.S. Department of Justice, Office of Community Oriented Policing Services, 2000).

49. B. Webster and E. Connors, "Police Methods for Identifying Community Problems," *American Journal of Police* 12, no. 1 (1993): 75-102; M. Buerger, "The Problems of Problem Solving: Resistance, Interdependencies, and Conflicting Interests," *American Journal of Police* 13, no. 3 (1994): 1-36; G.E. Capowich and J.A. Roehl, "Problem-Oriented Policing: Actions and Effectiveness in San Diego," in D. Rosenbaum, ed., *The Challenge of Community Policing: Testing the Promises* (Thousand Oaks, CA: Sage, 1994), pp. 127-146.

50. M. Scott, *Problem-Oriented Policing: Reflections on the First 20 Years* (Washington, DC: U.S. Department of Justice, Office of Community Oriented Policing Services, 2000).

51. J.E. Boydstun and M.E. Sherry, *San Diego Community Profile: Final Report* (Washington, DC: Police Foundation, 1975).

52. L. Sherman, C. Milton, and T. Kelly, *Team Policing: Seven Case Studies* (Washington, DC: Police Foundation, 1973); A. Schwartz and S. Clarren, *The Cincinnati Team Policing Experiment: A Summary Report* (Washington, DC: Police Foundation, 1977); S. Walker, "Does Anyone Remember Team Policing? Lessons of the Team Policing Experience for Community Policing," *American Journal of Police*, 12, no. 1 (1993).

53. A.M. Pate, W. Skogan, M.A. Wycoff, and L.W. Sherman, *Coordinated Community Policing: Executive Summary* (Washington, DC: Police Foundation, 1985); and M.A. Wycoff, W. Skogan, A.M. Pate, and L.W. Sherman, *Police as Community Organizers: Executive Summary* (Washington, DC: Police Foundation, 1985).

54. D.P. Rosenbaum, "The Theory and Research Behind Neighborhood Watch: Is It a Sound Fear and Crime Reduction Strategy?" *Crime & Delinquency* 33, no. 1 (January 1987): 103-134.

55. R.V. Clarke, ed., *Situational Crime Prevention: Successful Case Studies*, Second Edition (Guilderland, NY: Harrow and Heston, 1997).

56. The Police Foundation, *The Newark Foot Patrol Experiment* (Washington, DC: Police Foundation, 1981).

57. R.C. Trojanowicz, *An Evaluation of the Neighborhood Foot Patrol Program in Flint, Michigan* (East Lansing, MI: National Neighborhood Foot Patrol Center, Michigan State University, 1982).

58. Wilson and Kelling, "Broken Windows."

59. A.J. Reiss Jr., "Shaping and Serving the Community: The Role of the Police Chief Executive," in William A. Geller, ed., *Police Leadership in America: Crisis and Opportunity* (New York, NY: Praeger, 1985), p. 63.

60. The Police Foundation, *Newark Foot Patrol Experiment.*

61. M.A. Wycoff, W. Skogan, A. Pate, and L.W. Sherman, *Citizen Contact Patrol: Executive Summary* (Washington, DC: Police Foundation, 1985).

62. D. Brown and S. Iles, "Community Constables: A Study of a Policing Initiative," *NIJ International Summaries* (October 1986).

63. W.G. Skogan and S.M. Hartnett, *Community Policing, Chicago Style* (New York, NY: Oxford University Press, 1997).

64. G.W. Cordner, *The Baltimore County Citizen Oriented Police Enforcement (COPE) Project: Final Evaluation* (Baltimore, MD: Criminal Justice Department, University of Baltimore, 1985).

65. P.B. Taft, Jr., *Fighting Fear: The Baltimore County C.O.P.E. Project* (Washington, DC: Police Executive Research Forum, 1986).

66. M. Bard, *Family Crisis Intervention: From Concept to Implementation* (Washington, DC: U.S. Government Printing Office, 1973).

67. J. Meier, "Battered Justice," *Washington Monthly* (May 1987): 37-45.

68. L.W. Sherman and R.A. Berk, "The Minneapolis Domestic Violence Experiment," *Police Foundation Reports* 1 (April 1984): 1-8.

69. J.D. Hirschel, I.W. Hutchison, C.W. Dean, and A.M. Mills, "Review Essay on the Law Enforcement Response to Spouse Abuse: Past, Present and Future," *Justice Quarterly* 9, no. 2 (1992): 247-283.

70. K. Bannerman, "Domestic Violence Intervention Project: Charlotte-Mecklenburg Police Department," in *Excellence in Problem-Oriented Policing: The 2002 Herman Goldstein Award Winners* (Washington, DC: Police Executive Research Forum, 2002).

71. See http://www.missingkids.com/ and http://www.missingkids.com/html/amberplan.html.

72. J.E. Eck, "Drug Market Places: How They Form and How They Can Be Prevented," in C.S. Brito and T. Allan, *Problem-Oriented Policing: Crime-Specific Problems, Critical Issues, and Making POP Work*, Vol. 2 (Washington, DC: Police Executive Research Forum, 1999), pp. 91-111; Vancouver Police Department and Grandview-Woodland Community Policing Centre, "Showdown at the Playground: A Community Confronts Drug and Disorder Problems in a Neighborhood Park," *Excellence in Problem-Oriented Policing: The 2000 Herman Goldstein Award Winners* (Washington, DC: Police Executive Research Forum, 2001).

Suggested Reading

Alpert, Geoffrey P., and Alex Piquero, eds. *Community Policing: Contemporary Readings*, Second ed. Prospect Heights, IL: Waveland, 2000.

Peak, Kenneth J., and Ronald W. Glensor. *Community Policing and Problem Solving: Strategies and Practices*, Third ed. Upper Saddle River, NJ: Prentice Hall, 2002.

Sampson, Rana and Michael Scott. *Tackling Crime and Other Public-Safety Problems: Case Studies in Problem-Solving*. Washington, DC: U.S. Department of Justice, Office of Community Oriented Policing Services, 2000.

Scott, Michael. *Problem-Oriented Policing: Reflections on the First 20 Years*. Washington, DC: U.S. Department of Justice, Office of Community Oriented Policing Services, 2000.

Shelley, Tara O'Connor, and Anne C. Grant, eds. *Problem-Oriented Policing: Crime-Specific Problems, Critical Issues, and Making POP Work, Vol. 1*. Washington, DC: Police Executive Research Forum, 1998.

Police Organizational Improvement

14

The organization as we know it today is much different from the organization of 1950, when the traditional perspective on police administration reigned supreme. This is understandable. The fact that organizations are open systems means that they are affected by changing environmental influences. Organizations must necessarily change if they are to be responsive to changing societal demands.

In the 1970s many observers believed that the organizational turmoil and loss of respect for authority then evident were indicators of social and organizational disintegration that threatened the very foundations of society. Other observers saw these conditions as temporary aberrations of a society in a state of cultural lag, changing so rapidly that its institutions were unable to keep up with the change and respond to it meaningfully. Still others saw these trends producing an administrative revolution that would increase personal freedom as the organization became a "shelter without walls."[1]

In recent years, however, with less fear of social and organizational disintegration, organizational life has become more humane and, indeed, more considerate of the needs and concerns of employees. In addition, the tenor of the times has changed. Foreign competition and the trade imbalance have forced the United States into a more pragmatic posture, with emphasis on quality workmanship. Everyone now recognizes the necessity for improving their productivity in order to make their goods and services more competitive in the world market. In similar fashion, government agencies have begun to see the need to improve their productivity in order to provide more and better services at reduced cost to the taxpayer.

In this chapter we will briefly discuss some organizational improvement methodologies and applications that have been advanced in recent years and that apply to police management. Some of these approaches to improvement are embodied in specific police programs, while others are adapted from general management practices. Four approaches are presented: the human development approach, the structural design approach, the strategic management approach, and the learning organization approach.

The Human Development Approach

The Hawthorne studies of the 1920s introduced the concept that the worker is something more than a human machine. These studies provided a foundation for what eventually became the human relations movement, which characterized the worker as a social being with human needs and demanded that management treat its employees more humanely. An overview of human development approaches is given in Table 14.1.

Traditional theorists considered the human relations movement to be managerial permissiveness, branding it as an abdication of managerial authority, which had heretofore been considered the glue that held organizations together. Other theorists came to view the human relations movement as a cosmetic public relations gimmick and claimed that it involved no real changes in the patterns of organizational authority.

Table 14.1
Human Development Approaches

Approach	Key Theorist	Summary
Human Relations	Roethlisberger et al.	Hawthorne studies; recognition of the social needs of workers
Theory X and Theory Y	McGregor	Need hierarchy; worker self-direction and self-control
Management by Objectives	Drucker	Goals and objectives for direction and control
Job Enrichment	Herzberg	Importance of the work itself; motivation from work
Participative Management	Likert	Democratic management; supportive and advisory supervision
Organization Development	Bennis	Organizational improvement as change; integrated strategies

Neither group of theorists was correct. In retrospect, the human relations movement can be credited with improving the workplace considerably and with contributing to the improvement of employee compensation and other work benefits. Most important, the movement was the first step toward recognizing that the human element in an organization is not comparable to inert resources such as money, machinery, and raw materials. Organizational productivity became dependent on treating workers with dignity and with respect. The human relations movement was here to stay.

Theory X and Theory Y

Douglas McGregor was one of the first observers to suggest that the human relations movement and the debate about the relative merits of hard and soft management were missing the point.[2] He argued that the basic assumptions of management had not changed, and he forcefully contended that these basic assumptions were invalid.

McGregor called the conventional view of management's task *Theory X*. The assumptions behind Theory X are as follows:

1. people do not like to work and will avoid work whenever possible;
2. people must be forced to work; and
3. people are inherently unambitious and irresponsible, seek security, and expect to be directed in their work.[3]

McGregor conceded that most workers behaved just as the Theory X assumptions indicated, but he argued that the organizational climate created by Theory X managers caused workers' behavior. He believed that management's view of workers as lazy, stupid, and irresponsible, and management's treatment of workers on the basis of that view, made it all but impossible for workers to display interest, intelligence, and energy.

In arguing that the assumptions of Theory X did not accurately characterize the motivation and basic nature of organizational employees, McGregor drew on the findings of Abraham Maslow, whose findings were discussed in Chapter 8.[4] Basically, Maslow found that human behavior is motivated by a hierarchy of needs: basic needs, security needs, social needs, self-concept needs, and ideal self needs. Maslow contended that a satisfied need ceased to have any motivational value. The human need for oxygen, for example, is basic, but it does not motivate behavior except in circumstances in which a person's supply of oxygen is withdrawn.

McGregor saw that Theory X assumptions and management were based on the belief that workers are still motivated primarily by basic and security needs. Because Theory X assumptions were incorrect, management became frustrated when regular improvements in salary, fringe benefits, and job security did not result in increased productivity and higher morale. However, McGregor pointed out that for almost all workers, basic and security needs were satisfied. The major motivational needs of most workers, therefore, are social needs, self-concept needs, and ideal self needs.

McGregor also pointed out that for needs to have a motivating effect at work, the opportunity must be present to satisfy these needs at work. Although an individual's after-hours activities might satisfy certain needs, they have no motivating effect in the workplace. Although a man may be president of the Little League, a director of the Junior Chamber of Commerce, and a 32nd-degree Mason, and thereby satisfy some of his needs on the top side of the need hierarchy, such satisfaction plays no role whatsoever in motivating him to do his job; these needs must be satisfied where he works if he is to be motivated to do his job well.

Armed with Maslow's findings on motivation, McGregor proposed *Theory Y* as an alternative to Theory X. The general assumptions on which Theory Y is based are as follows:

1. It is natural for workers to expend energy in work that they enjoy.
2. If work is satisfying, it will be performed well; if it is not satisfying, it will be looked on as punishment and will be avoided.
3. Control and punishment are not the only methods to motivate work.
4. Workers are totally capable of directing themselves toward the accomplishment of goals and objectives to which they are personally committed.
5. There is a direct relationship between worker commitment and the rewards associated with the achievement of goals and objectives.
6. Rewards emanate from the satisfaction of motivational needs as these relate to the effort expended on the achievement of goals and objectives.
7. If conditions are right, workers will not only accept responsibility but also seek it.

8. Laziness and disinterest in work are the result of bad experiences, not innate human behavior.

9. Most people are ambitious and are capable of working innovatively and productively in organizational settings.

10. Modern management uses human potential to an extraordinarily limited degree.[5]

The essential difference between the two theories is that Theory X emphasizes external control of worker behavior, whereas Theory Y emphasizes self-control and self-direction. Theory X proponents treat employees like children; Theory Y proponents treat them like mature adults. Considering the fact that management has been treating employees like children for many generations, McGregor conceded that it would take considerable time for both managers and workers to grow accustomed to Theory Y. McGregor concluded that Theory X "fails because direction and control are useless methods of motivating people whose physiological and safety needs (what we have called basic and security needs) are reasonably satisfied and whose social, egotistic, and self-fulfillment needs (what we have called social, self-concept, and ideal self needs) are predominant."[6]

The applicability of Theory X/Theory Y to police organizations is obvious. The traditional hierarchical structure, proliferation of rules, and punishment-oriented management found in most police agencies clearly epitomizes Theory X assumptions. According to McGregor's thesis, it is only natural for police officers to respond with work-avoidance behavior. The irony of police administration is that, in spite of Theory X management, the street-level performance of police work is left largely to the discretion of police officers who are assumed to be lazy, irresponsible, and in need of direct supervision. Police administration is characterized by Theory X assumptions and the appearance of strict, tightly controlled management; actually, worker behavior is loosely controlled.[7] Police administration would benefit greatly from the adoption of Theory Y assumptions and a management system more honestly adapted to the realities of police work.

Management by Objectives

Another approach to management that differed sharply from Theory X was developed by Peter Drucker. He called his approach *Management by Objectives (MBO)*, which, like Theory Y, is based on self-control. Drucker saw his approach as a means of obtaining higher work standards and greater productivity along with stricter accountability.[8]

MBO is based on Drucker's observation that people work hardest when they have a clear goal in mind and when they can see a direct relationship between their efforts and the accomplishment of that goal. Moreover, Drucker argued, when employees have a clear understanding of the goals of the organization and when they see how their own work contributes to achieving those goals, they can then be counted on to establish objectives for their own work accomplishment. The task itself provides substantial direction and control, and employees will strive to achieve their objectives and hold themselves accountable to such objectives.

Drucker noted that the modern organization is characterized by factors that encourage misdirection. Specialization, as one example, tends to divert employee loyalty and effort away from the organization as a whole and toward the particular specialized areas. Instituting MBO, Drucker argued, can overcome factors of misdirection by emphasizing the goals of the organization as a whole, as well as ways that subunits contribute to their achievement.

Drucker points out that in order for employees to exercise self-control and self-direction, they need information on a regular basis by which to measure their progress. A semiannual or annual performance evaluation will not suffice. Employees need such information much more frequently, and it should be available to them without their having to go to an immediate superior for it. In short, the employee's job should be systematically structured so that direct feedback is periodically available to the employee for progress measurement.

Drucker also contends that there is nothing soft about MBO. With its emphasis on self-direction and self-control and its aim toward higher standards and greater productivity with stricter accountability, it requires much more from employees than they had previously been expected to give. Like McGregor, Drucker is convinced that, in general, people like to work, want to work, want a feeling of accomplishment, and are capable of intelligent direction. Drucker sees management's task as one of removing organizational impediments to motivation more than one of providing motivation.

In principle, MBO is as applicable to police agencies as to other organizations. The application is made difficult, however, by the problem of specifying meaningful, measurable goals and objectives for police officers and police units. Broad goals, such as protecting life and property and maintaining order, are meaningful but relatively vague and difficult to measure. More specific objectives such as "improve the Part I crime clearance rate from 20 percent to 30 percent" (one possible objective for a detective division) are more measurable but raise other difficulties. The clearance rate, for example, is affected by patrol officer activity, witness availability, the nature of crimes committed, and other factors beyond the control of the detective division. Moreover, the clearance rate statistic is susceptible to manipulation through practices such as convincing suspects to confess to numerous crimes in return for promises of immunity from prosecution.

Problems such as these do not negate the value of MBO for police administration; they simply make its utilization difficult. MBO can help a police organization focus its efforts on goal accomplishment, as long as the goals are perceived as meaningful by police officers and police managers. However, if the goals and the MBO program come to be perceived as meaningless, the entire process can become an empty paperwork exercise.

Job Enrichment

A third approach to management and organizational improvement that springs from motivational theory is *job enrichment*. The principal theorist for this approach has been Frederick Herzberg.[9]

Herzberg studied a number of techniques for motivating workers: increased wages, human relations training, and employee counseling. He found that such techniques served only as short-term motivators and that some even seemed counterproductive. He also studied work behavior and isolated two sets of workplace factors that bear on employee satisfaction and dissatisfaction. The dissatisfiers included company policy and administration, supervision, work conditions, salary, personal life, status, security, and work relationships with supervisors, subordinates, and peers. These he called *hygiene factors*. The satisfiers included achievement, recognition, the work itself, responsibility, advancement, and growth. These he called *motivators*. He found that the alleviation of the dissatisfiers tended to make employees happier but no more motivated. He concluded that motivation comes only from the satisfiers.

The implications of Herzberg's studies should be clear. Through salary increases and employee counseling, management may be able to decrease employee dissatisfaction; such decreases, however, will promote no motivation. Motivation can be achieved, according to Herzberg, only through those factors he calls motivators.

Job enrichment is the restructuring of work itself in terms of motivators. It is much different from *job enlargement*, which gives each worker more work to do, and it is much different from job rotation, which simply shuttles the worker from one unenriched job to another. Job enrichment can be accomplished, according to Herzberg, by taking the following steps:

1. reduce controls but increase accountability;
2. assign workers to established, definitive work units or projects;
3. provide sufficient authority for workers to accomplish tasks within a milieu of freedom;
4. furnish workers with productivity reports directly on a periodic basis without involving supervisors as intermediaries;
5. give workers tasks that are more difficult and challenging than tasks previously assigned; and
6. allow workers to become experts by giving them specialized tasks.[10]

Central to the job enrichment approach is the concept that needs that motivate work behavior should be satisfiable at the workplace. Robert Townsend, in agreeing with this approach, asks us to "look at the rewards we're offering our people today: higher wages, medical benefits, vacations, pensions, profit sharing, bowling and basketball teams. Not one can be enjoyed on the job. You've got to leave work, get sick or retire first."[11]

Jerry Robinson notes, however, that job enrichment is not an organizational panacea, although he and other managers have found that it is a useful approach to organizational improvement, particularly as it offers workers a greater sense of pride in their work.[12] Job enrichment must be considered an important input to the managing process.

One major effort toward job enrichment in the police service is the return of the investigative function to patrol personnel. This change in role allows patrol officers to follow preliminary investigations through to their ultimate conclusion rather than having to refer such investigations to others for follow-up. In job enrichment terms, such a procedure provides officers assigned to the patrol division a complete rather than a partial unit of work with which to become involved. Most police officers welcome this; there has always been a strong general resentment to surrendering interesting cases to investigative specialists.

Other job enrichment efforts that satisfy high-level needs and increase authority and accountability at the lowest operating levels of the organization are community policing and problem-oriented policing. Community policing, for example, views patrol officers as generalists who are responsible for "managing their beats." Problem-oriented policing encourages employees at all levels to work smarter by carefully identifying and analyzing problems and then designing and implementing systematic, tailor-made solutions.

Job enrichment is achieved only through the realization and satisfaction of upper-level hierarchical needs. The fact that these needs have not been recognized or satisfied is a sad reflection on the abilities of traditional police administrators. Police work is, for the most part, fascinating work. That police administrators have succeeded in making it humdrum, mundane, and lacking in rewards and recognition is a signal that something is terribly wrong. As Thomas Reddin puts it, "We give too little thought to the work itself. Work must be more than congenial; it must be absorbing, meaningful and challenging. There just isn't any 'work' as inherently rich in these qualities as police work."[13] Capable police administrators, anxious to achieve organizational goals and objectives, must look hard for ways to enrich the jobs of all those who work with them.

Participative Management

Another human development approach to organizational improvement that has received generous praise is *participative management*. This approach is based on including nonmanagerial employees in the management process.

The extent to which employees of an organization can be involved in the management process varies widely. Some factories in Europe, for example, are run by councils made up entirely of elected representatives of the employees. In other organizations, some members of the boards of directors are elected by the employees. Elsewhere, supervisors are appointed by employees. In some organizations, the appointment of supervisors is subject to employee veto.

Although the degree of involvement may vary, there are numerous examples of employee participation in management. To many traditional managers, the idea of employees participating in the management process has seemed radical, even revolutionary. Looking at the idea objectively, however, it is no more revolutionary than having citizens participate in their own governments, an idea that was also considered revolutionary when it was first advanced.

In studying a number of organizations, Rensis Likert found that a consensus existed among managers that the most effective organizations they had known were open, democratic ones.[14] Likert identified three key factors in participative management. The first was that the relationship between supervisor and subordinate should be a supportive type of relationship, with the supervisor emphasizing the helpful, rather than the authoritarian, aspects of his or her role. The second factor was that decisionmaking in organizations should be democratic and group-centered and that decisions made by groups under these circumstances should be forwarded to management by the democratically chosen group leader. The third and most important factor in participative management was the advisory role played by the supervisor in devising work goals and norms and in acting as a liaison between employees and management in attempting to accommodate the objectives of each.

There are two outstanding and practical reasons why management should involve its employees in the process of running the organization. One is that participation gives employees a greater feeling of belonging and a stronger commitment to their work. The second is that the involvement of employees in management tends to increase the efficiency and effectiveness of the organization.

Marjorie Boyd has noted that "businessmen have . . . known that workers can achieve extraordinary productivity increases by finding ways to do their jobs better or faster or cheaper."[15] The manager who wants to take advantage of employee ingenuity, initiative, and talent does so by involving employees as much as possible in the management of the organization.[16]

Participative management is not completely new to policing. The Police Foundation reported, for example, that the Kansas City (Missouri) Police Department, in connection with patrol strategy experiments, discovered great interest in the development of participative management models.[17] In 1973 the California Highway Patrol implemented a participative management effort in conjunction with a management-by-results program. When the program was introduced, the commissioner of that organization, pointing to the need for job satisfaction, stated: "Participative management recognizes that the greatest amount of untapped talent and ability is probably in the lower ranks in any organization. Traditional police authoritative methods of management tend to waste this potential."[18] Today, participative management is a common element of community policing.

Organization Development

Warren Bennis has described *organization development* (OD) as "an educational strategy employing the widest possible means of experienced-based behavior in order to achieve more and better organizational choices in a highly turbulent world."[19] OD is not actually a separate and distinct approach to human development in organizations. That is, OD programs include, in whole or in part, Theory Y, Management by Objectives, job enrichment, and participative management. Consider the following set of OD assumptions, for example, in light of the other approaches we have discussed:

1. people need to grow in their jobs and to realize their potentials;
2. once people's basic needs have been satisfied, they will work energetically, seeking challenge and assuming responsibility;
3. effectiveness and efficiency in organizations may be enhanced through the organization of work designed to meet human needs;
4. the more open organizational communications are, the greater the degree of personal and professional growth experienced by employees;
5. open confrontation as a means of resolving conflict achieves employee growth and the accomplishment of organizational goals far better than does unilateral conflict resolution;
6. as people begin to care for one another openly and honestly within group frameworks, it becomes easier to handle organizational problems in constructive rather than destructive fashion;
7. the structure of an organization and the kinds of job requirements within it can be changed to better meet individual, group, and organizational needs, goals, and objectives; and
8. problems relating to the design of organizations are directly responsible for personality problems within them.[20]

An important ingredient of OD is its treatment of growth and development as change. It takes note of the fact that many organizational employees are quite comfortable with the way things are presently done and therefore are resistant to changes, no matter how logically they are presented or how obviously advantageous they are to employee welfare.

A key figure in the OD process is the so-called *change agent*. Usually an objective and impartial outside consultant, the change agent is hired by the organization to oversee OD. Unlike the ordinary consultant, who is hired for a limited period of time to study organizational problems, the change agent (or OD consultant) contributes expertise on an ongoing basis, acting as a resource person and advisor to management and suggesting programs and strategies for organizational improvement, while at the same time developing the organization's own capacity to grow and to manage change. The OD consultant seeks to become fully aware of the organization's particular culture and to adapt OD assumptions and principles to the realities of the organization.

Quality Leadership

An approach to management that focuses primarily upon human development and incorporates aspects of Theory Y, job enrichment, and participative management is *quality leadership*. This approach also draws upon the characteristics of excellent organizations presented in Chapter 7 and on Total Quality Management.[21] The principles of quality leadership, as adopted by the police department in Madison, Wisconsin, are as follows:[22]

1. Believe in, foster, and support teamwork.
2. Be committed to the problem-solving process; use it, and let data, not emotions, drive decisions.
3. Seek employees' input before you make key decisions.
4. Believe that the best way to improve the quality of work or service is to ask and listen to employees who are doing the work.
5. Strive to develop mutual respect and trust among employees.
6. Have a customer orientation and focus toward employees and citizens.
7. Manage on the behavior of 95 percent of employees, and not on the 5 percent who cause problems. Deal with the 5 percent promptly and fairly.
8. Improve systems and examine processes before placing blame on people.
9. Avoid "top-down," power-oriented decisionmaking whenever possible.
10. Encourage creativity through risk taking, and be tolerant of honest mistakes.
11. Be a facilitator and coach. Develop an open atmosphere that encourages providing and accepting feedback.
12. With teamwork, develop with employees agreed-upon goals and a plan to achieve them.

In our view, these principles of quality leadership provide sound direction for improving police performance. They are solidly based on the latest studies of motivation and leadership, they recognize the need to harness both the hearts and minds of police employees, and they are very flexible. These principles are quite compatible with the overall approach to police administration advocated in this text and with the various methods for achieving police organizational improvement presented in this chapter.

Police Education

One of the first popular avenues to police organizational improvement, and one that directly focused on human development, was higher education for police officers.[23] Some of the presumed advantages of sending police officers to college and of accepting college graduates at the entrance level are listed below:

1. an enhanced understanding of police functions and the police role;
2. an increased knowledge of the importance of police in society;
3. an improved sensitivity for the problems of people;
4. a better ability to communicate;
5. the development of skills;
6. an improved capability for exercising discretion;
7. the refinement of analytical qualities;
8. the consideration of moral and ethical implications of police work; and
9. the development of personal values that are consistent with police organizational goals and objectives in a democracy.[24]

With the establishment of the Office of Law Enforcement Assistance in 1966 and later the Law Enforcement Assistance Administration, some strong impetus was given to making the need for police education a reality. The leading figure in the movement was Patrick V. Murphy, then the assistant director of the Office of Law Enforcement Assistance. Murphy prodded and guided a grant panel established by Attorney General Nicholas Katzenbach to provide seed money for various police educational efforts throughout the country. As a result, various regional and local training and educational programs were started with federal government money. Even on the grant panel, there was some strong opposition to sending police officers to college, a reflection of the time-honored assumption that only police officers should train police officers. Murphy won, however, and started what has become a massive influx of police officers to colleges and universities.

At about the same time, James Stinchcomb, a staff member of the International Association of Chiefs of Police, and Congressman William R. Anderson of Tennessee collaborated on a House bill that for the first time introduced the possibility of providing scholarships and government-supported loans to police officers interested in pursuing academic degrees. Anderson was successful in convincing the Johnson administration of the value of his proposal, and the Law Enforcement Education Program (LEEP) became incorporated in the Safe Streets Act. The rest is history. Primarily during the 1970s, thousands of police officers who otherwise never would have had a chance to go to college were given the opportunity to be exposed to ideas and techniques that were, for the most part, foreign to the heretofore isolated police subculture.

Today, the Police Corps program funded by the federal government provides some of the same types of educational opportunities, although the beneficiaries number more in the hundreds than in the thousands. Police Corps trainees can get their undergraduate educations for free (up to $30,000) if they work as sworn community police officers for at least four years after graduation. One twist in the Police Corps program is that participants must go to work for law enforcement agencies that are particularly "needy" as demonstrated by such criteria as crime rate and current police staffing level.

The evidence relating education to police organizational improvement today is inconclusive.[25] There is some evidence, though, that more educated officers have fewer citizen complaints made against them.[26] Perhaps the strongest argument for police officers to have a higher education experience is one of representativeness. Charles B. Saunders noted that "the most compelling argument for higher educational standards for police is the steadily rising educational level of the general population."[27] Ramsey Clark, former attorney general of the United States, agreed: "We need to draw more than half of our police from colleges merely to begin to reflect a common experience with the public served."[28]

Police Professionalization

An approach to police improvement that goes hand in hand with education is professionalization. This approach means many things to many people. Unfortunately, it has too frequently become merely a catchphrase for police requests for more respect, higher salaries, and better equipment, and for public demands for higher standards, more devotion to duty, and the elimination of corruption. As Michael Steinman and Chris Eskridge point out, "police departments rhetorically promote their preferred image of objective, highly rationalized professional operations while diluting it in their actual operating norms."[29]

To the extent that the police dream of professional status equal to that of doctors and lawyers, their dreams are unrealistic and even somewhat dangerous. They are unrealistic because the police service will never develop the bodies of knowledge, entrance requirements, or lucrative pay scales of these other professionals. They are dangerous because they imply that the police believe that they can be granted the same degree of self-regulation and autonomy that these other professions enjoy.

As a general description of efforts to upgrade personnel, professionalization is a worthy element of police organizational improvement programs, but professionalization methods must in no way be designed to wrest control of the police from the people and their elected representatives.

Police struggle with efforts toward professionalization and will continue to do so for a long time to come. James Q. Wilson indicates that professional people have a tendency "to govern themselves through collegial bodies, to restrict the authority of their nominal superiors, to take seriously their reputation among fellow professionals and to encourage some of their kind to devote themselves to adding systematically to the knowledge of the profession through writing and research."[30] Although they may hone their discretionary capabilities, develop job skills, and achieve certain educational levels (all of which are professional criteria), the very nature of their work in the public sector makes it extremely challenging for the police to completely meet the requirements on which professionalization is based.

Although efforts at professionalization are currently modest, strides have been made in a few states that are noteworthy. For example, in the state of Kentucky, the legislature passed the Peace Officers Professional Act in 1998, which requires that most law enforcement officers, with only limited exception, must be certified under the *Peace Officer Professional Standards (POPS)*.[31] Areas addressed in the certification include physical fitness testing, psychological testing, drug screening, polygraph, and medical screening. In recognition of the value of higher education, Kentucky has also begun to accept college courses in place of traditional police training to meet annual in-service training requirements.

Other mechanisms for instituting professionalization might include career development programs. Currently eight states have comprehensive career development programs that provide a more formalized structure to the training process through career tracking. One such program has law enforcement officer, specialist, and management tracks, as well as two comparable tracks for telecommunicators. [32]

New Approaches to Training

One standard approach to human development in organizations, including police agencies, has been training. In the past, however, police have tended to see training as too much of a panacea for curing all kinds of organizational ills.[33] Instead of recognizing the need to change organizational structures, reward systems, or management practices, police agencies have had a tendency to overrely on training.

This is not to say that police training might not be improved and therefore become more effective than it has been in the past. Perhaps the most significant police training development in recent years has been the shift toward more of an adult-learning approach.[34] This new approach puts the onus of responsibility for learning more on the student than on the instructor, which is particularly appropriate for a field claiming professional status. In-class sessions are more interactive, featuring group activities and individual research more often than lecture by the instructor, who is seen primarily as a facilitator. This new training style also fits nicely with community policing, as students spend much of their training time practicing how to solve realistic community problems instead of listening to lectures on laws and procedures. The experience so far seems to indicate that when trainees learn about law and procedure in the context of solving community problems, they learn it better and come away prepared to apply what they know to a greater degree than recruits trained in the traditional lecture style.

This adult-learning approach to training also encourages us to recognize that learning can take place in settings other than the formal classroom, with an instructor standing in front and students seated in uncomfortable hardback chairs. For example, police trainees might learn best about the work of social service and victim advocate agencies if they spent some time observing in those agencies. In addition, some police topics might be well suited for delivery using computer-based training in which trainees interact individually with scenarios and lessons presented by diskette, CD-ROM, or the Internet. Simulation training, which allows students, for example, to "virtually" drive automobiles or shoot weapons in seemingly "real-life" situations, has also increased in use. Another type of scenario-based training, such as that found in Hogan's Alley at the FBI Academy, allows students to interact with role players in real-life investigative and tactical activities. Through the use of a little imagination and creativity, the field of police training has experienced some dramatic changes in recent years.

Civilianization

Yet another human development approach to police organizational improvement is *civilianization*. On one level, civilianization can simply be an efficiency technique—replace relatively expensive sworn police officers with less costly civilian employees whenever possible. Some police agencies have successfully civilianized a wide range of positions, including front desk personnel, communications personnel, evidence technicians, telephone report takers, and numerous administrative jobs, saving substantial resources in the process.

Another benefit of civilianization, though, is that it brings different kinds of people into the police organization. Traditionally, civilian positions were the only police employment options for women. Today, women continue to hold the majority (67.7%) of lower-paid civilian jobs that offer little chance of promotion.[35] Most police agencies probably have a greater proportion of women in civilian positions than in the sworn ranks. Civilian positions, however, may be of particular interest to workers who simply are not interested in, or qualified for, sworn police positions. Bringing all kinds of people into police departments has the obvious and distinct advantage of making them more like the rest of society.

Cultural Diversity

As America becomes increasingly diverse ethnically and racially, it is critically important that police organizations both reflect that diversity and employ individuals who are skilled in dealing with a diverse clientele.[36] Diverse communities present major challenges to the police, including differences in language, culture, and historical experiences with police power. The need for police officers to be educated and trained about different cultures has been widely recognized since at least the 1960s, but today's society is even more diverse and complex than anything we imagined 20 or 30 years ago. Quite a few police departments now serve communities in which the dominant spoken language is Spanish. Others routinely encounter citizens who speak Russian, Czech, Korean, or Vietnamese.

Besides raising obvious education and training issues, this growing diversity has implications for police recruitment and selection. Police departments must seek applicants who already have experience in dealing with diversity, as well as applicants who are representative of various racial and ethnic groups in the community. It is not always possible or practical to have a police workforce that is precisely representative of every racial and ethnic group in the community, but it is vitally important (1) that no group see itself as barred from police employment, (2) that the police department make an honest effort to recruit throughout the community, and (3) that every group perceive the police department as responsive to its legitimate needs and problems.

The Structural Design Approach

In our concern for the people who make up an organization, we must be careful not to forget the organization itself. The way in which an organization is structured has an important bearing on its ultimate efficiency and effectiveness. In recent years the preeminence of behavioral scientists in the organizational-improvement field has tended to obscure the importance of structure.

Early structural theorists advanced a one-best-way approach to organizational arrangement. They relied on principles of hierarchy, such as chain of command, unity of command, span of control, and division of labor, to popularize the pyramidal organizational form. These theorists contended that this was the best way to organize any undertaking, whether it be a social club or a corporation such as General Motors; as a result, social clubs and General Motors were organized for years in much the same way. Structural theorists have had a tremendous influence on large numbers of organizations and the way they have developed.

Recently, however, a *contingency theory* of organizational structure has gained prominence. Much like situational leadership theory (see Chapter 10), contingency theory holds that situational factors require different organizational structures for different circumstances. Contingency theory will be discussed after a brief description of classical theory.

Classical Theory

James G. March and Herbert A. Simon have noted that classical organizational theory tends to view the employee as an inhuman instrument performing preassigned duties; employees came to be looked on, therefore, as constants rather than as variables.[37] It is easy to see how this conception of the worker leads to a one-best-way approach to organization and management.

In more recent years, the sheer size and complexity of organizations literally forced those in authority to share their authority. As authority is dispersed throughout an organization, that organization becomes decentralized. A pattern of decentralization currently in vogue is capsulized in the phrase "centralize policy making; decentralize decisionmaking."

Just as early classical theorists postulated that centralization was the only way to organize properly, many contemporary theorists now claim that decentralization is the only way to go. Even the Roman Catholic Church, in which centralized authority was for centuries always looked on as a key to its success, has decentralized in many respects. Bishops now make decisions that would have been looked on as being strictly within the province of the Vatican four decades ago. Parish councils have been established in many local Roman Catholic churches so that decisions affecting the local level can be made at the local level. Decisions about faith and morals are centralized in Rome; just about everything else is decentralized in dioceses and parishes. From an organizational standpoint, this increases effectiveness. Theorists who argue in favor of decentralization also claim that organizations should be as flat as possible, meaning that authority should be decentralized so that fewer levels of management are needed and so that decisions may be made where the action is.

These modern classical theorists are generally correct. However, the variety of tasks that different organizations perform, the differences in sizes of organizations, and the varying environments in which they operate provide substantial rationale for the position that no particular structure is best for all. Therefore, organizations should be structured in terms of their individual needs, goals, and objectives in accordance with factors that peculiarly characterize them and affect their productivity.

Contingency Theory

In 1964, Chris Argyris predicted that "organizations (of the future) will tend to vary the structures that they use according to the kinds of decisions that must be made."[38] More recently, Harold J. Leavitt asserted that there is no ideal structural design; structure, he said, must be contingent on variables such as tasks, environment, people, and technology.[39] He further suggested that organizations must be structured so that they are adaptable and capable of self-modification.

The principal proponents of the contingency theory have been Paul R. Lawrence and Jay W. Lorsch.[40] They studied a number of different organizations in a variety of fields, attempting to relate success to type of organizational structure. They concluded that there is no one best way to structure all organizations. The most efficient and effective organizations they found were structured to fit the environments in which they operated.

Lawrence and Lorsch advanced the theory that any organization can be located at some point along an environmental continuum that stretches from situations of stability and certainty to situations of instability and uncertainty. They suggested that traditional hierarchical structures tend to be more successful in stable and certain situations, whereas more decentralized and flexible structures are preferable in situations of instability and uncertainty.

Just as OD recognizes that approaches to human development must be tailored to organizational realities, the contingency theory forces abandonment of the one-best-way approach to structure in favor of the situational approach. In each organizational situation, the variables involved must be considered in structuring the organization to fit its environment. The contingency theory, therefore, is built around the proposition that an organization's structure should be contingent on the specific variables affecting the specific organization.

Police Organizational Structure

Many police organizations have benefited in recent years from simple reorganization. Reorganization, or *restructuring*, is basic to organizational improvement but is an impossible task if the police administrator is unfamiliar with the basic elements of police structure. In such cases, consultants from the outside are frequently used to make recommendations. Very often these consultants have an extremely difficult job, because they make recommendations based on principles of management that few in the police department understand. This constraint, coupled with the traditional police reluctance to change, makes departmental restructuring a difficult and sometimes even impossible job. Yet, as a rule, restructuring is essential for improvement.

Four key variables in police organizational structure are hierarchy, centralization, formalization, and specialization. The general trend with respect to hierarchy today is to try to "flatten" the organization by reducing the number of levels in the organization's structure. The rationale behind this trend is that unnecessary levels insulate executives from the actual work being done by front-line employees, distort communications, and waste resources. Flattening the organization may thus be a cost-saving move and may also create greater efficiency and effectiveness. A balanced approach is required, however. Too much flattening can create excessively wide spans of control to the point that supervisors and managers cannot keep track of what their subordinates are doing.

Many police departments today, especially larger ones, are also pursuing decentralization, often in conjunction with community policing. They are giving greater authority and responsibility to area commanders and squad supervisors so that they can be more responsive to the particular needs of neighborhoods and communities. Some departments are decentralizing not only their patrol divisions in this manner but also specialist units such as traffic and investigations.

It should be recognized, however, that enthusiasm for decentralization and centralization tends to run in cycles. A few decades ago, many police agencies pursued centralization as a means of combating police corruption and increasing organizational control. Some departments have centralized and decentralized their detective bureaus every 10 or 20 years in response to scandals or efficiency crusades. Right now decentralization is in vogue. In fact, though, neither approach is inherently more effective; it depends on the police organization's needs, environment, and overall situation.[41]

Formalization refers to the degree to which organizational activities are formalized—that is, governed by written directives, standard procedures, reporting requirements, and other formal systems. Clearly, police agencies have been undergoing substantial formalization in recent years.[42] Reasons for this increasing formalization include the accreditation program, developments in administrative law relative to employee discipline, and increasing police concern about vicarious civil liability. The ultimate benefits of formalization are uncertain, however. While more extensive formal systems do contribute to achieving accredited status, making disciplinary actions stick, and defending against lawsuits, their contribution to the quality of service provided by police agencies is simply unproven.

Recent trends in the area of police specialization seem contradictory. On one hand, increased patrol officer involvement in investigations and crime prevention is indicative of despecialization. Similarly, community policing and problem-oriented policing are seen by their advocates as strategies that reduce police specialization. On the other hand, though, many police departments have undergone substantial specialization in recent years, to include such activities as GREAT (Gang Resistance Education and Training), multijurisdictional drug squads, accident reconstruction units, mounted patrols, bicycle patrols, and so on. It is not clear at this stage how these contradictory urges for and against specialization will be worked out in police organizations.

One recent study of the implementation of community policing in two Illinois cities provides some of the best current evidence about the impact of police organizational structure.[43] In their study, Deanna Wilkinson and Dennis P. Rosenbaum came to six conclusions (excerpted here from the original):

1. A police organization that is heavily invested in . . . a centralized, hierarchical, and bureaucratized command structure will have difficulty creating an environment that is conducive to community policing strategies and that encourages creative problem solving.

2. Although community policing can survive within the constraints of special units, this does not mean that such activities will flourish or even survive for an extended period of time given the cultural and organizational forces that continue to work against this arrangement.

3. Participatory management is not an empty concept . . . when they are included, officers can emerge as motivated planners and problem solvers.

4. The depth of an organization's commitment to bureaucracy appears to be inversely related to the speed at which it is able to implement community policing. Too much concern with accountability and control can lead to significant program delays as new systems and procedures must be created and tested.

5. With regard to the policy question about whether bureaucratic reform should precede or follow the implementation of community policing strategies . . . when a department demonstrates a rigid adherence to the professional model of policing, it seems unwilling to give up this command and control for the sake of community policing. When the style of management is less rigid and more informal, the door is opened slightly for a gradual breakdown in the prevailing bureaucracy, especially when change is presented by the chief as inevitable.

6. Clearly, organizational structure and police culture are closely linked and mutually reinforcing; strategies for reform may need to approach them differently.

It is important to resist the temptation to accept one-best-way arguments pertaining to police organizational structure. Our own views are that flatter hierarchies are preferable to taller ones; that decentralization fits the basic nature of policing better than centralization; that some formalization is necessary, but that excesses should be avoided; and that specialization should be used only when absolutely essential. These, though, are generalizations that may not fit every situation. Each police executive must carefully tailor his or her department's structure to the particular circumstances faced by the organization. In addition, police executives should recognize that as organizational inputs change and as the agency's environment changes, alterations in the organization's structure may be required to maintain efficiency and effectiveness.

The Strategic Management Approach

The third general approach to organizational improvement is concerned with the processes of information and work flow and with the police organization's technology (its tactics and strategies) for accomplishing its goals and objectives. Rather than focusing primarily on the organization's people or on its structure, the strategic management approach focuses on the processes used in the organization to perform its work.

Part 4 of this text, with chapters on information systems, evaluating performance, and police strategies and tactics, has presented many of the latest developments in the strategic management approach to police organizational improvement. In this section we will touch on several additional considerations: patrol allocation, command accountability, total quality management, police organizational health, and corporate strategies for policing.

Patrol Allocation

A principal aspect of police administration amenable to systems analysis is *patrol allocation*. Recognizing that police departments will never have sufficient monetary resources to hire all the personnel they could use, the need for rational personnel allocation becomes clear. In the past police administrators often based their requests for additional personnel on highly questionable yet rarely questioned indicators such as crime rates, national average figures, and subjective evaluations of needs. In many instances they allocated their personnel according to traditional and political considerations. It is not at all unusual, for example, to find unnecessary police personnel assigned to city wards represented by politically powerful city council members or to sections of a community that are particularly vocal in their demands for community services. This has resulted in the expenditure of unnecessary funds and the irrational allocation of personnel.

In recent years, however, many police administrators have recognized the need for basing personnel requirements and allocation on established patterns of crime, activity statistics, and citizen requests for service according to time and place of occurrence. Through careful accumulation and analysis of activity data, the police administrator can allocate personnel when and where such personnel are actually needed and can authoritatively argue for personnel increases based on statistical evidence.

In large departments this process can be computerized and sophisticated analytical methods can be employed. In small departments the accumulation and analysis of activity data can be mathematically computed in relatively simple fashion. What this amounts to, in the most elementary terms, is:

1. documenting the total amount of patrol workload that occurs;
2. determining the time it takes to handle that workload;
3. translating the workload data into the number of patrol officers required to handle it;
4. determining how many patrol officers are needed at different times of the day (allocation);
5. determining how many patrol officers are needed on different days of the week (scheduling); and
6. determining how best to assign patrol officers to geographic areas (deployment).

Although this process may sound extremely involved, it is not very complicated. It is a process that can be handled by anyone who has achieved an eighth-grade proficiency in mathematics. It is also a process that is essential for police organizational improvement, because it helps assure that the police agency's largest chunk of resources, its patrol officers, are being utilized as efficiently as possible.

What police administrators often lose sight of, however, is the need to have patrol allocation serve the organization's strategy rather than vice versa. Because patrol allocation is somewhat mathematical and involves the use of data and formulas, it tends to be left to analysts or other experts. The analysts are allowed to do their calculations and make their determinations, after which the police executive says, "OK, what tactics and strategies can we employ, what can we accomplish, given this allocation of personnel?" Instead, police administrators should establish and articulate their organizations' strategies first; then the analyst should be instructed to determine how best to allocate personnel in order to handle the department's workload and support its overall strategy.

Command Accountability

Just as police supervisors have long found it difficult to hold police officers truly accountable, police chief executives have often wrestled with the task of holding their commanders accountable. In the last few years, owing largely to the popularity of the *COMPSTAT system* developed in the New York Police Department,[44] *command accountability* has received renewed attention. In the COMPSTAT process, area commanders (e.g., precinct captains) are regularly "put on the hot seat" in front of their peers, presented with the latest crime analysis information from their command areas, and expected to demonstrate intimate familiarity with ongoing problems and present solutions already undertaken to resolve those problems. The commander who is caught unaware or unprepared is not only embarrassed, but also may be looking at a different assignment if the performance is repeated.

Although this COMPSTAT system sometimes seems to be rather harsh in its implementation, and although it may sometimes be more about "the numbers" than actual community conditions, it addresses a real problem of police administration. Perhaps its greatest potential is that it shifts the focus of command accountability away from merely internal administrative issues (the budget, personnel, etc.) toward what really matters the most—substantive problems in the community. Any process that can successfully redirect police attention and accountability away from internal concerns and toward community problems is probably beneficial.[45]

Total Quality Management

One of the biggest developments in American management in the 1980s and 1990s was the popularization of *Total Quality Management* (TQM). This approach is based on ideas first presented many years earlier by W. Edward Deming.[46] He emphasized ideas such as quality control and continuous improvement and "believed that defects in manufactured goods were not due to poorly motivated employees or shoddy workmanship, but rather, to identifiable shortcomings in the production process itself."[47] Thus, in seeking organizational improvements, TQM focuses attention not so much on the human factor or on the organization's structure, but rather on the organization's work processes and other methods for accomplishing its goals and objectives. In doing so, it tends to emphasize such things as giving careful attention to customer satisfaction and systematically measuring the quality of performance.

As popular as TQM has been, its application to service-oriented organizations, such as police departments, has been quite challenging. Karl Albrecht and Ron Zemke identified 10 key differences between service-providing and product-making enterprises, and in each case the nature of service made TQM more difficult to apply in any meaningful manner. As an example, they pointed out that "service cannot be centrally produced, inspected, or stockpiled" as a manufactured product can be. Hoover further identified some difficulties in applying TQM to policing—he noted, for example, that "although we may want the police to delight the customer, prudent management of public resources demands that the police leave many customers explicitly unhappy."[48] Moreover, quality is simply very difficult to define or measure in policing.

These comments are not meant to indicate that TQM has no relevance for police administration but simply to warn against any unreasonable expectations about easily transforming policing through the application of TQM principles. Clearly, the central tenets of TQM, such as paying attention to the customer and trying to measure and monitor quality performance, have great value for improving police administration. The business of policing, however, is both service-oriented and decidedly more complex than most of the settings in which TQM has been successfully used.

Police Organizational Health

One recent project of the National Institute of Justice and the Office of Community Oriented Policing Services has been the "Measuring What Matters" initiative. In turn, one of the products of that initiative is a description of six attributes of the "healthy police organization."[49] As you can see below, these attributes include some human development concerns but are primarily strategic in nature.

1. The healthy police organization knows what it wants to accomplish. It has articulated goals . . . that can be expressed in an operational form. The goals can be assessed, meaning that there are measures, indices, of things that are reflective of the goals.

2. The healthy police organization needs to know its citizens. Are they getting what they want? There are a variety of user surveys that could measure transactions with citizens. We think it is important to break them down into units that matter.

3. The healthy police organization knows its business and the demands that are placed upon it.

4. The healthy police organization knows what it is doing about the demands of business. It has the ability to monitor resource allocations and officer activities.

5. A healthy police organization knows its people. Things that would tell us what people get from their jobs, what they are looking for from their jobs, what motivates them about their work . . . what demoralizes them.

6. The healthy police organization feeds back information to people and groups who need to know.

Corporate Strategies of Policing

The police field has reached a stage of maturity in which we now recognize that police departments have some basic choices open to them in deciding how best to achieve their goals and objectives, serve their communities, and improve their efficiency and effectiveness. This represents a big step forward from a time when few options seemed to be available. It also signals perhaps the major responsibility of top police executives—choosing and then implementing their agencies' basic strategies.

In Chapter 1 we presented a simple outline of police history based on the evolution of police strategy from political through professional to community eras.[50] This picture of police history has the virtue of simplicity, but it has been criticized for oversimplifying the 150-plus years of American policing.[51] It has also given rise to endless arguments about which of the three models is best and, in particular, whether the community model should replace the professional model.

In our view, this latter debate is naive and once again overly simplistic. The choice between the community and professional models is not an either/or decision, but rather is a matter of degree and emphasis. Moreover, there are more choices than just these two. For example, in the series that offered the three-stage vision of the evolution of policing, a later paper identified four contemporary "corporate" strategies of policing: professional crime fighting, strategic crime fighting, problem-solving policing, and community policing.[52] A brief description of each of these strategies will help illustrate the choices now open to police executives and their departments.

The *professional crime-fighting* approach heavily emphasizes the crime control function of policing, the law and professional standards as sources of police legitimacy, and the traditional tactics of motorized patrol, rapid response, and follow-up investigations. Under this model the police seek and accept the primary responsibility for crime control. Police officers are seen as professionals, with the attendant reliance on training and technology. Police executives seek maximum independence in running their departments.

The *strategic crime-fighting* approach accepts most of the tenets of the professional model outlined above, except for two modifications: the effectiveness of traditional police tactics is questioned, and more focus is placed on types of crime other than common street crime. The strategic model emphasizes such targeted techniques as directed patrol, case screening, differential responses, and repeat offender programs. This model also gives greater attention than the professional model to organized crime, white-collar crime, drug trafficking, and other specialized types of criminal activity.

The *problem-solving* approach varies from both the professional and strategic models in several respects. It recognizes the importance of the crime control function but also stresses other important functions of the police, such as fear reduction, dispute resolution, and control of disorder. It also emphasizes that law enforcement is but one method available to the police for controlling crime, fear, and disorder; other methods include prevention, mediation, education, and referral, to name just a few. The problem-solving approach urges police to reconceptualize their business away from incident handling and law enforcement and toward problem solving and prevention. This model gives the greatest importance to gathering and analyzing information as the bases for identifying and solving problems.

The *community policing model*, more than the others, insists on giving citizens a greater role in policing and police administration. The idea that the police can effectively assume the primary responsibility for crime control is rejected. Instead, police must work closely with citizens and communities in identifying problems, setting priorities, and solving problems. Community policing argues that policing must become more customer-oriented and that in the end the customer is always right. This model urges departments to assign police officers and commanders to geographic areas on a more permanent basis so that they will come to identify more strongly with communities and so that those communities can influence them more effectively. Ultimately, under community policing, community norms and values join the law as sources of police legitimacy. Creating positive police-community relations is seen as a valid and important objective of policing.

Many police executives, upon reading these descriptions, are inclined to say that they support all four strategies and that their agencies are guided by each one. This response is commendable in the sense that these executives recognize the merits of each strategy and want to avoid unnecessary either/or choices. However, any police agency will tend to emphasize some features of these strategies over others. In today's tight financial circumstances, most police agencies cannot afford to be all things to all people. In fact, whether by design or by default, police departments will adhere more to one or two of these strategies than to the others. The job of the police executive is to choose the organization's strategy consciously and carefully instead of letting it drift or emerge by default.

Which strategy is best? It all depends. The police executive should make every effort to adopt the strategy or combination of strategies that best fits the needs of his or her community and police organization. Just as critically, police executives must continually monitor developments within the field of policing, within their organizations, and within their communities in order to make strategic adjustments and changes when they are needed. For, as noted by Kenneth Andrews, "the highest function of the executive is . . . leading the continuous process of determining the nature of the enterprise, and setting, revising, and achieving its goals."[53]

The Learning Organization Approach

The final approach was popularized by Peter Senge in his book *The Fifth Discipline,* which describes the learning organization.[54] In this approach, you will see concepts that have been previously discussed throughout this chapter and have been developed into a contemporary multifaceted perspective by Senge. Learning organizations are those "where people continually expand their capacity to create the results they truly desire, where new and expansive patterns of thinking are nurtured, where collective aspiration is set free, and where people are continually learning how to learn together."[55] The fifth discipline that is necessary for the creation of learning organizations is *systems thinking*. Only when systems thinking is accompanied by building shared vision, mental models, team learning, and personal mastery, however, will it work to create a learning organization. With the adoption of community policing in contemporary police organizations, a potential exists to embrace the concept of the learning organization and direct efforts toward organizational improvement to overcome challenges that have hindered growth and improvement for years.

As we discussed earlier, systems thinking, or the systems approach, emphasizes the interrelatedness among different parts of the organization in working toward the unified goals and objectives of the organization. As Senge maintains, systems thinking, the fifth discipline is the framework for the learning organization. Shared vision is necessary for people to work toward common goals and objectives while learning and usually excelling at what they do. Mental models are deeply ingrained assumptions and generalizations through which individuals develop perspective and consequently view the world. Team learning is necessary because these are the fundamental learning units in organizations; without them, nothing can be accomplished. Finally, personal mastery is the cornerstone of the learning organization. It is the process of continually clarifying personal vision by maintaining patience and focusing one's energies in order to see reality objectively.

It is apparent how each discipline builds upon and supports the others. Each manager must be able to view the organization using the systems approach and to understand the importance of individual roles and his or her contribution to overall goals and objectives. Additionally, the manager must validate every employee's work and ensure that employees realize the impact of their performance on the organization.

William Geller (1997) suggests that applying the learning organization model to policing would be no easy task. Among obstacles he identifies are skepticism about research, unwillingness to encourage critical thinking among all members of the organization, and the belief that too much "thinking" prevents action. However, he maintains that while obstacles do exist, benefits from adopting a learning organization model may outweigh its costs. Geller identified 13 suggestions for fostering a learning police organization:

1. Create a Research and Development Unit that is well supported, actually does research, and is run by someone who actually understands policing.
2. Use geographical crime analysis that spans work units.
3. Involve senior police administrators in the process so as not to create turf battles; encourage collaboration.
4. Inventory the wealth of talent of all sworn and civilian employees.
5. Inventory the wealth of talent of citizens and groups in the community.
6. Use the SARA model for problem solving.
7. Encourage critical thinking and discourage group think.
8. Use middle managers to facilitate critical thinking.
9. Hold units accountable, measured against industry (CALEA) standards.
10. Institutionalize bottom-up evaluation of organizational performance.
11. Demonstrate practical results of previous police research.
12. Expand police-researcher partnerships.
13. Hire a "research broker" to enable the organization to become better consumers of research.[56]

Of course not all of these suggestions would be practical in every police organization. Additionally, resources may dictate the extent to which a police administrator can employ any of these suggestions. Those that present little or no cost to the organization are consequently easier to implement.

The size of an organization is a characteristic that may also affect the applicability of any of the above suggestions. For example, in a small police organization there may be little need or few resources to create a research and development unit. However, encouragement of critical thinking of all personnel seems reasonable and would probably be very useful.

In a review of Chris Argyris's work, Leanne Alarid examined the applicability of the learning organization to police agencies implementing community-oriented policing. [57] She maintains that because an essential element of community policing is organizational change, the learning organization framework could support the sometimes monumental changes involved in community-policing implementation. Going from a traditional law enforcement organizational structure to one that embodies tenets such as decentralization and individual empowerment can be quite overwhelming for a manager. By employing some of the principles of the learning organization such as shared vision and personal mastery, managers may find the task of organizational change not quite so daunting.

In a contemporary example using the learning organization in policing, the Colorado Springs Police Department developed the Police Accountability and Service Standards (PASS) Model to improve organizational effectiveness. This model is currently being tested in two of the department's divisions, the Falcon Patrol Division and the Metro Vice, Narcotics, and Intelligence Division. Preliminary findings indicate that using this model improves the quality of police services, perceptions of police effectiveness in addressing fear of crime, and perceptions of police effectiveness in working with neighborhood groups.

Summary

This chapter has outlined organizational improvement concepts that we regard as some of the most meaningful contemporary approaches to upgrading police organizations. There are literally hundreds of other significant efforts being made in departments all over the country that reflect the desire of police agencies to improve their services. The impetus for improvement has come from such organizations as the Office of Community Oriented Policing Services, the National Institute of Justice, the Police Executive Research Forum, the Police Foundation, and the International Association of Chiefs of Police. The fact that extensive research is being conducted and that innovative programs and strategies are being tried is a strong indication that the police service has made a meaningful commitment to progress. Improvements in productivity, organizational structure, work methods, and decision-making processes are all part of an ongoing effort to realistically prepare policing for the technological requirements of this century. Police administrators must develop a sound understanding of general approaches to organizational improvement, as discussed in this chapter, take a long look at their own organizations, and attempt to tailor programs of organizational improvement to fit the unique characteristics of their departments. In conclusion, we pass along the following advice offered by the Police Foundation in 1972, which is still valid today:

If new ideas for improving the delivery of police services are to be developed, and if good ideas are to be spread, "the need to build an organization capable of continuing change" is critical. Rank-and-file officers must, whenever possible, be involved in both the planning and implementation of each project. "Street insight" is a vital ingredient in initiating and evaluating any program. Such involvement also strengthens the ability of police agencies to manage the process of change. Unless the individual police officer regards himself, not as an outsider to the project taking place about him, but as an individual with a personal stake in the project's successful outcome, the prognosis for any experimental undertaking is poor.[58]

Discussion Questions

1. Do you agree that the physical and security needs of most Americans are satisfied? If you agree, how would you explain labor strikes and demands for higher wages?

2. Do you find that the presence of goals and objectives motivates you to work harder? Is there a difference between goals that someone else has set for you and goals that you have set?

3. Why do you think that we support democracy in government but question its usefulness in other types of organizations?

4. How do you react to change? Do you welcome it or dread it?

5. What do you think would be the ideal educational level for police officers? What do you think is a realistic level? In what ways do you think college education helps or hurts a police officer?

Cases

Two case studies at the end of this text present the basic techniques for determining patrol staffing needs. These techniques are introduced and explained in "Case 8: The Nervous Planner." In "Case 9: The Prescott Valley Project" you are put in the situation of having to calculate staffing needs based on workload information that is provided.

Notes

1. G.E. Berkley, *The Administrative Revolution: Notes on the Passing of Organization Man* (Englewood Cliffs, NJ: Prentice Hall, 1971).

2. D. McGregor, "The Human Side of Enterprise," *Management Review* 46, no. 11 (1957): 22-28.

3. D. McGregor, *The Human Side of Enterprise* (New York, NY: McGraw-Hill, 1960).

4. A. Maslow, *Motivation and Personality* (New York, NY: Harper, 1954).

5. McGregor, *Human Side of Enterprise*.

6. McGregor, *Human Side*, pp. 14-15.

7. G.W. Sykes, "The Functional Nature of Police Reform: The 'Myth' of Controlling the Police," *Justice Quarterly* 2, no. 1 (1985): 51-65.

8. P. Drucker, *The Practice of Management* (New York, NY: Harper, 1954).

9. F. Herzberg, "One More Time: How Do You Motivate Employees?" *Harvard Business Review* (January–February 1968): 53-62.

10. Ibid., p. 59.

11. R. Townsend, *Up the Organization* (New York, NY: Knopf, 1970), p. 140.

12. J.F. Robinson, "Job Enrichment: What It Is," *Supervisory Management* 18, no. 9 (September 1973): 5.

13. T. Reddin, "Are You Oriented to Hold Them? A Searching Look at Police Management," *The Police Chief* 33, no. 3 (March 1966): 20.

14. R. Likert, *The Human Organization: Its Management and Value* (New York, NY: McGraw-Hill, 1967).

15. M. Boyd, "How We Can Bring Back Quality: Sharing a Piece of the Action," *Washington Monthly* 5, no. 12 (February 1974): 24.

16. K. Blanchard and S. Bowles, *Gung Ho!* (New York: William Morrow, 1998).

17. The Police Foundation, *Experiments in Police Improvement: A Progress Report* (Washington, DC: Police Foundation, 1972), p. 31.

18. W. Pudinski, "Managing for Results," *Police Chief* 40, no. 1 (January 1973): 39.

19. W.G. Bennis, *Organization Development: Its Nature, Origins, and Prospects* (Reading, MA: Addison-Wesley, 1969), p. 17.

20. E.F. Huse and J.L. Bowditch, *Behavior in Organizations: A Systems Approach to Managing*, Second Edition (Reading, MA: Addison-Wesley, 1977), pp. 386-387.

21. W.E. Deming, *Out of the Crisis* (Cambridge, MA: MIT Press, 1986).

22. D.C. Couper and S.H. Lobitz, *Quality Policing: The Madison Experience* (Washington, DC: Police Executive Research Forum, 1991).

23. D.L. Carter, A.D. Sapp, and D.W. Stephens, *The State of Police Education: Policy Direction for the 21st Century* (Washington, DC: Police Executive Research Forum, 1989).

24. J.W. Sterling, "The College Level Entry Requirement: A Real or Imagined Cure-All," *Police Chief* 41, no. 8 (August 1974): 28.

25. D.W. Hayeslip Jr., "Higher Education and Police Performance Revisited: The Evidence Examined through Meta-Analysis," *American Journal of Police* 8, no. 2 (1989): 49-62; R.E. Worden, "A Badge and a Baccalaureate: Policies, Hypotheses and Further Evidence," *Justice Quarterly* 7, no. 3 (1990): 565-592.

26. V.E. Kappeler, A.D. Sapp, and D.L. Carter, "Police Officer Higher Education, Citizen Complaints and Departmental Rule Violations," *American Journal of Police* 11, no. 2 (1992): 37-54.

27. C.B. Saunders Jr., *Upgrading the American Police: Education and Training for Better Law Enforcement* (Washington, DC: Brookings Institution, 1970), p. 89.

28. R. Clark, *Crime in America: Observations on Its Nature, Causes, Prevention, and Control* (New York, NY: Simon & Schuster, 1970), p. 147.

29. M. Steinman and C.W. Eskridge, "The Rhetoric of Police Professionalism," *Police Chief* (February 1985): 26.

30. J.Q. Wilson, *Varieties of Police Behavior: The Management of Law and Order in Eight Communities* (Cambridge, MA: Harvard University Press, 1968), p. 30.

31. Kentucky Law Enforcement Council, "Peace Officer Professional Standards" (Richmond, KY: Kentucky Law Enforcement Council, 2001).

32. Kentucky Law Enforcement Council, "Career Development Program" (Richmond, KY: Kentucky Law Enforcement Council, 2002).

33. F. Himelfarb, "RCMP Learning and Renewal: Building on Strengths," in Q.C. Thurman and E.F. McGarrell, eds., *Community Policing in a Rural Setting* (Cincinnati, OH: Anderson, 1997), pp. 33-39.

34. C. Argyris, *Integrating the Individual and the Organization* (New York, NY: Wiley, 1964), p. 211.

35. "Equality Denied: The Status of Women in Policing, 2001" mimeo (Los Angeles, CA: National Center for Women and Policing, 2002).

36. J.E. Enter, "Police Administration in the Future: Demographic Influences as They Relate to Management of the Internal and External Environment," in G.W. Cordner and D.J. Kenney, eds., *Managing Police Organizations* (Cincinnati, OH: Anderson, 1996), pp. 175-188.

37. J.G. March and H.A. Simon, *Organizations* (New York, NY: Wiley, 1958), p. 29.

38. Argyris, *Integrating the Individual*, p. 211.

39. H.J. Leavitt, *Managerial Psychology* (Chicago, IL: University of Chicago, 1972), p. 309.

40. P. Lawrence and J. Lorsch, *Organization and Environment: Managing Differentiation and Integration* (Boston, MA: Harvard University Graduate School of Business Administration, 1967).

41. R.H. Langworthy, "Organizational Structure," in G.W. Cordner and D.C. Hale, eds., *What Works in Policing: Operations and Administration Examined* (Cincinnati, OH: Anderson, 1992), pp. 87-105.

42. G.W. Cordner, "Written Rules and Regulations: Are They Necessary?" *FBI Law Enforcement Bulletin* (July 1989): 17-21.

43. D.L. Wilkinson and D.P. Rosenbaum, "The Effects of Organizational Structure on Community Policing: A Comparison of Two Cities," in D.P. Rosenbaum, ed., *The Challenge of Community Policing: Testing the Promises* (Thousand Oaks, CA: Sage, 1994), pp. 124-125.

44. D. Anderson, "Why Crime Is Down," *New York Times Magazine* (February 1997): 47-62.

45. H. Goldstein, *Problem-Oriented Policing* (New York, NY: McGraw-Hill, 1990).

46. Deming, *Out of the Crisis*.

47. L.T. Hoover, "Translating Total Quality Management from the Private Sector to Policing," in L.T. Hoover, ed., *Quantifying Quality in Policing* (Washington, DC: Police Executive Research Forum, 1996), p. 2.

48. Ibid., op. cit., p. 15.

49. "Measuring What Matters Part Two: Developing Measures of What the Police Do," *Research in Action* (Washington, DC: National Institute of Justice, 1997), pp. 4-5.

50. G.L. Kelling and M.H. Moore, "The Evolving Strategy of Policing," *Perspectives on Policing* No. 4 (Washington, DC: National Institute of Justice, 1988).

51. F.X. Hartmann, ed., "Debating the Evolution of American Policing," *Perspectives on Policing* No. 5 (Washington, DC: National Institute of Justice, 1988); S. Walker, "Broken Windows and Fractured History: The Use and Misuse of History in Recent Police Patrol Analysis," *Justice Quarterly* 1, no. 1 (1984): 75-90; V.G. Strecher, "Histories and Futures of Policing: Readings and Misreadings of a Pivotal Present," *Police Forum* 1, no. 1 (1991): 1-9.

52. M.H. Moore and R.C. Trojanowicz, "Corporate Strategies for Policing," *Perspectives on Policing* No. 6 (Washington, DC: National Institute of Justice, 1988).

53. K.R. Andrews, *The Concept of Corporate Strategy* (Homewood, IL: Richard D. Irwin, 1980), p. iii.

54. P. M. Senge, *The Fifth Discipline: The Art and Practice of The Learning Organization* (New York: Doubleday, 1990).

55. Ibid., p. 3.

56. W.A. Geller, "Suppose We Were Really Serious about Police Departments Becoming Learning Organizations?" *National Institute of Justice Journal* (Washington, DC: December 1997).

57. L. Alarid, "Law Enforcement Departments as Learning Organizations: Argyris's Theory as a Framework for Implementing Community-Oriented Policing," *Police Quarterly* 2, no. 3 (September 1999): 321-337.

58. The Police Foundation, *Experiments in Police Improvements*, p. 23.

Suggested Reading

Goldstein, Herman. *Problem-Oriented Policing*. New York, NY: McGraw-Hill, 1990.

Hoover, Larry T., ed. *Quantifying Quality in Policing*. Washington, DC: Police Executive Research Forum, 1996.

Senge, Peter. *The Fifth Discipline: The Art and Practice of the Learning Organization*. New York, NY: Doubleday, 1994.

Sherman, Lawrence W., and the National Advisory Commission on Higher Education for Police Officers. *The Quality of Police Education*. San Francisco, CA: Jossey-Bass, 1978.

Silverman, Eli B. *NYPD Battles Crime: Innovative Strategies in Policing*. Boston, MA: Northeastern University Press, 1999.

Contemporary Issues in Police Administration

15

Learning Objectives

- Identify several community policing activities that have become commonplace among U.S. police departments.

- Explain why interorganizational collaboration is important for American policing.

- Explain the term "transnational crime" and why it is an increasingly important consideration in modern policing.

- Identify the most promising scenario for addressing the issue of racial profiling and racially biased policing.

- Identify several varieties of mass media that affect police and police administration.

- Identify three categories of computer involvement in criminal activity.

- Identify several of the most critical needs facing local law enforcement in combating computer crime.

- Identify five categories of technology utilization in law enforcement.

- Identify three elements of the mission of the new Department of Homeland Security.

- Explain the term "interoperability" and why it is a significant issue in modern policing and public safety.

This chapter presents information on several important themes and issues in contemporary police administration. These themes and issues attempt to capture present-day trends as well as future considerations affecting the police field. Three themes are highlighted: community engagement, collaboration, and globalization. Together, these themes emphasize the growing interdependence of modern policing—police are increasingly more connected to communities, other agencies, and even to events around the world. Five contemporary issues are then discussed: racial profiling, mass media, cybercrime, technology, and homeland security/terrorism. These issues present serious challenges to police departments today and promise to remain prominent issues well into the future.

Three Contemporary Themes

Community Engagement

It is generally accepted that many police departments had grown far too isolated from their communities by the 1960s and 1970s. Most officers patrolled in cars and had limited informal contact with the public. Calls for service and reported crimes were handled as quickly as possible; the "just the facts" approach was preferred. Police departments emphasized their crime-fighting role and advised the public to leave crime control to the police. The police expected to achieve crime control with the three-part strategy of preventive patrol, rapid response, and follow-up investigations.

Although we now realize that this model of "stranger policing" and the police-centered approach to crime control was fatally flawed, it developed for understandable reasons. Limiting police-public contact was expected to reduce police corruption and other abuses of authority. The professional model was also a method for administering the same level and quality of policing throughout the community—it showed no favorites. In addition, prior to research in the 1970s, preventive patrol, rapid response, and follow-up investigations were believed to be effective, especially in comparison to such antiquated techniques as the posse, the citizens' protective association, and foot patrol.

Police began to rediscover the value of community involvement in the 1980s. The forms of community involvement that have developed vary widely, from relatively passive participation in neighborhood watch groups to more aggressive action, such as confronting drug dealers and prostitutes, and from individual-level efforts to more organized activities, such as citizen patrols. Community crime prevention programs have become commonplace, as has community policing. One survey conducted in 2002 found that each of the following 12 activities had been implemented by at least 75 percent of the responding police agencies:

- Citizens attend police-community meetings
- Citizens participate in Neighborhood Watch
- Citizens help police identify and resolve problems
- Citizens serve as volunteers within the police agency
- Citizens attend citizen police academies
- Police hold regularly scheduled meetings with community groups

- Police have youth programs
- Police have victim assistance programs
- Agencies use fixed assignments to specific beats or areas
- Agencies give special recognition for good community policing work by employees
- Agencies do geographically based crime analysis
- Agencies use permanent neighborhood-based offices or stations[1]

More important than any particular programs, however, has been a fundamental change in policing philosophy and strategy. Individual police departments may or may not support foot patrol, citizens on patrol, or citizen review boards, but it is now universally recognized that police and citizens need to work together to be successful. Both police chiefs and beat patrol officers recognize this.

Community engagement in policing and crime control takes many forms and applies at several different levels. For example, the Seattle Police Department is undertaking a community-wide survey in 2003 to identify "friction points" between the police department and the community.[2] The department will then work with the community to address the issues of greatest concern to Seattle's citizens. This is an example of seeking community-wide input in order to improve police-community relations.

Many police agencies today utilize some form of civilian review of complaints against the police.[3] Appointed citizens may simply review the police department's internal investigations and decisions, they may serve as an appeals body, or they may even serve as the actual decisionmakers in meting out discipline to police officers. Many agencies also utilize community representatives on interview boards in the police officer hiring and promotion processes. These are examples of community involvement in the actual administration of the police agency.

Direct citizen participation in policing has also become more common. Some cities, such as Ft. Worth, Texas, have extensive citizen patrol programs.[4] Many jurisdictions also utilize police auxiliaries or reserves—these are generally citizens who have other jobs but who donate some of their spare time to the police or sheriff department. In some places these reserves are sworn and armed and perform regular police duties; in others they are non-sworn and assist in traffic control, youth programs, school programs, and similar supporting roles. These are examples of community involvement in police field operations.

Citizen participation in crime prevention activities is also quite common today. Perhaps the most powerful trend in this respect is toward community-based problem solving. When police officers and neighborhood residents work together to identify, analyze, and resolve persistent crime and disorder problems, stunning improvements are possible.[5] Clearly, citizens are in the best position to identify the chronic problems that really affect their lives—police are often surprised that abandoned cars and rowdy kids are of greater concern to neighborhood residents than burglaries and thefts. Engaging citizens in the problem-solving stages beyond problem identification (i.e., analysis and response) is more challenging but very rewarding.[6] This is the ultimate form of community involvement because it engages ordinary citizens in tackling the most serious problems in the neighborhoods where they live and work.

The importance of citizen involvement and community engagement for public safety has been reinforced in the aftermath of the events of September 11, 2001. Police, firefighters, and emergency medical service (EMS) personnel were assisted in their response to the World Trade Center by numerous citizen volunteers. Subsequently, law enforcement officials have recognized that they need the public's help in identifying suspicious activity that might be connected to terrorism. Although the U.S. Attorney General's "Operation TIPS" program was abandoned because it seemed too heavy-handed, there is no doubt that vigilant and engaged citizens are crucial to homeland security.

The underlying principle to all this is that ours is supposed to be a government of the people, by the people, and for the people. Because we the people are very busy these days, there are limits on our willingness and ability to participate in policing, crime prevention, and homeland security. Then too, we have professionals who are trained and paid to perform much of the work associated with public safety. It should not be forgotten, however, that our history teaches us that citizens will sometimes go too far and want to take the law into their own hands. Thus, there must be limits on the public's role in policing, and we must be careful to strike the proper balance between the roles of paid professionals and volunteer citizens. What we have learned is that it is essential for effective policing, and for the control of crime and disorder, that the police truly engage the community as partners. It is important that this fundamental principle not be forgotten.

Collaboration

The importance and necessity of collaboration has similarly become evident in recent years. Just as police departments are more effective when they work closely with the community, so too are they more effective when they collaborate with other public and private organizations.

Interorganizational collaboration is particularly crucial for American policing because of the extreme fragmentation of government resources and authority. Within a typical local community, the police department and fire department are separate agencies, and the ambulance service may also be a separate entity. Emergency communications (the 911 center) may be operated by the county or by a regional board. The county sheriff department is a separate agency that usually has jurisdiction within the local community, as does the state police department. Probation and parole may be one agency or two and may be operated by the county or the state. The same is true of juvenile services. Prosecutors may be employed locally, although it is more common for them to be county or state officials. Then there is the entire additional layer of federal law enforcement, federal probation, and U.S. attorneys arrayed on top of the local and state systems. In times of serious emergency, the National Guard and the military may also be deployed.

Because of the existence of all of these local, state, and federal public safety and criminal justice agencies with overlapping jurisdictions, coordination and cooperation are essential to avoid waste, interference, and conflict. The need goes even further today, though. Actual collaboration—working together to be more successful—is necessary. This involves sharing resources, expertise, and authority. Evidence of collaboration can often be found in everyday investigations and problem solving, in the formation of multijurisdictional task forces, and in joint training exercises.

Good examples of collaboration can be found today in the investigation of computer crime. Few departments have the necessary in-house expertise to address cybercrime at this point, so it is often provided by state or federal agencies or by a multiagency task force. If a local agency becomes aware of a computer crime or seizes computing equipment that might contain digital evidence, it may request assistance from one of these sources or just "hand off" the case.

Some effective problem-solving collaboration has recently begun to take place between police and probation, parole, and juvenile services agencies. For too long, many police departments and individual police officers did not work closely with these agencies. Police have found, though, that adult and juvenile probation officers, for example, have detailed information about their clients, as well as authority over them that in many instances exceeds police authority. Thus, police and probation officers working together may be able to address a gang problem, an after-hours nightclub problem, or a drug-house problem more effectively than either group working alone.

An excellent example of collaboration to improve police and public safety response is currently being implemented in a 40-county region in Eastern Kentucky.[7] More than 100 local law enforcement agencies, plus the state police and other state law enforcement agencies, are working together to implement a wireless data and voice communication system. Fire, ambulance, and other public safety agencies will be added to the system in later phases.

This project is designed to address what is referred to as the "interoperability" problem. This is the problem caused by different agencies having separate communications systems that cannot "talk" to each other. Lack of communications interoperability among public safety agencies was demonstrated most dramatically in New York and at the Pentagon on September 11, 2001, when responding agencies could not communicate effectively with each other. Lack of data interoperability was uncovered in the subsequent investigation into how the terrorists were able to enter the United States to plan and carry out their attacks—different federal agencies had pieces of information, but no one had the whole picture. It is now obvious that communications and data interoperability are essential prerequisites to effective collaboration to combat terrorism.

The Eastern Kentucky initiative includes a unique ingredient that will permit intensive collaboration among the 100-plus law enforcement agencies involved. Each of the agencies will adopt the same computer software to manage their dispatching and records data. This will enable agencies to share data much more easily than if different agencies used different software. It will also permit regional analysis of pooled data, a tool that is especially useful for small and rural agencies.[8] Through such regional analysis, police agencies and police officers will become familiar with real-time crime patterns that affect more than one town or county, enabling them to take more effective action in patrol, crime prevention, and investigation.

This discussion has centered on collaboration among police, public safety, and criminal justice agencies, but of course the police also need to collaborate with many other public and private agencies in order to address crime and disorder problems. Police departments have demonstrated the value of collaboration with schools, social services, mental health agencies, private security, and a wide variety of other activities over the past decade. The 2002 survey cited earlier in this chapter found that more than 75 percent of agencies had implemented three specific forms of collaboration:

- Police have interagency involvement in problem solving
- Police use regulatory codes in problem solving
- Police work with building code enforcement[9]

Similarly, a study of problem solving by individual patrol officers in San Diego found that it was common for officers to draw on resources from outside the department when responding to problems. The figures below indicate how often officers reported using different resources in the 227 problem-solving projects that were identified:

- 26% private sector
- 18% other city agencies
- 17% code compliance
- 6% other police including federal
- 6% county, state, or federal agencies (nonpolice)
- 4% social services[10]

It makes good sense for police agencies to engage in widespread collaboration with other public and private organizations. Collaboration can help the police be more effective in addressing crime and disorder problems. It can also contribute greatly to efficiency, through coordination of effort and elimination of redundancy and duplication. Collaboration is particularly crucial in a situation as fragmented as the American governmental system.

Globalization

The third theme that increasingly runs through modern policing is globalization. Trends in business, finance, trade, travel, communications, and computers really have "shrunk the world" in the last decade or two. It is far more likely now than 20 years ago that a local criminal investigation might involve international transactions and foreign individuals. These foreign individuals might have traveled to the local jurisdiction, or they might have played their roles (as witnesses, victims, or suspects) from afar.

Many traditional crimes can have international features today, such as drug distribution and theft. Much has also been made in recent years of international organized crime, especially involving Russians. Crimes committed with computers, including frauds, thefts, vandalism, and hacking, really know no boundaries. Then there are newer crimes (or perhaps crimes that are simply getting more attention today) such as human smuggling of women and children and illegal smuggling of immigrants, weapons, and even nuclear material. The term *transnational crime* has been coined to describe the increasingly international nature of crime.

International terrorism has become a huge concern for local, state, and federal law enforcement since the events of September 11, 2001. Americans, and people all around the world, witnessed the death and destruction that could be caused by a relatively small group of terrorists. These were far from the first acts of international terrorism committed against the United States, of course, and in fact other countries for a long time had been more seriously plagued by these kinds of attacks than had the United States. The attacks of 9/11 galvanized national and world attention, however, and drove home the new reality that crime and terrorism emanating from halfway around the globe could threaten American communities and American citizens.

Another aspect of globalization that has affected American policing has been the participation of local and state police in international policing missions in places like Haiti, Bosnia, and Kosovo.[11] As the United States, the United Nations, the European Union, and other bodies have accepted peacekeeping roles in war-torn countries around the world, it has become evident that a key element in the restoration of order and civil society is effective policing. Typically, police and military forces in these countries were previously aligned with repressive regimes. Once the initial military phase of peacekeeping has been accomplished, the country needs reliable, professional policing to maintain order and reassure the citizenry of their safety. While a policing system is being rebuilt along democratic lines, police officers are brought in from around the world to provide police service and help train the country's new police.

Many American police officers have now had the experience of serving in such international missions, and many American police departments now see that part of their responsibility is to support the development of more professional and democratic policing in other countries. This is a relatively new awareness for American police and contributes to their sense of being part of a global police community. It is also a fairly new realization for those in the U.S. government responsible for foreign relations "that security is important to the development of democracy and police are important to the character of that security. Assisting in the democratic reform of foreign police systems has become a front-burner issue in American foreign policy."[12]

It is difficult to predict all the future ramifications for policing of this trend toward globalization. Clearly, though, international issues and considerations that were once thought to be irrelevant for local American policing have become relevant and even significant. This trend can only continue.

Five Contemporary Issues

Racial Profiling

Racial profiling, or "driving while black," emerged in the 1990s as perhaps the most serious and sensitive issue facing police departments in the United States.[13] It was the subject of lawsuits, civil rights investigations, and consent decrees. It was discussed and debated in the U.S. Congress and in the 2000 presidential election. Many states mandated new police policies and data collection systems, and even more local communities did so. Only the events of September 11, 2001, deflected attention away from racial profiling, and when the issue reemerged, it was focused more on profiling of potential terrorists and the effects this might have on the rights of Middle Eastern and Islamic persons.

Two aspects of the racial profiling phenomenon merit its identification as one of the most important contemporary issues in American policing, despite its lower profile immediately following the terrorist attacks against the United States. One is that it underscores the continued salience of race for policing. Given the emphasis on community policing throughout the 1980s and 1990s, with its focus on community engagement and the improvement of police-community relations, it might have been expected that police-minority relations would have been greatly improved. During the same period, however, three well-publicized showings of police use of force—the Rodney King incident in Los Angeles and the Amadou Diallo and Abner Louima incidents in New York— and many other instances of questioned police use of force against people of color occurred in the United States. Understandably, uneasiness and suspicion continued to characterize the relationship between race and policing, creating the conditions for the dramatic rise of the racial profiling issue.

The racial profiling issue clearly struck a strong chord in minority communities and among those most concerned about civil rights and civil liberties in America.[14] While most police have ardently denied that they use, or support the use of, any such profiles, 40 percent of African Americans believe they have been profiled by police, and even a majority of whites believe the problem is widespread.[15] It seems likely that the term "racial profiling" has gradually expanded in the public mind and come to signify larger issues of racial bias and discrimination by police. Largely for this reason, the Police Executive Research Forum has encouraged police departments to address "racially biased policing," not just the narrower problem of racial profiling.[16]

As racial profiling–inspired data collection has continued around the country, it has frequently been discovered that minority drivers are overrepresented, in comparison to the total population, in vehicle stops by the police.[17] They are also typically more likely to have their persons and vehicles searched subsequent to vehicle stops.[18] Whether this overrepresentation of minorities in stops and searches is the result of police profiling (discrimination), or alternatively, a reflection of police deployment in lower-income neighborhoods, police efforts to address crime- and gang-related problems, or even differential driving habits, is currently not empirically known.[19] It is the subject of much discussion and debate, though. In the most promising scenario, police and citizens will work together to collect and analyze these data, interpret the results, discuss their implications, and fashion appropriate responses.[20] This approach employs the themes of community engagement and collaboration within the framework of community policing to encourage open conversation about a thorny and complex issue—something that has not happened often enough with respect to race and policing in America.

The other aspect of the racial profiling phenomenon that makes it a particularly salient contemporary issue is that it reflects the larger and even more endemic issue of police accountability. As discussed in Chapters 1 and 2, one of the most distinguishing features of policing is that ordinary police officers exercise substantial low-visibility discretion. Historically, officers have not been held to strict accountability in their use of this discretion. During the 1970s and 1980s some accountability began to be exacted for particularly serious police officer decisions, such as whether to use force against a person, the decision to engage in a high-speed pursuit, and the decision about whether to make an arrest in a domestic violence situation. Despite these developments, however, most police decisionmaking remained highly discretionary and not particularly accountable.

The racial profiling issue arises over concern about whether police officers make good and fair decisions when stopping people and cars and conducting searches. The common response of collecting and analyzing data on each stop creates conditions under which greater accountability can be established, especially if data collection includes information on each officer's identity. The types of cars and people that each officer stops can be scrutinized; patterns of discrimination and abuse can be identified. This represents a degree of supervision and accountability over everyday, ordinary police officer decisionmaking that has not previously been available or even anticipated. It might well be the harbinger of other forms of ever closer supervision over the actions of police officers, perhaps aided by modern technology (e.g., tiny cameras worn by officers, vehicle location systems, police car black boxes, etc.).

Will closer supervision lead to more effective and more just police work? Only time will tell us the answer to this question. Certainly, police have not always used their authority justly. It should be the case that greater supervision and accountability over police decisionmaking will reduce unnecessary use of force, improper searches, unjustified stops, and other forms of abuse of authority. If the net effect of such accountability measures is to reduce police discretion, however, it is possible that officer decisionmaking will become more legalistic (just following the law) and bureaucratic (just following the rules), which might or might not make policing more effective or just. If not properly implemented, such supervision could also greatly inhibit police officer initiative. The issue of accountability is one that we will surely wrestle with as long as we give some government employees police power and authority over the rest of us.

Mass Media

The mass media, both news and entertainment, have changed substantially over the last two decades. The media, and through them the public, seem to be increasingly interested in police work and crime. With increasingly more channels competing for the public's attention (thanks to cable and satellite TV), and the new medium of the Internet with unlimited "channels," it is easy to feel overwhelmed. At the very least, the attention of the mass media can definitely overwhelm a police agency that happens to find itself in the spotlight.

One example of the effect of the mass media was illustrated during a series of sniper slayings in the Washington, D.C., area in the autumn of 2002. For several weeks, area police departments had to contend with an army of news reporters representing local, national, and international news organizations. Some of these organizations, especially those providing 24-hour news shows, seemed to have unquenchable appetites for information. Such organizations need something new every few hours, whether the police have any real news to report or not. In addition, these news organizations compete vigorously (some would say viciously) with each other for readers, listeners, watchers and, ultimately, advertisers (i.e., money). Consequently, hundreds of reporters were constantly pestering witnesses, victims, families, Montgomery County Police Chief Charles Moose, and other police officials for new information. This led to leaks from the investigation team and the release of both inaccurate information and information that the police had hoped would be kept confidential while the investigation was underway.

Intense news attention can be beneficial as well. In the case of the sniper slayings, it is unlikely that an old acquaintance of the eventual suspects, who lived 2,500 miles away in Tacoma, Washington, would have known about the

D.C.-area crimes, put two and two together, and notified the authorities about his suspicions, if not for the intense, nationwide news coverage of the crimes. Similarly, it was an unauthorized leak about the suspect vehicle, broadcast over commercial radio, that led a trucker and another citizen to locate the suspects at an interstate rest stop in western Maryland within a few hours of the broadcast.

Another example of mass media effects was evident in Los Angeles at the end of 2002. New LAPD Chief William Bratton has focused on the phenomenon of police pursuits. Such pursuits are a serious consideration in most jurisdictions, of course. In Los Angeles, however, and a few other cities, it is common for police pursuits to be televised live through the use of TV helicopters and airplanes. The chief expressed concern that such live television coverage, often carried on several stations, emboldens those who are being chased, giving them the means to achieve their 15 minutes (or two hours) of fame. Giving chase on live television may also lead to poor police decisionmaking if officers feel pressure to perform bravely and capture their suspect at all costs.

"Reality TV" cop shows have joined 24-hour news and live TV coverage as means of presenting nonfictional accounts of policing to mass audiences.[21] These shows, from "Cops" to "Real Stories of the Highway Patrol," are typically filmed by riding along with police officers for hundreds of hours and then editing the film down to a 30-minute or 60-minute program. Thus, although the footage is realistic, the condensed form of presentation gives audiences an unrealistic sense of the pace of police work and an unrepresentative sample of police activity. These shows stand in contrast to the many fictional TV dramas based on police work, which audiences presumably understand to be fiction and not news or documentary.

A different application of the mass media is represented by the television show "America's Most Wanted." This network TV show is specifically designed to help police solve actual crimes and capture real suspects. It is essentially a bigger-budget, national version of Crimestopper shows that run regularly on many local TV stations. Unsolved crimes are dramatized in order to solicit the public's assistance in identifying and/or locating persons involved in the crimes.

As these examples illustrate, the entertainment and news media have complicated and complex effects on policing and police administration. These media, especially 24-hour TV and Internet news, create demands for information that are difficult to satisfy. They present a combination of live, edited, realistic, and fictional accounts of police work to millions of viewers that influence the public's perceptions and expectations. This in turn affects police officers, who are aware that the public (including victims, offenders, journalists, lawyers, and politicians) watches these shows, forms opinions about the police, and develops expectations that are often unrealistic.[22] The police sometimes then find themselves playing to roles defined by "Cops" or "NYPD Blue" instead of to roles defined by their agency's values, policies, and training.

For police administrators, the mass media are both a blessing and a curse; regardless, they are a reality. One hundred years ago, most police executives only had to deal with a local newspaper or two. Once television came onto the scene, most police chiefs still only had to deal with local TV news and reporters. This could be challenging, of course, but relationships could be developed, and the parameters were fairly well understood. As television matured, the LAPD and the FBI were early pioneers in working with Hollywood to influence fictional portrayals of their agencies, and a few other large police departments began to attract attention from national news organizations. Gradually, mass media began to affect policing through more intense news coverage and a seemingly endless array of TV shows and movies.

Only in the last 10 years or so, however, have the mass media really become a factor that the average police executive might actually have to work with and respond to. The Fox Network could show up at any time to film a reality show. Alternatively, following a significant crime or police shooting, a fleet of satellite TV trucks can be expected to park across the street from police headquarters. Any chief's worst nightmare would be to have an officer's questionable actions replayed every half hour on CNN. That scenario becomes increasingly more likely with the proliferation of mini-cams, surveillance cameras, and police car video systems. This all represents a revolutionary shift in the police-media relationship that is still developing. The effects that it will have on police-public relations, and on police officer behavior, are uncertain. What is certain is that police executives will have to become more sophisticated and savvy in their relationships with the mass media.

Cybercrime

Cybercrime is computer-mediated activity that is illegal or illicit and that can be performed through global electronic networks.[23] It can best be understood by examining the potential roles of the computer in criminal activity. Three useful categories are (1) the computer as a target, (2) the computer as a tool for the commission of a crime, and (3) the computer as incidental to the crime itself, or simply put, as evidence. Crimes in which the computer is the target involve individuals breaking into or attacking a victim's system and may include activities such as hacking, cracking, or sabotage. Crimes in which the computer is used as a tool for the commission of a crime typically involve traditional crimes, such as fraud, being committed in ways to which we are less accustomed. For example, theft, forgery, embezzlement, and even stalking are familiar crimes to us. However, any of these crimes may be committed using a computer today, consequently complicating their investigation. Finally, crimes in which the computer is incidental to the criminal activity could include using a computer to keep financial records of illegal business activities or perhaps sending a threatening e-mail message to someone.[24]

Although numerous efforts have been undertaken to give us a better description of the incidence and prevalence of cybercrime, what we know is limited. Long-term initiatives are viewed as key in obtaining a valid assessment of cybercrime. For example, the National Crime Victimization Survey has recently added questions to examine fraud, identify theft, and stalking among its respondents. The FBI has also included a question in the National Incident-Based Reporting System to indicate whether an offender used a computer in the commission of a crime. In other efforts, a recent Bureau of Justice Statistics national survey of state prosecutors found that 42 percent of these offices prosecute computer-related crimes under their state's computer statutes. As one might expect, in larger cities, prosecution of these crimes was even more likely, with 97 percent of full-time large offices indicating that they prosecute computer-related crimes. The most frequently prosecuted type of computer-related crime is child pornography, with three in 10 offices reporting prosecuting this type of offense. Credit card and bank card fraud represented the next most frequently prosecuted cases.[25]

The National Institute of Justice (NIJ) also conducted an assessment of the needs of state and local law enforcement in combating electronic crime and cyberterrorism. In this survey, respondents indicated what they perceived as being the 10 most critical needs:

- public awareness
- adequate data and reporting
- uniform training and certification courses
- onsite management assistance for electronic crime units and task forces
- updated laws
- cooperation with the high-tech industry
- special research and publications
- management awareness and support
- investigative and forensic tools
- structured computer crime units[26]

In response to some of the findings of this survey, the NIJ developed the Electronic Crime Program, which was designed to address any type of crime involving digital technology. The goal of the program is to help the criminal justice community build capacity for addressing electronic crime through collaboration among federal, state, and local law enforcement; industry; and academia.[27]

When addressing cybercrime, community engagement and community education are important. Citizens must know the extent of cybercrime so they will be less likely to become a victim. Anecdotal evidence indicates that a complicating factor about cybercrime is that oftentimes its victims go for long periods of time without knowing they are a victim. This is unlike most of the crimes with which law enforcement is familiar and accustomed to investigating. Collaborative efforts for dealing with cybercrime will require more partnerships among the private and public sector, specifically law enforcement and security. This may come in the form of assistance with investigations, training, and/or education. With increased and extensive Internet use, globalization has become a significant component of cybercrime. Today, we know no jurisdictional boundaries, which makes dealing with cybercrime an even greater challenge.

Technology

Technological advancement in the last decade has dramatically changed the way we work and the kind of work we do. This holds true for most occupations and certainly for law enforcement. While one might argue that technology makes our jobs easier, it also makes our jobs more challenging. It is true that technology can enable us to perform activities more efficiently and effectively, but that is assuming that we have the technology, understand its application, and have been trained to use it. Another complicating factor is that criminals have access to technology too, so this enables them to commit crimes using means they have not had in the past, or commit crimes they have not considered in the past.

The RAND Science and Policy Institute has categorized technology by its uses for law enforcement in an effort to assess current needs and capabilities and hopefully identify future directions in maximizing the appropriate technologies and finding technological gaps that must be filled. Law enforcement uses technology in the following areas, some of which might overlap:

- first response
- investigation and apprehension
- forensic analysis
- administration and management
- crime prevention

Examples of first-responder technology applications include those used for situation reporting, officer safety, officer deployment, and tactical communications. Digital crime scene photography and remote case filings are technologies that are used for criminal investigation and apprehension of suspects. Forensic analysis technologies deal primarily with the identification and analysis of physical evidence and include, for example, explosive residue analysis and ballistics analysis with the National Integrated Ballistics Information Network (NIBIN). Administration and management have broad-ranging technology applications in areas such as information processing, planning, training, and accountability.[28]

Technology can be a valuable asset, but can cause problems if used inappropriately or inadequately. Potential barriers to effective technology use include real costs, potential costs, technology risk, and human risk. Real costs include initial procurement costs and opportunity costs, as compared to the cost of other resources. Potential costs are those that are unanticipated and usually involve unintended consequences of the use of a technology. Technology risk is the risk that the technology will not work, either in its application to a problem or as it is intended to be used. Human risk typically deals with resistance to technology by personnel or their inability to use it appropriately. Occasionally, human risk may include potential danger with the use of a technology.

Community engagement for technology may mean encouraging the public to assess and embrace technology. Most of our efforts have been directed toward the law enforcement end user, but perhaps we might need to broaden our thinking with respect to how the public, with modern technology, might be able to assist in crime reduction efforts. Collaboration is accomplished more easily with the use of technology via multiple media. We might find ourselves "meeting" in a virtual conference room instead of at our local police department. Technology furthers the notion of globalization in that it not only creates worlds without boundaries, but also enables crimes to be committed anonymously from afar—crimes that might yield little or no evidence, or forms of evidence with which we are unfamiliar.

Terrorism and Homeland Security

Efforts to address terrorism and homeland security exemplify the needs for collaboration and community engagement, and emphasize the importance of our awareness of globalization. Since September 11, 2001, we have come to view terrorism and our responses to terrorism differently. The acts that occurred that day were unlike any we had ever seen before. While previous incidents at the World Trade Center and in Oklahoma City gave us pause, we had nothing of this magnitude that affected so many people and professions with which to compare these events.

The Homeland Security Bill, enacted in 2003, mandates that 22 previously existing federal agencies with combined budgets of about $40 billion and employing 170,000 workers, be collapsed into one, with additional new divisions being created to fill existing gaps. This represents the most sweeping federal reorganization since the creation of the Department of Defense in 1947. The Federal Bureau of Investigation and the Central Intelligence Agency, two premier intelligence-gathering agencies in the United States, will remain independent from the Department of Homeland Security. However, other agencies with intelligence-gathering capabilities, such as the Secret Service, will become part of the new department.

The mission of the new department is to: (1) prevent terrorist attacks, (2) reduce vulnerability to terrorism, and (3) minimize the damage from attacks that do occur. There are four divisions within the department, including Border and Transportation Security; Emergency Preparedness and Response;

Chemical, Biological, Radiological, and Nuclear Countermeasures; and Information Analysis and Infrastructure Protection. Although these divisions represent the department's primary focus, it will provide numerous other functions that are not directly related to homeland security. For example, it will also be responsible for responding to natural disasters, marine search and rescue, immigration and naturalization, counterfeiting, and drug smuggling.[29]

The divisions and major subunits in the new Department of Homeland Security are as follows:

- Border and Transportation Security
  - Immigration and Naturalization Service
  - Customs Service
  - Agriculture Department's Animal and Plant Health Service
  - Coast Guard
  - Federal Protective Service
  - Transportation Security Administration

- Chemical, Biological, and Nuclear Countermeasures
  - Health and Human Services Department—Civilian Biodefense Research Programs
  - Agriculture Department's Plum Island Animal Disease Center
  - National Biowarfare Defense Analysis Center (new)

- Emergency Preparedness and Response
  - Federal Emergency Management Agency
  - Chemical, Biological, Radiological, and Nuclear Response Assets
  - Domestic Emergency Support Team
  - Department of Energy's Office of Nuclear Security and Incident Response
  - Department of Justice's Office for Domestic Preparedness
  - FBI's National Domestic Preparedness Office

- Information Analysis and Infrastructure Protection
  - Department of Commerce's Critical Infrastructure Assurance Office
  - General Services Administration's Federal Computer Incident Response Center
  - Defense Department's National Communications System
  - FBI's National Infrastructure Protection Center
  - Department of Energy's National Infrastructure Simulation and Analysis Center

What does the creation of the Department of Homeland Security mean for local law enforcement? At this point, much is left to our speculation. Minimally, as Larry Hoover indicates, a new vision of their national security role and responsibility will be required of American police.[30] He identifies four challenges faced by local law enforcement in participating in efforts address-ing homeland security: technological, logistical, political, and ethical. The most significant technological challenge is interoperability. *Interoperability* is the ability to exchange information between organizations. Interoperability, or the lack thereof, can affect a variety of media, including but not limited to voice and Internet communications. Organizations may include not only local, state, and federal law enforcement but also public health, emergency medicine, and fire. The most problematic logistical issue is data entry. The necessity of this function is apparent, but if a majority of officers' time is spent here, then little time is left for other responsibilities.

Political issues take a variety of forms that focus on finances, role expec-tations, secrecy, and productivity, among others. Finally, ethical challenges include the issues of profiling and open records legislation. While technolog-ical, logistical, political, and ethical challenges are not new for the police administrator, those associated with homeland security are unlike ones faced before. The themes of community engagement, collaboration, and globaliza-tion are all apparent. Community engagement may be simply in the form of community awareness of the nature of the threats we face and how, as citi-zens, we can respond in a manner that will help law enforcement. Collabo-ration among so many levels of law enforcement and among so many disci-plines is new for us. Community policing broadened our perspective and taught us the value of collaboration, but not to this extent. Globalization implies a worldwide effect, which is what we are now faced with. What this means is that we may be dealing with issues that originate in another coun-try, but that also affect us locally, perhaps through the use of the Internet.

Summary

Three themes that run through modern policing at the start of the twenty-first century were discussed in this chapter. The community engagement theme refers to the importance of police working closely with individual cit-izens and neighborhood groups. The collaboration theme is similar—police need to collaborate with other organizations and agencies. These two themes, community engagement and collaboration, are not just feel-good programs, nor are they important merely because they tend to enhance pub-lic satisfaction with the police. Rather, research and the experience of recent decades demonstrates that they are central to effective policing—to control-ling crime and disorder and solving community problems.

The third theme is globalization. While most policing is still local, the rest of the world is slowly creeping into local police work, thanks to immigration, travel, free trade, modern telecommunications, computers, and related social and economic trends. Today's police executives must become more knowledgeable about global issues and international relations than their predecessors ever had to.

Five contemporary issues were also discussed: racial profiling, mass media, cybercrime, technology, and terrorism/homeland security. The diversity of these issues illustrates the growing complexity of police administration. While extremely challenging, this diversity also serves to keep the study and practice of police administration dynamic and vibrant. Modern police administration continues to need and deserve the best efforts of the best and brightest women and men who can be attracted to such an honorable calling.

Discussion Questions

1. What role do you think the United States, and U.S. police, should play in international police missions in places such as Bosnia, Kosovo, and East Timor?

2. When vehicle stop data are analyzed in a jurisdiction and it is found that African American and Hispanic drivers are overrepresented in stops and searches, what steps do you think should be taken?

3. As a police chief, what would you do if the Fox network approached you about filming a "Cops" television-style show in your department?

4. A lot of modern technology has been introduced into policing in the past decade or two. Which new technologies do you think have had the biggest impact on police work? On the effectiveness of police? Which do you think have had the least impact?

5. The movement toward protecting homeland security may have tremendous impacts on policing and American society. One is further blurring of the lines between police and the military. How much does this concern you? What issues does it raise?

Notes

1. L. Fridell and M.A. Wycoff, *The Future of Community Policing* (Washington, DC: Police Executive Research Forum, 2003).

2. Request for Proposal: Police-Public Contact Survey. City of Seattle, WA: Office of Policy and Management, 2002. Available at http://www.cityofseattle.net/mayor/docs/rfp.doc.

3. P. Finn, *Citizen Review of Police: Approaches and Implementation* (Washington, DC: National Institute of Justice, 2001).

4. See http://www.fortworthpd.com/communit.htm.

5. R. Sampson and M. Scott, *Tackling Crime and Other Public-Safety Problems: Case Studies in Problem-Solving* (Washington, DC: Office of Community Oriented Policing Services, 2000).

6. W.G. Skogan and S.M. Hartnett, *Community Policing, Chicago Style* (New York: Oxford University Press, 1997); M.E. Correia, *Citizen Involvement: How Community Factors Affect Progressive Policing* (Washington, DC: Police Executive Research Forum, 2000).

7. See http://www.centertech.com/letgrant/index.html.

8. N.G. La Vigne and J. Wartell, *Mapping Across Boundaries: Regional Crime Analysis* (Washington, DC: Police Executive Research Forum, 2001).

9. Fridell and Wycoff, *Future of Community Policing*.

10. G. Cordner and E. Perkins, "Problem-Oriented Policing in San Diego: A Study of POP in Practice in a Big City Police Department." Report to the National Institute of Justice, Washington, DC, 2002.

11. R.M. Perito, *The American Experience with Police in Peace Operations* (Clementsport, Nova Scotia: Canadian Peacekeeping Press, 2002).

12. D.H. Bayley, *Democratizing the Police Abroad: What to Do and How to Do It* (Washington, DC: National Institute of Justice, 2001), p. 5.

13. M. Buerger and A. Farrell, "The Evidence of Racial Profiling: Interpreting Documented and Unofficial Sources," *Police Quarterly* 5, no. 3 (September 2002): 272-305.

14. M. Alexander et al., *Driving While Black or Brown: The California DWB Report* (San Francisco: American Civil Liberties Union Foundation of California, 2002).

15. F. Newport, "Racial Profiling is Seen as Widespread, Particularly Among Young Black Men" (Princeton, NJ: The Gallup Organization, 1999).

16. L. Fridell, R. Lurney, D. Diamond, and B. Kubu, *Racially Biased Policing: A Principled Response* (Washington, DC: Police Executive Research Forum, 2001).

17. See, for example, G. Cordner, B. Williams, and A. Velasco, "Vehicle Stops in San Diego: 2001." Report to the San Diego Police Department, 2002.

18. E.L. Schmitt, P.A. Langan, and M.R. Durose, "Characteristics of Drivers Stopped by Police, 1999." (Washington, DC: Bureau of Justice Statistics, 2002).

19. R.S. Engel, J.M. Calnon, and T.J. Bernard, "Theory and Racial Profiling: Shortcomings and Future Directions in Research," *Justice Quarterly* 19, no. 2 (June 2002): 249-273.

20. A. Farrell, J. McDevitt, and M. Buerger, "Moving Police and Community Dialogues Forward through Data Collection Task Forces," *Police Quarterly* 5, no. 3 (September 2002): 359-379.

21. J.L. Worrall, "Constitutional Issues in Reality-Based Police Television Shows: Media Ride-Alongs," *American Journal of Criminal Justice* 25, no. 1 (fall 2000): 41-64.

22. D.D. Perlmutter, *Policing the Media: Street Cops and Public Perceptions of Law Enforcement* (Thousand Oaks, CA: Sage, 2000).

23. D. Thomas and B.D. Loader, "Introduction: Cybercrime: Law Enforcement, Security and Surveillance in the Information Age," in D. Thomas and B.D. Loader, eds., *Cybercrime: Law Enforcement, Security, and Surveillance in the Information Age* (London, England: Routledge, 2000), pp. 1-13.

24. S.W. Brenner, "Defining Cybercrime: A Review of State and Federal Law," in R.D. Clifford, ed., *Cybercrime, The Investigation, Prosecution, and Defense of a Computer-Related Crime* (Durham, NC: Carolina Academic Press, 2001). pp. 11-69.

25. C.J. DeFrance, *Prosecutors in State Courts, 2001* (Washington, DC: Bureau of Justice Statistics, 2002).

26. H. Stambaugh, D.S. Beupre, D.J. Icove, R. Baker, W. Cassaday, and W.P. Williams, *Electronic Crime Needs Assessment for State and Local Law Enforcement* (Washington, DC: National Institute of Justice, 2001).

27. National Institute of Justice Electronic Crime Program, http://www.ojp.usdoj.gov/nij/sciencetech/ecrime.htm

28. W. Schwabe, L.M. Davis, and B.A. Jackson, *Challenges and Choices for Crime-Fighting Technology: Federal Support of State and Local Law Enforcement* (Santa Monica, CA: RAND, 2001).

29. http://www.whitehouse.gov/deptofhomeland/

30. L.T. Hoover, "The Challenges to Local Police Participation in the Homeland Security Effort," *Subject to Debate* 16, 10 (October 2002): 1, 2, 4, 8-11.

Suggested Reading

Bayley, David H. *Democratizing the Police Abroad: What to Do and How to Do It* (Washington, DC: National Institute of Justice, 2001).

Fridell, Lorie, and Mary Ann Wycoff, *The Future of Community Policing* (Washington, DC: Police Executive Research Forum, 2003).

La Vigne, Nancy G., and Julie Wartell, *Mapping Across Boundaries: Regional Crime Analysis* (Washington, DC: Police Executive Research Forum, 2001).

Stambaugh, Hollis, David S. Beupre, David J. Icove, Richard Baker, Wayne Cassaday, and Wayne P. Williams, *Electronic Crime Needs Assessment for State and Local Law Enforcement* (Washington, DC: National Institute of Justice, 2001).

Thomas, Douglas, and Brian D. Loader, eds., *Cybercrime: Law Enforcement, Security, and Surveillance in the Information Age* (London, England: Routledge, 2000).

Case Studies

Harold Nubby was appointed chief of the Westerburg Police Department 15 years ago. A very principled person, Chief Nubby is looked on with great respect in his community of 15,000 people. He is a deacon in the First Methodist Church, a member of the Rotary Club, and a member of the board of directors of the local YMCA. Although approaching 60 years of age, he is physically fit and jogs four miles every day. A member of the department (which now numbers 28 officers and one civilian secretary) for the past 35 years, Nubby came up through the ranks to his present position.

Although he is well accepted in the community, he has great difficulty getting along well with his police officers and is considerably frustrated because the department is not functioning smoothly. Officers are often criticized in the press; although he has never been the focal point of such attacks, he would like to minimize the effects of this bad publicity. He would sincerely like to do a better job running his department and has almost given up. But not quite!

In an effort to improve the department, Nubby devotes almost all his time to its problems. He is at his desk promptly at 8:00 A.M., usually works right through his lunch hour, and never goes home to dinner before 7:00 P.M. Occasionally he jogs his four miles during the day, but most often he postpones this ritual to the late-night hours. It is not unusual to see him running through the streets of Westerburg at midnight. He almost always drops by the station after he finishes running, no matter what time that might be, and prowls the streets in his own departmental car, supervising the activities of his officers. On a Saturday night, he can usually be found in his car or in his office until 2:00 or 3:00 A.M.

Because his wife died five years ago and his four children are grown and settled, running the department efficiently has become almost an obsession with Nubby. The people of the community see this as overwhelming dedication on his part and feel grateful that they have a police chief of his caliber and commitment. Many of the citizens of the town, knowing him as they do, find it difficult to understand why their police department is not a better department and why the department is oblivious to citizen concerns. Nubby is so highly respected that no one has ever considered the idea that the department's problems stem from his own mismanagement.

The department's table of organization has one lieutenant, four sergeants, and 23 patrol officers. Lieutenant Augustino "Gus" Severino is commanding officer of the 4:00 P.M. to midnight shift. He is two years younger than the chief and joined the department two years after the chief. He and the chief have been traditional rivals for promotion over the years, and Severino has never succeeded in topping the chief in a promotional examination. This rivalry has caused a rift between the two men. Severino has become bitter and never misses an opportunity to be critical of Nubby, both as a police officer and as a person. The two men talk to each other only when it is officially necessary.

Although the chief feels hurt over this situation, he makes a concerted effort never to criticize the lieutenant. He has, however, given up on the possibility of developing a personal relationship with him. The chief is not personally bitter and would like to mend fences if possible.

Severino, on the other hand, has one ambition in life: to become the chief. However, he is not a particularly dedicated police officer and is much more interested in self-advancement than in the police department. Because he requires very little in the way of work from his officers, he gets along well with most of them and would generally have to be considered the leader of the emergent system. All four sergeants and most of the patrol officers are in his corner. As a result, what he does has the approval of most officers, and what he says is generally followed.

Departmental personnel see Severino as a "real cop" and the chief as a "do-gooder who was promoted beyond his capabilities." The chief fully understands how he is looked on by the department and believes firmly that the only way to combat the problem is to stay on top of it. In fact, the chief has taken only two vacation days in the last five years.

The chief is known as a strict disciplinarian, whereas Gus Severino bends over backward to cover up officers' mistakes. The sergeants fall in line behind Severino, thinking that one day he might become chief. A few citizen complaints are easier to handle than the wrath of subordinates. On one occasion, when a prisoner was brutalized, with two fellow prisoners and a newspaper reporter as witnesses, the shift sergeant, acting as commanding officer, and several patrolmen, lied under oath at the public hearing on the matter. The chief suspended the sergeant and all officers involved for 60 days, but the suspension was reversed on a technicality by the Civil Service Commission.

On another occasion, a citizen coming to the station to report that his car had been stolen discovered to his amazement that the desk officer, the only officer present in the station at the time, was sound asleep at the desk. When the chief investigated the matter, three patrol officers, the shift sergeant, and Gus Severino all signed written statements affirming that they were present at the station when the citizen came in and that the desk officer was wide awake and alert.

The most serious cover-up occurred when a 17-year-old high school student reported to Chief Nubby that she had been raped by an on-duty patrol officer. There were no witnesses. The incident occurred in the back of a police car in an isolated sand pit in the town. The officer involved had a considerable reputation as a "ladies' man," and had recently been divorced by his wife on the grounds of adultery. A physical examination of the girl supported her accusation that she had been raped. Chief Nubby's investigation of the incident included written statements from four patrol officers, the shift sergeant, and Gus Severino that the accused officer had been assigned to desk duties that night and never left the police station until he was relieved of duty because of illness at 10:00 P.M., one hour after the incident occurred. Although semen stains were found in the backseat of the police car that was allegedly involved in the rape, nothing could be proved against the officer. Chief Nubby was held in considerable contempt by his officers because he brought charges against the officer involved. Based on the testimony of the officers, the case was dismissed and the chief humiliated further.

"I've got to stay on their backs all the time," Chief Nubby is frequently heard to say. "Even if I leave town for a day or stay away from the department for a few hours to attend a Rotary meeting, all hell breaks loose."

Chief Nubby is a chief from the old school and is proud of it. "What's ruining the police service today is these young college kids," he says. "I don't know what they're teaching them in college these days; permissiveness, I think. Why, I'd take one good old-time cop to any 10 of these young punks any day."

The chief himself never took advantage of any educational opportunities. A 1936 graduate of Westerburg High School, his education stopped there. "You don't need an education to be a good police chief," he is fond of saying. "Education does nothing but confuse the issues. Look at me. I've done pretty well, and I've never received a day of police training in my life."

Yes, look at him. The fact that his police department is disorganized is evidenced by the fact that it has no organization chart. In fact, he has never seen an organization chart; he has no idea what one looks like, let alone what it is used for.

He does everything himself. He refuses to delegate authority to anyone else because he is afraid of what might happen. He and his secretary do all of what he calls the "paperwork" of the department. "There's no one in the department I can rely on," he says. "If I did, they'd just mess it up. It's easier to do myself."

His philosophy dictates that he controls everything. All official decisions are made by him. All equipment and supplies are handed out by him. If the members of the department need tear gas and riot equipment in an emergency situation, oxygen to refill empty oxygen tanks, bullets for their weapons, or even flashlight batteries, they have to see him. If he is unavailable, the equipment and supplies are unavailable. If a tire on a police car blows, the purchase of a new tire has to be cleared by him. In fact, he makes the purchase personally. Lieutenant Severino and the sergeants have no authority to make any meaningful decisions. The chief does not believe that they have the capability.

Additionally, there is no chain of command within the Westerburg Police Department. Officers communicate officially only when they are moved by the urge. The chief frequently gives direct orders to patrol officers and encourages them to bypass their supervisors in communicating with him. He calls this "keeping the lines of communication open" and envisions it as contributing to police effectiveness in the department.

The department has no established policies and procedures and uses as a guideline an outmoded (1947) set of rules and regulations. When the chief wishes to establish a policy or disseminate a procedure, he writes out a memorandum, which he usually types himself, and tacks it to a bulletin board that most officers rarely look at. Most of these policies and procedures are ripped off the bulletin board and thrown away shortly after they are posted.

The chief makes no effort to determine whether his policies and procedures are followed, unless a violation comes to his attention as the result of a citizen's complaint. When violations of policies and procedures are discovered inadvertently, perhaps by the chief in one of his nocturnal patrols, the officer or officers involved are reprimanded orally and no further action is taken. In most cases, the policy or procedure involved is missing from the bulletin board and cannot be found.

Although its chief is energetic, well-meaning, and dedicated, the Westerburg Police Department has some serious problems. What steps would you take to solve them?

Discussion Questions and Projects

1.   What is the department's major problem?

2.   If you were Chief Nubby, what steps, in what order, would you take to solve your problems?

3.   Draw an organization chart for the Westerburg Police Department, using what you know about the organization as a point of departure.

The Peripatetic Sergeant

John Crummerine is a sergeant on the Brushboro Police Department. Brushboro is a community of 40,000 people. The department consists of 45 patrol officers, eight sergeants, four lieutenants, two captains, and one chief. A simple organization chart of the department is given in Figure 1.

The department is an excellent organization. Chief Donna W. Slocum has a bachelor's degree in criminal justice from Michigan State University and is a graduate of the FBI's National Police Academy. Since becoming chief four years ago, after a national search to replace the retiring chief, she has been successful in shaping up the department, and it is now looked on as a model municipal police agency. Chief Slocum is fourth vice president of her state's association of police chiefs. She has written numerous articles for national police publications and is presently writing a book on police administration. She is considered by everyone who knows her to be a thoroughly knowledgeable and innovative police leader. She is well liked by her officers and commands the admiration of her community.

She has one problem: Sergeant John Crummerine. Crummerine, who has been in the department for almost 35 years, is the department's senior officer in terms of service. He was a close personal friend of the previous chief. John Crummerine has two problems: an aversion to work and a propensity for consuming large quantities of alcohol both on and off the job. Additionally, Crummerine is not at ease with the world unless he is walking. Police cars give him a feeling of claustrophobia, and he has never been able to adjust to the fact that police service today is necessarily highly mobilized.

As a patrol officer, a position in which he served for 30 of his 35 years on the job, he was always assigned to a walking beat, never to a car. When he became a sergeant five years ago because of his friendship with the former chief, he was the only sergeant in the department who was excused from mobile supervisory duties. He continued to walk his downtown beat and was assigned "supervisory responsibilities" over the one patrol officer who had the contiguous foot beat. It was common knowledge that the two men never saw each other. Crummerine was constantly on the move, strolling in his beat area. This also gave him frequent opportunities to visit and pass the time of day with his many friends in taverns, pool rooms, and liquor stores along the way. Toward the end of any given tour, John could usually be seen swaying to and fro in an alcoholic stupor on his way back to the station. Because he was a likeable fellow who never made an arrest and who never became involved in anything but a little light conversation with his beat clientele, he received very few complaints over the years and was generally accepted as the character he obviously was.

Figure 1 **Organization of the Brushboro Police Department**

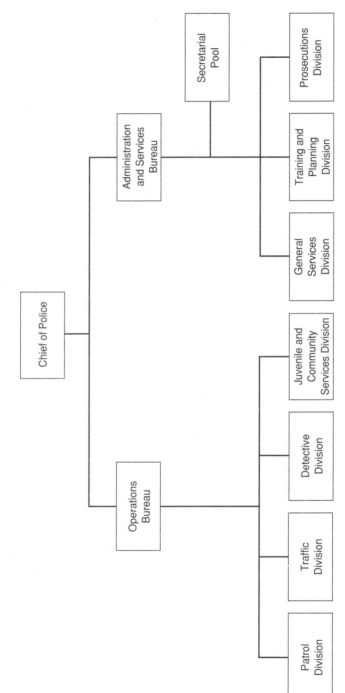

Enter Chief Donna W. Slocum. An advocate of motorized patrol and a critic of foot patrol in relatively peaceful communities of Brushboro's size, Slocum waited for six months before making any changes in the department. During those six months, she studied the department's problems. John Crummerine surfaced as a problem almost immediately. The first change made by Slocum was to eliminate walking beats and to assign all patrol supervisors and patrol officers to motorized responsibilities. The second change she made was to reassign the sergeant in charge of the General Services Division to the Patrol Division and replace him with Sergeant John Crummerine. He reasoned that the elimination of walking beats would increase the department's patrol capabilities, that all supervisory personnel should be mobile, and that Sergeant Crummerine, given his peculiar problems and interests, might become a more productive member of the department if he were given an inside job, which by its very nature would tend to curb the sergeant's wayward appetites. Although she anticipated that Crummerine might not be ecstatic about his new assignment and might not accept its challenge with relish and enthusiasm, in her wildest dreams she never anticipated what actually happened.

John Crummerine was a member in good standing of the Brushboro Police Brotherhood, a collective bargaining unit that was very strong in Brushboro and that, through its attorney, made absolutely certain that every provision of the contract between the Brushboro Police Brotherhood and the City of Brushboro was followed to the letter. The union contract contained a seniority clause stipulating that seniority would be the basis on which officers would choose both shift and work assignments. Sergeant John Crummerine was not only the senior member of the department, but also its senior sergeant. His seniority was indisputable. In no uncertain terms, the Brotherhood attorney spelled this out for Chief Slocum. Crummerine refused the transfer.

Slocum was forced to rescind her transfer order. She was not, however, forced to rescind her order eliminating all walking beats and assigning all patrol personnel, including supervisory personnel, to mobile units.

Slocum transferred Crummerine from his walking beat to a supervisor's car. In the meantime, the chief had issued policies and procedures governing the activities of patrol sergeants.

Slocum anticipated serious difficulties with Crummerine when the transfer had been effected, but to both her surprise and relief, Crummerine seemed to adjust to his new role very well. He could be seen at all hours darting about the city in his patrol car, meeting his every obligation and fully subscribing to the chief's new policies and procedures. Although there were a few unauthenticated reports that Crummerine was occasionally visiting his old haunts for a "quick one," his drinking never really surfaced as a problem. Not, at least, for four years.

The chief's first indication that Crummerine was back to his old tricks came about as a result of a late-night inspection of patrol operations by the chief herself. While touring the city, she noticed Crummerine's supervisor's car parked on Main Street. Inasmuch as no calls had been received for service in the Main Street area over the preceding hour, the chief felt that perhaps this situation warranted her attention. It was 10:00 P.M. as the chief pulled into a supermarket parking lot across the street from where Crummerine's vehicle was parked. There was no sign of Crummerine. In fact, there was no sign of Crummerine for the rest of the night. Shortly after midnight, when the shift changed, the chief saw the midnight shift sergeant, Henry Dalrymple, walking down the street toward the patrol supervisor's car. Arriving at the car, he got in, started up the motor, and drove off.

The following day, the chief, armed with this information, called to her office the commanding officer of the 4:00 P.M. to midnight shift, Lieutenant Nicholas Charos.

"Where was Crummerine last night, Nick?" he asked.

Charos gave the chief a sheepish grin. The grin asked the question: How much does she know?

"Why the grin, Nick? What do you know that I don't know?"

"Well, Chief, I guess you know," said the lieutenant.

"Know what?"

"I guess you know what's been happening with Crummerine."

"I don't know what's been happening with Crummerine unless you tell me what's been happening with Crummerine," said the chief.

"I don't want to get the old guy in trouble," said Charos.

"Well, why don't you assume that the old guy is already in trouble and we'll take it from there."

"Gee, Chief, I didn't think it was that serious. I would have brought it up before if I had. You know, the old guy is having trouble at home, and I just didn't want to add to his problems."

"But you know, Nick, that the old guy is a police officer—no, a police sergeant—and that makes him special in my book. That means he has responsibilities. If he's not meeting them, he should get in trouble."

"Yeah, but, gee, Chief, I—"

"Nick, stop pussyfooting around with me. You're his commanding officer and you have responsibilities, too."

"Okay, Chief. Okay. Don't start threatening me. I'm just an innocent party to this whole thing, and it's not that serious."

"What's not that serious?" demanded the chief.

"Okay, Chief, I'll lay it out for you. The old guy's wife is a lot younger than he is, and she wants to go out all the time, to the movies, dancing, out to dinner, to cocktail parties. She even wants to go to Disneyland and go on all the rides. Can you imagine the old guy going to Disneyland and going on all the rides?" Charos smiles. "I tell ya, Chief, she's drivin' him bananas. And then there's his kid, his only kid. Always was a nice kid, but the old lady is driving the kid right through the wall. The kid got on the sauce pretty bad, and that killed the old guy because the problem kinda runs in the family, and the kid got involved in a hit-and-run property damage over in Lakeport, and he's up on charges, so the roof's fallin' in."

"Too bad, but what's that got to do with what Crummerine is doing on the job?"

"Well, you know, Chief, he's sorta lettin' up. Nothin' serious, but sorta lettin' up."

"Where was he last night between 10 and 12?"

"You know about that?"

"Why don't you tell me about that?"

"If I *have* to."

"Look, Nick, I'm the chief. You're a lieutenant. You work for me, right?"

"Why don't you tell me what you know about last night, Chief, and then—"

"No, Nick. You tell me what *you* know about last night."

"Well, Crum came in late for work to begin with."

"How late?"

"An hour or maybe an hour and a half."

"Does that show on the attendance roster?"

"Well, Chief, no it doesn't. We didn't want to cause him any trouble, so—"

"So you covered for him?"

"Yeah, I guess you could say that we sorta—"

"*Sorta*! You *covered* for him. Go on."

"Well, Chief, you know that he's back on the sauce and that he—"

"Nick, how could I know he was back on the sauce if you didn't tell me he was back on the sauce?"

"I guess I just assumed you knew, Chief. Anyway, he's back on the sauce pretty good, and, you know, when he's on the sauce, all he wants to do is walk around—walk, walk, walk. He won't take a car. It's like the old days. He goes down on the old beat and walks all night. It's like he could solve all his problems by walking them off. What do you say to a guy when he tells you he's got problems and he needs to get away from the job for a while and walk them off.—Do you say, '*No, you can't; I'm not going to let you?*' Maybe you can be tough like that, Chief, but not me. I gotta go with the guy for awhile."

"How long has this been going on?"

"Couple of months. Maybe three. It's his wife, Chief. A real witch. We gotta help him. That's the way I see it."

"Did he take a car out last night?"

"Yeah. He took the patrol supervisor's car, like he always does."

"Then what?"

"Well, what he does, Chief, is park it someplace and go for a walk. You know, he visits his friends."

"What time did he go for a walk last night?"

"Gee, Chief, I really don't know."

"You *don't know*? You're his shift commander and you *don't know*?"

"Yeah, Chief, I really mean that. I don't know. I really don't."

"Did you have radio contact with him last night?"

"Gee, Chief, I really don't know. I could check the radio log."

"I have the radio log right here on my desk, Charos, and it doesn't show any contact at all. What do you have to say about that?"

"I don't know, Chief. I really don't know."

"So Crummerine left the station last night an hour or an hour and a half after you came on duty, and you haven't seen him or heard from him since?"

"I guess that you could put it that way, Chief. But I know he's okay. I know."

"You know he's okay? How do you know he's okay? You clairvoyant? Got ESP?"

"Come on, Chief. Crummerine does this all the time. He always shows up for work the next day."

"He does this all the time?"

"Yes, ma'am."

"You mean once he leaves the station, that's the last you see or hear from him, every night?"

"That's about it, Chief. I know it sounds a little screwy, but that's the way it is."

"Captain Wallbanger is commanding officer of the Operations Bureau, right?"

"Right."

"In the chain of command, you report to him, right?"

"Yes, ma'am. Right."

"I assume that Captain Wallbanger is fully apprised of this problem. Right?"

"Yes, ma'am, he is."

"He's *what*?"

"He knows all about it, ma'am."

"All about it?"

"Yes, ma'am. All about it."

"I can't believe it. Who told him?"

"I told him, ma'am. He's the officer I report to in the chain of command, like you said. Your policy is that we pass along to him any problems we can't solve. This problem has been passed along just like your policy says."

"I can't believe it. Wallbanger knew about this?"

"Yes, ma'am, he did. I assumed, I guess, that maybe he told you and that was how you knew about it."

"He didn't know about last night?"

"Yes, ma'am, he did."

"How did he know about last night?"

"I called him on the telephone and told him. That's your policy, ma'am. Every time Crummerine takes off, I always call the captain and tell him."

"And what does he do?"

"I guess he doesn't do anything. I had assumed that he at least told you about it. That's the policy, ma'am."

"Yes, Charos, I know, *that's* the policy."

Discussion Questions and Projects

1. Identify the specific problem or problems Chief Slocum has.

2. Should Chief Slocum take any action against Lieutenant Charos? Explain.

3. Should Chief Slocum take any action against Captain Wallbanger? Explain.

4. What should Chief Slocum do to strengthen the police department?

5. Do you believe that Lieutenant Charos's feedback will prove helpful to Chief Slocum? Why?

6. Is Chief Slocum's major problem Sergeant John Crummerine?

7. In a definitive fashion, outline your solutions to Chief Slocum's problems.

Case 3
The Yuletide Remembrance

Ever since becoming a member of the Midgeville Police Department, Patrolman Walter Whitty has had strong pangs of conscience whenever he saw his fellow officers of all ranks accepting gratuities. He not only knew that accepting gratuities violates the police officer's Canon of Ethics, but he also had been taught since childhood that nobody ever got something for nothing.

His education in practical police work got a severe jolt the first night he was assigned to duty. Teamed with partner John "Gunner" Paquette in a black-and-white, they left the station house at 4:10 P.M. and headed toward their sector in the northeast section of the city. Looking back on that first tour of duty, Walter often wondered how he was able to hide the pride he felt at actually becoming a police officer. It was something he had always wanted to be—ever since he was a kid. He sat there in the passenger seat with his brass polished and his shoes shined and felt a sudden sense of satisfaction; at long last he had achieved his goal. He *was* a police officer with a whole career of interesting, dignified, and rewarding work ahead of him. There would be no stopping him now. He would work hard, advance in rank, and become a truly professional law enforcement officer.

As the black-and-white pulled out onto Highway 19, heading north, Gunner was the first to speak. Gunner was an experienced officer and generally considered one of the department's best. At age 35, with 10 years of street experience behind him, he was a very self-assured, confident man.

"Just got out of the academy, right, kid?"

"I graduated last week," Walter replied.

"Then you understand what our relationship is going to be over the next eight weeks."

"Yes I do. You're my FTO. I learn it all from you."

"Right, kid. You learn it all from me. A field training officer can show you more in one week than you learned in 16 weeks at the academy."

"I believe it," said Walter, somewhat skeptically.

"The first thing I should tell you, kid, is that you forget everything they told you at the academy—everything."

"Everything?" asked Walter.

"Everything," said Gunner.

"I guess I don't understand exactly what you mean," said Walter.

"Well, kid, they do police work one way at the academy, and we do it another way on the street. There's a lot to learn on the street that don't exactly jibe with what they told you at the academy."

"Like what?" asked Walter.

"Like I'm gonna show you right now," said Gunner as he wheeled into the parking lot of a franchised hamburger restaurant.

"Let's go in and have a cup of coffee just to settle the nerves." Gunner pulled the car behind the restaurant. The two officers got out of the car and went into the kitchen of the restaurant.

"The first lesson you learn," said Gunner, "is that you always pull the car into the back of the restaurant, and you always go into the kitchen. As long as you have the portable radio with you, you never sign off the air."

"Why?" asked Walter. "I don't think I understand."

"The first rule of the road," said Gunner "is that the less they know about where you are or what you're doing, the better off you are."

"We sure didn't learn that at the academy," said Walter. "We were taught that we always went into restaurants through the front door and that we always signed off the air if we were going for coffee or for a lunch break."

"Right, kid," smiled Gunner. "Those are the policies, the rules we're *supposed* to follow. You will soon learn that the department's policies and the rules of the road are always different."

Gunner was right at home in the kitchen. He knew the restaurant manager and all the kitchen help. He took two large paper cups and filled them with coffee.

"How do you take yours, kid, cream and sugar?"

"Black," said Walter.

Gunner handed Walter a cup of steaming black coffee and put a generous supply of cream and three teaspoons of sugar into his own cup.

"Walter Whitty, meet Yancy Beauregard," said Gunner, pointing with his coffee cup toward the man with "Manager" in big red letters on his hat. "Yancy, this is Walter Whitty, one of our new men that I'm gonna train."

"Pleased to meetcha," said Yancy as he flipped a batch of burgers over on the grill. "You got a good teacher. Gunner here is the best. We got no trouble as long as Gunner's in a car nearby."

"That's right," Gunner laughed. "Our response time ain't bad when you got any problems here, right, Yancy?"

"Patrolman Gunner always gets here in a hurry."

"Good community relations, right kid?" Gunner was looking expectantly at Walter, his eyebrows raised and a big smile on his lips.

Walter nodded, thinking back on the lectures he had had at the police academy on good community relations. They had never covered what went on in the back rooms of hamburger joints.

"You stick with me, kid," said Gunner "and you'll learn a lot about good community relations."

"Right," said Yancy. "There's nobody knows more about good community relations than Gunner. When we need him, he's there."

"Right," said Gunner. "When you need me, I'm there, right, Yancy?"

"Right," said Yancy.

"By the way," said Gunner, "do you think I could swing by here in a couple hours and pick up some goodies for the wife and kids?"

"Sure," said Yancy. "If I'm not here, I'll leave word with Durk that it's okay. Anything you want Gunner, you know that."

"I know that," said Gunner. "I hate to put the bite on you so often, but the wife and kids are sick of fried chicken and fish and chips and pizza from all of those other restaurants all the time. Once in a while, they like a good hamburger feed."

"I hope they enjoy it," said Yancy.

"They'll *love* it," said Gunner. "The kids are wild about your hot apple pies. I usually swing by the Open All Nite and pick up a quart or two of ice cream for the pie. Nothin' like good, wholesome food for growin' kids."

"Right," said Yancy.

"Well, we gotta go fight crime," said Gunner. "Call us if you have any trouble with those motorcycle kids hanging around out front."

"I'll call you, Gunner, and thanks," said Yancy.

Walter reached for his wallet as Gunner moved toward the door.

Gunner looked around in disbelief. "What are you doing, kid?" he asked.

Walter fumbled for a bill.

"What are you doing, kid?" Gunner repeated.

"Just paying for the coffee," Walter said.

Yancy dropped three double cheeseburgers on the floor and stared at Walter.

"You gotta excuse him, Yancy," said Gunner. "He's just a rookie and they gotta lot to learn about street sense."

"It's always on the house here, young fella," said Yancy. "Least we can do for the officers in blue." Yancy picked the cheeseburgers off the floor and threw them back on the range. "We'll fry off the dirt," he said.

Walter left without paying, feeling a deep sense of remorse that he hadn't insisted.

Back in the black-and-white, Gunner said, "Don't ever do that again, kid. Don't ever embarrass me like that again."

Walter said nothing.

During the first night on the job, Walter learned what Gunner had meant by the *rules of the road*.

At 6:30, they returned to the restaurant and picked up 10 double cheeseburgers, seven orders of french fries, seven malts, and 14 hot apple pies. On their way to Gunner's house, they stopped at the Open All Nite. Walter watched Gunner through the large plate-glass window as he went to the ice cream freezer, picked up a gallon of ice cream, and waved at the cashier as he walked by without paying.

"Doesn't that bother you just a little?" asked Walter when Gunner was back in the car.

"Just a fringe benefit of the job, kid," said Gunner. "Everybody does it."

"But rules and regulations say that—"

"Kid, what'd I tell ya? Forget what they tell you in the academy. What you learn from your FTO is what's important. It'll save you a lot of headaches if you just go along with the system."

After they had made their delivery of "goodies," Gunner said, "Okay, kid. Now it's chow time for us. What'a ya feel like?"

"I'm not very hungry," said Walter.

"How about Chinese? Egg Foo Yung. Chicken Chop. Fried Rice. Pork Strips. Don't that make your mouth water?"

"Okay," said Walter.

"You don't like Chinese, kid?" asked Gunner.

"I love Chinese," said Walter.

Walter learned the rules of the road very thoroughly over the following two months. He paid for absolutely nothing he ate or drank while on the job, and he watched Gunner negotiate for a free lawn hose, grass seed, garbage can, wallpaper, cinder blocks, window panes, lawn chairs, and sport shirts.

"Look at it as good community relations," Gunner would say. "You couldn't *buy* better community relations."

After Walter left Gunner and the field training program, he became a full-fledged police officer. He was terribly confused about the wide gap that existed between departmental rules relating to gratuities and the rules of the road. Gunner did such a good job teaching him the rules of the road that he was convinced that all of the other officers subscribed to the "take-what-you-can-get" philosophy. Once on his own, however, he paid for everything. He found that this was extremely difficult to do, and he developed something akin to a guilt complex as a result. Rationally, this made no sense at all. Who ever heard of someone's developing a guilt complex because of scrupulously following departmental policy? But the department didn't care. Nobody cared. The policy was there for window dressing, nothing more.

After Walter had been on the job for two years, *he* became a field training officer. He gave his rookies a different kind of field training than he had received from Gunner. Rules and regulations and procedures were drummed into the heads of his recruits. For seven years, Walter remained a field training officer. Ever so gradually, Walter's image within the department began to change. Whereas he had always been ostracized for the fastidious manner to which he subscribed to departmental rules, now he was being looked on as a kind of hero by the younger members of the department.

The Midgeville Police Department was relatively small (38 total complement), and within nine years of Walter's becoming a patrol officer, he had been promoted to sergeant and had achieved considerable status as a no-nonsense, strictly-by-the-book professional. After years of worrying about how his fellow officers looked down on him, he was now in a position where he could enjoy his professional self-image. He had completed a community college program in law enforcement and was on his way to the baccalaureate degree when something happened that changed his life.

While at college, he heard a lecture on police unionization. He became interested in the idea and did a term paper on the police union movement. He presented the idea of a police union to his band of followers, who now numbered more than 50 percent of the department. They liked the idea and commissioned Walter to develop a union in Midgeville. When the chief heard about Walter's efforts, he chastised him severely and transferred him to the graveyard shift. Angered by the chief's actions, Walter's followers urged him to form a union immediately and assured him of their votes in an election. Walter became somewhat of a martyr and was elected first president of the union. The town of Midgeville challenged the right of the officers to organize. The case went to the State Board of Labor Arbitration for a decision. The board ordered a new election to be held under its supervision and assured the fledgling union that if more than 50 percent of the department's members voted for a union, a union could officially be established. When the final votes were counted, 73 percent of the department had voted for the union. Once again, Walter became its president.

Under Walter's direction the union flourished, winning for its members increased insurance benefits, higher pay, longer vacations, seniority for work shifts, and time-and-a-half for all overtime work. In a very short time, everyone in the department joined the union. Walter was a hero.

The time had come to challenge the rules of the road. Only a few officers now still followed those rules, Gunner Paquette among them. The worst offenders were the older officers. Even the chief violated his own gratuity policy. Every year at Christmastime, merchants would bring bottles and even cases of liquor to the chief's office.

The chief, after earmarking the select stock for his own liquor cabinet, played Santa Claus with the rest, doling it out equally among the officers who gathered at his door at 4:00 P.M. every Christmas Eve. Each year, fewer and fewer officers appeared at his door. Gunner and his pals, however, were always there waiting at the door. Everybody got at least seven bottles. Perhaps this was the opportunity that Walter had been waiting for.

He called a meeting of the union and proposed that the union write a letter to all the merchants in town who were traditionally accustomed to sending a so-called Yuletide remembrance and request that this year, instead, they make a contribution to the Children's Cancer Fund. This would be a way to eliminate the gratuity problem from the chief right on down the chain of command. A few of the old-timers grumbled at the rear of the room, but everyone else agreed with Walter that this was an excellent idea.

"Maybe this is a good way to remind the chief that he should follow his own policies," said one of the officers during the discussion.

"We'll make him eat that gratuity policy of his," said another officer. "And at the same time, we'll divert some much needed money to a good cause."

"And *that's* good community relations," said Walter, watching Gunner grimace at the rear of the room.

The letter went out:

> The Yuletide is upon us, and we, the members of the Midgeville Police Union, wish you and yours happy holidays as well as a healthy and prosperous New Year.
>
> Over the past several years, the merchants of this town have been very generous, and we have received large numbers of gifts from you. We have appreciated this very much. It is wonderful to know that we have so many good friends.
>
> Because our police department has a policy against accepting gratuities, we would like to ask you if you would take the money you would ordinarily spend on presents for police officers and, instead of buying us presents as is your custom, send this money to the Jimmy Fund to help the thousands of little children who have cancer.
>
> We pledge not to accept any gifts this year from the business community, and we ask you to pledge your support to the Jimmy Fund. Such a pledge would make us very happy.

This letter was sent on November 21, just 34 days before Christmas. It was signed by Walter Whitty. Ten days later, on December 1, merchants in Midgeville received the following mysterious, unsigned letter:

> We are writing this letter to inform you of the Midgeville Police Department Yuletide Gift Committee. This committee is being established to give you an opportunity to continue your generosity to police officers, as has been the tradition for so many years.
>
> We know that a few of our fellow officers have contacted you expressing their disinterest in receiving gifts. This, of course, is a free country, and our fellow officers have the right to take any posi-

tion they wish on the matter. We want you to know, however, that those of us who are members of the Yuletide Gift Committee are sincerely grateful to you for your many kindnesses of the past. Furthermore, we would like to see this wonderful tradition continued.

Therefore, we will continue to welcome your gifts and appreciate your generosity.

Happy Holidays!

On December 8, over the signature of the Midgeville Police Chief, the following notice appeared on the bulletin board at the police station:

Several businesspeople in the community have contacted me about whether or not officers in this department are receptive to accepting gifts during this holiday season. I would appreciate it if all officers who are interested in accepting gifts this year would sign this notice on or before December 12th.

The chief himself and six other officers signed, indicating that they would accept the gifts. One of the signatures was that of Gunner Paquette.

Discussion Questions and Projects

1. Discuss the ramifications of problems that exist within the Midgeville Police Department.

2. Discuss the department's required and emergent systems. How does each operate for or against the best interests of the organization?

3. What inputs does the Midgeville chief have to the basic functions of police management?

4. What relation does the chief's value system have to the way the department functions?

5. What inadequacies of leadership does the chief exhibit?

6. Of the five general styles of leadership, which one does the chief most closely follow?

7. Is Walter Whitty a leader? If yes, why? What style of leadership does he follow?

8. Discuss the organizational policies of the Midgeville Police Department.

9. Discuss the Midgeville Police Department in terms of Theory X and Theory Y.

10. Is there any hope for the Midgeville Police Department? Explain.

The Chief Who Played King

Walden Center, a town of 14,000, is 20 miles from Central City and serves as a residential bedroom community. It is a highly homogeneous community of relatively affluent citizens who take great pride in their town and local government. Before World War II, Walden Center had been a small, rural town of 6,000. Its rural character is still evident, and small farms, woodlands, and open space abound.

Until now, there have never really been any problems between Walden Center citizens and their town government. The town is administered by a town manager appointed by three elected selectmen. The town manager is the appointing authority for all town governmental departments, including the police department. Therefore, the town manager has the power to hire and fire.

Walden Center is the type of town that has grown slowly, so just about everyone in town knows everyone else. Disputes about how the town is run and how its fiscal affairs are handled are hammered out by its citizens at the annual town meeting, which is, in effect, Walden Center's legislative branch of government. This system of government has worked well for Walden Center because it has given every interested citizen a definite say in how the community is run. Because of the lack of bureaucracy, it has been relatively easy over the years to resolve any problems that might have arisen simply by calling the town manager or appearing before the board of selectmen at one of their weekly meetings.

Two years ago, Timothy "Hap" Emmet, who had been chief of police in Walden Center for about as long as anybody could remember, retired. An amiable, congenial man, Hap's door was always open to anyone who wanted to see him. He was a master at resolving disputes and had a knack for satisfying everyone's interests. The members of his police department both loved and respected him, and although he had no formal rules and regulations or policies and procedures, he was able to control the activities of his officers simply because they all "knew what Hap wanted." Although his given name was Timothy, everyone, including his officers, called him "Hap," a nickname that precisely fitted his personality.

When Hap retired, the town manager recommended to the board of selectmen that they conduct a national search for the chief's position, reasoning that they should seek out the best possible person for the job. Hap's act would be a hard one to follow, the town manager had said. Inasmuch as the new chief would be reporting directly to the manager, he wanted someone who knew something about the intricacies of police administration to handle the job.

The board was reluctant to agree to this request, and citizens were in something of an uproar about appointing a "foreigner" as their new chief. The issue centered on the concept of local control, and many people thought that this would be lost if a stranger

467

was appointed to the position. The officers in the department joined forces with the more vocally opposed citizens in demanding that the appointment be made from among those officers already in the department. The town manager persisted, quoting a textbook on police administration by Gary Cordner, Kathryn Scarborough, and Robert Sheehan to support his thesis.

Hap Emmet resolved the question by suggesting that the national search be conducted, but that all members of the department be given equal opportunity to be considered for the position.

At a meeting of the board of selectmen, when the controversy was at its height, Hap said, "I have never read this book the town manager talks about by Sheehan and Cordner. As a matter of fact, I've heard that the book is controversial and that a lot of chiefs don't like their approach, but I am in favor of getting the best person we can get. To tell you the truth, I think the next chief will come right from within the department. I know of a handful of Walden Center police officers who could take over the job tomorrow and probably do a better job than I'm doing right now." That was just like Hap, always praising his officers.

Hap carried the day, and the board voted unanimously to begin the national search. The board appointed a search committee consisting of five citizens and appointed Hap to chair the committee. Advertisements were placed in the *New York Times,* the *Central City Gazette* and the *Police Chief* magazine. Everyone was astounded that 178 applications were received for the position. Of the 178, 14 were from Walden Center's 26-member department. The choice was narrowed to seven candidates; one was from Walden Center, one was from Central City, two were from police departments in the state, and three were from out-of-state departments. Although Hap felt strongly that four candidates from the Walden Center Police Department should be considered, he was voted down by the majority of the members of the search committee.

Professor Michael Joseph from Central City University's Department of Police Administration was retained to write an examination to be administered to the seven finalists.

The out-of-state candidates were flown in at the expense of Walden Center and put up at the Tan Dog Inn, a local colonial hotel that boasted that Martha, not George, Washington had slept there. The examination was given at 8:00 A.M. on a Saturday and lasted two hours. By 1:00 P.M. on the same day, Professor Joseph handed the results to the search committee, which began interviewing candidates 30 minutes later. The committee had asked the town manager to become a member of the oral interview panel.

The Walden Center officer had scored lowest on the written examination, scoring 52 out of a possible 100. The Central City officer had a 61; the two candidates from in-state departments had 66 and 68, respectively. The three candidates from out-of-state departments received grades of 57, 76, and 98, respectively.

The interviews of candidates began with the committee armed with the test results. In a short meeting convened just prior to the start of the oral interviews, Professor Joseph briefed the committee on the examination results. He strongly urged that only the candidates with the 76 and 98 grades be considered seriously for the position. He indicated that the examination was a relatively easy test that anyone with a good understanding of police administration should have passed at a very high level. On the basis of this advice, the committee, in private session, decided to look seriously at only two candidates: those scoring 76 and 98 in the examination. The decision to do this was not unanimous. Hap Emmet was the lone dissenter. He believed that all of the candidates should be considered equally.

At the completion of the oral interviews late Sunday afternoon (the committee had adjourned at 7:00 P.M. on Saturday evening), the candidates were ranked by each committee member solely on the basis of the oral interviews; however, it can be assumed that the impact of the examination grades influenced the rankings. The officer from Central City was ranked seventh; the officers from in-state departments who received 66 and 68 were ranked fifth and sixth, respectively; the out-of-state candidate who received a 57 on the examination was ranked fourth; the Walden Center officer was ranked third; the out-of-state officer who received a 98 on the examination was ranked second; and the out-of-state officer who received a 76 on the examination was ranked first.

The appointing authority, the town manager, asked that each committee member seriously consider who, among the top three candidates, should be chosen for the position and called a meeting for the following Wednesday evening to advise him on a final decision. On Wednesday evening, the committee met with the manager and voted 4 to 1 to appoint the out-of-state officer who had achieved a grade of 76 on the examination and who ranked as first choice on Sunday evening. Again, Hap Emmet was the only dissenting voice. He voted for the Walden Center officer.

The town manager said that with all due respect to Hap's position, he would go along with the choice of the committee majority and expressed confidence that this type of new leadership (someone from the outside) would provide the department with the kind of leadership it needed. Although he said that he was impressed by the 98 score achieved by the out-of-state officer, he emphasized that the committee's feeling that this officer did not possess leadership qualities automatically eliminated him.

On the following day, after contacting each member of the board of selectmen, receiving their approval, and getting a commitment from them to offer the new chief a five-year contract, he made a public announcement in the local press. The news release read:

> Walden Center Town Manager Robert Gerard announced this morning the appointment of Luke P. Grinnel of Candlelight, California, as the town's new police chief. Grinnel was chosen after a national search in which 178 police officers applied for the position. He succeeds Chief Timothy Emmet, who will retire next month.
>
> Chief Grinnel is presently a lieutenant in the Candlelight Police Department and has come up through the ranks. He is a police science graduate of Long Beach State College and is currently pursuing studies for his master's degree at the University of Southern California.
>
> The new chief is the author of a number of articles in police journals and has served as a consultant on law enforcement to the governor of California.
>
> He and his wife, the former Terry-Anne Knapp-Sack, have five children. He will assume his new duties on August 1.

After the choice was announced, all of Walden Center was abuzz about the new chief. The reaction of the townspeople was decidedly favorable, and the board of selectmen commended the search committee and Hap Emmet for their efforts in "selecting the best person in the country for the job." Feelings were a little hurt in the police department, but Hap assured the officers that Chief Grinnel was "a good man with an excellent background."

"Things will work out just fine, you wait and see," said Hap.

In retrospect, history was to prove Hap, the search committee, the town manager, and the board of selectmen wrong. Things didn't work out just fine.

Luke Grinnel descended on Walden Center something like the 1938 hurricane. All spit and polish and armed with the latest theories of good police administration practice, he moved immediately to establish rules and regulations for the department. In a speech before the Rotary Club three weeks after his arrival, he criticized the department publicly, particularly Chief Timothy Emmet's leadership.

"The Walden Center Police Department looks to me like the Mexican Army," he said. "It is disjointed. It is disorganized. It has no procedures. It is a disaster. And I assure you, the townspeople of this great town, that things are going to change and change for the better at the Walden Center P.D."

Chief Grinnel's remarks, along with a picture of him in uniform, graced the front page of the *Central City Gazette* that night.

As one might expect, morale among police officers in Walden Center sank to a low ebb. No one had a good word to say about the new chief. For the first time in his life, old Hap looked down in the dumps.

"Hap, what have you done to us?" asked one officer who met him on the street. "We're supposed to get a professional police chief, and you went and gave us Adolph Hitler."

"I'm sorry, Randy," said Hap. "I'm truly sorry, but what can I do?"

"Maybe you could make a statement to the papers or see the board of selectmen or the manager and tell them you made a mistake."

But Hap was too principled a person to tell anyone that he had been the only member of the committee to oppose the new chief's nomination. He suffered in silence.

In the meantime, Grinnel issued new policies and procedures almost daily. "You're going to learn how to do it the right way even if I have to hammer it into your heads," he was fond of saying.

He had not been on the job a month before he had established an organization chart and a rigid chain of command. "If you want to communicate with me in the future," he said, "you do it through the chain of command. No more open-door policy here. Patrol officers report to their sergeants, the sergeants to their lieutenants, and the lieutenants to me. That's the way it's done in police departments all over the country, and that's the way it will be done here."

Once, after a roll call in which the new chief complained bitterly about the time-honored practice in Walden Center of allowing officers to get out of their patrol cars to carry on conversations with citizens on the street, a practice with which he thoroughly disagreed, he finished up the session by asking, "Any questions?" One officer, an old-timer who had been on the force for 21 years, asked, "But shouldn't we go through the chain of command if we want to ask you questions, sir?"

Without a bat of an eye, Grinnel retorted, "You've got three days of punishment duty for that. What's your name?"

"Blaney, sir."

"Three days punishment duty for your insolence, Blaney, and that will teach you who's running the show here."

Grinnel had not been on the job two months before the town manager and the board of selectmen were flooded with complaints. Not only police officers, but also citizens, were complaining.

One 80-year-old lady who had retired 15 years earlier as the town's librarian and who knew everyone in the community went to the police station by taxi to see the chief about finding her lost cat. She had tried to reach the chief by phone but was told by the officer answering the telephone that the chief didn't take complaints like that and that he'd "get into a peck of trouble" if he put the call through. When she arrived at the station, the desk officer told her that she would have to go through the chain of command to see the chief. She argued, but to no avail. In desperation, she wrote to the board of selectmen and to the town manager. On the following Monday evening, she appeared at the selectmen's meeting and wondered aloud, "What on earth, gentlemen, is this chain of command that a taxpaying citizen has to go through to talk to the chief of police?" She never did find her cat.

In another instance the president of a local bank, who was also scoutmaster of Troop 8, went to the station to meet with the chief to make plans for police coverage of the Boy Scout Council's annual regional jamboree, which was to be held the following week at the high school stadium. With more than 1,000 youngsters expected to be participating, the availability of emergency services and extra police coverage was of extreme importance. The desk officer informed the scoutmaster that the chief didn't handle such matters himself and that he would have to see Lieutenant Billingsley, who was head of the new Operations Division. Lieutenant Billingsley would be available in two weeks when he returned from vacation.

"But I can't wait two weeks," said the scoutmaster. "The jamboree is next Saturday."

"Sorry, sir," said the desk officer, "I can't help you. I'd like to, but I'd get into a lot of trouble if I did. It's not in my job description."

"Job description, hell," said the scoutmaster. "You tell the chief I want to see him now."

"Okay," said the desk officer, "but it won't do any good. Billingsley handles things like that. That's the chief's policy."

"The chief's policy be damned," said the irate scoutmaster. "Who does he think he is?"

"You wait here," said the timid desk officer, "I'll tell the chief you want to see him." He returned in less than a minute.

"Sorry, sir. Like I said, he said to see Lieutenant Billingsley."

"But Lieutenant Billingsley is on vacation. How can I see Lieutenant Billingsley?"

"The chief said he thinks he's home and to call him there. He'll take care of everything."

The scoutmaster called the town manager and issued a complaint against the chief. The town manager called the chief and asked him, as a special favor to him, if he would see the scoutmaster.

"He's an important guy in town," said the town manager. "He's president of the First National Bank and he's on the finance committee. I think it would be wise to see him."

Reluctantly, the chief agreed, explaining to the manager that he thought it unwise to interfere with the responsibilities of his people once he had delegated them the authority to carry out his orders.

At the meeting between the chief and the scoutmaster, the chief lectured the scoutmaster on the principle of delegation of authority. Then the chief called Lieutenant Billingsley, whom he found at home painting his house, and said, "Billingsley, get down here right away. Some scoutmaster is here about a jamboree this Saturday. Do you know anything about it? You don't? Well, you should, Billingsley. This is an annual affair, and you should have been on top of it. Get yourself down here right away and take care of it. What's whose name? The scoutmaster? I don't know, wait a minute. What's your name, mister? His name is Francini. He'll be here when you get here."

After he had hung up the telephone, the chief stood up, indicating that the meeting was over.

"He'll be down in about a half an hour, Mr.—, Mr.—"

"Francini."

"Yes, he'll be down in about a half an hour. Let me know if he doesn't handle everything to your satisfaction, and I'll get on his back."

"How will I let you know?" asked Francini. "Write you a letter?"

Discussion Questions and Projects

1. Did Walden Center make a mistake in hiring Luke P. Grinnel as its new police chief? Why?

2. What, specifically, are Chief Grinnel's problems?

3. If you were Chief Grinnel's best friend, what would you advise him to do?

4. Was the screening process through which Chief Grinnel was hired appropriate to the needs of the town?

5. Had you been chair of the search committee, what would you have done differently?

6. If you were a member of Chief Grinnel's police department, how would you personally react to his administration of the department?

7. Break up into small groups of four. Assume that one of you is town manager and that three of you are members of the board of selectmen. Discuss through role-playing how you would resolve the problem.

8. Inasmuch as the chief reports directly to the town manager, choose one of your classmates to role-play the town manager's position and another to role-play the chief's position. Conduct a meeting in which the two discuss the town manager's concerns.

Cod Bay is a summer resort community; its winter population of 19,000 expands to 60,000 in the summer. The Cod Bay Police Department has many problems controlling summer visitors. One persistent problem is illegal parking. Because there are numerous complaints from year-round residents about parking, the Cod Bay police chief arranged with several towing companies to tow all illegally parked cars to the police station parking lot. The towing companies did a brisk business, particularly on weekends, when the town was inundated with visitors. Part-time police officers, who were not professionally trained, were hired by the department to work weekends and were assigned to the downtown area specifically to enforce parking laws. All violators were towed; no one escaped the watchful eyes of the part-time downtown patrol officers, who were occasionally overzealous in their enforcement activities and who perceived some of the parking violators as wanton criminals. In their desire to carry out departmental policy and to compete for tows with fellow officers assigned to the same task, they occasionally made mistakes and towed cars that were not illegally parked.

Having one's car towed can be a traumatic experience, particularly if the car is not illegally parked. On one such occasion, an irate young man came to the police station to reclaim his car, a matter that involved paying the towing company a modest fee. Refusing to pay the fee, the young man asked to see the sergeant in charge. The burly sergeant was predisposed to dislike irate young men. At first, the sergeant attempted to determine the facts, and he summoned the part-time patrol officer back to the station to get his side of the story. After listening to the stories of the patrol officer and the young man, the sergeant realized that the young man's car had been legally parked. But even so, the sergeant sided with the patrol officer and informed the young man that if he wanted his car back, he would have to pay the towing charge.

The man refused, and a shouting match, precipitated by the sergeant, developed. When the man was told to leave the station, he demanded what he knew were his rights. He was told that if he did not leave the station, he would be arrested. Finally, he was taken bodily from the station by the patrol officer, who pushed him down a flight of steps to the sidewalk. The man regained his equilibrium and quietly walked off into the night, beaten by the system. He returned later, paid the fee, and reclaimed his car.

This situation illustrates two major problems involving the dominant police subculture and role expectations. Departmental policy dictated that the sergeant investigate the citizen's complaint, in this case the towing of a legally parked car. The dominant police subculture dictated that the sergeant back the officer whether he was right or wrong. The sergeant followed departmental policy to the degree that it existed and then reverted to the role expectation of the dominant police subculture. The sergeant was much more willing to stay on good terms with the officer, with whom he would have to deal continually, than with the young man, whom he would never see again. The officer, having received the backing of the sergeant, then reacted in terms of his own accurate perception of dominant police subcultural role expectations and pushed the young man down the flight of stairs. Although there are legal sanctions against such actions, the officer fully understood that subcultural role expectations would completely support the action that he took.

Discussion Questions

1.   If you were the sergeant in this situation, what would you have done?

2.   If you were the chief of police of this police department and this situation came to your attention, what would you do?

3.   In your opinion, what caused the Cod Bay Police Department to get into this situation of having a dominant police subculture that supports such actions by officers and supervisors?

4.   How widespread do you think this kind of behavior and police subculture are today?

Tulane City, an industrial urban community with a population of 97,000, has a large minority population and an unemployment rate of 19.3 percent. Its police department is administered traditionally and has very few binding policies and procedures. Police chiefs, who are selected politically from within the department, change with the election of each new mayor. Active political support of a successful mayoral candidate is the only real qualification needed to become chief.

Five disgruntled and politically active former chiefs are currently serving in the department's hierarchy. Almost all of their energies are directed toward embarrassing the present chief, who has limited education and training and no understanding of the principles of police administration. He sees himself only as a temporary caretaker of the office and realizes that soon, when a new mayor to whom he is not politically dedicated takes office, he will be back with the troops and subject to the role expectations of a dominant police subculture that is totally incompatible with the democratic principles of constitutional government.

The dominant police subculture in Tulane City condones and encourages beating prisoners, accepting gratuities, and taking a public-be-damned attitude; these subcultural values permeate the entire organization. Officers frequently refuse to answer calls, and a large detective force, grown lazy through the years, investigates only a small percentage of major crime, even though crime has risen 52 percent during the past year. Gambling is rampant throughout the city, and almost no effort is made to curtail it.

The department, although it consists of 168 sworn personnel and 12 civilians, has no organization chart, no internal affairs division, and no inspections unit. Except for personality conflicts between officers and supervisors, no one is suspended or otherwise punished unless involved in the commission of a serious crime that comes to public attention. The citizens of Tulane City are up in arms about their police department's ineffectiveness, but have discovered that no one within the department will listen to their complaints. The chief is coasting; he drives about the city in a new Cadillac and occasionally drops by the station to pick up his mail and luxuriate in his large, well-appointed office.

Police officers have successfully negotiated a contract that provides for time-and-a-half overtime pay for court appearances. Because court appearances mean additional income, exorbitant numbers of arrests are made, even for minor and insignificant violations. Many police officers, hiding away in the courthouse coffee shop, are unavailable when their cases are called and thereby increase their overtime incomes. One sergeant, the Breathalyzer operator on the early-night tour, appears in court almost daily. He is never called on to testify, because of a court policy that prohibits the prosecutor from introducing Breathalyzer evidence. His court appearances are solely for the purpose of collecting overtime. Another officer drops by the court-house frequently; he is allowed to sign an overtime chit for his services even when he has no case on the docket.

The Tulane City Police Department is in a shambles and works counterproductively to community interests. In every sense, the department is unsophisticated operationally and administratively. Officers drink, carouse, and sleep on the job. Very little is right with the Tulane City Police Department.

The Tulane City Police Department is a good example of a police department completely out of control as a result of role expectations established by the dominant police subculture. The acceptance of these role expectations by the chief provides the rationale for their acceptance by the whole department. If the chief had either the ability or the inclination to promulgate policies and procedures designed to change these role expectations, he would be ostracized from the department immediately on being relieved of command by a new mayor. Realizing that his life would be made unbearable and possibly even placed in danger when he returned to the ranks in a minor hierarchical position, he decided on the more comfortable approach of not rocking the boat. On the inevitable day when he will be fired as chief and replaced by another political caretaker, he will be welcomed back by his fellow officers.

Discussion Questions

1. If you were brought in from the outside to be chief of this department, where would you start?

2. Why do you suppose Tulane City has followed the practice of letting former police chiefs revert to their previous ranks and stay within the police department?

3. In your opinion, how did the Tulane City Police Department get into such a sorry state of affairs?

4. Suppose you were a middle manager in this department and wanted to perform your duties in a professional and responsible manner. How would you go about doing so within the organizational climate of the Tulane City Police Department?

Rixton is a small community of 16,000 people and has a police force of 23. Police Chief Walton Eager came up through the ranks and is a pleasant man, but he has little administrative ability. He promulgates all policy and procedures by tacking notices to a bulletin board already overcrowded with memorabilia dating back several years. He makes no effort to determine whether his officers understand his policies and procedures, and officers feel no need to pay any attention to them.

The department has many excellent officers who, despite poor leadership, conduct themselves in exemplary fashion. A small minority of six, however, causes some severe problems. These six officers have their own police subculture and peculiar role expectations. The dominant police subculture in Rixton, although not predicated on officially established rules and regulations, is generally accepted by most of the police officers and dictates role expectations that are consistent with democratic processes. The minority police subculture is in conflict with the dominant police subculture; each group thinks that the other is ineffective.

The officers in Rixton refer to the two subcultures as cliques. Each clique operates according to its own role expectations, with neither clique particularly constrained by Chief Eager's policies and procedures. The minority clique perceives the police role as being largely militaristic. The following situations, involving minority clique members, provide some interesting data on how role expectations and perceptions affect behavior.

1. Patrol Officer Luigi Pasternak, a former marine who collects guns and believes that most people are criminals, received a radio call to mediate an argument at a gas station. On receiving the call, Pasternak said, "Good. Maybe I'll get a chance to crack someone's head."

2. Patrol Officer Brodie Fishbaum, when asked what changes he would recommend to make the Rixton Police Department more professional, remarked, "I'd make it more military, have them all get haircuts, and have them wear combat boots." Commenting on his role, he said, "I like this [police work]. This is just like being in the military. At least I think so. Pasternak and I think we are."

3. Patrol Officer Moody Mickehaus, commenting on the fact that Brodie Fishbaum and Luigi Pasternak had been transferred to his shift, said, "Now that Fishbaum and Pasternak are back, you'll see a lot of arrests. We try to outdo each other."

These three conversations were typical of the way minority clique members felt about themselves. Their attitudes and behavior were dictated by their own subcultural role expectations and were reinforced by the members of their small, but influential, peer group. The fact that the dominant police subculture behaved differently in terms of different role expectations had very little effect on what they did.

Members of the minority clique were disturbed, however, that their group consisted of so few officers. Moody Mickehaus, for example, was forever comparing his own professionalism with that of other members of the department; he was terribly disturbed that they were not as professional as he perceived himself to be. He once remarked that he gets so upset about societal degeneration and his department's inability to deal with it that he sometimes has to drink himself to sleep. Although Mickehaus considered himself to be professional, he was looked on by officers subscribing to the dominant police subculture as being dangerous.

The Rixton Police Department, with its two cliques of patrol officers, illustrates a department in which there is more than one set of role expectations. The fact that the dominant police subculture in Rixton was service-oriented and not militaristic was a fortunate quirk of fate. The minority clique, however, caused tremendous problems for the chief and a great amount of internal disharmony within the ranks of those officers who were trying their best to do their jobs properly. The real problem with the Rixton Police Department was Chief Walton Eager, who simply had no understanding of the situation and believed that a system is a method used to pick winners at a racetrack.

Discussion Questions

1. If you became police chief in Rixton, what would you do to gain control over the minority police subculture?

2. In your opinion, why has Rixton been so fortunate in developing a fairly positive dominant police culture?

3. How can two such different subcultures coexist within one small police organization?

The Nervous Planner

You are one of 200 police officers assigned to the Randall City Police Department. You joined the department 10 years ago and have advanced in rank to lieutenant. During your career, you have been assigned to numerous responsibilities, including patrol, investigations, property, and communications. On receiving your baccalaureate degree this past June from Randall City College, you were called to the chief's office and informed that you were to be given one of the most responsible positions in the department, director of planning. Although you have many misgivings about your capabilities to handle such an assignment and are quite nervous about it, you accept.

Randall City has a population of 100,000 people. It is largely a residential community, but does have some light industry in the Friendly City Industrial Park area. Randall City has always been known as the "Friendly City" and pretty much lives up to that name. For a community its size, it has a relatively low crime rate and few real police problems. The police department is a good one and has few internal problems. Its officers are dedicated and extremely enthusiastic. Because of its lack of general police problems, it has never had a director of planning. You are its first.

The immediate situation that prompted the chief to appoint you came about as a result of the new mayor's concern about spiraling budget costs. In attempting to pinpoint areas in which money could be saved, the chief decided that his first effort will be made in the area of patrol personnel allocation. The department uses all two-officer patrol cars. Almost all of the patrol officers like the two-officer system, and although the chief has been tempted to do away with it in favor of one-officer cars, he has hesitated to do so in fear of what this might do to morale. Morale, incidentally, is at a very high level.

The department operates on a three-shift basis: midnight to 8:00 A.M. (Shift 1); 8:00 A.M. to 4:00 P.M. (Shift 2); and 4:00 P.M. to midnight (Shift 3). The city has nine patrol sectors, designated by letters; at least nine patrol cars are always on the road. Depending on the availability of personnel, usually several more are out as well. Citizens are very satisfied with the department and often comment on seeing patrol cars "all over the place." The department has 18 marked vehicles.

The chief believes that activity in the city does not warrant the number of officers currently assigned to the patrol function. He is certain that the midnight to 8:00 A.M. shift can be substantially cut and feels reasonably sure that the 8:00 A.M. to 4:00 P.M. shift can also be cut, but he needs figures to back up his feelings. Your first assignment is to provide him with these figures and to give him data that will indicate exact numbers of patrol officers needed to service activity on each of the three shifts.

An additional problem is the department's lack of capability to handle calls and to engage in general patrol activities when shifts change. There is sometimes a 20-minute delay in servicing calls that come in at 11:50 P.M., 7:50 A.M., and 3:50 P.M. You are requested to work out a system to alleviate this problem.

After thinking for several days about how to proceed, you finally decide that it will be necessary to collect data on the amounts of time that it takes patrol officers to service various types of calls, recognizing that certain types of calls take longer to service than others. Getting these times will be no problem, because the communications division has been time-stamping complaint cards for years. Information is available on what time each call was received, what time it was dispatched, what time the assigned officers went out of service at the scene, and what time the officers came back into service at the conclusion of the call. Your only problem is to attempt to categorize the different types of calls. After much study, you decide on the following categories: *Part I Crimes, Part II Crimes, Incidents, Accidents, Arrests,* and *Hospital Runs.* Patrol officers in your department are always assigned to calls that fall into one of these six categories.

Your next step is to determine what the average length of time is for servicing calls in each category. This is easy. You take the complaint cards for three months and add up all of the times time-stamped in each category and divide by the number of calls in each category. This gives you the average time for each category. Recognizing that some calls will take longer than others, and wanting to be fair, you decide to allot slightly more time on an average than your hard figures (the actual average time spent) indicate. After completing this task, you draw up a table showing your figures (see Table 1).

Table 1
Average Amounts of Time Spent in and Allotted to Servicing Activity Categories

Category	Time Spent	Time Allotted by You
Part 1 Crimes	22.3 min.	25 min.
Part 2 Crimes	16.2 min.	20 min.
Incidents	15.7 min.	20 min.
Accidents	23.5 min.	25 min.
Arrests	19.6 min.	20 min.
Hospital Runs	17.9 min.	20 min.

Now that you know how much time you will allot for each categorized activity, you must determine how many activities within each category occur each year on each of the three shifts. While gathering this information, it occurs to you that it might prove beneficial to determine the amount of activity per year by actual hourly time of occurrence. The possibility of recommending overlapping shifts to compensate for time lost during shift changes might be better accepted if this kind of detailed information were available. Additionally, if your study is to be a fully detailed personnel allocation effort, while you are in the process of determining how many officers you need per shift, why not use the same activity statistics to determine where and on what day of the week the activity takes place?

Rather than accumulating data for the year, you decide that three months of activity will be a sufficiently substantial sample. Inasmuch as three months represent one-quarter of a year, you can interpolate your annual activity statistics by multiplying your activity figures for three months by four. This should provide a reasonably accurate estimate of all activity for one year.

Wanting to estimate activity somewhat on the high side, you choose two relatively busy representative months to compensate for seasonal changes in activity. You choose July as a busy summer month, December as a winter month with high accident and crime frequency, and May as a month that is fairly representative of other months from an activity standpoint. These months are chosen on the basis of your experience as a police officer and not on the basis of any hard data that will support your position.

You collect your data by thoroughly reviewing daily radio logs for each of the three months chosen and compiling activity by category and by time of day for each of the three shifts (see Table 2).

Table 2
Three Months of Police Activity by Time of Occurrence, by Shift

Shift 1

Time of Occurrence	Part 1 Crimes	Part 2 Crimes	Incidents	Accidents	Arrests	Hospital Runs	Totals
12:00-1:00 A.M.	91	183	311	31	32	32	680
11:00-2:00 A.M.	72	146	264	32	24	26	564
12:00-3:00 A.M.	40	144	224	35	20	23	486
13:00-4:00 A.M.	37	72	129	11	19	9	277
14:00-5:00 A.M.	15	23	67	8	5	8	126
15:00-6:00 A.M.	12	12	56	7	1	8	96
16:00-7:00 A.M.	27	16	64	6	3	12	128
17:00-8:00 A.M.	31	13	61	14	5	10	134
Totals	325	609	1,176	144	109	128	2,491

Shift 2

Time of Occurrence	Part 1 Crimes	Part 2 Crimes	Incidents	Accidents	Arrests	Hospital Runs	Totals
18:00-9:00 A.M.	59	58	244	23	5	17	406
19:00-10:00 A.M.	44	55	212	20	9	13	353
10:00-11:00 A.M.	49	58	209	16	11	16	359
11:00-12:00 A.M.	50	57	203	18	15	18	361
12:00-1:00 P.M.	47	59	193	27	15	23	364
11:00-2:00 P.M.	59	74	221	21	32	22	429
12:00-3:00 P.M.	70	61	222	26	25	19	423
13:00-4:00 P.M.	63	59	172	21	18	25	358
Totals	441	481	1,676	172	130	153	3,053

Shift 3

Time of Occurrence	Part 1 Crimes	Part 2 Crimes	Incidents	Accidents	Arrests	Hospital Runs	Totals
14:00-5:00 P.M.	117	120	267	36	45	18	603
15:00-6:00 P.M.	103	126	200	47	38	30	544
16:00-7:00 P.M.	97	109	238	30	46	21	541
17:00-8:00 P.M.	100	115	274	22	59	25	595
18:00-9:00 P.M.	106	157	263	25	52	26	629
19:00-10:00 P.M.	113	166	287	27	78	29	700
10:00-11:00 P.M.	107	128	243	36	86	26	626
11:00-12:00 P.M.	73	142	186	31	95	21	548
Totals	816	1,063	1,958	254	499	196	4,786

You follow the same procedure for plotting activity figures for place of occurrence and day of occurrence (see Tables 3 and 4). Although the chief did not give you these specific assignments, this information will prove useful later in determining daily patrol personnel deployment.

Table 3
Three Months of Police Activity by Place of Occurrence, by Shift

Shift 1

Sector	Part 1 Crimes	Part 2 Crimes	Incidents	Accidents	Arrests	Hospital Runs	Totals	% of Total Activity
N.W.	52	74	167	13	14	9	329	13%
C.W.	44	66	129	13	6	9	267	11%
S.W.	18	47	110	10	2	8	195	8%
N.C.	43	119	139	20	17	23	361	14%
C.	42	46	135	24	16	21	284	11%
S.C.	34	102	145	19	9	11	320	13%
N.E.	37	68	119	20	14	12	270	11%
C.E.	31	45	115	11	27	22	251	10%
S.E.	24	42	117	14	4	13	214	9%
Totals	325	609	1,176	144	109	128	2,491	100%

Shift 2

Sector	Part 1 Crimes	Part 2 Crimes	Incidents	Accidents	Arrests	Hospital Runs	Totals	% of Total Activity
N.W.	62	45	168	20	8	15	318	10%
C.W.	63	49	291	28	5	18	454	15%
S.W.	52	40	141	22	8	11	274	9%
N.C.	43	71	191	22	3	28	358	12%
C.	27	51	217	16	3	17	331	11%
S.C.	44	73	157	10	3	15	302	10%
N.E.	55	61	191	20	5	17	349	11%
C.E.	51	49	183	18	92	16	409	13%
S.E.	44	42	137	16	3	16	258	9%
Totals	441	481	1,676	172	130	153	3,053	100%

Shift 3

Sector	Part 1 Crimes	Part 2 Crimes	Incidents	Accidents	Arrests	Hospital Runs	Totals	% of Total Activity
N.W.	138	94	194	28	26	15	495	10%
C.W.	108	109	212	51	15	18	513	11%
S.W.	59	86	194	15	15	14	383	8%
N.C.	94	179	256	28	57	33	647	13%
C.	75	108	189	16	23	29	440	9%
S.C.	77	127	234	29	24	27	518	11%
N.E.	79	123	211	21	24	10	468	10%
C.E.	103	150	276	38	296	34	897	19%
S.E.	83	87	192	28	19	16	425	9%
Totals	816	1,063	1,958	254	499	196	4,786	100%

Table 4
Three Months of Police Activity for All Three Shifts by Day of Occurrence

Day	Part 1 Crimes	Part 2 Crimes	Incidents	Accidents	Arrests	Hospital Runs	Totals
Sunday	231	328	699	74	115	62	1,509
Monday	242	249	594	77	82	67	1,311
Tuesday	252	289	656	77	112	79	1,465
Wednesday	192	253	626	52	84	55	1,262
Thursday	235	303	742	84	89	76	1,529
Friday	226	319	746	92	140	72	1,595
Saturday	204	412	747	114	116	66	1,659
Totals	1,582	2,153	4,810	570	738	477	10,330

You now take all of your activity by category for the three months, add it together on a per shift basis, and multiply by four. This gives you a reasonably accurate estimate of shift category for a year. Because different categories of activity require different amounts of time to service (see Table 1), you must then take the number of activities in *each* category and multiply that number by the number of minutes you have allotted in Table 1 for servicing each category of activity. For example, 325 Part 1 crimes have occurred on Shift 1 for the three-month period. Multiplying 325 by four gives you a projection that approximately 1,300 Part 1 crimes will occur in one year. By multiplying 1,300 by 25 minutes, you can determine that it takes 32,500 minutes for patrol officers to service all Shift 1 Part 1 crimes for the year. By dividing 32,500 by 60 (the number of minutes in an hour), you can determine that it takes 542 hours for Shift 1 patrol officers to service all Part 1 crimes for the year. Table 5 shows the number of hours spent by each shift in servicing activity in Randall City for one year.

Table 5
Hours of Police Shift Activity for One Year

Shift	Part 1 Crimes	Part 2 Crimes	Incidents	Accidents	Arrests	Hospital Runs	Totals
Shift 1	542	812	1,568	240	146	171	3,479
Shift 2	735	642	2,235	287	174	204	4,277
Shift 3	1,360	1,418	2,611	424	666	262	6,741
Totals	2,637	2,872	6,414	951	986	637	14,497

These figures, however, represent only the time needed to handle calls for service. Consideration must also be given to the fact that police officers are involved in many activities other than the servicing of calls. They direct traffic, check vacant buildings, write reports, patrol the community, enforce speed laws with radar, take coffee and lunch breaks, assist motorists, research laws, obtain search warrants, service patrol vehicles, check equipment, confer with fellow officers, check school bus operations, and become involved in myriad other activities that are not reflected in the time statistics that appear in Table 5. When determining personnel requirements for the patrol function, it is therefore necessary to build into officers' work schedules sufficient time to engage in these peripheral activities. Time must also be available to handle work overloads that are unpredictable and to provide assistance for fellow officers. Patrol officers must be available for unusual and unforeseen circumstances that require their availability on a moment's notice. Considering these factors, it is unrealistic to base shift personnel strength solely on the actual activity and called-for services reflected in the daily radio logs. Time must be allotted for the additional hours officers need to perform their additional responsibilities. This additional time is referred to as buffer time. Buffer time accommodates overload, relief, patrol, and incidental activities.

For every hour that patrol officers spend making investigations at the preliminary level and in servicing calls, two additional hours should be allowed each officer as buffer time. Multiplying the number of hours actually spent in servicing activity by three gives the number of hours needed to accommodate all buffer time and all actual activity on each shift by category for one year (see Table 6).

Table 6
Hours of Police Shift Activity for One Year Including Buffer Time

Shift	Part 1 Crimes	Part 2 Crimes	Incidents	Accidents	Arrests	Hospital Runs	Totals
Shift 1	1,626	2,436	4,704	720	438	513	10,437
Shift 2	2,205	1,926	6,705	861	522	612	12,831
Shift 3	4,080	4,254	7,833	1,272	1,998	786	20,223
Totals	7,911	8,616	19,242	2,853	2,958	1,911	43,491

Rather than working with annual figures, however, you determine that it would be easier to make your personnel calculations on a monthly basis. In order to ascertain the number of patrol hours needed on a per month basis, you simply divide your annual figures by 12 (see Table 7).

Table 7
Hours of Police Shift Activity for One Month, Including Buffer Time

Sector	Part 1 Crimes	Part 2 Crimes	Incidents	Accidents	Arrests	Hospital Runs	Totals	% of Total Activity
Shift 1	136	203	392	60	37	43	871	24%
Shift 2	184	161	559	72	44	51	1,071	30%
Shift 3	340	355	653	106	167	66	1,687	46%
Totals	660	719	1,604	238	248	160	3,629	100%

You can now see that Shift 1 (midnight to 8:00 A.M.) is approximately half as busy as Shift 3 (4:00 P.M. to midnight) and that Shift 2 (8 A.M. to 4 P.M.), although busier than Shift 1, is much less busy than Shift 3. It is apparent that a personnel adjustment is in order. Certainly the shifts should not be staffed with an almost equal number of officers, as is now the case.

In order to determine the exact number of officers needed to handle shift activity, it is first necessary to calculate the exact number of hours taken off each year by the 166 officers assigned to the patrol division. Because the amount of time taken off by patrol officers significantly affects the availability of officers assigned to the patrol function, a review of all time off taken by the 166 patrol officers must be made. You must establish a *time-off factor* for the patrol component of the department in an effort to determine the number of patrol officers necessary to be assigned to each shift to compensate for the time taken off by officers assigned to regularly established beats. Each shift must be staffed with a sufficient number of officers to compensate for all time taken off by all officers assigned to the shift. If this is not done, the chances of having shifts frequently understaffed can become a problem in attempting to provide a level of service consistent with identified needs.

Once this task has been performed and once shifts are properly staffed to compensate for the anticipated absence of personnel, a relatively consistent level of service can be maintained. The time-off factor is an instrument of measurement that you can use to determine the number of patrol officers needed to staff each shift fully, cover each patrol beat consistently, and compensate completely for all officers away from the job for whatever reason.

In calculating the time-off factor for Randall City, you work on the premise that every patrol beat assignment must be filled on a 24-hour basis, 365 days a year. Patrol officers, however, do not work 365 days a year. They work considerably less. In Randall City they take from 21 to 26 days off each year for vacations. In addition to the 104 days they would normally take off each year (two days out of each seven), Randall City police officers have been successful in negotiating a contract that places them on a four-and-two work week; this means that instead of taking two days off out of each seven, they actually take two days off out of each six. This gives them an additional 17 days off each year. They also take sick leave, injury leave, no-pay days, and leaves of absence. Occasionally, some officers are suspended. All of this time represents substantial time away from work. Each officer, therefore, is available for work many fewer hours than the maximum number of hours if he or she were to work eight hours a day, 365 days a year. The number of hours not worked, however, must be provided for by assigning a sufficient number of officers to each shift to compensate for time off.

You decide to determine the Randall City time-off factor before you determine the number of beats needed to accommodate activity on each of the three shifts. In order to do this, you must determine the number of workdays lost per year by all 166 officers assigned to the patrol function (see Table 8).

Table 8
Patrol Officer Time Lost by Day for One Year

Time-Off Category	Work Days Lost per Year
Vacation Leave	3,583
Days Off	17,264
Sick Leave	1,765
Injury Leave	663
4-and-2 Loss	2,822
Suspensions	103
No-Pay Days	131
Leaves of Absence	40
Total	26,371

The number of days lost per year by the 166 patrol officers is 26,371. The number of hours lost per year (210,968) is determined by multiplying the number of days lost per year (26,371) by eight (the number of hours in one workday). The number of hours lost every month by the 166 patrol officers (17,581) is determined by dividing the number of hours lost per year (210,968) by 12 (the number of months in a year). The average number of hours lost every month by each of the 166 patrol officers (106) is determined by dividing the number of hours lost each month (17,581) by 166 (the number of patrol officers).

If one patrol officer worked one eight-hour shift every day for one month, he or she would work 243 hours. These 243 hours are referred to as the *basic police officer month*. The basic police officer month is calculated by dividing 365 (the number of days in a year) by 12 (the number of months in a year). There are 30.4 days, or 243 hours, needed to cover each beat for each eight-hour shift each month. Put another way, there are 243 hours needed to staff one patrol beat fully for each one-month period.

Working with the basic police officer month as a standard, it is relatively easy, you discover, to determine the number of hours each patrol officer is available to work each month. By subtracting the average number of hours each patrol officer is off each month (106) from the number of hours needed for one patrol officer to cover one beat for a month (243), it can be determined that each Randall City patrol officer will be available for duty 137 hours per month. By dividing the number of hours in the basic police officer month (243) by the 137 hours each officer works on an average each month, the Randall City time-off factor (1.77) can be determined. This figure means, in effect, that .77 of one patrol officer is needed to compensate for time off taken by each officer.

By multiplying the time-off factor (1.77) by the number of beat officers needed to handle all activity on a given shift, you arrive at the number of officers who should ordinarily be assigned to that shift to compensate for time off. Although this might seem to be a rather involved process to determine shift strength, it is essential if any degree of consistency is to be achieved in staffing beats fully and providing services according to identified demands.

You now have the necessary information to make some preliminary estimates of the number of officers needed to staff your three shifts. You proceed by making use of information in Table 7.

1. *Shift 1*: A total of 871 hours is spent each month by patrol officers on Shift 1. By dividing 871 by the basic police officer month (243), it may be determined that 3.6, or 4, car beats are needed on Shift 1. If the department continues with its present policy to staff each patrol vehicle with two officers, eight officers will be needed to handle all patrol car activity on Shift 1. Adding the two walking beats to the four car beats gives a total of 10 patrol officers who will be needed to staff all beats. Multiplying the 10 patrol officers by the time-off factor (1.77) indicates that 18 patrol officers should be assigned to Shift 1. Fifty-five patrol officers are currently assigned to the shift.

2. *Shift 2*: A total of 1,071 hours is spent each month by patrol officers on Shift 2. By dividing 1,071 by the basic police officer month (243), it may be determined that 4.4, or 5, car beats are needed for Shift 2. If the department continues with its present policy to staff each patrol vehicle with two officers, 10 officers will be need-

ed to handle all patrol car activity on Shift 2. Adding the two walking beats to the five car beats gives a total of 12 patrol officers who will be needed to staff all beats. Multiplying the 12 patrol officers by the time-off factor (1.77) indicates that 22 patrol officers should be assigned to Shift 2. Fifty-five patrol officers are currently assigned to the shift.

3. *Shift 3*: A total of 1,687 hours is spent each month by patrol officers on Shift 3. By dividing 1,687 by the basic police officer month (243), it may be determined that 6.9, or 7, car beats are needed on Shift 3. If the department continues with its present policy to staff each patrol vehicle with two officers, 14 officers will be needed to handle all patrol car activity on Shift 3. Adding the three walking beats to the seven car beats gives a total of 17 patrol officers who will be needed to staff all beats. Multiplying the 17 patrol officers by the time-off factor (1.77) indicates that 31 patrol officers should be assigned to Shift 3. Fifty-six patrol officers are currently assigned to the shift.

Quite naturally, you are astounded by these calculations. They indicate that you need 71 police patrol officers to handle all of the activity on all three shifts. The department, therefore, is 95 officers overstaffed. You must have made some terrible error in mathematics somewhere along the way. You check and recheck your computations. They appear to be right. They couldn't be. If only you had a computer, maybe it would come out differently. You take a trip to Randall City College and run your figures through the computer there. The computer parrots back your own computations. No question about it, they are correct.

Having a large amount of excess personnel to work with, you refer to Table 9 and see that the shift workload is heaviest for all three shifts at shift changes. Table 9 also indicates that from 4:00 A.M. to 8:00 A.M., activity drops off markedly.

Table 9
Percentage Breakdown of Work Activity by Hour of Day

Shift 1

	May	July	Dec.	Total	% of Shift Activity	% of Daily Activity
12:00–1:00 A.M.	182	235	263	680	27%	7%
11:00–2:00 A.M.	140	183	241	564	23%	5%
12:00–3:00 A.M.	118	176	192	486	19%	5%
13:00–4:00 A.M.	71	97	109	277	11%	3%
14:00–5:00 A.M.	33	51	42	126	5%	1%
15:00–6:00 A.M.	35	31	30	96	4%	1%
16:00–7:00 A.M.	35	37	56	128	5%	1%
17:00–8:00 A.M.	38	34	62	134	6%	1%
Totals	652	844	995	2,491	100%	24%

Shift 2

	May	July	Dec.	Total	% of Shift Activity	% of Daily Activity
18:00-9:00 A.M.	120	122	164	406	13%	4%
19:00-10:00 A.M.	120	111	122	353	11%	3%
10:00-11:00 A.M.	114	119	126	359	12%	4%
11:00-12:00 A.M.	99	116	146	361	12%	4%
12:00-1:00 P.M.	105	130	129	364	12%	4%
11:00-2:00 P.M.	141	133	155	429	14%	4%
12:00-3:00 P.M.	117	151	155	423	14%	4%
13:00-4:00 P.M.	113	114	131	358	12%	3%
Totals	929	996	1,128	3,053	100%	30%

Shift 3

	May	July	Dec.	Total	% of Shift Activity	% of Daily Activity
14:00-5:00 P.M.	228	192	183	603	13%	6%
15:00-6:00 P.M.	198	180	166	544	11%	5%
16:00-7:00 P.M.	188	180	173	541	11%	5%
17:00-8:00 P.M.	196	199	200	595	13%	6%
18:00-9:00 P.M.	198	206	225	629	13%	6%
19:00-10:00 P.M.	201	263	236	700	15%	7%
10:00-11:00 P.M.	171	247	208	626	13%	6%
11:00-12:00 P.M.	156	210	182	548	11%	5%
Totals	1,536	1,677	1,573	4,786	100%	46%

It seems obvious that there is a need to have half the patrol officers assigned to Shift 1 report for duty at 11:00 P.M. and half at midnight; half the officers assigned to Shift 2 report at 7:00 A.M. and half at 8:00 A.M.; and half the officers assigned to Shift 3 report at 3:00 P.M. and half at 4:00 P.M. This will be one of your recommendations to the chief.

Although the total amount of activity does not warrant any additional patrol cars or the assignment of any more than a total of 71 patrol officers on all three shifts to accommodate all activity, the fact that patrol shifts are currently overstaffed suggests the possibility of assigning a number of additional officers to one-officer cars to not only increase patrol capability and visibility but also handle many of the routine calls that do not present any appreciable degree of danger and do not necessitate the services of more than one officer.

After thinking about the matter, you make the subjective judgment that 15 additional one-officer car beats can be created. You decide to distribute nine of these beats evenly among the three shifts. You add one additional one-officer car beat to Shift 2, two additional one-officer car beats to a new split shift from noon to 8:00 P.M. (Shift 2A), and three additional one-officer car beats to a new split shift to run from 8:00 P.M. to 4:00 A.M. (Shift 3A). Also, you reduce the number of two-officer cars on Shift 3 from seven to six and thereby put two additional one-officer cars on the road during Shift 3. Your new beat assignments for the patrol division appear in Table 10.

Table 10
New Patrol Assignments by Shift

	Assignment	No. of Patrol Officers Assigned to Beats
Shifts 1 and 3A	4 two-officer cars	8
	3 one-officer cars	3
	2 walking beats	2
	3 one-officer cars (midnight to 4 A.M.)	3
Total	12 beats	16
Shifts 2 and 2A	4 two-officer cars	8
	4 one-officer cars	4
	2 walking beats	2
	2 one-officer cars (noon to 8 P.M.)	2
Total	12 beats	16
Shifts 3 and 3A	6 two-officer cars	12
	5 one-officer cars	5
	3 walking beats	3
	3 one-officer cars (8 P.M. to midnight)	3
Total	17 beats	23

The time-off factor of 1.77 suggests that a total of 94 patrol officers be assigned to the patrol division. The breakdown of patrol assignments for each shift is given in Table 10. The full complement of officers assigned to each shift, computed by multiplying the number of patrol officers assigned to beats on each shift by 1.77, is presented in Table 11. It should be noted that you have been liberal in assigning an additional officer if the figure to the right of the decimal point is three or more.

Table 11
Full Complement of Officers Assigned to Shifts

	No. of Patrol Officers Assigned to Beats	Full Complement Assigned
Shift 1	13 (x 1.77 = 23.01), or	23
Shift 2	14 (x 1.77 = 24.78), or	25
Shift 3	20 (x 1.77 = 35.4), or	36
Shift 2A	12 (x 1.77 = 3.54), or	4
Shift 3A	13 (x 1.77 = 5.31), or	6
Total		94

According to your calculations and new personnel allocation plan, the Randall City Police department can be reduced by 72 patrol officers. You write a report, present all of this information to the chief, and suggest that your plan be implemented.

Discussion Questions and Projects

1. How do you think the chief should use the report?

2. Should the chief implement the recommendations contained in the report?

3. Knowing that you are the director of planning, how do think your fellow officers will respond to you once they learn that there is a possibility that 72 patrol officers will be laid off?

4. How will you respond to them?

5. If you were to change the recommendations in any way, what changes would you make?

6. Would it be possible to reduce the patrol force even further? How could this be done? Would it be wise? Would it result in significant financial savings?

7. Why, in your opinion, is Randall City so grossly overstaffed?

8. Do you think that the new mayor of Randall City will be pleased with your recommendations? Why?

9. How do you think that the information found in Tables 3 and 4 could be used?

10. By how many police officers could you reduce the force if you went all one-officer cars? Would this be a good move? Why or why not?

11. Do you think that you could conduct a personnel allocation study in your own police department if requested to do so by the chief? If you do, turn to Case 9.

The Prescott Valley Project

Prescott Valley is a town of 18,000 people and has a police department of 42 officers, 30 of whom are assigned to patrol duties in one-officer cars. This well-run town boasts the lowest property tax rate in the state. When its town manager, Janice Cady, hears about your personnel allocation study in Randall City, she seeks you out and asks if you will assist her in conducting a similar study in Prescott Valley. After clearing this request with your chief and getting his approval, you show Cady how to get the necessary activity information as well as the time-off information needed to determine the Prescott Valley time-off factor. Because Prescott Valley is considerably smaller than Randall City, you ask that she provide you with a four-month, rather than a three-month, sample of activity. You also request that this be done by shift.

In two months, Cady returns with the activity figures and time-off information for the Prescott Valley Police Department. You tell her that within a few minutes you will be able to determine what her personnel requirements are.

Although you question the amount of time allotted to servicing activity categories, Cady assures you that although these times seem to be excessively long, she herself conducted the time study and the figures are accurate. Because there is no investigations division in the department, patrol officers follow through themselves on all investigations involving Part I and Part II crimes. In addition, Prescott Valley is a large community geographically (67 square miles), and officers spend more time responding to calls. The community has no hospital, so the injured and sick must be transported to Randall City Hospital; this also increases activity time. The town has an ambulance that is staffed by the police department. Additionally, the town has no lock-up facilities, so prisoners must be transported to the jail at Randall City for booking; this increases the time allotted to the arrest category.

Table 1 shows the average amounts of time spent in servicing activity categories. Table 2 shows four months of shift activity by category. Table 3 shows the time lost by day for one year by the 30 officers assigned to the patrol function in Prescott Valley.

Table 1
Average Amounts of Time Spent in Servicing Activity Categories

Category	Time Spent
Part 1 crimes	4 hours
Part 2 crimes	2 hours
Incidents	.75 hour
Accidents	3 hours
Arrests	1 hour
Ambulance runs	1.5 hours

Table 2
Four Months of Police Activity, by Shift

Shift 1

Month	Part 1 Crimes	Part 2 Crimes	Incidents	Accidents	Arrests	Ambulance Runs
October	2	8	66	5	6	4
December	6	4	60	12	2	6
February	1	3	41	6	4	8
July	13	1	121	12	7	5
Totals	22	16	288	35	19	23

Shift 2

Month	Part 1 Crimes	Part 2 Crimes	Incidents	Accidents	Arrests	Ambulance Runs
October	8	33	99	26	20	16
December	13	37	97	44	10	19
February	7	23	87	30	7	27
July	13	15	150	28	8	11
Totals	41	108	433	128	45	73

Shift 3

Month	Part 1 Crimes	Part 2 Crimes	Incidents	Accidents	Arrests	Ambulance Runs
October	13	33	124	35	10	8
December	17	27	137	41	23	12
February	5	14	81	32	7	8
July	26	12	232	37	10	11
Totals	61	86	574	145	50	39

Table 3
Time Lost by Day for One Year

Individual Time-Off Factors	Officer Days Lost Per Year
Vacation Leave	325
Days Off	3,120
Bereavement Days	1
Sick Leave	317
Injury Leave	20
Military Leave	10
Holidays	116
Court Days	179
Total	4,088

Discussion Questions and Projects

1. What is the Prescott Valley Police Department's time-off factor?

2. How many car beats are needed to accommodate activity on Shift 1? How many patrol officers should be assigned to Shift 1?

3. How many car beats are needed to accommodate activity on Shift 2? How many patrol officers should be assigned to Shift 2?

4. How many car beats are needed to accommodate activity on Shift 3? How many patrol officers should be assigned to Shift 3?

5. Should the fact that the Prescott Valley Police Department provides ambulance service for the community affect personnel requirements? If so, how?

6. On the basis of Question 5, would you like to recalculate your figures?

7. Should the fact that Prescott Valley encompasses 67 square miles of area affect personnel requirements? If so, how?

8. On the basis of Question 7, would you like to recalculate your figures?

9. On the basis of any recalculations you may have made, how would you change your previous recommendations?

10. In your opinion, is the Prescott Valley Police Department overstaffed or understaffed? Explain.

Name Index

Subject Index